DEWEY AND HIS CRITICS

ESSAYS FROM

THE JOURNAL OF PHILOSOPHY

Selected, with an Introduction by
Sidney Morgenbesser

THE JOURNAL OF PHILOSOPHY, INC.
NEW YORK, 1977

iii

Dedicated to

Ernest Nagel and
John Herman Randall, Jr.

who edited the Journal
and interpreted Dewey
with great dedication
learning and illumination.

NOTE TO THE READER

Cross references within this volume may present a problem to the reader: the page references in the articles themselves refer to the original JOURNAL pages. Accordingly, the editors have provided (page 701) a listing of the articles in this volume with their original dates and pages, correlated with the pages of this volume. By using this list, the reader can decipher the cross references for him/herself. In a number of places, footnotes have been deleted, for reasons of space; wherever the first footnote of an article is deleted, it referred the reader to the article that immediately precedes in this volume.

Cloth: ISBN 0-931206-00-6   Paper: ISBN 0-931206-01-4

Library of Congress Catalog No. 77-94488

© Copyright 1977 by the JOURNAL OF PHILOSOPHY, INC.
Printed in U.S.A. by Lancaster Press, Inc., Lancaster, Pa.

CONTENTS

INTRODUCTION

DEWEY often called for a redirection of American philosophy, on some occasions beckoning philosophers to be concerned with the problems of men and on others questioning the genuineness of traditional philosophical questions under the current conditions of science and modern life. According to some of his students, Dewey thought that philosophers ought to be concerned with the problems of value, to furnish illumination and direction to our confused civilization; according to at least one very sympathetic interpreter, Dewey thought that the goal of philosophy was the reattainment of innocence and the divestiture of the culture of our times. One may go further. Hegelians often seem to suggest that philosophy should attempt a rational reconstruction of the culture of its time; Dewey, it may be claimed, wanted philosophers to engage in a reconstruction of their culture so that it might become rational and exhibit intelligence at work.

It becomes important, then, to understand how Dewey thought this could be done, how he thought his own philosophical work was related to its past, and how philosophers committed to Dewey's program will relate to philosophers who are not. An attractive answer—and one suggested by many recent metaphilosophical themes—would emphasize discontinuity. Dewey, it will be insisted, was a revolutionary: he and those influenced by him must become strangers to more traditional philosophers. On this view, Dewey and his followers would have to conclude that traditional philosophers should be by-passed, and so should their problems about the foundation of knowledge, privacy, and the given. By-passed, not criticized—for on what neutral philosophical ground should criticisms rest, especially those which involve metaphilosophical issues? Dewey aside, such strategy seems reasonable. After all, philosophers have apparently spent most of their time refuting each other and debating without decision, perhaps even without progress toward solution of their problems. Why not waive these and turn to other issues?

Reasonable or not, this was not the path that Dewey took. He did not think it was intellectually feasible to begin a reconstruction of philosophy by dismissing traditional philosophical issues, and he stressed continuity between old problems and new. Dewey engaged his contemporaries in debate, often on their own ground; he prized communication, even with philosophers who were loyal to traditions he questioned. Many of these debates between Dewey and his critics appeared in the JOURNAL OF PHILOSOPHY, and most of them, from the time of the birth of the JOURNAL till Dewey's death, are contained in this anthology. Dewey is its star; the supporting cast is admirable and impressive. Many justly famous philosophers appear, and so do many other very good, serious, and dedicated philosophers to whom history has not always been kind. It would not simply be an act of piety to suggest that, if we have made progress in American philosophy, it is in part due to the work of these philosophers. And in saying that we do not have to claim that they were gods or geniuses.

I

Dewey joined the Columbia Faculty in 1905; the JOURNAL was founded in 1904. It was an intellectually exciting time, with two native American philosophies: pragmatism and versions of realism, contesting for the rightful succession to the idealism that had dominated late nineteenth-century and early twentieth-century British and American philosophy. Dewey and the realists were at one in their criticism of subjective idealism, but differed in their account of the nature of knowledge (especially of our knowledge of the physical world), the senses, if any, in which reality is practical, the status of secondary qualities and of what Santayana and Dewey after him called "tertiary" ones, and the usefulness of correspondence to reality (or in Dewey's phrase, antecedent reality) as a criterion for the acceptability of hypotheses as credible —or as a requirement for knowledge. To recreate the mood of the time I have devoted a special section to the realist-pragmatist controversy. Since some of these issues have recently resurfaced, this section is also timely.

I will discuss each section of the collection separately, and begin here with Realism and its vicissitudes.

II. REALISM

Dewey objected to realism as a theory of knowledge, and offered many objections to realist views about perception and the acquisition of knowledge, objections which we will review below. But it is best to begin not with realism but with realists, who often disagreed with one another. There were diverse versions of realism and important distinctions among the New Realists—like Holt, Marvin, Montague, Perry, Pitkin, and Spaulding—and the Critical Realists—like Drake, Lovejoy, Pratt, Rogers, Santayana, Roy W. Sellars, and C. A. Strong. Furthermore, as the correspondence between William James and Dewey and especially the correspondence between James and Peirce reveal, pragmatists were at odds with one another over many important issues. The story is still more complicated. James influenced both the realists (American and British, especially the Russell of the teens) and Dewey. Dewey was criticized by many of the pragmatists and instrumentalists whom he influenced. C. I. Lewis's articles are self-explanatory: though he was influenced by Dewey, he differed with him about the given and about the grounds or foundations of knowledge. He shared with Dewey the pragmatist view that knowledge is for the sake of action, but did not believe that this thesis required or supported Dewey's quest against certainty. Although Ernest Nagel concurred with much of Dewey's theory of knowledge and his philosophy of science, he dissented strongly from some of Dewey's metaphysical views and from his account of the role of theory in science. And, as the articles by Dewey and Arthur Bentley reveal, later stages of Dewey criticized earlier ones. A story is told of Rudolf Carnap that once, when he was queried about one of his books, he answered that his grandfather had written it. Dewey had a kindred attitude toward some of his own work.

With these reservations in mind, it may be useful to consider first some aspects of the debates between Dewey and the New Realists and, second, the debates between Dewey and the Critical Realists. There is a received view about the New Realists which construes them as primarily concerned to argue against idealism that knowledge is an external relation, that things known are independent of their being known. Bernard Bosanquet and other idealists had argued that an object of thought always necessarily is in some degree a part of our psychical being, a particular mental state or occasion one with us in feeling and active in the total life of our mind. The New Realists objected; they affirmed that objects known and perceived are independent of us and are not mental states or entities; they relied on the view, advocated by Franz Brentano and by G. E. Moore, that, in every instance of the mental, there is a distinction to be drawn between act (which must be mental) and *object* (which need not be); and argued that the idealists, who had not carefully enough distinguished between the act and its objects, had gone wrong. The view I am summarizing contends that the New Realists, on the basis of this distinction, went on to construct a new epistemology or theory of knowledge, a new theory about thought and perception. There is, of course, much truth in this account; it captures an important part of the New Realists' contribution and focuses on an important part of the debate between them and Dewey. For Dewey did object to their use of the term 'knowledge' and argued against their use of the term 'awareness'. He did not merely claim—others did that too—

that there was no evidence for the existence of acts of awareness, or of our being aware, if only tacitly, of an act of awareness every time we are aware. He went further and claimed that 'awareness' and 'consciousness' are loaded terms that should be avoided in the theory of inquiry.

This account fails, however, to give an adequate picture of the New Realists' claims and goals. They had other arguments than Brentano's against the idealists, some of which are reviewed and criticized by Dewey in his comments on Perry and others. Again, the New Realists—at least some of them—were also concerned to construct a new metaphysics that would do away with dualism between the mental and the physical (see Dewey's "The Concept of the Neutral in Recent Epistemology," 228–230). The New Realists, then, were not only concerned to construct a new theory of knowledge or to offer new answers to standing philosophical questions. They often asked for a redirection of philosophy as Dewey himself did.

They argued that there was no general or genuine problem of how we get to know the real, and no need for "the science which investigates the nature, the possibility, and the limits of knowledge [and which] is fundamental to all other sciences."[1] Other philosophers may think there is such a need, but they are wrong. Many of the New Realists argued for the primacy of metaphysics, not epistemology; they suggested that philosophy should become constructive and analytic, analyze the use of language, concern itself with logical form, and engage in systematic analysis of the interrelation between wholes and parts. Too much concern with epistemology made the current state of philosophy intolerable to them: "philosophy . . . treats popularly and confusedly what modern logic treats with the painstaking thoroughness and the exactness of the expert."[2] The call for clarity was not first heard in the thirties.

Dewey, as I have stated, criticized the realists on their use of the terms 'knowledge' and 'awareness'. He noted the diverse uses of 'know' in ordinary language. Knowledge is used to "designate beliefs that are held with assurance especially with the implication that the assurance is justified, reasonable, grounded"; 'knowledge' is also frequently used as the equivalent of 'knowing-how', of skill, etc. In all such usages the terms are used differentially; they all

[1] Walter T. Marvin, "The Emancipation of Metaphysics from Epistemology," in *The New Realism: Coöperative Studies in Philosophy* by Edwin B. Holt, Marvin, William Pepperell Montague, Ralph Barton Perry, Walter B. Pitkin, and Edward Gleason Spaulding (New York: Macmillan, 1912), p. 45.

[2] *The New Realism*, Introduction, p. 26.

involve definite contrasts. But, in its epistemological use, in its use in the controversy between the realist and the idealist, Dewey argued that "the term 'knowledge' has a blanket value which is absolutely unknown in common life. It covers any and every 'presentation', of any and everything to a knower, to an 'awarer' if I may coin a word for the sake of avoiding some of the pitfalls of the term consciousness" ("Brief Studies in Realism, II," p. 99/100). He concluded that, once we use the term 'knowledge' this broadly, the knowledge relation becomes ubiquitous and the objective idealists can devise answers to the realists.

Nevertheless, Dewey did not conclude that the controversy between the realists and the idealists was meaningless. He tried to show that the realists were right—or basically so—about some issues, e.g., objects of perception, but wrong about other issues, about the nature of knowledge. It may be useful to note briefly some of the theses Dewey pressed in this period against some of the realists, for they reappear in slightly revised form in many other sections of this collection and are amplified in later stages of Dewey's life.

As the articles indicate, Dewey was at one with the realists in their contention that no idealistic conclusions follow from the well-known facts about the relativity of perception. He was also sympathetic with many of the arguments of the idealists against what F. H. Bradley called the "copy theory" of truth and perception. But Dewey did not, I think, defend a coherence theory of knowledge or justification, any more than he defended a coherence theory of truth. His approach was contextual. For Dewey, an agent is justified in acting upon his beliefs if he has encountered no difficulty while acting on them, even if it turns out that the beliefs were inconsistent. Should the agent, however, encounter a difficulty—or, in his terminology, a "problematic situation"—then of course he should—indeed must—formulate a consistent set of hypotheses and test them jointly. An agent may treat his beliefs as innocent and not in need of justification, later justifying change of belief as a result of inquiry. From the pragmatist's position, the request for justification is not always in order, and, as W. V. Quine has noted, the pragmatist "doesn't scratch when it doesn't itch." I have only indicated an approach to justification, which has been developed in a number of ways by other philosophers sympathetic to Dewey.

At all accounts, Dewey developed an experimental picture of the acquisition of knowledge. We start to inquire when we encounter a problem we cannot resolve simply by relying on our current beliefs; we acquire knowledge as a result of inquiry; and we use that knowledge to make sense out of what we experience or to act on now warranted belief. Dewey was thus pressing for a number of distinctions—getting to know, knowing, using knowledge—and arguing for the view that we get to know by acting in order to confirm hypotheses and to resolve problems encountered. Each term I have used needs amplification, and each part of the compound thesis needs development; Dewey did try to amplify and develop in many of the articles in this section. One of the important conclusions that emerges here is the pragmatic view that we should link cognitive significance not with impressions nor even with evidence, but with ways of getting to know. Dewey later claimed that his approach was vindicated when empiricists adopted the operational theory of meaning. (For comments and criticism of this part of Dewey, the reader is referred to the articles by Lewis, Randall, and Ratner.) There was another consequence that Dewey drew: that we cannot account for the acquisition of knowledge by reference to unique types of acts or experience that occur wherever we acquire knowledge. There are no unique acts of that sort, no unique acts of awareness that are "knowledge-acquiring" acts. Georges Dicker has recently developed some of these themes.

Nor is there any immediate knowledge. All knowledge is acquired as a result of inquiry. Lewis has reviewed some of these arguments and criticized them. Notice that Dewey was arguing primarily, if not exclusively, that we have no "immediate knowledge" of the causal properties of objects; he was not denying that we can often tell directly and without conscious inference that we are perceiving a specific physical object, and hence directly know that we are perceiving an object that has certain powers and capacities. There was of course no inconsistency; for he was not denying direct knowledge, only claiming that it was parasitic. "Knowledge-as-re-cognition" or "apprehension," as he put it in the *Logic*, is parasitic on knowledge we already have about the relevant physical objects and on other cognitive skills we have already developed. And I take it that Dewey thought it was part of the theory of knowledge to explain why we are able to re-cognize and how we originally acquired the relevant knowledge in question, and it seemed to him that the realists did not undertake to do that.

An additional note is in order. There are occasions when Dewey seems to say that, given language skills, we can tell by perception alone that a certain *quale* is present, but cannot tell by perception alone what object it is we are seeing—it is up to inquiry to inform us about that. Dewey put it this way: " 'The stick seems bent in water' does not mean that the appearing object *seems* bent. It means that what appears *is* something bent, though not necessarily the stick; perhaps it is light.''[3] Notice, however, that Dewey believed that we cannot confirm physical-object statements solely by appeal to statements about *qualia* or about appearances. He held that we must conjoin such sentences with other physical-object statements for testing purposes. For Dewey observation sentences in the sciences, even statements about ''qualia,'' are not theory-laden, but action-laden: to say that something is observable is to say that experimental conditions can be arranged for shared observation. The issues are not easy to disentangle, but they are discussed with profit by Dewey and McGilvary.[4]

In the course of defending his views about immediate knowledge or the lack of it, Dewey often distinguished between having an experience and knowing about it, or between primary and reflective experience. He put this distinction to many uses; here I want to note one epistemological use to which he put it, which figures strongly in his article on immediate knowledge of the mental (167–173) and in his debate with Rice.

Dewey often discussed this distinction and gave many examples from adult-behavior experience. But the epistemological point, I think, may perhaps be better put if we talk about babies and infants and understand Dewey to be claiming that a baby can experience pain and not know that it is in pain; similarly an infant may see and not know what it is seeing or even that it is seeing. Dewey, as I understand him, claims that it is not the case that a person who is in a mental state, knows that it is that state simply because

[3] *Philosophy and Civilization* (New York: Minton, Balch, 1931), p. 71.

[4] Notice in this connection that, despite his well-known critique of the sense-datum approach to perception, Dewey did not deny that it made sense to talk about the perception of *sensa*; often he insisted that their primacy had been misunderstood. ''The alleged primacy of sensory meanings is mythical. They are primary only in logical status; they are primary as tests and confirmation of inferences concerning matters of fact, not as historic originals. For, while it is not usually needful to carry the check or test of theoretical calculations to the point of irreducible sensa, colors, sounds, etc., these sensa form a limit approached in careful analytic certifications, and upon critical occasions it is necessary to touch the limit. The transformation of these ulterior checking meanings into existential primary data is but another example of domination by interest in results and fruits, plus the fallacy which converts a functional office into an antecedent existence. Sensa are the class of irreducible meanings which are employed in verifying and correcting other meanings. We actually set out with much coarser and more inclusive meanings and not till we have met with failure from their use do we even set out to discover those ultimate and harder meanings which are sensory in character.'' *Experience and Nature* (London: Allen & Unwin, 1929), p. 327.

it *is* that state. Hence he is arguing against one version of foundationalism, which would claim (1) that we can have knowledge only if it is based on premises or foundations that are certain and indubitable, (2) that we can get such knowledge by having knowledge of our mental states, and (3) that we can have such knowledge of our mental states simply because they are mental states. Dewey's argument against (1) above appears in his accounts of inquiry.

Notice that, on the account thus far presented, it was open to Dewey to agree that adults do have privileged "immediate" knowledge of at least some of these mental states and to claim only that such knowledge cannot be taken for granted, but itself must be explained. Whether Dewey took this position or the stronger one that we have no such privileged knowledge is, I think, open to question. The reader is referred to the interesting exchange between Rice and Dewey on this issue (see section VI).[5]

Dewey's views about the nature of inquiry are complex, and I shall be concerned with them below. Here it may be relevant to note that he appealed to his views about inquiry to rebut and criticize a number of related but distinguishable theses about the role of thought and confirmation which he thought the realists defended. He argued both that it is not the aim of thought to construct a theory that is in some suitable sense a mirror or a revelation of reality and that there is not and cannot be any general problem about the relation between thought and reality, or theory and reality. It is the aim of thought to construct and test theories that enable us to predict and explain, and any questions about the relationships between thought and reality or between theory and reality are idle. Notice that Dewey need not be interpreted to argue against a realist view of the nature of theoretical entities, to argue against their reality. His argument was rather that we can understand the significance and point of postulating theoretical entities or understand the role a theoretical term plays in a theory only if we understand the use to which the theory will be put and the specific problems to which it is addressed. A corollary follows: it is not the function of theories to offer a unique way of describing the world; the world may be described in many ways, and we

---

[5] I add a historical note. Dewey was often arguing against the thesis that we can, by direct inspection or by some special method of introspection, get to know the structure of mental phenomena; he was not denying that we can tell by "direct inspection" whether we are in pain or thinking. For a fuller discussion, see "Conduct and Experience," in *Psychologies of 1930* (Worcester, Mass.: Clark University Press, 1930), reprinted in *Philosophy and Civilization*, pp. 249-270.

also get to know the way the world is in ordinary perception—or rather the various ways the world is. For Dewey theory or inquiry begins when we confront a problematic situation, which, in his terminology, calls for reconstruction, and ends, at least temporarily, both with the adoption of a theory or hypothesis or judgment and with a reconstruction of the problematic situation. At all accounts we do not begin or end with a depiction of the given that is clearly structured or with direct knowledge of the facts. As Dewey put it,

> What makes the essential difference between modern research and the reflection of, say, the Greeks, is not the absence of "mere thinking," but the presence of conditions for testing its results; the elaborate system of checks and balances found in the technique of modern experimentation. The thinking process does not go on endlessly in terms of itself, but seeks outlet through reference to particular experiences. It is tested by this reference; not, however, as if a theory could be tested by directly comparing it with facts—an obvious impossibility—but through use in facilitating commerce with facts. It is tested as glasses are tested; things are looked at through the medium of specific meanings to see if thereby they assume a more orderly and clearer aspect, if they are less blurred and obscure.[6]

The realists thought that Dewey was unclear and unconvincing when he discussed the thesis that objects known are inquiry-dependent or, even more mysteriously, argued that knowledge or the acquisition of knowledge introduces changes in objects or situations. They argued that knowledge is independent of its objects, and that in no coherent sense can objects of knowledge be changed as a result of being known. But Dewey and the pragmatists disputed what they took to be a difficulty in the realist view. They took the realists to be arguing that, when we acquire knowledge, we acquire knowledge of that which was, is, or will be whether we get to know or not. And, if that be the case, the realists will have no reason to press for our acquiring knowledge in order to act. But we do acquire knowledge in the belief—which the pragmatists thought justified—that something occurs that would not have occurred had we not acted and that we would not have acted in the way we did had we not acquired the relevant knowledge. Dewey generalized and claimed that, when we get to know, something occurs in the world that would not have occurred had we not inquired; inquiry begins by our encountering an indeterminate situation, and, when we get to know, the problematic situation is

---

[6] *Essays in Experimental Logic* (Chicago: Chicago University Press, 1916; New York: Dover, 1966), p. 198.

altered. For Dewey, though it was not the case that to be is to be experienced, it was the case that to be experienced is to be. And if we experience a situation as "vague" or "confused" or indefinite, so be it; that is what it is.

Once again, the issues involved are complex; they are related to Dewey's views about contextual naturalism and objective relativism. It is therefore of interest to note that McGilvary, who was a major exponent of what was called "contextual naturalism" or "objective relativism" in the twenties and thirties, dissented from Dewey's views on these issues. I note briefly that the Objective Relativists thought that the New Realists fell into difficulty when they argued that when we perceive an object we perceive its real color or its real shape. For, once we argue thus, we are confronted with all sorts of problems having to do with that old philosophical puzzle: in what perception, if any, is the real shape or the real color revealed? Dewey and other philosophers who called themselves contextual naturalists or objective realists argued that we should drop the notion of the real shape or real color of an object and attribute to it many shapes and many colors—each one contextual and relational. For clarification of these issues I refer the reader to some of McGilvary's articles in the JOURNAL OF PHILOSOPHY.

Here then are some theses that Dewey argued for in his debate with the New Realists. As already indicated, Dewey presented himself as a slightly adverse ally of the New Realists and argued that they had been a useful corrective to idealism. He offered many formulas to indicate his agreement with the New Realists: perceived objects are not mental; we directly perceive physical objects; there are no intermediaries in perception between us and physical objects; objects known bear many relations to each other, independently of being known, etc.

Relations between Dewey and the Critical Realists were, I think, somewhat different—in his debates with them he seemed to be more adversary than ally. Perhaps we can put the case from the perspective of the Critical Realists. They were critical both of Dewey and of the New Realists, arguing that these philosophers failed to appreciate the fact that the "knowledge-relation" is dualistic. We think we get to know about objects in physical space by perception, but the "objects or relations" we directly experience or perceive are not those objects; we rely on memory, but the past is gone, and we can't be in direct relation to it. The Critical Realists affirmed that physical objects and the past are not themselves literally present in the consciousness of the knower, and the knower gets to know about physical objects or the past—x's which are not directly in consciousness—by being related to or directly aware of or by relying on y's which are. They offered diverse, often ingenious, philosophical theses, some of which still appeal to many philosophers.

Dewey offered many critical assessments of the theories of the Critical Realists. The debates were long and involved and often inconclusive. Dewey, as I understand him, argued that the Critical Realists had mistaken a functional distinction for an ontological one: there are y's (e.g., *qualia*) which function as signs for x's (physical objects); the presence of a *quale* may be taken as evidence for the occurrence of a body, but the x's and y's are not ontologically distinct. Dewey also claimed that the Critical Realists had committed a deeper mistake. They misdescribed the human agent as a disinterested spectator, one who somehow or other has experiences and then for some reason or other tries to account for them. He argued that they failed to appreciate not only the conceptual relations between knowledge and action, but also those between thought and action, and even experience and action.

Dewey took it to be the task of philosophy to explain how we get to know. He argued that we ought not to treat knowledge as a mystery, but should instead appeal to science not only as a paradigm case exhibiting how we get to know but also as a resource for explaining how we get to know.

Dewey was a tough critic, and the Critical Realists were made of stern stuff; they often answered his arguments with great acumen. Among other things they argued that some of Dewey's arguments about perception and those of the New Realists were irrelevant. The New Realists argued that we don't perceive mental entities; many of the Critical Realists agreed, but insisted that it was enough for their purposes to claim that we don't directly perceive physical objects or their surfaces. They further claimed that Dewey and the New Realists were not guided by the results of modern science as they claimed to be, for it is the results of modern science that force these dualisms upon us. There is no need to review all the issues—the reader can review and assess the articles by Drake and the debates between Dewey and Lovejoy at his/her own convenience.

There are two issues, however, that deserve some comment, because they have given rise to many discussions about Dewey's views about knowledge and its role and are still being discussed by commentators on Dewey. First, Lovejoy and many other philosophers claimed that Dewey was never clear about what happens when a scientist—or anyone else for that matter—acquires knowledge. According to some Critical Realists, if a person does acquire knowledge of a given proposition, he acquires a certain disposition, a disposition to be in a certain state of assurance when he thinks about that proposition; the acquisition of knowledge is the acquisition of that disposition. But Dewey, they claimed, was silent on what did occur and had little good to say about states of assurance or states of awareness, and hence little to say about "the knowledge relation."

Dewey did answer at least on some occasions that when a person acquires knowledge he acquires a certain ability to predict successfully. For a variety of reasons this answer will, I think, not do. Moreover, another answer seems to be the one he adopted in his later writings. I think we can interpret him as saying that, when a person gets to know, he acquires a certain disposition and a warrant, or a disposition to assert with warrant. I have only indicated part of Dewey's answer, and permit myself only a slight amplification. Dewey, as is well known, was primarily concerned to specify the conditions under which a person is in a position to make justified claims to knowledge or to assert with warrant, and hence often by-passed the problem of truth. For, clearly enough, a person may be justified in claiming that he knows and yet not know; though he took all precautions and reviewed all the evidence, the sentence he accepted turns out to be false. Nevertheless, Dewey did not by-pass the problem of truth, and he seemed on occasion to argue that, if we want to make truth an achievable aim and not merely a hope for inquiry, we must accept a verifiability theory of truth; we must be able to specify the conditions under which a person can know that a sentence is true. This is, I think, the intent behind his view that "the true means the verified and means nothing else." [7] It is quite clear that this thesis is not accepted by all pragmatists and is independent of many other pragmatic theses we have noted. In point of fact, Dewey himself often qualified it, e.g., in "Propositions, Warranted Assertability, and Truth."

I now turn to the second issue raised by the Dewey-Lovejoy exchange: Dewey's view about the roles or functions of knowledge.

Dewey was often interpreted (by many realists and others) as defending a normative thesis about knowledge, namely that we ought to pursue the acquisition of such knowledge as promises to

---

[7] *Reconstruction in Philosophy* (enl. edn., Boston: Beacon Press, 1948), p. 160.

satisfy our noncognitive interests. Dewey claimed that he was misunderstood, that he was defending no such normative thesis, but only a number of functional theses about knowledge. He claimed that knowledge plays two roles: it enables us to act on the basis of justified beliefs; it also enables us to experience what we do experience as making sense—knowledge accordingly enriches our direct experience. Dewey's views on sense and meaning and the way in which objects and events are experienced as making sense are complicated, and the reader is referred to some of the discussion of these issues in the exchange between Hall and Dewey in section V.

This point is related to another issue. Both the New and the Critical Realists complained that Dewey was obscure in defense of his view that the acquisition of knowledge changes objects. There is, I think, justice in these complaints. He meant, I think, a number of things. But often enough what he seemed to be saying was not that obscure. He was noting that, when we acquire knowledge of an object, we experience it differently than we did before, and so the object may be described as acquiring a new disposition, a disposition to be experienced as making sense. On other occasions Dewey called attention to the converse point: the fact that we change and grow as we acquire new knowledge and that we are enabled to change and grow as we acquire knowledge as a result of being members of a community. Dewey was the perennial educator, and his vision of society as an area of growth with all of us learning from each other is perhaps visionary, but it is, I think, an interesting challenge to one of the views he was contesting, namely that society is and must remain a marketplace where men and women with fixed resources, utilities, and beliefs meet only for the rational exchange of goods and services.

III. THEORY OF KNOWLEDGE

I have alluded to many themes and theses which are discussed more fully in many of the articles—thus, Dewey's criticism of idealism, in the articles by Hocking and Cunningham, and Dewey's criticism of classical empiricism, in the articles by Ratner, Russell, and Randall. There is no need here to comment on all these issues, but two deserve mention. They are Dewey's views about his philosophical predecessors and his views about inquiry. These are not disconnected issues, for Dewey often argued that major philosophical positions—empiricism, idealism—had mistaken views about inquiry and the acquisition of knowledge; he criticized them for paying exclusive attention to one phase of inquiry and for not developing views that accounted for all aspects of inquiry in an integrated way.

It would, however, be wrong to claim that Dewey argued against his predecessors simply on the grounds that they misunderstood the nature of inquiry. The issue is more complex.

As we have seen, Dewey's reactions to realism were varied; he was sympathetic with some but not all of the views of the New Realists, less sympathetic with the doctrines of the Critical Realists. Dewey's stance toward classical empiricism is also varied; he was sympathetic with some but not all of its theses—it would be silly to claim that he called for a total rejection of classical empiricism. I state this only because many have recently presented Dewey as a total revolutionary who wanted philosophers to begin afresh and develop totally new systems—or perhaps even wanted them to have no systemic views at all.

Dewey is not entirely at fault in this matter. In some of his popular articles and books he did sound as if he believed that philosophy should bury its past, but in his more systematic writings and in his teaching he kept the past alive for criticism and debate. It is reported that the Chinese philosopher Dr. Fung Yu Lan heard Dewey lecture at the University of Peking and came to believe that Dewey thought it was pointless to study the history of philosophy, that all traditional philosophy was defunct, superseded, and discardable. And so he came to Columbia to study Dewey on Dewey. But when he came and attended Dewey's courses, he heard him lecture on Aristotle and Locke, and he subsequently became a distinguished philosopher and historian of philosophy.[8] The truth, then, about Dewey the teacher and philosopher is more sober and less dramatic than the popular view to which I referred and which he occasionally encouraged.

There were some traditions, e.g., Cartesianism, for which Dewey had little if any sympathy. There were many philosophers whom he criticized for making some big mistakes—e.g., the mistake noted above of holding a spectator theory of knowledge—and whom he therefore approached with caution. But, with modification, some philosophical approaches, e.g., empiricism, were redeemable and in a sense basically right; other traditions, though in a sense basically wrong, were nevertheless to be credited with important theses that called for reinterpretation. Such was the case with objective idealism, which Dewey regarded as right in focusing on the teleological nature of the mind, but wrong to insist, as some idealists put it,

---

[8] Anecdote told by Walter B. Veazey, "John Dewey and the Revival of Greek Philosophy," *University of Colorado Studies in Philosophy*, II (1961), p. 1.

that the mind seeks a certain kind of understanding or fully understands something only if it comprehends it as a necessary part of a system, all of whose parts are internally related and necessitate each other.

For Dewey there is no such system—he was opposed to viewing nature as any form of system—but he was indebted to idealism in his teleological account of inquiry as goal-directed; he was also indebted to idealistic writings on ethics, especially the writings of T. H. Green.

I am of course making a plea that, in trying to understand Dewey's attitudes toward philosophical tradition, we should examine him at work and not concentrate too much on his popular pronouncements. And I use that plea to support another one. Dewey's views about the interconnections between perception, action, and cognition should not be oversimplified. He often argued that the notion of a disembodied perceiver is incoherent and that perception is a form of action, but he did not defend the view, which is often attributed to him, that all our knowledge of the external world is a result of experimentation on physical bodies. Still, he did emphasize the importance of experimentation on physical and changeable bodies, and did so for a number of justifiable historical reasons, some metaphilosophical and some methodological. He wanted to support his view that theories of knowledge ought to be influenced by developments in the sciences—a thesis he thought some of his contemporaries denied—by making the case for the view that major philosophies and theories of knowledge in point of fact have been so influenced; also that scientific practice supported his arguments against the dualism between knowledge and action.

Dewey went further and claimed that one of the jobs of philosophy is to facilitate the growth of knowledge. One of his early monographs, "Conditions for a Scientific Morality," was written in the hope of furthering the development of knowledge in the social sciences, to which, as we shall see below, he himself contributed. The major methodological thesis argued for in the article by Hook, Nagel, and Dewey is that the methods, aims, and theories of the social sciences should be continuous with those of the physical sciences, or that the pattern of inquiry in the social sciences ought to be similar in its main aspects to the pattern of inquiry in the physical sciences.

'Inquiry' was a key term for Dewey. What then did he mean by it? There is no simple answer, for he wrote many articles and books in the hope of specifying its main features. Often he used 'inquiry' loosely to apply to ordinary testing of hypotheses; in other writings and especially in the *Logic* he applied it to a pattern of interconnected acts and judgments exhibited in the sciences. Inquiry in the latter sense was teleological and creative; it set its aims by its previous results; its products were functional and could be understood only by reference to their role in inquiry. It had naturalistic import, since it resolved natural problematic situations. It was naturalistic in another sense as well: some of the habits that scientists exhibit are continuous with those exhibited by lower organisms.

But what, we may ask, is the pattern of inquiry? The story cannot be easily told, and only some of the main features of inquiry which are discussed in the articles in this collection will be mentioned.

For Dewey inquiry is a species of action: behavior guided by thought and especially by well-formulated hypotheses. It is carried out in accord with certain procedures which are justified by their previous success in inquiry. Similarly for reliance by scientists on theories and on rules of logic: these too are to be justified by their indispensable role in inquiry and by their successes. Inquiry is directed to specific problems, and scientists reach judgments when they think they have resolved their problems; to do so they must be in a position to deal with perceptual material in a conceptually perspicuous way. And they are in such a position, according to Dewey, because they can rely on two types of proposition—generic and universal—the one having existential import and being contingent, the other expressing necessary connections between characters or possibilities.

Dewey emphasized the social aspects of scientific work. Science is social in the sense that it is an organized community of researchers, united by the employment of a common method—or by commitment to the pattern of inquiry just baldly stated; it is also social in that scientists use not only first-order beliefs about nature but also second-order beliefs that require them to check their first-order beliefs with the beliefs of their colleagues. Among other things, they check whether they have proceeded in accord with scientific principles and rules—which are, however, as we have seen, not antecedent to inquiry; the procedures and rules are a product, not a presupposition, of inquiry. These are scientific ideals, occasionally violated in practice, but unless they were often followed, we could not achieve scientific progress.

These latter aspects of scientific work were of crucial importance to Dewey; he was describing a model for inquiry not only in the social sciences, but also for agents confronted with moral and ethical problems.

The themes and theses I have briefly sketched are discussed in the articles in section III. In the symposium on *Logic: The Theory of Inquiry,* placed here in section V, Nagel discusses Dewey's naturalism and his distinction between generic and universal propositions. Cunningham is critical (from an idealistic perspective) of Dewey's account of inquiry and its cumulative growth. As I understand Cunningham, part of what he is saying is that we can't account for scientific progress unless we make some metaphysical assumptions about Reality which Dewey does not make; and on this point, if I am right, Cunningham is perhaps closer to Peirce than Dewey was. McGilvary is critical of Dewey's views about the problematic "situations"; and Lewis raises some problems with Dewey's views about judgment and the termination of inquiry.

There is another objection to Dewey's position, raised by Jarrett. Inquiry in Dewey's sense is a relatively recent and special phenomenon. Men acquired knowledge before the rise of science, most of us getting to know by perceiving or by relying on testimony and not by inquiry in Dewey's sense. Why then the special attention to inquiry and science? Why put inquiry at the center of the theory of knowledge?

As I understand it, Dewey's answer is roughly as follows. Dewey took it to be evident to all except those who raise skeptical doubts about the possibility of knowledge, that science is good at getting knowledge and also good at presenting us with reasons for changing our beliefs, which we took to be warranted—if not obvious—prior to inquiry. That being the case, it is reasonable for philosophers interested in knowledge to study the institution best suited, as far as we know, for getting it.

Dewey seems to be saying that, were we to be asked to study firefighting, we would consider it reasonable to begin with the study of a well-run fire department justly renowned for its efficiency; we would study its history and the ways in which it had solved specific problems in the past, and we would examine the problems it still faces. We would not consider it reasonable to postpone inquiry because we had no clear criteria for fire, or reasonable to begin with a theory of ideal firefighters by reference to which we would judge and assess the work of the department in question. Again, most of us would not think it reasonable to say that there is nothing special about the firemen—come to think of it, we put out fires all the time, everytime we extinguish a match.

Dewey argued in a parallel way about inquiry and knowledge. But it is also the case, as I have tried to indicate, that he dealt with many traditional epistemological issues and criticized many traditional positions on so-called "philosophical" grounds—criticized them without reference to scientific findings. His position then seemed to be that, once certain dubious theories about knowledge are out of the way, we can get on with the major project of studying the nature of scientific inquiry. Finally, Dewey believed that many arguments for skepticism were meaningless or pointless. Russell answered in his review essay on *Essays in Experimental Logic.*

IV. METAPHYSICS AND AESTHETICS

Many of the distinctive traits of Dewey's metaphysics, which he took to be a description of the generic or ultimate traits of existence, are discussed in his exchange with Santayana. I note a few of the issues. Dewey's metaphysics is frequently classified as a process philosophy—according to which everything that is is an event-process; that is, no event is a sequence of nonchanging time-slices (see his article on Broad, "Events and the Future").

It can also be classified as a metaphysics of contingency, or a metaphysics of the contingent; for Dewey often described the world as a contingent one. He did not mean only that empirical laws are not necessary truths and events not fully predictable, although he meant that too. In describing the world, he did not begin with the notion of law. As I understand him, he intended to avoid the view that laws are true in virtue of the existence of regularities and that the world is a complex of two kinds of things: regularities and events. For Dewey there are only events and processes, many of which exhibit recurrent patterns of behavior and resemble one another. He described the world as an impressive mixture of suffering, tight completeness, order, recurrences which make possible prediction and control, ambiguities, processes going on to changes as yet indeterminate.

From this description of the world, which he took to be obviously true, Dewey drew a number of conclusions and, in consequence, introduced a number of requirements on a satisfactory form of naturalism. He tried to show that ideals and thinking and art can arise only in such a contingent world or have a function to perform only in such a world. He often contrasted our world with what he took to be the two possible contrary ones—a totally fixed and perfectly predictable world, and a purely random, chaotic world that allows for neither prediction nor control. And he tried to show that thinking and the having of ideas would have no place and would play no role in such noncontingent worlds.[9] In a totally fixed world or a world of beings who knew everything, there would be nothing to think about, no problems to solve. (This

[9] See, for example, *Art as Experience* (New York: Minton, Balch, 1934; New York, Capricorn, 1958), pp. 16/17.

was in a way an attack on the view that the aim of thought or of the thinking agent is to forge the perfect theory.) Dewey was not only defending the popular thesis that we would all be bored in a perfect world, but arguing that it would be incoherent to say that we could have ideas in a perfect world. It is tempting to go into greater detail and analyze Dewey's view, but it is best to send the reader instead to Dewey's and Santayana's essays. Santayana, though a naturalist, took Dewey's description to be parochial, too much a description of the world from a limited human perspective.

A brief reminder. It is obvious that Dewey was not saying, as some have suggested, that this is the best of all possible worlds, or that he was more or less content with the world as it is. Nor was he content with the contemporary social order or with the American scene or satisfied that the American social world was the best context in which ideas could flourish. As he once put it, "After all, the optimism that says that the world is already the best of all possible worlds might be regarded as the most cynical of pessimisms. If this is the best possible, what would a world that was fundamentally bad be like?" [10]

As indicated, Dewey required of a suitable naturalistic philosophy that it be able to show how complex human products, e.g., science and art, arise from the world as described in his way. It must make clear how "higher" human processes—like sophisticated forms of theory construction—arise and are continuous with nonreflective human activities or human actions undertaken or arising because the world is contingent in his sense. "A primary task," he writes, "is imposed upon one who undertakes to write about the philosophy of the fine arts. This task is to restore continuity between the refined and intensified forms of expression that are works of art and the everyday events, doings, and sufferings that are usually recognized to constitute experience." [11] Edna Aston Shearer has difficulties with this aspect of Dewey's view of art; so have some recent philosophers, notably Richard Wollheim.

Dewey's naturalism was a version of the emergent naturalism that was often debated in the twenties and thirties. It was also a version of contextualism—a position to which I have already alluded. It was an explanatory naturalism, explanatory not only in the sense that Dewey claimed that if events are explainable at all they are explainable by the sciences and that the basic explanations are to be provided by natural science. It was a form of explanatory naturalism in a stronger sense as well. Dewey offered

[10] *Reconstruction in Philosophy*, p. 178.
[11] *Art as Experience*, p. 3.

many naturalistic explanations or explanation-sketches of his own (e.g., of religious experience), and so there is no sharp divide between science and philosophy in Dewey's writings; indeed, many of what philosophers consider his philosophical works are also considered to be important contributions to psychology. At all events, in *Experience and Nature* and in *Art as Experience* Dewey offered explanations or explanation-sketches of diverse human phenomena as due to the interplay between the natural or, more specifically, the biological, and cultural phenomena, given that some aspects or parts of the cultural phenomena can themselves be shown to arise from biological phenomena. At one time he suggested that *Experience and Nature* should have been entitled *Nature and Culture*. There is a similar theme in his work on logic, where he tried to show that "there is no break in continuity between operations of inquiry and biological operations as well as physical ones" and again tried to exhibit how "rational operations of inquiry grow out of organic activities without being identical to them."[12]

Parts of *Experience and Nature* can, therefore, be viewed as a defense of alternative classifications of things and events which could serve as heuristic guides to explanations that would exhibit continuity and emergence. In one classification, some natural events come to an end and are histories—occurrences that have a beginning, a middle, and an end—other (higher) complex events and organisms behave teleologically, and still higher ones act with end in view. In another classification, some entities are described as physical, higher ones as physico-biological, and finally, still more complex entities as sociobiological organisms. These biological organisms live as members of communities and can share meanings because of their linguistic abilities and knowledge.

There are a number of overlapping themes: complex entities have traits that their parts do not have, yet these traits are dependent upon the arrangement and interrelations among those parts; the basic theories of the social sciences are not reducible to psychology, or, alternatively, men's behavior can be understood (if we may be allowed to put it somewhat tentatively) if man is approached as an animal with a unique linguistic ability which he can develop only as a member of a community.

It is hard to judge Dewey's success. Currently philosophers do not approach the issues of emergence in the way that seemed congenial to Dewey and his contemporaries. We are more accustomed to discussing these matters by considering the sense in which theories are reduced to each other. It is hard, therefore, to offer

---

[12] *Logic: The Theory of Inquiry* (New York: Holt, 1938), p. 19.

a simple verdict on the success of Dewey's and allied forms of emergent naturalism or to relate their views to current views about reduction. It is, I think, fair to say that some important aspects of Dewey's approach are supported in the work of such philosophers of science as Carl Hempel and Ernest Nagel. But it is perhaps best not to consider Dewey's approach in a wholesale manner, but to regard it as having specific theses on art and logic and ideas. His views may be interesting and true in some areas and disputable in others.

Before I continue to indicate a little more of the content of Dewey's naturalism, I observe that Dewey took his position to be correctable by reference to the work of the sciences. He was offering a hypothesis, or "a vision" in James's sense of the term. It may therefore be relevant to note that Dewey has on occasion been criticized for not satisfying his own requirements, criticized for offering views not supported by the sciences. Thus Nagel has criticized his work on time and individuality on exactly these grounds in his review of *Time and Its Mysteries*.

Neither is it evident that modern science denies, as Dewey seemed to claim, that there are a finite number of types of entities of which everything is composed. Dewey's view on that matter is, I think, not very persuasive; his related view that there is no fixed privileged way of describing the world is much more compelling. And that view, as we have already seen, is related to his views about inquiry: that it is not the aim of science to offer *the* only way of describing the world, and the related view that scientific theories do not reveal or describe a world of theoretical entities that have ontological status superior to that of the entities and events that are directly experienced. It should also be evident from the quotations I have cited that Dewey's metaphysical theory is an account of what he took to be empirical things; it is not an account of what may perhaps misleadingly be called his "ontology." It especially does not contain Dewey's views on abstract entities like classes and propositions and universals. Dewey's treatment of these matters is placed here in the section on Mind, Meaning, and Logic.

These quotations also indicate that Dewey distinguished between thing-events and objects—objects are events with meaning [13] —and, having done so in what he took to be a perspicuous manner, he allowed himself, in the classifications to which I have alluded, to refer to processes, organisms, situations, etc.

I think it is fair, however, to say that one could accept or re-

---

[13] *Experience and Nature,* p. 318.

ject Dewey's classifications without commitment to his views about the primacy of events or his views about process, and accept or reject his classification even if we begin by taking events and things as different besic kinds of entities. In the main Dewey was opposed to the view that things are substances in the sense that they could exist independently. He tried to show that we have no real understanding of what it would mean to describe an entity as one that could exist all by itself.

In other sections of his writings Dewey stresses the slightly different thesis that we have knowledge of the world only as an arena of interacting things and that many if not all of the interesting "properties" of things are dispositional and contextual; we understand things only as entities that are disposed to manifest certain types of behavior under some conditions and not others, and to specify those conditions we must introduce reference to other things. Given Dewey's naturalism, all the thing-events are natural; given his metaphysics, there is no purely disembodied mind, even in principle.

This theme figures strongly in his contextualistic naturalism and in his account of the reality of tertiary qualities and properties, to which I will refer again. Things and events are terrifying or soluble in similar but not identical ways. The disposition of a soluble thing or a thing soluble in water is made manifest when it is placed under suitable conditions in a "natural" object; similarly for terrifying events—they too have their disposition made manifest in the lives of natural organisms, not in the lives of disembodied minds. In addition, as we have seen, the terror event is not mental, in any interesting epistemological sense.

There is a prima facie asymmetry between experience and inquiry for Dewey: in inquiry we make entities exhibit their dispositions; in experience dispositions of natural entities are made manifest in us. But this asymmetry holds only under certain conditions, when we are passive and merely have experiences. Under other conditions we use our knowledge to enrich our experience, and in general experience is due to our actions or our interactions with nature. But, as already noted, late in his life Dewey tried to offer a more refined version of this thesis, with emphasis upon transaction, and he did so in his papers with Bentley (see section III).

V. Mind, Meaning, and Logic

There are then all sorts of dualisms that are being attacked in Dewey's metaphysics and in his theory of the mind, which we have begun to consider. So it is not surprising that Dewey's views about the nature of mind have often been described as a critique of Cartesian dualism. This way of putting Dewey's position is slightly misleading. Dewey was not, I think, primarily a foe of Descartes; often he described himself as inheriting and modifying rather than starting a tradition. Neither is it evident that Descartes held the views that are often labeled Cartesian and dualistic. Still, I think the phrase 'Cartesian dualism' is convenient, and at all events there is no need to introduce new names beyond necessity. I shall therefore try to specify a sense for the phrase 'Cartesian dualism' and employ it as a name for a body of doctrine which Dewey did criticize and which figures in the debates here considered.

But before I do so I think there is a more general issue that deserves attention. It was Lovejoy, I think, who once wittily suggested that Dewey hated the number 2, implying that Dewey was opposed not merely to dualisms but even to important distinctions. Recently Dewey has been presented by a very suggestive and sympathetic critic as a philosopher who wants "the distinction between art, science, philosophy to be rubbed out and replaced with the vague and uncontroversial notion of intelligence trying to solve problems and provide meaning." Properly qualified, this thesis may be true. Dewey often tried to show that there were important similarities between various kinds of activities; he also tried to show that both scientists and artists try to solve problems and that the products of both provide meanings. Still, similarities allow for differences. Thus Dewey did not think it was helpful or true simply to say that artists and scientists think in the same way, and he tried to specify the difference in *Art as Experience*. He thought it important that we distinguish between the roles that symbols play in art products and in scientific products. Thus we avoid thinking of art products and scientific products as competing sources of knowledge. He argued for the thesis that "science states meanings, art expresses them" (p. 84). Again, Dewey made certain claims for art that he did not make for other cultural products.

"Art," he said, "is the living and concrete proof that man is capable of restoring consciously, and this on the plane of meaning, the union of sense, need, impulse, and action characteristic of the live creature. The intervention of consciousness adds regulation, power of selection and redisposition. Thus it varies the arts without end. But its intervention also leads in time to the idea of art as a conscious idea—the greatest intellectual achievement in the history of humanity" (p. 25).

Once again Dewey can be understood as inheriting and modifying a tradition, here a form of Hegelian idealism. For idealists art is of supreme importance because it is a revelation of reality that is basically spiritual; for Dewey it is vital because it is proof of what men at their best can do. For neither is art simply a form of entertainment or a source of delight valuable only as an expression of genius. Dewey naturalized Hegel, in the sense that he tried to give a naturalistic account of all major types of experience, but there is no "phenomenology" for Dewey. "Experiences" are not to be ordered, with one more real or more important than another; each major type of experience—art, ethics, cognition—has its own reality and its own finality. We will return to this theme after considering Dewey's critique of Cartesian dualism.

Dewey's Cartesian-dualist may be understood as maintaining (a) that man is best viewed as a compound of two substances, (b) that all mental-events are private and inner, and that their owners have immediate knowledge of them, (c) that emotions and feelings are expressions of inner events or sensations, and (d) that all actions are caused by mental events that are contemporaneous with them or close to them in time.

We noted some of Dewey's criticisms of (a) and (b) when we considered his metaphysical writings and his controversy with the Realists. As also noted, (b) was further criticized by Dewey in various articles and in the article he wrote jointly with Hook and Nagel. Here the authors tried to show that there are no disembodied events and that the methods of the social sciences including psychology are continuous with those of the natural sciences. They further argued that a Deweyan type of naturalism is a viable alternative both to dualism and to materialism. Sheldon demurred; the controversy over dualism, naturalism, and materialism continues to this day.

Dewey's criticism of (c) appears in his article on Stevenson (676–687) and is reviewed in the article by Jarrett; parts of the critique have already been referred to in my brief comments on contextual naturalism. For Dewey, some emotions can be viewed as "expressions of inner states," or perhaps better, as the release or venting of inner states, but not all. Complex emotions can be understood only by reference to the beliefs and actions of the agent and are modified by the agent's actions and his reflection. Dewey's critique of (d) figures in his "Psychological Doctrine and Philosophical Teaching" and "The Objectivism-Subjectivism of Modern Philosophy" (66–75). In that article he reiterates some themes from his important early paper on the Reflex Arc Concept, where he tried to show that analogues of (d) were also defended by the behaviorists of his day. Dewey suggested that behaviorists had often substituted responses for actions and stimuli for inner private events and reasoned that actions can be viewed as sequences of responses each of which is caused by an appropriate stimulus. Dewey argued that actions, especially those undertaken to solve specific problems, must be understood and described teleologically, that specific stimuli cause specific responses which in turn cause other stimuli, and that they function as causes because the agent is trying to reach a goal or resolve a specific problem.

I should like to expand slightly on the issues alluded to here, as they relate to the "social behaviorism" to which all the authors in this volume refer.

Notice first that much of what Dewey says is relevant to the explanation and description of animal behavior. But this is no objection to his view. Dewey did stress the continuity between the animal and the human and, as he often put it, between the biological and the cultural. For all we know, when animals try to deal with their problems they have images, but images function mentally for Dewey only if they are taken as signs of or representations of certain possible states of affairs. They act, as it were, as surrogates for hypotheses. Animals have minds, since they can take events as signs of other events; humans have more complex minds, since they can engage in both sign and symbol behavior and since they have skills to acquire mastery of symbolic systems, especially linguistic systems. For Dewey there are no private minds because there are no private languages, but this is a slogan that acquires sense and significance only if we already find convincing much of what Dewey says about belief, decision, and problematic situations in many of his writings, including his *Logic*, or perhaps especially his *Logic*.

Psychology was opening up at the turn of the century, and, as is usually the case when a discipline begins, it was open both to philosophers and philosophical influences. Dewey's functional approach has been very influential and has remained of interest to psychologists, as is evident in the work of George Miller, Eugene Galanter, and K. H. Priban. Behaviorists can argue that Dewey's approach may be relevant for the explanation of why we do certain things, but not for the explanation of how we do them, and it is possible to argue against Dewey that we are able to do what we do because of appropriate stimulus-response bonding brought about by learning. But if K. S. Lashley is right, teleological considerations must be introduced even to account for how we do what we do.

Dewey's emphasis on the teleological and his view of thinking as rehearsal has, I think, been misunderstood. Some authors have argued that, for Dewey, consciousness or mind is primarily if not exclusively teleological. But this is wrong. Psychologists like G. T. Ladd have insisted that consciousness may be viewed as a recurrent grappling with problems and have been criticized by E. R. Titchener and others. It was in part to avoid this type of criticism that Dewey developed his distinction between reflective and primary experience, or the distinction between those experiences in which we are trying to test hypotheses and those in which we are not. Dewey's thesis on these points is, I think, best understood by reference to some of the debates in the late nineteenth and early twentieth century among philosophers and psychologists.

As a corollary to the point just reviewed, we note that it is misleading to say that Dewey argued that, in every experience, emotion, thought, and action are interconnected, or for some complex thesis to the effect that whenever we act we think or get to know, that thinking itself is emotional, and that emotions are always best understood as modified by and modifying action. The point for Dewey was the reverse: far too often we are only reacting; many of our beliefs do not guide action but block it; some beliefs about ultimate ends are inhibitory to inquiry in matters moral rather than contributory to it. Experiences exhibiting the union of thought, action, and emotion—to which I referred in mentioning his views about art—are for Dewey far too rare, and are rare because of unfair social arrangements or because men hold dubious theories as to what ought to be the case. In much of Dewey's writings there is a lament over the fact that, for cultural or social reasons, men have misused the gift of thought and intelligence; we are not even as "alive" as some animals are.

It is therefore wrong to conclude that Dewey was offering us a "Yankee theory of the mind," as Russell and others seem to suggest, or thought that we are always trying to solve problems—and in the most efficient manner at that. We do waste time, and it is misleading to approach the wasting of time teleologically or to ask whether we are wasting time wasting time. Dewey knew that as well as the rest of us. He did not look upon a certain kind of liberalism as an a priori codification of rationality.

Many liberals have insisted that we should try to solve specific social problems in piecemeal fashion, never challenging the basic social framework, and some have regarded Dewey as a liberal in this sense. Dewey did often ask for clear specification of a social problem before we act to solve it, but he never thought that all social problems call for piecemeal solutions. Well-defined questions in science often call for major complete overhaul of theories, and Dewey took science as a model. In point of fact he became more radical with age and called for basic social changes from at least 1929 on. His version of liberalism, which will concern us below, is compatible with radicalism. As he put it, "liberalism must now become radical, meaning by 'radical' perception of the necessity of thorough-going changes in the set-up of institutions and corresponding activity to bring the changes to pass."[14]

VI. ETHICS AND SOCIAL PHILOSOPHY

Dewey's psychological theory, or theory of the mind, contained, as we have seen, a number of distinguishable but compatible elements, conceptions of how the mind works and of how it works at its best, recommendations that we acquire certain habits, among them that of deliberation. Similar theses are involved in Dewey's defense of some of his ideals, e.g., growth. Also, of his vision of a free society, within which men and women work together to solve their problems in the interests of all, guided by the results of science, a society to be approached as we extend "the application of democratic methods, methods of consultation, persuasion, negotiation, communication, co-operative intelligence, in the task of making our own politics, industry, education, our culture generally, a servant and an evolving manifestation of democratic ideas."[15]

In each case Dewey was trying to show either that his ideas and recommended procedures are better than competing ones, more reasonable or natural, or that alternative approaches to morality are based on dubious psychological premises. Among other things, he tried to show that, in a society where men and women freely cooperate, they would voluntarily restrain themselves in those ways which most moral thinkers take to be essential; they would want to be moral. Conversely, if in our society we have to worry about how to motivate people to be moral, we should at least entertain the hypothesis that there is something amiss with the activities we are engaged in—the point here being similar to the point Dewey repeatedly made about education: if educators need to worry about how to motivate learning, there must be something amiss in the activities or institutions their students are engaged in.

Morality, therefore, for Dewey, is doubly social: some of the

---

[14] *Liberalism and Social Action* (New York: Putnam, 1935), p. 62. See, further, R. Alan Lawson, *The Failure of Independent Liberalism* (New York: Capricorn Books, 1971), pp. 99–121.

[15] *Freedom and Culture* (New York: G. P. Putnam's Sons, 1939), p. 175.

moral rules we do follow can be explained by reference to some obvious features of social life—men do not live by threat alone—some restraints on action are needed in any society—and mutual interests must be considered to assume cooperative action, which in turn is required in any society. However, the fact that men far too often ask why they ought to be moral, or all too frequently are told that they must be moral, shows that society has failed to be cooperative; some individuals have had no real role in the shaping of morality. This recurrent Deweyan theme is illustrated in the following passage:

> . . . As we have said, men did not begin to shoot because there were ready-made targets to aim at. They made things into targets by shooting at them, and then made special targets to make shooting more significantly interesting. But if generation after generation were shown targets they had had no part in constructing, if bows and arrows were thrust into their hands, and pressure were brought to bear upon them to keep them shooting in season and out, some wearied soul would soon propound to willing listeners the theory that shooting was unnatural, that man was naturally wholly at rest, and that targets existed in order that men might be forced to be active; that the duty of shooting and the virtue of hitting are externally imposed and fostered, and that otherwise there would be no such thing as a shooting-activity—that is, morality.[16]

Above I have stated that Dewey's ideal is to be realized as we apply or extend our democratic methods and procedures. Notice that there was no need, therefore, for Dewey to justify his ideal; for in addressing his fellow Americans, he took it as evident that they were already committed to democracy as a way of life. What required justification was his thesis that democracy could be saved only by extending it; and that he tried to show in a number of books and articles. This was a kind of internal criticism, for he appealed to certain American ends and ideals which he thought were already accepted, in criticizing American practice.

Theses to the effect that social events are "in principle" not controllable, which were defended by Santayana and others against both James and Dewey, seemed to Dewey to be a priori dogmas. So did the thesis that the social world is too complex for scientific enquiry and thus we can never develop adequate theories to guide action. Dewey was not haunted by the fear that social control of economic or social systems would inevitably lead to social control of people; that problem seemed to him to be soluble in a democratic society. He often presented himself as working in the tradition of

---

[16] *Human Nature and Conduct* (New York: Holt, 1922), p. 232.

Jefferson or Emerson—and what he said about Emerson could be applied to himself: "Against creed and system, convention and institution, Emerson stands for restoring to the common man that which, in the name of religion, of philosophy, of art and morality, has been embezzled from the common store and appropriated to sectarian and class use." [17]

I have alluded to many major themes and theses which are related to Dewey's ideal of a liberal society and how it is to be based on face-to-face small communities—themes and theses which are developed in Dewey's "The Future of Liberalism" and in Hocking's interesting review of *The Public and Its Problems*. It remains to show how some of these themes are related to Dewey's social psychology and other aspects of his ethical theory. In his social psychology, especially as developed in *Human Nature and Conduct*, Dewey tried to supplement his account of mental abilities and human action with a theory of native human endowment and human learning. He tried to show not merely how habits are learned but also how they are relearned by members of a society which has as one of its tasks to go from need to satisfaction, to develop habits and institutions that promise to satisfy human needs.

Needs play a role, impulse another. We are naturally endowed not only with needs, but also with a stock of impulse or energy which can manifest itself in various ways. We are also naturally endowed with a set of second-order dispositions to acquire dispositions to behavior or to desire (desire is impulse guided by intelligence), with certain native tendencies that can be directed in all sorts of ways, and we acquire habits by the redirecting of impulse. Impulse, which is a crucial and often criticized part of Dewey's theory, reappears at times of conflict to provide energy for the redirection of habit.

Dewey's theory was, thus, a type of learning model in social psychology. But, unlike other models, it stressed that habits are not only learned but continually relearned. It stressed that human habits have a certain kind of structure to them, that they are interanimated in conduct, and that appeal to habit is never sufficient to explain behavior or action. Habits often conflict, and we have to be directed by intelligence. Dewey's theory denies what has been called the "infinitely elastic," or "plastic" theory of human nature, the theory that human beings can always be taught to be satisfied with their lot or to acquire satisfactory habits, and the related view that all societies have devised the best possible habit structures, given their resources and knowledge. In addition,

---

[17] *Character and Events* (New York: Holt, 1929), pp. 75/6.

Dewey emphasizes a number of social aspects which are occasionally by-passed by other theorists. He notes, as we have seen, that certain kinds of restraints on behavior must arise because of social arrangements and, hence, that it is misleading to say that morals ought to be social: they are. He also takes it as obvious that all societies will face some similar tasks—providing food and shelter, for example—and that all societies must be designed to deal with the contingent, about which he spoke in *Experience and Nature* and elsewhere. A major point for Dewey is that intelligence must be understood in terms of the making and breaking of habits. His celebrated naturalistic analysis of "good" and his defense of the means-ends continuum are, as it were, theorems in his theory of intelligence.

In passing Dewey develops many mini-theories to support the claim that various social arrangements to deal with these invariant tasks both reflect and reinforce class differences and hierarchical social arrangements. There is much in Dewey reminiscent of Marx, and Sidney Hook has written at length and in considerable detail about some of the differences and similarities between Marx and Dewey.

Intelligence or deliberation can play a role when habits, many of which exhibit our preferences, conflict. It can also play a role when there is conflict between desires and, more generally, when we are faced with problems that cannot be solved simply by relying on already entrenched habits. In either case choice seems to presuppose preference, and might for Dewey be causally impossible or incoherent without it; for what could we appeal to when we choose? In any given case of deliberation we are deliberating on how to resolve conflict between desires, or "values" if one wishes, and hence in any given case we are taking certain values or preferences for granted—in that context these do not call for justification. But 'values' is not to be taken ontologically, as naming entities that explain preferences.

There is no realm of values whose members are cognized and whose cognition motivates choice—so Dewey argues in his debate with David Prall. He adds that the "essence" approach to value runs afoul of various epistemological arguments he has already used against the Critical Realists. There is no room for Reason to cognize the Desirable and then use its findings to criticize desire; reason or intelligence uses information about desires to find the desirable. It tries to "harmonize"—to use the ancient word—desires; I use this word with purpose, because in much of his theory Dewey goes back to Greek traditions; indeed he once identified himself as a member of the School of the revival of Greek thought. But it was not harmony he recommended here, but growth. "Not health as an end fixed once and for all, but the needed improvement in health—a continual process—is the end and good."[18] So he wrote about natural ends and also about moral virtues. For Dewey's views about growth as an ideal, see the article by Sidney Hook in section I.

For use at times of conflict, Dewey recommended the habit of deliberation—among other reasons, because, if we deliberate, we have a better chance of being rational than if we act impulsively. I say "among other reasons," for it seems to me that Dewey attributed direct utility to the use of the method of deliberation and did not justify it only by its fruits. But, like all habits, it may be overused; we may overdeliberate and fail to move from deliberation to action. Dewey, however, gave no precise rules for determining the misuse of deliberation.

Deliberation is more reasonable than alternative ways of dealing with conflict, and it is carried out in a morally acceptable way if it addresses itself to or at least takes into consideration the relevant moral factors. In his ethical writings Dewey tries to specify the kind of factors that a morally sensitive agent must take into consideration when he tries to maximize the good. The problem— the main one, perhaps, in Dewey's ethics—is to specify the features that must be taken into consideration when an agent makes direct moral judgments on what to *do* in specific cases; derived moral judgments criticizing or assessing the moral action taken will make sense only if we attend to the situation that the agent confronted. Perry and other writers find fault with Dewey's account.

I shall consider the issues by abstracting from some of the moral issues involved, and also allow myself to refer both to the articles in this collection and to some of Dewey's other writings, especially *Human Nature and Conduct*. The situation appears to be roughly this. Perry and others argue that, when an agent deliberates, he (1) considers his long- and short-term interests, (2) tries when rational to "maximize" his chances for satisfying these interests, and (3) when rational and fortunate, does so. Does Dewey have room for other theses? He seems to argue that he does, and specifically, to be arguing for the following: (4) that when an agent deliberates he may think of alternatives he would not have thought of before he deliberated; similarly, he may change his mind about what he "really" desires; (5) that, as a result of action after choice, a new interest or preference may develop, and hence it is misleading to say that choice when rational and reasonable "maximizes" short- and long-term interests which

---

[18] *Reconstruction in Philosophy*, p. 177.

are fixed, or which are not changed as a result of choice and action; and (6) that when we are in conflict we may have the power to revise our preference rankings.

It is, I think, thesis (6) that Dewey defended when he argued that "the thing actually at stake in any serious deliberation is . . . what kind of person one is to become, what sort of self is in the making, what kind of a world is making."[19] But I am not at all sure of all this and invite the reader to form his own judgment. If I am right, Dewey is arguing against two views: that action can be explained by reference to beliefs and desires fixed before deliberation, and that an agent can set ends for himself and then start desiring them because they seem to him desirable or right.

I have been discussing individual choice and deliberation. Dewey's thesis that intelligence ought to be socialized and that social institutions ought to be established that would serve the purpose of deliberating for society about its problems, raises issues analogous to those just reviewed about rationality and freedom. There seems to be a difference, however, between Dewey's account of social intelligence and that of personal intelligence. For his projected social institutions would not wait for actual conflicts to arise, but would anticipate them. In the lives of individuals, on the other hand, the role of deliberation seems to be restricted: it plays a causal role only when conflicts or difficulties are directly encountered. However, in some of his writings on educational theory, Dewey tried to show how reflection on our preferences could play a causally efficacious role even when we are not in conflict; this would be possible if habits were originally acquired in a critical way. Israel Scheffler has dealt with many of these issues in great detail.

I have noted some of Dewey's themes and views about ways of dealing with conflicts between desires and attitudes. Analogues of these appear in Dewey's views about moral conflict—conflict between obligations, or between obligation and desire, or interpersonal conflict. Once again the distinctive Deweyan theme appears: these conflicts should be seen not as a threat but as an opportunity for inquiry and an enlarged morality; the conflicts may show that there was something antecedently amiss with our commitments. Deliberation about moral matters has its own distinctive problems and patterns, which Dewey tried to specify. In many of his writings, and especially in the *Ethics* written jointly with Tufts, Dewey tried to show how one can interpret traditional moral theories as either making recommendations as to how to deal with conflict or as specifying suitable restraints on what may vaguely be called

---

[19] *Human Nature and Conduct*, p. 217.

moral deliberation. Each school of ethics can be seen to make a sound point. The non-ideal observer theory is important for noting that we must try to consider the total evidence, utilitarianism for insisting that not every attitude is a moral attitude—only one that concerns human needs and interests—and Kantianism for correctly noting the requirement of generality. We abide by these restraints in trying to deal with conflict morally in the same way as scientists try to develop a general theory that will be in accord with the data and will have explanatory content. Dewey's critique of traditional moral theories is to be found in his *The Quest for Certainty*.

Dewey's conception of moral theory is therefore different from others current. He does not think that it is the task of the moral philosopher to offer a general moral theory that will systematize and explain "our" moral beliefs. The moral beliefs of any genuine community elude systematization, because of conflict. Of course there are some moral beliefs that are shared—it is wrong to cut off babies' ears for fun—but they are too weak to build on. Neither does he think that it is the task of the moral philosopher to try to specify a moral theory that all men and women would share were they completely rational and reasonable and totally informed. There is no way a philosopher can know what such a moral theory would look like. But the task of the moral philosopher was not only analogous to the task of the philosopher of science—to specify criteria for reasonable moral theories that change over time. Dewey thought that the moral philosopher should also try to make clear the relevance of his criteria by dealing with specific moral problems and testing his criteria thereby. There is a continuity between Dewey's moral philosophy and his involvement with public affairs.

A few additional comments may be in order. In many of his writings Dewey seemed to attribute to people a desire for a unified method of dealing with moral and factual claims; he often argued that deep social problems arise when—in light of developments in the sciences—that desire seems unsatisfiable. He further argued that much in traditional philosophy can be understood as an attempt to deal with the problem of specifying a unified method for dealing with the justification of fundamental moral beliefs and "deep" factual ones. Given this approach, it is clear why Dewey repeatedly tried to show the analogies between justification in science and in matters moral—pointing out that in neither is justification based on indubitable and certain foundations, nor need it be. Naturalism plays a role in explaining convergence in scientific belief and possible convergence in moral. In the Preface to the second edition of *Human Nature and Conduct* Dewey indicated that his work in ethics is continuous with Hume's. One difference can be put as follows. Hume appealed to sympathy to account for aspects and parts of much of our morality; Dewey argued that social institutions don't allow our native sympathies to have full play.

There is also a continuity between Dewey's general moral theory and his ideal of a free cooperative society. As indicated, the hope or expectation was that, when we deal with our problems in our present society in a morally acceptable way, we will approach Dewey's ideal society.

There would be a sort of foundation for Dewey's ideal of a free cooperative society guided by intelligence if he could show that there is some deep human longing for it. But his account of native endowments (see xxxvii above) precluded that belief; there was not enough structure in original human nature to allow such a conclusion. Dewey derived some consolation from the view that the contrary could not be proved either. He saw no evidence that a liberal free society would inevitably frustrate some deep human need for authority or that a cooperative society could not flourish because men are basically self-interested; and so he argued that we must have faith in human nature and act on the belief that nothing natural makes it impossible that democratic, free societies satisfying his ideas would be self-sustaining.

Dewey was not troubled by the recognition that a liberal society begins with faith and without adequate knowledge of the truth about human nature. A liberal society is self-correcting and committed to being guided by inquiry. Hence, as the sciences develop, faith will be replaced by more adequate knowledge, which of course will always remain corrigible. There are no fixed foundations for a liberal society any more than there are fixed foundations for science.

On these points Dewey adds a characteristic twist. A liberal society committed to being guided by inquiry must become an experimental society, for only by adequate social experimentation will adaptive social scientific knowledge be available. This last thesis is not novel; related theses were defended by Bentham, Marx, and Mill. It would be good to have a comparative study of their differences and similarities in depth.

VII

Until very recently many of Dewey's theses, e.g., that of the supremacy of method, would have struck many philosophers as obvious or trite. That such reactions were widespread may perhaps be a tribute to Dewey's influence. Today some of Dewey's theses about the unity of science are being attacked from the left, as it were, and it is up to philosophers who are convinced of the basic soundness of Dewey's general approach to science as unified by its method, to meet these criticisms as I think they can be met. Others of Dewey's theses that I have mentioned are vague and others still debatable, subject to legitimate criticisms brought against him even by philosophers committed to pragmatism or instrumentalism. Dewey once wrote, "every genuine accomplishment instead of winding up an affair and enclosing it as a jewel in a casket for future contemplation, complicates the practical situation." [20] The practical situation in philosophy, for those convinced of Dewey's accomplishment, then, is to build on his work even while questioning it. For many Dewey has complicated the philosophical picture, if only because he tried to broaden its scope and significance. For him not only epistemology, but also aesthetics, metaphysics, ethics must be naturalized; in addition it is not enough for the philosopher to criticize various dubious dualisms—e.g., those between thought and action, means and ends, examine theory and practice; a philosopher should try to explain the social origin of these dualisms and note whether they reflect or buttress unfair and undesirable social arrangements.

But Dewey is capable of many interpretations, and I want briefly to consider one which has been entrenched. The belief is widespread that, according to Dewey, there is no such thing as philosophy; there are philosophers of X or Y, of science, of art. Philosophy is, as it were, a second-order activity—hard to describe, but perhaps easy enough to recognize. Furthermore, it is often claimed that Dewey's conception of the role of philosophy has not been sufficiently accepted and that philosophy suffers thereby. Randall, I think, has spoken for many when he said, "In Pasternak's book *Dr. Zhivago*, there is a character, the old uncle, who says, 'Philosophy is like horseradish. It is good if taken in small portions, and added to something else. But it is not good if taken in large portions by itself.' This gentleman would have understood Dewey. It is Dewey's genius that he knew just how to mix a small proportion of philosophical horseradish with other intellectual concerns. . . . Now there are some philosophical movements popular today [this was in 1959] that might well be judged to be 'pure horseradish'." [21]

It is interesting to note that even philosophers who hold alter-

---

20 *Human Nature and Conduct*, p. 285.

21 "The Future of John Dewey's Philosophy," JOURNAL OF PHILOSOPHY, LVI, 26 (Dec. 17, 1959): 1005–1010, p. 1006.

native views about the nature of philosophy often make their peace with Dewey by agreeing that he is important because he was a philosopher of many X's and a great philosopher of public affairs. This is intended as tribute, and so it is. Dewey was a model philosopher of public affairs—his range of interests and his ever-readiness to participate on behalf of a decent and humane society were dazzling. Dewey was not without his faults—his comments about the pacifists in World War I were disappointing to many—but on the whole he was a noble, perceptive, kind, and considerate philosopher—a philosopher of amazing energy and devotion to the common good.

Now it may very well be that all philosophy is philosophy of X, but it is very doubtful that that was Dewey's view or that his actual practice was in accord with that view. Not only did he offer general naturalistic theses, but he often tried to specify a unique function for philosophy and to deal, as I have indicated, with the problem of whether one can have a unified approach to the justification of moral and factual beliefs. This was one of the reasons why Dewey was known as a philosopher of science and freedom.

Science was of importance to Dewey not only because it was the court of appeals for theories about knowledge; it also supplied a model of a community that was stable even if its members did not share common theories or ideologies, a model of a community where cooperative action resulted in shared standards rather than presupposed them. The greater community could also progress, Dewey thought, if its members shared certain second-order attitudes about their moral beliefs analogous to the higher-order attitudes that scientists hold toward their theories. At all accounts the moral unit for Dewey was the good society, and a society is good only if its members can choose between alternative careers and ways of life and have a voice in determining what alternatives are available to them among which they can choose. Much in Dewey can be understood as trying to make sense of that view and to justify it.

Still, as I have already noted, much in Dewey is independent of the specific metaphilosophical theses just reviewed. His views about language, his critique of Cartesian dualism, his functional theories about thinking, can be judged—and ought to be judged—on their own merits. So one can appeal to Dewey's own work to justify philosophical concern with distinctive philosophical theses. Moreover, one can accept Dewey's metaphilosophy without accepting his own views about the interconnections among science, ethics, and democracy. Should one? I don't know the answer. Dewey's program, which calls for an examination of the possibilities of an integrated view about scientific knowledge and moral theory as a basis for social action, is a very difficult program; it is hard enough to work out responsible views about the nature and content of scientific knowledge. The obvious answer is a philosophical community whose members learn from one another—but philosophical communities are rare and becoming decimated. There is another problem. Dewey often appealed to many who believed that the human wish for brotherhood can, through cooperative action, become a want manifested in habit. It is hard to sustain that belief at the moment. Well, perhaps the time has come to let Dewey speak again.

We have no right to appeal to time to justify complacency about the ultimate result. We have every right to point to the long non-democratic and anti-democratic course of human history and to the recentness of democracy in order to enforce the immensity of the task confronting us. The very novelty of the experiment explains the impossibility of restricting the problem to any one element, aspect, or phase of our common everyday life. We have every right to appeal to the long and slow process of time to protect ourselves from the pessimism that comes from taking a short-span temporal view of events— under one condition. We must know that the dependence of ends upon means is such that the only *ultimate* result is the result that is attained today, tomorrow, the next day, and day after day, in the succession of years and generations. Only thus can we be sure that we face our problems in detail one by one as they arise, with all the resources provided by collective intelligence operating in co-operative action. At the end as at the beginning the democratic method is as fundamentally simple and as immensely difficult as is the energetic, unflagging, unceasing creation of an ever-present new road upon which we can walk together (*Freedom and Culture*, p. 176).

SIDNEY MORGENBESSER

JOHN DEWEY PROFESSOR OF PHILOSOPHY
COLUMBIA UNIVERSITY

Section I

DEWEY: GENERAL ORIENTATION

THE JOURNAL OF PHILOSOPHY

JOHN DEWEY, 1859–1952

THE following remarks were made at a memorial meeting in tribute to John Dewey held by the Department of Philosophy of Columbia University. They were designed primarily to give the present students in that department some sense of the quality of mind of the teachers and thinkers of an earlier generation. It is hoped that former students of these men, and perhaps even other candid minds, may find of some interest these comments, made by one to whom the intellectual personalities spoken of are still living realities. All three were connected intimately with the work of this JOURNAL, Woodbridge and Bush as founders and editors, Dewey as a faithful contributor. It has hence seemed not inappropriate for these remarks to appear in our pages.

* * *

We are met together as a department this evening in an act of piety. Piety has been defined by Santayana as devotion to the sources of one's being. And the sources of our being, as a department, in the philosophical acceptation, are the three great minds to whom this department owes whatever reputation for distinction it may have achieved, and to whom those now teaching in it owe whatever substance they may exhibit. These three great minds are Frederick J. E. Woodbridge, Wendell T. Bush, and John Dewey.

Philosophically, these three men were in very close agreement, though they employed very different languages, and hence their agreement was not always apparent at first hearing. Woodbridge employed the simple, classical Greek language of the philosophy of being; Bush, the lively, imaginative, witty language of William James, to which he added his own genius for apt figures and illustrations, always employed with what he called "metaphorical propriety." Dewey used—the language of John Dewey, which owed its difficulty primarily to being the language of the idealistic philosophy of social experience in which he grew up—a language now happily, but confusingly, forgotten.

These three were in such close agreement that when students came, after one of them had taken a potshot at the other's way of putting the truth, asking just what the difference was, I always had great difficulty in clarifying the issue, and finally gave up the

1

attempt—where they thought they differed no longer seemed to me of much consequence.

But these three men were very different in temperament and personality. Bush once remarked to me, "Woodbridge is a traditionalist, he is backward-looking. He really ought to have been a bishop. Dewey is the investigator in the laboratory, pushing always beyond the present frontiers of knowledge." This was not quite just to Woodbridge—nor was it intended to be: Bush was speaking of Dewey primarily. It was not just, because it overlooked the controlling strain of iconoclasm in Woodbridge, which made him break with all the conventions of scholarship in Greek philosophy, in the interpretation of the early Greeks, of Plato, and of Aristotle, to brush them impatiently aside, and to approach their thought freshly and directly. It made him break with all the sacrosanct dogmas of modern philosophy, and use the sanity and sobriety of Aristotle to criticise the epistemological strain that runs through it, to arrive in the end at a position difficult to distinguish from Dewey's.

But Woodbridge was definitely in the classic tradition, though he looked beyond it to much broader horizons. He saw the truth, and he made you see it too. There was no nonsense about asking your opinion. The truth didn't belong to you. But neither did it belong to him—he hated disciples who would spread "his" truth. Truth was there, impersonally, something to be discovered. That is the classic tradition.

Woodbridge was the iconoclastic institutionalist. He belonged to the best college, he belonged to the best country, he belonged to the best church. He had the best family, he had the best philosophy, and—what we all appreciated—he had the best students. He was loyalty incarnate.

Bush was the man of the world, the true Cyrenaic, who enjoyed and mastered all the world had to offer. He was a collector of essences, like his teacher Santayana. But unlike Santayana's, all his essences existed; for him, nothing that did not exist was given. His mind was utterly objective and social. But he was the student also of William James—the James whose thought he well characterized as "scientific method conscious of itself and its implications." Bush's mind was scientific method incarnate—though he directed it toward his major interests, the achievements of art, like Plato, and the objective and artistic achievements of religion. His was the temper of the true experimentalist.

One thing all three men possessed in common—the power of attracting intense personal loyalty and devotion, quite apart from any ideas they may have inculcated. They were all three magnificent teachers, though in very different ways; and all three were far more interested in doing something to their students—in making them see something, making them think—than in spreading doctrines or turning out disciples. This was true even of Dewey, who wanted above all co-workers and fellow-investigators who could help him to go further, and who had to bear the cross of disciples who hadn't gotten nearly so far as he. The loyalty and devotion each of these men evoked was to a teacher, not to a master; to a thinker, not to a system; to a personality, not to an idea.

Bush said that Dewey was the laboratory investigator. He added, in the most perceptive review written of Dewey's best book, *Experience and Nature* (which appeared in this JOURNAL), in which he characteristically avoided every one of Dewey's technical terms and talked instead about the man in the moon, that Dewey insisted on carrying on all his investigations in an historical museum, on coming to terms with all past wisdom before going on to the next point.

Dewey was not, like Woodbridge, inside the classic tradition looking out. He stood outside it, looking in. Bush was right— he was fascinated by it. That is why the two perspectives could sound very different, and at the same time be very similar—they had the same ingredients. Dewey once said, "If a philosopher ignores traditions—the classic tradition of Greece and the Middle Ages, the tradition of eighteenth-century rationalism, the tradition of German idealism, the religious and philosophic traditions of Europe—his thoughts become thin and empty [like the logical positivists']. But traditions are something to be employed. If a philosophy declines to observe and interpret the new and characteristic scene, it may achieve scholarship; it may erect a well equipped gymnasium wherein to engage in dialectical exercises [like the symbolic logic and the logical positivism against which he warned students as a "new scholasticism," in the last talk he gave to them, in this room]. It may clothe itself in fine literary art [he was thinking of Santayana]. But it will not afford illumination or guidance to our confused generation. These can proceed only from the spirit that is interested in present realities and that faces them frankly and sympathetically."

"The classic tradition" and "present realities"—for Dewey both were essential, and each was to be used to illuminate and to criticise the other. This is the source of the power of Dewey's thought. He was neither the mere traditionalist, blind to the new world and to our new intellectual resources, like Chancellor Hutchins; nor the mere contemporary experimentalist, confining his bibliography largely to his own writings, like Carnap or Reichenbach. He was what may be called an "experimental traditionalist," or a "traditional experimentalist." I prefer the former emphasis, for I think that Dewey's enduring contribution to philosophy is not to be found in those places where he exhibits himself primarily as the critic of a too narrow tradition. To be sure, the immediate impact of his thought on American civilization came from his liberating it from the rigidities and stratifications (favorite epithets of his) of the narrow Puritanism of his youth—a function performed in England, *mirabile dictu,* according to the testimony of Keynes, by G. E. Moore. But Dewey's enduring contribution is to be found where he extends and broadens the classic tradition, by setting it in the context of the wider experience of modern knowledge.

That is why *Experience and Nature* is likely to prove the book that will wear best—more so than *The Quest for Certainty,* which is too much an attempt to illustrate and prove his "position" in a field in which he was not very competent, the theory of physical science; and more so than the *Logic,* which, besides maintaining a conception of logic and its nature which belonged to his youth, and has been since repudiated by more recent logicians—who have, to be sure, their own blindnesses and limitations—is too much concerned with defending his own terminology, and too unwilling to accommodate itself to the demands of the coöperative inquiry he so rightly extols.

We all know Dewey the philosopher of education, and Dewey the social and political philosopher. What he has accomplished, in freeing American education from a narrow traditional classicism; and what he has accomplished, in introducing into social thinking the anti-formalism, the concern with concrete facts, the institutionalism, the vivid historical sense of the Hegelian tradition—and also the pluralism and the democratic feeling bred of American experience—these achievements belong to history. Dewey will remain a great spokesman of American liberal democracy of the first half of this century, and a great advocate of the direction of philosophic reflection to the "problems of men," rather than to the narrow and technical concerns of the professors of philosophy. No other philosophy in the world today can claim to offer such immediate "illumination and guidance to our confused generation," except dialectical materialism—which, as a dialectical monism, has little to offer to American experience in comparison with Dewey's experimental pluralism.

But Dewey's influence on American education has been limited to one historical era, and in the long run what will remain of it is very problematical. It may well turn out in the future that our culture will require not primarily freedom from the tyranny of the past, but the necessity of learning what is, and what has been so, and that we shall find we shall have to teach our children something—that mere education in coöperation will not be enough, and mere open-mindedness will not suffice, if there is nothing in the open mind.

And Dewey's social thought, even his epoch-making *Human Nature and Conduct,* will surely be transcended, as we gain further detailed knowledge about human nature. Dewey's famous course on social philosophy is the one major course of his he unfortunately never wrote up—though at one time he promised to do it for Howard Odum. The book in this field that will endure best, I am convinced, is *The Public and its Problems,* for there Dewey is closest to the American experience of cultural and institutional pluralism. Its fertility has not yet begun to be exhausted by social thinkers who have been recently whoring after false European gods.

What will remain, I am persuaded, will be Dewey's contribution to metaphysics. He didn't like the name, and he preferred another language—though he learned from Woodbridge what metaphysics is. But I am convinced that *Experience and Nature* is the greatest new addition to metaphysical knowledge since Spinoza—Hegel for all his insights is incredible—with its reading of the traditional metaphysical issues in terms of Dewey's functional conception of existence as experienced. Dewey took what is living in Hegel, and rejected what is dead, and reconstructed what he took in terms of his biological functionalism. Ernest Sutherland Bates, in a very penetrating review of *Philosophy and Civilization,* rightly called Dewey's thought "a pluralistic Hegelianism immersed in the concrete."

With *Experience and Nature* belongs of course *Art as Experience,* as the amplification of the culminating ninth chapter of the earlier work, in which art is exhibited as the most inclusive metaphysical category, the context in which all other distinctions in experience are ultimately made. Dewey chose the philosophy of art as the theme of his William James Lectures at Harvard, saying, "I'll show them that I am not concerned merely with means." For Dewey, art is far from being relegated to the appendix—it is the central core of his thought. And he had a first-hand familiarity with and a fine sensitivity to certain of the arts—to poetry, and, under the stimulus of A. C. Barnes, to painting, though never to music. But his book on art is primarily a metaphysical analysis, a placing of art in its context in other natural human activities.

A few years ago, when Russell's *Human Knowledge* had just come out, I had a phone call. "This is Margaret Mead. I am reading Russell's book, and I wonder whether you could tell me briefly just what is the difference between Russell and Dewey." We poor professors all get calls like that. But Margaret Mead is an intelligent girl—though she puts too much faith in improved diapers for my taste—so I made the attempt to answer her. The reply ran something like this: Dewey's greatest theoretical contribution to philosophy in general, and to metaphysics in particular, is his working out of the implications of taking "experience" as primarily the social experience of human communities. This makes "experience" all that the anthropologist includes as belonging to human "culture," instead of identifying it, as most philosophers still do, with the supposed fruits of an antiquated introspective psychology, based on isolated sensory "data." Indeed, in recent years Dewey often said he wished he had used the term "culture" instead of "experience"—it would at least have made his professional colleagues realize he was talking about something different from what they mistakenly supposed.

This anthropological—and, Dewey stoutly claimed, commonsense and broadly human—way of conceiving "experience" sets Dewey's technical philosophy off sharply from the other professed "empiricisms" of the day. Bush and Woodbridge shared this conception of experience; that is why all three were in fundamental agreement—Bush for anthropological and temperamental reasons, Woodbridge because of what he called naïve common sense. Hence, while Dewey, like so many of his generation, appealed to "experience" to criticise traditional metaphysical distinctions and concepts—to "criticise" them in the sense of putting them in their setting, in the context in which they function and have validity—he did not, like Bertrand Russell, appeal to "canoid patches"—the epistemologist's name for a dog—but to social and cultural experience, the experience of groups, to their shared experience—with very fruitful results. This is why the concepts and methods of the best anthropologists, like the critical school of Boas, for dealing with the experience of human communities, seemed so promising to Dewey. Hence on the theoretical side his thinking can be called the philosophic expression of our most successful and critical sciences of man, of anthropology.

Dewey called his philosophical position "experimentalism," and he had great faith in the "experimental methods" of science. This awakened little enthusiasm in those who had already found the Truth—from rival professional philosophers with systems of their own, to the followers of the various party lines—little enthusiasm among all those who know just what other people need and what is really good for them. Dewey hadn't found the Truth, and he was not sure he knew what is best for men. He was still looking for more wisdom. He had a good deal of confidence in scientists and their methods, because they too are looking for more truths— that is what "science" meant to him, not a logical system, a formalized set of conclusions, but looking, "inquiry."

Dewey thought, if you can learn more it ought to make a dif- ference in the way you do things. Knowledge for him seemed to have a relevant contribution to make to wisdom. He probably would not have emphasized the Greek and Hegelian background of this insight. He liked to impute it to simple common sense—it's helpful to think about human problems, and to talk them over. This notion, that knowledge and thinking have any relevance to "values," is of course anathema to all theologians, and to most professional philosophers today.

What the evangelists of the various ready-made faiths call Dewey's "scientism" is not an admiration for a hard, "value-free" technical efficiency. It is not even the American faith in gadgets. Dewey was no mechanical genius, and his struggles with a Model-T Ford are among my earliest memories of him. He was the kind of Vermonter who becomes a school teacher, not the kind who becomes an inventor or industrialist. Next door to his birthplace in Bur- lington is a house with a bronze tablet indicating that here Atwater Kent was born. Dewey's house has no tablet. Kent will probably need his.

No, Dewey was hopeful of scientific methods because they help you find out something you didn't know before. Surprisingly enough, in view of our present fashion today of regarding science and knowledge as the source of all our evils, this struck him as a good thing. He was convinced we don't know enough yet, not nearly enough, especially about human affairs, about wisdom. It's easy to feel that way about other people—most of us do. But Dewey felt it about himself. Unlike most intellectuals, he was not even sure he knew what other people need better than they do themselves. Far too intelligent to be an intellectual, he thought you might find out more about what people need by asking them, by talking it over with them. They know where the shoe pinches better than you do.

This respect for the experience of other men, this willingness to learn from them what they have found out, above all, to learn by working with them, is the very core of John Dewey the man, and it is the core of his philosophy as well. From the point of view of the assorted absolutists—chancellors, commissars, or cardinals— who already know all the answers, this has been Dewey's unforgivable sin. He hadn't found The Truth, and he actually thought that other men were as likely to discover more of it as he or you or I. He had a curious, faintly old-fashioned faith, that men can really hope to learn something of wisdom by working together on their common problems. Think what this idea would do to original sin, or the true church, or the dialectic of history!

It is easy for our sophisticated young intellectuals today to feel that philosophy, like the world, has passed beyond Dewey. Those who never knew him personally have been known to assign him to the Age of Innocence—that simple, unpretentious, genuine, but incredibly shrewd and sharp Vermonter! In the thirties, of course, Dewey was only a "liberal"—while the bright young set had just discovered Marx, and now knew the Truth. The same set today is not so sure about that Truth. The brilliant young Neo-orthodox theologians, who had just discovered that Santa Claus isn't going to bring the Kingdom of God this Christmas, turned up their noses at Dewey—he still hoped we might make some progress, he had never heard of Sin—Dewey, who grew up in the heart of Calvinism! It is the fashion today, in certain philosophical circles, to be disdainful of Dewey's contention that philosophers should concern themselves with the problems of men. They find the problems of logicians so much easier! And most recently of all, even the problems of logicians and mathematicians seem too useful and too vulgar for the latest crop of analysts.

Whenever you went to Dewey, and asked him why he didn't adopt the latest jargon, why he didn't try to translate his thought into the prevailing fashionable terminology, so that he might be more clearly understood, he would smile that inimitable smile of his, and say, "I want to leave something for you young fellows to do." He has left something for us. He has left a liberalism that is opposed to all absolutistic totalitarianisms, a faith that intelligence and education can do something about "sin"—that individuals can become more individual by working together and sharing their experience, a faith that there was never a more crying need for philosophy than today—for technical philosophy—if only it doesn't sink into a sterile scholasticism, but has the imaginative sweep of the great thinkers, and the courage to work out new theories—a philosophy that is genuinely experimental, willing to push out into the unknown.

The best way of honoring Dewey is to work on Dewey's problems—to reconstruct his insights, to see, if need be, farther than Dewey saw. If it may be given to us to see farther, it will be largely because he pointed out to us where to look. In that way, you and I can be really working with Dewey, as he always wanted us to do, and sharing in that enjoyed meaning that was, and is, and will continue to be John Dewey.

JOHN HERMAN RANDALL, JR.

COLUMBIA UNIVERSITY

VOLUME LVI, No. 26   DECEMBER 17, 1959

JOHN DEWEY—PHILOSOPHER OF GROWTH *

ONE of the most endearing features of John Dewey's personality was his openness to ideas and suggestions whatever their source. At the very height of his philosophical career and even towards its very close, he was always sensitive to the possibility of new facets and dimensions of experience, to new problems and to new aspects of old problems. He was rarely satisfied with his own formulations. What he sent to the press was never a final version of his ideas but the latest draft of a position which was not yet completely thought out in his own mind and which he sincerely hoped would be developed by others. A few months after his 90th birthday had been celebrated, he remarked: "Only in the last two years have I come to see the real drift and hang of the various positions I have taken." And when death came, it interrupted him in the midst of a new interpretation of the history of modern philosophy. The world for him was more than we can ever say about it and he was convinced that every reflective mind could refract the many-colored scene of human activity in a distinctive and interesting way.

* A talk delivered in the Rotunda of the Low Memorial Library, October 20, 1959, on the occasion of the presentation of the letters of John Dewey, written to Mrs. Corinne Frost, to Columbia University.

Some of John Dewey's theories in philosophy were revolutionary, so much so that his conception of thinking and of mind could only with difficulty be expressed in terms of the inherited incoherencies of the traditional philosophical vocabulary. But his conception of philosophy was as old fashioned as that of Socrates. Philosophy for him was a quest for wisdom, a survey of existence from the standpoint of value, a criticism of the methods by which we appraise the modes and values of experience. What the professional philosopher does—or should do—systematically, other men and women do episodically. He was therefore prepared to heed and follow up any intimation of truth, any insight or vision that lit up the human scene, in complete independence of its academic credentials. It was the authenticity of the experience which engaged his interest, and he had a rare feeling for it.

John Dewey's correspondence with Mrs. Frost differs only in volume and duration from the vast correspondence which he carried on with many others. There is hardly anyone who wrote to Dewey who did not receive a reply from him. This was not only because of his innate courtesy but in most cases because of the enkindling effect of what others said and thought upon him. He often told me that he was indebted for some of his seminal ideas to men and women who had tried to make sense of their own experience without the benefit of the technical idioms of the philosophical schools and traditions. If he had any partiality it was for those who wrestled with problems at first hand in the thick of life-situations. The fact that others, with whom he sometimes sought to share his discoveries, could not always see the glimmer of light in the dark and obscure passages of the manuscripts and letters he received, led to no alteration in his judgment, to no weakening of his confidence. For, judging all things by their fruits, he was convinced that anything which suggested fresh thought to him must be itself inherently or potentially thoughtful.

The same attitude which John Dewey displayed toward his correspondents he revealed during his long career as a teacher. Judged by the external trappings of the dynamic classroom teacher, John Dewey was among the worst teachers of the world. He was completely devoid of the histrionic arts which a good teacher, even when he follows Dewey's principles, must summon up to awaken interest or command attention, and which always facilitate communication between teacher and student when attention is lagging. It is not likely that he would ever have been chosen as a master teacher for television, especially at an hour when the audience is struggling to stay awake. Nonetheless John Dewey was a great teacher for those students whose interests had already been aroused in ideas and who were struggling to articulate their philosophical insight. Dewey's reaction to his students' efforts to see and to say things freshly was not to refute but to encourage, to help ideas get stated. He was more patient with his students than they were with each other. In one of his letters he says that "delaying is one manifestation of the active potency of time"—and he charitably interpreted groping and obscure formulations as such delay. Teaching for him (when he wasn't lecturing) was a kind of intellectual collaboration. Students were helped to overcome their native self-doubt by an unexpected accession of unsuspected intellectual power that often provided the momentum to surmount what had seemed formidable obstacles. With the rarest of exceptions, this was Dewey's unfailing attitude even to those of his students who had come to Columbia University innoculated against his philosophy by previous teachers and who used his ideas as scratching posts for the development of their dialectical teeth and claws. Having been trained by Morris R. Cohen as an undergraduate to believe that pragmatism was a philosophy which made our wishes, which were real, into horses, which were imaginary, I constituted myself the official opposition for an entire year in one of Dewey's large lecture classes, to the annoyance not of Dewey but of my fellow students who objected to the constant interruption of their slumber. I became converted to pragmatism in the most unpragmatic way. With Dewey's encouragement I sat down to write what I thought would be the definitive refutation of pragmatism on the basis of Peirce's theory of leading principles. The argument carried me to conclusions I did not wish to reach—and protesting all the way, I went to Dewey himself, after Morris Cohen failed me, to tell me what was wrong in where I was coming out. This time, too, Dewey encouraged me but with a grin. He could find nothing wrong with the argument.

There is no doubt that Dewey encouraged too many, and I suspect that he sometimes realized this. But he knew what he was doing. He was more fearful of encouraging too few, of withering with chill winds of criticism or imperious demands for immediate clarity insights struggling to be born, of inhibiting powers on the verge of development. Some of his professional colleagues felt there was enough error and nonsense in the world and that what could not stand up against the sharp sickle of criticism was hardly worth cultivating. Dewey's attitude was that one genuine insight or fruitful vision was worth the risk of many errors. It was not that he was tolerant of error. He believed, however, that in honest inquiry even errors could play a constructive function, that we could learn from them to devise "the means of invention and circumvention'' which marks creative intelligence at work in the process of growth. What he prized above all was the quality of *becoming* in human beings.

All who knew John Dewey have at one time or another said that he lived his philosophy as well as taught it. In his living and in his teaching he regarded growth as the key educational and moral value. I am firmly convinced that when all the dust of controversy settles, John Dewey will be regarded as the philosopher of human growth in the age of modern science and technology, as the philosopher who saw man not as a creature with a fixed nature, whether conceived as a fallen soul or a soulless configuration of atoms, but as a developing mind-body with an historical career, who because he does something in and to the world, enjoys some degree of freedom, produces consequences never witnessed before, and leaves the world different from the world into which he was born.

The concept of growth, as John Dewey understood it, is not a simple one and some analysis is necessary to see its central position in his thought. As everyone knows, in his *Democracy and Education* Dewey maintained that there was no one end or goal in education to which everything else was subordinate. The closest to an all-inclusive educational end was the principle of growth itself conceived participially as the process of *growing*. This brought the retort that there are all sorts of growth in experience, some of them vicious, some even fatal to their subjects as well as, so to speak, to their objects, or victims. Unless growth has a direction, there is no genuine development. Unless we have antecedent knowledge of what is good, we do not know if the development is even desirable. We sometimes find ourselves wishing not only that something wouldn't grow but that it had not come to be.

Dewey used to reply to this that growth in education as in life develops the standards by which its direction and desirability are judged. There is growth and growth. There is the growth which generates obstacles to further growth, and the growth which creates the conditions for further growth. There is growth which prevents and growth which encourages the processes of education. The important thing, said Dewey, is that ''the conception of growth must find universal and not specialized limited application.''

It is questionable whether this ever satisfied Dewey's critics. But it is obvious that for Dewey growth is an inclusive and not a single exclusive end. It embraces *all* the positive intellectual, emotional, and moral ends which appear in everybody's easy schedule of the good life and the good education—growth in skills and powers, knowledge and appreciation, value and thought. For

Dewey, however, it is not enough to list these ends; they must be brought into living and relevant relation to the developing powers and habits and imagination of the individual person. We grow not by worshiping values but by realizing them in our daily behavior. The pattern of realization is an individual thing even when the values are common. There are different rates of growth, different styles of growth; but when they maximize our powers to grow they are all ways by which we grow in maturity. We are mature to the extent that we form habits of reasonable expectation on the basis of what we know about the world, our fellows, and ourselves—to the extent that we can cope with an ever-changing environment, make sense of new experience, and escape both the petrifactions of routine and the blind outburst of impulse. The growth, consequently, which Dewey identifies with genuine and desirable education is a shorthand expression for the direction of change in a great variety of growths—intellectual, emotional, and moral. It excludes, therefore, the kinds of growth which interfere with or reverse the direction of change in this variety of growths— it excludes growths in prejudice, arbitrariness, hate, invidious prestige, power and status, and even that miscellany of knowledge which burdens a mind not in training for a quiz show. More important still, it becomes clear why in the interests of growth Dewey became a critic of specialized and narrow vocationalism, of merely professionalized education, and why he became the protagonist of a liberal and general education for *all*. The same analysis that has been made of growth as an educational end can be extended to Dewey's assertion that in ethics "Growth itself is the only 'moral' end." Dewey should not have said "only" but "central" or "most inclusive."

Dewey's concern with growth and the emphasis he gives it, flowed in part from his post-Darwinian naturalism. Man is as authentic a part of nature as other things which have careers in time, but he is a part of nature which, to keep its very equilibrium and to remain alive, must enter actively into the processes that condition its very nature. Man must grow with the things which challenge him in this contingent and dangerous world or else he dies. Dewey had the courageous but not unqualified optimism of a man embattled in perpetual struggle for a *better* world. The effort and risk were worth making even against odds. His optimism was never on that stupendous cosmic scale of his supernaturalist critics who believed that man could find a final peace by a faith in or a leap to some transcendental source. Although the world can be made less contingent and less dangerous, it will never be a safe place for man because of the very differences his own growth, especially the growth of his knowledge, makes to the world. Dewey believed that in a world of rapid change man must find peace in action rather than withdrawal. Events have a way of breaking in the doors by which we would seek to escape them. To be serene in the very midst of affairs is the "top of sovereignty."

Because there are various kinds of growth and failures to grow, there are various kinds of death. In one of his letters to Mrs. Frost, Dewey writes of "that large class of people who live on the physical plane and who find such ease in their dogmas of habituation that for all practical purposes they are lifeless." Dewey would have said the same thing about those whose mental life is lived only in the after-glow of their memories, memories of past triumphs and achievements. They, too, have effectively ceased living. To live is to grow with the problems and challenges of the present, and whatever helps realize the processes of growth helps us to stay alive and intellectually young. "Keeping young," writes Dewey, "seems to be a function of using maturity as a source of new [experiences] and contacts."

There is another aspect of Dewey's concept of growth and another sense in which he intended the conception of growth to be given "a universal and not a specialized limited application." We tend to think of growth as primarily a biological or psychological category, but *human* growth cannot be understood without going beyond biology and psychology whose terms are abstracted from the inclusive social and cultural matrix. The organism grows not only in and with its natural environment; it grows with other organisms in society. There are societies (perhaps it is better to say there are families, for as yet there is only a vision of such societies) in which growth is the ideal norm *for all*. It was because he took the growth of every individual person as his moral ideal that Dewey committed himself so wholeheartedly to democracy. Discussing the idea that the object of learning should be continued capacity for growth, he writes: "This idea cannot be applied to all the members of a society, except where the intercourse of man with man is natural, and except when there is adequate provision for the reconstruction of social habits and institutions by means of wide stimulation arising from equitably distributed interests. And this means a democratic society!" He links the ideas of growth and democracy more explicitly in a passage in which he says: "A society of free individuals in which all, through their own work, contribute to the liberation and enrichment of the lives of others is the only environment in which any individual can really grow normally to his full stature." This is an overstatement—for if it were true we should have to conclude that no individual has ever grown to his full stature. But its very over-emphasis should indicate how important for Dewey democracy as a moral ideal is. It indicates also that "the liberation and enrichment" of life is integral to the meaning of desirable growth. The phrase "the liberation and enrichment" of life signifies a great many values which when stated abstractly sound platitudinous and preachy but which taken in the context of Dewey's philosophy of education, art, society, religion, and conduct are immensely suggestive. The "liberation and enrichment" of life consists in the experiences of happiness and delight, intellectual adventure, friendship and love, knowledge and art, of unity with the world and ourselves—and of many other things. But to aim at these values for all involves a program of profound social reconstruction.

Long before the discovery of nuclear energy and its vistas of tremendous power were even dreamed of, Dewey was convinced that modern science and technology had given man an unprecedented opportunity to reconstruct his social world. Man can no longer be reasonably considered as an object of historical forces but as a co-determiner of his own history. Granted the importance of natural resources, armed with science men themselves become the most important of all natural resources provided only that they have the desire and resolution to make use of their knowledge. Dewey maintained that once men set out to put knowledge and intelligence to use, the relevant test of all social institutions becomes their impact upon the quality of human life and experience. No more radical criterion can be envisaged, for it applies not only to the operation of the *status quo* but just as much to all proposals to modify it or revolutionize it.

One of the ironies of intellectual history is that despite Dewey's sharp indictment of industrial society in America and his criticism of the cult of the practical and useful, he himself has been charged with an easy acquiescence in the values of machine civilization, and of elaborating a philosophy of practice which lends itself to its justification. It is true that Dewey regarded the periodic complaints against the industrialization of culture as a romantic nostalgia for times that were not recoverable. But only a perverse misreading of what Dewey understood by "the useful" can account for the rest of the criticism. His meaning was made clear in his demand during the days of the depression: "Regiment *things* and free *human beings.*" He believed the first could be achieved through scientific technology and the second by scientific social inquiry and the arts of democratic government. He dared our age, which worships science almost superstitiously but ignores its rationale, and the social implications of its logic and ethics, to apply scientific method to the problem of making industry serve men, to the problem of liberating human energy and humanizing its expression, to the problem of organizing industrial relations in order to meet the imperatives of educational growth.

For Dewey, scientific method or planning in the interests of efficiency and production is one thing—and by far not enough. Here commodities, their quantity and rate of output, are king— and everything which bears upon the quality of life of the maker and the user of commodities is disregarded as irrelevant. Scientific method in the interests of the humanly useful is quite another thing for Dewey—and the only rational basis for social criticism. It is instructive to note, as the critics have *not* done, how Dewey defines the useful. "To be useful," he says, "is to fulfill need. The characteristic human need is for possession and appreciation of *the meanings* of things." From this point of view "the only thing essential to the idea of utility is its inherent place and bearing in experience." It remains only to relate that inherent place and bearing in experience to the needs of personal growth.

In one of his early popular writings Dewey describes the lot of most members of industrial society in terms of a contrast between "living one's life" and "earning one's living." He implies that a society worthy of men would be one in which, as men earned their living, they would have opportunity for the growth and self-fulfillment which are required both for a sense of significance and a sense of enjoyment in life. This explains why Dewey placed such great emphasis on the importance of vocations—on life callings —and why he considered an education conducted without any reference to it a leisure class pursuit. But for all of Dewey's optimistic expectations about the power of applied science, the effects it wrought were greater, if not better, than he had imagined. It is an open question whether all or even most work in modern industrial society can be made meaningful, whether it can engage the individual's interest and creative capacity so as to make possible that feeling of significant achievement which the good teacher or physician or skilled craftsman has. The prospective consequences of applied science, once the danger of war is lifted and full use can be made of nuclear energy, make problematic not so much the achievement of meaningful vocations as the meaningful use and enjoyment of leisure.

Far from undermining, this reinforces the importance Dewey gives to growth as the encompassing and justifying end of education. During his life Dewey was just as keen a critic of the leisure-time activities of our society as of its mechanical and industrial processes whose impress they reflected. To what extent, he asked, do the leisure-time activities of the great masses of individuals contribute to their intellectual and emotional growth, to a liberal and humane outlook on affairs, to a deeper sympathy for all suffering creatures, to a wider appreciation and more reflective judgment of values, beliefs, and conduct, to a richer and more diversified personal experience? Very imperfectly, is his answer. Life is certainly easier than it used to be; and as far as the burden of physical toil is concerned, it will be much easier in the future. But it is far from obvious that human lives will by that fact alone be more meaningful and satisfying than they used to be.

For these and other reasons Dewey's philosophy of growth possesses a continuing *actualité* not only to basic problems of education and public policy but to the whole of human experience. Dewey is the philosopher of human freedom in this our revolutionary age of modern science, whose faith in man is rooted in faith in the arts of intelligence. Alfred North Whitehead in assessing Dewey's influence once said that the magnitude of his achievement "is to be estimated by reference to the future"—a future in which Whitehead confidently asserted that "for many generations the North American Continent will be the living center of human civilization." Events since Whitehead wrote have made that prediction another illustration of how contingent the universe is. The living center of human civilization has shifted many times and in the future there may be more than one center. But we can with assurance predict that wherever that center is, if those who live in it are imbued with a passion for human freedom and an equality of concern for all persons to reach their maximum growth as human beings, it will find a guiding and coherent philosophy in the thought of John Dewey.

SIDNEY HOOK

NEW YORK UNIVERSITY

The following five articles, by William Ernest Hocking, C. I. Lewis, Joseph Ratner, Frederick J. E. Woodbridge, and John Dewey, were read at a symposium on The Philosophy of John Dewey at a joint meeting of the Eastern and Western Divisions of the American Philosophical Association, December 30, 1929, at Columbia University, New York City.

The Journal of Philosophy

ACTION AND CERTAINTY [1]

DEWEY'S philosophy is not a set of propositions: it is a national movement. On good instrumental grounds this is what it ought to be. To this extent Dewey might be willing to agree that the real and the ideal are one! At any rate, on his own theory, the right way to estimate his philosophy would be to examine, not the propositions, but the movement.

Before I grasped this point I wasted much labor in the attempt to criticise Dewey's propositions. In 1897 or thereabouts I published a complete refutation of the Dewey-McClelland method of teaching number. That method proposed to define numbers by ratios, so that the number one was expounded, not as the first cardinal integer, but as the ratio of anything to another thing of the same size. It thus required two objects to define "one." Pointing this out in my first philosophical essay, I received my first philosophical shock in the perfect impassivity with which Dewey received his theoretical ruin. I doubt whether to this day he is aware of the disaster, or of the existence of my article. Occasional subsequent onslaughts on my part have been equally conclusive.

I might be inwardly troubled, even now, by this godlike calm of Dewey's under fire if I had not recently witnessed his equal serenity under a great wave of world-wide good-will—not untouched, but adequate and unperturbed. Living as he does in a sphere beyond the good and evil of praise and criticism, I have come to regard him as an authentic human symbol of The Absolute! I shall therefore not hesitate, on this occasion, to renew the discussion. That, I think, is what he would desire. I can imagine him saying, as Socrates—under less happy circumstances—once said: "To-day, if we can not revive the argument, you and I will both shave our locks"!

But let me begin by saying something of what I have learned from this philosophy. I owe much to the habit, painfully acquired, of looking for the meaning of terms and propositions in what they lead to, and especially in what they lead us to do. The blank face of a proposition is deceptive: its very self is in its working out. I venture even to embroider a little upon this theme. The work of a proposition is often less a construction than a fight. It has been of

[1] Read at the meeting of the American Philosophical Association, December 30, 1929, New York City.

the greatest help to me, especially in reading the history of ideas, to consider propositions in terms of their *fighting-value*.

Take the proposition, All men are created equal, as it came from the pen of Thomas Jefferson. What did Jefferson suppose that to mean? Mr. Archibald Grimke accuses Jefferson of insincerity because he was, and remained, a slave-holder. But Jefferson's eye was on another battle. His dictum had nothing to do with the fight against slavery, but with the fight against a governing class, pretending a natural superiority and a divine right. This was the fighting-meaning of his thesis, and he can not on this count be called insincere.

Or consider the doctrine of Nationality as it appeared in the nineteenth century. The foreign ministers of Great Britain evoked this principle in order to support the efforts of Greece and Italy to become autonomous. It did not occur to them that zealous formal logicians would extend the same principle to India and other portions of the Empire. That doctrine was intended by them to do specific work in Europe; an indiscriminate extension to other fields and other campaigns, however true to the verbal surface, was false to the fighting-sense of the idea.

In public law and in theology, the interpretation of all general formulae must be sought in their original fighting-purport, and logical extension runs the risk of complete impertinence. The Monroe Doctrine in its own day had specific work to do: for Roosevelt, by logical extension, it did vastly different work; and now, still other and unexpected work—as in raising misunderstanding with our neighbors to the South and in hindering our coöperation with the League of Nations. The charge of insincerity here rests rather upon the logicians than upon those who look to the original fighting-value of the formula.

I presume that instrumentalism itself has a fighting-value, and that much of its meaning lies therein.

It has clearly some important work to do, not solely in the minds of the philosophical fraternity, but in the minds of wide masses of the American people. Now this people has been, and is, a vigorously active people; and it has been widely assumed that this practical bent has predisposed us to be pragmatists. This, I believe, is the precise reverse of the truth. It is a commonplace of social psychology that the active temper tends to dogmatism: the active man, like the active crowd, needs to assume something as fixedly true, beyond the reach of enquiry, a *pou sto* that justifies and supports a strong thrust. Common action nourishes itself on slogans, not on hypotheses, and the typical "man of action" displays a set jaw and an unyielding maxim. It is because we are dominantly a people of deeds that we are inclined to be a dogmatic nation, believing stiffly in eternal principles, final conventions, natural rights, an unchanging Constitution and mechanical theologies. The great public work of the instrumental philosophy has been to limber up the ways of knowing of this people, to reduce fixed dogmas to working-hypotheses fit for experiment; to give the intellectually traditional, authority-seeking, hero-worshipping American the courage of his own experience. As a people we do believe in the dignity of labor (and so far as I can see, we are the only people under the sun, unless it be Russia, who really have that belief in their bones). We must carry this belief over into the dignity of *a laboring philosophy*, arising out of and pertinent to existing crises, not to ancient ones.

It is because America is *not* instinctively pragmatic that pragmatism has had, and still has, much fighting work to do.

Among the professionals likewise, it has to combat those traits which lend support to this impulsive popular dogmatism, such as the idle securities and finalities of abstract truth, or the lingering traces of those gods of Epicurus who do not concern themselves with human affairs. Especially it has been charged to widen the scope of the inductive methods, hypothesis and verification, in the field of social philosophy, and thereby to render our moral thinking flexible and contemporaneous—not to destroy the law and the prophets, nor yet to fulfill them (for that, too, would be looking backward in a way), but to endow them with the divine capacity of perpetual self-regeneration.

This is to make philosophy a highly responsible undertaking, indeed the most responsible of human enterprises. It is at once a promise to the common man that philosophy shall mean something to him; and it is a promise (not without an admonition) to the philosopher that when he has given his thinking its due prospective significance, philosophy will once more bear its due part in the national life. When our work becomes so much a matter of public importance that some one of us is asked to drink the hemlock, solely on account of his philosophical teaching, then at least we shall have learned a part of the lesson of instrumentalism.

These, in my judgment, are some of the continuing good works of instrumentalism; they constitute its instrumental truth.

And now I have to record why I am not wholly satisfied with this variety of truth. I believe that we must continue to judge the validity of propositions in some independence of their working. If this is true, it will not be out of place to look once more at the propositions of instrumentalism apart from their working- or fighting-value.

(The mere fact that we can make this distinction goes to illustrate the argument. And if the instrumentalist should be so unwary as to defend these propositions, merely as propositions, his defense would amount to a surrender of his position. For he would be recognizing meaning apart from working. In this case, the theoretical critic has the field to himself, and the argument comes to an abrupt end. Let us waive this point!)

It would hardly be necessary to restate these familiar propositions except to show what limited portion of Dewey's philosophy I plan to deal with, and to make clear what version of his doctrine I am taking for discussion. The central thesis of instrumentalism I take to be this:

(1) That the meaning of conceptions and propositions is always functional. They spring, not out of blank presentation, but out of hesitation, perplexity: they are projects of solution, promissory and hypothetical in character. Their validity or truth consists in doing what they thus claim to do, namely, in resolving the difficulty, and in being, in this sense, verified.

From this would necessarily follow these corrollaries:

(2) That there is no strictly immediate truth;

(3) That there is no strictly stable or eternal truth;

(4) That there is no *a priori* truth; and, in sum,

(5) That there can be no significant theoretical certainty.

My effort will be, not to introduce novelty into the examination of these doctrines, but simply to express as clearly as possible my persisting difficulties, and to reduce them, where I can, to a principle.

My difficulty with the first proposition, the definition of trueness, tends to condense itself into a principle which we might call *the non-correspondence of meaning and working.* To every conception and to every general proposition there may be attached an indefinite variety of workings; to every working, in turn, a variety of meanings. If the meaning were to be found in the working, there should be a unique and unambiguous correspondence betweeen these entities: this correspondence does not exist.

Our proposition, All men are equal, will serve to illustrate the point. Not all of this proposition was at work in Jefferson's day: more and other work was capable of coming out of it. In spite of Jefferson's pre-occupation, it was legitimate to set that same generality to work on the slavery business: it still has work on hand, far beyond Jefferson's horizon, in the treatment of backward peoples, and who knows what further, to the end of time. Its identity and life as a proposition can not be limited by the special perplexities of any one age. Nor can it be identified with the sum of a series of the indefinitely many possible workings it may sponsor. For it has a present meaning of some sort, whereas many of these possible programs of action are, at any given time, not so much as contemplated.[2] If we only know a thing when we see what comes of it, then indeed, we never know anything; for we never have in hand what is yet to eventuate.

Look at this non-correspondence from the other end. Assume (what is not highly improbable) that Jefferson began first with his fight and then cast about for a generality to sanction the conflict he felt to be inevitable. Is it logically required that he should have lighted on just this maxim about human equality? If we knew by inspection just what universal is exemplified in a given particular, law, induction, and living would be much simpler than they are. The versatility of mathematicians and physicists in setting up divergent hypotheses which lead to the same phenomena has prepared us to believe that no course of action is uniquely dependent upon any one theoretical premise. If the meaning is to be found solely in the progress from problem to solution-in-action, we should have to agree that any one of a number of "rationalizations" of this process would be verified by its success. This conclusion being eminently unacceptable, we are driven to locate the center of meaning in the proposition, and to regard it as separable from any specific course of action.

The non-correspondence between meaning and working begins in the process of conception, as an incommensurableness between *objects* and *interests*.

I am hungry: that is a state of dissatisfaction, favorable for starting a thinking process. I see a red apple: I at once conceive it as a possible food. That conception is clearly functional: it is a promissory hypothesis and carries a plan of action definitely related to my hunger. But I note that the redness of the apple, or for that matter its apple-ness, has no essential relation to its food-interest. A baked potato would do the same. I can not, therefore, regard the apparition of the apple as being just covered by, or

---

[2] The class of all the possible programs of action derivable from a given generality is a class which is in fact never contemplated, and which is probably in strict logic not contemplable. But the meaning of the proposition is contemplable, otherwise it would be impossible to "apply" it to new circumstances, or to "deduce" from it further plans of action. From what are the new applications derived? Surely not from previous programs, such as Jefferson's. Then from something distinguishable therefrom: that something different is the meaning of the proposition.

It must be noted, too, that some programs may lead to auspicious, others to inauspicious conclusions; some may eventuate as they promise, others may lead to disappointment. The solving, or verifying, outcome of any one group of programs can not guarantee that of others. Hence no finite series of verifications can constitute the truth.

exhausted in, that food-interest; nor is my food-interest exhausted in the apple. There is something in the apple-fact, and therefore in the apple-idea, which extends beyond any interest and any process which I then and there project. The active-meaning omits much of the fact-meaning: the fact-meaning (or object-idea) appears primary, admitting the active-meaning as a temporary rider, due to a momentary and somewhat accidental relationship. The fact-meaning, based on presentation, contains indeed the possibility of much as yet unimagined use and interest, and also the exceptional possibility of uselessness. But the two, object and interest, clearly have no common measure and there is no way to make them precisely congruent. Thus the instrumental element in idea-making presupposes an immediate or presentational element as more fundamental.

In his notable chapter on "The Play of Ideas,"[3] Dewey recognizes the absence of one-to-one correspondence between ideas and plans of action. He does not, however, draw the consequence which seems inescapable, namely, that the working-test of truth is in a perilously loose relation to the proposition tested, and will yield to a more direct test when we can get it.

The lover, unable to perceive directly how he stands in the regard of his beloved, is driven to the method of hypothesis and verification: "If she loves me, she will make a friendly response to this advance, appear at the window when I sing, answer this letter." He must rest his case for the moment on a succession of progressively bolder pragmatic tests. The beloved, in the same situation, if she finds herself forbidden the initiative implied in all experiment, may be momentarily reduced to plucking the petals from daisies—I am not sure whether this is instrumental! But both maintain a hope for the more nearly immediate evidence of avowal, and the ideal of telepathic perception. Such immediate evidence is indeed dangerous evidence, in this case, without a long-continued series of good works; but clearly that series of works might attain pestilential length unless it could sometime soon reveal its essential inwardness by direct expression.

Or take an instance like this: In the study of radioactivity, it early became a question whether these so-called "rays" are really vibrations or discrete particles shot off from radio-active elements at high velocity. Somebody is led to suspect that the *alpha*-rays are nothing more nor less than positively charged atoms or helium. But there is no hope of observing directly any such ray, still less an individual atom of helium. So one tests deductions from the hypothesis, such as this, that the atomic weights of elements in the uranium-

---

[3] *The Quest for Certainty,* pp. 156, 158.

radium series ought to differ by multiples of the atomic weight of helium, which turns out to be the case. This and other verifications tend to confirm the hypothesis; but they still leave it possible (and widely believed) that these hypothetical atoms are merely signs for reckoning, with only a remote symbolic relationship to any spatial fact.

Now one day Sir William Crookes invents the spinthariscope. And here under a lens one perceives, not the atoms to be sure, but the individual sparkles which occur when these minute entities bombard the screen of zinc sulphide there focussed. The collisions can be located and counted. The helium atom takes on a numerical and spatial individuality. This kind of corroboration of the hypothesis has a wholly different cogency from that of successful practical prediction. It is presentational. Manipulative activities are required to get it; but they are *irrelevant to its force.* The primary meaning of verification lies there, and we resort to it whenever we can get it.

Since only a part of a general proposition can do work at any time, an instrumental confirmation can always be had for a proposition which is only partially true.

Half-truths actually do a vast amount of valiant service in the world, namely, when they announce that half which is for the time being ignored. Thus, if men are too well steeped in tradition, it is in order to preach the gospel that "All things change." This half-truth will for a time be instrumentally justified. Then, when under this teaching men have become so flexible and shifty as to lack all spine and consistency, its star begins to set, and the times are ripe for the complementary half-truth, that "Whatever is real is permanent," which may then receive the same kind of confirmation.

This epochal variability in the working-power of partial truths (and most of the working-truths of history I judge to have been of this sort) tends to bring our perceptions of truth into that rhythm in which some sort of "dialectical" process can begin. Such a process is bound to commence when one observes his own vacillation, and tries to remedy it. What requires the revision is not any failure of the instrumental working—the half-truths could continue to labor in alternate shifts—it is the demand for inner consistency. The structural principle thus announces itself as something again independent of the pragmatic principle. Not at odds with it: for there can be no hostility between Dewey and Barbara. Only, the interest in trueness tends to migrate away from the periphery of consequences to the center where Barbara spins out the materials of immediacy into a coherent, continuous fabric.

So far, I have dealt with the first two propositions, the instrumental definition of truth, and the thesis that there is no strictly immediate truth. Now consider the third thesis, that there is no eternal truth.

It is evident that the demand for consistency is at the same time a demand for *stability* in propositions. That is, the kind of truth we want is one we can hold to in all circumstances. The business of the dialectic is to find a conception of things which will *hold good,* and not for a little while, nor for an epoch, but always. If we prefer to translate stability by eternity, by way of indicating the limit to which stability tends, there is no harm done. The demand is the same whether there is much or little or no such ideally stable truth available.

And let us note that the need in question, while it is a logical need, is not merely logical. Nor is it merely a psychological oddity, such as marks the temperamentally active type of humanity, of which we were earlier speaking: it lies in the nature of all action. For all action intends to change something in particular: and in order to effect just this alteration in the world, the frame of action must hold still! The maxim for action is: Regard the universe as static except where you want it to budge. The ideal situation for the man who wants to move things is to have an unalterable conviction at his back: "Here I stand, I can not otherwise, God help me." The man who can say that will either make things happen or be himself obliterated.

Nothing to my mind more strikingly illustrates, and at the same time criticises, the instrumental principle than the immense working qualities of propositions supposed to be not only eternal but transcendent as well. Theological orthodoxies and heterodoxies have sometimes been stupidly adored in that detached and footless contemplation which is the *bête noire* of the instrumentalist. But they have at least as often appeared in history as *things done!* Thus Carlyle writes of those intractable heathen, the Wends, in the early days of Brandenburg: "Being highly disinclined to conversion," he says, "they once and again burst up, got hold of Brandenburg, and *did frightful heterodoxies there"!* After two centuries of clash these Wends were either blown up like dry powder or else "damped down into Christianity," which implies that they began to *do orthodoxy,* and that the new deeds were of a markedly different cast. In either case, it was a *doxy* that they did: good instrumentalism, but with an absolute for an implement or battle axe.

Is it not a momentous thing for our theory of truth that all major plans for human action, whether or not we who look backward, can see them tied to half-truths, have tried to get hold of absolutes and universals? And please note: it is *not for moral holidays* that these absolutes have been required.

Why, to fight British Torydom or slavery, do Thomas Jefferson and his successors reach out for a formula about "All men," instead of taking some legend that will snugly fit the moment's case? Is it because they do not want this day's business to be itself temporary and abstract and to be all undone and done over? And is it because they know that *the fruit of action can be no more permanent than the sight it comes out of* that they need to see the momentary effort in its setting and make the whole of things a party to what they now propose to do? I suspect that nothing short of a true property of all men would have *worked* for Jefferson's revolution: it was an eternal verity of some sort that King George was disowning, and it would take that same eternal verity to defeat him. Let us say, if we think so, that Jefferson got only a relative and approximate truth: I only remark that such a suspicion on his part would have lamed him for the moment, and sent him searching for another and more durable universal. It is not the scorn of action, it is the love of it, which prompts the quest for theoretical certainty, such as one can have before action begins. No one can be mad, of anger or devotion, unless he is first sure of something.

I suspect that at bottom Dewey is as little enamored of incessant change and relativity in the world of judgment as anyone. In commenting on Charles Peirce, he dwells approvingly on Peirce's idea of reality: "Reality," he says, "means the object of those beliefs which have after prolonged and coöperative enquiry become stable; and truth is the quality of those beliefs."

What is meant by a belief "becoming stable"? If we can identify the belief during the period of its variation, there would appear to be a core of it that is not affected by the variation. There is, of course, no incompatibility between the persistence of a truth, and its change in the sense of clarification and growth. We may agree with Dewey that "the scientific attitude, as an attitude of interest in change instead of interest in isolated and complete fixities, is necessarily alert for problems,"[4] and its work forever unfinished. But it is equally evident that the whole scientific and experimental undertaking aims at and believes in permanence. For unless experiment can establish something, and unless something of what we suppose "established" stays established, endures, accumulates, the whole experimental business becomes a fool's paradise.

The corpus of knowledge is at no moment static: but we know this, that *change does not eat out what is true in it*. From this two things follow. First, that survival becomes an empirical criterion of trueness, so that for instrumentalism also the only truth which fully deserves the name is eternal truth. Second, that whatever

---

[4] *The Quest for Certainty.*

turns out by survival to have been the true element in our present beliefs, we *now have that truth,* and have had it, whether or not we can now extricate it from its adulterants.

But of what advantage is this present possession of eternal truth, if we never know certainly what it is?

The answer lies in that aspect of truth which we call the *a priori.* If there is any *a priori* truth, it is presumably of the durable variety; and might conceivably furnish something to hold to, for purposes of action, while we are waiting for the rest of our durable truth to survive! But is there any such truth?

It is hard to see how anyone who places faith in scientific method can doubt the *a priori.* For scientific method (which we may allow to be the only fruitful method, because it is a composite of every method) necessarily makes appeal to truths which can never be tested.

Take the assumption that the standard measure of length remains constant. About the standard meter-stick in Paris, or any other physically extant measure, I may refuse to make that assumption. I may imagine it subject to FitzGerald Contractions, or any other type of distortion I please. But in that case I conceive myself as measuring the altered length in terms of a measure which does not vary. An assumption which we can not avoid making, and which we assume when we try to test it, may fairly be called an *a priori* proposition.

Kant in his pragmatic moments made use of another variety of *a priori* judgment. His postulates of practical reason, as he thought, were such as to make very tangible differences in behavior and experience: but these eventualities need not be waited for, inasmuch as they were *necessary consequences* of the postulates. They could be known in advance. Instrumentalism seems to adopt the view that we do not know what results are going to be until we reach them. But why? Why must the relation between a belief and its working-out be purely factual? If the consequences really pertain to that belief, the connection is not accidental, and it must be theoretically possible to foresee them. As an ancestor of pragmatism, Kant's method here seems to deserve reconsideration. Wherever necessary consequences can be perceived and evaluated in advance, we have an *a priori* judgment.

Our more general ethical standards seem to be of this nature. With all the immense force of experience and social tradition in molding our ethical sense, it is not yet obvious to me that the experience of eventualities can ever instruct us in the primitive distinction between right and wrong. We can hardly adopt the view (to quote a colleague) that Cain did not know it was wrong to kill Abel until after he had done so. Unless the discovered consequence confirmed an uneasy foreboding of his own, already ethical, it could teach him nothing except that he had made an unfortunate decision. Nor can we adopt the view that the "lost causes" of mankind are proved by the outcome to have been somehow illicit. I am wholly convinced that it is wasteful, and may be vicious, to contemplate impossible ideals; that an ideal ought to be a pressure toward technical embodiment; that if ends are holy, the use of means is not less so. But how are we to know which ideals are possible and which are not? If we are to avoid the vice of cherishing impossible ideals, we must be guided either by an *a priori* knowledge of what ideals are possible or impossible, or by an *a priori* knowledge of what ideals are right. If we assume (with Joan of Arc, for example) that what is right must be somehow possible, we are relieved of the effort to foresee ultimate outcomes; the whole burden of judgment rests on the prior assurance of rightness. The event of failure reacts, not on the validity of the ideal, but on the wisdom of the means used or the energy of the agent. The defeated reformer, lover, patriot may have to curse himself as a fool: but he has still to say, "That for which I tried had the quality of goodness in it: my knowledge of that quality was prior to eventualities, and remains unmoved by them."

An element of knowledge may be *there* and may be effective long before it can be isolated, as children cut corners long before they can announce that the straight line is the shortest distance. It is not absurd to suppose that *a priori* knowledge may have a *de facto* existence, and yet a very belated official recognition. I wish to commend to your judgment a view of *a priori* knowledge which sees it as *growing out of experience*. We all want to be good empiricists; we have all grown humble in respect to the value of abstract rational anticipations of experience. Most of us, I believe, would like to join Dewey in getting away from the old passive copying empiricism, and in uniting with a better brand some recognition of the active contribution of the thinker: we believe Kant was right in seeking a synthesis of the empirical and the rational, and we further agree in not being satisfied with his proposals. May I suggest, then, that the office of experience is not solely to supply raw material, nor to provide simple ideas, nor yet to tease knowledge out into the ventures of action, but to present connections as factual in which we may, by slow degrees, recognize the necessary. The *a priori* is an element of knowledge which shells out of our changing empirical judgments as something implicitly presupposed and invariant. We may call it the *uncovered a priori*. And if the principle of this uncovering be admitted, we may willingly consult experience until the end of time for ascertaining the full measure of that *a priori* knowledge which even now we are using.

One such *a priori* element I seem to find uncovered in Dewey's *Quest for Certainty*. It occurs in a passage which, rejecting "fixed beliefs about values" so far as their contents are concerned, mentions one value which no future experience can dislodge. This invariant value is, to put it briefly, the value of trying to realize value. More fully, it is the value "of discovering the possibilities of the actual and striving to realize them."[5] Devotion to this value is declared invincible; it is the fit kernel for a forward-looking religious attitude toward the world. I need not emphasize the importance of this passage.

It constitutes of itself a comment on another thesis of instrumentalism, namely, that all values are immanent, human-born and man-achieved; and that we do well to get rid of their traditional transcendent moorings.

To me this doctrine often comes with a sense of relief; as if we would take a distinct step ahead in replacing the primordial value-reservoir of a certain type of idealism by those prospective and possible values which stir millions of finite beings to continued effort. Surely the best qualities of experience are things achievable, not antecedently there. The equality of men of Jefferson's faith,—who can say it is *there?* Suppose we regard it rather as something to be brought about. To treat men as equal is to bring equality to pass. We can *confer* equality: the responsibility falls on our shoulders, and the world, which seemed a monstrous enigma under the doctrine of the is-ness of equality, becomes once more a hopeful place.

But this change does not dispel the metaphysical horizon. If value is creatable, the universe *is* already the entertainer of this possibility. Possibility is neither a human product, nor a mere form of expectancy: it is an objective property of things, antecedent to our action. Further, it is not there by accident: the universe which contains it can not be conceived as indifferent to its actualization. Possibility thus takes on the hue of obligation; and no single value in the human scene remains unaffected by this relationship. For a value which in our cosmic setting we are due to work out acquires a momentousness not attainable by a value which we merely *may* work out if we are so disposed and have the needed energy.

The value of trying to realize value appears to me to belong to this metaphysical setting of action; and if we wished to apply to it the opprobrious terms, "transcendent," "eternal," or even "absolute," the objections would arise chiefly, I think, from the traditional connotations of these words. I will confine myself to calling it a case of the uncovered *a priori,* and to making a plea that we extend the use of the principle by which this invariant is uncovered.

5 P. 304.

For we are going to get truth by endless experimenting, and there is presumably a charter for this experimenting which is not itself establishable by experiment. We are going to get truth by induction, and whatever the inductive postulate is, we can not prove *it* by induction. To my mind, experiment and induction are ways of trying to unearth necessities; and there is a prior necessity laid on us for continuing this search for necessity, whose authority no success can confirm and no failure unsettle. Here we have a small group of *a priori* elements, which are in a way formal and transcendent; that is, they are not in the fight, because they constitute the arena and the urge which makes the fight go on! I am disposed to see in them available theoretical certainties which underly all human action. To them the more concrete certainties may attach themselves in proportion to that power of genius which, in the midst of incoherent and disagreeing empirical cases, can discern the universal element, not perfectly but clearly enough to do a man's work in the world.

Dewey recommends a philosophy "willing to abandon its supposed task of knowing ultimate reality and to devote itself to a proximate human office." [6] This can never happen: for philosophy can not perform the second function without the first. Men are like tigers in one respect which is to the credit of both: they can't enjoy food until they can see their way out of the trap. The amelioration of details leaves them ill at ease while they are without confidence in the frame of things,—if only a negative confidence that its uncontrollable reaches are not certainly brewing the spume of death to them and their works. In any case, we shall do the human offices with all the wisdom we can muster; but it is the peculiar province of philosophy to read and truly report the ultimate auspices of these deeds, be these auspices good or ill.

I plead for the recovery of a Platonic element in our way of knowing. A renewed grip of the changeless vein in things and an inkling of totality, so far from veiling the transitional, or withering experiment, or drugging the spirit of enterprise, would show themselves the very nerves of action. There is nothing infusible in these two things, the great work of Dewey and the Platonic vision. Knowing and doing are not the same thing: nothing but confusion can be got from identifying them, for in that case activity itself could not be known. No doubt they are of a piece, inseparable: they reach their culmination together; knowing is at its height at the point where the present deed plays against the outer reality. But as doing, like the galloping hoof, gathers the earth into it and puts the earth behind it, so about the moment's knowledge

---

6 *The Quest for Certainty*, p. 47.

born in that same contact, there spreads the horizon and the stable arch of the sky.

When Dewey accepts for himself somewhat tentatively the designation "experimental idealist," then we who have been thinking of ourselves as idealistic experimentalists, may be permitted to recognize a kinship and to join in the long quest for the remainder of our certainty, some of which we think we have in hand.

WILLIAM ERNEST HOCKING.

HARVARD UNIVERSITY.

PRAGMATISM AND CURRENT THOUGHT[1]

IT is somewhat difficult in the case of pragmatism to determine what are its essential and distinctive theses. That there should be thirteen distinguishable pragmatisms, however, is not a peculiarity: these could be set alongside the thirty-seven idealisms and fifty-one realisms. William James is reported to have said that he was pleased to find that pragmatism had this wealth of meaning; he accepted all thirteen. In any case, such variety merely marks the fact that pragmatism is a movement, not a system. Its beginnings are attributable to Charles Peirce. But Peirce has something the quality of a legendary figure in American philosophy. His originality and the wealth of his thinking are not fully evident in his published writings. Apart from a few persons—amongst whom were James and Royce—some of his most important conceptions can have had little influence, because they have never been printed: and the coincidence of these doctrines with the views of later pragmatists is distinctly limited. James's enthusiasm for them must in part be set down to that catholicity of appreciation which was so notable a part of his character. James called himself a "radical empiricist" as well as a pragmatist, and the connection, or lack of it, between these two aspects of, or strands in, his philosophy, has been a matter of some question. We must, of course, look to Professor Dewey's writings for the integration and systematic elaboration of pragmatism. But no one could have exercised the quite unparalleled influence which he has had upon American thought without giving rise to a wealth of resultant views which is a little confusing when one tries to grasp their coincidence or central meaning. Hence it is not a matter for surprise if those most deeply influenced by him show a tendency to drop the term, lest a too extended agreement with one another be suggested, and that those of us who still have ventured to use it are doubtful of our right to the designation.

If, then, I venture to suggest what is the core of pragmatism, and

[1] Read at the meeting of the American Philosophical Association, Dec. 30, 1929, New York City.

what I think may be the chief significance of it, both in philosophy and for other branches, I hope it will be understood that I do not take myself too seriously in the matter. This view is presented to those who will best know how to correct my mistakes.

Pragmatism is, as James indicated, not a doctrine but a method: viewed logically, it can be regarded as the consequence of a single principle of procedure. But this principle, though by itself it says nothing material in the field of metaphysics or epistemology, and though its application is by no means confined to philosophy, has nevertheless a wealth of philosophic consequences. It implies at least the outline of a theory of knowledge; and if it dictates no metaphysical theses, at least it rules out a good deal which has been put forward under that caption, and it operates as a principle of orientation in the search for positive conclusions.

I refer, of course, to the pragmatic test of significance. James stated it as follows: "What difference would it practically make to anyone if this notion rather than that notion were true? If no practical difference whatever can be traced, then the alternatives mean practically the same thing, and all dispute is idle." [2] Peirce formulated it with respect to substantive concepts rather than propositional notions—though the two come to the same thing: "Our idea of anything is our idea of its sensible effects. . . . Consider what effects that might conceivably have practical bearings, we conceive the object of our conception to have. Then, our conception of these effects is the whole of our conception of the object." [3] It is one importance of this pragmatic test that it is so obviously valid and final: once it has been formulated, there can be no going back on it later without conscious obscurantism. Any consequence of it, therefore, shares in this imperative and binding character. Peirce's dictum draws our attention to the fact that there is a kind of empiricism which is implicit in the pragmatic test: What can you point to in experience which would indicate whether this concept of yours is applicable or inapplicable in a given instance? What practically would be the test whether your conception is correct? If there are no such empirical items which would be decisive, then your concept is *not* a concept, but a verbalism.

If one does not find in Professor Dewey's writings any terse

[2] *Pragmatism*, p. 45.

[3] "How to Make Our Ideas Clear," *Chance, Love and Logic*, p. 45. Compare: ". . . Since obviously nothing that might not result from experiment can have any bearing on conduct, if one can define accurately all the conceivable experimental phenomena which the affirmation or denial of a concept could imply, one will have therein a complete definition of the concept, and *there is nothing more in it*. For this doctrine he [the writer, Peirce] invented the name pragmatism."—"What Pragmatism Is," *Monist*, Vol. 15, p. 177.

formulation which is exactly parallel (and of that I am not sure), this is only because here the pragmatic test is clothed with its consequences; it pervades the whole, and is writ large in the functional theory of the concept. Ideas are plans of action; concepts are prescriptions of certain operations whose empirical consequences determine their significance. This connotation of action is not, of course, a new note; it appears in Peirce's emphasis upon conduct and experiment, and in James's doctrine of the "leading" character of ideas. Is this functional theory of the concept implicit, like empiricism, in the pragmatic test?

So far as Professor Dewey himself is concerned, it would appear that this doctrine antedates his explicit pragmatism, and may have been the root of it. (Perhaps he will tell us.) It appears in his paper on "The Reflex Arc Concept in Psychology," the first important document for "functional psychology," published in 1896.[4] He there criticises current psychological theory as not having sufficiently avoided the fictitious abstractions of sensationalism. "The sensation or conscious stimulus is not a thing or existence by itself; it is a phase of a coördination."[5] "A coördination is an organization of means with reference to a comprehensive end."[6] "The stimulus is that phase of the forming coördination which represents the conditions which have to be met in bringing it to a successful issue; the response is that phase of one and the same forming coördination which gives the key to meeting these conditions, which serves as instrument in effecting the successful coördination. . . . The stimulus is something to be discovered. . . . It is the motor response which assists in discovering and constituting the stimulus."[7] Substitute "sensation" or "sense data" for "stimulus," "operation" or "action" for "motor response," and what is here quoted will be found occupying a central place in all Professor Dewey's subsequent expositions of his pragmatic doctrine. Three years later, he wrote: "I conceive that states of consciousness . . . have no existence as such . . . before the psychologist gets to work." "Knowing, willing, feeling, name states of consciousness not in themselves, but in terms of results reached, the sorts of value that are brought into experience."[8]

[4] *Psychological Review*, Vol. 3, pp. 357–370. My attention was drawn to this by its citation in Boring's *History of Experimental Psychology*, pp. 540–541.

[5] *Loc. cit.*, p. 368.

[6] *Loc. cit.*, p. 365.

[7] *Loc. cit.*, p. 370.

[8] "Psychology and Philosophic Method," address before the Philosophical Union of the University of California, 1899, pp. 6 and 10. It is interesting to remember that in the preceding year, James presented the first statement of *his* pragmatism, "Philosophical Conceptions and Practical Results," under the same auspices.

If, then, I am right in the derivation here assigned, Professor Dewey's functional theory of knowledge is the necessary consequence of a methodological principle applied to psychology; namely, that concepts used should designate something concretely identifiable in experience, not abstractions apart from that which serves for their empirical discovery. Sensations, or sense data, are condemned as not thus identifiable apart from the responses to which they lead and the ends such action serves.

The functional theory of the concept has, as I have tried to show elsewhere, other grounds, of a more purely logical sort. Viewed in this way, however, and apart from psychological considerations, it is not, I think, a simple consequence of the pragmatic test, but has a conceivable alternative, namely, immediatism or the presentation-theory of knowledge. By this logical approach, one has to adduce reasons for repudiating the conception that empirical knowledge—or *some* empirical knowledge—is immediately given, in order to reach the conception that activity and its issue are indispensable and characterizing factors in empirical cognition. The theory that meanings connote action and truth connotes prediction, is implicit in the notion that truth and meanings are something *to be tested*; hence, that they do *not* bring their own warrant in being simply given.

I believe we here arrive at a turning-point in pragmatic theory.[9] On the one side, the pragmatic principle seems to stress the directly empirical. Put enough emphasis on that, and one might conceivably —though not validly, I think—arrive at a highly subjectivistic theory, of knowledge as immediate. On the other side, it stresses the limitation of meaning to what makes a verifiable difference, and of truth to what can be objectively tested. Follow out the consequences of *that*, and of the functional theory of knowledge which it implies, and I believe one is inevitably led to the doctrine that concepts are abstractions, in which the immediate is precisely that element which must be left out. To this point, I should like to adduce certain illustrations, drawn from contemporary science.

The new physics is, in good part, based upon certain applications of the pragmatic test. And to these physicists the validity of this methodological principle and the functional interpretation of conceptual meanings seem to be simply synonymous. One main premise of physical relativity is, of course, the impossibility of deciding which, of two bodies in relative motion, is at rest with respect to an absolute space. (We may remind ourselves that James's illustration

---

[9] When this was written, Professor Burtt's paper, "Two Basic Issues in the Problem of Meaning and of Truth," contributed to *Essays in Honor of John Dewey*, had not yet come to hand. I note with pleasure that a part of his paper and part of what is here written run parallel.

of the pragmatic test—the man and the squirrel—is simply an example of the relativity of motion to frames of reference.) In elaborating the consequences of this relativity of motion, it became necessary to repudiate other absolutes, such as length, time, simultaneity, etc.; and this was done by identifying these with the actual modes by which they can be tested—the pragmatic test once more. The resultant methodology may be generalized in what Bridgman calls "the operational character of concepts." "We evidently know what we mean by a length if we can tell what the length of any and every object is, and for the physicist nothing more is required. To find the length of an object we have to perform certain physical operations. The concept of length is therefore fixed when the operations by which length is measured are fixed: that is, the concept of length involves as much as and nothing more than the set of operations by which length is determined. In general we mean by any concept nothing more than a set of operations; *the concept is synonymous with the corresponding set of operations.*" [10]

Why does the physicist thus identify his concepts with operations of testing? Is it because the properties he is concerned with are peculiarly those which are difficult or impossible of immediate apprehension? Not at all. Suppose a critic to observe: "But of course your concept of length goes back to an immediately given somewhat. You test the relation of a particular length to the yardstick, but unless your yardstick were an immediate so-longness, directly apprehended, your concept of length would be entirely empty." He will reply that this immediate so-longness has nothing to do with physics, because it can not be tested. The *yardstick* can be tested; as it happens, the measurement of it will differ for different relative motions. But any immediate so-longness of it is something which makes no difference to physics: if it had one so-longness to A and another for B, that would be unverifiable and ineffable. It is the significance of the operational character of concepts to extrude such ineffables from physics. Subjectively it may be that A and B both seem to themselves at rest in the center of the universe, directly apprehending certain so-longnesses, so-heavinesses, felt endurances of things, and what not. But physical position and motion are simply relations to a frame of reference, physical time a relation to clocks; physical properties in general consist in those operations and relations by which they are assigned and tested. The standards are absolutely standards—that is, arbitrary—but they are not absolute in any other sense. The standard yardstick, or clock, or whatever, has its length or the measure of its seconds, etc., in an entirely similar and verifiable set of relations to other things, and only so. Any immediate

---

[10] *The Logic of Modern Physics*, p. 5; italics are in the text.

content of the concept is extruded by the principle of the pragmatic test. If your hours, as felt, are twice as long as mine, your pounds twice as heavy, that makes no difference, which can be tested, in our assignment of physical properties to things. If it *should* thus make a difference in our predication of properties, we should at once decide that one of us must be mistaken. Such decision would reveal our implicit recognition that our concept of the predicated property excludes this subjective element, and includes only the objectively verifiable relations.

The physical concepts are not, by this extrusion of the immediate, emptied of meaning. Their meaning is, as Bridgman says, in the operations of verification and their results; it is contained in that complex network of relationships which constitute the laws and equations and physical predications of which the science consists. The concept is, thus, merely a sort of configuration or relational pattern. Whatever the immediate and ineffable content which is caught in that net may be—for John Jones or Mary Doe or anybody—it does not enter into the science of physics. The resultant conception of the content of the science is admirably expressed by Eddington: "We take as building material *relations* and *relata*. The relations unite the relata; the relata are the meeting points of the relations."[11] The conceptual in knowledge is the element of pure structure or operational construction.

Thus the pragmatic test becomes a kind of law of intellectual parsimony, and leads, in science, to what might be called "the flight from the subjective." Physics is by no means an isolated example: the parallel thing has happened, or will happen, in every science, because it is simply the extrusion of what the science can not finally and conclusively test. Mathematics, being the oldest science, did it first. Geometry begins with rope-stretching and ends as the deductive elaboration of purely abstract concepts, the problem of the nature of space being handed over to physics and philosophy. Arithmetic begins with counting empirical things and ends in the logical structure of *Principia Mathematica*, for which the existence of the number 8 (for a certain type) requires an extraneous assumption. Just now mathematics threatens to go further and restrict itself to systems of operations upon marks. Psychology first got rid of the ineffable soul; a pragmatic psychologist then asked, "Does consciousness [as distinct from its content] exist?"; and now we have behaviorism, based on the methodological principle of restriction to what is objectively verifiable. If some of these movements go beyond what is necessary or valid, at least they exhibit the tendency, and the ground of it.

[11] *The Nature of the Physical World*, p. 230.

Professor Dewey seems to view such abstractionism in science as a sort of defect—sometimes necessary but always regrettable; an inadequacy of it to the fullness of experience. In various ways, it seems to him to threaten the relations between knowledge and life. Professor Eddington's book suggests that a doubt on this point besets him too when, as physical scientist, he finds himself also constrained to assess philosophical significances. That the world as experienced and life as lived are not going to be thrown out of the window, goes without saying. Particularly for Professor Dewey, it seems to me that this apprehensiveness is misplaced, because he has himself indicated the main considerations essential for the solution of the problem which results—the problem of the relation of abstract concepts to the concrete and directly empirical. Time does not permit attention to all the pertinent considerations. But I wish to suggest one which is important, by a final illustration, drawn once more from physics.

As an eventual result of subatomic and quantum phenomena, the new physics has abolished imaginable matter. Analysis of the physical emerges finally in something like Schrödinger's Ψ-functions, in mathematical expressions of probability, concrete representation of which can only be approached in terms of an admittedly fictitious sub-ether of variable dimensions. Immediately apprehensible matter dissolves into mathematics. Two other expressions of this same abstractness of the physically ultimate occur in Eddington's later chapters: one is that statement about relations and relata, already referred to; the other is to the effect that physics reduces the concrete object to pointer-readings.[12] The elephant sliding down the grass slope is at once an immense flock of Ψ-functions getting integrated, and a set of pointer-readings. The two interpretations do not seem interchangeable. Let us fasten on the pointer-readings. Why reduce the elephant to pointer-readings? In the first place, because physics can not deal with the elephant as a whole. It comprehends a good many—perhaps most—of the elephant's properties, but that he is, for example, a wonderful fine fellow and very intelligent, must be omitted from physical consideration. Let us call that organization of properties which physics *can* deal with "the physicist's elephant." Why is the physicist's elephant reduced to pointer-readings? First because, with the apparatus oriented upon the elephant, the elephant *determines* the pointer-readings. Second, because such pointer-readings are a conveniently hybrid sort of reality: the apparatus and pointers being physical, their readings correlate with the properties of the elephant; and the readings being numerical, they translate those properties into mathematical values. The

[12] Pp. 251 ff.

significance of the pointer-readings is merely for the purpose of such translation. The last state of the physicist's elephant, like the last state of the electron, is in mathematical functions. But this last stage for the *physicist* is merely an intermediate stage of operations with respect to the elephant. The numerical values given by the pointer-readings are substituted for the variables in some mathematical equation expressing physical law. They thus determine a numerical value of some other mathematical function. This last can be translated back into something of the order of pointer-readings, and hence back into some other and previously undetermined property of the elephant—with the eventual result, perhaps, that we get the elephant safely into a box-car. Such eventual result is the reason for being of the whole set of operations. If it be asked, then, "Why reduce the elephant to mathematical functions?" the answer is that this is the best way known to man for getting him into the box-car.

The physicist's elephant is an abstraction, but a rather palpable sort of abstraction. All of him that the physicist finally deals with is what is common to the elephant and the pointer-readings; namely, a more abstract, a *very* abstract, configuration of relationships. This structure of relations is what, in general terms, the mathematical equations of physics express.

Thus if the last conceptual stage of the elephant—and of the physical in general—is in mathematics, or a set of relations of relata, it is not necessary to try to follow this transmogrification of the elephant, or of matter, with the imagination. Nor is it appropriate to cry shame upon the physicist for leaving the world of palpable elephants in favor of such unimaginable abstractions. The physicist's concept represents simply an intermediate stage in a process which begins and ends with elephants and such—not with the physicist's elephant even, but the one which slid down the bank and got put in the box-car.

As Professor Dewey points out, the physicist and mathematician simply take this intermediate stage off by itself and deal with it on its own account.[13] Thus if we reflect upon the functional theory of knowledge, I think we may come to the conclusion that there is no implication of it which is incompatible with the notion that concepts in general are abstractions—are even very thin abstractions. Because the function of concepts is not to *photograph* elephants but to get them into box-cars. Concepts represent simply that operational function of cognition by which it transforms the something given, with which it begins, into the something anticipated or something done, with which it ends. That they may have lost, or discarded as irrelevant, those elements of the concrete and immediate which char-

[13] See *The Quest for Certainty*, pp. 156 ff.

acterize direct perception and imagination, is nothing to the point. Goodness in a concept is not the degree of its verisimilitude to the given, but the degree of its effectiveness as an instrument of control. Perhaps Professor Dewey might even, with entire consistency, find less occasion to regret that the relatively undeveloped sciences of human affairs show a tendency to imitate this abstractness. When the social sciences attain that degree of abstractness, and consequent precision, which already characterizes physics and mathematics, perhaps they will have less trouble getting their social elephants into their social box-cars. Economics is the best developed of the social sciences, and a fair illustration.

To conclude: the fact that the pragmatic test seems, on the one hand, to demand that all meaning be found eventually in the empirical, and on the other, seems to induce a flight from the immediate and directly apprehensible into abstractions, is not, in reality, any contradiction or any difficulty. In one sense—that of connotation—a concept strictly comprises nothing but an abstract configuration of relations. In another sense—its denotation or empirical application—this meaning is vested in a process which characteristically begins with something given and ends with something done—in the operation which translates a presented datum into an instrument of prediction and control.

C. I. LEWIS.

HARVARD UNIVERSITY.

The Journal of Philosophy

JOHN DEWEY'S THEORY OF JUDGMENT [1]

KEYNES opens his *Formal Logic* with the statement: "Logic may be defined as the science which investigates the principles of valid thought. Its object is to discuss the character of judgments regarded not as psychological phenomena but as expressing our knowledge and beliefs." It is clear from this that logic, though formal, does not intend to be inhuman. Though it is not concerned with the psychology of our judgments, it is nevertheless concerned with the judgments *we* make, with *our* "knowledge and beliefs." Now what is this judgment which is independent of our psychology, but yet, strangely enough, expresses *our* knowledge and beliefs? "Judgment proper," to quote Bradley of this time, "is the act which refers an ideal content to a reality beyond the act. A judgment says something about some fact or reality. A judgment must be true or false." Examples of judgment are "*A* is *B*," "I see my finger," or, to use the summary expression for all possible judgments, "*S* is *P*."

Logicians since the days of Bradley and Keynes are given more to using the term "proposition" than the term "judgment" for denoting the central fact of their science. Johnson begins his extensive treatise on logic by explaining and defending this change. "A systematic treatment of logic," says he, "must begin by regarding the proposition as the unit from which the whole body of logical principles may be developed. The natural use of the term "judgment" is to denote an act or attitude or process which may constitute an incident in the mental history of an individual. As so conceived, we should have further to distinguish the changing phases of a process (which might alternately involve interrogation, doubt, tentative affirmation or negation) from the terminus of such process in which a final decision replaces the variations undergone during what is commonly called suspense of judgment. It would thus be more natural to speak of passing judgment upon a proposition proposed in thought, than to identify judgment as such with the proposition. . . . Now as regards the relation of the proposition to any such act as may be called judgment, my special contention is that the proposition can not usefully be defined in isolation, but only in con-

[1] Read before the American Philosophical Association, Columbia University, Dec. 30, 1929; a few slight additions have been made.

nection with some such attitude or act of thought; and I prefer to take the notion of asserting as central amongst these variations of attitude.'' And the proposition which judgment asserts is, to continue the quotation, ''that of which truth and falsity can be significantly predicated.'' Johnson's examples of propositions have again the general form of S is P.

In spite of metaphysical and terminological differences, Bradley and Johnson hold essentially the same views as to the nature of the central fact of logical science. And Johnson, like Bradley, like Keynes, and like all other logicians, affirms that ''logic is most comprehensively and least controversially defined as the analysis and criticism of thought.''

Since thought is the universally accredited subject-matter of logic it is of the very first importance to find out what the analysis and criticism of thought involve. Clearly, they do not involve an analysis and criticism of the psychical experiences of the mind when reflectively thinking—an account of its *erlebnisse*. If this is what is meant by ''psychological phenomena,'' then the realist contention is sound. But the process of reflective thinking has a logical structure as well as a psychical content and source. And the logician, if he is to take his task seriously, though he must not concern himself with the latter, must concern himself with analysing and explaining the former. That is, the logician must give an account of the procedure and technique of the mind in its reflective operations. And this is necessarily preliminary to any account he may wish to give of the nature and relations of the intellectual tools the mind employs.

Johnson admits as much in the passage quoted. He says, ''The proposition cannot usefully be defined in isolation but only in connection with some act or attitude of thought''; and for his system he *prefers* ''to take the notion of asserting as central amongst the variations of attitude, possible in judgment.'' Preferences where legitimate always claim respect. But is it legitimate to base a logical system on a preference? Dewey, as you all know, maintains that ''interrogation, doubt, tentative affirmation'' (to use Johnson's own expressions) are more centrally characteristic of judgment than is assertion. How can these rival claims be settled if logicians do not analyze the acts and attitudes of the mind when reflectively engaged? Does not, indeed, the mere statement of Johnson's preference presuppose on his part some sort of knowledge, if not analysis, of the nature of actual human thought? And it pre-supposes this in his capacity of logician for, on his own account, his logical system is developed from this preference or assumption. It is folly for the logician to think he can escape the necessity of inquiring into the form and content of human thinking by disparagingly calling such inquiry "psychology." If it is psychology—in the sense meant by psychologists (which is more than highly questionable)—then, obviously, psychological analysis—whether logicians like it or not—is the necessary precondition of even the most formal kind of logical analysis.

This issue is raised again, and the same conclusion is forced upon us when we consider another part of the citation from Johnson. Once more it is willingly granted that it is advantageous for Johnson to assume that judgment passes "upon a proposition proposed in thought," but again it must be asked, What warrant has he for this assumption? As is well known, Dewey claims that what is proposed in thought for judgment is not a proposition at all, but a problem. And a problem is not an object we cognize, but a state of affairs we experience in a variety of non-cognitive ways. How can logicians possibly determine which of these rival accounts is true, how can they ever possibly come to know what *is* actually proposed in thought for judgment unless, as logicians, they analyze the logical processes of the mind when it is forming and passing judgment? It bears repeating, that if this is psychology, then it is high time all logicians recognized that logic has its psychological foundations.

This summary disposal of so important an issue can not help but be unsatisfactory. But the issue is introduced here not so much for treatment as for use as an avenue of approach. It has enabled us, on the one hand, to state with the authority of quotation the premises on which idealist and realist logicians found their logical systems; and, on the other hand, to state with the strength of contrast, the premises of instrumental logic. These alternatives are distinguished from one another in no indifferent way. The character of our whole logical theory is determined by that set of premises we feel justified in taking. It would be an act of supererogation, if not of impertinence, for me to expound to you the consequences for logical theory of taking the alternative Dewey has developed and espoused. The task of this paper is not that of expatiating on the long familiar. Within the possibilities of this occasion, the task is to indicate rather how we may re-think afresh the consequences of the alternative idealist and realist logicians have taken, and to show how the results we will reach re-inforce the validity of Dewey's contention that his theory is a successful way out of the morass of contemporary logical problems.

Before proceeding further, it will be well to assemble what has been said so far about the two crucial features of Dewey's theory of judgment and their vital differences from rival theories. According to Dewey: (1) the original datum proposed for judgment is not a simple assertion, but a problem to be solved: (2) judgment is not a simple assertion, a sawed-off act of the mind, a trigger-response to stimulus, but a complex process of inquiry, involving several types of mental activity—a process of weighing, discovering, estimating, assembling, testing, developing, analysing, and criticising facts and hypotheses contributory to the solution of the problem. It is judg*ing*—the whole complex procedure of arriving at a definitive solution that is the essential epistemic element without relation to which, as Johnson himself rightly maintains, "the proposition can not usefully be defined"; the passing of the judgment—the assertion of the solution obtained—is merely, to quote Johnson again, "the terminus of such process." And this terminal act of reflection really falls, as we shall see, outside judgment proper.

It may sometimes be unimportant whether we take as our original datum the terminus of the process we are concerned with or take the whole process itself. But in logic and metaphysics this condition of happy immateriality does not, alas, obtain. What we take as our original datum makes all the difference in the world: the difference between clarity and confusion, between success and failure, between truth and falsity. The original datum of idealist and realist logicians is the proposition—the terminus of the process of judgment. The proposition is torn out of all context of origin and purpose in the process of human inquiry and made the object of a primary act of assertion. The central fact of logical science is treated as being determinate in content and final in form.[2]

The original datum of realist logic has a remarkably faithful parallel in the original datum of realist metaphysics. The sense-datum, too, is torn out of all context of origin and purpose in the process of human perception, and made the object of immediate sensory cognition. The central fact of metaphysical science is also treated as determinate in content and final in form. The sense-datum has the character and function in realist epistemology and metaphysics that the proposition has in realist logic.

Contemporary discussion has been more thorough and more fruitful in epistemology and metaphysics than in logic. Dewey especially has amassed a more forceful array of criticisms of the metaphysics of sense-data than he has of the logic of propositions. It will therefore be, I think, as valuable as it is interesting to adapt Dewey's criticisms of the former for the purposes of criticising the latter. To do this it will, of course, be necessary to consider realist

---

[2] This paper has chiefly in mind English philosophers. In so far as American idealists and realists hold views identical with those of their English brethren, the remarks apply also to them. As it is impossible within the limits of this paper to go into all the shades of American differences, I have been forced to make the English schools the direct, and when necessary the exclusive, objects of attention.

metaphysics and logic together. The task is large, but our treatment fortunately can be brief, since the fundamental issues and arguments are known to you all.

Dewey has pointed out time and again that sense-data are not the originally "given" in perception, but the derivatively "taken" in reflection, that they are developed and used for their evidential value. They are not immediate intuitions of sense, but the highly-refined products of thought. They are not the initial subject-matter of thought, but the residual elements of its analysis. Sense-data are not isolated in their own existence, nor atomic in their constitution. They are isolated, when isolated, only in the intellectual uses to which they are put; and they are atomic, when atomic, only in the artificial sense that our investigations are most productive when we proceed step by step, when we employ the most elementary sense-data seriatim, or atomically, if you like. To summarize, in Loewenberg's excellent terminology, sense-data are primarily not pre-analytical, but post-analytical data. It is to be recognised, of course, that the post-analytical data of one inquiry may become the pre-analytical data for a subsequent inquiry. Indeed, it is just this possibility and ever-recurring actuality that makes rational inquiry a continuous never-ending developmental process. Inquiry can grow and progress only as it uses attained results as the basis for further achievement. And it is as much a matter of growth and progress when attained results are used as data for more refined analysis of the starting point, as when they are used as "facts" for more extensive exploration of the subject-matter involved. This dual procedure of constantly going back to re-analyse and revise first principles and of constantly going forward to discover new spheres of the subject-matter is the very life-blood of inquiry, the indispensable condition of its having a significant and fruitful career. Neither idealist nor realist logic can, without ignoring or distorting its own principles, account for these living features of scientific inquiry because neither logic treats of scientific method in its own natural matrix. It must, however, also be recognized—which is never done by idealist or realist—that when the post-analytical sense-data of one inquiry become the pre-analytical data of another inquiry, they by that fact lose their achieved intellectual status *qua* sense-data or *objects* of cognition, since they lose their evidential value. For instead of being instrumental to the solution of a problem, they now, by hypothesis, constitute the problem to be solved. And just as soon as sense-data set instead of solve a problem, they cease to be, in Dewey's technical terminology, *objects* of cognition, and become *data* of non-cognitive experience.

These criticisms of the metaphysics of sense-data have equal force and validity when directed against the logic of propositions. The proposition is, by the realist, rent out of its natural context and treated as if it had an isolated existence; even the ideology of atomism is not wanting in propositional logic to make the parallel complete. The real isolation of the proposition, however, is like that of the sense-datum, an isolation, when isolated, in intellectual use— we sometimes find it best to deal with one proposition at a time; and, likewise, the proposition is atomic, when atomic, only in intellectual use—we always find it safest and easiest to deal with the simplest propositions we can obtain. We have already pointed out that the proposition is not the original subject-matter of thought, but the highly refined product of analysis. And what has been said about the possibility of sense-data functioning in one context as post-analytical and in another as pre-analytical data, applies without modification to propositions. To summarize again, instead of treating the proposition in relation to the process of inquiry of which it is the terminus—and in which relation it is alone properly understandable—idealist and realist logicians have treated the proposition as a self-sufficient entity isolated in its essential character, and sometimes even atomic; and instead of seeing the proposition as a product of intellectual construction they have seen it as a wraithlike courier from another world, a spectral evangel of a place better than any on earth.

From this way of viewing the proposition, derive all those problems and perplexities among which idealist and realist logicians flounder about, sorely assailed. The main problem that confronts them with forever new difficulties is that of truth; and to this problem consideration of time restricts us. With characteristic exactitude, the problem of truth is, as they say on the street, "the spittin' image" of the main problem the metaphysicians of sense-data are faced with—the problem of discovering what, precisely, the sense-datum is a sense-datum of, to what it is related and how.

The sense-datum is, by its metaphysicians, taken as the immediate object of sensory intuition, as a piece of "infallible knowledge," to use Whitehead's confessional expression. But like all "infallibilities" the sense-datum, too, alas, betrays the trusting mind. When so ordinary a sense-datum as the one we perceive when we look at our finger is scrutinized by a merciless analytic mind such as G. E. Moore pre-eminently possesses, its innocent appearance of being infallibly true is exposed as a sinful reality that is treacherously false. It is shown that at most the sense-datum gives us knowledge only of its own inconsequential self. It does not give us any knowledge, let alone infallible knowledge, of its relation to the finger it is presumably a sense-datum of; nor does it tell us whether it is part of the finger or part of the surface of the finger; nor even what relation it bears to either or both. The only shred of consolatory knowledge we can wrest from its mischievous infallibility is that in some sense—some very peculiar Pickwickian sense—it bears some relation—some very peculiar Pickwickian relation—to the finger or part of the surface of the finger. This is a very inadequate account of even the most elementary form of this persisting problem. As you all know, for those metaphysicians of sense-data who are addicted to seeing double, or seeing sticks that are thoughtlessly left standing in ponds, the difficulties, unlike the images, multiply, in both number and severity, in a geometric ratio. In all the turmoil that ensues it is a strong philosopher indeed who can keep his head. For it is a cause of terrible disappointment, a source of deep disillusion, if not of fatal despair, to be at first buoyed up preternaturally by an "infallible knowledge" that quite soon lands you, no matter how ceremoniously, in a bottomless quagmire where no knowledge is to be found and where ignorance is not bliss. Small wonder some English philosophers have flung themselves headlong into the wily arms of dogmatic scepticism. Especially small wonder when we remember they have no animal faith as anodyne!

Now just as the realist metaphysician naïvely accepts the sense-datum as a piece of "infallible knowledge" and so starts on a journey of sorrow, so the realist logician as naïvely accepts the proposition as the bearer of eternal truth or falsity and starts on a similar journey. With equally increasing disillusion, and equally in vain, does he attempt to discover what, precisely, his proposition is a proposition of, what lies behind it, to what it corresponds and how.

Dewey's diagnosis of the ailment of sense-data metaphysics is, briefly, that far from immediate perception giving us "infallible knowledge" it gives us no knowledge whatever. Our senses are not organs of knowledge; perception is a non-cognitive relation we enter into with the things about us. On this doctrine of the non-cognitive character of perception stands or falls most of Dewey's other contributions—those of prognosis as well as diagnosis. When, therefore, we seek to carry Dewey's critical and constructive arguments in metaphysics over into the field of logic we would be leaving behind what is most vital if we did not take this doctrine with us. And we would be totally unworthy of the spirit his philosophy inspires, if we did not have the courage to say that the immediate intellectual apprehension of propositions is, no more than the immediate sensory perception of sense-data, a case of knowledge.

If the immediate relation of the mind to propositions is not a knowledge-relation, what then *do* we know. The answer is as simple as the question is profound. We do *not* know propositions taken individually and in isolation from their functional context—i.e., in their immediate relation to the mind; what we *do* know are propositions taken together in their relationships to one another and to the context in which their evidential value is developed and used—i.e., we know propositions in their mediate relation to the mind. We *immediately* apprehend propositions (as we do sense-data) in much the same way we apprehend a person by the arm or the throat. Sometimes we are mistaken or, as Dewey prefers to say, do mis-take; the person apprehended may look like the one we are after, but he may not have the same voice or the same fingerprints. But that he is not the person we want, we discover only *after* we have examined the person we apprehended; that is, only *after* we have made our apprehended datum the basis of analysis and investigation, only *after* we have converted the brute *datum* of experience into an *object* of knowledge.

In instances of error, everyone admits our apprehension is not a case of knowledge, no matter what we may have thought at the time; and in instances of correct apprehension, it is no more a case of knowledge, even though realists and idealists have erected logical systems to the vanity that causes most of us to say "We *knew* it was you all the time." This vanity, as you know, is the source of some of the most insuperable difficulties in these logics.

Propositions like sense-data, in their primary character, are *had*, not known. They are the termini of inquiry, the depositories of conclusions reached. They are the results of inference, not, in the first instance, factors in the process of inferring. The unit of thought has, as Dewey has shown, three fundamental phases or moments; it arises in non-cognitive experience, passes through an intermediary phase of judgment which alone is cognitive and finds its euthanasia in a return to non-cognitive experience. The proposition which is the terminus of the process of judgment belongs to the third non-cognitive phase. And, therefore, as we stated at the beginning, it falls outside judgment proper.[3]

It follows that if propositions which are the terminations of the process of judgment, the post-analytical data of inquiry, are not objects of knowledge, they also are not either true or false. This conclusion, though seemingly perhaps startling, is really not so—nor

---

[3] I would like to suggest that instead of proposition, the term "statement" be used. Etymologically and intrinsically it is a much superior term; it is void of the ambiguity of the term "proposition"; and its meaning is, predominantly, that of denoting or something to be denoted, rather than of asserting, or something to be asserted. It also gives us two pairs of symmetrical expressions—judgment and statement, and judging and stating. Judging clearly connotes a *process;* stating as clearly connotes an *act.* There are other advantages to be derived from this suggested change in terminology, but this is not the place to argue for it.

is it altogether new. We have been repeatedly instructed in recent years that definitions and postulates are neither true nor false; and we have been told this by realists the most hardened of whom will admit that definitions and postulates are, by virtue of their own logical doctrine, also propositions. Now instead of making definitions and postulates exceptional, and creating a whole raft of inexplicable theories to explain why they are to be favored, it is the conclusion of this paper, to which the whole argument leads, that all propositions, as above defined, like definitions and postulates, are neither true nor false. Proof more than that implied in the foregoing is precluded now. Time does not allow either for anything more than this brief indication of the way out of contemporary logical problems Dewey's philosophy affords us. For it is also contended here that this conclusion only expresses rather more explicitly what is implicitly involved in Dewey's philosophy of the mind and epistemology as well as in his theory of judgment. In this latter contention I may be wrong, but I do not believe I am because, as already stated, judgment, for Dewey, takes place within a non-cognitive context of experience, and is essentially hypothetical, in contrast to the judgment of the idealists and realists which takes place within an experiential vacuum and is essentially assertoric or categorical.

Since assertoric propositions in their primary character as termini of the process of judgment are neither true nor false, it remains that these predicates must be attributed solely to hypothetical judgments. And nothing so convincingly testifies to the validity of this conclusion as the realist logic itself. For that logic takes its propositional datum as being "either true or false"—and wherever we have "either—or" we have a hypothetical involved. Of course, this logic has no business to treat its propositional datum hypothetically because, as Johnson says, the proposition is, for it, the "terminus of the process of judgment"; and since in the process of judgment the hypothetical element is eliminated, the only proper attitude to be taken to the terminal proposition is "assertive" (or, as I would prefer to say, denotative or declarative). But the practice of treating the conclusion *of* inquiry, independent of any context as the beginning *for* inquiry, of treating isolated termini *of* the process of judgment, as the original subject-matter *for* judgment—this practice is indeed the basic confusion of this logic—if we may single out one confusion as being more basic than another. And this confusion does not diminish but increases in intensity as its consequences spread throughout the ramifications and complexities of the logic. It has its source in the fundamental contradiction Dewey has summed up in *The Quest for Certainty*—a contradiction realism has in common with the classic tradition which "asserted that knowledge is determined by the objective constitution of the universe. But it did so only after it had first assumed that the universe is itself constituted after the pattern of reason." Whence the result that, although propositions are, in realist theory, derivatives of their corresponding subsistential facts or esssences, in practice they are made the determinants for the putative discovery of their correspondents and the criteria of their validity. Every realist is harassed by his professional obligation to find corresponding "eternal" facts or essences for propositions positive and negative, atomic and molecular, true and false. He is in much the same pathetic predicament as is the person who first accepts the doctrine that appearances in the physical world are all ectoplasmic manifestations, and then on the basis of this unwary acceptance, sets out to discover for every appearance he meets, a mediumistic or astral source. This pathetic predicament idealists and realists can escape only if they adopt the instrumentalist method of taking a hypothetical judgment in its functional context, considering it alone the object of knowledge or cognition, capable of either truth or falsity; and of taking the completed and isolated proposition as being a datum, even though not brute, of non-cognitive experience and therefore neither true nor false.

It has no doubt occurred to most if not all of you that if starting with "I see my finger" or "*A* is *B*" thrusts philosophers into ever more complicated difficulties, it is sheerest folly to persist in making such rash statements. They should, rather, start more modestly, exercising some of that intellectual restraint they extol as high virtue in the scientist. Everyone will grant that it is a perverse doctrine that starts with "infallible knowledge" and ends in questionable opinion and ignorance; and that it is a perverse method that can establish the validity of its arguments only at the cost of invalidating the source from which those very arguments are derived. Such a doctrine and such a method are an insult to the laws of scientific progress so firmly established. Philosophers should start with a question, with a hypothetical judgment instead of an assertoric proposition alleged to be eternally true. Questions bespeak problems, and problems, to be sure, bespeak difficulties for the philosopher. But these difficulties would be simpler and far easier to solve. Moreover, coming at the start, they would strengthen, not weaken and demoralize, the intellectual fibre. And once the difficulties are overcome, and the problems solved, the philosopher would then be able to announce with the confidence that is born of tested knowledge, the discovery of his eyes or mind. With the final statement, "I see my finger" or "*A* is *B*," he could rest from his weary labors and enjoy the laurels of victory hard won.

To make problems and the method of their solution, instead of propositions and the method of their formal deployment, the subject-matter of logic, is no trivial change. The whole history of thought proves it is of utmost importance to get the right start. Definitions or formal propositions lead only to more definitions or more formal propositions as the Platonic dialogues and symbolic logic abundantly demonstrate; they give us no entrance into the real subject-matter itself. In the degree that we are exact logicians, we are forever boxed up in the narrow confines of our formal starting point; our method is rigidly restricted to unravelling dialectical implications—a stultifying occupation that always makes the mind quite vicious. Problems, on the contrary, lead us directly into the heart of the natural subject-matter, and the technique of investigation takes on the ample form of experimental method. Dialectic is kept on a leash, and the mind of man, free to find nourishment in the pastures of knowledge which contain only the salt of wonder, grows in wisdom and increases to the fulness of its power.

The metaphysics of sense-data, for all its initial forthright realism, comes, when developed, dangerously near being a variation in metaphysical idealism. G. E. Moore has to resuscitate Mill's vacuous doctrine of matter as the possibility of sensation—a doctrine that belongs with Spencer's Unknowable in the medical cabinet of philosophical abortions. And Russell's theory of perspectives, especially in the hands of Eddington, is as definite a return as one could maliciously desire to the idealism Moore and Russell started out to demolish. The realist logic of propositions is, likewise, in essential nature the idealistic logic over again. At the start, it was the same logic minus its super-idealistic head; but since Whitehead's God has been substituting for Bradley's Absolute it is minus that head no longer.

Finally, the claim of the symbolic branch of realist logic that it is a genuine departure from the Aristotelian mold, is unfounded. Symbolic logic, like Aristotelian logic, takes the finished statement, the terminal proposition, as its datum; and any logic that does this, is in its major features essentially like any other logic that does this; and symbolic logic, like the ancestor it denies, concerns itself solely with dialectical implications. Because symbolic logic has a wider range of implications and relations than the syllogistic ones, does not make it non-Aristotelian. Symbolic logic is certainly an advance on Aristotelian logic; but it is an advance on the same road with the same type of logical army. Instrumental logic, on the other hand, is, as we have tried to show, a new type of logic. Although it has not been unheralded—and recently at any rate not been unsung—it is none the less a new line of advance with a new set of ideas on a new road that it has broken into service for the greater glory of logic and the greater benefit of mankind.

JOSEPH RATNER.

NEW YORK CITY.

EXPERIENCE AND DIALECTIC [1]

EVEN a misguided comment on Professor Dewey's philosophy may be instructive. Opinions have a social as well as an individual character, with the obvious consequence that one man's understanding of another is at least one instance of how that other is understood. Otherwise, why should we comment on great philosophers, and tell the world what they thought, when they have already told the world themselves? In the present case, malice could suggest that a philosophy should be defined and judged in terms of the effects it produces, but malice would be confused if confronted with a multiplicity of effects, and might find the criterion that a philosophy is what it is experienced to be, forcing it, in the interest of justice, to distinguish between appearance and reality. A commentator is embarrassed in making the distinction, for what he finds the philosophy to be is what he concludes it to be. His commentary is, then, at least as instructive as personal revelations usually are. He exhibits himself. He is an appearance. If the reality, as it may very well do, mocks him, that is the penalty of being an appearance, and, perhaps, some justification for being it, some evidence that the reality is antecedent to the appearance and should control it. Haunted by this perplexing circumstance, I proceed with this paper. I shall state what I have to say in summary at the beginning, and then illustrate it in two particulars.

Professor Dewey has had an eminently practical effect. He has profoundly influenced the way many people think and act and teach. When his writings are stripped of dialectic and controversy, and freed from contact with certain of the traditional problems of philosophy, there remains a positive and substantial pronouncement on human life in its immediate practical character. This pronouncement has had on many minds the effect of a genuine liberation from obstacles which warped their thinking and clogged their action. It proposes to substitute courage for uncertainty and hopefulness for fear. That is a very practical substitution. Certainty, or the claim of it, might have been offered as the substitute for uncertainty, and courage might have been offered as the substitute for fear. This, however, is not what the pronouncement offers. The soul is not to be cured of uncertainty and fear by becoming certain and courage-

---

[1] Read at the meeting of the American Philosophical Association in New York, December 30, 1929.

ous. It is to be made immune to its vices by means of a revised alignment of opposites, an alignment revised in view of the exigencies of living. The shift involved is naturally described as a shift from the theoretical to the practical. And I suspect that the major difficulties found in construing the philosophy of Professor Dewey arise from attempts to justify that shift on theoretical grounds. It is difficult for me to think that Professor Dewey himself does not attempt to provide such a justification. I find this less in what he affirms than in what he denies. His affirmations impress me as keeping close to a progressive development of a central theme. His denials, however, often impress me as requiring the acceptance of the opposite of what is denied as the ultimate theoretical ground which supports the practical affirmations. I seem at times to be asked to substitute courage for certainty on the ground that there is no certainty, and hopefulness for fear on the ground that there is nothing of which to be afraid. In such moments I find myself involved in a dialectic of theories of knowledge and existence. I become myself a controversialist, and find myself leaving the solid ground of experience.

There are two sentences in *Experience and Nature* [2] which express concisely and without controversial implications that pronouncement on human life to which I have referred. They are these: "Because intelligence is critical method applied to goods of belief, appreciation, and conduct, so as to construct freer and more secure goods, turning assent and assertion into free communication and sharable meanings, turning feeling into ordered and liberal sense, turning reaction into response, it is the reasonable object of our deepest faith and loyalty, the stay and support of all reasonable hopes. . . . What the method of intelligence, thoughtful valuation, will accomplish, if once it be tried, is for the result of trial to determine." I have said that these sentences are without controversial implications. They receive, moreover, in Professor Dewey's manifold expansion of them, an emphasis which puts them in a position of philosophical dignity. They are not left without an expert analysis which aims to make them of primary importance, and to exhibit their entire independence of any attitude which can be defined as antecedent or more fundamental. This analysis, when freed from dialectical and controversial entanglements, impresses me as wholly convincing. The attempt to bring intelligence to bear on life in the manner described, is an attempt which is, and can be, made, without first having solved any antecedent problem whatever. Least of all does it wait on the solution of such problems as the existence of God, immortality, freedom *versus* necessity, mechanism

[2] Pp. 436–437.

versus teleology, and the like. Problems do not exist to be solved before we can live: they arise in the process of living, and in that process are solved and resolved. Professor Dewey has driven that fact home with untiring persistence; and he has made that fact the starting-point of all fruitful thinking. As a consequence, he has made many of us intolerant of any other attitude. He has made it quite impossible for many of us to believe that life can generate any problem the solution of which would be life's undoing. And he has made this impossible because he has shown us in a wholly convincing manner that if we are to philosophize profitably we must begin with the concrete operations of intelligence as these promote more satisfactory living, and not with some antecedent scheme of things which is supposed to explain or justify these operations. Life with its exigencies is fundamental, and this fundamental can not be explained by any solution of life's problems, nor deduced from any system of things which our ingenuity may devise. Whatever one thinks of all this, it is a very definite and a clearly intelligible philosophy. And it is natural for it to recommend courage in the face of uncertainty and hopefulness in the face of fear.

It is natural, too, perhaps, that among its analyses it should give a prominent and even a distinctive place to the analysis of reflective thinking and the operation of ideas. Its premise, it may be said, forces it to look upon thinking as inquiry, and upon ideas as the intellectual instruments of inquiry which find their validity in what they effect or accomplish. Here is a thesis which can stand on its own bottom. It seems to be a major thesis of Professor Dewey, which he uses to frame a logic of practice, to give moral tone to actions, and to humanize education. In his development of it, however, he seems to me to support it far less by an appeal to its natural source, than by using it dialectically to confound every analysis of knowledge which implies an antecedent reality to which intelligence must conform in its operations if it is to be successful. Now, the question I would raise here is not whether there is such an antecedent reality, nor whether there are grounds for believing that there is. Such questions, like Professor Dewey's major thesis, seem to me to stand on their own bottom. Surely we can ask with as complete intelligibility as we can ask any question, whether or not reflective thinking implies an antecedent reality to which knowledge must conform to be successful. It is a question to be settled by inquiry fully as much as any other. To make it a wholly illegitimate question, and to read the whole history of philosophy down to very recent times as if it were vitiated by attempted answers to this question, give to Professor Dewey's thesis a character extraordinarily difficult to construe. I repeat, the question is not whether there are objects antecedent to knowledge to which knowledge must conform to be successful. The question is, rather, whether Professor Dewey's thesis would be vitiated in proportion as one believed in such objects and operated accordingly, and whether, if there were such objects, that thesis would be wholly destroyed? I ask the question because I have failed to discover that the existence or non-existence of such objects has anything to do with the essential character of the thesis. I can not find that the problem of their existence has to be settled first, before validity can be claimed for the thesis. Yet I am forced to believe that Professor Dewey thinks that such a settlement is essential. As I follow his settlement, I find myself in a dialectic which sets antecedent objects over against eventual objects to the confounding of both.

To be more specific, in *The Quest for Certainty* [3] Professor Dewey says in italics, *"only the conclusion of reflective inquiry is known."* This forces me to reply, "The conclusion of reflective inquiry is currently said to be knowledge; am I then to identify knowledge with the known." If I do this, I am thrown into the arms of the idealists, whose embrace I dislike. So I distinguish between knowledge and its object; I conceive the object to exist prior to its being known. Then I am confronted with the charge that this robs knowing of practical efficacy. To avoid this I must recognize that objects of knowledge exist only after the act of knowing; they are eventual objects. That there are eventual objects after the act of knowing, and that, unless there are such objects, the act of knowing is futile, are propositions which are for me both clear and acceptable. But if any objects whatever are known, it seems to me to be irrelevant whether they exist prior or subsequent to the act of knowing. What knowing eventuates in is a known object. I suppose no one disputes that, at least no one disputes it so far as the intent of knowledge is concerned. If that eventuation is made to depend on the prior settlement of the problem of antecedent as against eventual object, I can see nothing left but a dialectic which settles nothing. I do see, however, that an analysis of knowing as a concrete operation with subject-matter, makes such a dialectic quite unnecessary. Why, then, play eventual objects over against primary subject-matter, making of the former reconstructions of the latter, and making these reconstructions the objects of knowledge? I am quite ready to agree that it is the important business of knowing so to deal with subject-matter that more satisfactory objects are substituted for less satisfactory, and that, thereby, greater security, control, and happiness are secured; but I fail to see how this warrants the statement that *only the conclusion of reflective inquiry is known.* That statement seems to me to come from another source. To find that source I am

[3] P. 182.

driven back on Professor Dewey's dialectical and controversial arguments. These drive me, in spite of all he says, to try to frame some conception of existence which is wholly independent of the act of knowing, and yet the justification of that act and the source of its efficacy. Yet this seems to be precisely what I am forbidden to do by the dialectic.

The matter may be made still more specific. In the chapter on "The Seat of Intellectual Authority" in *The Quest for Certainty*, Professor Dewey uses the example of a physician called in to diagnose the disease of a patient. He has the physician do what a physician would do, examine the patient and bring to bear his medical knowledge on the case. But the whole discussion drives me to ask: Must we conclude that it is only after the physician has found out what is the matter with the patient that the patient has anything the matter with him? So to conclude would be to caricature. Is, I venture to ask, the caricature only the result of the reader's stupidity, or is it the result of being forced to decide whether antecedents or consequents are the objects known? One must ask: Do what things are and the ways they operate depend on the eventuation of inquiry? Must we conclude that they do so depend because intelligence does, as a matter of fact, participate in the order of events, and so operate that more satisfactory objects are substituted for less satisfactory? Is this caricature? What saves us from the confusion here involved except a metaphysics of the kind which the dialectic of prior and eventual objects tends to destroy?

The questions are not asked to try to convict Professor Dewey of contradiction. They are asked because one reader at least finds no clue to an answer to them except in the dialectic, and that clue leaves him in the dialectic. The best he can do is to conclude that existence is essentially dialectical, and that the dialectic is incidentally resolved by the practical operations of intelligence. This may be a sound conclusion. If, now, we try to settle the question whether it is or not, we discover in ourselves a close intellectual kinship with Plato, Aristotle, Spinoza, Locke, Kant, Hegel, and all that array of names which the history of philosophy holds up for admiration.

Again I take sentences from *Experience and Nature*.[4] "A naturalistic metaphysics is bound to consider reflection itself a natural event, occurring *within* nature because of traits of the latter. . . . The world must actually be such as to generate ignorance and inquiry, doubt and hypothesis, trial and temporal conclusions. . . . The ultimate evidence of genuine hazard, contingency, irregularity, and indeterminateness in nature is thus found in the occurrence of

[4] Pp. 68–70.

thinking. The traits of natural existence which generate the fears and adorations of superstitious barbarians, generate the scientific procedures of disciplined civilization.'' Sentences like these abound in Professor Dewey's writings. They impress me as being fully as characteristic of his philosophy as the instrumental doctrine of intelligence. At times, they impress me as more characteristic, because they define an attitude from which instrumentalism may be derived, but which itself is not derived from instrumentalism. It is a challenging attitude which nowhere else in my reading have I found so vigorously set forth.

It is not unusual among philosophies to be what is called anthropomorphic. It is very unusual, however, to be that in Professor Dewey's sense. There is a vast difference between constructing nature out of human traits and finding in human traits clues for inferences regarding what nature is. According to Professor Dewey's attitude, we are just as much forbidden to put man over against nature as an ultimate contrast as we are forbidden to put the sun, the moon, or the stars, over against it as such a contrast. If the latter are good grounds for inference, so also is man, and every part of man's make-up and activity.

I dislike to leave this feature of Professor Dewey's philosophy with so bare a statement of it. The importance of it is so great that it deserves far more attention than it has received. It involves an attitude difficult to describe by those pet isms with which we philosophers love to deal, and in which we think we feel at home. And ''nature'' is a very troublesome word. One thing, however, seems clear. Limited by our location and by our length of days, we do try to form some conception of that context within which we ourselves are so evidently incidents. ''Nature'' may not be that context; it may be only a part of it; but who is going to decide for us all? Shall we let a word cramp the challenging significance of an utterance which affirms that man, when he tries to pass beyond the limits of the evident situation in which he finds himself, must not neglect anything within that situation? Let us, then, for the present at least, accept ''nature'' as the name for that which includes us as events within itself. What, then, is nature like? The answer is, it is, in some measure at least, like what we are. If we are unstable, there is instability in it; if we are contradictory, there is contradiction in it; if we are hopeful, there is possibility—one might dare to say, hope—in it; if we err, there is something like error in it; if we are incomplete, there is incompleteness in it. And all this does not mean that we are the exclusive instances of all such traits of nature. We are samples of them. In short, man is a sample of nature, and just as good a sample as the solar system or an atom. Consequently, we should never suppose that the latter afford better grounds for inferring what nature is like than the former affords. Here is a road which philosophers rarely travel with unencumbering luggage.

The acceptance or rejection of this conception of nature is not here in question. Nor is the method by which it is approached. These matters are left to the disputatious. The thing that troubles me is the limitation which Professor Dewey seems to put upon what we are entitled to infer from the samples of nature which we may study and analyze. Clearly man is not the only sample. There is the solar system also, and, if not the atom, at least that which admits an atomic theory. Why, then, should inference to anything permanent and unchanging be forbidden? Such inferences may be unsound, but they suggest themselves repeatedly as we explore the varied samples of nature. I do not find, however, that Professor Dewey rejects them because there is not evidence for them. He seems, rather, to argue them into illegitimacy. The ground of the argument seems to be, I repeat, not lack of evidence; it seems, rather, to be the conviction that any recognition of the permanently fixed or unchanging is bad. It implies a disastrous preference. *The Quest for Certainty* seems to me to read the history of philosophy in terms of that disaster, and to turn that history into an argument against the recognition of anything but relative permanency. And in *Experience and Nature* [5] we read: "One doctrine finds structure in a framework of ideal forms, the other finds it in matter. They agree in supposing that structure has some superlative reality. This supposition is another form taken by preference for the stable over the precarious and incompleted." Are we to conclude, therefore, that to avoid disaster, we must take a preference for the precarious and incompleted? Why is one preference better than the other, and why should the question be one of taking preference at all? I get no answer in terms of evidence of the same kind that warrants the emphasis on change. I get a dialectical answer, as if dialectic, and not the method by which nature is inferred, is to decide what inferences are to be admitted. And when I examine the dialectic, I find it motivated by the insistent claim that the recognition of the permanent gives it a metaphysical superiority to the changing. This makes it possible to play the one off against the other in the interest of proving that the permanent is but the relatively stable in a nature which is change through and through.

Now nature may be just that. I am not questioning that conception of what nature is. I am only pointing out that I find that conception supported finally, not by empirical evidence, but by a dialectical argument. That, again, may be the way to support it. If it is, then I am forced to conclude that dialectic is a better sample

[5] P. 72.

of nature's processes than any other. This also may be true. Then, to consider its truth, I find myself owning kinship with Heraclitus and Parmenides and their illustrious followers. I must carry the debate into that atmosphere; and when I do, I find no help whatever in terms of that practical procedure which marks the development of securer knowledge.

Such are the two illustrations I venture to give of the general statement I made in the beginning of this paper. They represent a conclusion I am led to by reading the writing of Professor Dewey. It is what his philosophy ultimately looks like in my own mind: a philosophy with a doctrine of experience and nature which admits of a positive and progressive development in its own terms, which stands, as I have said, on its own bottom; but which, in spite of this, is made to depend on a dialectic which runs back in the history of philosophy very far indeed. We should expect, as I see it, a metaphysics which is wholly inferential. We have, instead, a metaphysics which is a matter of preference. And this preference—we may even say that the empirical fact of preference—implies that nature is essentially dialectical, and that one way, at least, by which the dialectic is incidentally obviated, is through the practical procedure of intelligence. Experience appears to be, therefore, not something which is justified by its fruits, but which is justified by a dialectic which determines what experience is like.

FREDERICK J. E. WOODBRIDGE.

COLUMBIA UNIVERSITY.

IN REPLY TO SOME CRITICISMS [1]

IT is inevitable, on an occasion like this, that the adverse criticisms be selected for discussion and reply. This fact gives an unduly controversial character to this article. So I wish to begin by expressing my grateful appreciation of not only the attention given by critics to my thought, but especially of their considerate tone, and their words of generous recognition of some value in my thinking.

I

There are, I take it, two main points and one that is subsidiary, in the article by Professor Woodbridge. Of the main points, one concerns the attitude taken by me toward the antecedents and the consequents of reflection with respect to objects of knowledge; the

[1] See the articles read at the meeting of the American Philosophical Association, New York, December, 1929, by Prof. W. E. Hocking ("Action and Certainty"), and Prof. C. I. Lewis ("Pragmatism and Current Thought"), both printed in this JOURNAL in the preceding issue, No. 9, and the article by Prof. F. J. E. Woodbridge, which appears in this issue.

other concerns the method by which my position is reached—Mr. Woodbridge conceiving it to be purely dialectical and not, as I have maintained and believe, empirical. The point that seems to me subsidiary, deals with the place of the permanent and the changing in existence. With regard to this problem also, Professor Woodbridge believes that I reach my position by dialectic rather than derive it from experience.

Although Mr. Woodbridge's two main points are related to each other, it will be better to consider the question of the nature of the antecedents and consequents of reflection first and independently of the question of method, because I find attributed to me a somewhat different view from that which I hold. Perhaps the difference in view may be most directly approached through the instance of the patient and the physician (employed by me) to which Mr. Woodbridge refers. I began the discussion of this illustration with the statement, "it is evident that the presence of a man who is ill is the 'given.'" Then I went on to say that *this* "given" is not as such a case of knowledge at all; the particular point I was making being that the given in the sense of data of *knowledge* is the product of reflective analysis of that which is given or had in direct perceptual experience, and which, as such, is not a case of knowledge. Moreover, data for knowledge when once arrived at, define the problem, and hence are not identical with the *object* of knowledge. As I said, in the context referred to, "The original perception furnishes the *problem* for knowing; it is something *to be* known not an object of knowing." But, as I also tried to show, the original experience does not furnish the problem in the sense of constituting it in a defined way; the resolution of the experience into those particulars called data accomplishes this task. The patient having something the matter with him is antecedent; but being ill (*having* the experience of illness) is not the same as being an *object of knowledge;* it is identical, when the further experience had by the physician supervenes, with having a subject-matter *to be* known, to be investigated. If the distinctions (upon which I have insisted at considerable length) between something *had* in experience and the object *known,* between this something and data of knowledge, and between the data and the final object of knowledge, be noted, I do not understand why any one should think I was denying the existence of antecedent things or should suppose that the object of knowledge as I conceive it does away with antecedent existences. On the contrary, the object of knowledge is, according to my theory, a re-disposition *of* the antecedent existences. After quoting a statement of mine that "only the conclusion of reflective inquiry is known" Mr. Woodbridge goes on to say, "I conceive the object to exist prior to its being known.'' I, too, conceive that things had in direct experience exist prior to being known. But I deny the identity of things had in direct experience with the object of knowledge *qua* object of knowledge. Things that are *had* in experience exist prior to reflection and its eventuation in an *object* of knowledge; but the latter, as such, is a deliberately effected re-arrangement or re-disposition, by means of overt operations, of such antecedent existences. The difference between Mr. Woodbridge and myself, as I see it, is not that he believes in the existence of things antecedent to knowledge and I do not; we differ in our beliefs as to what the character of the antecedent existences with respect to knowledge is. While Mr. Woodbridge says "the object exists prior to *its* being known," I say that "*the* object" is the eventual product of reflection, the prior or antecedent existences being subject-matter *for* knowledge, not *the objects* of knowledge at all.

The foregoing remarks are not intended, of course, to prove that my position is correct, they are meant to show what the position is. The question of correctness brings up the question of the method by which is reached the conclusion that the object consequent on reflective inquiry differs from the antecedently experienced existences, since it is their re-disposition. Mr. Woodbridge thinks that the method is purely dialectical, not empirical. Now, of course, I employ dialectic. I do not suppose that any one could write on philosophy without using it. If I could take the reader by the hand and lead him to see the same things I think I see and have the same experience I have, I would do it. Short of that possibility, I use dialectic. But this is so obvious, it can not be what Mr. Woodbridge objects to. As far as I can make out, the objectionable dialectic consists in laying it down as a premiss that knowledge must have practical efficacy, and then arguing from this premiss to the conclusion that the object of knowledge must differ from what exists antecedent to knowing. If I had been guilty of this practice I should agree with Mr. Woodbridge's criticisms.

As matter of fact, however, I have depended upon empirical evidence. The evidence which I have cited at considerable length, running, in fact, through several chapters, is drawn from the experimental sciences. The argument may be stated in a simple way. The sciences of natural existence are not content to regard anything as an object of knowledge—in its emphatic differential sense—except when the object in question is reached by experimental methods. These experimental methods involve overt operations which re-dispose the existences antecedently had in experience. Q.E.D. Dialectic is used, of course, but it is used in order to invite the reader to experience the empirical procedure of experimental inquiry and then draw his own conclusion. If I am wrong, it is because my empirical analysis is wrong. I regret that none of my critics offered his own interpretation of experimental knowledge and its object. In any case, the practical efficacy of reflective thought (rather than of knowledge) is the conclusion of my empirical analysis, not the premiss of a dialectic.

I have called the criticism regarding my preference for the changing over the immutably fixed, subsidiary. This is because it does not seem to be so important in the criticism nor so well established as that just dealt with. In one respect, my argument on this point is frankly dialectical. The history of thought seems to me to disclose that the belief in immutable existence is an emotional preference dialectically supported. Dialectic is obviously in place in dealing with a position as far as that is itself dialectical. In any case, I have not meant to deny the theory of immutable substances because it is "bad," although it is pertinent to the dialectic to point out that bad consequences have resulted in morals and natural science from its assumption. In addition to this negative reason, derived from dialectic, I find a positive reason in the history of science for my hypothesis that the difference between the apparently permanently permanent and the obviously changing is one of tempo or rate of change. For science seems to have moved constantly away from acceptance of everlasting unchangeable elements. Its continually increasing emphasis upon interaction seems to be compatible empirically only with the fact that things are modified in their interactions. While, then, I would not call the hypothesis in question proved, it appears to me more reasonable than the contrary doctrine.

II

To reply adequately to the points raised by Professor Hocking would involve a substantial statement of my theory of meaning and truth. Consequently, I am compelled to engage in a series of rather summary remarks.

1. In arguing for the non-correspondence of meaning and working, Mr. Hocking says "if we only know a thing when we see what comes of it, then indeed we can never know anything; for we never have in hand what is yet to eventuate." For, as he points out, when ideas are taken as plans of action, they develop later into other plans not even contemplated, much less in process of execution, when the idea was originally conceived. This is an objection which is natural when truth is conceived of as an inherent property of some meanings, ideas, or propositions. By converting my position in terms of his own, Mr. Hocking naturally finds my position unsatisfactory. But if it is taken in its own terms, it is seen that any idea

or proposition is relevant to its *own* problematic situation in which it arises and which it intends to resolve. As far as it does resolve it, it is validated or is "true." This resolved situation may produce *another* situation that then requires to be resolved, a further meaning and further truth, and so on. There is continuity between these different situations, in so far as the *subject-matter* is continuous. Looking *back*, it is easy to suppose that there was a single idea or meaning (like that of freedom in Mr. Hocking's illustrations) which has remained identical through a series of partial realizations. But this retrospective survey and the meaning it yields is always in fact —according to my conception—a new meaning arrived at in dealing with a new empirical situation.[2] Without going into detail, I would say that much of Professor Hocking's argument and illustrations (the case of the lover, radio-activity, etc.) seems to me to rest on an identification of truth with meaning which is necessary from his point of view, but which is denied from mine. What he calls "half-truths," "partial-truths," are from my point of view *meanings* in process of development; the question of truth arises only when the question of experimental verification enters in. Part of the meaning may be verified, but such verification is not a half-truth; it is the whole truth of that part of the meaning.

2. The same line of argument applies to the question of the immediacy of truth. There is a sense in which truth, as the solution of problems, is immediate; it is the same sense in which a solution *when it is arrived at* is immediate; it immediately exists. But it is arrived at through mediation or reflection involving operations; it is, in good Hegelian language, a mediated immediacy. What is denied is that meanings, apart from their application through operations, are more than *claims* to truth. More specifically, what is denied is that immediate properties, such as clearness, so-called self-evidence, etc. (the properties insisted upon by the rationalistic schools as marks of truth) are more than properties of *meanings*.

3. It is an old story that "eternal" is an ambiguous word. It means both irrelevancy to time and enduring through all time. Taking the word in the latter sense as Professor Hocking's argument seems to require, I should say that stability of truth, like "reality" as defined by C. S. Peirce, represents a *limit*. Of course we want truths to be as stable as they can be. That is to say, we want meanings which have been confirmed in a comprehensive variety of empirical situations and that accordingly offer us the promise of further applications. What is objected to is the conversion of this ideal limit into an inherent and antecedent property

---

[2] In connection with this point I would call especial attention to the argument *against* the agnostic inference that Mr. Hocking draws from my theory which is found on pp. 192–194 and elsewhere in *The Quest for Certainty*.

of meanings. Such conversion appears to me the essence of dogmatism. And some of Mr. Hocking's illustrations in exemplifying such dogmatisms, also exemplify, to my mind, the objectionableness of the conversion of an ideal limit into an eternal truth. These fixed dogmas work, of course, but I can not share—taking the light of history as a guide that reveals the way in which they have worked —Mr. Hocking's enthusiasm for the "absolute as a battle-ax." The fixed truths of paranoiacs also work—but rather disastrously.

4. That there are *a priori meanings* in an empirical sense, I have never denied or doubted. It is the nature of a genuine meaning to be prospective and thus *temporally a priori*. When the nature and function of these meanings are clarified they form what may be called postulates. The value of postulates in science is undoubted. The conversion of meanings-as-postulates into truths, already alluded to, is, once more, natural in the philosophy of Mr. Hocking, but from my point of view it is fallacious. I would have postulates recognized for what they are and not frozen into dogmatic truths. The assertion that "necessary consequences can be perceived and evaluated in advance" rests, to my mind, on an ambiguity in the term "necessary consequences." It may signify either logical implications or existential outcomes. The fallacy of such ethics as the Kantian, consists, as I see it, in supposing that the former is identical with the latter, or that the latter *ought* to be identical with the former. It therefore leads to a rigidity which is favorable not only to dogmatism in thought, but to fanaticism in action: since the consequences follow logically from the principle they *must* be right and *must* be fought for at all costs. Experience seems to me to testify to the need of an ethics more humble toward existential consequences. Such humility is quite consistent with firm attachment to hypotheses that have had a wide confirmation in the history of the race and of the individual, provided pains are taken to examine the relation between the hypothesis and its consequences so as to give assurance that the latter are genuine confirmations. "The value of trying to realize value" is such a hypothesis—provided one join with it (or interpret it as) a constantly renewed endeavor at "*discovering* the possibilities of the actual."

I recognize the quite summary character of these comments. But as I said at the outset, Mr. Hocking's points raise a large number of fundamental issues in logic and morals, and to do justice to them would require not a few paragraphs, but a treatise.

III

I find myself in such sympathy with the article of Mr. Lewis that I shall confine my comment upon it to one minor point. He says "Professor Dewey seems to view such abstractionism in science as a sort of defect—something necessary, but always regrettable; an inadequacy of it to the fullness of experience." I fear that on occasion I may so have written as to give this impression. I am glad, therefore, to have the opportunity of saying that this is not my actual position. Abstraction is the heart of thought; there is no way—other than accident—to control and enrich concrete experience except through an intermediate flight of thought with conceptions, relations, abstracta. What I regret is the tendency to erect the abstractions into complete and self-subsistent things, or into a kind of superior Being. I wish to agree also with Mr. Lewis that the need of the social sciences at present is precisely such abstractions as will get their unwieldy elephants into box-cars that will move on rails arrived at by other abstractions. What is to be regretted is, to my mind, the tendency of many inquirers in the field of human affairs to be over-awed by the abstractions of the physical sciences and hence to fail to develop the conceptions or abstractions appropriate to their own subject-matter.

In conclusion I wish again to thank the participators in the discussion for their sympathetic treatment of my intellectual efforts. If I have omitted reference to the paper of Mr. Ratner, it is because in his case a sympathetic understanding is manifest which calls for no reply—indeed, his paper seems to me to answer by way of anticipation some of the criticisms upon which I have commented, especially the one concerning the nature of antecedent existences.

JOHN DEWEY.

COLUMBIA UNIVERSITY.

The Journal of Philosophy

THE OBJECTIVISM–SUBJECTIVISM OF MODERN PHILOSOPHY

I

IN his *Adventures of Ideas,* Whitehead writes as follows: "It is customary to contrast the objective approach of the ancient Greeks with the subjective approach of the moderns. . . . But whether we be ancients or moderns we can deal only with things, in some sense, experienced."[1] Since I agree fully with this statement, my only comment is that it involves repudiation of the view that approach through experience is *ipso facto* subjective. There is a further statement of Whitehead's which I wish to use as a peg from which to hang some remarks of my own, as preachers use a text. "The difference between ancients and moderns is that the ancients asked what have we experienced and the moderns asked what can we experience."[2] I propose to develop the distinction between "what *has* been" and "what *can* be" experienced, in explanation of the difference between ancient and modern philosophy, in a way that has no authorization in Whitehead's treatment. In fact, my development is in a direction contrary to what Whitehead goes on to say. For that reason I feel the more bound to say that the particular interpretation he gives the distinction commands, within the limits set by the point he is making, my full assent. For he is concerned to show how the notion of experience was narrowed by the criteria set up by some moderns for judging what *can* be experienced. There can be no doubt as to the existence of this criterion nor as to its restrictive consequence.

The limitation is due, as Whitehead justly says, to two errors. "The first error is the assumption of a few definite avenues of communication with the external world, the five sense-organs. This leads to the pre-supposition that the search for data is to be narrowed to the question, what data are directly provided by the activity of the sense-organs. . . . The second error is the presupposition that the sole way of examining experience is by acts of conscious introspective analysis."[3] When applied to such writers

[1] P. 287.

[2] *Op. cit.,* p. 288.

[3] *Op. cit.,* p. 269 and p. 290. Cf. the following from p. 269, "Warping has taken the form of constant reliance upon sensationalist activity as the basis of all experiential activity."

as Locke and Hume on one side and Kant on the other side nothing could be truer than these statements. The outcome was a definite and to my mind disastrous narrowing of the field of experience. Upon the face of the matter, then, the view I am going to advance seems to be contradicted by facts. For what I wish to say is that ancient philosophy is the one which is restricted, since it could not venture beyond what had already been accomplished in the way of experienced things—using "things" to designate activities and institutions as well as "objects," while modern experience is expansive since it is marked off by its constant concern for possibilities of experience as yet unrealized, as is shown, for example, in its interest in discovery and invention. In consequence what *can* be experienced stands for something wider and freer than what *has* been experienced.

II

There is an undeniable discrepancy involved in admitting the justice of what Whitehead says about the way in which the idea of what "can be experienced" was used to narrow the experiential field and the position I am here taking. As to the views about experience literally expressed by modern philosophers of both the experiential and the *a priori* schools, I have no desire to explain away the discrepancy. What I intend to point out is that the spirit and direction of modern philosophy is of quite another sort, since it has been occupied with breaking down fixed barriers, with novelty, expansion, growth, potentialities previously unforeseen; in short, with an open and "infinite" world instead of the closed and finite world of the Greeks. If this statement does not apply to the general movement and implicit intent of modern philosophy, we are faced with a much greater discrepancy than the one just mentioned: that between the actual tendencies of modern experience and the philosophy that has been produced on the ground of this experience.

Accordingly, I do not think it is a necessary part of my task to account for the view nominally taken by modern philosophers about what *can* be experienced. At the same time, I do not believe the paradox is as great as it seems to be on the surface. The very fact that modern philosophy has been concerned with possibilities of experience which lie beyond the range of what *has been* experienced in the past made it peculiarly sensitive to the existence of certain barriers to their acceptance and realization, namely, the barriers that are products of past culture and are sanctioned by the philosophy which reflected that culture. In behalf of their own interest in the prospective, in possible expansion, philosophers were obliged to assail the beliefs and habits which stood in the way. They needed a criterion and method for carrying on their battle. In short, the positive side of modern philosophy, what I have called its spirit and direction of movement, was such as to give great importance to the negative work that had to be done. The readiest instrumentality of destructive criticism was identification of valid beliefs with those authorized by experience when experience is reduced to material of direct observation; namely, to simple ideas, impressions, sense data. The incompatibility of this reduction to the positive faith which animated the modern philosophers was concealed from view by their intense belief that if only obstructions inherited from the past were once done away with, the forces inhering in experience would carry men forward. Even more instructive than what was explicitly said about experience is the revolution that took place as to the respective outlooks of "experience" and "reason." In ancient philosophy, experience stood for the habits and skills acquired by repetition of particular activities by means of selection of those which proved successful. It was a limiting principle, while reason, insight into reasons, was emancipatory of the bonds that were set by acquired habits. Francis Bacon and his experiential followers took exactly the opposite view. The "rational," when disassociated from personal experience, was to them the lifeless, the secondhand. Personal "experience," irrespective of any technical definition, was the means of initiation into living realities and provided the sole assurance of entering pastures that were fertile as well as fresh. Empiricism and liberalism were allies; the possibility of growth, of development, idealization of change as progress, were all, whether rightly or wrongly, connected with faith in experience. Technically, or in strict formal logic, the *tabula rasa,* the blank sheet of paper, view of mind to be written upon by "external" impressions, should have led to the conclusion that human beings are passive puppets. Actually, the feeling that if hampering and restrictive traditions and institutions could be got rid of, firsthand experience would ensure that men could and would go ahead, was the dominant factor.

III

If we consider Greek thought in an analytical way, we shall be persuaded, in any event, that from its own standpoint it can not be called *objective.* If the term is used, it is from our own present standpoint; that is, on the ground of the contrast of Greek thought with subjectivistic tendencies of modern philosophy, tendencies which, however, could not be identified as such, were it not that the distinction between the cosmological and the psychological, the "objective" and the "subjective," had been consciously made and become current. And it is precisely this distinction which does not appear in Greek thought. "Being" was set over against becoming, the latter containing an element of non-being or imperfection; the everlasting, immutable, and immortal were marked off from the transitory, and mortal imitations or images were set over against their originals. But the nearest approach to anything like the modern distinction of subjective-objective was between that which is by *nature* and that which is by *institution* or *convention*.

What may be truly said of ancient philosophy in contrast with modern is that it is naïve, using that word to designate a condition in which the distinction between the subjective and the objective is not made. Since naïveté suggests freshness and directness of approach, due to absence of artificial sophistication, one may apply the word "naïve" eulogistically to Greek philosophy. Of the Greek attitude, we could say that it fused qualities we now distinguish, were it not that fusion suggests prior differentiation, and it is just this antecedent differentiation that is lacking. In every characteristic expression of the Greek genius, the qualities we call emotional and volitional, and hence attribute to persons, are used to clothe things that we call physical and lacking in such qualities. The atomists, literally interpreted, are an exception to this statement. But one has only to read Lucretius (or Santayana today), and to reflect upon what is known regarding Democritus, to see that their interest in cosmology was a moral interest rather than a scientific one in the modern sense. In all influential and widely held ancient cosmologies, the physical world was marked by qualitative and teleological traits which modern physics has stripped away. Until this stripping had taken place there was no ground for anything like sharp opposition of the animate and inanimate; the human and the non-human; the "subjective" and "objective." In the matter of accounting for human traits in terms of generic cosmological qualities, there is no difference between Plato and Aristotle on one side and Democritus on the other.

There is a positive point involved in the foregoing negations. Greek philosophy moved and had its being in and among the things, the subjects, of *direct* experience, the world in which we human beings act, suffer, and enjoy. There is no particular point in saying their attitude was *animistic,* as if they had *first* discriminated certain qualities as psychic and personal and had *then* projected them into an "external" and purely physical (in our sense) world. As a contemporary writer has said in a criticism of the idea about animism entertained by such writers as Tylor, Spencer, and Lang:

Our present day dichotomy of *behavior* has isolated two types: the type directed toward things, which follows strictly a cause and effect sequence; and the type directed toward persons, which runs the gamut from love to manipulation. . . . Animism considered as *behavior* is nothing more than this; properly speaking, it is only the expression of a state of mind that has not made our distinction between *behavior* toward persons and behavior toward things, but which brings the whole field under one rubric, treating the entire external world according to the pattern learned in dealings with fellow beings.[4]

The fact that philosophers refined and systematized what is involved in this habitual attitude does not militate against the other fact that they retained it intact as far as its fundamental moral and qualitative implications are concerned. Until the type of physical science which we call modern had become established, what alternative did philosophy have save to describe the world in terms of basic properties of the material of direct experience? If we did not have an alternative in the *pou sto* provided for us by present-day physical science, we too should "naturally" describe the world in teleological and qualitative terms. Any other procedure would strike us as artificial and arbitrary. I was strongly reminded of this fact in reading recently a book by a writer deeply imbued with the spirit of classic Greek philosophy. He uniformly refers to "philosophies of experience" in a disparaging tone. But, as uniformly, his own account of Nature is couched in moral and poetic terms appropriate only to Nature as it is directly presented in experience and inappropriate to nature as disclosed to us in physics.

IV

For the purpose of the present article, the point of the foregoing is the necessity of distinguishing between the things of *direct* experience (which may also be called everyday experience if the latter word is extended to include the relatively extraordinary experiences of poets and moral seers), and something else. What name shall be given to this something else? It may be called *physical* subject-matter in the sense of material of the physical sciences. But this name only makes the *problem* more precise; it offers no solution. And here I recur to the special postulate of this particular discussion: The postulate, namely, that "whether we be ancients or moderns, we can deal only with things, *in some sense,* experienced." From the standpoint of this postulate, the problem is to discover *in terms of an experienced state of affairs* the connection that exists between physical subject-matter and the common-sense objects of everyday experience. Concern for the *con-*

---

[4] Article, by Ruth Benedict, on "Animism" in the *Encyclopaedia of the Social Sciences,* Vol. I, p. 66. I have italicized "behavior" in order to emphasize the point made.

ditions upon which depend the activities, enjoyments, and sufferings, constituting direct experience, is an integral part of that very experience when it is marked by faith in the possibility of its own indefinite expansion. The hypothesis here offered is that physical subject-matter represents in its own distinctive nature the *conditions* upon which rest the having, and the averting, of things in direct experience. What other method of getting outside and beyond the things of direct experience is conceivable save that of penetration to the conditions upon which they depend?

It is a commonplace that the sole method of controlling the occurrence of specific events—whether as to production or prevention—is by means of knowledge of their causal conditions. It is also a commonplace that modern science, as distinct from ancient, is occupied with determination of such conditions, and also that their discovery has been attended with creation of all sorts of technologies by means of which the area of things experienced and experienceable has been indefinitely widened. Every student of philosophy knows that Greek philosophy subordinated its account of things in terms of "efficient" causation to the account of them in terms of "formal" and "final" causation: that is, it was concerned with stating, by means of definition and classification, *what* things are and *why* they are so (in terms of the ends they serve), rather than with the quite subordinate question of *how* they come into being. The habit of viewing the history of philosophy in isolation from the state of culture in which philosophical theories are produced explains why this undeniable fact has not been linked to the fact that technologies for production and prevention of specifiable objects did not then exist; at least not outside of certain arts and crafts which, in any case, were products of past experiences, or of what *had* been experienced, not of scientific insight. Under these circumstances, the part of intelligent persons was to make as much as possible of characters, of natures, or essences, that "make things to be *what* they *are*" in their own alleged non-relational or "inherent" being. The connections of space, time, motion, that are so important in modern science could not possibly have appeared to be of more than secondary significance until the use of these connections in making possible a control of experience had been demonstrated in experience.

It is not a new discovery that the word "object" is highly ambiguous, being used for the sticks and stones, the cats and dogs, the chairs and tables of ordinary experiences, for the atoms and electrons of physics, and for any kind of "entity" that has logical subsistence—as in mathematics. In spite of the recognized ambiguity, one whole branch of modern epistemology is derived from the assumption that in the case of at least the first two cases, the word "object" has the same general meaning. For otherwise the subject-matter of physics and the things of everyday experience would not have presented themselves as rivals, and philosophy would not have felt an obligation to decide which is "real" and which is "appearance," or at least an obligation to set up a scheme in which they are "reconciled." The place occupied in modern philosophy by the problem of the relation of so-called "scientific objects" and "common-sense objects" is proof, in any case, of the dominating presence of a distinction between the "objective" and the "subjective" which was unknown in ancient philosophy. It indicates that in the sense at least of awareness of an ever-present problem, modern philosophy is "objective-subjective," not just subjective. I suggest that if we gave up calling the distinctive material of the physical sciences by the name "objects" and employed instead the neutral term "scientific subject-matter," the genuine nature of the problem would be greatly clarified. It would not of itself be solved. But at least we should be rid of the implication which now prevents reaching a solution. We should be prepared to consider on its merits the hypothesis here advanced: namely, that scientific subject-matter represents the *conditions* for having and not-having things of direct experience.

Genuinely complete empirical philosophy requires that there be a determination *in terms of experience* of the relation that exists between physical subject-matter and the things of direct perception, use, and enjoyment. It would seem clear that historic empiricism, because of its commitment to sensationalism, failed to meet this need. The obvious way of meeting the requirement is through explicit acknowledgment that direct experience contains, as a highly important direct ingredient of itself, a wealth of *possible* objects. There is no inconsistency between the idea of direct experience and the idea of objects of that experience which are as yet unrealized. For these latter objects are directly experienced *as* possibilities. Every plan, every prediction, yes, every forecast and anticipation, is an experience in which some non-directly experienced object is directly experienced *as a possibility*. And, as previously suggested, modern experience is marked by the extent to which directly perceived, enjoyed, and suffered objects are treated as signs, indications, of what has *not* been experienced in and of itself, or/and are treated as means for the realization of these things of possible experience. Because historic empirical philosophy failed to take cognizance of this fact, it was not able to account for one of the most striking features of scientific method and scientific conclusions—preoccupation with generality as such.

For scientific methods and scientific subject-matter combine highly abstract or "theoretical" considerations with directly present concrete sensible material, and the generality of conclusions reached is directly dependent upon the presence of the first-named type of considerations. Now in modern philosophy, just as scientific "objects" have been set over against objects in direct experience, thereby occasioning the *ontological* problem of modern philosophy (the problem of where "reality" is to be found), so identification of the experiential with but one of the two factors of the method of knowing has created the *epistemological* problem of modern philosophy: the relation of the "conceptual" and "perceptual"; of sense and understanding. In terms of our hypothesis, the distinction and the connection of the distinguished aspects rests upon the fact that what *is* (has been) experienced is of cognitive importance in connection with what *can* be experienced: that is, as evidence, sign, test, of forecast, anticipation, etc., while, on the other hand, there is no way of valid determination of objects of possible experiences save by employing what *has* been experienced, and hence is sensible. Anticipation, foresight, prediction, depend upon taking what is "given" (what has indubitably been experienced) as ominous, or of prospective reference. This is a speculative operation, a wager about the future. But the wager is subject to certain techniques of control. Although every projection of a possible object of experience goes beyond what has been experienced and is in so far risky, this fact does not signify that every idea or projected possibility has an equal claim. Techniques of observation on one side and of calculation (in its broad sense) on the other side have been developed with a view to effective co-operation. Interactivity *of the two factors* constitutes the method of science. Were it not for the influence of the inertia of habit it would be fairly incredible that empiricists did not long ago perceive that material provided by direct sense-perception is limited and remains substantially the same from person to person and from generation to generation. Even when we take into account the additional sense data furnished by artificial instruments, the addition bears no proportionate ratio to the expansion of the subject-matter of the sciences that is constantly taking place. Were it not that "rationalist" theories of knowledge are in no better case with respect to accounting for increase in scientific knowledge (which is its most striking trait in modern times), the marked impotency of sensationalist empiricism would long ago have effected its disappearance.

V

I have presented the more difficult aspect of my position and argument first. Few persons, I take it, would be rash enough to deny that an *actual* experience of a definite thing depends upon the operation of factors which have to be distinguished from those of physical subject-matter. It is better at first to refer to these latter factors denotatively, rather than to apply the word "subjective." From the denotative point of view, no one will deny that an experience of light involves an optical apparatus and not simply the existence of certain physical vibrations and quanta, and similarly with experiences of sound, temperature, solidity, etc. In the logical sense of "objectivity," these organic conditions are as objective as those described in physics. The organism is one "object" among others. However, the function of organic factors is so distinctive that it has to be discriminated. When it is discriminated, it is seen to be so different in kind from that of physical subject-matter as to require a special name. As a candidate for the name, "subjective" has one great disadvantage, namely, its traditional use as a name for some sort of existential stuff called psychical or mental. It has, on the other hand, the advantage of calling attention to the particular agency through which the function is exercised: a singular organism, an organism that has been subjected to acculturation, and is aware of itself as a social subject and agent.

The difference in function is, in any case, the important matter. Physical subject-matter consists of the conditions of *possible* experiences in their status *as* possible. It does not itself account for any actual experience. It is general and remote. Objects of direct experience are singular and are here and now. The "subjective" factor (using the word to designate the operations of an accultured organism) is, like "objective" (physical subject-matter) a *condition* of experience. But it is *that* condition which is required to convert the conditions of *kinds* of objects, which as kinds represent generic possibilities, into *this* object. Since every actual or direct experience is of some *this,* here and now, it is imperative to distinguish this type of condition from the type supplied by generic "objective" subject-matter. Greek thought failed to recognize the existence of this "subjective" factor as a condition of positive control. It took account of it only as a ground for indiscriminate scepticism. Or, when convention and institution were regarded as more important than "nature" (as it was by one Greek school) it was because nature was regarded as so crude, raw, wild, that the most arbitrary escape from it was better than subjection to nature. What is not sufficiently noted is that definite differentiation of personal-social factors in their function in production of objects of experience is now part of the technique of controlling the experienced presence of objects; with further advance of behavioral psychology it will become of constantly increased importance. The old stock-in-trade of wholesale scepticism, namely, dreams, illusions, hallucinations, the effect of organic defects, of beliefs locally current, is now in practical fact a positive resource in the management of experience.

I hope what has been said will at least serve to explain the title I have given this article. It is true that modern philosophy is "subjective" as ancient philosophy was not.

In its concern with what *can* be experienced whether or not it *has* been experienced, it has systematically taken account of the operation of *specific* personal-social factors. But it is equally true that modern philosophy has been "objective" in a way in which ancient philospohy was not. It is impossible to make sense of the problems with which modern philosophy has been pre-occupied unless this fact is recognized in its full force. The outstanding defect of modern philosophy is that these problems have taken form by means of setting the two sets of conditions in opposition to one another. This fact is explicable only in terms of the projection into the modern situation of certain heritages from the earlier philosophy which originated in and reflects a different state of culture. Philosophy will become *modern* in a pregnant sense only when the "objectivism-subjectivism" involved is seen to be one of coöperative interaction of two distinguishable sets of conditions, so that knowledge of them *in their distinction* is required in order that their interaction may be brought under intentional guidance. Without such knowledge, intelligence is inevitably held down to techniques for making mechanical permutations and combinations of things that *have* been experienced, and mankind is dependent upon accident for introduction of novelty. The fact that mankind is still far from realization of the power contained in its ability to distinguish certain conditions of experience as physical and others as socio-psychological is true enough. This fact indicates the special responsibility of philosophy today.

Columbia University.   John Dewey.

Section II

REALISM

THE JOURNAL OF PHILOSOPHY

PSYCHOLOGY AND SCIENTIFIC METHODS

REALISM AND PRAGMATISM[1]

AN acquaintance with the prevailing ambiguity in philosophical terminology prepares us in advance to find that the term realism has a number of diverse connotations. In this case, however, the diversity is offset, in a measure, by a certain degree of unanimity. All forms of realism appear to agree in the assertion that the consciousness of the individual is not a constituent element of extramental objects. The realism with which we are specifically concerned asserts, moreover, that in experience such objects may be presented to us precisely as they are; in other words, that the qualities which are revealed to us in experience inhere in, or belong to, these objects independent of the fact that they are known.

For the sake of brevity I shall assume without argument the contention that conscious states are not constitutive of extramental realities, but that the two are numerically distinct. This much being granted, we at once reach the central question of realism if we inquire into the nature of the conscious processes involved in the attainment of knowledge. It appears, *prima facie,* that there are two modes of knowing, designated usually as sensation and thought, and more descriptively by James as 'acquaintance-with' and 'knowledge-about.' The distinction usually drawn between the two will be sufficiently described for our purposes if we say that in the former the object of awareness is supposed to be a modification of the conscious state itself, while in the latter it is not.

That this distinction is insufficient as a final statement of the facts is a conviction which is apparently gaining ground at the present time. To this conviction we owe the recent attempts to reinterpret the concept of consciousness. So far as realism is directly concerned, the issue thus raised is in a sense a very simple one. It has reference solely to that form of knowing which was just now indicated by the

[1] Read before the Western Philosophical Association, at Madison, Wisconsin, April, 1906, as a contribution to a discussion of the topic: 'Recent Arguments for Realism, with Special Reference to the Relations of Realism and Pragmatism.'

term 'acquaintance-with.' Among contemporary realists some appear to regard 'acquaintance-with' and 'knowledge-about' as distinct and irreducible forms of knowing, while others attempt to reduce all knowing to the type of 'knowledge-about.'

While this distinction of types is easily made, it seems true that, as a matter of fact, the first type of realism is able to maintain itself only by occasional lapses into the second. Knowing is indeed declared to be of two kinds, but at critical points the two are merged into one. A flagrant illustration of this is found in Locke, who may be regarded as the historical representative of this form of realism. Ideas are stated to be the object of thinking, but the term idea does duty for both conscious state and extramental fact. And of course in so far as 'idea of sensation' is merely a name for such a fact, we have not two kinds of knowing, but only one. In a more subtle form the same confusion may be traced in Hobhouse, who has more recently taken up arms in behalf of this general type of realism. The confusion argues an inherent difficulty in the whole position, as even a brief elaboration will perhaps suffice to show.

In the opening chapters of his 'Theory of Knowledge' Hobhouse presents a vigorous defense of simple apprehension as a unique mode of knowing. Furthermore, it is claimed that simple apprehension brings us face to face with an independent external order. Its differentia, however, is not sought in the fact that the object known is a qualification of a conscious state, but in the fact that it asserts only the present, whereas other states, such as memory, assert what is not present.[2] In this presentation everything turns upon the phrase 'assertion of the present.' Both 'assertion' and 'present' are ambiguous terms. If the assertion concerns a fact which may properly be described as a qualification of the asserting consciousness itself, then we do indeed have a unique mode of assertion, but it is not the assertion of an extramental fact. On the other hand, if the fact *is* an extramental fact, then the uniqueness does not pertain to the assertion, but to the fact asserted. The fact is unique because it is present, but the consciousness which takes cognizance of such a fact has no peculiar differentia. And similarly with regard to the term present. 'Present' has an acceptable meaning if used to indicate a qualification of consciousness. But if not used in this sense, the term signifies nothing that is unique in the way of knowing. In fact, no other possible meaning will fit the case. The assertion of the present can not mean the spatially present, for its object may be anything within the range of vision; it can not mean the temporally present, for then it would include objects such as tigers in India or the opposite side of the moon.

[2] Cf. pp. 15 *et seq.*, 531-6.

The insistence, in short, that simple apprehension is a distinct form of knowing implies that the object known is a qualification of consciousness, whereas this implication is denied by the doctrine that an extramental reality is immediately present. And that, apart from the contradiction involved, this immediate presence of objects is for Hobhouse essentially an arbitrary view, is further evident from the fact that some contents or objects are unquestionably regarded merely as qualifications of consciousness. Of feelings, such as a headache, this is expressly asserted; and the distinction which is recognized between primary and secondary qualities appears to admit of no other interpretation.

It follows, then, that of the two propositions advanced by Hobhouse, one or the other must be abandoned. If we hold to a twofold form of knowing, we must surrender the direct perception of the external order and label all qualities as secondary; while if we maintain that this direct perception is a fact, we must locate all qualities in the extramental world and resolve the experience of 'acquaintance-with' into that of 'knowledge-about.' In the latter case that which is known is always other than the knowing state; in other words, consciousness as such is completely exhausted in the function of knowing.

Of these alternatives the latter is the one that is adopted by Mr. G. E. Moore, in a comparatively recent article in *Mind*.[3] The gist of his contention is that in sense experience, as such, we must distinguish between the (objective) quality and the consciousness of the quality. "When we refer to introspection and try to discover what the sensation of blue is, it is very easy to suppose that we have before us only a single term. The term 'blue' is easy enough to distinguish, but the other element, which I have called consciousness—that which sensation of blue has in common with sensation of green—is extremely difficult to fix. . . . That which makes the sensation of blue a mental fact seems to escape us; it seems, if I may use a metaphor, to be transparent—we look through it and see nothing but the blue; we may be convinced that there is *something*, but *what* it is no philosopher, I think, has yet clearly recognized" (p. 446).

That consciousness is a *what*, a 'stuff' or reality of some sort, differing as to existence from other realities, this writer does not attempt to dispute. Although extremely elusive in introspection, consciousness nevertheless 'can be distinguished if we look attentively enough, and if we know that there is something to look for' (p. 450). His main concern is to eliminate the distinction between 'acquaintance-with' and 'knowledge-about,' as appears unmistak-

[3] October, 1903, 'The Refutation of Idealism.'

ably from the following passage: "The awareness which I have maintained to be included in sensation is the very same unique fact which constitutes every kind of knowledge: 'blue' is as much an object, and as little a mere content, of my experience when I experience it, as the most exalted and independent real thing of which I am ever aware" (p. 451).

According to this view, conscious states exist, indeed, but the object known is never a mere qualification of the conscious state itself. This distinction, however, between object and conscious state involves a serious difficulty. As a matter of terminology we may, if we like, designate as object whatever is in any way apprehended in consciousness. But if we do so, it seems necessary, as is urged by Professor Strong,[4] to acknowledge that objects such as pain are not on the same footing as other objects. If it be asserted that all objects, pain included, possess the essential nature revealed in consciousness, whether they are known or not, this can only mean, in the case of pain, that pain is pain, irrespective of any 'knowledge-about.' It can not mean that pain is pain, independent of all sentiency. And if not, the contention that consciousness is reducible to the type of 'knowledge-about' must be abandoned, and 'acquaintance-with' still remains as a distinct category of experience.

But if Moore's distinction between object and consciousness will not serve to reduce immediate experience to the form of 'knowledge-about,' another resource still remains for this second form of realism. It may be held that Moore's device is insufficient because he does not rid himself of the notion that consciousness is a something which has 'states.' If, however, we avoid this initial fallacy, we may still manage to accomplish the proposed reduction. According to this other view, consciousness is neither a substance nor a quality, but a relation. It is 'a kind of continuum of objects.' This conception assimilates consciousness to other types of existence, such as space, time and species. Consciousness is, in short, simply a name for a certain kind of relation among objects; it is a continuum in which things become representative of one another.

This view, as compared with that of Moore, appears to differ in the fact that it places the emphasis upon the representative function of consciousness. For Moore the experience of 'blue' requires no explanation further than the simple distinction between object and consciousness. For this view, however, a mere 'blue' would apparently be no experience at all. It is an experience only in so far as the blue is representative of some further fact. As a blue it is indeed an object, but not an object for a consciousness, since

[4] *Mind*, April, 1905, 'Has Mr. Moore Refuted Idealism?'

consciousness is limited by definition to the representative functions of objects.

A very clear presentation, in outline, of this position has been given by Woodbridge[5] and Montague.[6] Unfortunately it has not yet been presented in detail, so that criticism must necessarily be tentative. With this proviso, I may venture to note a few points. In the first place, while it is true that this theory reduces all knowing to one type, it is not clear wherein it can lay claim to any special advantage in the case of objects such as pain. And secondly, it seems, in the end, to bring us no nearer to the world of objects than the most extreme form of subjectivism. If blue is nothing to us, except in so far as it is representative of some other fact, and if this other fact in turn derives its entire significance from its reference to a third fact, there seems to be no possibility of escape from the realm of symbols to that of the symbolized. On this basis, objects as known are placed in a position as precarious as that of certain islanders, who were said to eke out a scanty living by washing one another's clothes. There is no starting-point or datum, such as the first general type of realism finds in the experience of 'acquaintance-with.'

Essentially the same conclusion seems to emerge when we approach the subject from a different side. Thus it is stated by Montague: ''Air waves stimulate the auditory nerve, and sound is manifested; hydrogen unites with oxygen, and water is manifested —a substance differing from its components both in primary and in secondary qualities. Yet we do not hold that water is subjective and hydrogen and oxygen objective. Why should we hold that sound is more subjective than water?'' (p. 315). In this passage it seems to be implied that the quality of sound has no existence apart from the physiological conditions which also determine consciousness. And if the conditions which determine sound coincide with those which determine consciousness, the same must doubtless be inferred in the case of other qualities, such as color, taste and smell. It would seem, then, that the qualities which pertain to objects when the conditions of consciousness are not realized correspond in general to the qualities historically known as primary. But, furthermore, it is obviously necessary to distinguish between the real and the apparent sizes, shapes, etc., of objects, since the apparent size and shape depend upon the accidental conditions of perception. The real size, then, implies a reference to certain standardized conditions of perception. Apparent size is treated as

[5] This JOURNAL, Vol. II., p. 119, 'The Nature of Consciousness.'

[6] *Ibid.*, Vol. II., p. 309, 'The Relational Theory of Consciousness and its Realistic Implications.'

a symbol of such reference, *i. e.*, as an indication of what we should see under standard conditions. But since the standard, or criterion, is selected solely with reference to convenience and is not determined by the intrinsic nature of the object, it appears to give no clue whatever to real or absolute size.

It seems necessary, then, to conclude that whether realism recognizes 'acquaintance-with' as a factor in consciousness or limits consciousness to the form of 'knowledge-about,' it fails to make out a case. At this juncture pragmatism offers its services as a mediator. To give to the specific contention of each party a certain measure of justification and to maintain at the same time the fundamental proposition of both that in experience we encounter objects directly and not mere symbols of objects—both these ends, it is held, may be attained by the adoption of a more adequate conception of experience.

From the point of view of pragmatism it may be said that the element of truth in the realism of Hobhouse lies in its recognition of an element or factor in experience other than representative knowing. And yet the truth of the realism of Woodbridge and Montague lies precisely in its doctrine that consciousness is not substantive nor adjectival, but relational. These apparently contradictory assertions may be reconciled by means of a distinction between experience and consciousness, a distinction which realism neglects to make. As we have seen, neither form of realism succeeds in the attempt to lay hold of the object directly. And the reason is that the object in question is essentially a phantom object, enveloped in all the mystery of a ready-made datum. Regarding such an object we can have neither 'acquaintance-with' nor 'knowledge-about.' But the difficulties disappear if in the place of such objects we substitute 'concrete ways of living' as the terminal points in which the conscious relations inhere. In this way objects may be experienced immediately, as the first form of realism contends. On the other hand, if we limit the term consciousness to experiences of an 'essentially dualistic inner constitution,' then all consciousness is relational, as the second form of realism maintains.[7] Furthermore, it may be asserted that objects in this sense do not depend upon consciousness, but that sense and thought are merely functional differentiations which arise in certain critical situations. The objects or 'concrete ways of living' to which consciousness refers can not be characterized as possessing either sense or thought, as being either subjective or objective. They involve no reference to a beyond, no opposition between agent and external order, no distinction between noumenon and phenomenon. In such an experience we have a bit of ontolog-

[7] Cf. James, 'Does Consciousness Exist?' This JOURNAL, Vol. I., p. 477.

ical reality; it is *reine Erfahrung*, immediate experience, or, if you prefer, a thing; and thus the previous contention that experience gives us reality itself, and not merely a symbol or copy of reality, is in principle sustained.

And the immediate correlate of this doctrine is the proposition that sense and thought are derivative and not ultimate, that physical world and experiencing individual are terms of purely functional import. Upon this proposition pragmatism stakes the issue. In order, therefore, to secure recognition for its claims, pragmatism must show that an account of consciousness in terms of function is adequate; in other words, it must furnish a satisfactory explanation of the origin of consciousness.

For the consideration of the explanation which is offered, we may take as our point of departure the statement that consciousness is 'the function which makes possible the reorganization of the results of a process back into the process itself, thus constituting and preserving the continuity of activity.'[8] So long as we are on the plane of the concrete ways of living, activity proceeds without hesitation or conflict. But when the process leads to results which are undesirable and unforeseen, it becomes necessary to determine the significance of the total situation. Thus the first unhesitating reaction of the child upon the lighted candle gives place to a process of inquiry as to the precise significance of the stimulus or object, when it is presented a second time. The candle becomes representative of the pain-experience and the reaction is modified accordingly. This function of representation is consciousness, and its work is done as soon as the new significance of the candle has become incorporated in the total situation, so that activity proceeds uninterruptedly as before.

As a final explanation, however, of the origin of consciousness, this presentation is open to serious criticism. If consciousness is merely a name for this revising of the scale of values or for the process by which a readjustment is secured, it obviously implies an antecedent scale of values or a previous adjustment. Every situation is the outcome of a preceding situation, for it is in possession from the outset of a certain adjustment, or of an environment which has acquired its present character as the result of previous struggles and achievements. This is true even of those situations which involve instinctive reactions, for since a philosophy of pure experience can not start out with a nervous mechanism, instinct must be historically a product of conscious endeavor. And for this reason the usual appeal to biological analogy, such as the foregoing illustration

---

[8] 'Studies in Logical Theory,' p. 375.

of the child and the candle, merely places the problem of consciousness a step further back.

In view of this fact a dilemma seems inevitable. If we reduce experience down to a completely undifferentiated starting-point in which there are no objects or extraneous factors of any sort, a maladaptation is impossible from the nature of the case. Unless a Fichtean *Anstoss* be postulated, the process can not be got under way. On the other hand, to start with a certain degree of differentiation is likewise a confession of failure. Such a procedure assumes that consciousness has already done its work, for the adjustment with which we start implies that the significance of the various elements within the environment is thoroughly understood or appreciated. We are obliged to assume a foresight of ends or an appreciation of values in terms of activity, antecedent to all experience whatsoever.

But even if we disregard this dilemma, the postulates of consciousness present a further and similar problem. It has been argued, indeed, that these can be derived from antecedent pure experience or concrete ways of living. Thus the postulate of identity is said to be suggested by 'the felt sameness of the continuous conscious life.'[9] The continuous conscious life, however, can scarcely mean the fragment which is included within the time span of the individual. But if more is intended, there is already a tacit postulation of the validity of memory. And memory, in turn, involves the postulate of identity. The assertion that there is a 'felt sameness' or 'felt identity' begs the whole question, for it implies that the identity which is 'felt' is the same sort of fact as a color or a sound. That an entirely unique factor is tacitly introduced, which for pragmatism appears *wie aus der Luft gegriffen,* is a circumstance which is obscured by the ambiguity of a term.

It appears, then, that the endeavor of pragmatism to derive both sense and thought from a more fundamental category is no more successful than the attempts already noted to reduce all 'acquaintance-with' to the category of 'knowledge-about.' That these are not ultimate and irreducible forms of knowing and that experience gives us objects directly, are propositions which still await satisfactory demonstration. This fact, however, does not leave pragmatism without a certain measure of suggestiveness and value. Its insistence upon the instrumental character of sense and thought has done much to make prominent the purposive character of our mental life, and it has thrown light upon the process whereby the character of sense-stimuli becomes differentiated and significant. Experience may properly be regarded as a process of progressive

[9] Schiller, 'Personal Idealism,' pp. 97, 98.

differentiation, provided that we distinguish between psychological genesis and ontological reality.[10] The error of pragmatism lies, as I venture to think, in the fact that this distinction is disregarded, with the result that we are offered a hypothetical pure experience as the primordial stuff from which all things proceed, and a functional psychology which arrogates to itself the proud rank of queen of the sciences, once held by medieval theology.

In conclusion I may add that this view of knowing as twofold in form is not necessarily final. My contention is only that it is more adequate than those which have been offered as substitutes for it. Doubtless such phrases as 'modifications of consciousness' contain a suggestion of hypostatization. But this is due to historic associations rather than to intrinsic reasons. Whether consciousness is less mysterious from these other points of view seems much open to doubt. And, lastly, the effect of these conclusions upon realism as such is not so much a disproof as a removal of the positive grounds for belief. The conclusions are indeed opposed to the view that extramental realities are the direct object of experience. But whether objects are ever reflected in consciousness as in a mirror is a question which may be raised anew. Or to put the matter more generally, the metaphysics involved in the assumption of a twofold mode of cognition is a question which undeniably affords room for different antecedent possibilities and which remains as a matter for separate treatment.

B. H. Bode.

University of Wisconsin.

---

[10] Cf. Baldwin, 'The Limits of Pragmatism,' *Psychological Review,* 1904, p. 30.

THE JOURNAL OF PHILOSOPHY

PSYCHOLOGY AND SCIENTIFIC METHODS

KNOWLEDGE AND PERCEPTION

TO maintain that we accumulate knowledge about a great variety of things that discovery and observation provide us with would seem a thesis sufficiently commonplace. It was the burden, nevertheless, of a recent article which I believed to have a certain pertinence to current perplexities.[1] To say that the subject-matter of knowledge of existence is revealed by perception is only to say that there is a subject-matter about which such knowledge may, under favorable conditions, be accumulated. The purpose of the article referred to was to claim that the subject-matter of existential knowledge must be provided by perception, and that the knowledge relation is one that occurs subsequent to perception, being a relation within what I ventured to call the existential universe of discourse. As the subject-matter of all existential discussion must, if I am right, belong to the class of discovered things, things known and things unknown do not differ from each other in the matter of *percipi*. A thing which has no place in the universe of discourse is not unknown in any logical sense. Accordingly, to treat the problem of defining knowledge as a problem of perception is, to say the least, an abuse of language,[2] for something that we have come upon may be an object of total ignorance. In fact it might be said that we are continually seeking to convert objects of ignorance into objects of knowledge. Before the deciphering of the Rosetta stone, Egyptian hieroglyphics could hardly be called objects of "knowledge" in any reasonable sense; but they are no longer the objects of ignorance that they formerly were: which is to say that they were objects of perception long before they were objects of knowledge. Knowledge of electricity is something which the electrician has got because he knows how certain things in the existential universe of discourse

---

[1] "The Existential Universe of Discourse," this JOURNAL, Vol. VI., p. 175.

[2] It is not claimed that the stricter usage of the word "knowledge" here advocated will, of itself, solve any problems. The epistemological problem of perception takes for granted the subject matter of empirical knowledge, and has to do with the interpretation of that subject matter. I have already argued that such an effort at interpretation is logically vicious.

affect one another. An object of ignorance would be one, not that we failed to discover, but one which bore no significant relation to any other member of its universe of discourse. Such an object would be an object of perception merely, and thereby, not an object of knowledge because not a term in any cognitive relation.

In the previous article much emphasis was put on distinguishing what I there called the immediacy and the causality aspects of things. I wish now to try to indicate the relation which these two aspects bear to one another. I must resort to the terminology of the preceding discussion.

I

If we replace the formula for sodium chloride by its more analytic equivalent intended to distinguish immediacy and causality we have $I_{Na}C_{Na} + I_{Cl}C_{Cl}$ produce salt. As the formula describes the determinate cooperation of causal factors, it is evident that the sign $+$ connects Na and Cl, not in virtue of their immediacy, but in virtue of their causality. This can be made more evident to the eye by writing the formula as follows:

$$\frac{I_{Na}}{C_{Na}} + \frac{I_{Cl}}{C_{Cl}} \text{ produce salt.}$$

What now is the relation of I_{Na} to C_{Na}? It must not be forgotten that C_{Na} is not something *überhaupt*, but an instance of a particular causal efficacy operating under determinate conditions. The empirical relation of I to C should be evident to any one who admits that a blind man would not make the best assistant in a laboratory. A mutilated power of perception would interfere with the success of experiments and demonstrations. One who is going to use sulphuric acid must be able to tell that chemical from other chemicals. Salt and sugar resemble each other in one respect but not in another, and trouble has sometimes resulted from omitting the simple test of perception to learn which was which. If a particular immediacy did not serve to identify a particular causality there could be no science of the empirical world where causality was in question. And where the immediacy of one thing is very much like that of another, mistakes are frequent, and sometimes tragic. Immediacy is the sign of causality, but what causality is predicted by a given immediacy must be empirically found out. The chemist is the man who has learned to read a certain group of signs and to take advantage of them. It is a pleasure to acknowledge an obligation to Hobbes. He says: "A mark, therefore, is a *sensible object* which a man erecteth voluntarily to himself, to the end to *remember* thereby somewhat past, when the same object is objected to his sense again: as men that have passed a rock at sea, set up some mark thereby to remember their former danger and avoid it."[3] So we might say that immediacy is a sensible aspect of a thing which, under the conditions of human experience, operates as a sign of whatever causality has been discovered to go along with it. If immediacy did not "mean" causality there could be no such thing as a science of nature. A critic might, however, reply: "To be sure, the immediacy of a thing is a sign of whatever causality the thing has been discovered to have. It may, however, be the sign of a great deal of causality as yet undiscovered. How can we say that the thing has been tried in all possible combinations?" Such a comment would express a relapse into the very point of view which appears to the present writer logically illegitimate. Undiscovered causality is something not within the existential universe of discourse. Within that universe immediacy has no relation to unobserved causality, for it can have no relation to a term devoid of content. If, then, we recognize that in situations where there is an exercise of causality, things combine to generate results because of their causality characteristics, and that the results are unaffected by the immediacy of the factors, but that immediacy, after experience has learned its lesson, is the sign of what may be expected if certain other familiar cases of immediacy are brought into conjunction, is not the real meaning of Hume's analysis of the causal relation more evident? "No object ever discovers by the qualities which appear to the senses either the causes which produced it or the effects which will arise from it; nor can our reason, unassisted by experience, ever draw an inference concerning real existence and matter of fact."[4] Hume's analysis recognizes that there is nothing about I_{Na} and I_{Cl} to enable us to predict in advance of experience how C_{Na} and C_{Cl} will operate. It will not be maintained, I suppose, that the explosiveness of gunpowder, the adhesive power of cement, the various utility of iron, is identical with the present "appearance" of any of these things. But immediacy, *after experience,* does enable us to tell cement from gunpowder. And that seems to be all that Hume was trying to say about causality.

II

A large part of the capital of "epistemology," indeed its initial motive, has been the supposed difficulty of distinguishing between immediacy and possible illusion. If any case of immediacy can be either hallucination or normal perception, how shall we tell by any *a priori* definition which a given case of immediacy shall be? It is

[3] "Human Nature," chapter V.
[4] "Inquiry," Section IV.

a problem of distinguishing between a real and a counterfeit, and this problem occurs often enough in practical affairs. In the world of flux and method, we test the sign function of immediacy. Dr. Johnson did so when he kicked the stone. The stone was an affair not merely of present sense-qualities, but of consequences to be arrived at in a particular way, and which might be expected by anybody familiar with stones. It is sometimes said that the difference between illusion and fact is that the latter presents us with "existence" while the former does not. Such an illusion is a case of pure immediacy. The fact comprises this same immediacy plus something else called "existence." If the letter E stand for existence, illusion and fact will be represented by I and I + E respectively. What now is the criterion for determining whether or not I is married to E? What are the tests for E? If experience can produce no information out of her store, there can be no test, for there will be no way of knowing what I alone empirically lacks, and hence no possibility of testing for it. What I alone empirically lacks is nothing on the side of immediacy, but it is the causality of which that immediacy is normally a sign. Such a case of illusion is synonymous with causal emptiness. The question, Have we or have we not here a case of existence? is the question, Does the immediacy here observed function as a sign of determinate consequences?

III

The aspects represented by I and C are both genuine aspects of the things that make up the empirical world. That is only to say that the empirical world is characterized by time and process. Metaphysicians have, it is true, not yet ceased to imagine a reality in which the calm of eternal self-identity leaves no place for the genesis of consequences. The theological conception of a changeless divine will survives in the metaphysical notion of a changeless absolute. But in the less exalted regions where empirical verification is possible and where methods are tested by facts, a complex future is generated by a complex present; and it is precisely the relation of present to future which C is intended here to represent. Of course, when the future arrives it will present itself in terms of immediacy, but it will include not merely that, but the conditions out of which its future must be generated, and of which that present immediacy is a sign for those who have learned to read it. Yet if immediacy is never worth appreciating on its own account, there can be no intrinsic values anywhere. Both I and C, present and future, are real aspects of experience and we can be interested in either one by itself. It sounds quite natural to ask, "Do you know the Sistine Madonna, or the coloring of Turner, or the style of Tennyson?'' The question means, have you a direct and immediate acquaintance with these things? Have you appreciated their immediacy and do you preserve something of the impression? Thus the epistemologist frequently doubts whether you ''know'' the table or the inkstand. He does not doubt for a moment that you know it is a table or an inkstand, *i. e.*, that you know how to apply some of its causality. Such an epistemologist evidently uses the word knowledge in a sense that can not include the knowlege of the engineer, the geologist, the historian, the navigator, or the man of affairs. It is, of course, merely a question of terminology, but it is, in philosophy, worth some trouble to use one word to mean one thing, and when the word knowledge has come to mean two things we should consider which meaning we shall retain. There is no excuse for giving the word knowledge one meaning in science and another in metaphysics. What the imagined epistemologist really questions is not the range of our knowledge, but the authority of our perceptions. The word ''perception'' is a good word. When we mean perception let us say perception. Then we can use the word knowledge consistently to designate such things as the knowledge of the chemist, the physician, and the astronomer.

Those writers who have most systematically cultivated epistemology of the classic type have begun by taking the objective world in the relation of perception, but not in a normal and empirical relation.[5] They have described the world in terms of immediacy and formulated a ''representative'' theory of knowledge. To do so, however, is to leave out of account just the factors which signify the genesis of the future, that is, the factors with which that knowledge that is humanly most important is primarily concerned. Such a description can give no picture of a world in which anybody could do anything, or one thing affect another. To use again the formula

$$\frac{I_{Na}}{C_{Na}} + \frac{I_{Cl}}{C_{Cl}} \text{ produce salt.}$$

what the ''representative'' theory accomplishes is to eliminate C_{Na} and C_{Cl} as distinct aspects of sodium and chlorine. With them goes the relation of causal cooperation, leaving I_{Na} and I_{Cl} each standing alone by itself. The existence of I_{Na} and I_{Cl} is, of course, synonymous with perception, but the relation which provided the content of the chemist's knowledge has been lost. If we would do justice to the ''representative theory'' we should speak of a representative theory of perception, but not of a representative theory of knowledge. To define the problem of knowledge as the

[5] ''The Existential Universe of Discourse,'' this JOURNAL, p. 181.

problem of a representative, or copying, function in which the mind or consciousness mirrors its objects, is to make the chemistry of carbon irrelevant to the knowledge of carbon, and to forget, apparently, that the knowledge of nature is something to be accumulated, transmitted, and used. Knowledge of nature is skill in reading the signs of nature, and a point of view which is unable to treat immediacy as the sign of causality can provide no basis for a theory of knowledge.

WENDELL T. BUSH.

COLUMBIA UNIVERSITY.

The Journal of Philosophy

Psychology and Scientific Methods

BRIEF STUDIES IN REALISM. I

Naïve Realism vs. Presentative Realism[1]

I

IN spite of the elucidations of contemporary realists, a number of idealists continue to adduce in behalf of idealism certain facts having an obvious physical nature and explanation. The visible convergence of the railway tracks, for example, is cited as evidence that what is seen is a mental "content." Yet this convergence follows from the physical properties of light and a lens, and is physically demonstrated in a camera. Is the photograph, then, to be conceived as a psychical somewhat? That the time of the visibility of a light does not coincide with the time at which a distant body emitted the light is employed to support the same sort of conclusion, in spite of the fact that the exact difference in time may be deduced from a physical property of light—its rate. The dislocation in space of the light seen and the astronomical star is used as evidence of the mental nature of the former, though the exact angular difference is a matter of simple computation from purely physical data. The doubling of images of, say, the finger when the eyeball is pressed is frequently treated as a clincher. Yet it is a simple matter to take any body that reflects light, and by a suitable arrangement of lenses produce not only two but many images, projected into space. If the fact that under definite *physical* conditions (misplacement of lenses), a finger yields two images proves the psychical character of the latter, then the fact that under certain conditions a sounding body

---

[1] I am indebted to Dr. Bush's article on "Knowledge and Perception," this Journal, Vol. VI., p. 393, and to Professor Woodbridge's article on "Perception and Epistemology" in the "James Memorial Volume," as well as to his paper on "Sensations," read at the 1910 meeting of the American Philosophical Association. Since my point of departure and aim are somewhat different, I make this general acknowledgment in lieu of more specific references.

yields one or more echoes is, by parity of reasoning, proof that the echo is made of mental stuff.[2]

If, once more, the difference in form and color of a table to different observers, occupying different physical positions, is proof that what each sees is a psychical, private, isolated somewhat, then the fact that one and the same physical body has different effects upon, or relations with, different physical media is proof of the mental nature of these effects. Take a lump of wax, and subject it to the same heat, located at different positions; now the wax is solid, now liquid—it might even be gaseous. How "psychical" these phenomena! It almost seems as if the transformation of the physical into the mental in the cases cited exemplified an interesting psychological phenomenon. In each case the beginning is with a real and physical existence. Taking "the real object," the astronomical star, on the basis of its physical reality, the idealist concludes to a psychical object, radically different! Taking the *single* object, the finger, from the premise of its real singleness he concludes to a double mental content, which then takes the place of the original single thing! Taking one-and-the-same-object, the table, presenting *its* different surfaces and reflections of light to different real organisms, he eliminates the one-table-in-its-different-relations in behalf of a multiplicity of totally separate psychical tables! The logic reminds us of the story of the countryman who, after gazing at the giraffe, remarked, "There ain't no such animal." It almost seems, I repeat, as if this self-contradiction in the argument created in some minds the impression that the object—not the argument—was undergoing the extraordinary reversal of form.

However this may be, the problem indicated in the above cases is simply the good old problem of the many in one, or, less cryptically, the problem of the maintenance of a continuity of process throughout differences. I do not pretend that this situation, though the most familiar thing in life, is wholly without difficulties. But its difficulty is not one of epistemology, that is, of the relation of known to a knower; to take it as such, and then to use it as proof of the psychical nature of a final term, is also to prove that the trail the rocket stick leaves behind is psychical, or that the flower which comes in a continuity of process from a seed is mental.

[2] Plato's use of shadows, of reflections in the water, and other "images" or "imitations" to prove the presence in nature of non-being was, considering the state of physical science in his day, a much more sensible conclusion than the modern use of certain images as proof that the object in perception is a psychical content.

II

Contemporary realists have so frequently and clearly expounded the physical explanation of such cases as have been cited that one is at a loss as to why idealists go on repeating the cases without even alluding to the realistic explanation. One is moved to wonder whether this neglect is just one of those circumstances which persistently dog philosophical discussions, or whether something in the realistic position gives ground (from at least an *ad hominem* point of view) for the neglect. There is a reason for adopting the latter alternative. Many realists, in offering the type of explanation adduced above, have treated the cases of seen light, doubled imagery, as perception in a way that ascribes to perception an inherent cognitive status. They have treated the perceptions as *cases of knowledge,* instead of as simply natural events having, in themselves (apart from a *use* that may be made of them), no more knowledge status or worth than, say, a shower or a fever. What I intend to show is that if "perceptions" are regarded as cases of knowledge, the gate is opened to the idealistic interpretation. The physical explanation holds of them as long as they are regarded simply as natural events—a doctrine I shall call naïve realism; it does not hold of them considered as cases of knowledge—the view I call presentative realism.

The idealists attribute to the realists the doctrine that "the perceived object is the real object." Please note the wording; it assumes that there is *the* real object, something which stands in a contrasting relation with objects not real or else less real. Since it is easily demonstrable that there is a numerical duplicity between the astronomical star and the visible light, between the single finger and the doubled images, when the former is dubbed *"the"* real object the latter evidently stands in disparaging contrast to its reality. *If* it is a case of knowledge, the knowledge refers to the star; and yet not the star, but something more or less unreal (that is, if the star be "the" real object), is known.

Consider how simply the matter stands in what I have called naïve realism. The astronomical star is *a* real object, but not "the" real object; the visible light is another real object, found, when knowledge supervenes, to be an occurrence standing in a process continuous with the star. Since the seen light is an event within a continuous process, there is no point of view from which its "reality" contrasts with that of the star.

But suppose that the realist accepts the traditionary psychology according to which every event in the way of a perception is also a case of knowing something. Is the way out now so simple? In the case of the doubled fingers or the seen light, the thing known in perception contrasts with the physical source and cause of the knowledge. There *is* a numerical duplicity. Moreover the thing known in perception is in relation to a knower, while the physical cause is not as such in relation to a knower. Is not the most plausible account of the difference between the physical cause of the perceptive knowledge and what the latter presents precisely this latter difference—namely, presentation to a knower? If perception is a case of knowing, it must be a case of knowing the star; but since the "real" star is not known in the perception, the knowledge relation must somehow have changed the "object" into a "content." Thus when the realist conceives the perceptual occurrence as a case of knowledge or of presentation to a mind or knower, he lets the nose of the idealist camel into the tent. He has then no great cause for surprise when the camel comes in—and devours the tent.

Perhaps it will seem as if in this last paragraph I had gone back on what I said earlier regarding the physical explanation of the difference between the visible light and the astronomical star. On the contrary, my point is that this explanation, though wholly adequate as long as we conceive the perception to be itself simply a natural event, is not at all available when we conceive it to be a case of knowledge. In the former case, we are dealing with a relation between natural events. In the latter case, we are dealing with the difference between an object as a cause of knowledge and an object as known, and hence in relation to mind. By the "method of difference" the sole explanation of the difference between the two objects is the absence or presence of relation to mind.

In the case of the seen light,[3] reference to the velocity of light is quite adequate to account for its occurrence in its time and space difference from the star. But viewed as a case of what is known (on the supposition that perception is a case of knowledge), reference to it only increases the contrast between the real object and the object known in perception. For, being just as much a part of the object that causes the perception as is the star itself, it (the velocity of light) *ought* to be part of what is known in the percep-

---

[3] It is impossible, in this brief paper, to forestall every misapprehension and objection. Yet to many the use of the term "seen" will appear to be an admission that a case of knowledge is involved. But is smelling a case of knowledge? Or (if the superstition persists as to smell) is gnawing or poking a case of knowledge? My point, of course, is that "seen" involves a relation to organic activity, not to a knower, or mind. Furthermore, the seen light is not in relation *to* an organism. We may speak, if we will or if we must, of the relation of vibrations of the ether to the eye-function; but we can not speak, without making nonsense, of the relation of the perceptual light to an eye, or an eye-activity. For the joint efficiencies of the eye-activity and of the vibrations condition the seen light.

tion, while it is not. Since the velocity of light is a constituent element in the star, it should be known in the perception; since it is not so known, reference to it only increases the discrepancy between the object of the perception—the seen light—and the real, astronomical star. The same is true of any physical conditions that might be referred to: *The very things that, from the standpoint of perception as a natural event, are conditions that account for its happening are, from the standpoint of perception as a case of knowledge, part of the object that ought to be known but is not.*

In this fact we have, perhaps, the ground of the idealist's disregard of the oft-proffered physical explanation of the difference between the perceptual event and *the* (so-called) real object. And it is quite possible that some realists who read these lines will feel that in my last paragraphs I have been making a covert argument for idealism. Not so, I repeat; they are an argument for a truly naïve realism. The presentative realist, in his appeal to "common sense" and the "plain man," first sophisticates the umpire and then appeals. He stops a good way short of a genuine naïveté. The plain man, for a surety, does not regard noises heard, lights seen, etc., as mental existences; but neither does he regard them as things *known*. That they are just things is good enough for him. That they are in relation to mind, or in relation to mind as their "knower," no more occurs to him than that they are mental. By this I mean much more than that the formulæ of epistemology are foreign to him; I mean that his attitude to these things *as* things involves their *not* being in relation to mind or a knower. Once depart from this thorough naïveté, and substitute for it the psychological theory that perception is a cognitive presentation of an object to a mind, and the first step is taken on the road which ends in an idealistic system.

III

For simplicity's sake, I have written as if my main problem were to show how, in the face of a supposed difficulty, a strictly realistic theory of the perceptual event may be maintained. But my interest is primarily in the facts, and in the theory only because of the facts it formulates. The significance of the facts of the case may, perhaps, be indicated by a consideration which has thus far been ignored. In regarding a perception as a case of knowledge, the presentative realist does more than shove into it a relation to mind which then, naturally and inevitably, becomes the explanation of any differences that exist between its subject-matter and the constitution of some real object with which it contrasts. In many cases—very important cases, too, in the physical sciences—the contrasting "real object" does not become "known" by perception or presentation. It is known by a logical process, by inference—as the case of the contemporary position of the star is determined by calculations from data, not by perception. This, then, is the situation of the presentative realist: If perception is a case or mode of knowledge, it stands in unfavorable contrast with another indirect and logical mode of knowledge; *its* object is less valid than that determined by inference. So the contrast of *the* (so-called) real object with the fact "presented" in perception turns out to be the contrast of an object known through a logical way with one directly "apprehended." I do not adduce these considerations as showing that the case is hopeless for the presentative realist;[4] I am willing to concede he can find a satisfactory way out. But the difficulty exists; and in existing it calls emphatic attention to a case which is certainly and indisputably a case of knowledge—namely, propositions arrived at through inference—judgments as logical assertions.

With relation to this unquestionable case of knowledge, the logical or inferential, perceptions occupy a unique status, one which readily accounts for their being regarded as cases of knowledge, although in themselves they are merely natural events. (1) They are the sole ultimate data, the sole media, of inference to all natural objects and processes. While we do not, in any intelligible or verifiable sense, know *them*, we know all things that we do know *with* or *by* them. They furnish the only ultimate evidence of the existence and nature of the objects which we infer, and they are the sole ultimate checks and tests of the inferences. The visible light is the evidence on the basis of which we infer the existence, place, and structure of the astronomical star, and some other perception is the verifying check on the value of the inference. Because of this characteristic use of perceptions, the perceptions themselves acquire, by "second intention," a knowledge status. They *become* objects of minute, accurate, and experimental scrutiny. Since the body of propositions that forms natural science hangs upon them, *for scientific purposes* their nature *as* evidence, *as* signs, entirely overshadows their natural status, that of being simply natural events. The scientific man, as scientific, cares for perceptions not in themselves, but as they throw light upon the nature of some object reached by evidence. And

---

[4] This is the phase of the matter, of course, which the rationalistic or objective realist, the realist of the type of T. H. Green, emphasizes. Put in terms of systems, the difficulty adduced above is that in escaping the subjectivism latent in treating perception as a case of knowledge, the realist runs into the waiting arms of the objective idealist. And as a matter of fact, it is extremely difficult to find any differences—save verbal and psychological ones—between contemporary propositional realists—as G. E. Moore and Bertrand Russell—and the classic type of objective idealists. Propositional realism I shall deal with in a later paper.

since every such inference tries to terminate in a further perception (as its test of validity), the *value* of knowing depends on perception. (2) Independent of science, daily life uses perceptions as signs of other perceptions. When a perception of a certain kind frequently recurs and is constantly used as evidence of some other impending perceptual event, the function of habit (a natural function, be it noted, not a psychical or epistemological function) often brings it about that the perception loses its original quality in acquiring a sign-value. Language is, of course, the typical case. Noises, in themselves mere natural events, through habitual use as signs of other natural events become integrated with what they mean. What they stand for is telescoped, as it were, into what they are. This happens also with other natural events, colors, tastes, etc. Thus, *for practical purposes,* many perceptual events are cases of knowledge; that is, they have been *used* as such so often that the habit of so using them is established or automatic.

In this brief reference to facts that are perfectly familiar, I have tried to suggest three points of crucial importance for a naïve realism: first, that the inferential or evidential function (that involving logical relation) is in the field as an obvious and undisputed case of knowledge; second, that this function, although embodying the logical relation, is itself a natural and specifically detectable process among natural things—it is not a non-natural or epistemological relation, that is, a relation to a mind or knower not in the natural series; third, that the *use,* practical and scientific, of perceptual events in the evidential or inferential function is such as to make them *become* cases of knowledge, and to such a degree that this acquired characteristic quite overshadows, in many cases, their primary nature.

If we add to what has been said the fact that, like every natural function, the inferential function turns out better in some cases and worse in others, we get a naturalistic or naïvely realistic conception of the "*problem* of knowledge ": Control of the conditions of inference—the only type of knowledge detectable in direct existence—so as to guide it toward the better.

IV

I do not flatter myself that I will receive much gratitude from realists for attempting to rescue them from that error of fact which exposes their doctrine to an idealistic interpretation. The superstition, growing up in a false physics and physiology and perpetuated by psychology, that sensations-perceptions are cases of knowledge, is too ingrained. But—*crede experto*—let them try the experiment of conceiving perceptions as pure natural events, not as cases of awareness and apprehension, and they will be surprised to see how little they miss—save the burden of confusing traditionary problems. Meantime, while philosophic argument such as this will do little to change the state of belief regarding perceptions, the development of biology and the refinement of physiology will, in due season, do the work.

On concluding my article, I ought to refer, in order to guard against misapprehension, to a reply that the presentative realist might make to my objection. He might say that while the seen light is a case of knowledge or presentative awareness, it is not a case of knowledge of the star, but simply of the seen light, just as it is. In this case the appeal to the physical explanations of the difference of the seen light from its objective source is quite legitimate. At first sight, such a position seems innocent and tenable. Even if innocent, it would, however, be ungrounded, since there is no evidence of the existence of a knower, and of its relation to the seen light. But further consideration will reveal that there is a most fundamental objection. If the notion of perception as a case of adequate knowledge of its own object-matter be accepted, the knowledge relation is absolutely ubiquitous; it is an all-inclusive net. The "ego-centric predicament" is inevitable. This result of making perception a case of knowing will occupy us in the second paper of this series.

VOL VIII. No. 20   II   SEPTEMBER 28 1911

EPISTEMOLOGICAL REALISM: THE ALLEGED UBIQUITY OF THE KNOWLEDGE RELATION

AT the close of my previous paper I pointed out that if perception be treated as a case of knowledge, knowledge of every form and kind must be treated as a case of a presentation to a knower. The alleged discipline of epistemology is then inevitable. In common usage, the term knowledge tends to be employed eulogistically; its meaning approaches the connotation of the term science. More loosely, it is used, of course, to designate all beliefs and propositions that are held with assurance, especially with the implication that the assurance is reasonable, or grounded. In its practical sense, it is used as the equivalent of "knowing *how*," of skill or ability involving such acquaintance with things and persons as enables one to anticipate how they behave under certain conditions and to take steps accordingly. Such usages of the term are all differential; they all involve definite contrasts—whether with ungrounded conviction, or with doubt and mere guesswork, or with the inexpertness that accompanies lack of familiarity. In its epistemological use, the term "knowledge" has a blanket value which is absolutely unknown in common life. It covers any and every "presentation" of any and every thing to a knower, to an "awarer," if I may coin a word for the sake of avoiding some of the pitfalls of the term consciousness. And, I repeat, this indiscriminate use of the term "knowledge" is absolutely unavoidable if perception be regarded as, in itself, a mode of knowledge.[2] And then—and only then—the problem of "the possibility, nature, and extent of knowledge *in general*" is also inevitable. I hope I shall not be regarded as offensively pragmatic if I suggest that this undesirable consequence is a good reason for at least not accepting the premise from which it follows unless that premise be absolutely forced upon us.

At all events, upon the supposition of the ubiquity of the knowledge relation in respect to a self, presentative realism is compelled to accept the genuineness of the epistemological problem, and thus to convert itself into an epistemological realism, getting one more step away from both naïve and naturalistic realism. The problem is especially acute for a presentative realism because idealism has made precisely this ubiquity of relationship its axiom, its short cut. One sample is as good as a thousand. Says Bain: "There is no possible knowledge of a world except in relation to our minds. Knowledge means a state of mind; the notion of material things is a mental fact. We are incapable even of discussing the existence of an independent material world; the very act is a contradiction. We can speak only of a world presented to our own minds."

On the supposition of the ubiquity of the relation, realism and idealism exhaust the alternatives; if the relationship itself is a myth, both doctrines are unreal because there is no problem of which they are the solution. My first step in indicating the unreality of both "solutions" is formal. I shall try to show that *if* the knowledge relation of things to a self is the exhaustive and inclusive relation, there is no intelligible point at issue between idealism and realism; the differences between them are either verbal or else due to a failure on the part of one or other to stick to their *common* premise.

I

To my mind, Professor Perry rendered philosophic discussion a real service when he coined the phrase "ego-centric predicament." The phrase designated something which, whether or no it be real in itself, is very real in current discusion, and designating it ren-

---

[2] As I suggested in an earlier article, "Some Implications of Anti-intellectualism," this JOURNAL, Vol. VI., p. 477, the conception of the ubiquity of the knowledge relation in all that has to do with a self is one of the things included in the term intellectualism, when that is taken in a pejorative sense.

dered it more accessible to examination. In terming the alleged uniform complicity of a knower a predicament, it is intended, I take it, to suggest, among other things, that we have here a difficulty with which all schools of thought alike must reckon; and that consequently it is a difficulty that can not be used as an argument in behalf of one school and against another. If the relation be ubiquitous, it affects alike every view, every theory, every object experienced; it is no respecter of persons, no respecter of doctrines. Since it can not make any difference to any particular object, to any particular logical assertion, or to any particular theory, it does not support an idealistic as against a realistic theory. Being a universal common denominator of all theories, it cancels out of all of them alike. It leaves the issue one of *subject-matter*, to be decided on the basis of that subject-matter, not on the basis of an unescapable attendant consideration that the subject-matter must be known in order to be discussed. In short, the moral is quite literally, "Forget it," "Cut it out."

But the idealist may be imagined to reply somewhat as follows: "If the ubiquity were of any other kind than of precisely the kind it is, the advice to disregard it as a mere attendant circumstance of discussion would be relevant. Thus, for example, we disregard gravitation when we are considering a particular chemical reaction; there is no ground for supposing that it affects a reaction in any way that modifies it as a chemical reaction. And if the 'ego-centric' relation were cited when the point at issue is something about one group of facts in distinction from another group, it ought certainly to be canceled out from any statement about them. But since the point at issue is precisely the statement of the most universally defining trait of existence as existence, the invitation deliberately to disregard the most universal trait is nothing more or less than an invitation to philosophic suicide."

If the idealist I have imagined making the above retort were up in recent realistic literature, he might add the following argument *ad hominem:* "You, my realistic opponent, say that the doctrine of the external relation of terms expresses a ubiquitous mark of every proposition or relational complex, and that this ubiquity is a strong presumption in favor of realism. Why so uneven, so partial, in your attitude toward ubiquitous relations? Is it perchance that you were so uneasy at our possession of an ubiquitous relation that gives a short cut to idealism that you felt you must also have a short cut to realism?"

If I terminate the controversy at this point, it is not because I think the realist is unable to "come back." On the contrary I stop here because I believe (for reasons that will come out shortly) that both realist and idealist, having the same primary assumption, can come back at each other indefinitely. Consequently, I wish to employ the existence of this *tu quoque* controversy to raise the question: Under what conditions is the relation of knower to known an intelligible and discussable question? And I wish to show that it is *not* intelligible or discussable if the knowledge relation be ubiquitous and homogeneous.

The controversy back and forth is in fact a warning of each side to the other not to depart from their *common* premise. If the idealist begins to argue (as he constantly does) as if the relation to "mind" or to "consciousness" made some difference of a specific sort, like that between error and fact, or between sound perception and hallucination, he may be reminded that, since this relation is uniform, it substantiates and nullifies all things alike. And the realist is quite within the common premise when he points out that every special fact must be admitted for *what it* is specifically known to be; the idealistic doctrine can not turn the edge of the fact that knowledge has evolved historically out of a state in which there was no mind, or of the fact that knowledge is even now dependent on the brain, provided that specific evidence shows them to be facts. The realist, on the other hand, must admit that, after all, the entire body of known facts, or of science, including such facts as the above, is held fast and tight in the net of relation to a mind or consciousness. In specific cases this relation may be ignored, but the exact ground for such an ignoring is precisely because the relation is not a specific fact, but the uniform presupposition of fact.

Imagine a situation like the following. The sole relation an organism bears to things is that of eater; the sole relation the environment bears to the organism is that of food, that is, things-to-eat. This relation, then, is exhaustive. It defines, or identifies, each term in relation to the other. But this means that there are not, as respects organism and environment, two terms at all. Eater-of-food and food-being-eaten are two names for one and the same situation. Could there be imagined a greater absurdity than to set to work to discuss the relation *of* eater *to* food, of organism *to* the environment, or to argue as to whether one modifies the other or not? Given the premise, the statements in such a discussion could have only a verbal difference from one another.

Suppose, however, the discussion has somehow got under way. Sides have been taken; the philosophical world is divided into two great camps, "foodists" and "eaterists." The eaterists (idealists) contend that no object exists except in relation to eating; hence that everything is constituted a thing by its relation to eating. Special sciences indeed exist which discuss the nature of various sorts of things in relation to *one another,* and hence in legitimate abstraction from the fact that they are all foods. But the discussion of their nature *an sich* depends upon "eatology," which deals primarily with the problem of the possibility, nature, and extent (or limits) of eating food in general, and thereby determines what food in general, *überhaupt,* is and means.

Nay, replies the foodist (realist) : Since the eating relation is uniform, it is negligible. All propositions that have any intelligible meaning are about objects just as they are as objects, and in the relations they bear to one another as objects. Foods pass in and out of the relation to eater with no change in their own traits. Moreover, the position of the eaterists is self-contradictory. How can a thing be eaten unless it *is,* in and of itself, a food? To suppose that a food is constituted by eating is to presuppose that eating eats eating, and so on in infinite regress. In short, to be an eater is to be an eater of food; take away the independent existence of foods, and you deny the existence and the possibility of an eater.

I respectfully submit that there is no terminus to such a discussion. For either both sides are saying the same thing in different words, or else both of them depart from their common premise, and unwittingly smuggle in some other relations than that of food-eater between the organism and environment. If to be an eater means that an organism which is more and other than an eater is doing something *distinctive,* because contrasting with its other functions, then, and then only, is there an issue. In this latter case, the thing which is food is, of course, something else besides food, and is that something in relation to the organism. But if both stick consistently to their common premise, we get the following trivial situation. The idealist says: "Every philosophy purports to be knowledge, knowledge of objects; all knowledge implies relation to mind; therefore every object with which philosophy deals is object-in-relation-to-mind." The realist says: "To be a mind is to be a knower; to be a knower is to be a knower-of-objects. Without the objects to be known, mind, the knower, is and means nothing."

Our result is that the difficulties attending the discussion of epistemology are in no way attendant upon the special subject-matter of "epistemology." They are found wherever any reciprocal relation is taken to define, exclusively and exhaustively, all the connections between any pair of things. If there are two things that stand solely as buyer and seller to each other, or as husband and wife, then that relation is "unique," and undefinable; to discuss the relation *of* the relation *to* the terms of which it is the relation, is an obvious absurdity; and to assert that the relation does not modify the "seller," the "wife," or the "object known," is to discuss the relation *of* the relation just as much as to assert the opposite. The only reason, I think, any one has ever supposed the case of knower-known to differ from any case of an alleged exhaustive and exclusive correlation is that while the knower is only one—just knower—the objects known are obviously many and sustain many relations to one another that vary independently of their relation to the knower. This is the undoubted fact which is at the bottom of epistemological realism. But the idealist is entitled to reply that the objects in their variable relations to one another nevertheless fall within a relation to a knower—that is, if that relation be exhaustive or ubiquitous.

II

Nevertheless, I do not conceive that the realistic assertion and the idealistic assertion in this dilemma stand on the same level, or have the same value. The fact that objects vary in relation to one another independently of their relation to the "knower" *is* a fact, and a fact recognized by all schools. The idealistic assertion rests simply upon the presupposition of the ubiquity of the knowledge relation, and consequently has only an *ad hominem* force, that is a force as against *epistemological* realists—against those who admit that the sole and exhaustive relation of the "self" or "ego" to objects is that of knower of them. The relation of buyer and seller is a discussable relation; for buyer does not exhaust one party and seller does not exhaust the other. Each is a man or a woman, a consumer or a producer or a middle man, a green-grocer or a dry-goods merchant, a taxpayer or a voter, and so on indefinitely. Nor is it true that such additional relations are borne merely to *other* things; the buyer-seller are more than, and other than, buyer-seller to *each other*. They may be fellow-clubmen, belong to opposite political parties, dislike each other's looks, and be second cousins. Hence the buyer-seller relation stands in intelligent connection and contrast with other relations, so that it can be discriminated, defined, analyzed. Moreover, there are specific differences *in* the buying-selling relation. Because it is not ubiquitous, it is not homogeneous. If wealthy and a householder, the one who buys is a different buyer —*i. e.*, buys differently—than if poor and a boarder. Consequently, the seller sells differently, has more or less goods left to sell, more or less income to expend on other things, and so on indefinitely. Moreover, in order to be a buyer the man has to have been other things; *i. e.*, he is not a buyer *per se*, but *becomes* a buyer because he is an eater, wears clothes, is married, etc.

It is also quite clear that the organism is something else than an eater, or something in relation to food alone. I will not again call the roll of perfectly familiar facts; I will lessen my appeal to the reader's patience by confining my reiteration to one point. Even in relation to the things that are food, the organism is something more than their eater. He is their acquirer, their pursuer, their cultivator, their beholder, taster, etc.; he *becomes* their eater *only* because he is so many other things. And his becoming an eater is a natural episode in the natural unfolding of these other things.

Precisely the same sort of assertions may be made about the knower-known relation. If the one who is knower is, in relation to objects, something else and more than their knower, and if objects are, *in relation to the one who knows them*, something else and other than things in a knowledge relation, there is somewhat to define and discuss; otherwise we are raising, as we have already seen, the quite foolish question as to what is the relation of a relation to itself, or the equally foolish question of whether being a thing modifies the thing that it is. And, moreover, epistemological realism and idealism both say the same thing: realism that a thing does not modify itself, idealism that, since the thing is what it is, it stands in the relation that it does stand in.

There are many facts which, *prima facie*, support the claim that knowing is a relation to things which depends upon other and more primary connections between a self and things; a relation which grows out of these more fundamental connections and which operates in their interests at specifiable crises. I will not repeat what is so generally admitted and so little taken into account, that knowing is, biologically, a differentiation of organic behavior, but will cite some facts that are even more obvious and even more neglected.

1. If we take a case of perception, we find upon analysis that, so far as a self is concerned in it at all, the self is, so to say, inside of it rather than outside of it. It would be much more correct to say that the self is contained in a perception than that a perception is presented to a self. That is to say, the organism is involved in the occurrence of the perception in the same sort of way that hydrogen is involved in the happening—producing—of water. We might about as well talk of the production of a specimen case of water as a presentation of water to hydrogen as talk in the way we are only too accustomed to talk about perceptions and the organism. When we consider a perception as a case of "apperception," the same thing holds good. Habits enter into the *constitution* of the situation; they are in and of it, not, so far as it is concerned, something outside of it. Here, if you please, is a unique relation of self and things, but it is unique, not in being wholly incomparable to all natural relations among events, but in the sense of being distinctive, or just the relation that it is.

2. Taking the many cases where the self may be said, in an in-

telligible sense, to lie *outside* a thing and hence to have dealings with it, we find that they are extensively and primarily cases where the self is agent-patient, doer, sufferer, and enjoyer. This means, of course, that things, the things that come to be *known,* are primarily not objects of awareness, but causes of weal and woe, things to get and things to avoid, means and obstacles, tools and results. To a naïve spectator, the ordinary assumption that a thing is "in" experience only when it is an object of awareness (or even only when a perception), is nothing less than extraordinary. The self experiences whatever it *undergoes,* and there is no fact about life more assured or more tragic than that what we are aware of is determined by things that we are undergoing, but that we are not conscious of and that we *can not* be conscious of under the particular conditions.

3. So far as the question of the relation of the self to known objects is concerned, knowing is but one special case of the agent-patient, of the behaver-enjoyer-sufferer situation. It is, however, *the* case constantly increasing in relative importance, and from both sides. That is to say, the connections of the self with things in weal or woe are progressively found to depend upon the connections established in knowing things: on the other hand, the progress, the advance, of science is found to depend more and more upon the courage and patience of the agent in making the widening and buttressing of knowledge a chief business.

It is impossible to overstate the significance, the reality, of the relation of self as knower to things when it is thought of as a *moral* relation, a deliberate and responsible undertaking of a self. Ultimately the modern insistence upon the self in reference to knowledge (in contrast with the classic Greek view) will be found to reside precisely here.

My purpose in citing the above facts is not to prove a positive point, viz., that there are many relations of self and things, of which knowing is but one differentiated case. It is less pretentious: viz., to show what is meant by saying that the problems at issue concern matters of fact, and not matters to be decided by assumption, definition, and deduction. I mean also to suggest, but only to suggest, what kind of matters of fact would naturally be adduced as evidential in such a discussion. Negatively put, my point is that the whole question of the relation of knower to known is radically misconceived in what passes as epistemology, because of an underlying unexamined assumption, an assumption which, moreover, when examined, makes the controversy verbal or absurd. Positively put, my point is that since, *prima facie,* plenty of connections other than the knower-known one exist between self and things, there is a context in which the "problem" of their relation concerns matters of fact capable of empirical determination by matter-of-fact inquiry. The point about a difference being made (or rather making) in things when known is precisely of this sort.

III

That question is not, *save upon the assumption of the ubiquity of the knowledge relation,* the absurd question of whether knowledge makes any difference to things already in the knowledge relation. Until the epistemological realists have seriously considered the main propositions of the pragmatic realists, viz., that knowing is something that happens to things in the natural course of their career, not the sudden introduction of a "unique" and non-natural type of relation—that to a mind or consciousness—they are hardly in a position to discuss the second and derived pragmatic proposition that, in this natural continuity, things in becoming known undergo a specific and detectable qualitative change.

In my prior paper I had occasion to remark that if one identifies "knowledge" with situations involving the function of inference, the *problem* of knowledge means the art of guiding this function most effectively. That statement holds when we take knowledge as a relation of the things *in* the knowledge situation. If we are once convinced of the artificiality of the notion that the knowledge relation is ubiquitous, there will be an existential problem as to the self and knowledge; but it will be a radically different problem from that discussed in epistemology. The relation of knowing *to* existence will be recognized to form the subject-matter of no problem, because involving an ungrounded and even absurd preconception. But the problem of the relation of an *existence* in the way of knowing to *other existences*—or events—with which it forms a continuous process will then be seen to be a natural problem to be attacked by natural methods. The question of whether the knowing-event marks a qualitative distinctive difference in the career and destiny of things is a secondary matter; one that may be allowed to take care of itself, once the problem is shifted from the alleged epistemological relation to that of naturalistic existences.

JOHN DEWEY.

COLUMBIA UNIVERSITY.

VOL. IX. No. 13.   JUNE 20, 1912

DISCUSSION

PROFESSOR DEWEY'S "BRIEF STUDIES IN REALISM"

IN the interesting "Studies in Realism," which Mr. Dewey has recently published, he has done two things. In addition to presenting more fully than he had done before his own view of the nature of perception, he has criticized the doctrine of perception held by "epistemological" and "presentative" realists. It is this criticism of realism that I wish to examine in this paper.

The cardinal error Mr. Dewey finds in this realism is perhaps best summed up in these words: "Until the epistemological realists have seriously considered the main propositions of the pragmatic realists, viz., that knowing is something that happens to things in the natural course of their career, not the sudden introduction of a 'unique' and non-natural type of relation—that to a mind or consciousness—they are hardly in a position to discuss the second and derived pragmatic proposition that, in this natural continuity, things in becoming known undergo a specific and detectable qualitative change" (p. 554). The realists criticized are guilty, then, of believing that knowing is a sudden introduction of a "unique" and non-natural relation.

There are three adjectives in this charge, but I presume that only one of them has any dyslogistic significance. The suddenness of the introduction of any relation can hardly be objected to by any empiricist who sticks to his last. Nor can the recognition of the uniqueness of any relation be reasonably considered by Mr. Dewey as an anti-empirical procedure. He has himself recognized at least one unique relation and has given an excellent statement of what a unique relation is: "Here, if you please, is a unique relation of self and things, but it is unique, not in being wholly incomparable to all natural relations among events, but in the sense of being distinctive, or just the relation that it is" (p. 552). This sentence shows that the adjective that really is meant to count in Mr. Dewey's indictment is the adjective "non-natural."

Now why should the consciousness relation, which "epistemological" and "presentative" realists recognize, be considered non-natural? The answer seems to be that for them this relation is a relation "*to a mind.*" A very cursory glance over the pages of Mr. Dewey's articles will show that the realists he is criticizing, whether "presentative" or "epistemological," are constantly represented as holding that the thing known in perception is in relation "to a knower" or "to consciousness." Every criticism he passes against these realists presupposes for its validity that these realists are committed to the doctrine that there is a non-natural "mind" or "consciousness" or "knower," and that anything in order to get known must get into a non-natural relation to this non-natural term. It is possible that these criticisms could be stated in other forms which should leave out of account this presupposition, so thorough-going in the form in which Mr. Dewey has stated them, but what the criticisms would then be would largely be a matter of conjecture. As the criticisms now stand they have direct pertinence only to some type of non-naturalistic realism which is based on the recognition of "mind" as an indispensable "knower" in every perception.

Relation to a mind or consciousness or knower! This is a thesis which some years ago was quite generally supported, and among realists even now Messrs. Bertrand Russell and G. E. Moore still maintain this thesis. But most of the American thinkers, whom the American Philosophical Association's "Committee on Definitions" would class as "epistemologically monistic realists," have been as outspoken against this thesis as Mr. Dewey himself. For instance, Mr. Woodbridge and the contributors to the "First Program and Platform of Six Realists" have made it fundamental to their respective realisms that consciousness is a relation *between* things and not a term of a relation or a relation of things to mind.

Now Mr. Dewey has, in the commendable way so characteristic of him, made his criticisms as impersonal as possible. With two or three exceptions he has named no names; but he has made it, nevertheless, quite obvious that the "epistemological" and "presentative" realists he has in mind are those whose views are similar to Mr. Perry's. His reference to Mr. Perry's phrase, "ego-centric predicament,"[2] near the beginning of his second paper, seems to be a clear indication of his meaning, so far as "epistemological" realism is concerned. As regards "presentative" realism his position is made unmistakable. "Many realists . . . have treated the cases of seen light, doubled imagery, as perception in a way that ascribes to perception an inherent cognitive status. They have treated the perceptions as *cases of knowledge,* instead of as simply natural events having, in themselves (apart from a *use* that may be made of them), no more knowledge status or worth than, say, a shower or a fever. What I intend to show is that if 'perceptions' are regarded as cases of knowledge, the gate is opened to the idealistic interpretation. The physical explanation holds of them as long as they are regarded simply as natural events—a doctrine I shall call naïve realism; it does not hold of them considered as cases of knowledge—the view I call presentative realism" (p. 395). All epistemologically monistic realism, thus, is explicitly brought within the scope of his criticism.

Now how does Mr. Dewey show that when perceptions are regarded as cases of knowledge the gate is opened to the idealistic interpretation? After stating his own "naïve" realistic position he says: "But suppose that the realist accepts the traditionary psychology according to which every event in the way of a perception is also a case of knowing something. Is the way out now so simple?

[2] Of the bearing of which on the realistic position I have written elsewhere, *Philosophical Review*, Vol. XXI., pages 351 ff.

In the case of the doubled fingers or the seen light, the thing known in perception contrasts with the physical source and cause of the knowledge.   There *is* a numerical duplicity.   Moreover, the thing known in perception is *in relation to a knower,* while the physical cause is not as such *in relation to a knower.*   Is not the most plausible account of the difference between the physical cause of the perceptive knowledge and what the latter presents precisely this latter difference—namely, *presentation to a knower?* If perception is a case of knowing, it must be a case of knowing the star; but since the 'real' star is not known in the perception, the knowledge relation must somehow have changed the 'object' into a 'content.' *Thus* when the realist conceives the perceptual occurrence as a case of knowledge *or of presentation to a mind or knower,* he lets the nose of the idealist camel into the tent.   He has not great cause for surprise when the camel comes in—and devours the tent'' (pp. 395–6; most of the italics mine).

It is as clear as anything can be that here the gate is opened to the idealistic interpretation by the introduction of the phrases and clauses I have italicized.   Once deny that a case of knowledge is a presentation of the thing known to a ''mind'' or ''knower,'' and the proof that an idealistic interpretation is involved in the treatment of perceptions as cases of knowledge loses all cogency.   But this is just the denial that is made by many realists who still regard perceptions as cases of knowledge.   These realists, however, in so regarding perceptions are ''presentative'' realists according to Mr. Dewey's definition.   In other words, Mr. Dewey's proof of the essentially idealistic character of ''presentative'' realism requires two premises. One is that perceptions are cases of knowlege, and the other is that perceptive knowledge is presentation to a ''knower.''   Without the latter premise the proof halts, and Mr. Dewey must do without this premise if he is to represent the position of these realists correctly. Mr. Dewey's proof then leaves untouched the question whether these realists have given ground for the idealists' neglect of the physical explanation given by realists of such cases as doubled imagery (p. 395).

Now everything that is further urged in these two articles against ''presentative'' and ''epistemological'' realism assumes that all the advocates of this realism believe perception to be a presentation of objects ''to a mind.''   Hence the whole argument is void as against these realists who, while being ''presentative'' and ''epistemological,'' deny the existence of a ''mind'' to which objects are presented. It is quite possible, as I have already suggested, that some of the reasons urged against this type of realism can be restated so as to bear against it, but it is evident that in the form in which they have been stated by Mr. Dewey they are beside the mark, if the mark is this type of realism.[3]

But there is one specification of the charge against "presentative" realism which it is possible here to examine without regard to the fact that it is implicated in the general misunderstanding already alluded to. Mr. Dewey says that if "presentative" realism be true the physical conditions which cause perception ought to be perceived along with other objects. "In the case of the seen light, reference to the velocity of light is quite adequate to account for its occurrence in its time and space difference from the star. But viewed as a case of what is known (on the supposition that perception is a case of knowledge), reference to it only increases the contrast between the real object and the object known in perception. For, being just as much a part of the object that causes the perception as is the star itself, it (the velocity of light) *ought* to be part of what is known in the perception, while it is not. Since the velocity of light is a constituent element in the star, it should be known in the perception; since it is not so known, reference to it only increases the discrepancy between the object of the perception—the seen light—and the real, astronomical star. The same is true of any physical conditions that might be referred to: *The very things that, from the standpoint of perception as a natural event, are conditions that account for its happening are, from the standpoint of perception as a case of knowledge, part of the object that ought to be known but is not*" (pp. 396-7).

The simplest way to answer this criticism is to challenge the statement. Why *ought* anything to be perceived that is not perceived? Either we have an empiricist theory of perception or we have an apriorist theory. Apriorism can, from its own presuppositions, lay down the law as to what ought to be. The genuine empiricist may also be concerned with what ought to be, but, in matters theoretical, what ought to be is for him only what he is led by experience to expect. If these expectations are not realized, he does not decline to accept what comes instead; he merely tries next time not to cherish such vain expectations. Now our past experience does

---

[3] The fact that such an acute thinker as Mr. Dewey can criticize an adverse view without realizing that he is thoroughly misapprehending it should make him more sympathetic with the failure of the critics of instrumentalism in understanding its presuppositions. It may also be suggested that perhaps one reason for Mr. Dewey's misunderstanding questions asked of him by a realist, questions that concern his view of consciousness, is that Mr. Dewey misunderstands the questioner's view of consciousness and is thus led to impute to the questioner an imputation to Mr. Dewey of a view which the latter has first erroneously imputed to the questioner. (See Mr. Dewey's "Reply," this JOURNAL, Vol. IX., pages 19 ff.)

not justify us in saying that whenever anything is perceived the physical conditions which give rise to our perception of it are all perceived. If then we persist in saying that nevertheless they *ought* to be perceived, this "ought" is evidently not an "ought" of empirically warranted expectation, but an "ought " of *a priori* legislation. It is a bit of sheer dogmatism, of licentious intellectualism; and the use of such an "ought" by an avowed opponent of dogmatism and intellectualism for the purpose of demolishing an empirical realism comes as a startling surprise, not unrelieved by a touch of humor.

"Presentative" realists who regard consciousness as a selective relation among things, a relation unique in the sense of being the distinctive relation it is and comparable to other natural relations,[4] have in this conception of consciousness a means of explaining why the physical conditions of perception as a case of knowledge are not themselves perceived. This explanation consists in showing that what has to be explained is an instance of a general characteristic of selective relations. This characteristic is exemplified when the chisel of the sculptor, though it is the physical condition of the marble's assuming a similitude to the model, does not itself enter into the relation of similarity with statue and model. Suppose, for another instance, that my room-mate at college invites me to spend the holidays at his home and that there I meet his sister whom I subsequently marry. When I thus enter into the matrimonial relation with the girl of my choice, must she and I include her brother in the family constituted by our marriage, because forsooth he was the condition of our coming to know and love and wed each other? Must we likewise marry the clergyman who officiated at the ceremony, and also marry the marriage-license which authorized it, because they too are the conditions of the marriage? What a monstrously redundant polygamy such an "ought" requires every bride and groom to commit! It seems the most "natural" thing in the world that new relations should arise and sometimes arise suddenly, and yet that the conditions, physical and otherwise, which brought about these relationships should not be included in the specific relational complexes produced by them. Why should we deny to the consciousness relation a similar privilege of obtaining among just the terms its conditions see fit to assign to it, without intruding ourselves upon it with the arbitrary demand that it should be more catholic in its terms than it naturally is?   EVANDER BRADLEY MCGILVARY.

UNIVERSITY OF WISCONSIN.

4 "Experience and its Inner Duplicity," this JOURNAL, Vol. VI., page 232: "In answering this question I beg the reader not to allow the term 'togetherness' as I have employed it to prejudice him. Like every general term, it emphasizes common features and slurs over peculiar features."

DISCUSSION

IN RESPONSE TO PROFESSOR McGILVARY

WITH the editors' kind permission, I shall group together my responses to the three articles which Professor McGilvary has been kind enough to devote of late to my writings.[1] I shall take them in the order of their publication.

1. Regarding my article in which I argued that if the ego-centric predicament marked a ubiquitous fact and so was a true predicament, it left the controversy between the idealist and the realist insoluble and, in fact, meaningless, I should like to say that so far as I know there is nothing in that article which attributes to Professor Perry the belief that it is a true predicament. I had no such intention; it was the situation, not Professor Perry's views, that I was dealing with; and besides I was not sure what his attitude was, as there are things in his writings that could be interpreted both ways. I certainly never thought of arguing that a realist *must* accept the

[1] "Realism and the Ego-Centric Predicament," *Philosophical Review*, May, 1912; "Professor Dewey's Awareness," this JOURNAL, Vol. IX., page 301; and "Professor Dewey's Brief Studies in Realism," this JOURNAL, Vol. IX., page 344.

predicament as real; although I was convinced (and still am) that any realism which regards the self, ego, mind, or subject as necessarily one of two terms of the knowledge relation can not escape the predicament. So far as Professor McGilvary's argument is concerned, *if* the predicament is a predicament, he has fallen into a fallacy which, upon retrospection, I think he will find as amusing as he finds, upon occasion, my logic. He quotes the following from Professor Perry: "The same entity possesses both immanence by virtue of its membership in one class, and also transcendence, by virtue of the fact that it may belong also indefinitely to many classes." In comment, Professor McGilvary adds: "This means that when T stands in the complex $TR^c(E)$ it had 'immanence': but when this same T stands in some other complex TR^nT', it has 'transcendence' with respect to the former complex." *If* the predicament is genuine, a moment's reflection will make it obvious that the last formula is not complete. It should read $TR^nT'R^c(E)$. Any known relation among things, *if* knowledge involves a relation to an ego, is itself in relation to the ego.[2] That with respect to the subject-matter of knowledge, realism has the advantage over idealism of recognizing the importance of the relations that things sustain to one another was explicitly recognized in my article.[3]

2. In the second article, Professor McGilvary asks me two questions. In reply to his first, I would say that he is right in suggesting that I included "organic inhibitions" within the generic term "organic releases"—a careless way of writing. His second question is not so easily disposed of: namely, "Why are these 'organic releases' called 'the conditions of awareness' rather than awareness itself?" The passage of my own upon which Professor McGilvary bases his question reads as follows: "Of course on the theory I am interested in expounding the so-called action of 'consciousness' means simply the organic releases in the way of behavior which are the conditions of awareness, and also modify its content." Professor McGilvary's

[2] Since the text was written, Professor McGilvary's review of Perry's "Recent Philosophical Tendencies" has appeared (*Philosophical Review*, July, 1912). In this review Professor McGilvary states the point succinctly and vividly in this way: "How can we discount what is *ipso facto* counted in the very act of discounting?" (p. 466). This relieves Professor McGilvary from any imputation of incurring the fallacy mentioned above. But it makes me even more uncertain than before as to just why and how my article fell under his criticism.

[3] "Nevertheless, I do not conceive that the realistic assertion and the idealistic assertion in this dilemma stand on the same level, or have the same value. The fact that objects vary in relation to one another independently of their relation to a 'knower' *is* a fact, and a fact recognized by all schools." This JOURNAL, Vol. VIII., page 551—the article with which Mr. McGilvary is here dealing.

difficulty is a natural one: the passage should either have expanded or not appeared at all. I was alluding to the views of those who hold that "consciousness" acts directly upon objects. Since my own view appears similar to this doctrine and has, as matter of fact, been identified with it, I threw in the above-quoted passage. My intention was to state that the difference made in objects was made not by a distinct or separate entity or power called consciousness, but by the distinctive type of behavior that involves awareness. The passage as I wrote it is worded with an unfortunate accommodation to the view I was criticizing. What I should have brought out was, first, that "consciousness" is short for conscious or intelligent behavior; and, secondly, that this kind of behavior makes its own distinctive difference in the things involved in its exercise. The unfortunate accommodation to which I refer (and which gives point to Professor McGilvary's query) is the seeming acceptance on my part of a dualism between organic action and awareness of an object. Cancelling this concession and remaining true to my own point of view, the distinction between organic action and the object known is replaced by the distinction of unconscious and purposive behavior with respect to objects. Strictly speaking, accordingly, upon my view the "organic releases" are neither conditions of awareness nor the awareness itself. They are a distinguishable element in intelligent behavior, "awareness" being another distinguishable element. I hope this makes my real meaning clear.

3. I have to confess that I am surprised by Professor McGilvary's last article. It starts by quoting from me (p. 345) a passage in which I state that until the epistemological realists have "considered the main proposition of the pragmatic realists, viz., that knowing is something that happens to things in the natural course of their career, not the sudden introduction of a 'unique' and non-natural type of relation—that to a mind or consciousness—they are hardly in a position to discuss the second and derived pragmatic proposition that, in this natural continuity, things in becoming known undergo a specific and detectable qualitative change." So far the quotation from my article. Then follows immediately this amazing statement of Professor McGilvary. "The realists criticized are guilty, then, of believing that knowing is a sudden introduction of a 'unique' and non-natural relation." I call it amazing because I know of no principles of conversion, obversion, contraposition or any other mode of interpreting a proposition by which the passage quoted is transformable into what Professor McGilvary makes out of it. *Idealists* hold that knowledge is a unique and non-natural relation of things to mind or consciousness, and they make this belief

the basis of the doctrine that things thereby have their seemingly physical qualities changed into psychical ones. This idealistic doctrine has been attributed to pragmatists; at least it has been attributed to me, as possibly Professor McGilvary may recall. That realists are not in a position to consider the actual nature of the pragmatic doctrine that knowing makes a difference in things till they have dissociated the premises upon which it rests from the premises upon which the idealistic conclusion rests, may, I think, be stated without being turned into a statement that realists are "guilty" of holding the obnoxious doctrine.

So far as this portion of his article is concerned, it seems to rest upon the supposition that I was hitting at some person or persons, instead of examining a position. In talking about presentative realism, I thought I made it clear that by presentative realism I meant the doctrine that knowledge is presentation of objects, relations, and propositions to a knower, such presentation occurring (according to this kind of realism) both by perception and by thought. I can assure Professor McGilvary (and others, if there be others that need the assurance) that I never supposed that my criticism applied to any except to those to whom, by its terms, it does apply. Mr. McGilvary says: "Mr. Dewey has, in the commendable way so characteristic of him, made his criticisms as impersonal as possible." I could gladly have foregone the compliment if this impersonal examination of a problem had been taken as, in good faith, of the essence of the article. The identification of mind, soul, with the self, the ego, and the conception that knowledge is a relation between the object as one term and the self as the other, are perhaps the most characteristic and permeating traits of the doctrines of modern philosophy. As yet the realists, with two partial exceptions, have not explicitly developed a theory regarding the self—or subject—and its place or lack of place in knowledge. The problem seems to me important enough to repay attention.

In the latter part of Mr. McGilvary's article, there is a point presented which does not depend upon dubious mind-reading of my intentions. In my earlier article I had stated "the very things that, from the standpoint of perception as a natural event, are conditions that account for its happening, are from the standpoint of perception as a case of knowledge, part of the object that ought to be known, but is not." Mr. McGilvary questions the "ought"—questions, in fact, is a mild term. It denotes, according to him, "*a priori* legislation," "sheer dogmatism," "licentious intellectualism." Before doing penance in sackcloth and ashes, I will remark that *ought* sometimes means "ought as a matter of logical conclusion from the premisses." It was in that sense the ought is used in this passage, so that if I am in error my sins are not of the kind mentioned, but consist of inability to connect premiss and conclusion properly. To go into that matter would involve pretty much a recapitulation of my entire article. I content myself here with pointing out that I was dealing with the doctrine that a seen light is, *ipso facto,* a knowledge (good or bad) of its cause, say an astronomical star, and with the bearing of this doctrine upon the idealistic contention concerning the numerical duplicity of the star and the star as "known" in perception—that is, the immediately visible light. And my point was that if the seen light is *per se* knowledge of the star as a real object, the physical conditions referred to can not be appealed to (this "can not" is intended in a purely logical sense) in explanation of the deficiencies and mistakes of the perceptual knowing, since they are, according to the doctrine, part of the object known by the perception. Mr. McGilvary's illustration regarding a wedding and the events that lead up to it is interesting, but not relevant, as there is no contention, so far as I am aware, that the event called a wedding is, *ipso facto,* a knowledge of that which caused it. It is somewhat "amusing" that the illustration fits perfectly what I said about the adequacy of the naturalistic explanation when applied to the happening of the perception as an event, but has no visible tie of connection with the doctrine that the perception is, *ex officio,* a knowledge of the "real" object that produced it.

JOHN DEWEY.

COLUMBIA UNIVERSITY.

VOL. XIV, No. 18.   AUGUST 30, 1917

DUALITY AND DUALISM

IN what follows I am not to be understood as arguing in behalf of epistemological monism. So far as I know I have not a chemical trace of interest in it. And if my argument does not on that account run in behalf of epistemological dualism, it is because dualism appears to me only two monisms stuck loosely together, so that all the difficulties in monism are in it multiplied by two. If my position must be labeled, I should prefer to call it empirical pluralism, for it is actuated by respect for the plurality of observable facts.

To my mind the logic of Dr. Drake[1] is unduly simplified. It amounts to assuming that wherever you have numerical duality in perceiving there you have epistemological dualism. Now there is numerical duality in perception, namely, the difference in time and place, *etc.*, of the organic event of sensing, imagining, *etc.*, from that of its extra-organic cause. Consequently there is epistemological dualism. Q.E.D. Whether this argument affects the monistic realists or not is for them to determine. But an empirical pluralist is certainly untouched by it. To him the duality is also a triplicity, a fourness, a fiveness, . . .; and in addition the numerical diversity, however great or small, has nothing to do with knowledge. It is of precisely the same nature as the numerical diversity in any train of events which is construed as causes-effects—or antecedents-consequents. The affair of knowledge enters in only when one of the series is *used* as evidence for inferring some other one in the series, whether antecedent to it or consequent upon it. Only when the numerical diversity of evidence and what is inferred from it becomes an adequate ground for epistemological dualism, will the numerical duality of extra-organic cause and intra-organic event, which is found in all perceptions, even set a problem for an empirical pluralist.

I might well leave the matter here. But it happens that Dr. Drake uses terms which show what the cause of his difficulty is. He says: "The question is: Do the images exist in the object, are they numerically identical with some parts of it, or, are they numerically different, existing at other points in space, and only similar to it and representative of it"? Now so far as his reference to me is concerned (and the same holds as to his earlier article),[2] the last clause, "similar to it and representative of it," shows that he has missed the point of my analysis of perception and of knowledge by means of perception. For Dr. Drake assumes that I must hold what he holds; namely, that the organic sensory-cerebral event (sensation-image in the usual phraseology) *is* intrinsically *representative* of its extra-organic cause; in short, is in its very occurrence a fact of the knowledge order or genus. Now this is just what I deny, holding that the event *becomes* cognitive only when *used* as representative, that is to say, as evidence for inferring some other event. Smoke is numerically different from fire, has (or may have) a different locus in space, exists at a different time, *etc.* But it is not inherently representative of fire, although we learn to use it as sign or evidence or representation of fire. This sort of physical numerical duality is literally that which I find figuring in all knowledge. And as I have already said, there is always *more* than duality. The smoke affects my nostrils—there is a smell; my eyes—there is a sight. The smell, the

[1] This JOURNAL, Vol. XIV., especially pp. 368–69.
[2] This JOURNAL, Vol. IX., p. 152.

sight affect my brain, my muscles. A whole series of physical effects is found in every case of the happening of sensory responses. A popular account would be content to say that we go direct from smoke to inferring fire. A more careful one will say that we go from an intra-organic event to smoke and from that to fire. But this is the difference between a more careful and extensive account and a rougher, more summary account. It is a difference in the detail of a series continuously physical in all its constituents. At no point is there a switch from one order or genus of Being to another. And without such a switch there is neither epistemological dualism nor does the demand for an epistemological monism arise. The key to the notion that there is such a switch (to be formulated in a dualism or explained away in a monism) arises from failing to note that representation is an *evidential function* which supervenes upon an occurrence, and from treating it as an inherent part of the structure of the organic events found in sensings. There are no physical events which contain representation of other events as part of their structure. Hence a separate world called psychical is provided for these hasty products of elision and telescoping.

To avoid misunderstanding let me say that the retort that the smoke is not a "conscious datum" while sensations and cerebral events are conscious data is not a reply, but a repetition of the same ignoring of the position. For the position herein recapitulated holds that to call anything "conscious" (so far as the requirements of this argument concern the word) is simply to say that it figures within the inferential or evidential function.

JOHN DEWEY.

COLUMBIA UNIVERSITY.

VOL. XIV, No. 24.   NOVEMBER 22, 1917

DR. DEWEY'S DUALITY AND DUALISM

DR. DEWEY'S "Duality and Dualism" furnishes another depressing bit of evidence that even the ablest philosophers sometimes can not grasp the simplest distinctions of those who hold views alien to their own. At the outset of the article whose logic Professor Dewey criticizes I had taken pains to explain the distinction between what many of us call epistemological dualism and what we call ontological dualism. I had tried in earlier articles (to one of which he also refers) to make clear that my view, although epistemologically dualistic, was ontologically monistic. My distinction had been ignored by several critics, who attacked my doctrine as an ontological dualism. In this article, therefore, I wrote: "I wish to leave no excuse for any further confusion of my epistemological dualism with ontological dualism." "In order to avoid any misunderstanding, I wish to state as explicitly as possible that I personally side with the dominant tendency in American realism in denying the existence

of a non-physical stuff or realm or awareness or subject or ego—
'there ain't no sech animal.' The 'mental' is a subclass of the
physical, or refers, if you prefer, to a relation between certain physical entities. This is ontological monism.''

This distinction, and this use of terms, is no idiosyncrasy of
mine. All of these terms are, of course, open to objection and misunderstanding. But it has seemed to me wisest to keep to the terms used
by those whom I know to hold the doctrine which I hold. I recently
discussed this matter of terminology with four leaders of philosophic
thought in this country, frequent contributors to these columns, who
hold the doctrine. It was their unanimous feeling that these are the
best terms to use for the doctrines to which I refer, and that the distinction which I have emphasized, and which Dr. Dewey persists in
ignoring, is important. I must ask, then, in all courtesy, to have my
terms accepted in this sense, in which they are currently used by responsible writers, and which I have been careful to explain.

We have often offered evidence that our sense-data constitute information (even when not recognized as such) concerning existents
outside of consciousness. The perceiver gains his knowledge of these
outer existents through his sense-data. They may be said to represent those outer existents, in the sense that they vary concomitantly
with them, and act as substitutes for them in guiding the organism.
If this is the situation, our term ''epistemological dualism'' seems to
us warranted. Professor Dewey does not discuss the evidence we
offer; and I must not here repeat it. Nor am I concerned to defend
our terms as the best available. All that I wish to do is to clear them
from an evident misinterpretation, and thereby to defend myself
from the accusation of logical fallacy.

My logic, my critic says, ''amounts to assuming that wherever
you have numerical duality in perceiving there you have epistemological dualism.'' But we do not say ''wherever,'' nor do we say
that *any* ''numerical duality'' implies epistemological dualism.
What we say is that *in certain situations* (perception, memory, *etc.*)
there is numerical duality (*viz.*, between sense-datum, memory-
datum, *etc.*, on the one hand, and object-perceived, object-remem-
bered, *etc.*, on the other hand), *of a certain sort* (described above);
and any theory which clearly recognizes this kind of duality in these
situations we *call* epistemological dualism. That is what we who
hold the doctrine *mean* by it.

Professor Dewey's misunderstanding seems to be twofold. In
the first place, the ''numerical duplicity'' which he speaks of is apparently not that which we are speaking of, not that which leads
us to call our doctrine by the name which he thinks unwarranted.
The numerical duplicity which he recognizes is ''the difference in

time and place, *etc.*, of the organic event of sensing, imagining, *etc.*, from that of its extra-organic cause . . . a difference in the detail of a series continuously physical in all its constituents." This duality he has often spoken of, apparently supposing that this is the duality which we epistemological dualists are talking about. We have replied, in effect, that we recognize that physical series, and rejoice in it, but that our doctrine rests upon another duality entirely, the duality, namely, which I have mentioned in the preceding paragraph. By "object perceived" we refer to what he is apparently referring to by the phrase " extra-organic cause." But by "sense-datum" we mean something else than "the organic event of sensing." Hence the statement that the two items of which he chooses to speak (together with various other items of which we are likewise not speaking) stand in a continuous physical series is an irrelevance.

Even, however, if he were speaking of the same two items as we, it would be still irrelevant to show that they stand in a continuous physical series. Suppose they do! We shall none the less call ourselves epistemological dualists. For the meaning of that term has nothing to do with the question whether or no our two items stand in such a series. It is just the simple *fact* of the duality plus the fact of the use by the organism of the one item as if it were the other, that leads us to adopt that term, in contradistinction to those who deny or ignore that duality.

But his chief misunderstanding is that of which I spoke at the outset, the assumption that I mean by the term "epistemological dualism" the belief in two kinds or realms of Being, that I believe in "a separate world called psychical." After admitting a duality (*his* duality, not mine) in perception, he says, "At no point is there a switch from one order or genus of Being to another. And without such a switch there is neither epistemological dualism nor does the demand for an epistemological monism arise." Here, as throughout, he seems to be reading into the term "epistemological dualism" what, in the very article he is criticizing, I explicitly declared to be not its meaning for me. His confusion results no doubt from the fact that many, perhaps most, epistemological dualists are also ontological dualists; and some of them on occasion have made the very illogical leap which he attributes to me. The distinction, however, between the two senses of the word "dualism" is clear enough; and the failure to recognize it leads him to misread my conclusion as well as my premise. It is small wonder that he finds my logic faulty!

The incident deserves this attention, not for the sake of protecting the honor of my logic, but in order to win a better comprehension for a doctrine held by not a few, and persistently misrepresented by its opponents. The whole issue between us and the epistemological monists evidently seems factitious to Professor Dewey; he declares he has not a "chemical trace of interest" in the one doctrine, and no more in the other. If it is not discourteous, I should like to suggest the possibility that the pragmatist's lack of interest in certain problems with which other workers are grappling may occasionally be due, like the sense of superiority of the contemporary pacifist who is "above the battle," not to an actual transcendence of the problems, or discovery of their unreality, but to obsession by an inhibiting idea which prevents their acuteness from being felt.

DURANT DRAKE.

VASSAR COLLEGE.

THE JOURNAL OF PHILOSOPHY

REALISM WITHOUT MONISM OR DUALISM—I

KNOWLEDGE INVOLVING THE PAST

IN his contribution to the volume of *Essays in Critical Realism* Professor Lovejoy maintains that pragmatism can make good a profession of realism only by aligning itself with a dualistic epistemology such as is presented by his collaborators and himself. He supports this contention largely by an examination of passages drawn from my writings. The least I can do is either to express my assent or state the grounds for witholding it. Certain of his points, and those perhaps of the more fundamental character, though occupying less space, concern the conception of experience. This phase of the matter is reserved for independent treatment. Other points seem, however, to adapt themselves to separate discussion, and to them I address myself. The first has to do with knowledge of the past, or, as from my standpoint I should prefer to say, knowledge about past events or involving them.

This kind of knowledge is taken by Mr. Lovejoy, as by many others, to constitute a stronghold for a representative or dualistic theory of knowledge. Even the monistic epistemologists appear to accept some kind of transcendent pointing to and lighting upon some isolated thing of the past, carrying, apparently, its own place in the past or date in its bosom, though they deny the existence of an intermediate psychical state and fall back on a knower in general or a brain process to make the specific transcendent reference. To me, this latter difference seems a minor matter compared with the question of a leap into a past which is treated as out of connection with the present. Consequently, I have tried to show that knowledge where the past is implicated is logically knowledge of past-as-connected-with-present-or-future, or stating the matter in its order, *of* the present and the future as implicating a certain past. After several pages which seem to me largely irrelevant to my own conception, Mr. Lovejoy states what my conception actually is and says of it (p. 68) that it is "the most effective and plausible part of the pragmatist's dialectical reasoning against the possibility of strictly 'retrospective' knowledge." It certainly should be; it expresses the gist of my discussion.

The point concerns the relation of verification to thought and hence to knowledge. Verification of thought about the past must be present or future; unless, then, thought about the past has a future reference in its meaning, how can it be verified? With reference to this question, Mr. Lovejoy is good enough to state that my "paradox" involves an attempt to escape from a real difficulty or at least what appears as a difficulty. Before coming to Mr. Lovejoy's specific objections, let me develop this point. Quite apart from pragmatism, an empiricist who is empirical in the sense of trying to follow the method of science in dealing with natural existences, will feel logically bound to call nothing knowledge which does not admit of verification. To him, then, judgments about the past will present themselves as hypothetical until verified—which can take place only in some object of present or future experience. In contemplating the possibility of applying this conception to ordinary "memory-judgments," he will be struck by what is going on in the natural sciences. He will see that many zoölogists have ceased to be satisfied with theories about past evolution which rest simply upon a plausible harmonizing of past events, that they are now engaged in experimentation to get present results, that the tendency is to find present, and hence observable, processes which determine certain consequences. He finds geologists attempting verification by experiment as well as by search for additional facts. Turning to another field of judgments about the past he finds that "literary" historians are influenced by the striking or picturesque or moral phases of the events they deal with, and by their lending themselves to composition into a harmonious picture, while "scientific" historians are not only more scrupulous about the facts, but search for new, as yet hidden, facts, to bear out their inferential reconstructions. There is nothing inherently paradoxical in saying that such emphatic scientific cases should give us our clew to understanding the logic of everyday cases which are not scientifically regulated.

I see a letter box; there is an observed thing. It is a commonplace that every recollection starts, directly or indirectly, with something perceived, immediately present. It suggests a letter. This may remain a mere suggestion. The thought of a letter written yesterday or last year may become simply something for fancy to sport with—an esthetic affair, what I call a reminiscence. Truth or falsity does not enter into the case. But it may give rise to questions. Did I actually write the letter or only mean to? If I wrote it, did I mail it or leave it on my desk or in my pocket? Then I do something. I search my pockets. I look on my desk. I may even write the person in question and inquire if he received a letter written on a certain date. By such means a tentative inference gets a categorical status. A logical right accrues, if the experiments are successful, to assert the letter was or was not written. Generalize the case and you get the logical theory concerning knowledge about the past which so troubles Mr. Lovejoy.[1]

So far, however, the gravamen of Mr. Lovejoy's objection is not touched. He replies that the *meaning* of the judgment concerns the past as such, so that verification even if future is of a meaning about the past. Only the *locus* of verification is future: means of proof, but not the thing proved. Consequently, my argument confuses what the original judgment meant and knew itself to mean with an extraneous matter, the time of its verification (see p. 69 of *E. C. R.*). It may be doubted whether dialectically the case is as clear as Mr. Lovejoy's distinction makes it out to be. In what conceivable way can a future event be even the means of validating a judgment about the past, if the meaning of the future event and the meaning of the past event are as dissevered as Mr. Lovejoy's argument requires? Take the case of questions about the past which are intrinsically unanswerable, at least by any means now at our command. What did Brutus eat for his morning meal the day he assassinated Cæsar? There are those who call a statement on such a matter a judgment or proposition in a logical sense. It seems to me that at most it is but an esthetic fancy such as may figure in the pages of a historic novelist who wishes to add realistic detail to his romance. Whence comes the intellectual estoppal? From the fact, I take it, that the things eaten for breakfast have left no consequences which are *now* observable. Continuity has been interrupted. Only when the past event which is judged *is a going concern having effects still directly observable are judgment and knowledge possible.*

The point of this conclusion is that it invalidates the sharp and fixed line which Mr. Lovejoy has drawn between the meaning of the past and the so-called means of verification. So far as the meaning is wholly of and in the past, it can not be recovered for knowledge. This negative consideration suggests that the true object of a judgment *about* a past event may be a past-event-having-a-connection-continuing-into-the-present-and-future. This brings us back, of course, to my original contention. What can be said by way of fact to support its hypothetical possibility?

---

[1] Mr. Lovejoy remarks in passing that ''we have even developed a technique by means of which we believe ourselves able to distinguish certain of these representations of the past as false and others as true'' (pp. 67–68 of *E. C. R.*). I do not see how an account of this technique could fail to confirm the position taken above; I am willing to risk it.

Let us begin with what is called reminiscence. The tendency to tell stories of what has happened to one in the past, to revive interesting situations in which one has figured, is a well-known fact. So far as the stories are told to illustrate some present situation, to supply material to deal with some present perplexity, to get instruction or give advice, they exemplify what is said about prospective meaning. But there are only a few persons who confine themselves to what is intellectually pertinent, who cut down reminiscence to its bare logical bones. Esthetic interests modify the tale, and personal, more or less egoistic, interests fill it up and round it out. The development of reminiscence in old age is doubtless in part compensatory for withdrawal from the actual scene and its imminent problems, its urgencies for action.

Taking, however, whatever intellectual core there may be, such as the material that is employed to give advice to another as to how to deal with a confused and unclear situation, there appears a clear distinction between subject-matter employed and object meant. The past occurrence is *not* the meaning of the propositions. It is rather so much stuff upon the basis of which to predicate something regarding the better course of action to follow, the latter being the object meant. It makes little difference whether the past episode drawn upon is reported with literal correctness or not. Imagination usually plays with it and in the direction of rendering it more pertinent to the case in hand. This does not necessarily affect the value of the judgment—the advice given—as to the course of action which it is better to pursue, or the *object* of judgment. The facts cited, the illustrative material adverted to in support of the conception that a certain course is better, are subject-matter, but not the meaning or object.

Such a case does not directly and obviously cover judgments *about* the past. If the one giving advice began to reflect upon the pertinency of his own past experience to the new issue, we may imagine him going back over the past episode to judge how correctly he has reported it. Just what was it that happened, anyway? This sort of case is crucial for my theory. It exemplifies the situation in which Mr. Lovejoy claims that the meaning to be verified is exclusively concerned with the past even though the locus of means of verification be future. It is worthy of note that, by illustration, this examination of the correctness of the present notion about the past arises out of a problem about the present and future. It is conceivable that specific reference to the past is, after all, only part of the procedure of making judgment about the present as adequate as possible.

This point is not stressed, however, for it is, at this stage of discussion, an easy retort that such an inference follows only because the illustration has already been loaded and aimed in that direction. As a suggestion, however, it may be borne in mind. What does positively emerge from the prior discussion is a distinction between *subject-matter* and *object* of judgment and knowledge. How far is the distinction a general one? It is not one introduced *ad hoc* for the discussion of judgments about the past. It characterizes by logical necessity any *inquiry*. For if the object were present, there would be no inquiry, no thought or inference, no judgment in any intellectual sense of that word. On the other hand, there must be subject-matter, there must be accepted considerations, or else there is no basis for constructing or discovering the object. A verdict represents the judgment in a court of law; it contains the object, the thing meant. Evidence presented and rules of law applied furnish subject-matter. These are diverse and complicated and only gradually is the object framed from them. A scientific inquiry about Einstein's theory, the nature of temperature, or the cause of earthquakes presents the same contrast of an ultimate object, still unattained and questionable, and subject-matter which is progressively presented and sifted till it coheres into an object, when judgment terminates.[2]

If we apply this generic and indispensable distinction to analysis of judgments about the past, it seems to me that the following conclusion naturally issues: The nature of the past event is subject-matter required in order to make a reasonable judgment about the present or future. The latter thus constitutes the object or genuine meaning of the judgment. Take the illustration of the letter. Its *object* must be described in some such terms as the following. What *is* the state of affairs as between some other person and myself? Is his letter acknowledged or no; is the deal closed, the engagement made, the assurance given or no? The only subject-matter which will permit an answer to the question is some past episode. Hence the necessity of coming to close quarters with that past event. In the subject-matter there are always at least two alternatives, while the object is singular and unmistakable. Either I wrote the letter or I did not. Which thought or hypothesis is correct? There can be no inquiry without just such incompatible alternatives present to mind. I have to clear up the question of what is the *object* of judgment by settling its appropriate subject-matter: what *has* happened. The *object* of the judgment in short is the fulfillment of an intention.

---

[2] Subject-matter is not to be confused with data. It is wider than data. It includes all considerations which are adduced as relevant, whether by way of factual data or accepted meanings, while data signifies such facts as are definitely selected for employment as evidential.

I intended or meant to enter into certain relations with a correspondent. Have I done so or is the matter still hanging fire? Certainly, whether or not my analysis is correct, there does not appear to be anything forced or paradoxical about the view that in all such cases the actual thing meant, the object of judgment, is prospective.[3]

To protect the conclusion from appearing to depend upon the quality of the particular illustration used, namely one involving a personal past and personal course of action, we need an impersonal instance of a past episode. That provided by Mr. Lovejoy may be employed. "When I point to this morning's puddles as proof that it rained last night, the puddles are the means of proof but not the thing proved. For verification-purposes their sole interest to me is not in themselves, but in what they permit me to infer about last night's weather. If someone shows me that they were made by the watering-cart, they become irrelevant to the subject-matter of my inquiry—though the same proposition about the future, 'there will be puddles in the street,' is still fulfilled by them" (p. 69 of *E. C. R.*). One wishes that Mr. Lovejoy had subjected his statement to the same critical scrutiny to which he has exposed mine. When it is examined, certain interesting results present themselves.

In the first place, my conception is not contained or expressed by any such judgment as that "there are or will be puddles in the street." The implication of my hypothesis is that the object of judgment is that "prior rain has present and future consequences," such as puddles, or floods, or refreshment of crops, or filling of cisterns, *etc.* In denying that the past event is as such the object of knowledge, it is not asserted that a particular present or future object is its sole and exhaustive object, but that the content of past time has "a future reference and function."[4] That is, the object is some past event in its connection with present and future effects and consequences. The past by itself and the present by itself are both arbitrary selections which mutilate the complete object of judgment. What appears in the above case of the letter as a fulfilment of intention, appears here as a temporal sequence of condition and consequence. In each case, the past incident is part of the subject-matter of inquiry which enters into its *object* only when referred to a present or future event or fact.

In the second place, analysis reveals that the proposition "there

---

[3] The argument does not depend upon any ambiguity between objective and object. As long as inquiry is going on the object is an objective because it is still in question. The final object represents some objective taking settled and definitive form.

[4] As Mr. Lovejoy quotes from me (p. 67 of *E. C. R.*). I do not wish to claim, however, that I have previously made this point as clearly as I am now making it.

will be puddles in the street'' is *not* the same in case the passage of the watering-cart is the past event which properly enters into the subject-matter of inquiry. It is by further investigation of present and future facts that it is determined whether a watering-cart or a shower *is* the actual past event. Not all streets will have puddles if the watering-cart was the cause, or at least roofs won't be wet, cisterns won't be replenished, farmers' soil moistened. If we consult the value of accurate weather reports to a mariner or a member of the Chicago Board of Trade, we get light upon the real object of a judgment involving past weather conditions. The point is the connection of past-present-future, a temporal continuum. Precisely to avoid such incomplete inferences as are manifested in the conclusion ''there will be puddles in the street'' on the basis of considerations like those adduced in Mr. Lovejoy's illustration, we make the exact nature of the past event the theme of exact and scrupulous inquiry.[5] The importance of the present as basis of inference about the past is seen in the growing importance in science of contemporary records, registrations, devices for carrying over the past event into things which can be inspected in the present, devices for measuring and registering the lapse of time, *etc.* This makes the difference between scientific thought and loose popular thought. The reference to or connection with the present and future comes in at the completing end. The present not only supplies the only data for a correct inference about the past, but since the potentialities or meanings of the present depend upon the conditions of the past with which they are correlated, future events are also implied as part of the meaning. If a watering-cart, or a local shower, then no effect upon crops, no effect upon the prices of grain; or, on a lesser scale, no needed precautions as to wearing rubbers.

The logical bearing of the earlier reference (p. 311) to the impossibility of judgments about the past without continuing and present consequences ought now to be clearer. My analysis may be correct or incorrect: that is a question of fact. But the account given does not involve an arbitrary paradox undertaken in behalf of some pet theory. The real point at issue is whether, as long as we are dealing with isolated, self-sufficient events or affairs, anything which is properly called knowledge and object of knowledge can exist. The real point of Mr. Lovejoy's argument is that isolated, self-complete things are truly objects of knowledge. My theory denies the validity of this conception. It asserts that mere presence in experience is quite a different matter from knowledge or judgment, which always involves a *connection,* and, where time enters in, a connection of

[5] That is, we examine present things more carefully and extensively.

past with past and future. The reader may not accept this theory, in spite of its congruity with all the best authenticated cases of knowledge of matter of fact, namely, the objects of science. But when the secondary matter of inconsistency or arbitrary paradox is concerned, it is essential to grasp this point. The case of judgment involving past events is but one case of the general (logical) theory as to knowledge. And as I have pointed out before, it makes it possible to drop out the epistemological theory of mysterious "transcendence," and deal with problems on the basis of objective temporal connections of events, where we never are obliged, even in judgments about the remotest geological past, to get outside events capable of future and present consideration. Once recognize that thoughts about the past hang upon present observable events and are verified by future predicted or anticipated events which are capable of entering into direct presentation, and the machinery of transcendence and of epistemological dualism (or monism) is in so far eliminated.

What is the alternative to my conception? Mr. Lovejoy makes it clear what the alternative is. After all, we have not got very far when we have postulated a psychical somewhat that somehow transcends itself and leaps back into the past. How do we know that it is not leaping into the air or into some quite wrong past? In speaking of this point, and denying the possibility of fulfilling meanings about the past, or of their verification proper, he mentions "an *irresistible propensity* to believe that *some* of them are in fact valid meanings" (p. 70, italics mine). An irresistible propensity which applies to "some" meanings and not to others is, to say the least, a curious fact. It suggests that perhaps the propensity is most unreliable when it is most irresistible. He speaks also of indirect verification based on "instinctive assumptions" (p. 71). He says that a truly pragmatic analysis "would include an enumeration of the not-immediately-given-things which it is *needful for the effective agent, at that moment, to believe or assume* . . . if the process of reflection is to be of any service to him in the framing of an effective plan of action" (p. 70). He charges me as a pragmatist of failing to live up to pragmatism and "trying to transcend one of the most inescapable limitations of human thought" (p. 70).

There are pragmatists who fall back on instinctive assumptions and propensities, as a ground for accepting and asserting meanings to be valid. They will welcome Mr. Lovejoy to the fold. But the author of "Thirteen Varieties of Pragmatism" should be cognizant that there is a variety not of the "will to believe" type. If his conception is such a fixed part of the definition of pragmatism that refusing to admit it is inconsistent with pragmatism, then, as I have said before, I have no claim to be called a pragmatist. I am even hopeful that his clear statement of instinctive propensity *versus* logical verification as the alternatives will help convert some non-pragmatists to my account of knowledge involving past events.

Enumeration of the things needful to assume in framing an effective plan of action is an undoubted part of the process. But it is a hypothetical enumeration. Part of the operation of intelligent formation of a plan of action is to note what the needs of the situation are. But the needs of an agent can themselves be judiciously estimated only in connection with other matters which enter into the situation along with the agent. To isolate the needs or propensities of the agent and regard them as grounds of belief in the validity of meaning seems to be the essence of subjectivism. And when the plan of action is framed it is still tentative. It is verified or condemned by its consequences. A propensity without doubt suggests a certain view and plan: when employed in connection with environing factors it makes a view or plan worthy of acceptance *for trial*, acceptance as a working hypothesis. Beyond this point, the notion that a propensity, however practically irresistible, or an assumption, however instinctive—if there be such things apart from habit—warrants belief that a meaning is valid commits us to a subjectivism which is, to my mind, the most seriously objectionable thing in idealism.

It is Mr. Lovejoy, it seems to me, who is committed to a subjective pragmatism.

JOHN DEWEY.

COLUMBIA UNIVERSITY.

VOL. XIX., No. 13   JUNE 22, 1922

REALISM WITHOUT MONISM OR DUALISM—II

A PREVIOUS paper discussed the nature of knowledge involving past events. The paper tried to show that the *object* of knowledge in such cases is a temporal sequence or continuum including past-present-future. While this analysis may be taken on its own merits or demerits, it was also indicated that its acceptance renders unnecessary the epistemological machinery of psychical states possessed of so-called transcendent capacity. Mr. Lovejoy's discussion in the *Essays in Critical Realism* considers, in addition, the case of anticipatory thought, judgments involving expectation, forecasts, prediction. He tries to show that in their case, at least, a mental state must be admitted, a representation which is psychical in its existence. He also questions the point in my own discussion (contained in the *Influence of Darwin, etc.*, in the essay on "The Experimental Theory of Knowledge'') which claims that such anticipatory reference is involved in all knowledge.

In principle, the problem of anticipatory knowledge introduces nothing not contained in the prior discussion where reference to the future was shown to be involved in knowledge involving the past. But a discussion of the problem shifts somewhat the points of emphasis and it affords an opportunity to make explicit some of the implications of the prior discussion, with reference especially to the place of verification and of representation and ideas in a naturalistic realism which involves neither monistic nor dualistic realism. We may first consider the nature of representation.

In any judgment concerning the future or the past, there is something to which the name representation is appropriate. A present stone stands for an animal living in the past, ashes, for a fire that has died down, an odor for a flower still to be smelled, a sudden oscillation of a needle for an event still to be discovered, and so on.

Now the piece of rock, the ashes, the odor, the oscillating needle are first of all things present in experience on their own account, or noncognitively; then they may become implicated in a reflective inquiry. We may ask what they stand for or indicate, what they give witness to or are evidence of, or what they portend. In this situation and also when it is asserted that they mean or support a certain conclusion, they acquire a representative capacity which they did not inherently possess. The piece of rock is still a piece of rock but it is taken, either hypothetically or categorically according to the stage of reflection reached, as sign or evidence of something else, a fossil. It exercises a representative *function*, although it is not in its own existence a representation. Just so a poem may be not just enjoyed, but used as evidence of being written by a particular author or as an indication of a certain crisis in the life of its author; an esthetic object in its first intention is not of this sort, but it becomes such when and if it enters as a datum into a judgment about something else. Just so a board may become a sign, a column of mercury an index of temperature, a spire of smoke a clew to fire, a stain the evidence of some chemical reaction. There is a well-known rhetorical device by which a function is transferred to a thing, and we call the thing by the name of its function. Just so we call sounds or marks on paper, words; or a stone, a fossil; just so we may call things having the representation function, representations. In the first case we are not likely to forget that the term used implies a connection, not a self-possessed quality. In the second case, we too easily forget this fact and get into trouble.

This is stated somewhat dogmatically because an argument is not at issue, but rather a recapitulation of a criticized position which it is necessary to bear in mind if the force of the criticism is to be estimated. It brings us to the question of "mediatism" and "immediatism" in knowledge.[1]

Mr. Lovejoy says that two opposing views of the knowledge situation may "be named 'immediatism' and 'mediatism.' According to the former, whatever kind of entity be the object of knowledge, that object must be actually given, must be itself the directly experienced datum. According to the latter view, it is of the essence of the cognitive process that it is mediate, the object being never reached directly, and, so to say, where it lives, but always through some essence or entity distinguished from it, though related to it in a special way."[2] To this statement he adds the acute remark that both idealists and monistic realists are immediatists. He conducts his discussion on the assumption that I am an immediatist in the sense defined and as excluding all mediatism. Then he has no difficulties in finding inconsistencies in my treatment. I should go further and say that upon this assumption everything I have written about knowledge is one huge inconsistency.

For, as the remarks about representation indicate, wherever inference or reflection comes in (and I should not call anything knowledge in a logical or intellectual sense unless it does come in), there is, clearly, mediation of an object by some other entity which points to or signifies or represents or gives witness to or evidence of. Nevertheless, thought or inference becomes knowledge in the complete sense of the word only when the indication or signifying is borne out, verified in something directly present, or immediately *experienced*—not immediately known. The object has to be "reached" eventually in order to get verification or invalidation, and when so reached, it is immediately present. Its cognitive status, however, is *mediated;* that is, the object known fulfils some specific function of representation or indication on the part of some other entity. Short of verificatory objects directly present, we have not knowledge, but inference whose content is *hypothetical.* The subject-matter of inference is a candidate or claim to knowledge requiring to have its value tested. The test is found in what is finally immediately present, which has a meaning because of prior mediation which it would not otherwise have.

There is, I think, nothing fundamentally new in this view, although it goes contrary to the more usual belief that knowledge is

---

[1] The immediacy of *experience* concerns one of the reserved questions.

[2] P. 48 of *Essays in Critical Realism.*

some kind of direct apprehension or perception of some thing or event. There is a certain sense in which Mr. Lovejoy is much more of an immediatist than I am. I mean that for him the psychical representation is but an organ or extraneous means of grasping or pointing to some entity immediately complete in itself as an object of knowledge—as was pointed out in the prior article dealing with "knowledge of the past." While from my point of view the relation, connection or mediation of one thing by another is an essential feature of the *subject-matter* of knowledge. The conception is not, as was said, intrinsically novel. It is not inherently pragmatic. It results from carrying over into the logical theory of knowledge, the methods universally adopted at present by natural science, or inquiry into natural events. It is as appropriate to this kind of science as the assumption that the objects of knowledge are forms or essences which must be directly inspected, was to the Aristotelian science. The "pragmatic" feature comes in when it is noted that experiment or action enters to make the connection between the thing signifying and the thing signified so that inference may pass from hypothesis to knowledge. It is then seen that some "consequences," namely those of the experiment, are an integral part of the completing or fulfilling or leading out of the "representation" into final objects.[3] Thus we again arrive at a union of immediate and mediate in knowledge, instead of their sharp distinction.

These considerations appear pertinent to a discussion of the nature of intellectual anticipations, predictions, *etc.* In my essay on the "Experimental Theory of Knowledge," I pointed out that there is an internal complication in such cases; on the one hand, there is something indubitably present, say, smoke; on the other hand, this is taken to mean something absent, say, fire. Yet it is not a case of sheer absence, such as total ignorance would imply. The fire is presented *as* absent, as intended. Its subsequent presence is required in order to fulfil the reference of the smoke. Mr. Lovejoy says that this presented-as-absent is what epistemology has always signified by "representation" (*Essays* p. 51). So far, so good, bearing in mind what has been said about the meaning of representation. But Mr. Lovejoy introduces a further qualification. I had said that in order to fulfil the meaning of what is given-as-present, the given-as-absent must become present, and this involves an opera-

---

3 Confusion arises sometimes, I think, because Mr. James accepted an "immediate" knowledge, "acquaintance," and applied the conception of transitive leading only to "knowledge about." In the latter he did not emphasize the experimental production of consequences, although he did not deny it. Hence follows the importance of discriminating varieties of pragmatism in discussing theories of knowledge.

tion which tries to bring the inferred fire into experience in the same immediate way in which the smoke is present. Mr. Lovejoy denies the need of any operation or act. He says that we may dream of a windfall of fortune about which one can do nothing. Of course one can, just as one may construct day-dreams without end. But are these thoughts, in any cognitive sense, of the future, or are they just fancies whose function—so far as they have any—is esthetic enrichment of the present moment? He also denies the necessity of an act to bring the meant object into actual experience on the ground that the thing present, smoke, may merely remind us of a past object; it may merely beget a reminiscence (p. 53). I should not think of denying this fact. The claims of my theory begin when we ask what is the cognitive status of this reminder or reminiscence. I may be reminded of something beautiful which I have read in a poem. Does this make the reminder knowledge? Does it give the smoke or the poem a place in some existential landscape? Does it even depend upon my being able to place the poem with respect to its author, the book where I read it or the time when it was read? What my theory is after is precisely the differentia between a reminder or reminiscence which is esthetic and one which is cognitive or a reminder of *fact*. My theory involves no slurring over of the existence of reminders. It claims that when we take them *as* knowledge we proceed to act upon them, and that the consequences of the acting test the validity of the claim of a recollection to be true knowledge. Mr. Lovejoy may hold that every dream and every reminder is a case of knowledge. But I do not see how he can attribute the implications of that doctrine to a theory which holds that some experienced objects are self-enclosed esthetically, and therefore lack cognitive status. Moreover, his inference that my theory is false, since we do not act upon a dream, may appear to some to throw doubt upon the theory that a dream is a case of knowledge rather than upon *my* theory.

In discussing my criticism of monistic realism, Mr. Lovejoy has no difficulty in finding numerous passages which indicate that I am not a monistic realist. Considering that I was criticizing monistic realism for its monism, his discovery does not surprise me. The converse discovery would have given me a shock. Mr. Lovejoy then argues that if I am not a monistic realist I must be a dualistic one. "That, then, is the alternative to which he [the present writer] is limited—*either* idealism or else dualism. . . . . A conception of knowledge which should be at once realistic and monistic is barred to him" (*E. C. R.*, p. 62). Mr. Lovejoy appears fond of the use of the principle of excluded middle. But this principle is two-edged as well as sharp. Unless handled carefully, it cuts the fingers of the one who uses it. We have already noted how Mr. Lovejoy makes an exhaustive disjunction between the immediate and the mediate in knowledge on the basis of which he convicts me of inconsistency. We have also noted that the gist of my theory about the object of knowledge is that it is mediate in one *respect* and immediate in *another,* so that the alleged inconsistency is due to failure to grasp the theory. Neither is the disjunction between monistic and dualistic realism exhaustive. There remains pluralistic realism, which is precisely the theory I have advanced. The things which are taken as meaning or intending other things are indefinitely diversified, and so are the things meant. Smoke stands for fire, an odor for a rose, different odors for many different things, mercury for atmospheric pressure or heat, a stain for a biochemical process, and so on *ad infinitum.* Things are things, not mental states. Hence the realism. But the things are indefinitely many. Hence the pluralism. It all hangs together with the hypothesis which has been outlined concerning the nature of knowledge.[4]

Mr. Lovejoy, however, has another shot in his locker. Since I admit that in anticipatory inference—in all reflection from my point of view—something is present-in-experience-as-absent and as-to be-brought-into-presence-of-a-direct-kind, he holds that I have admitted the psychical or mental as a term in the judging process, and hence am committed to dualism. His dialectical argument in support of this view appears to manifest another instance of addiction to uncritical use of the principle of excluded middle. Present-as-absent, or the presence of the absent, is an impossibility as regards any physical thing. Hence there is an admission of a psychical entity. For, he says, the adjectives mental and psychical as he uses them "simply designate anything which is an undubitable bit of experience, but [which] either can not be described in physical terms or can not be located in the single objective or 'public' spatial system, free from self-contradictory attributes, to which the objects dealt with by physical science belong" (*E. C. R.*, p. 61).

This assumption of an exhaustive disjunction between the physical and psychical is significant. It disposes, by a single sweeping gesture, of the growing number of persons, not pragmatists, who

---

4 There is nothing original on my part in this view. It is held by some whose realistic standing is probably less open to suspicion than is mine, Professor Woodbridge for example. See his "Nature of Consciousness," this JOURNAL, Vol. II, p. 119. He has drawn some inferences from this conception which I have found myself unable to accept, and I have drawn some which I fear do not command his assent. But I am glad to acknowledge indebtedness to him for much clarification of my own thought on the subject.

hold that certain entities are neutral to the distinction of psychical and physical. It asserts, by implication, that all meanings, relations, activity systems, functions, affairs like mathematical entities, like a constitution, a franchise, values, operations, conceptions, norms, *etc.*, are psychical. Such a position is peculiarly striking in the context of a volume which makes constant use of the notion of essence. Mr. Lovejoy, himself, refers on the very page from which the passage is quoted to "a common character or essence" found in the thing representing and the thing represented.

From the standpoint of argument, I am entitled, I think, to leave the matter here, till Mr. Lovejoy and his collaborators have wrestled with the question of essence in its bearing upon the exhaustiveness of the disjunction between the physical and the psychical, and till many non-pragmatists have been disposed of. The situation certainly puts the burden of proof upon Mr. Lovejoy. But it is better to take advantage of this opportunity to make a brief restatement of my own view as to the nature of "ideas" or the mental. Mr. Lovejoy starts with a ready-made psychical existence which assumes the function of reference or of signifying, and that the future thing which is presented as absent is, itself, psychical, or if not in itself, at least in its presence-as-absent. My hypothesis reverses the notion. It starts with a thing, *res*, actually present, smoke, rock, and with the present fact that this something refers to something else of the same order of existence as itself, a fire, or geologic animal. It bases itself upon the undoubted occurrence of inference from one present thing to another absent thing of the same non-psychical kind. It thus avoids the breach of continuity, the dualism, involved in dividing existence into two orders, physical and psychical, which are defined only by antithetical attributes, and of such a nature that reference and intercourse between them is an affair totally unlike any other known matter. It also has the advantage of starting from a *vera causa*, the undubitable fact of inference.[5]

According to hypothesis, then, the future thing meant is objective—a fire, possibility of finding additional traces of extinct organisms, a rain storm, penalization of certain modes of behavior, or an eclipse of the sun. It is stood for or represented by something equally objective, mathematical figures, words, heard or seen things, *etc.* That one objective affair should have the power of standing for, meaning, another is the wonder, a wonder which as I see it, is to be accepted just as the occurrence in the world of any other quali-

---

5 *Essays in Experimental Logic*, p. 225.

tative affair, the qualities of water, for example.[6] But a thing which has or exercises the quality of being a surrogate of some absent thing is so distinctive, so unique, that it needs a distinctive name. *As exercising the function we may call it mental.* Neither the thing meant nor the thing signifying is mental. Nor is meaning itself mental in any psychical, dualistic, existential sense. Traditional dualism takes the undoubted logical dual*ity*, or division of labor, between data and meanings, and gets into the epistemological predicament by transforming it into an *existential* dual*ism*, a separation of two radically diverse orders of being.[7] Starting from the undoubted existence of inference, or from a logical function, "ideas" denote problematic objects so far as they are signified by present things and are capable of logical manipulation. A probable rain storm, as indicated to us by the look of the clouds or the barometer, gets embodied in a word or some other present thing and hence can be treated *for certain purposes* just as an actual rain storm would be treated. We may then term it a mental entity. Such a theory, it will be noted, explains the mental on the basis of a logical function. It does not start by shoving something psychical under a logical operation.[8]

The matter is so important that perhaps it is worth while to try to state it in another way. Meanings are the characteristic things in intellectual experience. They are the heart of every logical function. They are not physical nor are they (pace Mr. Lovejoy's disjunction) psychical.[9] A meaning is not necessarily such that it can be called an idea or thought. But a meaning may be adopted hypothetically, as a basis for instituting inquiries, or as a point of departure in connection with other meanings for reasoning, an experiment in combining meanings together to see what develops. Such a tentative acceptance of meanings is all that is possible in a problematic situation, unless we make either a dogmatic assertion or a dogmatic denial. What is the meaning of some event? What is it all about? Something suggests itself as a possible answer or solution. It is as yet,

---

[6] That is to say, it is a metaphysical or cosmological or scientific question—as the case may be—which effects all schools of epistemological thought alike. It is not a problem which bears more heavily on one than on another, though on the face of it there are more difficulties for a dualistic school than for others because of the implied breach of continuity.

[7] This point has been developed, not to say labored, in the essay entitled "Data and Meanings" in the *Essays in Experimental Logic*, pp. 136–156.

[8] See the essay on the "Logical Character of Ideas," pp. 220–229 of *E. E. L.*

[9] Of course upon my theory they are, existentially speaking, the *operations* involved in any situation having cognitive reference.

however, only a possible, a conjectural meaning. How is it to pass beyond conjecture and be definitely asserted or rejected? Inquiry proceeds by taking a stand, as it were, upon the meaning and using it as a base for new observations and reasonings. *If* so and so, *then* so and so. We look to see if the "then so and so" can be actually presented in experience. In the degree in which we can thus find what is hypothetically demanded and can determine that *only* the "if so and so" implies it, we make assertion categorical. Such is the course of any legitimate reflection. But the operation demands that the meaning be embodied in existence, that it be a "concretion in discourse" to borrow Mr. Santayana's apt term. The usual method is a word or diagram, but in any case, there must be some physical thing to carry the meaning, if the latter is to be employed for intellectual manipulation and experimentation, or as an effective hypothesis. The hypothetical meaning thus embodied constitutes *a* thought or *an* idea, *a* representation.

This is the theory which I have put forth.[10] The theory is, of course, conceivably incorrect. But if so, it is incorrect because of matters of fact. It is not arbitrary nor paradoxical, and while it is obviously inconsistent with presentative dualism or transcendent immediatism it does not appear to be inconsistent with itself when it is taken in its own terms.

I close with a general remark on the main point at issue, the question of the method appropriate to investigation of the problem of knowledge. This, rather than "pragmatism," *is* the point at issue. Professor Rogers, in his contribution to *Essays in Critical Realism,* has stated the matter in such a way as to define the issue. He says "that the quarrel between the critical realist and the pragmatist is due, primarily, to the fact that they are not dealing with the same problem. Professor Dewey's concern is with the technique of the actual advance of knowledge in the concrete—its linear dimension in relation to other knowledge past and future, as this enters into the texture of conduct. The critical realist, on the contrary, is interested in its dimension of depth—its ability to present to man's mind a faithful report of the true nature of the world in which he has to act and live" (p. 160).

I am grateful to Professor Rogers for putting the case so clearly from his point of view. It marks a genuine advance in fruitful discussion. It gives me an opportunity to say that from my own standpoint the quarrel is not due to the fact that we are discussing different problems. We are discussing the same problem. The

---

[10] See, in addition to references already given, pp. 430–433 of *Essays in Experimental Logic.*

difference concerns the method by which the problem is to be approached and dealt with. The objection is to the epistemological method as distinct from a method which accepts logical procedure as a fact and then tries to analyze it. My contention is that the problem of a faithful report of the world in which we have to act and live can be fruitfully approached only by means of an inquiry into the concrete procedure by which actual knowledge is secured and furthered. In most matters, we have painfully learned that the way to arrive at a sound generalization is by examination and analysis of specific, concrete cases. Why not apply this lesson of scientific procedure to the problem of reaching a conception of knowledge, to the problem of the nature of a faithful report of the world? If we do enforce this lesson, the disjunction between the critical realist's problem and the "pragmatist's" problem, as stated by Mr. Rogers, vanishes.

What does "faithful" denote and signify? What does "report" denote and signify? And, more important still, by what method shall we seek an answer to these questions? Mr. Pratt in his contribution quotes a saying of Mr. Santayana's that "an opinion is true if what it is talking about is constituted as the opinion asserts it to be constituted" (p. 99 of *E. C. R.*). With all my heart; assent can not be too unqualified. But is the statement a solution or does it contain the gist of a problem? What is an opinion, existentially speaking, and what does it mean? And so of the terms "talking about," "assert," and so of the connection between the talking about and the "what" talked about, implied in the term "as." These are things to be investigated if we are to reach a satisfactory conclusion concerning the nature of a faithful report. And I see no way to answer them except to adopt the same procedure which we employ in investigating other subject-matters: analyze special cases of knowledge secured and advanced, and generalize the outcome of the analysis. My objection to the epistemological method is that it ignores the only method which has proved fruitful in other cases of inquiry; that it does so because it accepts, uncritically, an old and outworn psychological tradition about psychical states, sensations and ideas,[11] and because, in so doing, it states the problem in a way which makes it insoluble save by the introduction of a mysterious transcendence plus a naïve confidence in irresistible propensities and unescapable assumptions. And when it comes to any particular case of alleged knowledge we find the epistemologists abandoning their epistemological machinery and falling back upon the logical procedure ac-

11 See an article in this JOURNAL, Vol. XI, p. 505.

tually employed in critical investigations which terminate in experimental verifications. Why not begin, then, at this point?

We are trying to know knowledge. The implication assuredly is that there is knowledge. The procedure which I have tried to follow, no matter with what obscurity and confusion, is to begin with cases of knowledge and to analyze them to discover why and how they are knowledges. If this procedure can be successfully undertaken, then we can tell what knowledge is. What other method is reasonable? We are trying, be it remembered, to know knowledge, to get at and formulate its character. What is the likelihood of success in the undertaking if we rule out specific cases of knowledge and try to investigate knowledge at large? If we have no case of knowledge upon which to go, and upon which to base judgments as to the value of a proferred knowledge of knowledge, what meaning has the term knowledge? Why not call it abracadabra, or splish-splosh, or anything else that comes into your head? How does knowledge, at the best, mean something different from poesy or fancy or dreams? For my part if we wish to know what a faithful report of the world in which we live means, I prefer to take the best authenticated cases of faithful reports which are available, compare them with the sufficiently numerous cases of reports ascertained to be unfaithful and doubtful, and see what we find. Starting in this way, we have a method by which we can also discriminate and identify poesy, reverie, dreams, sensations, ideas, hypotheses, data, and all the rest of it. The principle of parsimony has claims which all tell in behalf of the use of the logical method.

JOHN DEWEY.

COLUMBIA UNIVERSITY.

THE JOURNAL OF PHILOSOPHY

TIME, MEANING AND TRANSCENDENCE

I. THE ALLEGED FUTURITY OF YESTERDAY

I AM greatly obliged to Professor Dewey for the careful and extended comment[1] with which he has honored my contribution to *Essays in Critical Realism*. Philosophers of eminence have not always been equally ready to enter the lists and join issue directly, and point by point, with their critics. Mr. Dewey's two papers, therefore, are an encouraging manifestation of belief in that conception of the philosophic quest of truth which makes it consist in an essentially social and coöperative process of intellectual experimentation, wherein all philosophical theses, arguments and distinctions are cast into the alembic of searching, patient, analytic discussion by many and diverse minds. I do not, indeed, find that, in the present instance, great progress has as yet been accomplished towards actual agreement. But that, doubtless, is a result which could hardly be expected after a single exchange of views. Meanwhile Mr. Dewey's articles seem to me to do a good deal to make more clear the nature, the grounds and the causes of disagreement. And I am hopeful that a continuance of the discussion may still further clarify not merely these matters, but the important philosophical issues which they involve.

What those issues are it is doubtless well to remind the reader. In the essay with which Mr. Dewey's articles are concerned I attempted to vindicate, among others, the two following theses: (*a*) that all practical or instrumental knowledge is, or at least includes and requires, "presentative" knowledge, a representation of not-present existents by present data; (*b*) that "pragmatically considered, knowledge is thus necessarily and constantly conversant with entities which are existentially transcendent of the knowing experience." As the simplest and least dubitable example of such

---

1 "Realism without Monism or Dualism," this JOURNAL, XIX, pp. 309–317, 351–361. These papers will be here cited as *R. M. D.*, and the *Essays in Critical Realism* as *E. C. R.*

transcendent reference, and therefore as a crucial instance, I cited our judgments of retrospection and anticipation. In them, it seems obvious to most men, we "mean" and know entities which are not directly given in experience at the moment when they are known, inasmuch as they do not then form a part of the existing world. In justifying both the general theses mentioned, and the particular instance of judgments about the past, I was under the necessity of controverting views which had been expressed by Mr. Dewey and which seemed to me an aberration from the true logic of his own pragmatic doctrine. Though not without some ambiguity of language, he had seemed to maintain that the object meant or known in valid judgments must always be "directly experienced"—an assertion which, if taken literally, would imply the impossibility of intertemporal cognition, of the knowing of one moment's experience at another moment. And in fact, with respect to the special case of knowledge of the past, Mr. Dewey had been led by his "principle of immediate empiricism" into an apparent denial of its possibility.[2] Because the past object *is* transcendent of the experience that knows it, is "past and gone forever," Mr. Dewey had in numerous passages betrayed a curious reluctance to admit that the past as such can be said to be "known" or "meant" at all. This paradox is in truth, as I have previously contended, an inevitable consequence of the attempt to escape epistemological dualism by denying the transcendence of the object known.

The same paradox the first part of Mr. Dewey's reply seems to reaffirm and even sharpen; for its argument leads up to such assertions as: "the present or future constitutes the object or genuine meaning of the judgment about the past";[3] in retrospective judgments "the actual thing meant, the object of judgment, is prospective";[4] "the past occurrence is *not* the meaning of propositions" of this type.[5] And since he has, as he thinks, overthrown this supposed crucial instance of the transcendent reference of knowledge, Mr. Dewey concludes that he has proved it "possible to drop out the epistemological theory of mysterious 'transcendence.'" While, for reasons to be mentioned later, I doubt whether these propositions mean what they say, I shall first assume that they do so, and shall review Mr. Dewey's argument as an attempted proof of them.

[2] For example see *E. C. R.*, pp. 42–4, 52–4, 63–71.
[3] See *R. M. D.*, p. 313.
[4] *R. M. D.*, p. 314.
[5] *R. M. D.*, p. 312; italics in original.

1. The first argument consists in the contention that it is "only when the past event which is judged is a going concern having effects still directly observable" that "judgment and knowledge are possible." But this proposition, which is given the emphasis of italics, is, I suppose, denied by no one; I, at least, am far from disputing it. Obviously, the ground of present belief must be a present ground; the evidence which can to-day justify a judgment about yesterday's events must be evidence existing to-day, not yesterday. Nor do I see any objection to converting this truism into Mr. Dewey's proposition that " the true object of a judgment *about* a past event may be" (I should even add: in the case of scientifically verifiable judgments, must be) "a past-event-having-a-connection-continuing-into-the-present-and-future." Since we do not regard as now knowable (in the usual sense of "knowledge") past matters of fact which have left no now discoverable trace of or witness to their reality, we may properly enough say that the *complete* "object" of any genuine piece of verified knowledge of the past is a past having effects, direct or indirect, surviving in the present (memories being included among these effects). In other words, continuity—usually of the causal sort—with the present is undeniably a *part* of the meaning of the expression "known past event." But the part is not the whole; and it is upon a distinction so simple as this that Mr. Dewey's first argument breaks down. For the matter at issue has to do solely with that part of the total object of a judgment about the past which *is* past. Mr. Dewey seems to suppose that when it is shown that any valid and verified retrospective judgment contains at least an implicit reference to the present and future, we are thereby relieved of all logical concern about its primary reference to the past. It is as if an astronomer, observing in the spectrum of a star both red and yellow rays, should say to himself: "This red is evidently merely a red-in-connection-with-yellow; it will therefore suffice, in my study of the star, if I consider only the yellow, disregarding any problems which may have to do solely with the red." But, as Mr. Dewey's own expressions inevitably and repeatedly concede, the past reference still remains, an essential aspect of the present cognitive experience; and with it remains the justification for the contention of the portion of my paper under discussion.

2. Mr. Dewey, however, seeks to justify the monopoly of his philosophic attention enjoyed by the present and future part of a retrospective judgment's reference, by means of a distinction between "object" and "subject-matter"; and it is upon the application of "this generic and indispensable distinction" to that class

of judgments that he seems finally to rest his case. By "subject-matter" he signifies the "accepted considerations" in any inquiry, the things known, or taken as known, in order that they may lead to a knowledge of something else which at the outset of the inquiry is not known. The "object" is this something else, which *becomes* a "thing known," an accepted consideration, at the successful conclusion of the inquiry. Thus in a court of law the verdict "contains the object, the thing meant; evidence presented and rules of law applied furnish subject-matter." The distinction itself is unexceptionable, though more sharply contrasted terms might have been found to express it; but Mr. Dewey's way of applying it "to analysis of judgments about the past" seems to me really very odd. In such a judgment it is "the nature of the past event" which he identifies with the "subject-matter," on the ground that it is "required to make a reasonable judgment about the present or future"; the latter *"thus constitutes the object or genuine meaning of the judgment."* Hence, "there is nothing forced or paradoxical about the view that in *all* such cases the actual thing meant, the object of judgment, is prospective."[6] *Q. E. D.* The paleontologist will thus learn, with some surprise, that when he is seeking to determine whether a certain fossil animal was contemporaneous with paleolithic man, the "actual thing meant" by his inquiry, the "object or genuine meaning" of the judgment which he reaches at the end of it, is not an organism that has been extinct for ages, nor even present fossil remains, but something "prospective." As for that class of judgments about the past which are the specialty of courts of criminal law, Mr. Dewey's previous application (cited just above) of his distinction to these judgments now manifestly requires not merely revision but reversal. In a coroner's inquest, for example, the "nature of the past event" under inquiry is the manner in which the deceased came to his death; which is therefore the "subject-matter" of the inquiry; which in turn means, by Mr. Dewey's definition, that it constitutes the "accepted considerations" in the case; while "the evidence presented"—though *it* is classified as "subject-matter" only a few lines earlier in Mr. Dewey's paper—must in the light of his present conclusion be removed from that class (and so from that of "accepted considerations") and be described as the "still unattained object" of the inquiry!

    6 *R. M. D.*, pp. 313, 314; italics mine. The distinction between object and subject-matter, as here used, seems to be merely another phrasing of that between "reference" and "content" employed for the same ends in *The Influence of Darwin upon Philosophy*, p. 61. *Cf.* my comment on this, *E. C. R.*, p. 67.

How has it come about that Mr. Dewey thus reverses, in the course of a single page, the meaning of his own terminology for expressing this "indispensable distinction"? The origin of the confusion is perhaps not beyond the reach of analysis. If he had adhered to his original definitions, it would have been obvious that, in any inquiry into the nature or reality of a past event, the "accepted considerations," and therefore the "subject-matter," must, as he himself in other passages often reiterates, consist of present data—the testimony of the witnesses, the character and situation of the fossil. Thus the superior status of "object" would have fallen to the lot of the past event to which the inquiry relates. This result, however, would be contrary to Mr. Dewey's main thesis; and consequently, another distinction seems to have been unconsciously substituted for the original one, while the same pair of terms is retained to express it. The new distinction actually seems to turn upon a play on the double meaning of the word "object." In the original distinction the word, of course, meant simply the thing referred to in a judgment; it now means the purpose or interest which leads one to ask the question which the judgment answers: "the object is the fulfilment of an intention." Thus—as Mr. Dewey illustrates—if I ask myself whether I mailed that letter yesterday, the "object" of my inquiry is to get answers to such questions of present or future interest as these: "What *is* the state of affairs between some other person and myself? Is his letter acknowledged or no; is the deal closed, the engagement made, the assurance given or no?" Now, of course, the "object" of an inquiry or judgment—*i.e.*, of the raising of the inquiry or the making of the judgment—in this sense of the term is undeniably always present or future. My object, the fulfilment of my intention, in doing anything is necessarily synchronous with or subsequent to the doing. But the illicitness of the substitution of this sense of "object" for the former needs no pointing out. Yet it is solely by means of this unconscious pun that Mr. Dewey gives even a semblance of plausibility to his conclusion that "the object of a judgment is always prospective."

When we revert to his original, and only pertinent, definition of object—"the true object of a judgment about a past event [must] be a past-event-having-a-connection-into-the-present-and-future"[7] —it becomes evident that it is not only arbitrary but absurd to single out from that total "true object" of the judgment one part, the present and future part, and apply to it exclusively the eulogistic descriptions of *"the* object or genuine meaning of the judg-

[7] *R. M. D.*, p. 311.

ment," "the actual thing meant." The absurdity, of course, consists in the fact that, if any part were to be singled out for such preferential treatment, it would be precisely the part to which Mr. Dewey, in his final conclusion, refuses recognition; as his own language shows, the judgment is, after all, "a judgment *about* a past event." In other words, the present and future facts included in what he regards as the total object of such a judgment are admittedly *logically* instrumental to a knowledge of the past fact. True, the past fact, once known, may in a subsequent moment, when reflection is directed to other issues, serve as the means of proof of something else. But to let this obscure the respective logical rôles of past fact and present and future facts in the original, actually retrospective, inquiry is to fall into the fallacy against which Mr. Dewey himself has warned us—that of failing "properly to place the distinctions and relations which figure in logical theories in their temporal context," of "transferring the traits of the subject-matter of one phase to that of another, with a confusing outcome."[8] Having arrived at the retrospective conclusion that A killed B, a court may then proceed to the prospective conclusion that A ought to be hanged. Doubtless—if Mr. Dewey insists on his pun—the court's "object" in the former inquiry was to determine whether or not A shall be hanged. But this does not alter the fact that during the trial the court's function consists in looking backward, and that the distinction between the verdict, which is mainly the business of one set of men, and the sentence, which is usually the business of another man, is that the former constitutes an assertion about what has happened and the latter implies an assertion—in American courts, of a rather low order of probability—about what is going to happen. If, indeed, pragmatist writers could only be persuaded to master. the distinction between a verdict and a sentence, they might discover why it is that their critics find in their writings a constant and baffling confusion of temporal categories.

Let me now briefly recapitulate. Mr. Dewey's attempt to justify the thesis that in judgments about the past "the actual thing meant, the object of judgment, is prospective," consists of two arguments: (*a*) He observes that the "true," *i.e.*, the total, object of any retrospective judgment, if regarded as verifiable, *includes* present and future facts which are the means of its verification. This is true but irrelevant. The object of such a judgment *also* includes past facts; these do not lose their pastness by their "connection with the present"; and it is with them that the issue raised in my paper had to do. (*b*) His other argument resolves itself into the

---

[8] *Essays in Experimental Logic*, p. 1; cited in *E. C. R.*, p. 78.

substitution of one sense of the expression "object of a judgment" for another sense—namely, of the sense "fulfilment of the intention which prompted the making of the judgment" for the sense "thing or event logically referred to by the judgment." The proof of the "prospectiveness" of the judgment's reference is based upon the former meaning, but the conclusion is illicitly transferred to the latter. Both arguments thus fall to the ground. Yesterday, *quâ* yesterday, still remains irreducibly external to to-day, existentially transcendent of all the present thinkings and knowings which have to do with it and all the present, immediately experienced data which give circumstantial evidence concerning it. Mr. Dewey, therefore, has in fact done nothing to "eliminate the machinery of tanscendence and of epistemological dualism," or to show (in the sense required by the argument) that "we are never obliged, even in judgments about the remotest geological past, to get outside events capable of future and present consideration." [9]

3. The sentence just quoted, however, is worth dwelling upon; for it excellently illustrates a certain elusiveness of import which seems to me highly characteristic of the entire argument. The reader will have observed that everything, in the interpretation of the sentence, depends upon the meaning assigned to the words "capable of future and present *consideration*," and that these words may bear either of two meanings. They may most naturally be taken to mean "capable of being *thought of* in the present and future." So taken, the sentence embodies the most harmless of truisms; undeniably, "even in judgments about the remotest geological past," we never "get outside events" which may be objects of present or future thought. But here it is the thought and not the thought's object that is present or future; and therefore, so taken, the sentence has no pertinency to its context. It is by no means equivalent to the proposition with which it seems supposed to be synonymous, viz., that "the *actual thing meant*, the *object* of judgment, is prospective." To make it fit the context, therefore, the reader's mind is likely to transfer the futurity or presentness mentioned from the thought to the object. So taken, the sentence becomes pertinent but it also becomes the most glaring of paradoxes. And it is, so far as I can see, from this quick and delicate,—and, of course, unconscious—shifting of meanings and of matters-referred-to, that the argument must gain whatever interest and plausibility it can conceivably possess, for Mr. Dewey or anyone else. It is the paradoxical sense of the ambiguous proposition which gives it its interest, its appearance of novelty and importance, and it is

[9] *R. M. D.*, p. 316.

its platitudinous sense which gives it its appearance of truth and even self-evidence; and either end of the thing, or both in rapid alternation, may be turned towards the bewildered critic of pragmatism, as the exigencies of controversy require. It is just such an unwitting shift of meanings that renders in some degree intelligible (certainly nothing else can do so) Mr. Dewey's insistence that "there is nothing forced or paradoxical" about his principal thesis. Taken as stated and in the natural sense of its terms, the proposition that the "actual thing meant" by a retrospective judgment is prospective, is as evident and as queer a paradox as philosopher ever penned. But taken with certain qualifications which are sometimes suggested—and which really reverse the meaning—it is indeed no paradox, but a commonplace. The qualified meaning of the statement seems to be that already discussed, namely, that *among* the things at least implicitly "meant" by a judgment about the past, *in so far as that judgment is conceived as verifiable,* are present and prospective data of experience. But for this simple and unimpeachable statement is speedily substituted language which, by the usual rules of English speech, should signify that the *sole* "actual thing meant" in such a judgment is something present or prospective. And here again the truth of the first proposition throws its mantle over the paradoxicality of the second, while, reciprocating the service, the paradoxicality of the second gives to the truth of the first an air of unfamiliarity, of deep and stirring revelation.

And in this lies, I think, the real nub of the difficulty in the present discussion. It is, I am convinced, this fashion of treating as equivalent and interchangeable the two meanings of an ambiguous proposition that gives the pragmatist the illusion of having discovered a new way of escape from old dilemmas; and it is this, he ought at any rate to be told, which makes his reasonings, to some of his readers, puzzling and elusive to the last degree.[10] And now that the point has been made explicit, I venture to hope that Mr. Dewey will face the distinction indicated and will tell us plainly which of these two very different things he means to assert: (*a*) the flagrant paradox that the only "thing meant," in a judgment about the events of yesterday, is future or "prospective"—"a blank denial that we can think of the past," as a philosophical correspondent of mine puts his understanding of Mr. Dewey's meaning; or (*b*) the familiar commonplace that we form judgments which relate to actual past events, but that these judgments constitute

10 The play upon the meaning of "object," already noted, is another case in point.

verifiable knowledge only in so far as the past events are causally connected with present or future existents which can serve as means of verification, and that our motive in judging is always some present interest. The choice of either alternative would compel Mr. Dewey to abandon one part or another of the complex of propositions making up his form of pragmatism. If he elects the first, he will thereby deny such judicious observations as he himself has often made, to the effect that "detached and impartial study of the past is the only alternative to luck in assuring success to passion"; and, in general, will repudiate not merely a primary conviction of common sense, but a necessary presupposition of the method of the empirical sciences. If he elects the second meaning of his equivocal thesis, he is—as has already been sufficiently shown—then faced with the admitted existential externality of the past object—or, if he prefers the phrasing, the past part of the object—of the judgment. The case for epistemological dualism based upon the actual pastness of the object, or an object, of the retrospective judgment would therefore remain unshaken. And, it must be added, even if the more extreme version of his contention about these judgments were made out, the main issue concerning transcendence would not be vitally affected; for a "prospective" object is as manifestly transcendent as a past object. In short, all that Mr. Dewey even attempts to do is to substitute one mode of transcendence for another.

4. Mr. Dewey concludes his first paper with a counter-attack, charging me, and apparently critical realists generally, with a "subjectivism" [11] from which he represents his own version, though not all versions, of pragmatism as free. The subjectivism alleged consists in the view that, since our retrospective judgments mean but do not actually include and possess the past, belief in their validity, in the existence of the past to which they refer, involves an element of alogical faith, explicit or implicit. At any given moment of reflection the testimony of his memory is the only evidence any man possesses as to any empirical fact whatever, beyond the immediately present sense-data; but the testimony of memory can not itself be empirically verified. My entire store of recollec-

---

[11] It is unnecessary to comment at length on Mr. Dewey's assertion that my view—and any dualistic or monistic realism—implies that "isolated, self-complete things are truly objects of knowledge." "Isolated" past events are, in the sense that they are external to the present; isolated they are not, and are not by the realist held to be, in any sense which denies their "connection with past and future." Mr. Dewey is here (p. 315, foot) attacking a man of straw, the misdirection of his attack being due to a failure to discriminate between logical distinction and lack of causal connection.

tions may conceivably be illusory; that they are not can not be proved, and belief in their general trustworthiness is therefore an instinctive and practically necessary assumption which outruns proof. This I had always supposed to be a universally accepted, though an important, truism. But Mr. Dewey rejects it. Never will the true pragmatist "isolate the needs or propensities of the agent and regard them as grounds of belief in the validity of meaning." As against the realist's weak yielding to "instinctive propensities," the pragmatist insists austerely upon "logical verification."

Now if Mr. Dewey has really discovered a way out of this ancient *impasse* of thought, has found a strictly "logical" means of verification of the reality of yesterday and the validity of retrospection *as such*, he has, assuredly, made a most momentous contribution to philosophy. But the discovery, if made, is not disclosed in his paper. None of the three considerations which he adduces prove the possibility of any such verification. (*a*) He apparently thinks that those who deny the possibility of a strict verification of the *general* belief in a real past and of the *general* trustworthiness of memory, as it exists from moment to moment, must dispense with logic altogether and follow merely their "instinctive propensities" in deciding what *particular* judgments about the past they will believe and what reject. But this by no means follows. The structure of any logical system of empirical beliefs is obvious enough. We first postulate, or implicitly assume, that there *was* a past and that our present memories constitute a source of knowledge concerning it, except in so far as they are subject to certain conflicts *inter se*. We then find these memories exhibiting certain prevailing uniformities of sequence and coexistence among the things remembered; from these we derive our conception of a regular order of nature; and finally we reject as spurious any memory-content which conflicts with this order, and as doubtful any which our present memories of the fortunes of former rememberings render suspect. But the necessity for that initial postulation the pragmatist can as little escape as any other man who will take the trouble to reflect at all upon the logical grounds of his beliefs. (*b*) Mr. Dewey, however, seems to suppose that he has escaped it by his "account of knowledge involving past events"—which presumably refers again to the proposition that "the actual thing meant" in such knowledge is "prospective." But this proposition must, once more, be taken either in its literal and paradoxical, or in its qualified and truistic sense. In the former, it signifies that we never mean, and therefore never have as objects of our knowledge, any past events whatever. Such a thesis is hardly favorable to the view that knowledge of the past is "logically verifiable." In the qualified sense, the proposition, as we have seen, means that we do actually know the past, with the aid of present memory-images and sense-data. But *how* the present existences constitute a true "logical verification" of past existences, the proposition does not explain. (*c*) Finally, Mr. Dewey tells us, in familiar pragmatistic language, that a belief about the past is "verified or condemned by its consequences." This, however, is another example of the error from which the pragmatist, of all men, should be most free—the confusion of the traits of one temporal phase of experience with those of another. When the consequences of a prior belief arrive, that belief is already "past and gone forever"; and how, at the later moment, we can—except by means of a faith in memory—know even that there *was* a prior belief of which these are the consequences, Mr. Dewey does nothing to make clear.

Considered as historical phenomena, most of the aspects of Professor Dewey's view about judgments of the past which I have here criticized seem to me to be simply manifestations of the working of the old leaven of epistemological idealism, and of the wrong sort of intellectualism, of which pragmatism has not yet purged itself— expressions of an obscure feeling that nothing ought to be treated as "known" which is not immediately given, actually present, totally verified on the spot. For the critical realist, on the contrary, all our knowledge (beyond bare sensory content) is a kind of foreign commerce, a trafficking with lands in which the traffickers do not live, but from which they may continually bring home good store of merchandise to enrich the here-and-now. And like all such traffic, it requires first of all a certain venture of belief, instinctive with most men, deliberate and self-conscious with those who reflect.

ARTHUR O. LOVEJOY.

JOHNS HOPKINS UNIVERSITY.

The Journal of Philosophy

SOME COMMENTS ON PHILOSOPHICAL DISCUSSION

IN a contribution in the volume entitled *Essays in Critical Realism,* Mr. Lovejoy criticized a theory I had advanced concerning the nature of knowledge, using the case of knowledge about past events as crucial. In articles in this JOURNAL (Vol. XIX, pp. 309–317 and pp. 351–361) entitled "Realism Without Monism or Dualism" (referred to as R.M.D.), I replied to his strictures, endeavoring to develop my theory about knowledge involving past events in greater detail, both in itself and in its bearing upon the general theory of knowledge. Mr. Lovejoy then replied in articles entitled "Time, Transcendence and Meaning" (referred to as T.M.T.), in this JOURNAL, (Vol. XIX, pp. 505–515 and pp. 533–541). Mr. Lamprecht also commented on my theory of knowledge involving past events in this JOURNAL (Vol. XX, pp. 488–494) in an article entitled "A Note on Professor Dewey's Theory of Knowledge" (referred to as N.T.K.).

The present article is a continuation of this discussion, though for reasons which it is hoped will be apparent in the sequel, it only incidentally discusses the precise theme of the previous articles, being devoted to raising a prior question as to certain obstacles which seem to limit fruitful, controversial discussion of philosophical issues. For I agree with Mr. Lovejoy both in expressing satisfaction at willingness to engage in coöperative discussion, and in his conviction that "in the present instance great progress has not as yet been accomplished toward actual agreement" (T.M.T., p. 505). So instead of continuing a discussion wherein almost every sentence might only afford occasion on both sides for new specific criticisms, variants of former ones, it may be more profitable to ask why so little progress toward agreement has been effected, especially as the difficulties and unsatisfactory outcome do not seem confined in philosophical discussion to this case as between Messrs. Lovejoy, Lamprecht, and the present writer.

Philosophers have a quite human way of interpreting the statements of others in terms of conceptions and preconceptions underlying their own problems; that is, of stating the position of the one criticized in terms of what it would mean if held by one's self. Whatever does not fit into the framework then appears as an inconsistency.

Mr. Lovejoy prefaces his comments on a certain quotation from me with the following remark: "While, for reasons, to be mentioned later, I doubt whether these propositions mean what they say, I shall first assume that they do so" (T.M.T., p. 506). I doubt very much whether any one in that attitude of *a priori* rejection *can* actually "assume" that a passage means what it says. It appears psychologically impossible for one in such a condition to sympathize with its purport enough to grasp it. So I am not surprised to find that in Mr. Lovejoy's statement the passage cited is given a meaning very different to that which it bears to one who actually holds it.

In my first article, I said that the point under discussion has to do "with knowledge of the past, or, as from my standpoint I should prefer to say, knowledge about past events or involving them" (R.M.D., p. 309). Again, a certain "consideration suggests that the true object of a judgment *about* a past event may be a past-event-having-a-connection-continuing-into-the-present - and - future" (R.M.D., p. 311: p. 312, "judgments *about* the past"; italics in original). On p. 310, "thought about the past" is twice referred to as the theme of discussion; on p. 313, the phrase, twice employed, reads "judgments about the past." On p. 315, in addition to such phrases as "correct inference about the past," "judgments about the past," there is the specific statement, "we make the exact nature of the past event the theme of exact and scrupulous inquiry." On p. 316 the matter is stated as follows: "once recognize that thoughts about the past," *etc.;* "judgments involving past events" (p. 317); "knowledge involving past events." Finally, on the only page of the entire discussion not included in the prior citations appears the following: "In denying that the past event is as such the object of knowledge, it is not asserted that a particular present and future object is its sole and exhaustive object, but that the content of past time has a future reference and function" (p. 314).

The enumeration is tedious, but appears necessary. I do not know how it could be more explicitly stated that the existence of thought, knowledge, judgment about past events (or "involving" them, the other term repeatedly used) is taken for granted, so that the problem under discussion is the logical or cognitive meaning of such thought, judgment, or intellectual reference. And the last quotation—the import of which can be duplicated from many other passages—makes explicit that the point asserted is that the *content* of the past event, its intellectual significance, involves *its* future reference. Antecedently to experience of adverse criticism, it would have been incredible to me that any one could have conceived that I was engaged in denying or slurring over the existence or possibility of intellectual, cognitive reference to past events, or doing anything except raising the question of what occurs, *logically, when* such reference is made.

But the caption of Mr. Lovejoy's reply is "The Alleged Futurity of Yesterday." And the quirk given my hypothesis by this caption runs all through his article. Instead of discussing my thesis his criticism wins (on paper) an easy victory by assuming that I am doubting or denying the possibility of any cognitive reference to yesterday at all. Yet unless one starts from something as fact, there is no sense in raising a question as to the import or meaning of that fact. Again he says "Mr. Dewey had in numerous passages betrayed a curious reluctance to admit that the past as such can be said to be 'known' or 'meant' at all" (T.M.T., p. 506).

The looseness of writing evinced here in making "known" and "meant" equivalent terms in my theory is not only characteristic of Mr. Lovejoy's reply, but indicative of his reluctance to take my hypothesis seriously enough to understand whatever point it may have. For I expressly discriminated between the two functions of "meaning" a past event and that *valid* (verifiable or verified) way of meaning it which constitutes knowledge. I had asserted—and still believe—that the kind or manner of meaning it, which is entitled to the name of *knowledge*—in the eulogistic sense defined—is impossible if the past event be isolated and be taken as the complete and exhaustive object of reference. My regret is that a discussion intended to be coöperative and occupying many pages should not have discussed this distinction, which undoubtedly requires criticism in order that it may be clarified.

Again, Mr. Lovejoy says, "As Mr. Dewey's own expressions inevitably and repeatedly *concede,* the past reference still remains an essential aspect of the present cognitive experience" (T.M.T., p. 507, italics not in original). Here a fact assumed as basis of inquiry into its logical status and import is transformed into a concession on my part. Again, "As his own language shows, the judgment is, after all, a judgment *about* a past event," as if this also were a concession forced unwillingly from me, instead of being the explicit premise of inquiry (T.M.T., p. 510). Again, "Yesterday, *qua* yesterday, still remains irreducibly external to-day" (T.M.T., p. 511) —as if my thesis implied a denial of this fact.[1] And, in one quotation, Mr. Lovejoy even suggests that perhaps I have intended to

---

[1] Of course, the phrase "irreducibly external" may be ambiguous. In its obvious sense I never thought of doubting it; the only *question* is whether this "irreducible externality" is taken in a sense which denies the existential continuity of yesterday and to-day—the fact that yesterday is the yesterday *of* to-day. For I do hold that when this existential continuity is ignored or denied yesterday can not be an *object of knowledge.*

make "a blank denial that we can think of the past" (T.M.T., p. 512).

With this reversal of my explicitly stated theme and thesis, is it surprising that Mr. Lovejoy finds in my article "elusiveness of import," "shiftings of meaning," "most glaring of paradoxes," "reasonings puzzling and elusive to the last degree," "as evident and as queer a paradox as philosopher ever penned," *etc?* It would have been shorter and simpler to have pointed out a flat and total contradiction—unless something led the critic to re-read the article in its own terms instead of in terms of his own theories and preconceptions.

Mr. Lamprecht's misconception of my position, while not so extensive, is equally as discouraging in view of our much larger store of common premises. He says, indeed, that his difference is "terminological," since, although I restrict the meaning of knowing more narrowly than he thinks advisable, I have a right to make the verbal limitation. When he states the difference, it assumes this form: "Not only does he [the present writer] confine knowledge to the knowing-process instead of also including the information we may thereby accumulate, but also he confines knowledge to those knowing processes which look to or mean the future" (D.T.K., p. 491). Here are two statements about my position. Mr. Lamprecht cites no evidence in support of either of them; they must, accordingly, seem to him matters-of-course. I can accordingly only declare in a somewhat brutal fashion that neither of them is either relevant to the article he is discussing or is correct. As to the assertion that I restrict knowledge to the knowing-process, it is curious that on the same page in which occurs the passage just cited, Mr. Lamprecht quotes my statement of the thesis of my paper which begins: "The *object* of knowledge, *etc.*" (italics in original). My whole discussion concerned the object of knowledge in its import for an empirical logic. If Mr. Lamprecht finds in the article even a single incidental reference to the knowing-process, he will do more than I can. The other statement contains a misapprehension which is similar to that dealt with in the case of Mr. Lovejoy. He asserts that I limit knowledge to processes that "mean or look to the future." I can only, accordingly, repeat the references already given to passages in the article, which explicitly state that, assuming given cases where a past event is looked to and meant, the inquiry concerns the logical status of such meanings or lookings in cases where the reference is cognitive (not esthetic), and where, accordingly, the factor of truth and falsity enters in.

Just why Mr. Lamprecht should have failed to note the basic feature of my discussion, it is somewhat idle to speculate upon. But in his article appears a significant shift that may throw light upon the matter. He says: "I should wish to use the term 'knowledge' for those processes of scientific investigation in which we seek to discover what happened in the past for the sake of *interest* in the past itself" (D.T.K., p. 491, italics not in original). Again, "in spite of being *interested* in social reforms and hence in the past as a source of advice about the present, I am also *interested* in the past for its own sake" (D.T.K., p. 492, italics mine). And again, "Sometimes I am afraid that Professor Dewey would regard my *interest* in the past as a fault of *character*" (*Ibid.*, p. 492, italics mine). There is, so far as I am aware, not a word about interest or personal attitude in my discussion, and there certainly is no point or sequence in my argument which implies or depends upon the matter of interest. The issue, if stated so as to involve interest, would be stated as follows: "*When* one is interested in knowing the past for its own sake, in what kind of object, logically speaking, is he interested? What is the meaning of the past event as entering into knowledge?" Now my answer that the object is a temporal continuum in which the past event is but one portion, a portion that becomes logically meaningless if it be isolated and made exhaustive, may be wrong. But the question has nothing to do with questions of personal interest or of character, but with the logical or cognitive nature of the *object* involved.

I may remark, though it is, perhaps, aside from the point, that I have been increasingly struck by the fact that interest in strictly logical analysis is rare in comparison with personal, moral, and esthetic interest, and that articles written from the former standpoint are usually criticized from the latter, a fact presenting a certain irony in view of the fact that the critics usually profess a certain disinterested objectivity. [2] In any case, to recur to Mr. Lamprecht's article, there is an obvious difference between a conception of knowledge which begins with a limitation of the signification of the word to cases where something future is meant or looked to, and a theory which holds *as the result of analysis* that when a past event is cognitively meant and looked to, that event itself in its intellectual status and import looks toward something future to *it*, in virtue of which future event an idea about the past event is verifiable. If one began with such a terminological restriction, as is imputed to me, reflection will, I am sure, convince Mr. Lamprecht, and others interested, that it would hardly have been needful to write an article to show that,

[2] Compare criticisms of instrumentalism which ignore the fact that it is a theory about the characteristic object of knowledge as such, and who think they have disposed of it by pointing to "disinterested" knowledge, or to the fact that knowing is enjoyable and worth while for its own sake. Compare my article in this JOURNAL, "Tradition, Metaphysics and Morals, Vol. XX, pp. 187–192.

upon this basis, mere reference to past events in their bare pastness is not knowledge.

If my comments stopped here, they would be guilty of serious injustice to Mr. Lovejoy. He does, in a number of cases, refer to my actual thesis. But he finds it a truism, a platitude, a commonplace, and hence dismisses it with a conviction that it can not be my thesis, which is accordingly identified with the self-contradictory absurdity previously considered. In one passage, indeed, Mr. Lovejoy expressly asks me to "tell us plainly" which of two alternative positions I do hold (T.M.T., p. 512), the "familiar commonplace" or the absurdity. Unfortunately, however, he states the position which he regards as commonplace in terms of his own conception, not in terms of my hypothesis, so I can not reply plainly with a yes or no. His words are: "And now that the point has been made explicit, I venture to hope that Mr. Dewey will face the distinction indicated and will tell us plainly which of these very different things he means to assert: (*a*) the flagrant paradox that the only 'thing meant' in a judgment about the events of yesterday is future or 'prospective'—a blank denial that we can think of the past, as a philosophical correspondent of mine puts his understanding of Mr. Dewey's meaning; or (*b*) the familiar commonplace that we form judgments which relate to actual past events, but that these events constitute verifiable knowledge only in so far as the past events are causally connected with present or future existents which serve *as means of verification,* and that our motive in judging is always some present interest" (T.M.T., p. 513, italics mine).

The last clause in the quotation sums up one part of Mr. Lovejoy's discussion, based upon the following quotation from me: "The *object* of the judgment in short is the fulfillment of an intention." Mr. Lovejoy, carrying in this case his tendency to ignore context and tease out isolated sentences to an almost incredible length, takes this sentence to be general and comprehensive in significance, instead of specific and local, and hence charges me with a flagrant fallacy of ambiguity, of making my conclusion rest upon an "unconscious pun." I have confused, he says, "object" in the sense of "thing or event logically referred to by the judgment" with "object" in the sense "fulfillment of the intention which prompted the making of the judgment" (T.M.T., pp. 509, 510, 511).

Let me say that a moderately careful reading of my text will show (1) that the scope of the sentence quoted is confined to a particular illustration used, and is not a statement of my general position; (2) that in the specific illustration used, the phrase "fulfillment of intention" has absolutely nothing to do with the interest, aim, motive, or intent that prompted making the judgment (any more than an inquiry into the intent of Julius Cæsar in crossing the Rubicon and its fulfillment would have anything to do with the intent of the one making the inquiry); (3) that in at least three passages, remarks are made which, apart from ordinary regard for context, protect the sentence from such a construction as Mr. Lovejoy has given it. (*a*) In a foot-note it is stated that "the argument does not depend upon any ambiguity between object and objective." (*b*) The next paragraph begins with the following words: "To protect the conclusion from appearing to depend upon the quality of the particular illustration used, namely, one involving a personal past and personal course of action, we need an impersonal instance of a past episode." The conclusion concerns the validity of the distinction between subject-matter and object; the personal case was one involving the question of past fulfillment of a past intention, not that of the intention of the one making the judgment. And it is expressly stated that the validity of the distinction will be shown by taking an impersonal case, in which fulfillment of any intention does not appear as any part of the object. (*c*) And with respect to the two illustrations it is then expressly said: "What appears in the above case of the letter as fulfillment of intention appears here as a temporal sequence of condition and consequence." I respectfully submit that if I had foreseen the possibility of this misunderstanding by Mr. Lovejoy, I could hardly have done more to protect the text against it.

What has just been said relative to the last clause in Mr. Lovejoy's request for a plain statement is by way of a parenthetical excursus. We return now to the main point. It will be noted that in the quotation from him the alternative to the self-contradictory notion imputed to me is the commonplace that present and future events supply "means of verification" of propositions about the past event as such. Before comparing this conception with what I actually meant and said, attention may be called to some other passages of Mr. Lovejoy's of the same general tenor. On p. 507, he goes as far as to say that he accepts my statement that "the true object of a judgment *about* a past event" *must* be "in the case of scientifically verifiable judgments a past-event-having-a-connection-continuing-into-the-present-and-future." This he finds to be a "truism." On p. 512, he refers to a correct statement of my own position as "a simple and unimpeachable statement." Again he refers (p. 510) to a statement of my own position as "true but irrelevant." In this case, however, he misstates the position just as he does in the passage to be discussed in the text. For he says that the true or total object *includes* present and future facts which are the *means* of its [idea of past event] verification" (italics mine).

I now invite the reader to compare the statements of the (b) alternative, given by Mr. Lovejoy, with the following quotation from the article of mine to which Mr. Lovejoy is nominally replying. "So far, however, the gravamen of Mr. Lovejoy's objection is not touched. He replies that the meaning of the judgment concerns the past as such, so that verification even if future is of a meaning about the past. Only the locus of verification is future: *means* of proof, but not the thing proved" (R.M.D., p. 311, italics not in original). An illustration is then used which is asserted to "invalidate the *sharp and fixed line* which Mr. Lovejoy has drawn *between the meaning* of the past *and the so-called means* of verification" (italics not in original). This conclusion brings us back, it is expressly said, to my "original contention." And the rest of the article is devoted to answering the question, "What can be said by way of fact to support its hypothetical possibility?" (*ibid*).

In other words, in his earlier article Mr. Lovejoy held that in my theory of knowledge of temporal events I had confused the status and import of the object meant with that of the means used to verify the thought about that object. My reply is devoted to trying to show that the "so-called means of verification" are in truth integrally constituent parts of the object meant. Aside from this point my argument has *no* point; the argument about the nature of transcendence in knowledge is the development of its logical implications. But I failed to make the point clear to Mr. Lovejoy. For there is not even an incidental allusion in his whole article to it, much less a serious consideration of it as the gist of the issue between us. So I repeat that the burden of my theme is as follows: There should be substituted for Mr. Lovejoy's conception that present and future events are "means of verification" of judgments about past events logically complete in themselves, the notion that, in the complete object of knowledge, past-present-future events form an integral continuum, so that no part can be taken logically as complete and exhaustive "as such" or "solely" without a mutilation amounting to falsification; that in *inquiry,* aiming at the constitution of such a complete object, a *distinction* between reference to past events as such and present and reference to future events as such is both legitimate and inevitable —a distinction in which future events supply the point or "meaning," the significance, of the reference to the past event, which functions as subject-matter for determining the status and connections of the future event in the complete object of knowledge.

To make sure that I am not even now beating the air in vain I wish to say explicitly that if Mr. Lovejoy actually accepts this position of mine, whether under the caption of platitude or however, even then there is no difference between us on the point of knowledge about a past event and the difference that remains between us concerns the bearing of this proposition upon the problem of the nature of transcendence. As it stands, however, I do not feel entitled to make the statement of agreement regarding the object of knowledge in cases involving past events more than hypothetically. For in spite of Mr. Lovejoy's apparently unqualified agreement in one passage cited, in two of the other passages he changes its meaning by introducing the notion of "means of verification." In addition there are such passages as the following: "The matter at issue has to do *solely* with that *part* of the total object of a judgment about the past which is past" (T.M.T., p. 507). From my point of view, the matter at issue is precisely whether the past can be severed, in the manner indicated by the introduction of the word "solely."

However this matter of agreement may stand between us, it is incumbent upon me to point out that on every page but one of my first article the proposition regarded by Mr. Lovejoy as a platitude and commonplace, is explicitly stated to be the thesis of my argument. On the opening page occurs the passage: "I have tried to show that knowledge where the past is implicated is logically knowledge of past-as-connected-with-present-or-future, or stating the matter in its order of the present and future as implicating a certain past" (R.M.D., p. 309). In commencing my second article, I summed up the prior article as follows: "The paper tried to show that the *object* of knowledge in such cases [involving past events] is a temporal sequence or continuum including past-present-future" (R.M.D., p. 351).[3]

These definite and formal statements appeared, it seems, to Mr. Lovejoy to express such truisms that he could hardly believe them to represent my conception. The burden of his criticism centres, accordingly, about three passages which occur within a consecutive two pages of my article—with what purport will appear below. " 'The past occurrence is *not* the meaning of propositions' of this type"; "the present or future constitutes the object or genuine meaning of the judgment about the past"; in "retrospective judgments 'the actual thing meant, the object of judgment, is prospective' " (the passages in double quotation marks are from p. 506 of T.M.T.; those in single quotation marks are from pp. 312, 313, 314, respectively, of my article R.M.D.).

Taking these passages just as they stand and without regard to their context, the reader of Mr. Lovejoy's article would have been justified in at least thinking that they are in such flat contradiction to my explicitly stated thesis that there is something radically wrong

---

[3] See also explicit statements on pp. 311; 314; 315; 316; p. 312 has a less formal statement to the same effect.

in my article. But if he was sufficiently interested, or sufficiently puzzled, by the fact that I should have fallen into such a contradiction to turn to my article and examine the context of the quotations, he would have discovered that I was *not* engaged in stating my thesis in any one of these quotations. The first quotation is found where the material, by description, is some past incident used as basis of advice regarding the question of what course of action is to be followed. By description, therefore, the object judged is the future course of action: "the past occurrence is not the meaning of the propositions." *That* statement *is* a truism in this particular context. If I had employed it even to support my main theme, to say nothing of conveying it, it would have been an obvious begging of the question. But it is expressly stated that "such a case does not directly and obviously cover judgments about the past" (R.M.D., p. 312). So much for Mr. Lovejoy's first citation.

What was the point of the illustration? "The facts cited, illustrative material adverted to in support of the conception that a certain course is better to pursue, are subject-matter, but not the meaning or object"—since, by express statement, the object in the case selected is "the better course to pursue." In other words, by use of a case in which there can be no dispute that the object of judgment is prospective (and where, accordingly, the futurity of the object can not be cited in support of any general proposition), it was indicated that, nevertheless, intellectual reference to a past event may be involved. The past event is involved in making the judgment about the future object; not being the *object*, it was termed *subject-matter*.

The next two passages quoted occur in development of this distinction between past event as subject-matter and something else as object. The statement about "object" quoted by Mr. Lovejoy, applies explicitly, as well as by context, to "object" in distinction from subject-matter in *inquiry*. "What does positively emerge from the prior discussion is a distinction between *subject-matter* and *object* of judgment and knowledge. It is not introduced *ad hoc* for discussion of judgments about the past. It characterizes of logical necessity any *inquiry*" (p. 313. Since the italics are in the original, and since it is expressly stated to be a distinction applicable to inquiry rather than just to knowledge involving past events, I hardly see how I could better have guarded myself against the misconstruction of Mr. Lovejoy). Then it is stated "If we apply this generic and indispensable distinction to judgments about the past, it seems to me that the following conclusion naturally issues: The nature of the past event is subject-matter required to make a reasonable judgment about the present or future. The latter thus constitutes the object or genuine meaning of the judgment'' (p. 313).   It was undeniably unfortunate that I employed the word ''object'' in two senses, one for the complete object of the completed judgment, the existential connection of past-present-future event, and the other for the object, during the operation of *inquiry*, in contrast with subject-matter. But it is certainly plainly indicated that the final and complete object includes in an integrated whole both ''subject-matter'' and ''object'' as they appear in distinction during inquiry.

The third passage quoted by Mr. Lovejoy is even more explicitly limited in scope. It is found in a discussion of a particular case where—by description—the point at issue is what is my present relationship to a certain correspondent, and where by description the question of whether a certain letter was written and mailed by me in the past must be settled in order to determine the question of present relationship. The full passage is: ''Certainly whether or no my analysis is correct, there does not appear to be anything forced or paradoxical about the view that in all such cases, the actual thing meant, the object of judgment, is prospective'' (R.M.D., p. 314). The words ''whether or no my analysis is correct'' draw a line about as explicitly as it could be drawn between my general thesis and a proposition applied to a particular type of case. (In one of the many passages where Mr. Lovejoy cites the above passage, he italicizes the word ''all'' in the phrase ''all such cases.'' Clearly, the emphasis fell upon the word ''such.'') If the passage had the general meaning Mr. Lovejoy attaches to it, the expression ''whether or no my analysis is correct'' would have been sheer nonsense.

The very next sentence reads: ''To protect the conclusion from appearing to depend upon the quality of the particular illustration used, namely, one involving a personal past and personal course of action, we need an impersonal episode of a past event.'' An instance used by Mr. Lovejoy is selected and analyzed, and within twenty lines of the third stock passage cited by Mr. Lovejoy occurs the following: ''The implication of my hypothesis is that the object of judgment is that 'prior rain has present and future consequences,' such as puddles, or floods, or refreshment of crops. . . . In denying that the past event is as such the object of knowledge, it is *not asserted that a particular present or future object is its sole and exhaustive object,* but that the content of past time has a future reference and function. That is, the object is some past event in its connection with present and future effects and consequences. The past by itself and *the present by itself* are *both* arbitrary selections which mutilate the complete object of judgment. . . . The past incident is part of the subject-matter of inquiry which enters into its object only when referred to a future event or fact'' (R.M.D., p.

314, italics not in original. To avoid further misconception it should be expressly stated that the "future fact" in the last sentence means future to—because a consequence of—a past event, not future to the time of making the judgment; it might be contemporaneous with the latter).

In short, having selected passages which occur in making a distinction to be later employed in statement of my positive thesis, Mr. Lovejoy quotes them as if they were final statements of my theory, and then that part of my argument in which the distinction is employed to state my thesis is wholly passed over. I regret, but am not surprised, that so little approach is made towards agreement. For his discussion leaves the issue just what and where it was: Are present and future events integral parts of the objects of knowledge where a past event is meant, or are they merely means of verifying judgments about past events, which judgments are logically complete in themselves?

In the foregoing there is no suggestion that Mr. Lovejoy has intentionally misconstrued meanings or has isolated passages from their context because of a controversial intent. I have dealt with the prior arguments at such tedious length in order to illustrate how preconceptions as to problems and issues result in misunderstandings. Such passages as the following may throw light on the nature of his preconception. At the outset he states his main propositions as follows: "All practical or instrumental knowledge is, or at least includes, 'presentative' knowledge, a representation of non-present existents by present data," and "knowledge is thus necessarily and constantly conversant with entities which are existentially transcendent of the knowing experience" (T.M.T., p. 505). It will be noted that in this passage "representation of not-present existents by present data" is converted, as if a matter of course, into existential transcendence of the "knowing experience." And this *is* a matter of course on the assumption that present data constitute "presentative knowledge," and are the "knowing experience." In his concluding paragraphs Mr. Lovejoy states the matter in this wise: "The doctrine that the present content of a cognitive experience and the absent object 'meant' by that experience are two entities, not one, is unescapable" (T.M.T., p. 541). Here we have the same implication. There is a purely immediate knowledge of a given thing, which is the knowing or cognitive experience; then there is the absent object meant by this "knowing experience."

Having thus stated the problem, Mr. Lovejoy assumes that I am dealing with a problem capable of being stated in like terms, and that since my theory differs from his, I must be denying his conclusion. But what I was and am primarily denying is the statement of the *premises,* or rather the conceptions in terms of which Mr. Lovejoy approaches and states the *problem.* I have not denied that practical or instrumental knowledge involves a representation of non-present existents by present data; I have devoted a good deal of space to enforcing that proposition. What I have denied is that there exists anything to be called "presentative" knowledge in contrast with what Mr. Lovejoy terms instrumental knowledge. I have held that all knowledge whatever involves an inferential or mediational function. I have also denied (what Mr. Lovejoy asserts) that present data, which stand for or mean the "absent" thing, are psychical. Hence my conception of what Mr. Lovejoy calls the "knowing" or "cognitive experience" is radically different from his. To him it is confined to presence of data which are psychical in character; hence any physical contemporaneous thing as well as any past or future event must be external to the "knowing experience." If I had the same premises, I should assert the same conclusion. But my whole point lies in an assertion that this description of the "knowing experience" is mythological. I assert that the "knowing experience" always involves a referential connection between present-non-psychical data and something absent, meant or signified by these non-psychical data. My theory about knowledge involving past events is that it is one case of such reference. But let Mr. Lovejoy or any one else come to my argument with a preconception that I have the same notion of "knowing experience" as identical with present data which he accepts, and misconstruction of every further statement I may make is bound to occur.

JOHN DEWEY.

COLUMBIA UNIVERSITY.

Section III

THEORY OF KNOWLEDGE

The Journal of Philosophy
Psychology and Scientific Methods

THE POSTULATE OF IMMEDIATE EMPIRICISM

THE criticisms made upon that vital but still unformed movement variously termed radical empiricism, pragmatism, humanism, functionalism, according as one or another aspect of it is uppermost, have left me with a conviction that the *fundamental* difference is not so much in matters overtly discussed as in a presupposition which remains tacit: a presupposition as to what experience is and means. To do my little part in clearing up the confusion, I shall try to make my own presupposition explicit. The object of this paper is, then, to set forth what I understand to be the postulate and the criterion of *immediate empiricism*.[1]

Immediate empiricism postulates that things—anything, everything, in the ordinary or non-technical use of the term 'thing'—are what they are experienced as. Hence, if one wishes to describe anything truly, his task is to tell what it is experienced as being. If it is a horse which is to be described, or the *equus* which is to be defined, then must the horse-trader, or the jockey, or the timid family man who wants a 'safe driver,' or the zoologist or the paleontologist tell us what the horse is which is experienced. If these accounts turn out different in some respects, as well as congruous in others, this is no reason for assuming the content of one to be exclusively 'real,' and that of others to be 'phenomenal'; for each account of what is experienced will manifest that it is the account *of* the horse-dealer, or *of* the zoologist, etc., and hence will give the conditions requisite for understanding the differences as well as the agreements

[1] All labels are, of course, obnoxious and misleading. I hope, however, the term will be taken by the reader in the sense in which it is forthwith explained, and not in some more usual and familiar sense. Empiricism, as herein used, is as antipodal to sensationalistic empiricism, as it is to transcendentalism, and for the same reason. Both of these systems fall back on something which is defined in non-directly-experienced terms in order to justify that which is directly experienced. Hence I have criticized such empiricism (*Phil, Rev.*, Vol. XI., No. 4, p. 364) as essentially absolutistic in character; and also ('Studies in Logical Theory,' p. 30, 58) as an attempt to build up experience in terms of certain methodological checks and cues of attaining *certainty in* knowledge.

of the various accounts. And the principle varies not a whit if we bring in the psychologist's horse, the logician's horse or the metaphysician's horse.

In each case, the nub of the question is, *what sort of experience* is meant or indicated: a concrete and determinate experience, varying, when it varies, in specific real elements, and agreeing, when it agrees, in specific real elements, so that we have a contrast, not between *a* Reality, and various approximations to, or phenomenal representations of Reality, but between different reals of experience. And the reader is begged to bear in mind that from this standpoint, when 'an experience' or 'some sort of experience' is referred to, 'some thing' or 'some sort of thing' is always meant.

Now, this statement that things are what they are experienced to be is usually translated into the statement that things (or, ultimately, Reality, Being) *are* only and just what they are *known* to be or that things are, or Reality *is,* what it is for a conscious knower —whether the knower be conceived primarily as a perceiver or as a thinker being a further and secondary question. This is the root-paralogism of all idealisms, whether subjective or objective, psychological or epistemological. By our postulate, things are what they are experienced to be; and, unless knowing is the sole and only genuine mode of experiencing, it is fallacious to say that Reality is just and exclusively what it is or would be to an all-competent all-knower; or even that it *is,* relatively and piecemeal, what it is to a finite and partial knower. Or, put more positively, knowing is one mode of experiencing, and the primary philosophic demand (from the standpoint of immediatism) is to find out *what* sort of an experience knowing is—or, concretely how things are experienced when they are experienced *as* known things.[2] By concretely is meant, obviously enough (among other things), such an account of the experience of things as known that will bring out the characteristic traits and distinctions they possess as things of a knowing experience, as compared with things experienced esthetically, or morally, or economically, or technologically, etc. To assume, because from the standpoint of the knowledge experience things *are* what they are known to be, that, therefore, metaphysically, absolutely, without qualification, everything in its reality (as distinct from its 'appearance,' or phenomenal occurrence) is what a knower would find it to be, is, from the imme-

---

[2] I hope the reader will not therefore assume that from the empiricist's standpoint knowledge is of small worth or import. On the contrary, from the empiricist's standpoint it has *all* the worth which it is concretely experienced as possessing—which is simply tremendous. But the exact *nature* of this worth is a thing to be found out in describing what we mean by experiencing objects as known—the actual differences made or found in experience.

diatist's standpoint, if not the root of all philosophic evil, at least one of its main roots.

For example, I start and am flustered by a noise heard. Empirically, that noise *is* fearsome; it *really* is, not merely phenomenally or subjectively so. That *is what* it is experienced as being. But, when I experience the noise as a *known* thing, I find it to be innocent of harm. It is the tapping of a shade against the window, owing to movements of the wind. The experience has changed; that is, the thing experienced has changed—not that an unreality has given place to a reality, nor that some transcendental (unexperienced) Reality has changed,[3] not that truth has changed, but just and only the concrete reality experienced has changed. I now feel ashamed of my fright; and the noise as fearsome is changed to noise as a wind-curtain fact, and hence practically indifferent to my welfare. This is a change of experienced reality effected through the medium of cognition. The content of the latter experience cognitively regarded is doubtless *truer* than the content of the earlier; but it is in no sense more real. To call it truer, moreover, must, from the empirical standpoint, mean a concrete *difference* in actual things experienced.[4] Again, in many cases, it is only in retrospect that the prior experience is cognitionally regarded at all. In such cases, it is only in regard to contrasted contents *in* the subsequent experience that the determination 'truer' has force.

Perhaps some reader may now object that as matter of fact the entire experience *is* cognitive, but that the earlier parts of it are only imperfectly so, resulting in a phenomenon which is not real; while the latter part, being a more complete cognition, results in what is relatively, at least, more real.[5] In short, a critic may say

[3] Since the non-empiricist believes in things-in-themselves (which he may term 'atoms,' 'sensations,' transcendental unities, *a priori* concepts, *an* absolute experience, or whatever), and since he finds that the empiricist makes much of change (as he must, since change is continuously experienced) he assumes that the empiricist means that *his own* non-empirical Realities are in continual flux, and he naturally shudders at having his divinities so violently treated. But, once recognize that the empiricist doesn't have any such Realities at all, and the entire problem of the relation of change to reality takes a very different aspect.

[4] It would lead us aside from the point to try to tell just what is the nature of the experienced difference we call truth. Professor James's recent articles may well be consulted. The point to bear in mind here is just what sort of a thing the empiricist must mean by true, or truer (the noun Truth is, of course, a generic name for all cases of 'Trues'). The adequacy of any particular account is not a matter to be settled by general reasoning, but by finding out what sort of an experience the truth-experience actually is.

[5] I say 'relatively,' because the transcendentalist still holds that finally the cognition is imperfect, giving us only some symbol or phenomenon of Reality

that, when I was frightened by the noise, I *knew* I was frightened; otherwise there would have been no experience at all. At this point, it is necessary to make a distinction so simple and yet so all-fundamental that I am afraid the reader will be inclined to pooh-pooh it away as a mere verbal distinction. But to see that *to the empiricist* this distinction is not verbal, but real, is the precondition of any understanding of him. The immediatist must, by his postulate, ask what is the fright experienced *as*. Is what is actually experienced, I-know-I-am-frightened, or I-*am*-frightened? I see absolutely no reason for claiming that the experience *must* be described by the former phrase. In all probability (and all the empiricist logically needs is just one case of which this is true) the experience is simply and just of fright-at-the-noise. Later one may (or may not) have an experience describable *as* I-know-I-am- (-or-was) and improperly or properly, frightened. But this is a different experience—that is, a different *thing*. And if the critic goes on to urge that the person 'really' must have known that he was frightened, I can only point out that the critic is shifting the venue. He may be right, but, if so, it is only because the 'really' is something not concretely experienced (whose nature accordingly is the critic's business); and this is to depart from the empiricist's point of view, to attribute to him a postulate which he expressly repudiates.

The material point may come out more clearly if I say that we must make a distinction between a thing as *cognitive*, and one as *cognized*.[6] I should define a cognitive experience as one which has certain bearings or implications which induce and fulfill themselves in a subsequent experience in which the relevant thing is experienced *as* cognized, *as* a known object, and is thereby transformed, or reorganized. The fright-at-the-noise in the case cited is obviously *cognitive*, in this sense. By description, it induces an investigation or inquiry in which both noise and fright are objectively stated or presented—the noise as a shade-wind fact, the fright as an organic reaction to a sudden acoustic stimulus, a reaction which under the given circumstances was useless or even detrimental, a maladaptation. Now, pretty much all of experience is of this sort (the 'is' meaning, of course, is experienced *as*), and the empiricist is

(which *is* only in the Absolute or in some Thing-in-Itself)—otherwise the curtain-wind fact would have as much ontological reality as the existence of the Absolute itself: a conclusion at which the non-empiricist perhorresces, for no reason obvious to me—save that it would put an end to his transcendentalism.

[6] In general, I think the distinction between -*ive* and -*ed* one of the most fundamental of philosophic distinctions, and one of the most neglected. The same hold of -*tion* and -*ing*.

false to his principle if he does not duly note this fact.[7] But he is equally false to his principle if he permits himself to be confused as to the concrete differences in the two things experienced.

There are two little words through explication of which the empiricist's position may be brought out—'*as*' and '*that.*' We may express his presupposition by saying that things are what they are experienced *as* being; or that to give a just account of anything is to tell what *that* thing is experienced to be. By these words I want to indicate the absolute, final, irreducible and inexpugnable concrete *quale* which everything experienced not so much *has* as *is*. To grasp this aspect of empiricism is to see what the empiricist means by objectivity, by the element of control, a principle of guidance and selection, the normative or standard element in experience. Suppose we take, as a crucial case for the empiricist, an out and out illusion, say of Zöllner's lines. These are experienced as convergent; they are 'truly' parallel. If things are what they are experienced as being, how can there be the distinction that we draw between illusion and the true state of the case? There is no answer to this question except by sticking to the fact that the experience of the lines as divergent is a concrete qualitative thing or *that*. It is *that* experience which it is, and no other. And if the reader rebels at the iteration of such obvious tautology, I can only reiterate that the realization of the *meaning* of this tautology is the key to the whole question of the objectivity of experience, as that stands to the empiricist. The lines of *that* experience *are* divergent: not merely *seem* so. The question of truth is not as to whether Being or Non-Being, Reality or mere Appearance, is experienced, but as to the *worth* of a certain concretely experienced thing. The only way of passing upon this question is by sticking in the most uncompromising fashion to *that* experience as real. *That* experience is that two lines with certain cross-hatchings are apprehended as convergent; only by taking that experience as real and as fully real, is there any basis for or way of going to an experienced knowledge that the lines are parallel. It is in the concrete thing *as experienced* that all the grounds and clues to its own intellectual or logical rectification are contained. It is because this thing, afterwards adjudged false, is a concrete *that*, that it develops into a corrected experience (that is, experience of a corrected thing—we reform things just as we reform ourselves or a bad boy) whose full content is not a whit more real, but which is experienced as true or as truer.

[7] What is criticized, now as 'geneticism' (if I may coin the word) and now as 'pragmatism' is, in its truth, just the fact that the empiricist does take account of the experienced 'drift, occasion and contexture' of things experienced—to use Hobbes's phrase.

If *any* experience, then a *determinate* experience; and this determinateness is the only, and is the adequate, principle of control, or 'objectivity.' The experience may be of the vaguest sort. I may not see any thing which I can identify as a familiar object—a table, a chair, etc. It may be dark; I may have only the vaguest impression that there is something which looks like a table. Or I may be completely befogged and confused, as when one rises quickly from sleep in a pitch-dark room. But this vagueness, this doubtfulness, this confusion is the thing experienced, and, *qua* real, is as 'good' a reality as the self-luminous vision of an Absolute. It is not just vagueness, doubtfulness, confusion, at large or in general. It is *this* vagueness, and no other; absolutely unique, absolutely what *it* is.[8] Whatever gain in clearness, in fullness, in trueness of content is experienced must grow out of some element in the experience of *this* experienced *as* what it is. To return to the illusion: If the experience of the lines as convergent is illusory, it is because of some elements in the thing as experienced, not because of something defined in terms of externality to this particular experience. If the illusoriness can be detected, it is because the thing experienced is real, having within its experienced reality elements whose *own mutual* transcendence effects its reconstruction. Taken concretely, the experience of convergent lines contains within itself the elements of the transformation of its own content. It is *this* thing, and not some separate truth, which clamors for its own reform. There is, then, from the empiricist's point of view, no need to search for some aboriginal *that* to which all successive experiences are attached, and which is somehow thereby undergoing continuous change. Experience is always of *thats;* and the most comprehensive and inclusive experience of the universe which the philosopher himself can obtain is the experience of a characteristic *that.* From the empiricist's point of view, this is as true of the exhaustive and complete insight of a hypothetical all-knower as of the vague, blind experience of the awakened sleeper. As reals, they stand on the same level. As trues, the latter has by definition the better of it; but if this insight is in any way the truth of the blind awakening, it is because the latter has, in its *own* determinate *quale,* elements of real continuity with the former; it is, *ex hypothesi,* transformable through a series of experienced reals, without break of continuity into the absolute thought-experience. There is no need of logical manipulation to effect the transformation, nor *could* any logical consideration effect it. If effected at all it is just

---

[8] One does not so easily escape medieval Realism as one thinks. Either every experienced thing has its own determinateness, its own unsubstitutable, unredeemable reality, or else 'generals' *are* separate existences after all.

by immediate experiences, each of which is just as real (no more, no less) as either of the two terms between which it lies. Such, at least, is the meaning of the empiricist's contention. So, when he talks of experience, he does not mean some grandiose, remote affair which is cast like a net around a succession of fleeting experiences; he does not mean an indefinite total, comprehensive experience which somehow engirdles an endless flux; he means that *things* are what they are experienced to be, and that every experience is *some* thing.

From the postulate of empiricism, then (or, what is the same thing, from a *general* consideration of the concept of experience), nothing can be deduced, not a single philosophical proposition.[9] The reader may hence conclude that all this just comes to the truism that experience is experience, or is what it is. If one attempts to draw conclusions from the bare concept of experience, the reader is quite right. But the real significance of the principle is that of a method of philosophical analysis—a method identical in kind (but differing in problem and hence in operation) with that of the scientist. If you wish to find out what subjective, objective, physical, mental, cosmic, psychic, cause, substance, purpose, activity, evil, being, quantity—any philosophic term, in short—means, go to experience and see what it is experienced *as*.

Such a method is not spectacular; it permits of no offhand demonstrations of God, freedom, immortality, nor of the exclusive reality of matter, or ideas, or consciousness, etc. But it supplies a way of telling what all these terms mean. It may seem insignificant, or chillingly disappointing, but only upon condition that it be not worked. Philosophic conceptions have, I believe, outlived their usefulness considered as stimulants to emotion, or as a species of sanctions; and a larger, more fruitful and more valuable career awaits them considered as specifically experienced meanings.

JOHN DEWEY.

COLUMBIA UNIVERSITY.

[9] Excepting, of course, some negative ones. One could say that certain views are certainly *not* true, because, by hypothesis, they refer to nonentities, *i. e.*, non-empiricals. But even here the empiricist must go slowly. From his own standpoint, even the most professedly transcendental statements are, after all, real as experiences, and hence negotiate some transaction with facts. For this reason, he can not, in theory, reject them *in toto*, but has to show concretely how they arose and how they are to be corrected. In a word, his logical relationship to statements that profess to relate to things-in-themselves, unknowables, inexperienced substances, etc., is precisely that of the psychologist to the Zöllner lines.

Vol. II. No. 21.   October 12, 1905.

DISCUSSION

OF WHAT SORT IS COGNITIVE EXPERIENCE?

PROFESSOR DEWEY'S recent article in this JOURNAL has definitely contributed to a clearer understanding of what the term 'real' means to many advocates of immediate empiricism and pragmatism. The real is simply *that* which is experienced and *as* it is experienced. It would seem that there could be little further misunderstanding on that point. The challenge to the pragmatist to tell what he means by reality appears, thus, to have been met successfully. If it were necessary to lend external authority to Professor Dewey's exposition, one might cite the ancient statement of Aristotle that reality is whatever can be the subject of investigation. From such a definition of reality it is evident that reals may differ from one another in any way in which they are found to differ; and that, consequently, there may be 'true' reals and 'false' reals if warrant can be found for such a distinction among the things which may be investigated.

There is no need of an elaborate proof to show that this definition, in spite of—rather, just because of—its simplicity and obviousness, is the only fruitful definition of reality. The history of thought is in evidence. To the metaphysician it is a real blessing, for it frees him from the trivial question whether there is anything real at all, and turns him to the more fruitful and important question, what is the nature of the real, when is it most fittingly and appropriately defined?

Now, it is just that question which seems to cause confusion and dilemma. And it is here that further clarification is needed. For the natural and obvious answer to the question when is reality most fittingly and appropriately defined, seems to be this: when it is *truly* defined. That this answer is the cause of the greater part of current controversies about pragmatism is obvious enough. It seems worth while, therefore, to say something about it, and elicit, possibly, further discussion from Professor Dewey and others.

The dilemma in question is apparent. If reality as true is but one sort of reality or one sort of experience, how can it possibly be affirmed that the nature of reality is most fittingly defined, when we have that sort, when, that is, reality is experienced as true? The answer occasionally given that it is thus most fittingly defined because defined in a way which most usefully meets the needs which raise the demand for definition, seems to many minds to be unsatisfactory. The reasons for dissatisfaction vary much, from quaking fear for the possible loss of an absolute to a genuine conviction that the whole knowing experience is a transcendent kind of experience, related to all other kinds in a way in which they are not related to it. I willingly leave the absolutist to his fears, but would say something in favor of the transcendence of knowledge.

As what I have to say has been definitely shaped in its formulation by Professor Dewey's article, I use some of his expressions to bring out the point I would raise for discussion:

"In each case," says Professor Dewey, "the nub of the question is, *what sort of experience* is meant or indicated: a concrete and determinate experience, varying, when it varies, in specific real elements, and agreeing, when it agrees, in specific real elements, so that we have a contrast, not between *a* Reality, and various approximations to, or phenomenal representations of, Reality, but between different reals of experience. And the reader is begged to bear in mind that from this standpoint, when 'an experience' or 'some sort of experience' is referred to, 'some thing' or 'some sort of thing' is always meant.

"Now, this statement that things are what they are experienced to be is usually translated into the statement that things (or, ultimately, Reality, Being) *are* only and just what they are *known* to be, or that things are, or Reality *is,* what it is for a conscious knower —whether the knower be conceived primarily as a perceiver or as a thinker being a further and secondary question. This is the root-paralogism of all idealisms, whether subjective or objective, psychological or epistemological. By our postulate, things are what they are experienced to be; and, unless knowing is the sole and only genuine mode of experiencing, it is fallacious to say that Reality is just and exclusively what it is or would be to an all-competent all-knower; or even that it *is,* relatively and piecemeal, what it is to a finite and partial knower. Or, put more positively, knowing is one mode of experiencing, and the primary philosophic demand (from the standpoint of immediatism) is to find out *what* sort of an experience knowing is—or, concretely how things are experienced when they are experienced *as* known things."

Again, Professor Dewey says in a foot-note, "The adequacy of any particular account [of the truth-experience] is not a matter to be settled by general reasoning, but by finding out what sort of an experience the truth-experience *actually* is." I have italicized the word 'actually.'

Now, my difficulty in getting a clear understanding of these and similar statements gets sharply pointed in the question: In what sort of experience do I find out what any sort of experience is, and is *actually* or otherwise? Is the answer to that question this: In the sort of experience you are having at the time? If so, I find out what sort of an experience a moral experience is by having it, and what sort a cognitive experience is by having it. But how shall I distinguish a moral experience from one that is cognitive? By having, I suppose the answer would run, a new experience in which the two are experienced as different.

Such an answer—and let it be kept in mind that I am not burdening anybody with such an answer, but am using it as one which seems to be implied in the statement under consideration—deserves to be pushed to its full limit in order to get a clear view of the sort of experience which it indicates. So pushed it appears to me to be this: If I am to find out what the different sorts of experience are, how they are related to one another, how they are distinguished, what sorts of objects constitute them, what has been their history, what their promise is, which of them may be called true, and which false, I must have an experience in which what I desire to find out is to some extent, at least, experienced. But this desired experience, which would contain within it all the possible riches of science and philosophy, is just the sort of experience which is generally called a cognitive experience. If, therefore, the suggested answer is the correct one, it appears to me clear that in cognitive experience all other sorts of experience may exist without alteration; for, otherwise, how could we find out what sort they are? How could they be identified as the concrete, particular sorts of experience indicated? In other words, in the cognitive sort of experience all other sorts appear to be transcended. The nub of the *question*, to use Professor Dewey's words once more, is, undoubtedly, what sort of experience is meant or indicated. But it would appear that this question can be *answered* only in a cognitive experience!

As I have said, I burden no one with the answer which appears inevitably to lead to this conclusion. Yet I willingly take the burden myself. While I do not like the word 'experience' as an ultimate term in metaphysics, I can find little objection to it when it is used as equivalent to 'some thing' or 'some sort of thing,' when 'thing' may be, apparently, any term or any relation. Thus using the word, I can readily assent to such expressions as this: There are many sorts of experience of which the cognitive sort is only one and one which can be confused with the others only to the detriment of all. But I must now add that the cognitive experience is of such a 'sort' that it enables us to tell what the others *actually* are when we ask the question about *their* sort. This question may not be asked and may not be answered. In that case no one sort of experience is identified or distinguished. And what sort of an experience would that be if not precisely what we should mean by an unconscious experience?

I do not know whether those philosophers who bear by choice or by imputation the name of pragmatists deny, as a rule, the transcendence of the cognitive experience as here defined. When it is denied, I see no alternative but to assert that in the cognitive experience all other experiences become altered. But if we must have cognitive experience in order to have science and philosophy, and cognitive experience alters things, why then it appears to me that science and philosophy will be hugged to the bosom of the absolute idealist as his legitimate offspring!

In the endeavor to escape from the barren consequences of the position that *all* experience is in its nature cognitive and cognitive only, or, in other words, that all *things* are 'states of consciousness,' there appears danger of running to the opposite extreme. That is why, as it seems to me, the revolt against absolutism fails to convince many who are by no means absolutists. We attempt to give an account of experience which will commend itself to thought. How can we succeed if we raise the suspicion that any account of experience for thought must necessarily be, not only partial and inadequate, but radically different from what experience is? Surely here is a point where discussion can not fail to be important and profitable.   FREDERICK J. E. WOODBRIDGE.
        COLUMBIA UNIVERSITY.

VOL. II. No. 24.   NOVEMBER 23, 1905.

DISCUSSION

THE KNOWLEDGE EXPERIENCE AND ITS RELATIONSHIPS

PROFESSOR WOODBRIDGE'S recent article in this JOURNAL raises clearly and effectively certain questions involved in the conception of philosophy and its problems, which, in my mind, associate themselves with the ideas set forth in the first chapter of 'Studies in Logical Theory.' At all events, I am going to make some points in his article an excuse for reverting to the position there taken, *viz.*, that the characteristic problem of philosophy is the relationships to one another borne by certain typical functions or modes of experience, *e. g.*, the practical, cognitional, esthetic, etc. Objectively put, philosophy arises because the reals which are the distinctively appropriate subject-matters of these different types get into conflict with one another, a conflict so thorough as to leave us no choice except (*a*) to doubt all, (*b*) somewhat arbitrarily to select one as the standard and norm for valuing the others, or (*c*) to effect a harmonization of their respective claims through a more thorough consideration of their respective historic and working positions and relationships.[2]

Woodbridge's article presents a special case of the general problem, *viz.*, how to justify the peculiar claims of knowledge to provide a valid account of other modes of experience. "If reality as true is but one sort of reality or one sort of experience, how can it possibly be affirmed that the nature of reality is most fittingly defined, when we have that sort, when, that is, reality is experienced as true?" (p. 574). And again: "We attempt to give an account of experience which will commend itself to thought. How can we succeed if we raise the suspicion that any account for thought must necessarily be not only partial and inadequate, but radically different from what experience is?" (p. 576).

1. Certainly any empirical statement which ends up in the implication that the knowledge account is radically different 'from what experience is' has committed suicide. But when we say, with Woodbridge, (1) that 'the real is simply *that* which is experienced and *as* it is experienced' (p. 573), and (2) that 'there are many sorts of experience of which the cognitive sort is only one' (p. 576), we seem to be committed to the conviction that the knowledge-experience is of things which, in some sense, are different from what the things of other experiences *were*, and from what they would continue to be in the future were it not for an intervening knowledge-experience. As I interpret the history of thought, it is precisely the fact that the knowledge account *is* different from what the things of other experiences are, contemporaneously with those experiences, which has been

---

[2] One of the many merits of Bradley's 'Appearance and Reality' is the way in which it thrusts this conception virtually, if not intentionally, to the foreground. It leaves but three alternatives: to accept Bradley's result; to explain *away* satisfactorily the seeming discrepancies of the various functions; or to find another method and scheme of harmonization than his.

the main motivation of the transcendental non-empirical conception of knowledge.

Because the things of experience *are* so many different things, it has been thought that reality to be one, single and comprehensive, must be *exclusively* identifiable with the content of the perfected knowledge account; and this is then set over against the things of other experiences (of all experience *qua* experience), as the absolute against the phenomenal, the really real against the world of appearances. Hence the attacks made by the transcendentalists upon recent empiricisms (however denominated), because they deny exclusive or isolated jurisdiction to the knowledge function. Hence also the charges by the empiricists upon the 'transcendent' concept of knowledge, claiming that the isolation in which knowledge is placed leaves it an arbitrary, brute dictum (none the less arbitrary and even solipsistic because referred to a knower *termed* Absolute), or else a subjectivistic esthetic indulgence, since such isolation excludes verification in all the senses of verification hitherto employed by man. When, therefore, we have, as in Professor Woodbridge's account, a 'transcendence' notion of knowledge put forth with an empiristic motivation and basis, we have the problem in an especially interesting form: How can the knowledge-experience connect with other experiences in such a way as not to justify itself at *their* expense? How can, at one and the same time, knowledge be transcendent of other experiences, and the things of other experiences be real?

2. What, concretely, is the knowledge-experience? Three sets of facts are designated by the term knowledge: (1) It may denote the *de facto* presence in experience of a discriminate or outstanding quale or content. Some degree of distinction is necessary to any experienced thing, and such determinateness in experience one may agree to call knowledge. This sort of thing can hardly be referred to as transcendent—for what does it transcend? Not the things of other experiences, for it *is* the things of all experiences. It is a name for them in their determinate character. If transcendence refers to the relationships between such things, and things not *at all* determinately present in experience, then it has an intelligible meaning, but appears to involve a theory of the existence of reals apart from experience— or to be non-empirical. And transcendence as a relationship of that which is in experience to out-of-experience things would certainly make wholly meaningless *any* statement as to whether knowledge does or does not modify the out-of-experience. Such a statement can have intelligible meaning only when said of the things of knowledge in contrast and connection with other experienced things. Knowledge

in this sense (apart from the question of the appropriateness of the term) does not seem, then, to be anything more than a restatement of the postulate of immediate empiricism: that things are that which they are experienced to be, recognizing that some sort of distinctiveness is necessary to any thing. All things, truth and error, the obscure and the clear, the practical, the logical, the esthetic, are thus present, and all equally real—though *not* equally valuable and valid.

(2) Reference as a contemporaneous empirical trait is not an inevitable accompaniment of presence as just defined. The quale or content which discriminates a thing may not be referred explicitly to any other, nor any other to it. Connection may exist, however, practically: one thing may be found subsequently to affect, influence or control, favorably or unfavorably, the quality of some other present thing. Reference as an empirical fact is then established—that is, becomes a discriminate element in the constitution of something which is complex. Hence a second sense of knowledge. It is the experience in which the nature of such reference is investigated and defined. This involves such transformation of the character of antecedent things as makes possible the ascription to them and the maintenance by them of the relevant references.

Recognize that practical bearing or influence becomes explicit as reference in case of conflicting and therefore uncertain and contradictory bearings, and we get knowledge as Woodbridge has defined it when he says: "It is of such a sort that it enables us to tell what the others actually are when *we ask the question about their sort.*"

The practical conflict of experiences in bringing to light the problem of their reference, also brings to light the question of their nature as fitted to sustain such and such a reference; it makes their old characters suspicious, doubtful, precarious—in a word, problematic. This inherent dissentience is always, as to its *terminus ad quem,* a movement of inquiry, of institution or definition. This constitutes an answering or 'telling' experience in which an unquestioned thing replaces the dubious thing. Hence, while it would not do to say that the statement quoted above is an innocuous truism —there are too many subjectivistic theories of knowledge abroad to render its realistic implication other than important—it may do to say that its excellence lies in the fact that it identifies knowledge as a doubt-inquiry-answer experience.

When Woodbridge adds (to what was last quoted): "The question may not be asked and may not be answered. In that case no one sort of experience is identified or distinguished. And what sort of an experience would that be if not precisely what we should mean by an unconscious experience?" (p. 576), there appears to be a relapse to the first sense of knowledge set forth. It is one thing to say that distinctive character is necessary to any experience, in order not to fall into the contradiction of an unconscious experience; it is another thing to say that *that kind* of identification and distinction, namely, of reference, which follows from express questioning and constitutes express answering, is necessary to a conscious experience. Only of the first sense of knowledge can the contradiction be relevant; only of the second sense is the reference to question and answer relevant.

Bearing these things in mind, I do not appreciate the difficulty in the statement that reality is most fittingly defined as true 'because defined in a way which most usefully meets the needs that raise the demand for definition' (p. 574, the 'needs,' however, do not 'raise' the demand, they *are* the demand). For the 'needs' and their 'usefully meeting' are neither of them extrinsic to the situation. The needs *are* the unstable, dissentient characters constituting an intolerable condition; while 'usefully' *is* the meeting of this demand, that is, their transformation into a stable, dependable state of affairs. Needs are not met more or less usefully; they are met more or less successfully, and the successful fulfillment defines the useful thing of the situation. There is no other measure of use.

I am convinced that the charges of subjectivism and of an arbitrarily utilitarian practicalism brought against current empiricism are due to the fact that the critic, because he himself retains a belief in the independent existence of a subject, ego, consciousness or whatever, external to the subject-matters, ascribes similar beliefs to the one criticized; and hence suppose that the latter, when he talks about genesis in needs, and outcome in success or fulfillment, is talking about something resident in a subject or consciousness which arbitrarily pounces in, picks out its plum and withdraws triumphant. But to the thoroughgoing empiricist, the self, the ego, consciousness, needs and utility, are all alike interpreted in terms of functions, contexts or contents in and of the things experienced.

3. The empiricist (of the immediate type) will prefer to use the term knowledge-experience, or cognitional experience, concerning the sort just described. For here things are *contemporaneously* experienced as known things. It is now and here that they have 'knownness' as one of their discriminated properties—just as they may have that of hardness or unpleasantness or monetary value. But 'knowledge' is also used to denote the function or result of the doubt-inquiry-answer experience in its outcome of critically assured presence, with respect to further experiences. By the nature of the case, dissentiency of conflicting things reaches an end when the

nature of reference is defined, and the character of things altered so that they may sustain such reference. Hence, when Woodbridge says (p. 575) "in cognitive experience all other sorts may exist without alteration," he says something which seems obviously false if said of knowledge in the second sense discussed (since transformation is the salient trait of *its* things), but ideally true of knowledge in this third sense. That is, the precise and defining aim of knowledge in the second sense is to *secure* things which are permanent or stable objects of reference; which may be persistently employed without thereby introducing further conflicts. Unalterability means precisely capacity to enter into further things as secured points of regard, established contents and quales, guaranteed methods.[3]

We are thus enabled to give a precise statement of the relationship of the knowledge-experience to alteration and to validity. In its second sense, knowledge arises because of the inherent discrepancy and consequent alteration of things. But it gives that alteration a particular turn which it would not take without knowledge—it directs alteration toward a result of security and stability. Hence it is because knowledge is an experience, in organic connections of genesis and destiny with other experiences, that the validity of knowledge or truth has an assignable meaning. Because it is an affair of meeting the concrete demands of things, the demand of dissentient things for consensus, harmony, through defining reference and through redefining things which sustain the reference in question, validity or invalidity is a trait or property of facts which may be empirically investigated and instituted. But validity is not definable or measurable in terms of the knowledge-content if *isolated*, but only of the *function* of the knowledge-experience in subsequent experiences. So knowledge tells us the 'nature of the real when it is most fittingly and appropriately defined,' because it is only when a real is ambiguous and discrepant that it needs definition. Its peculiar fitness is functional, relative and empirical, not absolutistic and transcendental. Yet we may admit a certain empirical transcendence. The outcome of the doubt-inquiry-answer experience literally goes beyond the state of suspense and dissentience out of which it originates. So far as the knowledge experience fulfills its function, it permanently transcends its own originating conditions. It puts certain things out of doubt, rendering them reliable, economical and fruitful constituents in other more complex things. *This* transcendence is the very essence of the pragmatic empiricist's account of truth.

JOHN DEWEY.

COLUMBIA UNIVERSITY.

[3] Knowledge might thus be roughly defined as the function of economically (or efficiently) securing increasing complexity in experienced things.

DISCUSSION

THE KNOWLEDGE EXPERIENCE AGAIN

I OWE an apology to the editor and to the readers of this JOURNAL for returning a third time to the defense of my article on 'Immediate Empiricism,'[1] but Dr. Bode's recent article[2] is so clear and compact that I can not refrain from again taking a hand.

Dr. Bode points out that since I recognize that an experience (which is not itself a knowledge experience) may be cognitive, $i.\ e.$, have bearings which lead out into a distinctively knowledge experience, I can not readily be charged with making such a gap between the (dominantly) non-knowledge experience and the knowledge experience as deprives the latter of all point when it comes. But he claims (1) that this later experience which identifies the thing of the first as being thus and so (a fearsome noise as a wind-curtain fact) is essentially a 'pointing' experience, a 'knowledge about,' and hence does not give the full meaning or truth of the first, which can be found only (2) in an experience which is wholly of the 'acquaintance with' type, having neither the 'leadings' of the first nor the 'pointings' of the second. And this he claims must be (3) an 'unconscious experience,' a term which can have no other meaning assigned to it than the implication or presupposition of an object out of experience, conscious experience being then confined (on this basis) to relations between final out-of-consciousness terms. This position is (4) acutely identified with Woodbridge's definition of consciousness as a continuum, with its realistic implications.

I agree wholly with the first two points (save that empirically the 'complete acquaintance' thing need not necessarily be an entire experience, but may be an element in a more complex experience, and this, *as a whole*, may have cognitive leadings). But if this third point is correct, empiricism, in presupposing things which can not be experienced, has hanged itself on the topmost bough of the tree whose seed and fruit it meant and pretended to be. I marvel that Dr. Bode, in seeing so clearly the first two implications, did not follow the empirical clue; and, instead of arguing conceptually that the

[1] Vol. II., No. 15, p. 393.
[2] Vol. II., No. 24, p. 658.

terminal experience *must* refer to something unexperienced, did not look about for some experience which should meet the conditions of complete cognitive fulfillment in a thing which itself is neither a 'leading on' nor a 'pointing back.' Take again the case of the fearsome noise which develops into a wind-curtain fact. What is its appropriate career? Surely not into an 'unconscious experience,' but into an experience which in so far forth is practical (or moral) and esthetic. The complete acquaintance which is self-adequate is, one might say, a relationship of friendship or affection (or of contempt and disregard) and of assurance or control. The complete 'acquaintance' determines the attitude of, say, management of the thing as a means to an end; or of, say, amused recollection—not remembrance as logical pointing; *i. e.*, you are what once fooled me (an S-P experience, or judgment), but remembrance as recreation, or revival, in their literal immediate senses.

I am enough of a Hegelian to believe that 'perfect' knowledge is not knowledge (in its intellectual or logical connotation) at all, but such a thing as religionists and practical people have in mind; an attitude of possession and of satisfaction,—the peace that *passes* understanding. It means control of self, because control of the object on which the status of the self contemporaneously depends. Here, if anywhere, the pragmatic is justified, like wisdom, of its children; and if we have something more than the pragmatic, it is because this attitude of attained adjustment is so saturated with emotional, or morally and esthetically conscious, content. If one will realize how largely discursive knowledge empirically fulfills itself in a coloring or toning—an immediate value element—in subsequent experiences,[3] one will, I think, be fully guarded against supposing that 'unconscious experience' is the sole alternative to intellectualized experience. 'Unconscious' the experience is with respect to logical determinations; but immediate experience is saturated with values that are not logical determinations. The epistemological idealist can not deny this as a fact, because it is precisely this fact which makes him discredit immediate experience, and insist, therefore, upon its absorption into an 'absolute' which is just and wholly logical.

Such a position also differentiates itself from the realism which Bode criticizes. If consciousness were just cognitional awareness, Woodbridge would seem to have said the last word in calling it a 'continuum of objects'—of objects which are, as objects, out of consciousness. For as cognitional or intellectual, it is surely the business, so to say, of consciousness to be determined (that is, deter-

---

[3] There is much in Dr. Gordon's articles on 'Feeling' (this JOURNAL, Vol. II., Nos. 23 and 24) which I should gladly adopt as exegetical of my position.

minate) solely in and through objects. Otherwise common sense is crazy and science an organized insanity. But the 'things' of which knowledge constitutes a continuum may be precisely immediate values which are not constituted by logical considerations, but by attitudes, adjustments, coordinations of personal activities. Knowledge, in the strict or logical sense, mediates these activities (which include, of course, passivities), establishing certain 'leadings' and 'pointings,' certain equivalences, and thereby certain intermediaries and transitional points of immediate valences or worths; and, when it has completely wrought out a certain equivalence, finds its own surcease in a new value, expressive of a new esthetic-moral attitude. From this point of view, knowledge is not, but develops, a continuum; an emotional content being, as substrate, the continuum of which knowledge 'pointings,' or discriminated-identities, are the discretes.[4]

Have we not the elements of a reconciliation of what is significant in realism and in idealism? We have something which is beyond consciousness *as cognitional* and which determines consciousness as cognitional—*literally* determines it in the sense that the practical-esthetic attitude, in order to maintain itself, evokes the reflective attitude; and *logically* determines it, in that the content of knowledge must conform to conditions which the knowledge consciousness does not itself supply.[5] But this 'efficient' and 'formal' cause presents a situation in which a conscious agent or person is indispensably present. It is not a non-empirical thing-in-itself (against which idealism has stood as a protest); and it is something in which a conscious being plays a part. Is epistemological idealism anything but a transfer into the knowledge situation of a relation which actually holds in the practical-esthetic situation—a mistranslation which always calls out 'realism' as a counterbalance; which tends, in the end, to destroy the peculiar individuality that is the essence of such situations (resolving individuality into terms of the universal, objective content which is alone appropriate to knowledge); and which hopelessly complicates the treatment of the knowledge situation itself by deliberately throwing away the key to its interpretation?

I wish to take this occasion to say a few words also about Professor Bakewell's interesting contribution to this discussion.[6] My original contribution was intended, as Bakewell sees, to bring into sharper relief what seemed to be the fundamental point at issue, so that the

---

[4] See, again, Dr. Gordon's articles, and also her thesis, 'The Psychology of Meaning,' pp. 22–26.

[5] See 'Studies in Logical Theory,' p. 85, and, for a statement in psychological language, pp. 253–256.

[6] This JOURNAL, Vol. II., No. 25, p. 687. The preceding paragraphs stand as written prior to the appearance of Professor Bakewell's article.

artillery of the opponents of recent empiricism (for whose range and shot I profess the greatest respect) might fire there, rather than at bogey-men or side-issues. I must confess I did not succeed in so presenting it to Professor Bakewell. He says the idealist denies that 'any single actual experience, as existent or as known, is immediate, and simply immediate' (p. 690). By turning to p. 394 of my original article, it will be seen that I there declare the nub of *immediate* empiricism to be precisely the thoroughgoing fallacy of the absolute identification, for metaphysics, of experience '*as known*' with experience '*as existent.*' This is the point at issue; hence objections which rest upon the fact that all *knowledge* involves a mediate element, are just non-relevant. That the distinction between the immediate *content* and the mediate *content* (together with their reference to one another) is necessary in and to the knowledge experience *as such*, I not only fully accept, but have been at considerable pains to expound and to attempt to explain (in 'Studies in Logical Theory').

So when 'the idealist' (p. 688 of Bakewell's article) says that 'experience is always a complex of the immediately perceived and the mediately conceived' he is saying something which the empiricist accepts so far as the content of a *distinctively* knowledge, or logical, experience is concerned, while he (1) takes fundamental issue with the implication that experience is 'always' distinctively logical, and also (2) points out that even the distinctively logical experience is still 'always' *in toto* an immediate experience; or, more specifically, that the distinction between 'immediate perception' and its material ('data') and 'mediate conception' and its methods ('thinking') is always within and for the sake of a value in experience which is 'pragmatic' (personally, I should add esthetic), not reducible to cognitional terms. Since it is only *as elements in the content* of an immediate experience that the distinction between the immediately perceived (the sensibly given) and the mediately conceived (the relationally thought) occurs, it is obvious that immediate empiricism does not identify the immediacy for which it stands with one of the *terms* of its own content at a special juncture.[7]

When Professor Bakewell says that 'immediacy in this enlarged and general sense, as noting that aspect of direct ownership, of personal appropriation, which is always found in concepts and principles of mediation . . . is a fact fully taken into consideration by idealism,' he is saying something which doubtless *his* idealism takes due account of, but which many of us believe epistemological idealism is wholly impotent to take account of. It gladly assumes the benefit

---

[7] I repeat what I have said before: it is the essential vice of *sensationalistic* empiricism to make this identification between a *functionally determined instrument and test of knowledge* and experience as such.

of such facts, but only by introducing elements which are not, and can not be reduced to, cognitional terms and relations; which connote emotional and volitional values; and to which 'humanism,' 'pragmatism,' 'radical empiricism,' are desirous of assigning their metaphysical weight. If Professor Bakewell's idealism takes *such* facts into consideration, then, I believe, he is, for all intents and purposes, an immediate empiricist, though seemingly one not yet entirely free from epistemological bondage.

JOHN DEWEY.

COLUMBIA UNIVERSITY.

The Journal of Philosophy

Psychology and Scientific Methods

THE CONTROL OF IDEAS BY FACTS. I

I

THERE is something a little baffling in much of the current discussion regarding the reference of ideas to facts. The not uncommon assumption is that there was a satisfactory and consistent theory of their relation in existence prior to the somewhat impertinent intrusion of a functional and practical interpretation of them. The way in which the functionalist logician has been turned upon by both idealist and realist is suggestive of the way in which the outsider who intervenes in a family jar is proverbially treated by both husband and wife, who manifest their complete unity by berating the third party.

I feel that the situation is partly due to various misapprehensions, inevitable perhaps in the first presentation of a new point of view, and multiplied in this instance by the coincidence of the presentation of this logical point of view[1] with that of the larger philosophical movements, humanism and pragmatism, which resulted in interpreting the logic partly in terms of additional misconceptions of these philosophies, and partly in terms which, even if pertinent with reference to them, were not exactly relevant to the less ambitious logical theory. In the hope that the atmosphere is now more favorable, I wish to undertake a summary statement of the logical view on its own account, hoping it may receive clearer understanding on its own merits.

In the first place (apart from the present frightful confusion of logical theories), it was precisely the lack of an adequate and generally accepted theory of the nature of fact and idea, and of the kind of agreement or correspondence between them which constitutes the truth of the idea, that led to the development of a functional theory of logic. A brief statement of the difficulties in the traditional views may therefore be pertinent. That fruitful thinking—thought that terminates in valid knowledge—goes on in terms of the

[1] 'Studies in Logical Theory,' University of Chicago Press, 1903.

distinction of facts and ideas, and that valid knowledge is precisely genuine correspondence or agreement, *of some sort*, of fact and idea, is the common and undeniable assumption. But the discussions are largely carried on in terms of an epistemological dualism which renders the solution of the problem impossible in virtue of the very terms in which it is stated. The distinction is at once identified with that between mind and matter, or consciousness and objects, or the psychical and the physical, where each of these terms is supposed to refer to some fixed order of existence, a world in itself. Then, of course, there comes up the question of the nature of the agreement, and of the recognition of it. What is the experience in which the survey of both idea and existence is made and their agreement recognized? Is it an idea? Is the consistency ultimately a matter of self-consistency of ideas? Then what has become of the postulate that truth is agreement of idea with existence beyond idea? Is it an absolute which transcends and absorbs the difference? Then, once more, what is the test of any idea qua idea? What has become of the correspondence of fact and thought? Or, more urgently, since the pressing problem of life, of practise and of science is the discrimination of the *relative*, the *superior* validity of this or that theory, plan or interpretation, what is the criterion of truth within present non-absolutistic experience, where the distinction between factual conditions and thoughts and the necessity of some working criterion of their correct adjustment persist? Putting the problem in yet another way, either both fact and idea are present all the time or else only one of them is present. But if the former, why should there be an idea at all and why should it have to be tested by the fact? When we already have what we want, namely, existence, reality, why should we take up the wholly supernumerary task of forming more or less imperfect ideas of those facts and then engage in the idle performance of testing them by what we already know to be real? But if only ideas are present, then it is idle to speak of comparing an idea with facts and testing its validity by its agreement. The elaboration and refinement of ideas to the uttermost still leaves us with an idea, and to common sense and science while a self-consistent idea stands a show of being true in a way in which an incoherent one can not, a self-consistent idea simply *as* an idea is still but a hypothesis, a candidate for truth. Ideas are not made true by getting bigger. But if only 'facts' are present, once more the whole conception of agreement is again given up—not to mention that such a situation is one in which by definition there is no thinking or reflective factor at all.

This suggests that a strictly monistic epistemology, whether idealistic or realistic, does not get rid of the problem. Suppose, for example, we take a sensationalistic idealism. It does away with the ontological gulf supposed to exist between ideas and facts, and by reducing both terms to a common denominator seems to facilitate fruitful discussion of the problem. But the problem of the distinction and reference (agreement, correspondence) of two types or sorts of sensations still persists. If I say the box there is square, and call 'box' one group of ideas or sensations and 'square' another sensation or 'idea,' the old question comes up, Is 'square' already a part of the 'facts' of the box, or is it not? If it is, it is a supernumerary, an idle thing, both as an idea and as an assertion of fact; if it is not, how can we compare the two ideas, and what on earth or in heaven does their agreement or correspondence mean? If simply that we experience the two 'sensations' in juxtaposition, then the same is true, of course, of any casual association or hallucination. What we still have on the sensational basis, accordingly, is a distinction of something 'given,' 'there,' brutally factual, the box, and something else which stands on a different level, ideal, absent, intended, demanded, the 'square,' asserted to hold good or true of the thing 'box.' The fact that both are sensations throws no light on the logical validity of the proposition or belief because by theory a like statement holds good of every possible conjunction.[2]

The same problem recurs on a realistic basis. For example, there has recently been propounded[3] the doctrine of the distinction between relations of space and time and relations of meaning or significance, as a key to the problem of knowledge. Things exist in their qualitative character, in their temporal and spatial relations. When knowledge intervenes, there is nothing new of a subjective or psychical sort, but simply a new relation of the things—the suggesting or signifying of one thing by another. Now this seems to be an excellent way of stating the logical problem, but, I take it, it only states and does not solve. For the characteristic of such situations, claiming to terminate in knowledge, is precisely that the

[2] Mill's doctrine of the ambiguity of the copula ('Logic,' Bk. I., Ch. IV., § 1) is an instance of one typical way of evading the problem. After insisting with proper force and clearness upon the objective character of our intellectual beliefs and propositions, *viz.*, that when we say fire causes heat we mean actual phenomena, not our ideas of fire and heat (Bk. I., Ch. II. and Ch. XI., § 1, and Ch. V., § 1), he thinks to dispose of the whole problem of the 'is' in judgment by saying that it is only a sign of affirmation (Ch. I., § 2, and Ch. IV., § 1). Of course it is. But unless the affirmation (the sign of thought) 'agrees' or 'corresponds with' the relations of the phenomena, what becomes of the doctrine of the objective import of propositions? How otherwise shall we maintain with Mill (and with common sense and science) the difference between asserting 'a fact of external nature' and 'a fact in my mental history'?

[3] 'Studies in Philosophy and Psychology,' article by Woodbridge on 'The Problem of Consciousness,' especially pp. 159–160.

meaning relation is predicated *of* the other relations; it is referred to them; it is not simply a supervention existing side by side with them as do casual suggestions or the play of phantasy. It is something which the facts, the qualitative, space and time things, must bear the burden of, must accept and take unto themselves as part of themselves. Until this happens, we have only the continuance of 'thinking,' not accomplished knowledge. Hence, logically, the existential relations play the rôle of fact, and the relation of signification that of idea,[4] distinguished from fact and yet, if valid, to hold *of* fact.

This appears quite clearly in the following quotation: "It is the ice which means that it will cool the water, just as much as it is the ice which does cool the water when put into it." There is, however, a possible ambiguity in the statement, to which we shall return in the last paper of this series. That the 'ice' (the thing regarded as ice) *suggests* cooling is as real as is a case of actual cooling. But, of course, not every suggestion is valid. The 'ice' may be a crystal, and it won't physically cool water at all. So far as it is already certain that this *is* ice, and also certain that ice, under all circumstances, cools water, the meaning relation stands on the same level as the physical, not being merely suggested, but part of the facts asserted. It is not a meaning-relation as such at all. We already have truth; the entire work of knowing as logical, is done. In other words, we have no longer the relation characteristic of reflective situations. Here again, the implication of the thinking situation is of some 'correspondence' or 'agreement' between two sets of distinguished relations; the problem of its nature and valid determination remains the central question of any theory of thinking and its relation to facts and to truth—that is, of any logic.[5]

I hope this statement of the difficulty, however inadequate, will serve at least to indicate that a functional logic inherits the problem in question and does not create it; that it has never for a moment denied the *prima facie*, working distinction between 'ideas,' 'thoughts,' 'meanings' and 'facts,' 'existences,' 'the environment,' and the necessity of a control of meaning by facts, if there is to be any question of truth and error. It is concerned not with denying, but with understanding. What is denied is not the genuineness of the problem and of the familiar terms in which it is stated, but the

---

[4] In other words, 'ideas' is a term capable of assuming any definition which is logically appropriate—say, meaning. It need not have anything to do with the conception of them as little subjective entities.

[5] Of course, the monistic epistemologies have an advantage in the statement of the problem over the dualistic—they do not state it in terms which presuppose the impossibility of the solution.

value of the orthodox intellectualistic interpretation. What it insists upon is the relative, instrumental or working character of the distinction—that it *is* a *logical* distinction, instituted and maintained in the interests of intelligence with all that intelligence imports in the exercise of the life functions. To this positive side I now turn.

In the analysis it may prove convenient to take an illustration of a man lost in the woods, taking this case as typical of any reflective situation in so far as it involves perplexity—a problem to be solved.[6] The problem is to find a correct idea of the way home—a practical idea or plan of action which will lead to success, or the realization of the purpose to get home. Now the critics of the experimental theory of logic make the point that this practical idea, the truth of which is evidenced in the successful meeting of a need, is dependent for its success upon a purely intellectual idea, that of the existent environment, whose validity has nothing to do with success but depends on agreement with the actual state of affairs. It is said that what makes a man's idea of his environment true, is its agreement with the actual environment, and 'generally a true idea in any situation consists in its agreement with reality.' I have already indicated my acceptance, in a general way, of this formula. But it was long my misfortune not to be possessed offhand of those perfectly clear notions of just what is meant in this formula by the terms 'idea,' 'existence' and 'agreement' as have most writers on epistemology; and when I analyzed these notions I found the distinction between the practical idea and the theoretical not fixed or final, and I found a somewhat startling similarity between the notions of 'success' and 'agreement.'

Just what is the environment of which an idea is to be formed? *i. e.*, what is the intellectual content or objective detail to be assigned to the term 'environment'? It can hardly mean the actual visible environment—the trees, rocks, etc., which a man is actually looking at. These things are there and it seems superfluous to form an idea of them when the genuine article is at hand; moreover, the wayfaring man, though lost, would have to be an unusually perverse fool if under such circumstances he was unable to form an idea (supposing he chose to engage in this luxury) in agreement with these facts. The environment must be a larger environment than the visible facts; it must include things not within the direct ken of the lost man; it must, for instance, extend from where he is now to his home, or to the point from which he started. It must

---

[6] See Professor Russell's article, in this JOURNAL, Vol. III., p. 599, entitled 'The Pragmatist's Meaning of Truth.' (It should perhaps be added that this article was in manuscript before I saw the comment of Mr. Schiller on Professor Russell's article, in this JOURNAL, Vol. IV., p. 42.)

include the unperceived elements in their contrast with the perceived, or else the man would not be lost. Now we are at once struck with the facts that the lost man has no alternative except either to wander aimlessly or to conceive this inclusive environment, and that this conception is just what we here mean by idea. It is not some little psychical entity or piece of consciousness-stuff, but is the interpretation of the locally present environment in reference to its absent portions, that part to which it is referred as another part so as to give a view of a whole. Just how such an idea would differ from one's plan of action in finding his way, I do not know. It is a map constructed, with one's self lost and one's self found, whether at starting or at home again, as its two limits. If this map in its specific character is not also the only guide to the way home, one's only plan of action, then I hope I may never be lost. It is the *practical* facts of being lost and desiring to be found which constitute the limits and the content of the 'environment.'

As to the *agreement* of the idea and the environment. Supposing the individual stands still and attempts to compare his idea with the reality, with what reality is he to compare it? Not with the presented reality, for *that* reality is the reality of himself lost; not with the complete reality, for that at this stage of proceedings is the idea itself. What kind of comparison is possible or desirable then, save to treat the mental layout of the whole situation as a working hypothesis, *as* a plan of action, and proceed to *act* upon it, to use it as a director and controller of one's divagations instead of stumbling blindly around until one is either exhausted or accidentally gets out? Now suppose one uses the idea—that is to say, the present facts projected into a whole in the light of absent facts—as a guide of action. Suppose, by means of its specifications, one works one's way along until one comes upon familiar ground—finds one's self. *Now,* one may say, my idea was right, it was in accord with facts; it agrees with reality. That is, acted upon sincerely, it has led to the desired conclusion; it has, *through action,* worked out the state of things which it contemplated or intended. The agreement, correspondence, is between purpose, plan, and its own execution, fulfillment; between a map of a course constructed for the sake of guiding behavior and the result attained in acting upon the indications of the map. Just how does *such* agreement differ from success?

I can hardly hope that this brief account will be as convincing to others as it is to me; its very simplicity and brevity will—such is the reputation philosophy has made for itself—be odorous with the suggestion of hocus-pocus. But before entering upon a more detailed analysis, let me summarize the situation as a whole. The import of the discussion is that the terms environment, idea and agreement are all of them essentially *practical* terms, denoting distinctive functions or operations, the term 'practical' having no reference to any *fixed* utility, but simply to certain values to be sustained or transformed through an operation.

Every reflective situation has the problem of discovering the intent or meaning appropriate to the management or development of a troubled situation, its pertinency being proved by its capacity to administer the difficulty through the use of the idea as a method or plan. The woods of the scientist and the philosopher, his paths and sign-boards and miscues, the unfamiliar surroundings into which he wanders, his home, his schemes for getting there—all of these differ infinitely in local color and setting from those of the wayfarer in question. But the situation in its diagrammatic features remains the same. Types of agency and response differ according to the different sorts of disturbed organizations, interrupted universes of value, that present themselves; but the category of the problematic; the contrast of the given and the intended; the use of the given to form a conception or hypothetical view of an inclusive situation in which both it and the wanted are contained; the use of this conception as guide to experimental activity in transforming, through degrees, the given into the intended; the use of the results thus obtained to confirm and revise the guiding idea; final verification (if at all) through actively instituting or bringing about a condition of affairs which 'agrees with' the intent of the situation because it fulfills it— these characteristics are found in every reflective process and are found only in a reflective process.   JOHN DEWEY.

COLUMBIA UNIVERSITY.

THE JOURNAL OF PHILOSOPHY
PSYCHOLOGY AND SCIENTIFIC METHODS

THE CONTROL OF IDEAS BY FACTS. II

IN a previous portion of this paper I endeavored to show, first, that every situation of reflective knowledge involves a discrimination and a reference of existence and meaning, of datum and ideatum; and secondly, that the significance to be assigned to these categories, as well as to their correspondence, is thoroughly instrumental or 'pragmatic,' being relative to the problem of reorganizing a situation of disturbed values. In this portion of the article I propose to go over the ground in more detail, dealing with some explicitness with each phase of the situation. Before taking up the interpretation of the logical categories of fact, meaning and agreement, it may be well to say a few words on the nature of the disturbed and disordered situation for the sake of rectifying which the reflective process takes place. A quotation from a recent critic affords a convenient point of departure. I quote from the first volume of Baldwin's 'Thought and Things': "In the writings of Dewey and his colleagues the case made much of is that of embarrassment and confusion, due to failure of habitual dispositional processes to establish themselves; this is made the starting-point of all new constructions, which come as the establishment of new equilibrium after these crises. But I am pointing out the further case that often such embarrassment or disintegration is not the extreme case; for it often happens that a new and unwelcome object simply forces itself upon us. It is not content with knocking down our fortifications and necessitating our building new ones; it rides full-armed through our walls, and compels its recognition in certain of its characters, *for what it is*—say, for example, a round stone which a child takes for an apple and attempts to bite" (p. 50, note).

I do not profess wholly to understand the supposed bearings of this, but it is clear enough that Baldwin takes the instance of the child's performance as in some way presenting the sort of fact before which the theory breaks down. Since it is precisely this unwelcome fact that Chapter III. of 'Studies in Logical Theory' (on the 'Datum') deals with, it is clear that Baldwin must have totally misapprehended its point. I accordingly append the following remarks in the hope that they may prevent, for some readers, the perpetuation of misapprehension.

1. 'Confusion and embarrassment' are not terms characteristic of the 'Studies.' Stress, tension, interruption *in* the organized system of value (or in the functions which sustain this value) are the usual phrases. If the terms 'confusion and embarrassment' are employed as equivalents, they must be taken in the same sense; *i. e.,* they must *not* be interpreted as emotions or states of consciousness of any sort, but as applying to a system of action and its values—as when we say the *affairs* of a banker are embarrassed. The emotional perturbations that may accompany this in the banker's personal history are not conceived as primary, but as the organic reverberations of the 'confused' state of a system of activities, in which all sorts of things and persons are involved; prior to reflective analysis, the emotions belong to the conflicting situation, but they never make it up.

2. The system of activities so far as organized or harmonious (having its various elements mutually reinforcing each other) both underlies and overlies the dualism between thought and datum. It is in the conflicting situation that they get set over against each other, the thought being purpose and the object obstacle to realization of purpose. It is child-reaching-and-putting-object-in-mouth that is the total situation in the instance cited—an operation including a variety of values in themselves characterized prior to conflict neither as ideative nor as factual. But when *in* this activity various factors actively conflict with each other, then some stand out as purpose, intent, end: others as data, obstacles, which *through* thinking—through the ideational—are to be reinterpreted and readjusted.

If the child does not interpret the 'hard stone' with reference to an incompatible purpose, end, plan of action, there is no overriding object at all—many a child puts hard stones in his mouth for the sake of doing so. On the other hand, it is only as he sets some result conceived as desirable or intended over against the thing, that he goes on to perform those testing activities, *guided by the intent*, that will result in giving any intellectual content, any character, to that which at first is just interruption in the activity, so that finally the interruption is delimited and defined as round stone. Let the reader put this question to himself: *At what stage of proceedings and how* does the child determine that which forbids his purpose (which *is* purpose once more only in the conflict of activity) to be round hard stone? Not by hypothesis, at the outset; and in the degree that the purpose does not function as a plan of action in directing exploring (experimental) activities with reference to the nature of the interruption, the thing is not intellectualized at all, but is merely practically rejected—spewed out of the mouth. The normal conclusion of this investigating tentative process is the formation of a new total situation of harmonized values on the basis of mutually reinforcing, instead of conflicting, activities. When one wishes to eat an apple, it is not an overriding but a fulfillment of purpose to throw away what one has found out to be a stone.

3. The references to 'habitual dispositional processes' and to 'forcing itself upon *us*' seem to give the clue to the source of the misunderstanding. Strictly speaking, the 'us' is irrelevant to the logical problem, which is the problem of the relation of fact and idea. But if one chooses to *shift the issue* from the logical question to the question of the relation of 'external object' and 'me,' the mode of analysis just indicated serves. In any organized system, *qua organized*, there is no dualism of self and world. The emergence of this duality is within the conflicting and strained situation of action; the activities which subtend purpose and intent define the 'me' of that situation, those which constitute the interruptive factor define its 'external world.' The relation *prima facie* is purely practical; its transformation into a reflective or intellectual duality of fact—with described character—and purpose— of characteristic content—is precisely the process of rationalization by which a brute practical acceptance-rejection gets transformed into a *controlled directed evaluated system of action*, in which the duality of me and object is again overcome.

I should like here to refer to what is said in the 'Logical Studies' (pp. 16–17) about the evil of confusing the dualities of different types of situation, the technological, the intellectual, the esthetic, the affectional, with one another. The moment, for example, it is recognized that the logical fact-meaning duality is not to be identified with the technological object-agent duality, a large part of the present confusion of logic and of psychological epistemology clears itself up—it simply evaporates. It is this confusion which is, I believe, responsible for what Woodbridge in the article already referred to[1] calls the end-term conception of mind—which I may paraphrase as the putty-magical-faculty conception; putty, in so far as 'consciousness' is regarded as receptive of impressions; magical-faculty, in so far as it is supplied with a Lockean or Kantian or Lotzean machinery for synthesizing, ordering and objectifying these impressions.

[1] 'The Problem of Consciousness,' in 'Studies in Philosophy and Psychology,' p. 140 ff.

The significance, in the scheme of reality, of an active and centered self or agent or 'me' is a precious product of modern as against ancient life and philosophy. But the offhand identification of this practical agent with 'consciousness' is the source of endless woes. There is, as intimated above, a real point of connection, indeed, between the 'object-me' and the 'fact-meaning' relationships. Through the intellectual function, the 'me' becomes a rationalized, a truly purposive and investigating activity. From something just brutely accepting or brutely rejecting, it becomes something which is directed and put into action on the basis of relevantly conceived aims and relevantly characterized facts. It is precisely this intermediary power, inhering in the reflective, fact-meaning situation, which is meant by the instrumental function of knowledge. In my conception the whole matter reduces itself to this: Is it with respect to reality as inert objects that intelligence functions, so that its duty is simply to copy or repeat them in another realm, or does it exercise its office in respect to reality as activity, so that its duty is to develop this activity in the direction of increased discriminations of value, into more complex and richer situations? If the condition in which reflective knowledge appears is already adequately real, thinking is futilely gratuitous; if it is real so far as it goes, if its lack is simply quantitative, the appearance of thinking, of significance relations, is miraculous and there is no possible test of the validity of any extension or amplification of the given narrow reality which they may happen to effect. Finally the activities that do, as undeniable fact, result from intelligence are on this basis mere tail-pieces, deforming rather than ornamental in character, hitched on to reality as accidental by-products of knowledge. But if reflective thought presents itself as a developing phase of a situation inherently lacking in full reality and has for its purpose to delimit and interpret this situation, transforming its practical conflicts first into recognition of ambiguities and then into a clear conception of alternative possibilities—of intents—which may be experimentally tested, reflective knowing is natural in its origin, verifiable as to its contentions and contents, and fruitful in issue of reality. It lies, at every stage, within the processes of reality itself.

From this sketch of the disturbed or disordered situation within which and for the sake of which knowing occurs, I turn to the various terms of this knowing function as it energizes. The nature of 'fact' or 'existence' first presents itself. Since it is a not uncommon assumption that the theory which interprets knowing pragmatically supplies only a changed phraseology for a Berkeleian idealism, let the point be emphasized that we are dealing here with an intellectual or logical matter, the determination of a true description or delimitation, the assignment of a correct τὸ τί ἦν εἶναι of a given environment or set of facts. It is not the nature of existence or reality *ueberhaupt* which is under consideration, but of *that* reality of which, by assumption, there is an idea, and with respect to which there is to be a true idea. There may be, if you please, hundreds of realities both existing and existing in experience which are of any sort you please, and which are just what they are and just as they are. But we are not discussing such presences, for with respect to them we have and need to have no idea; as to them there *is* no problem of a true or valid idea; they do not at all come within the scope of reflection as such, or of logic or of any theory of knowledge as an intellectual operation.

Hence, however it may be in psychology and epistemology (I throw this concession in for the benefit of those whom it may concern, rather than on my own account, since I believe that any 'ology at least pretends to be logical), in logic there *is* no idea so long as there are nothing but realities as such, for logic does not demand the absurdity of duplicating in idea what we already have in reality. But, on the other hand, as soon as there is question of anything which is to be passed upon as true or false, of knowledge in the intellectual sense of that term, there is a reality which is not full reality, since it requires its own supplementation—which is not outward and quantitative, but inward and qualitative—through fulfillment of its intent. If the universe as complete reality is exhaustively present at one time to God or man, then neither God nor man has an idea or thought of it—and this even if the universe itself be only an idea. But if one has an idea of something which is there, then what is there is precisely that which needs for its own reality first interpretation and then transformation through that idea. Any given set of facts of which there is an idea is not yet fully real in itself, but is something which is to be made real through the transformation it receives in the process of fulfilling its own meaning or intent on the deliberate basis of that intent. On the other hand, so far as any one has a portion of reality present to him at any time in such fashion that this portion is adequate or self-included in value, there is no idea or thought of that thing—no knowledge in any reflective sense of the term knowledge. One has then to be constantly on one's guard against slipping the category of reality first in and then out of the reflective situation, not noting the different imports that the term inevitably receives according as it falls within or without reflective knowledge.[2] So

---

[2] In the hope that constant dripping may wear down the stony-hearted, I repeat once more that the idealistic fallacy is the assumption that 'real' reality, *the* 'Truth,' is just what reality is in and for the thought situation;

long as one is not dealing with the knowledge-situation at all, one may have perfectly good realistic systems—realities which are what they are entirely apart from any relationship to the function of intelligence; but an intellectualistic realism—that is to say, a realism which conceives facts within the reflective situation as identical with reality irrespective of it—totally ignores the fact that it is only because independent reality has lost something of its full characteristic of reality that it enters into reflection at all; and that in being set over against its own meaning or intent it is inevitably modified from what it is when it is in complete possession of its value, and that in its reference to this meaning it demands precisely its own further requalification. It ought, I should say, to be axiomatic in logic that the reality concerned in any intellectual situation, in so far as intellectual, is not true and good reality in a final objective sense, but is a sign with respect to it, a sign whose significance still requires to be made out, and whose value (as in the case of any sign) is in the value of the consequences to which it may direct one.

When, accordingly, it is said that fact and meaning, environment and conception, are functional distinctions, it is meant that they are divisions of labor or discriminations of status with respect to the problem of control of activity. Once more any strictly intellectualistic view of the relation of fact and idea is in this dilemma. Idea is either an idea of present fact, in which case it is superfluous, or else it is an idea of some fact not present, with respect to which it is idle to talk of agreement. There is no epistemological straddle by which one can compare an idea with an unknown reality so as to pass upon its truth; while if the fact is already known, it is silly fooling to invent an idea and go through the form of comparing it. But if we take the matter practically, an idea may be formed on the basis of presented fact (which is not the reality of which there is the idea) which may succeed in transforming the given fact, the fact *there*, into a complete reality, the reality in which the idea is true.

The environment is, as we have already noted, not identical with presented fact. If it were, the individual in the woods would not be lost. Or, generically, if the facts, the truths, which the scientist already owns, were *the* fact, *the* truth, he would not be a scientist;

while that of realism is that it is just the same in and for thought as it is outside. The central contention of the account I am presenting is that it is in the reflective situation, and there alone, that reality receives requalification and development of values in a directed way, and that the criterion of knowledge-validity is not accurate reproduction of reality already there—the common assumption of both the idealistic and realistic epistemologies—but the effectual rendering of a value-transformation office. Labels are dubious matters, but it is in this sense that pragmatism is to be understood, if pragmatism is to develop into an acceptable theory of knowledge.

there would be no inquiry, no reflection. Presented facts define the lost traveller; the scientist perplexed. They directly determine a problem, not a solution. Moreover, the contrast with the total reality is a part of the internal content of the given facts, not something external or additional. If it is not a part of them, as given, then at once they monopolize the whole field; the man is no longer a lost soul seeking salvation through reflection. He may esthetically enjoy what is before him. It is as good as anything else. But if there is thinking, aiming at 'making good,' then environment involves the absent as well as the present; and this not externally, say from our standpoint as distinct from that of the traveller (we recognizing that what he sees has to be pieced together with what he does not see), but internally, since relation to the absent is an inherent part of the very quality of that which is present. In other words, that which is present or given is inherently self-discrepant, self-irreconcilable, or actively ambiguous, meaning differing things by turns. That which is most positive or unquestionable is set in a context, and this context colors through and through what is set in it. The absent may determine the presented fact, as presented, either from the standpoint of ground which has been traversed, with which the present territory is continuous—a *Hinterland*—or from that which the traveller wishes to traverse, a foreground. The given, the 'local environment,' so to say, is apprehended as a portion of a larger whole in which, however, it is disjointed. It is given as an element in a disordered reality. And such is the character of all 'facts' about which we think. They are pragmatic, 'things done,' but, as yet, badly done.

JOHN DEWEY.

COLUMBIA UNIVERSITY.

VOL. IV. No. 12.   JUNE 6, 1907.

THE JOURNAL OF PHILOSOPHY

PSYCHOLOGY AND SCIENTIFIC METHODS

THE CONTROL OF IDEAS BY FACTS. III

IN the preceding paper, under this title, I gave a sketch of the
situation within which the distinction of fact and meaning is
instituted, and an interpretation of the category of 'fact.' I shall
conclude, in this portion, with an account of the categories of meaning and of agreement, or correspondence.

The 'facts,' as we have seen, refer to something absent. This, of
course, is the ideal or ideative aspect of the situation. Now this
absent, which is intended by the presented or factual, is asserted to
be just as real as the presented itself. This assertion, moreover, is
not a declaration on the part of an outsider who has the entire reality
before him; it is the assertion of the given qua given, since it *is*
given only *as* pointing to, intending, something beyond itself.[1] The
reality of the absent can be questioned only by questioning the
reality of the presented. This is present, then, *in idea* or *as idea*.
As such it is contrasted with the given facts of disordered system.
But as realities, the reality of presented fact and of idea stand on
exactly the same level.[2] What we call idea denotes the way in which
the *entire* reality, to which the local self-discrepant fact is referred

---

[1] The 'given' is an ambiguous term. It means sometimes the whole situation, *not* as taken reflectively or for knowledge at the time, but just as it is in
the total experience of it—what I have elsewhere termed the immediate. (See
this JOURNAL, Vol. II., p. 393.) But it also means this total experience as
contemporaneously intellectualized or delimited, as setting the terms for thought,
the data, the 'facts.' It is, of course, in the latter sense that the term is here
consistently used.

[2] The fallacy of orthodox logical empiricism is right here. It supposes
there can be 'givens,' sensations, percepts, etc., prior to and independent of
thought or ideas, and that thought or ideas may be had by some kind of compounding or separating of the givens. But it is the very nature of sensation
or perception (supposing these terms to have any knowledge-force at all, such
as Lockean empiricism ascribed to them) already to be, in and of itself, something which is so internally fractionized or perplexed as to suggest and to require an idea, a meaning.

for its own reality, is present[3] (it isn't, once for all, a bit of sublimated psychical stuff); while what we call facts denotes this entire situation presented in its disrupted, fragmentary elements.

While, however, the entire reality as entire can be present, under such circumstances, only in idea, it does not follow, of course, that the idea is real in the same mode as are the presented facts. When we say the idea stands on the same level of reality as the given facts, we refer only to the idea as idea, as existent, not to the details of its content. These *may* be false; at best, they are hypothetical. We have, then, a very pretty situation. The presented facts are brutely, unquestionably, stubbornly, there,[4] but they present themselves as *not* the whole and genuine reality, but as a distorted and perverse portion of it, requiring absent portions in order to be made sound and whole. On the other hand, this total reality, or environment, is present only as an idea—an intention, suggestion or meaning. In claim, it is *the* real; in performance, it is the doubtful, problematic, hypothetic; just as the 'given' facts are real in execution, but uncertain in value and unstable in pretension. Yet the idea, while it may be contrasted with brute, given fact, can not be set over against the total reality, for it *is* that total in the only way in which, *under the circumstances,* it can be realized. The relationship of given fact and idea stands, then, as follows. Neither is real in the sense that it can be cut off from the other and *then* taken to be the total reality, since this latter is precisely the tension in which one stands out against and yet for the other. Both are real in the sense that they present that reality as a condition of disturbed or disordered values. *Both present one and the same reality: but, as distinguished from one another, present it from different stand-*

---

[3] Hence, to return, in passing, to the statement in terms of the discrimination and reference to one another of physical relations and significance relations (see Vol. IV., p. 200), it is not strictly true that, in the first instance, or from the standpoint of the reflective situation itself, the meaning relation is one relation among or along with others. Rather the *thing meant* is that inclusive whole in which *physical* relations would realize coherently, instead of expressing ambiguously, their *physical* relations to one another: water-quenching-thirst, ice-cooling-water are just integrated situations of physical elements, which mean *it* only by meaning to modify one another so as to abrogate their discrepancies as given. The discrimination of a meaning relation along with and over against the physical relations as another relation of the same elements takes place not in the situation itself, but in that situation in which the logician reflects upon a reflective situation: a new and interesting type of situation, the implications of which can not be followed out here.

[4] It may turn out, of course, that something taken to be *there* was in truth suggested or intended, and hence this may be transferred to the ideal side. But this affects only the specific contents; something immediately *there*, and hence not idea, there must be in order that something may be meant, or be ideative.

points, or in different functions. The 'given' facts are the reality in its *existent* disorganized state of value. The 'idea' or intended is this same reality in its *projected* rectification. In this practical sense, fact and idea necessarily have a certain agreement or correspondence with one another from the start. They correspond as a disease and its diagnosis, or as the diagnosed disease and its proposed remedy, or as a statement of a problem and the suggested method of its solution, as an obstacle and an end which functions that obstacle. To correspond is to respond to one another—to incite and answer one another.

Here, then, we have two aspects of control. On the one hand, the total situation, postulated as fundamentally real in form, but now present only as intended or suggested (and hence hypothetical in content), controls the determination of the 'given' facts. It sets the limits of what shall be taken as given and what not; of what is a relevant and proper element in the determination of presented fact and what not. The given or fact of the lost traveler is obviously different in constitution from that of a botanist, or lumberman, or hunter, or astronomer, whom we might put into his boots. Apart from reference to the kind of total reality which is demanded as the rectification of the troubled or internally discrepant situation, there is no control over the τὸ τι ἦν εἶναι or intellectual content of the facts. If reference to this demanded total reality is dropped out, then the given becomes self-sufficient, an object of esthetic admiration or curious elaboration. Or, when it is forgotten that the function of observation is to define the facts that describe the problem of a situation, we get an indefinite accumulation of detail which intellectually is totally insignificant, save *per accidens.* It is the idea then as purpose, as end in view, which prescribes the selective determination of the constitution of the 'given' facts.[5] The environment varies, in intellectual definition, as the organism, character or agent varies. If this be taken to mean that the world is the sport of the organism, merely subject to its whims, or only a collection of its own states, this overlooks, first, the fact that the constitution of the agent is itself a correlative determination in the same system of values that is undergoing reorganization through internal dissension; and secondly, the point already mentioned that what we mean by fact is just that which, as problem, controls the correct formation of the idea as intent and method of action. It is not some indifferently existing world totally irrelevant to the development of the true idea of *this* situation. An indiscriminate universe, one

[5] This, once more, is the truth omitted by the rigid or structural type of empiricism. It is, of course, also the truth emphasized by idealistic logics. (See, for example, Royce, 'The World and the Individual,' Vol. I., Ch. VII.)

without selective determination, one, that is, not arranged for the sake of building up and testing an idea, could never be an object of knowledge; at its worst, it would be total reminiscence on a vast scale, a vast mirage or pointless anecdote; at its best, something better, perhaps, than any knowledge—an esthetic delight and free play.[6]

The other aspect of control is that exercised by the given facts over the formation of the *content* of the end, purpose or intent. The fact of being lost is the fundamental given fact; that which simply can not be got rid of. This may suggest a blind struggle, aimless wandering. But in the degree in which the aim of finding home is used to define the problem set by being lost, there is study, investigation, accurate observation; the content of 'being lost' is more or less reconstructed; certain features drop out as irrelevant and misleading—especially the grossly emotional ones; others are emphasized, new features are brought to light. *That* 'given' is gradually determined which shall be most likely to suggest the total situation, or rearranged harmonized whole of discrepant details, in the way most likely to be effectual as standpoint and method of action. The end first operates, so far as the situation is rationalized, as a basis of inspection and analysis of the situation in its given or disturbed form. The result of this analysis states the obstacles of which the end must take account, if it is to be realized. Thus the end is intellectualized in its content; for it assumes detail in accordance with the needs of the situation defined as obstacles. From mere end, it becomes a systematic plan of action, a method of procedure in overcoming obstacles by utilizing them. The disturbed values constitute the brute, the obdurate, the stubborn[7] factors, because they evidence the obstructive factors which must be reckoned with if success—harmonization of elements—is to occur. In this practical sense, they are coercive as regards the idea, and control its formation as to specific content. As the method of action is put into effect, it, so far as successful, changes the obstacles into resources; they lose their obtrusively coercive practical quality, and become cues, sign-boards and real means to the end. In this change

[6] Once more, the total absolutely completed, unified, harmonious reality, the absolute fact which is also absolute meaning, is a case of esthetic fallacy when treated as the reality which is involved in knowledge. Esthesis may be 'better' than gnosis, but to substitute it for gnosis is to translate, from the esthetic side, a delight into an illusion, and from the cognitive, a possible good intent into a certain self-imposture.

[7] This involuntary stubborn character as reality-exponent is valid when taken in relation to succeeding reactions—as that which must be reckoned with; when interpreted in an intellectualistic, ontological fashion, it always gives rise to the end-term or putty conception of mind.

of practical function, the brute character of the given is transformed into luminous or significant character—it not merely *means* to signify, but it *does* signify. In the same degree, of course (because it is the same process), the idea ceases to be just an intention of the given and becomes an inherent, constituent value of reality. The individual who is really finding his way sees his original givens, or data, assuming new and positive imports as they cease to be evidences of being lost and become evidences of being found; as they cease to be obstacles and become effectual and energizing conditions in a total situation. When the situation which has been represented in its disrupted character by facts as given, and in its total character by the idea or meaning, is realized as an effectively harmonized situation, the original brute datum is transformed through the acquisition of the meaning which it had previously simply pointed to,. while the guessed-at meaning is verified by becoming a structural value of the facts. This reciprocal transformation is the signal and seal of their agreement or correspondence. It is possible that one and the same reality should be brute and inconsistent in fact while harmonized and one in idea, precisely because the situation, being an active one, is reality in transition, and, so far as reflective, is in process of *directed* transformation. Moreover, we escape wholly from the intellectualistic dilemma of having to compare an idea with a fact which is present, or having to compare the idea with a fact which is merely absent, because their correspondence is witnessed in the eventual construction of a harmonized scheme of meanings. The objective reality which tests the truth of the idea is not one which externally antecedes or temporally coexists with the idea, but one which succeeds it, being its fulfillment as intent and method: *its* success, in short.

In these last remarks we have, of course, passed on to the subject of agreement. If we exclude acting upon the idea, no conceivable amount or kind of strictly intellectualistic procedure can confirm or refute an idea, or throw any light upon its validity. How does the non-pragmatic view consider that verification takes place? Does it suppose that we first look a long while at the facts and then a long time at the idea until by some magical process the degree and kind of their agreement become visible? Unless there is some such conception as this, what conception is there of agreement save the experimental or practical one? And if it be admitted that verification involves action, how can that action be relevant to the truth of an idea, unless the idea is itself already relevant to action? If by acting in accordance with the experimental definition of facts, *viz.*, as obstacles and conditions, and the experimental definition of the end or intent, *viz.*, as plan and method of action, a harmonized situation effectually presents itself, we have the adequate and the only conceivable verification of the intellectual factors. If the action indicated be carried out and the disordered or disturbed situation persists, then we have not merely confuted the tentative positions of intelligence, but we have in the very process of acting introduced new data and eliminated some of the old ones, and thus afforded a fresh opportunity for the resurvey of the facts and the revision of the plan of action. By acting faithfully upon an inadequate reflective presentation, we have at least secured the elements for its reinterpretation. This, of course, gives no absolute guarantee that the reflection will at any time be so performed as to prove its validity in fact. But the constant self-rectification of intellectual content and intent through the modification introduced by acting upon them in good faith is the absolute of reflective knowledge, loyalty to which is the religion of intellect.

The intellectual definition or delimitation assigned to the 'given' is thus as tentative and experimental as that ascribed to the idea. In form both are categorical, and in content both are hypothetical. The facts really exist just as facts, and so the meanings exist just as meanings. One is no more superfluous, more subjective, or less necessitated than the other. In and of themselves as existences both are equally realistic and compulsive, but on this basis, as just existences, there is no element of content in either which may be strictly described as intellectual or cognitional. There is only a practical situation in its most brute and unrationalized form. The moment we recognize the element of uncertainty in the contents unreflectively supplied for facts and meanings and set to work to redefine those contents with reference to the requirements of their adequate functioning in the transformation of the situation, reflective knowledge, rationalization, begin. What is uncertain about the facts as given at any moment is whether the right exclusions and selections have been made in determining them. Since that is a question which can be decided finally only by the experimental issue, this ascription of character is itself tentative and experimental. If it works, the characterization and delineation are found to be proper ones; but every introduction of unquestioned, categorical, rigid objectivity into the structure compromises the probability that it will work, save accidentally. The character assigned to the datum must be conceived as hypothetically as possible in order to preserve the elasticity needed for easy and prompt reconsideration and requalification at the bidding of the needs of the developing situation. Since the logical force and function of the facts are not ultimate and self-determined, but relative to suggesting an intent in the form of an approved method of action, the reflective situation is adequately reflective only in so far as the thought of the purpose to be attained is consistently utilized to recharacterize the fact. Any other procedure virtually insists that all facts and details anywhere happening to exist and happening to present themselves, since all are equally real, must all be given equal status and equal weight; and their outer ramifications and internal complexities be indefinitely followed up. The complete worthlessness of this sheer accumulation of realities, its total irrelevancy, the lack of any way of judging the significance of the accumulations, are good proof of the fallacy of any theory which ascribes objective logical content to fact wholly apart from the needs and possibilities of a practical situation. Supply an end to be reached, a purpose to be fulfilled, and at once there is a basis for supplying internal individuality and external restriction to the facts in question, while so long as the end is tentative the character, inherent and external, assigned to facts must also be provisional.

It has been suggested that the controlled development through reflection of a disordered situation into a harmonized one is compromised and hindered in just the degree in which the facts and meaning are permitted to assert, as fixed and final within the reflective situation, the contents which they bring to it from without. The more stubbornly one maintains the full reality of either his facts or his ideas, just as they stand, the more accidental is the discovery of relevantly significant facts and of valid ideas—the more accidental, the less rational, is the issue of the knowledge situation. Due progress is reasonably probable in just the degree in which the intent, categorical in its existing imperativeness, and the facts, equally categorical in their brute coerciveness, are assigned only a provisional and tentative nature with deliberate reference to the control and reordering of the situation. That this surrender of a rigid and final character for the content of knowledge on the sides both of fact and of meaning in favor of experimental and functioning estimations, is precisely the change which has marked the development of modern from medieval and Greek science, seems undoubted. To learn the lesson one has only to contrast the rigidity of both phenomena and conceptions (Platonic ideas, Aristotelian forms) in Greek thought with the modern experimental selection and determining of facts and experimental employment of ideas. The former have ceased to be ultimate realities of a nondescript sort and have become provisional data; the latter have ceased to be eternal meanings and have become working hypotheses. The fruitful application of mathematics and the evolution of a technique of experimental inquiry have coincided with this change. That, indeed, realities exist independently of their use as intellectual data, and that values and meanings exist apart from their utilization as hypotheses, are the permanent truths of Greek realism as against the exaggerated subjectivism of modern philosophy; but the conception that this existence is of the intellectualistic type, *i. e.*, is to be defined in the same way as are contents of knowledge, so that perfect being is object of perfect knowledge and imperfect being object of frustrate knowledge, is the fallacy which Greek thought projected into modern. Waiving the question whether this existence of independent realities and meanings signifies anything at all apart from participation and position in systems of well-ordered activity, it is certain that science has advanced in its methods in just the degree in which it has ceased to assume that prior realities and prior meanings retain fixedly and finally, when entering into reflective situations, the characters they had prior to it; in which it is realized that their very presence within the knowledge situation signifies that they have to be redefined and revalued from the standpoint of the needs and intent of just the new situation.

This conception does not, however, commit us to the view that there need be any conscious situation which is totally non-reflective. It may be true that any experience which can properly be termed such involves within itself something which is meant over and against what is given or there. None the less, since every reflective situation is a specific situation (one having its own disturbance and problematic elements and its own demanded fulfillment in the way of a restored harmony), it is true that the contents carried over from one reflective situation into another are at the outset nonreflectional with reference to the new reflective situation, entering primarily as *practically* determining or alogical elements; and this remains true of the outcome of the most comprehensive thought so far as that becomes datum for another intent. Because the stated condition of fact or meaning is a satisfactory solution with respect to the concrete problem of one concrete situation, its functioning as the disturbing and uncertain element in some other concrete situation is not thereby prevented. Hence the requirement of requalification within each new specific intellectual process. In the second place, there are many situations into which the rational factor—the mutual distinction and mutual reference of fact and meaning—enters only incidentally and is slurred, not deliberatively accentuated. Many disturbances of value systems are relatively trivial and induce only a slight and superficial redefinition of contents. This passing tension of facts against their meaning may suffice to call up and carry a wide range of inherently valuable and meaningful facts which are quite irrelevant to the intellectual problem and to the specific purpose now entertained, and which accordingly require no redefinition. Such is the case where the individual is finding his way through any field which is upon the whole familiar, and which, accordingly, requires only an occasional resurvey and revaluation at moments of relative and slight perplexity. We may call these situations, if we will, knowledge situations (for the reflective function characteristic of knowledge is present), but so denominating them does not in the least do away with their sharp difference from those situations in which the critical qualification of facts and definition of meanings constitute the central problem. To call the passing attention which a traveler has occasionally to give to the indications of his proper path in a fairly familiar and beaten highway while his main attention is elsewhere, knowledge, in just the same logical sense in which the deliberate inquiry of a mathematician or a chemist or a logician is knowledge, is as confusing to the real issue involved as would be the denial of *any* reflective factor in the former. If, then, one bears in mind these two considerations—(1) the unique problem and purpose of every reflective situation, and (2) the difference as to range and thoroughness of logical function in different types of reflective situations—one need have no difficulty with the doctrine that the primary difficulty of critical or scientific knowing is that facts and meanings enter such situations with stubborn and alien characteristics imported from situations which, in their contrast with the requirements of reflection in *this* case, may be fairly termed non-reflective; so that the essential problem of intelligence so far forth as intelligence, is precisely the reassignment of content in accordance with the needs and purposes of this situation: it is just this resurvey and revaluation which constitutes rationality.

This affords an opportunity to speak again of the logical problem to which reference and promise of return were made earlier in this paper (Vol. IV., pp. 199–200). Facts may be regarded as existing qualitatively and in certain spatial and temporal relations; when there is knowledge there is another relation added, that of one thing meaning or signifying another. Water exists, for example, as water, in a certain place, in a certain temporal sequence. But it may suggest or signify the quenching of thirst; and this signification relation constitutes knowledge.[8] This statement may be taken in a way con-

---

[8] This view was originally advanced in the discussion of quite another problem than the one here discussed, *viz.*, the problem of consciousness; and it may not be quite just to dissever it from that context. But as a formula for knowledge it has enough similarity with the one brought out in this paper to suggest further treatment; it is not intended that the results reached here shall apply to the problem of consciousness as such.

gruous with the account developed in this paper. But it may also be taken in another sense, consideration of which will serve to enforce the point regarding the tentative nature of the characterization of the given, as distinct from the intended and absent. Water means quenching thirst; so it is drunk, and death follows. It was not water, but a poison which 'looked like' water. Or it is drunk and is water, but does not quench thirst, for the drinker is in an abnormal condition and drinking water only intensifies the thirst. Or it is drunk and quenches thirst; but it also brings on typhoid fever, being not merely water, but water plus germs. Now all these events demonstrate that error may appertain quite as much to the characterization of existing things, suggesting or suggested, as to the suggestion qua suggestion. There is no ground for giving the 'things' any superior reality. In these cases, indeed, it may fairly be said that the mistake is made because qualitative thing and suggested or meaning relation were *not* discriminated. The 'signifying' force was regarded as a part of the direct quality of the given fact, quite as much as its color, liquidity, etc.; it is only in another situation that it is discriminated as a relation instead of being regarded as an element. It is quite as true to say the fact is called water because it suggests thirst-quenching as to say that it suggests thirst-quenching because it is characterized as water. *The knowledge function becomes prominent or dominant in the degree in which there is a conscious discrimination between the fact relations and the meaning relations.* And this inevitably means that the 'water' ceases to be *surely* water, just as it becomes doubtful or hypothetical whether this thing, whatever it is, really means thirst-quenching. If it really means thirst-quenching, it is water; so far as it may not mean it, it perhaps is not water. It is now just as much a question *what* this *is* as what it means. Whatever will resolve one question will resolve the other. In just the degree, then, in which the existence or thing gets intellectualized force or function, it ceases to be just reality as such and becomes a fragmentary and dubious reality to be circumscribed and described for the sake of operating as *sign* or clue of a *future* reality to be realized through action. Only as reality is reduced to a sign, and questions of its nature as sign are considered, does reality get intellectual or cognitional status. The bearing of this upon the question of the practical character of the distinctions of fact and idea is obvious. No one, I take it, would deny that action of some sort *does* follow upon judgment; no one would deny that this action *does* somehow serve to test the value of the intellectual operations upon which it follows. But if this subsequent action is *merely* subsequent, if the intellectual categories, operations and distinctions are complete in themselves, without inherent reference to it, what guarantee is there that they pass into relevant action, and by what miracle does the action manage to test the worth of the idea? But if the intellectual identification and description of the thing are as tentative and instrumental as is the ascription of significance, then the exigencies of the practical situation are already operative in all the categories of the knowledge situation. Action is not a more or less accidental appendage or after-thought, but is undergoing development and control in the entire knowledge function.

Reality in its characterization as fact, in the logical force which it has in the regulation of the formation and testing of ideas, is not, then, something outside of or given to the reflective situation, but is given or determined *in* it. Reality as such is the entire situation, while fact is a specific determination of it. If the reflective situation were purely intellectualistic, then the objective idealist would have logic on his side; but since it is a focusing of a disturbed system of activities and divided values on their way to a unified situation of harmonized values, we have a dynamic realism. Similarly the idea is not a fixed thing, an entity existing in some ontological psychical region, and then happening to get caught in a reflective situation. If it were, either the subjective idealist would be right, or else the determination of truth would by its nature be impossible. But idea is a logical determination, ultimately practical in origin and function. What on one side is a name for operative realism, names on the other an experimental idealism.

In conclusion, I remark that the ease with which the practical character of these fundamental logical categories, fact, meaning and agreement, may be overlooked or denied is due to the thoroughly organic way in which practical import is already incarnate in them. It can be overlooked because it is so involved in the terms themselves that it is assumed at every turn. The pragmatist is in the position of one who is charged with denying the existence of a certain reality, because in pointing out a certain fundamental feature of that reality which previously had not been stated but assumed, he puts the affair in such a strange light as to appear arbitrarily to change its character. Such a confusion always occurs when the familiar is brought to definition. The difficulties are more psychological,—difficulties of orientation and mental adjustment,—than logical, and in the long run will be done away with by getting used to the different view-point, so as to see things from it, rather than by argument. Meanwhile the argument of this paper is proffered in the hope that it may, with some, facilitate the process of habituation. JOHN DEWEY.

COLUMBIA UNIVERSITY.

The Journal of Philosophy

Psychology and Scientific Methods

A REVIEW OF PRAGMATISM AS A THEORY OF KNOWLEDGE[1]

IN preparing this paper I have become aware in myself of a certain habit of mind. It has arisen, I imagine, from repeated attempts to clarify obscure issues in lecturing to students: but whatever its psychological source, it seems worth while to describe it for the light which it throws upon the theory of knowledge to which I shall be more or less explicitly appealing in my criticism of pragmatism. I find myself attempting to demonstrate, in the sense of *showing* or *making to appear*. Philosophical topics, to be sure, do not readily lend themselves to this mode of treatment; nevertheless I find myself imagining that the object of inquiry may somehow be set down between my hearers and myself where we can survey it together and perhaps eventually agree because we are both looking at the same thing. In other words, I always try to simulate the presence of the experience to which the problem refers. The present task, involving both my readers and myself, would thus seem to me to be the joint examination of a complex but familiar experience wherein Messrs. James, Schiller, Dewey *et al.* have found certain elements and relations which they take to be highly significant, and

[1] In making this study of pragmatism, I have relied mainly on the following sources: William James: 'Humanism and Truth,' *Mind*, N. S., Vol. XIII.; 'Pragmatism's Conception of Truth,' this JOURNAL, Vol. IV., p. 141; 'A Defense of Pragmatism,' *Popular Science Monthly*, Vol. LXX., Nos. 3 and 4. Schiller: 'Humanism'; 'In Defense of Humanism,' *Mind*, N. S., Vol. XIII. John Dewey: 'Logical Studies'; 'The Reflex Arc Concept,' *Psychological Review*, Vol. III.; 'The Experimental Theory of Knowledge,' *Mind*, N. S., Vol. XV. A. W. Moore: 'Existence, Meaning and Reality in Locke's Essay,' University of Chicago Decennial Publications; 'The Functional *versus* the Representational Theories of Knowledge in Locke's Essay,' University of Chicago Contributions to Philosophy. G. H. Mead: 'The Definition of the Psychical,' University of Chicago Decennial Publications. H. H. Bawden: 'The Functional View of the Relation between the Psychical and the Physical,' *Philosophical Review*, Vol. XI.; 'The Functional Theory of Parallelism,' *Philosophical Review*, Vol. XII.; 'The Meaning of the Psychical from the Point of View of the Functional Psychology,' *Philosophical Review*, Vol. XIII.

which they have more or less consistently and intelligibly described in their theory of truth. Does the same experience reveal to us what it has revealed to the pragmatist? Will what the pragmatist sees there stand the light of renewed examination; will it resolve itself into something else, or will it vanish away like a ghost at the approach of dawn? Is pragmatism a reality, an illusion or a hallucination? In thus formulating the question I am supposing that truth is discovered and critically inspected experience; that to know is to see, whether with the bodily eye or with the eye of the soul; and that knowledge is perfected when the idea coincides with its object in direct apprehension. Whatever the outcome of our inquiry, there is a certain immediate advantage in the use of this method; for it makes negative criticism impossible. If we are unable to confirm the finding of the pragmatists, it must be because we have found something else.

If pragmatism is to be examined in the manner which I have indicated, it is necessary that we should first discover its locus in experience. What is pragmatism a description *of*, or a theory *about?* Now it is entirely clear that pragmatism is not, primarily, at least, a theory of reality, but a theory of knowledge. The term truth is here used as qualifying thought rather than being. At the very outset there is danger of confusion because of the ambiguity of such a term as truth. It is of the very nature of knowledge that at the point where it is true it sustains relations of peculiar intimacy with being. It is both true *for* a knower and true *of* being. Indeed, the same ambiguity attaches to the term knowledge, for knowledge is not held to be really knowledge until it is true. But it is clear that the pragmatist arrives at what he calls truth by following the series of thought rather than the series of being. There is a stage in thought at which the thinker possesses the assurance of truth, after the raising of some question, the trial of alternatives and the affirmation of some one of them. The thinker at length believes or makes up his mind; and in this experience thought is concluded. The enterprise is finished, and the activity suspended, even though at some later time the thinker may be compelled to judge retrospectively that he was in error. "What we want," says Professor Dewey, "is something that takes itself as knowledge, rightly or wrongly."[2] Since, then, the truth which the pragmatist is talking about is the concluding phase of thought, we may properly refer his description to the experience of *arriving at belief*. This may be said to be the locus of pragmatism; and in examining this experience we ought either to see what the pragmatist sees or something which accounts for it while correcting it or

[2] 'The Experimental Theory of Knowledge,' *Mind*, N. S., Vol. XV., p. 20.

replacing it. I have found the pragmatist's description of the thought-process highly obscure, but shall venture a brief preliminary outline of what I have been able to understand and verify for myself. He marks in the first place what we may call a prediscursive experience wherein knowledge and its object are not as yet distinguished. In this experience the controlling principles are practical. Life is going on, consisting in attitudes appropriately expressing desires and purposes. The organism is herein well adapted to its environment; it possesses sufficient familiarity with the environment to run smoothly and act unhesitatingly. But there now appears a new phase of experience in which the properly cognitive situation stands revealed. The transition is described by Professor Dewey as 'a disintegration of coordination,' by Professor Moore as an 'interruption in the continuity of habit' and by Professor Bawden as a condition of 'tension.' This, as I understand it, is the state of thought as that arises in the course of conduct. A situation puzzles me, and I require so to conceive it as to be enabled to resume my action. Such a moment is analyzable into the following factors:

1. *Reality, or Beliefs already Fixed.*—This element of experience is the object (this term now appearing for the first time) in so far as already known. The pragmatists would seem to disagree among themselves as to whether sensation belongs to this category or to the next. Let us designate this factor of the situation by the letter M.

2. *The Object as Problematic.*—This is the disturbing factor, consisting in a sensation as yet unresolved, or in a general discord which makes the situation practically unworkable. Let us designate this factor as x.

3. *Ideas*, or, to quote Professor Moore's phrase, '*Instruments of Reconstruction.*' These elements, which we may designate as a', b', c', are tentative interpretations of x, and mark the period of deliberative hesitation.

4. *The Noetic Interest.*—Herein appears for the first time the subject or the knower himself, experienced as a particular need actively attempting to relieve itself. Let us designate this as S. S is not to be identified through its content so much as through its 'polar' relation to O.

The interest S will be realized when, x having been assimilated to M, conduct is resumed and experience enters upon a postdiscursive immediacy. The resolution of the situation will take place in something like the following manner. S projects judgments x *is* a', x *is* b', x *is* c', etc. Of these x *is* a' alone proves compatible with M. In the selected affirmation x *is* a, a' loses its ideal status and becomes homogeneous with M, but at this point $M + a$, or object believed, loses its objectivity or difference from S, and the cognitive experience is replaced by the normal practical immediacy.

Now, the locus of truth, as the pragmatist describes it, is the point at which this complex cognitive structure begins to collapse or shut up. Some such process indubitably occurs, and the pragmatist is correct in directing our attention to its critical moment. The locus of true knowledge is doubtless at the point of transition from discursive to immediate experience. But *what in this moment constitutes its truth?* To answer that question correctly is to answer the question which pragmatism, as a theory of truth, explicitly raises. Unfortunately, the answer of the pragmatist is not clear or unequivocal. Indeed, there seem to be many answers which are not reciprocally necessary, if, indeed, they are compatible. To the end of clarifying the issue I shall from this point forth discuss seven distinct propositions, all of which refer directly or indirectly to the situation just described, and all of which are to be found in the current writings of the pragmatists.[3] Some of these propositions seem to me to be a correct reading of the situation, others not. Whether pragmatism requires that they shall all be true or can identify itself with some of them, I shall leave it to the reader to conclude.

I. *Truth in Knowledge is always Relative to a Particular Intention.* The pragmatist together with the idealist has done well to insist upon this proposition. The truth or falsity of any judgment depends, as every one will readily agree, upon what is meant. No one attempts either to verify or to refute any conclusion until one has identified its reference. One can always escape a specific charge of error by saying, 'I did not mean that.' One who does not mean anything or who can not distinguish what one means from what one does not mean, may from the critical point of view be disregarded entirely. However, it is important to guard this generalization. The truth or error of knowledge is relative to an intention to know some one thing rather than some other thing, to know x rather than y, and not upon an intention to put the knowledge to some use. Thus, I may intend to vote for the man with the cleanest record, and proceed to discover him; but it is the latter intention alone, the intention to discover that one among the candidates who has the cleanest record, to which my ensuing belief is relative as respects its truth or error. It is clear that the truth or error of one's judgment depends upon what one wants to know, but there is no ground for saying that it depends upon what one wishes to do with the knowledge when one gets it. One may always reserve beliefs for subsequent uses that

---

[3] Three of these propositions will be examined in the present paper, and the others in a paper entitled ' A Review of Pragmatism as a Philosophical Generalization '—to appear in a later number of this JOURNAL.

at the time of their formation are highly problematic. It may be true that one always wants knowledge for some other than cognitive purpose, but such ulterior purposes, vague and tentative as they are, clearly have nothing to do with that *specific* intention upon which the proof of a judgment turns.

We may follow the pragmatist, then, so far as to agree that the truth or error of a judgment involves reference to the particular situation in which it arises. The truth or falsity of the judgment x *is a* could not be proved by any knower who was not in possession of x. There is still, it is true, a very significant question which the pragmatist has not clearly answered. How is an intention to be identified? How is the question 'What is x?' to be distinguished from the question 'What is y?' Questions can not be identified merely through identifying the thinker, for the same thinker may ask many questions, and many thinkers may ask the same question. Reverting to the general thought process as described above, I can find no answer to this question unless we are willing to designate the intention by its real content. I find that an intention to know some particular thing is identified only through that particular thing which one intends to know. In other words, a problematic x can be distinguished from a problematic y only so far as x has a being, or real quality, different from that of y. In this case, then, x in the above analysis must always be homogeneous with M, except as respects clearness or adequacy. The significance of this will, I trust, appear later. There is a certain verification of it in the fact that whenever we are in doubt as to our cognitive intention, we deal with experience as realistically as possible. I can best indicate to you what I am thinking about by pointing to the thing itself or setting it down between us.

II. *The Proof of Knowledge Must be Contained in the Process or State of Knowledge.* Professor James says: "Is it not obvious that even though there be . . . absolute sailing directions in the shape of prehuman standards of truth that we *ought* to follow, the only guarantee that we shall in fact follow them lies in our human equipment? The ought would be a *brutum fulmen* unless there were a felt grain inside of our experience that conspired."[4] Although this is an important and far-reaching proposition, I do not hesitate to accept it; for it appears to me to be self-evident. It means, for our purposes, that all the elements for the proof of knowledge must be contained within the thought process itself, as analyzed above. The guarantee of knowledge as true can not consist in any *ab extra* verification. If I am to know at all, I must be cognitively self-sufficient.

4 'Humanism and Truth,' *Mind*, N. S., Vol. XIII., pp. 464–465.

The verification of my knowledge must be internal, an experienced relation between my intention and my progressive enlightenment. All of the elements which enter into my conviction of truth must be elements of my own experience. I can be convicted of error only through being led to correct my own initial experience in the light of my own wider experience. To suppose the contrary is equivalent to declaring of every particular state of knowledge that in itself it is not true knowledge. Even if we prefer to conceive of one absolute knower as alone typical, we must suppose even such a knower to rely upon his own internal conviction, even for the knowledge of his own finality. If the absolute is to know that he is absolute, the proof of it must lie among the elements of his own experience. But if we thus restrict knowledge to the absolute knower, we involve ourselves in a predicament as embarrassing as it is unnecessary. For it would then follow that only an absolute knower could know that there is an absolute knower. Indeed, such a proposition as is involved in the judgment 'I know that only God knows' (equivalent to 'I know that I can not know') is a flat contradiction. We can not even attribute to an absolute knower any superior qualifications for knowledge except such as arise from a completer experience of the particular things which he proposes to know; and similarly the sufficiency of my own experience will always be determined by the degree to which I have covered the particular things which I propose to know. There is no virtue in irrelevant experience, no matter how widely it may be extended. The way to adequate knowledge is not the general increase of experience, but close application to the matter in hand. We conclude, therefore, that if knowledge is not to be pronounced absurd *a priori*, the so-called finite or human knower must glean truth out of his own experience; must, in short, find among the elements embraced in the cognitive experience as above analyzed the certification of his own knowledge.[5] This is, of course, far from saying that the proof of truth must be referred to the caprice of the individual, for among the elements contained in the individual experience are certain elements which possess the status of reality or being. These are as proper parts of the cognitive process as is the alleged active interest which distinguishes itself from them. Our conclusion thus far means only that to know truly involves nothing beyond what is covered by the knower's own experience.

The issue is sometimes obscured by phrasing the question: How do I know that I know? But this complexity of phrase contributes

---

[5] It could easily be shown, following out what has been said above, that unless one could know within the bounds of one's own experience, one could not even *intend* to know.

absolutely no additional meaning. I know that I know in precisely the same way that I know anything else. What we are seeking is not a description of that particular kind of knowledge in which knowledge is also the object known, but a description of that which is common to all cases of knowledge. How do I know that x is a, that y is b, or, in general, *how* do I know?

Now thus far I find in pragmatism nothing from which experience forces me to dissent. In every case of knowledge there is an intention, and the proof of truth must be an experienced sequel to that intention. In every case of true knowledge there is one who intends, and it is he, if any one, who knows the truth concerning his intention. It is revealed to him. True knowledge is sought and found by a knower in one identical and self-sufficient process.

III. *The Mark of the Truth of Knowledge is the Satisfying Character of the Practical Transition from Cognitive Expectation to Fulfillment, or of the Resolution of Doubt into Practical Immediacy.*—I have had no little difficulty in thus phrasing what I believe to be the crucial thesis in pragmatism, but I trust that this proposition when elucidated will prove acceptable. In the analysis with which I first presented the problem, I indicated what we may all agree to be the moment at which knowledge becomes true. There is a period of arrest followed by a moment of release. This series may with entire propriety be construed in practical terms. It possesses all the characteristics of a practical enterprise,—interest, desire, hope, fear, suspense, excitement, delight, and a satisfaction which gradually loses its feeling intensity. If I describe the moment of truth according to its place in this series, it will undoubtedly be that moment in which suspense is relieved and replaced by satisfaction. Now the pragmatist, as I understand him, conceives that when that moment is thus described the element of truth is defined. The truth of belief, in other words, is to be marked by its place retrospective and prospective in the enterprise of thought. Thus Professor James says that, according to pragmatism, 'the truth of any statement *consists* in the consequences, and particularly in their being good consequences.'[6] Now it must be observed that the essence of the matter is the degree to which the satisfying character of the crucial moment *constitutes* its truth. That the truth when sought and found is satisfying, no one will be disposed to deny; but to say that the satisfaction element is identical with the truth element is another matter. And it would seem to me that the frank empiricism of the pragmatist here provides a disproof of his conclusion. Having insisted properly enough that true knowledge belongs to a practical context, he neglects the fact that precisely at the point where

[6] *Op. cit.*, pp. 31–32.

knowledge is true, it belongs to another context, namely, that of reality. In the very analysis of the pragmatist himself, we may find that which *conditions* the satisfaction to which the pragmatist attaches so much importance. It is because x when construed as a may be assimilated to M that the tension is relieved. It is because the statement is verified through being found consistent with reality, that its consequences are good. There is, in other words, a ground for the satisfaction taken in truth. The knower is satisfied with a certain condition into which his experience is resolved. Truth satisfies because of what it is; the knower, if he is but faithful to his own intention, will be satisfied with nothing else. The pragmatist admits that knowledge is true in so far as verified, but emphasizes the adventure of *verification* to the neglect of that in which verification consists. Now if we examine closely into the nature of the verification, and keep in mind what has been said concerning the intention of the knower, the facts seem to be clear. I can not intend to know x without already experiencing, to the extent of distinguishing, the object which I propose to know. My intention, in other words, is a partial knowledge of the object. My tentative judgments, since they must refer to the object, must be intermittent and equivocal experiences *of it*. When some one of these judgments is verified, some such partial experience steadily persists and develops into the object. But let us refer more explicitly to our introductory analysis. M is reality accepted as such; x designates my intention and must belong to the same context, because it is (though problematically) an object known to be real. When my judgment x *is* a is verified, the experience $M + x$ gives way gradually to the experience $M + a$. Now M is described by the pragmatist as reality. If we substitute for the term 'reality' the phrase 'funded belief,' we have only postponed the issue; for we are supposed to be analyzing a typical instance of the formation of belief and the typical instance involves the acceptance of something as real. We may say, then, that whenever a belief is formed or knowledge is taken to be true, some problematic or confused element of experienced reality is through further examination completed and coordinated with other elements of experienced reality. The essential factors, *consistency* as well as *reality* and *quality,* are all objective, given and not supplied. A judgment is verified when upon further inspection and confrontation with reality it stands its ground. In other words, a judgment is true in so far as it coincides with a proposition or complex entity which is found with its distinguishing characters upon it, and its consistency about it.

The processes of knowledge which for the pragmatist are most typical, are those in which there is a high degree of indirection. The greater the pomp and circumstance of knowledge, or the dramatic interplay of interests, the more important the element of satisfaction. But it is clear that this does not in itself determine truth. I may put experience behind me and make a game of finding it without thereby enhancing the truth of my discovery; for upon the showing of pragmatism itself it is the moment of confirming experience in which the truth shows its face, and there are many such moments in which circumlocution and anticipation play a very small part. It is in perception, enriched and made adequate by thought, that the cognitive moment is seen to the best advantage; and there one knows truly because one's knowledge merges into its object. Now, undoubtedly, indirection is characteristic to a greater or less degree of all knowledge. As I can not know, neither can I, humanly speaking, think, without the use of language and various other expedients for substitution; but it is a fact which the pragmatist is far too inclined to overlook that in cognition symbols can not be employed without an antecedent and explicit knowledge of their reference. It has been possible for me to use verbal symbols in the present discussion only because they may put the reader in mind of the same object which I am contemplating in my own thought; and the truth or falsity of what I say has reference not to the existence or consistency of the words, but to the existence or consistency of certain elements of experience which all parties to the discussion may directly have in mind. So far as I am able to see there are only two legitimate kinds of substitution in knowledge. In the one case, the substitute serves as an index, as a means of communication or record, which will point the thinker to a certain region of experience. In the other case, as when I study social movements in statistical tables, the substitute is partially identical with the object. In both cases my thinking, in so far as true or false, is in terms of the object itself. I think about that to which the verbal symbols point me or about that which is common to the representation and to the object. If this be true, the proof of truth must be sought not in any relation between the terms of discourse as such, but directly in the elements and systematic relations of real experience.

The realistic view which I have here briefly indicated, is, I understand, held by some pragmatists to be consistent with that doctrine; but if this is to be the case it would seem to me that pragmatism must be so reworded as to lose its radical character. It would then mean that truth, since it is an attribute of knowledge, must always be related to a cognitive interest and have characteristics which are derived from that context. This is a very different thing from saying that one is to look to these characteristics for its proof. For pragmatism as a radical doctrine truth is held to *consist* in an experience of satisfaction, such as 'All's well, now I can act.' For realism truth consists in an experience of identification, such as 'Here is a or $M + a$.' These two theories strictly held and strictly interpreted are not compatible. The pragmatist insists that true knowledge is a function of the process of knowledge. The critic of pragmatism insists, firstly, that true knowledge is also a function of the thing known; secondly, that in this latter functional relation is to be found the element of truth. Truth, because it is a part of the cognitive interest, must satisfy; but because it is *truth* it must envisage reality.

In this criticism I have not resorted to a general and vague insistence that true knowledge must 'correspond' to its object. I agree with the pragmatist that this is to take refuge in confusion. At the same time I would insist upon emphasizing the object as the element which plays the determining part in the constitution of truth. Experience seems to me to reveal the identity of true knowledge and its object. The object with what is true of it, and knowledge when true for the thinker, are one and the same thing. But this thing may be regarded in two ways because it belongs to two different series. If the object is approached along the cognitive series, then its uniqueness, its distinction in that series, is due not to its place in that series, but to its belonging to another series. The term *true knowledge* in the cognitive series is marked by its being the term in which this series intersects the series of reality. If the pragmatist is willing to accept this conclusion, then the issue is greatly clarified; but he can not, I believe, do so without largely abandoning those generalizations and philosophical corollaries of which he makes so much.

RALPH BARTON PERRY.

HARVARD UNIVERSITY.

DISCUSSION

PROFESSOR DEWEY'S VIEW OF AGREEMENT

THE article by Professor Dewey on the 'Control of Ideas by Facts' presents such an opportunity for definite questions by reason of its analysis of a specific situation that I can not forbear stating, in an interrogatory form, the difficulties I experience. My agreement with his logical position is so fundamental that any outstanding divergence on minor points must be capable of amendment.

Foregoing preliminaries, I shall plunge into the heart of the matter. Suppose, to use his illustration of the man lost in the wood (p. 201), the man has been hunting and, having bagged enough game, decides to return home. Presently he discovers an unfamiliarity in the appearance of things. We have now desire on the man's part to get home and a recognition that he is lost. Temporarily his action is stopped. He must reflect; but this reflection is for the purpose of enabling him to fulfill his primary desire to get home. Under the new conditions, the old desire has given place to a more complex one involving, consciously, means and end. This signifies that the focus of attention has been shifting gradually. He must find the *way* home. This gives a very complex reflective situation. Observation follows. He sizes up the surroundings, attempting to take in all the relevant facts, such as the lay of the land, the presence of conspicuous objects, the direction of the sun, etc. If he recognizes a landmark, a more or less definitely organized idea of the environment arises. "It is not some little psychical entity or piece of consciousness-stuff, but is the interpretation of the locally present environment in reference to its absent portions . . . " (p. 202). It may be that he isn't certain of the correctness of his idea. If he reaches by its means, however, a place he is sure of, he remarks, if he is reflective, "That idea of mine *was* true." I would lay considerable stress upon the past tense of the proposition.

First, I would raise the question of a possible ambiguity in the use of the term 'plan of action' as synonymous with idea. I admit frankly that the thinking has been purposive, but is the idea a purpose? "That is, acted upon sincerely, it has led to the desired conclusion; it has *through action* worked out the state of things which *it contemplated* or *intended*" (italics mine). Now I would submit that the *man* intended to go home, not the *idea*. Referring back to the analysis above,—in order to get home (primary desire) he discovered that he must find the way (secondary desire). The idea is connected with *that*, not *directly* with the getting home. "The agreement, correspondence, is between purpose, plan and its own execution, fulfillment." Here, again, purpose is made synonymous with plan, and plan, apparently, with idea. It strikes me there are two purposes in the case, one subordinate to the other: (1) to get home, and this is not the idea; (2) to get a true idea of the way, and this again is not the idea.

'As to the agreement of the idea and the environment' (p. 202), Professor Dewey shuts out, first, presented reality, 'for that reality is the reality of himself lost.' I should say, because, by the terms of the problem, presented reality is not the reality wanted. "Not with the complete reality, for that at this stage of proceedings is the idea itself." No, once more, for the reality sought is not present by the very nature of the search. The conscious experience is, I submit, more complex than Professor Dewey realizes. The individual is, in all probability, a practical realist. He has just come from home and believes that the forest stretches away beyond his ken and then gives place to the fields which lead up to his home. Now an adult has certain organized constructs; one of these is the impersonal physical world. I would refer in this connection to James's doctrine of the many worlds. These constructs always have gaps in them when a problem arises concerning them. The man's construct of the physical world is of this kind. He may know the plan of the next village or the direction of New York from Albany, but, just now, he wants to know the way home. Consequently he disregards his other geographical knowledge, because it isn't relevant. It is to fill this particular gap that the idea arises. Until it drops into place, so to speak, it is psychical, personal, *his* idea. If it is admitted to be true, it flows over and, behold! we have our construct with the 'aching void' filled; the problem has disappeared. My terms must remind the reader of James's description of remembering a name, and it is built upon analogy with that. What, then, is the agreement? It would be paradoxical to say 'agreement with this gap,' and yet, in a sense, that is the fact. If it were not for this functional relation of idea as psychical and the physical, impersonal world, postulated but not completely known, the idea would not, when its truth is recognized, fill the gap, in the physical construct, just where it does. This is the movement in what I would call the organization and building up of the physical world. We say the idea *is* true. Why? Because it agrees with the now constructed physical world. We can look at the *same reality as physical and as psychical*. But, natural realists that we are, we believe that the world was that way all the time. We say the idea *was* true. This is where an unconscious duplicity or straddling enters, which I believe accounts for a good deal of the trouble with 'correspondence.' 'Agreement' represents an endeavor to harmonize structure and function, the past and the present. Now this is a perhaps unduly technical way of asserting that we seek to *disregard the fact of reconstruction and growth because we are dealing with a construct that we look upon as non-temporal and impersonal and common.* I do not think this dialectic movement in the erection of an impersonal and *common* world is adequately recognized in discussions of truth. Extreme pragmatists emphasize too strenuously the fact of function, of reconstruction, of change, the personal side. Extreme intellectualists see only the formal, the structural, the timeless, and thus *may* fall into the copy view. As in most controversies, a middle position is more likely to be right. 'Agreement' involves an unconscious attempt by our thought at a reconciliation. Common sense believes 'it was that way all the time if we had only known it.' A warning may prevent misinterpretation. This is a logical question, primarily, and logic has nothing to do, directly, with realism and idealism as metaphysical systems.

Early in this article I criticized Professor Dewey for a confusion of idea and purpose, asserting that the term 'plan of action,' so much used to-day, is ambiguous. An illustration occurs to me that may bring out my position better. Suppose I am standing at one side of a house with a friend, a house we are both acquainted with, and the question arises about the structure of another part of the house, not visible from where we stand. Both of us have ideas which until they are proved by actual observation we regard as personal, while the house is common and impersonal. Later we may have the purpose of going around to see which of us is right, but that is not the idea, nor does the idea guide us. Our 'plan of action' will be to walk around. Before we seek to verify our ideas, what do we believe? If I am not mistaken, that the house there is of a certain form and the invisible portion 'hangs on' the part seen by us. The question before each is, Have I filled it out properly?

Perchance, a side-light can be thrown on this problem by a contrast. Some ideas are plans of action, literally, and yet not concerned with truth. I have a problem at present. It is this, Shall I go to the library or down town? It is surely a reflective situation, and I can think of myself as doing either, but I do not raise the truth question. Why? After I go down town I do not say, I was right. Why, again? Because I am dealing here *with another sort of reality.* Ordinarily people do not regard themselves as determined, as the house is. The very nature of this sort of reality is to be changing, active. It strikes me that genetic analysis of the various constructs we make, would go a long way towards solving logical problems.

R. W. SELLARS.

UNIVERSITY OF MICHIGAN.

THE DILEMMA OF THE INTELLECTUALIST THEORY OF TRUTH

IS the intellectualist in his theory of truth an anarchistic subjectivist? Considerably to my own surprise, reflection has convinced me that he usually is. He insists that truth is a property of ideas (the term is used to include judgments, beliefs, all mental functions having cognitional value) *antecedent* to any process of verification; he insists that this antecedent self-possessed, self-contained property determines the working of an idea, or its verification. It follows that truths come into existence (arise or first subsist) when certain ideas are entertained. Until Columbus (or somebody else) entertained the idea that the world was round, the truth (being a self-contained property of the idea) that the world was round was nonexistent. When the idea that the value of π is 3.1415926 arose in some one's mind, *this* truth was then and there created, and so on.[1] Such is the logical implication of this "antecedent property" theory. Note, further, the accidental and arbitrary way in which ideas arise, if truth is an independent property of them. They just happen. For the intellectualist can not deny that a large share of the ideas of men possess an antecedent property of falsity rather than of truth. If these properties of truth and falsity are ultimate, self-contained, and unique properties; if an idea is as likely to have one kind of property as the other; and if there is nothing in an idea which reveals upon bare inspection which of the two kinds of property is possessed, surely the intellectualist is committed to a belief in the thoroughly atomistic nature of truths.

A reply which the intellectualist might presumably make to these statements will be found only to enforce them. The reply is that the intellectualist holds that the self-contained truth-property of ideas consists in their relation of agreement or correspondence to things. Precisely: he makes the relation of agreement with things which constitutes truth a self-contained property of ideas. It is this very fact which commits him to the baldest kind of psychical idea-ism —not to dignify it with the title of idealism. If there were anything in the so-called cognitive self-transcendency of ideas which concretely lighted upon their intended objects so that their truth or falsity was self-luminous, the appeal of the intellectualist to "agreement with reality" would have some bearing; but since such phosphorescence is notoriously lacking, this so-called "self-transcendency" is obviously, after all, only an internal property of an idea *qua* idea.

I shall, however, be properly reminded that not all intellectualists

[1] I do not raise the question whether truths cease to exist when their ideas vanish, though this would seem also to follow.

make truth a property of ideas. Some make it a property of things, events, objects. That Columbus discovered America, that water is H_2O, are truths independent of *any* ideas. Well then, is not *this* type of intellectualism committed to absolutistic rationalism? If things, events, are properly called truths, then the universe must be conceived as a truth-system, *i. e.*, a system of relations of reason, or as "objective thought." The frantic disclaimers of many contemporary anti-pragmatists of sympathy with the Hegelian theory of truth (or that of Bradley or Royce) seem rather amusing. What escape from sophistic subjectivism have they except this theory? The other day I ran across the following quotation from Bossuet in Janet's Final Causes: "If I now ask where and in what subject these truths subsist, eternal and immutable as they are, I am obliged to own a being wherein truth eternally subsists and is always understood; and this being must be the truth itself, and must be all truth; and from it is derived the truth in all that is."[2] Why not, if truths exist *per se* in the order of nature?

The non-pragmatist, if logical, thus appears as either a pure subjectivist or as an objective absolutist. Usually he is not logical, but oscillates at will between the two positions, using one at need to cover up the weakness of the other.

JOHN DEWEY.

COLUMBIA UNIVERSITY.

[2] English translation, page 395.

THE CONCEPT OF THE NEUTRAL IN RECENT EPISTEMOLOGY

ABOUT the time in which the concept of neutrality was going out of favor in politics it came to the front in epistemology. Some ambiguity seems to attach, however, to the concept of neutrality in the latter as in the former realm. In the interest of clarity, not in that of any particular school of thought, I wish to set forth two meanings which certainly *may* attach to the concept, with the hope that some of those who profess themselves believers in neutral entities may be led to greater explicitness.

In one sense to call anything neutral means neutral *in a specified respect or reference;* that is, with respect to the application of a particular set of alternatives. In this sense, I do not see that "neutral" means more than that a certain conception in either of its forms is inapplicable. To say, for example, that certain things are neutral with respect to the distinction of mental and material would be to say that there are things such that intelligent discussion of them is not forwarded by applying to them, without further specification, the distinctions marked out by the terms "mental-material." What is asserted is the irrelevancy of a certain type of distinction. Thus, before discussing whether a certain term, say "experience," has subjectivistic or objectivistic implications, we might have to consider whether, taken without specific qualifications, it was not rather a neutral term, a term to be used "without prejudice." Such neutral terms, understood to be aloof with reference to certain large antitheses which have had a great rôle in the history of thought, would certainly be a great aid in clearer discussion. For there is always a tendency to assume that the question is which one of two current antitheses is to be applied, when perhaps the primary question is whether either one is applicable.

In contrast with this conceivable meaning of the term neutral, which might be called the logical, stands another which might be called the metaphysical or ontological, namely, that there is a certain sort of stuff which is, intrinsically, neutral. Consequently, it is not necessary to specify any particular *respect* or *reference* in which it is taken as neutral. Rather the attempt is made to discover and describe a particular kind of material or stuff which may be called neutral exactly as a certain stuff may be called lead or wood.

It seems to me clear that nothing is gained (while there is danger that much in clarity and pertinency may be lost) in trying to bring social facts as such under the captions of "subjective" or "objective," or under those of "physical" or "mental." They are both or neither, according to the respect in which they are taken for discussion. To assert that they are "neutral" entities would then be a way of asserting one's conviction of the irrelevancy of introducing the question whether they are mental or material. The same might be said of mathematical terms. But while one might be glad to employ the term neutral if he thought that this was its connotation, one might hesitate to use it if he thought the term meant to convey something positive about the nature and structure of social things and mathematical things, something "metaphysical" over and above what the competent sociologist or mathematician would specifically discover.

Perhaps others share in my feelings that greater explicitness as to the sense in which writers use the term would conduce to clearness. It seems to me, for example, that I noted both senses in the recent discussions of the Philosophical Association. Historically speaking, the ambiguity may be detected, I think, in James's conception of pure experience, a conception having presumably certain affiliations with the contemporary conception of the neutral. At times Mr. James identifies a pure experience with experience of a peculiar subject-matter or stuff; it is of something which *antecedes* all reflection. It is a presence of a *that* which is not a *what*. Its description is highly reminiscent of some of the things said about sensation in his *Psychology*.[1] But the term pure experience is also given a radically different meaning. Contrast with the doctrine just laid down the following: "The instant field of the present is always experience in its 'pure' state, plain unqualified actuality, a simple *that*, as yet undifferentiated into thing and thought, and only virtually classifiable as objective fact or as some one's opinion about fact."[2] According to this passage, the experience in which a distinction is made between fact and opinion is itself, as a direct occurrence, "pure" of the distinction; it is "neutral" in reference to it. In this sense, pure experience is not characterized by possessing or presenting any peculiar subject-matter. The experience of any subject-matter, whether perceptual or conceptual, simple or complicated, elementary or systematized, just *as* an experience is pure or neutral. Only later on can it be referred to or classified, and so be treated as mental or physical. The following passage is, if possible, even more explicit in the same sense: "Let the reader arrest himself in the act of reading this article now. *Now* this is a pure experience. . . . Reading simply is, is there; and whether there for some one's con-

---

[1] Compare *Essays in Radical Empiricism*, p. 93, and its assertion that only the new born babe has pure experience, with *Principles of Psychology*, Vol. II., p. 7, and its assertion that "pure sensations can only be realized in the earliest days of life."

[2] *Radical Empiricism*, p. 74.

sciousness, or there for physical nature, is a question not yet put."[3] And he sums up by saying that the *point* of the pure experience theory is that any experience (not simply that of the new born babe) is in itself innocent of the "inner" or "outer" quality. The "inner-outer" distinction has to do with a classification made for a specific purpose and need. If we do not have the purpose, we do not classify; the distinction is irrelevant. In present language, in itself *any* experience is neutral. Consequently neutrality is not a matter of a peculiar stuff or distinctive element. This position seems to me as sound as appeal to the hypothetical experience of the new born babe is trivial or misleading. Such "purity" as the latter possesses is something to outgrow as rapidly as the baby in fact does outgrow it. It is not something to which to appeal as philosophically enlightening, much less as a philosophical norm or standard.

I venture to add that the contemporary conception of neutral entities as in themselves a particular kind of being seems to be derivable from a combination of this notion of James (which, as he pointed out, was influenced by Mach) with one obtained by an excursion of Münsterberg into the epistemology of psychology. In his article on "Psychological Atomism" he held that distinguishable sensations are molecules as it were of which the elementary atoms are not distinguishable, but which have to be assumed to satisfy certain scientific requirements.[4] Mr. Münsterberg assumed indeed that these "inexperiencable" psychical atoms were radically different from physical atoms. But bring the pure and neutral sensation of the infant (taken from James) to bear upon these elements which determine the material and processes of our complex experience (according to Münsterberg) and you get something extraordinarily like the neutral entities out of which, according to Holt, physical and mental entities are both built up.

JOHN DEWEY.

COLUMBIA UNIVERSITY.

---

[3] *Radical Empiricism*, p. 145.
[4] *Psychological Review*, Vol. VII., pp. 1–17.

THE JOURNAL OF PHILOSOPHY
PSYCHOLOGY AND SCIENTIFIC METHODS

PROFESSOR DEWEY'S "ESSAYS IN EXPERIMENTAL LOGIC"

IN reading this collection of essays, I have been conscious of a much greater measure of agreement than the author would consider justifiable on my part. In particular, in passages dealing with my own views, I have often found that the only thing I disagreed with was the opinion that what was said constituted a criticism of me. There seems to me quite clearly to be, in Professor Dewey's outlook, a misunderstanding of some, at least, of the "analytic realists." I shall try, in what follows, chiefly to remove this misunderstanding. Philosophical writing, as a rule, is to my mind far too eristic. There are various classes of difficulties to be dealt with in philosophy, each fairly easy to solve if it stood alone. Each philosopher invents a solution applicable to his own problems, and refuses to recognize those of others. He sees that the theories of others do not solve his problems, but he refuses to see that his theories do not solve the problems of others. I do not wish to offer merely another example of this kind of blindness, since I consider that it constitutes a most serious obstacle to the progress of philosophy. In return, I would beg Professor Dewey to believe that certain questions which interest me can not be solved unless his doctrines are supplemented by theories brought from a region into which, as yet, he has not thought it necessary to penetrate.

A misunderstanding, as between him and those who hold views more akin to mine, is likely to arise through different use of terms. What he calls "logic" does not seem to me to be part of logic at all; I should call it part of psychology. He takes the view—for which there is much better authority than for mine—that logic is concerned with thought. The ways in which we become possessed of what we call "knowledge" are, for him, questions of "logic." His book is said to consist of studies in experimental "logic." Now in the sense in which I use the word, there is hardly any "logic" in the book except the suggestion that judgments of practise yield a special form—a suggestion which belongs to logic in my sense, though I do

231

not accept it as a valid one. A great deal of his criticism of my views on the external world rests, I think, upon this difference of terminology. He insists that what I call data are logical, not psychological, data, and in his sense of these words I entirely agree. I never intended them to be regarded as data which would be psychological in his sense. The subject which I call "logic" is one which apparently does not seem to Professor Dewey a very important one. No doubt he feels that I attach too little importance to matters which he regards as vital. This differing estimate of relative importance is, I think, the main source of differences between him and me. I hope that, if both recognize this, the differences may come to be greatly diminished. It is in this hope, and not in a spirit of controversy, that the following pages are written.

I. LOGICAL AND PSYCHOLOGICAL DATA

I will try first of all to set forth what I conceive to be the most important features, from my point of view, in Professor Dewey's doctrine as regards data. To a great extent I am in agreement with his doctrine; but I shall leave the critical consideration of it until I have endeavored to state it. Let us begin with some quotations.

1. "That fruitful thinking—thought that terminates in valid knowledge—goes on in terms of the distinction of facts and judgment, and that valid knowledge is precisely genuine correspondence or agreement, *of some sort*, of fact and judgment, is the common and undeniable assumption" (p. 231).

2. "A functional logic . . . has never for a moment denied the *prima facie* working distinction between 'ideas,' 'thoughts,' 'meanings,' and 'facts,' 'existences,' 'the environment,' nor the necessity of a control of meaning by facts" (p. 236).

3. "The position taken in the essays is frankly realistic in acknowledging that certain brute existences, detected or laid bare by thinking but in no way constituted out of thought or any mental process, set every problem for reflection and hence serve to test its otherwise merely speculative results" (p. 35).

4. *Perceptions* are not themselves cases of knowledge, but they are the source of all our knowledge of the world: "They are the sole ultimate data, the sole media, of inference to all natural objects and processes. While we do not, in any intelligible or verifiable sense, know *them*, we know all things that we do know *with* or *by* them. They furnish the only ultimate evidence of the existence and nature of the objects which we infer, and they are the sole ultimate checks and tests of the inferences. Because of this characteristic use of perceptions, the perceptions themselves acquire, by 'second intention,' a knowledge status. They *become* objects of minute, accurate, and experimental scrutiny" (pp. 259–260).

5. But this cognitive function of perceptions is derivative. It is a "superstition" that "sensations-perceptions are cases of knowledge. . . . Let them [the realists] try the experiment of conceiving perceptions as pure natural events, not as cases of awareness or apprehension, and they will be surprised to see how little they miss" (p. 262).

6. "To find out *what is* given is an inquiry which taxes reflection to the uttermost. Every important advance in scientific methods means better agencies, more skilled technique for simply detaching and describing what is barely there, or given" (p. 152).

7. "According to Mr. James, for example, the original datum is large but confused, and specific sensible qualities represent the result of discriminations. In this case, the elementary data, instead of being primitive empirical data, are the last terms, the limits, of the discriminations we have been able to make" (pp. 298–299).

These quotations may serve for the moment to illustrate Professor Dewey's doctrine as regards data.

The first three raise no point of controversy as between him and me. The sixth and seventh, though I believe he would regard them as affording an argument against some of my views, certainly do not say anything that I disagree with, except in so far as there is an ambiguity in the second sentence of the seventh: "primitive empirical data" may mean primitive in time, or primitive in logic. The logical articulation of a man's knowledge changes as his knowledge increases; at every stage, there will be parts of his knowledge that are logically more primitive and parts that are logically less so. What, at an advanced stage of knowledge, is primitive in logic, may be very far from primitive in time. The last terms in our discriminations are very likely to become *logically* primitive in our knowledge very soon after we have reached them. But if Professor Dewey means "primitive in time," there is no matter of disagreement between us so far.

The different senses in which things may be "data" need to be considered somewhat more fully, if misunderstandings are to be removed. When I speak of "data," more particularly of "hard data," I am not thinking of those objects which constitute data to children or monkeys: I am thinking of the objects which seem data to a trained scientific observer. It is quite consciously and deliberately, not by mistake, that I am thinking of the trained observer. The kind of "datum" I have in mind is the kind which constitutes the outcome of an experiment, say in physics. We have reason to expect *this* or *that; this* happens. Then *this* is what I call datum. The fact that *this* has happened is a premiss in the reasoning of the man of science; it is not deduced, but simply observed. The state of mind that I am imagining in investigating the problem of the physical world is not a naïve state of mind, but one of Cartesian doubt.

The confusion between the two kinds of primitiveness[1] is not

---

[1] When Professor Dewey speaks (p. 406) of "Russell's trusting confidence in 'atomic' propositions as psychological primitives," he is imagining that I mean one sort of primitiveness when in fact I mean another. I mean what would be a premiss to a careful man of science, not what is a premiss to a baby or a gorilla.

always easy to avoid. In those whose knowledge has not reached a high level of logical articulation, there will be comparatively little that is logically derivative. The habit of reasoning and inferring and binding together different pieces of knowledge into a single logical system increases the proportion of logically derivative knowledge, and the deductive weight that has to be supported by what remains logically primitive. One thing that makes the problem exceedingly confusing is that even what we are calling the *logical* articulation of a man's knowledge is still a question of psychology, in part at least. If a man believes two propositions p and q, and if p implies q though he has never noticed this fact, then p and q are separate pieces of his knowledge, though not separate in abstract logic. The logical articulation of a man's knowledge is subject to restrictions imposed by logic, since we shall not regard one part of his knowledge as logically derivative in relation to another unless it is logically inferable, as well as psychologically inferred by him; but although logic thus enters in as controlling the possible articulations of a man's knowledge, logic alone can not determine them, and his individual psychology is required in addition in order to fix the actual logical order among his beliefs.

We have thus three different problems, one of pure psychology, one of mixed psychology and logic, and one of pure logic. We may illustrate the three problems by means of the science of physics.

1. The problem of pure psychology is this: How do we, as a matter of history, come by the beliefs we have about material objects? What earlier beliefs preceded those which we now entertain, either in the individual or in the race? What vaguer state than "belief" precedes the growth of even the earliest beliefs? And what vaguer objects than those presented to a trained observation are to be found in a less sophisticated experience? All these are questions of psychology. They are questions which I, for my part, have not attempted to discuss. Nothing that I have said on the problem of the external world is intended to be applicable to them.

2. The problem of mixed psychology and logic is this: How do we, ordinary persons with a working knowledge of physics, organize our physical beliefs from a logical point of view? What, if we are challenged, and an attempt is made to make us doubt the truth of physics, shall we fall back upon as giving a basis for our belief which we are not prepared to abandon? Take, say, the facts out of which modern physics grew: Galileo's observations on falling bodies. We have in Galileo's work a mixture of argument, inference, mathematics, with something else which is not argued or inferred, but observed. For him, this something else constituted part of what was logically primitive. To those who are troubled by skepticism, the

discovery of what is logically primitive in their own beliefs (or half-beliefs) appears important as a possible help in deciding as to their truth or falsehood. We will call the primitive in this sense the "epistemological primitive." It is the primitive in this sense that I mean when I speak of "data." I agree entirely with Professor Dewey when he says (p. 428): "To make sure that a given fact *is* just and such a shade of red is, one may say, a final triumph of scientific method;" but when he goes on to say: "To turn, around and treat it as something naturally or psychologically given is a monstrous superstition," we shall no longer agree if we are speaking of "data" in the sense of "epistemological primitives" rather than temporal primitives.

3. In addition to these, there is, or may be, a third kind of primitive, namely, the *pure* logical primitive. This, when it can be defined, can only be defined by logical simplicity or deductive power. A deductive system is preferable when its premisses are few and simple than when they are many and complicated, but this seems to be mainly an esthetic question. There is, however, something beyond this in logical simplicity. The law of gravitation, for example, implies Kepler's three laws, and much besides; in this sense, as a premiss, it is logically preferable to them. Although, often, in a deductive system, there will be a certain element of arbitrariness in the choice of premisses, yet the arbitrariness is restricted: there will be, usually, a fairly small collection of propositions from among which it is clear that the logical premisses should be chosen. And the more advanced the logical organization of the system, the more restricted will be the choice of premisses. But this sense of "primitive" does not enter into inquiries of which the purpose is to find out whether the grounds for believing some body of scientific propositions are sufficient. In such inquiries, it is the second sense of "primitive," the epistemological sense, that is important. The pure psychological and the pure logical are alike irrelevant. And it is in the second sense that I speak of "data" in discussing the problem of the external world. As an example of the search for the logical primitive in physics, we may take Herz's *Principien der Mechanik*. In this book the author is not concerned to persuade us that physics is true, but to find the best way of stating premisses from which physics (supposed known) can be deduced.

There is a problem as regards the comparative merit of the differing psychological data at various levels. The common-sense view is that greater discrimination and more analytic observation yield more knowledge. It is supposed that we know more about an object which we have inspected closely, with attention to parts and differentiation, than about an object of which we have only what is called a "general impression." The successes of science, whose observation of facts is highly analytic, have confirmed the view that observation of this sort yields the most information. But as against this common-sense view we have a sort of artificially archaistic view, which opposes analysis, believes in a faculty of "intuition" possessed by peasant women, dogs, and ichneumon wasps, loves savage religions, and maintains that the progress of intellect has driven wisdom away from almost all men except the few immovable philosophers among whom intellect has not progressed. Those who adopt this artificially archaistic view believe that the large confused data spoken of by James (in the seventh of our above quotations) have more capacity for revealing truth than is to be found in scientific observations. I do not think that Professor Dewey belongs to those who take this view. Accordingly he does not regard the vaguer data as giving more knowledge than those that are more analyzed. But there are aspects of his theories which might mistakenly suggest that he took this view.

I do not wish, at the moment, to consider Professor Dewey's views so much as to consider the problem in itself. The problem concerned is what we may call the problem of "vagueness." It may be illustrated by what occurs while we watch a man walking towards us on a long straight road. At first we see only a vague dot; we can not tell whether it is moving; we only guess that it is a human being because it seems about the right size. Gradually it passes through various grades of growing distinctness: we recognize it as so-and-so, and at last we see what sort of expression he has on his face, and whether he looks well or ill. In this case, it is clear that the more analyzed apprehension enables us to know more. We can more or less infer what a man would look like a long way off when we see him near at hand; but the converse inference is much more circumscribed. Now although, in the case of the man approaching along a road, our attention remains throughout equally analytic in character, and the changes that occur are due merely to the fact that the object comes nearer, yet I think that there is a close analogy between the quick changes in this case and the slow changes in the case of increasing powers of analytic attention. In these changes also, I think, what happens is that more differentiations exist in the new datum, and that the new datum allows more inferences than the old one. At the same time, as in the case of the man approaching, what (to save trouble) we may call the same physical object gradually comes to occupy a larger portion of the field of attention, so that, although more is known about an object which remains within the field of attention, there are fewer such objects at any one time. A man who is reading sees differences on the printed page which are probably more minute than any that a dog ever sees, but while he is seeing them he may miss other things which the dog would never miss, for instance a person speaking to him. There seems no reason to reject the common-sense view that, through trained attention, we acquire more knowledge about the things we attend to, but become more restricted as regards the area of attention.

Following the analogy of the man on the road, whom I will now suppose seen simultaneously by a number of people at different distances, I suggest that it is possible, theoretically at least, to distinguish elements, in the perceptions of all these people, which are correlated and may be called perceptions "of" the one man. For the moment I do not wish to go into the meaning of this "of"; it is enough that these elements are correlated in the way that leads to their being said to be "of" one object. It is not necessary that the element which is a perception of the man in question should be consciously isolated and attended to by the person who has it: it is enough that it occurs, regardless of whether anybody knows that it does. (But of course the hypothesis that it sometimes occurs without anybody's knowing is based upon what *is* known.) Now among the correlated occurrences which we call perceptions of the one man, some allow more inference as to the others and some less. Those that allow less we will define as "vaguer;" those that allow more, as "less vague." Those that are less vague are more differentiated: they consist of more parts. In a very vague perception of the man, he is an undifferentiated dot. In a still vaguer perception, the whole man may be absorbed into the smallest discriminated element: we may see a distant regiment as a speck, without being able to distinguish its component men. In all this, I am accepting common sense. It may be necessary to abandon common sense on some points, but in all that concerns vagueness what I wish to maintain is in the closest agreement with common sense.

We may lay down the following common-sense propositions. (1) All that we learn through the senses is more or less vague. (2) What we learn by careful analytic attention of the scientific kind is less vague than what we learn by causal untrained attention; what we learn by seeing things close at hand is less vague than what we learn by seeing them at a distance. (3) Even the vaguest perception has *some* value for purposes of inference, but the vaguer it is the smaller becomes its value for inference. From these characteristics we may advance to those implied in the above definition of vagueness. The inferences drawn from what we perceive (or the expectations aroused) are motived by habitual correlations.[2] And the correlations of this sort (*e. g.*, those between what are called appearances of a given object at different distances) are many-one correlations: many different appearances near-to will all correspond to the same appearance further off. Wherever we have a many-one correlation, the "one" can be inferred from any of the "many," but not vice versa; we have the "one" determined by any of the "many" but not any of the "many" by the "one." It seems to me that the vague data of unanalytic attention are just as "true" as the more precise data of trained observation, but allow fewer inferences. We might illustrate the matter by an analogy. If you are told that a man is descended from Adam, that gives you the vaguest possible information as to his ancestry; if you are told that he is descended from William the Conqueror, that is still pretty vague; but as the generations grow later, the information that a man is descended from so-and-so becomes more and more significant. The reason is that the relation of son to father is many-one: when you are told that B is a son of A, and Z is descended from B, you can infer that Z is descended from A; but when you are told that Z is descended from A, you can not infer that he is descended from B, because he may be descended from one of A's other children. So it is with correlated perceptions: the vaguer correspond to the earlier generations and the more precise to the later. But of course in the case of perceptions there is possible continuity instead of the discreteness of generations.

I claim for the above view of the relation between psychologically primitive data and the precise data of science various merits which, as I shall try to show, do not seem to be possessed by Professor Dewey's theory.

(*a*) The transition, as we have been explaining it, is a continuous one, and is one not having a terminus in either direction. No perception can be so precise as to be incapable of greater precision— unless, indeed, we were to accept, in regard to all physical things, the theory of *quanta*, and hold that all physical quantities are discrete, in which case there would be a theoretical limit of complete exactitude, though of course far below the threshold of our perceptions. And at the other end of the scale, no perception can be so vague as to be incapable of greater vagueness, unless, indeed, the world appeared always just the same whatever the environment might be. Perhaps absence of life might consist in this absolute vagueness; but where there is life, even so low in the scale as the amoeba, an environment which contains food will seem different from one

---

[2] These inferences are not logically cogent, and are sometimes mistaken, but that is a point that need not concern us at this moment.

which does not (to judge by behavior), and will therefore be perceived with less than the maximum of vagueness.

(*b*) Another advantage of our definition and theory is that it allows *some* inferential value to even very vague data. It does not have to say: The precise observation of the scientist gives truth, and the vague feeling of the infant gives error. Still less does it have to say the opposite. Assuming a common-sense world, and leaving aside all doubts as to causality, induction, *etc.*, our perceptions always give tolerable ground for *some* expectation or inference; but though the vaguer perceptions may give inferences which (in some sense) cover a wider field, the more precise perceptions allow more inferences within the field they cover. That is to say, suppose what is originally one vague object of attention A (a crowd, say) is correlated with what are later ten more precise objects of attention (ten men, say), then regarding any one of these ten (Z, say) the system of its correlates can be better known when Z is perceived than it could when only A was perceived.

(*c*) Connected with this is one of the great merits of our theory: namely, that it does not involve an Unknowable, either at the beginning or at the end, because the differences involved are differences of degree, and it is not necessary to assume the existence of an unattainable limit in either direction. There will doubtless be degrees that are *unknown*, but that is a different matter from having to declare them *unknowable*. Any one of them might become known at any moment. The case is analogous to that of a large finite integer which no one has ever happened to think of: any one *might* think of it any moment. In like manner any degree of vagueness or exactitude might be attained, and there is no need to suppose that there is such a thing as an absolute exactitude, which would be unattainable.

There are, not unconnected with our last point, certain other questions which, to my mind, raise difficulties as to Professor Dewey's instrumentalism. It would seem to follow from what he says that, although we can know that there are crude data, yet we can never know any particular crude datum, because objects of *knowledge* have to be objects of a certain kind, and crude data are not of this kind. Now I do not say that such a view is impossible, but I do say that it is difficult, and that, before it can be accepted, something must be done to show that the difficulties are not insurmountable. This brings us, however, to a general discussion of what Professor Dewey calls "instrumentalism."[3]

[3] I leave on one side, for the present, the question raised in the fourth and fifth of the quotations with which we began this section, namely, the question whether sensations and perceptions are cases of knowledge. I do not myself

II. Instrumentalism

The theory which Professor Dewey calls instrumentalism is a form of pragmatism, but (as appears by the twelfth essay, on "What Pragmatism Means by Practical") it is a pragmatism which is not intended to be used for the support of ancient superstitions or for bolstering up common prejudices. Some quotations, again, will serve to state the position which he advocates.

1. "If we exclude acting upon the idea, no conceivable amount or kind of intellectualistic procedure can confirm or confute an idea, or throw any light upon its validity" (p. 240).

2. "Instrumentalism means a behaviorist theory of thinking and knowing. It means that knowing is literally something which we do; that analysis is ultimately physical and active; that meanings in their logical quality are standpoints, attitudes, and methods of behaving towards facts, and that active experimentation is essential to verification" (pp. 331–332).

3. "The thesis of the essays is that thinking is instrumental to a control of the environment, a control effected through acts which would not be undertaken without the prior resolution of a complex situation into assured elements and an accompanying projection of possibilities—without, that is to say, thinking. Such an instrumentalism seems to analytic realism but a variant of idealism. For it asserts that processes of reflective inquiry play a part in shaping the objects—namely, terms and propositions—which constitute the bodies of scientific knowledge. Now it must not only be admitted but proclaimed that the doctrine of the essays holds that intelligence is not an otiose affair, nor yet a mere preliminary to a spectator-like apprehension of terms and propositions. In so far as it is idealistic to hold that objects of knowledge *in their capacity of distinctive objects of knowledge* are determined by intelligence, it is idealistic" (p. 30).

4. "Again, the question may be asked: Since instrumentalism admits that the table is really 'there,' why make such a fuss about whether it is there as a means or as an object of knowledge? . . . Respect for knowledge and its object is the ground for insisting upon the distinction. The object of knowledge is, so to speak, a more dignified, a more complete, sufficient, and self-sufficing thing than any datum can be. To transfer the traits of the object as known to the datum of reaching it, is a material, not a merely verbal affair" (pp. 44–45).

The view of Professor Dewey, if I understand him rightly, might be restated roughly as follows: The essence of knowledge is *inference* (p. 259), which consists in passing from objects present to others not now present. In order that this may be possible, one of the essentials is that the material originally given should be so shaped as to become an available tool for inference. After this shaping, it becomes what *science* calls a datum; it is then something different from what was there before. The essence of a belief is the behavior which exemplifies it (which *is* it, one is tempted to say); this behavior is such as is intended to achieve a certain end, and the

believe that this question is of great importance to the issue between him and me. I shall return to this topic briefly at a later stage.

belief is shown in the behavior adopted for that purpose. The belief is called *true* when the behavior which exemplifies it achieves its end, and false when it does not—omitting refinements due to cooperation of different beliefs. Knowledge is like a railway journey: it is a humanly constructed means of moving from place to place, and its matter, like the rails, is as much a human product as the rest of it, though dependent upon a crude ore which, in its unmanufactured state, would be as useless to intellectual locomotion as iron ore to locomotion by train.

There is a great deal that is attractive in this theory. I am not prepared dogmatically to deny its truth, at any rate in great part. But there are some problems which it *seems* to be unable to deal with.

First and foremost, we have the problem of the crude datum. The crude datum, in Professor Dewey's view—the "large but confused" original datum of William James—is something which lies outside knowledge. This has to do with the other thesis, exemplified in the fourth and fifth quotations of our previous section, that sensations and perceptions are not cases of knowledge, but inference alone is a case of knowledge. This, further, has to do with the practical bias—the view that knowledge must be treated as a means to something else. It is true, I think, that as a help in practical life the sort of knowledge we need is the sort that embodies or suggests inference. We want to know what will help or hinder, which is always a question of inference in a behaviorist sense. And here, further, if we are to take behaviorism seriously, we must contend, for example that a man or animal who eats something believes (unless he is tired of life) that it is nourishing food, however little he may reflect —for he has adopted the behavior appropriate to that belief, and belief must not depend for its existence upon anything except behavior. Thus in every case of eating there will be a case of inference. But the sort of knowledge that would be called "contemplation" has to be abandoned on this view.

Let us develop the point of view which is suggested, rather than fully stated, by Professor Dewey. It might with advantage, I think, be brought into connection with the thesis which the "neutral monists" have taken over from William James, that there is no such thing as "consciousness," and that what are called the mental and the physical are composed of the same material. It is not difficult to make sensation and perception fit into this view, by means of the thesis, urged in some of the above quotations, that they are not cases of knowledge at all. It is more difficult to fit in judgment and inference. But judgment is practically denied by Professor Dewey, as something distinct from inference; and inference is interpreted on behavioristic lines. Interpreting him, we might say: "Inference is behavior caused by an object A and appropriate if A is succeeded or accompanied by B." I do not say that this definition would be accepted: it is schematic, and artificially simplified, but it may serve to exemplify the theory we are examining. We thus arrive at some such picture as the following: Man, an animal struggling for self-preservation in a difficult environment, has learned to behave towards objects as "signs"—a practise which exists also among other animals, but in less developed forms. An object which is not in itself either useful or harmful may come to be a "sign" of something useful or harmful which is frequently found in its neighborhood, that is to say, it may come to promote behavior appropriate to that of which it is a sign, rather than to itself. Such behavior may be said to embody inference, or the "knowledge" that the object in question is a sign of the inferred object. Objects which are useful as signs acquire a special interest, and it is an essential part of the business of science to perfect the manufacture of such objects out of the material presented in nature. Such, it seems to me, is Professor Dewey's theory in outline.

I do not wish to maintain that this theory is false; I wish only to suggest that the reasons for thinking it true are far from adequate.

The first criticism that naturally occurs to any one who has endeavored to ascertain the truth about causality is, that the theory is amazingly light-hearted in its assumption of knowledge as to causality.[4] The writings of Hume, I know, are inconvenient. There are two recognized methods of dealing with what he has to say on Cause: one is to maintain that Kant answered him, the other is to preserve silence on the matter. I do not know which of these is the more inadequate. The second is the one adopted by Professor Dewey (in common with other pragmatists). His conception of signs and inference, his whole notion of knowledge as instrumental, depends throughout upon acceptance of the ordinary common-sense view of causation. I do not wish to be misunderstood in this criticism. I am willing to believe that there may be a great measure of truth in the common-sense view of causation, and I am incapable of saying or writing much without assuming it, at least verbally. The point is not that this view must be false, but that, for instrumentalism, it must be *known* to be true. We must actually know particular causal laws. Our beliefs will be beliefs in causal laws, and we must know what effects are caused by our beliefs, since this is the test of their value as instruments. The very conception of an "instru-

---

[4] "The term 'pragmatic' means only the rule of referring all thinking, all reflective considerations, to *consequences* for final meaning and test" (p. 330). "Consequences" is a causal word.

ment" is unintelligible otherwise. For those who are troubled by Hume's arguments, this bland ignoring of them is a difficulty, suggesting, at least, that a good deal of re-statement and further analysis is necessary before instrumentalism can take its place among articulate possible philosophies.

The second criticism which occurs to me is closely allied to the first. It is, that Professor Dewey ignores all fundamental skepticism. To those who are troubled by the question: "Is knowledge possible at all?" he has nothing to say. Probably such a question would appear to him otiose; he would argue (no doubt justly) that to a *fundamental* skepticism there can be no answer except a practical one. Nevertheless, a theory of knowledge should have more to say on the matter than he has to say. There are different levels of skepticism; there are popular prejudices which are easily dissolved by a little reflection, there are beliefs which we can just succeed in feeling to be doubtful by prolonged destructive analysis (such as the law of causation for example), and there are beliefs which it is practically impossible to doubt for more than a moment, such as the elementary propositions of arithmetic. But the beliefs which are epistemologically primitive in Professor Dewey's system will have to involve propositions which even the most hardened antiskeptic could be made to doubt without much trouble. For, if the truth of a belief is proved by its being a good instrument, we have to know what effects the belief has, what effects other beliefs would have had, and which are better. This sort of knowledge is surely about as doubtful as any that would ever be called knowledge. We also assume to begin with, in Professor Dewey's system, the whole of what is involved in the biological position of man: the environment, the struggle for existence, and so on. Thus our theory of knowledge begins only after we have assumed as much as amounts practically to a complete metaphysic.

This might be admitted, since Professor Dewey considers that "theory of knowledge," as a subject, is a mistake. I suppose he would say, what I should agree to in a certain fundamental sense, that knowledge must be accepted as a fact, and can not be proved from outside. I find, however, both in this respect and as regards data, an insufficient realization of the importance of degrees and continuous transitions. The passage from crude data to the most refined data of science must be continuous, with truth at every stage, but *more* truth in the later stages. So there is a gradation of truths; and similarly there is a gradation of beliefs, a continuous passage from what we feel to be very uncertain up to what we can not doubt, with some degree of belief at each stage, but more at the later stages. And theory of knowledge exists as a subject which endeavors to organize our beliefs according to the degree of conviction, and to attach as many as possible to those that have a high degree of conviction. If it be asked: "Is a belief of which I feel strong conviction more likely to be true than one of which I feel a good deal of doubt?" we can only answer that, *ex hypothesi*, we *think* it more likely to be true. And there is no miracle by which we can jump outside the circle of what we *think* to be true into the region of what *is* true whether we think so or not.

Professor Dewey, in an admirable passage, points out the effect of bias in forming the theories of philosophers. He says:

"It is an old story that philosophers, in common with theologians and social theorists, are as sure that personal habits and interests shape their opponents' doctrines as they are that their own beliefs are 'absolutely' universal and objective in quality. Hence arises that dishonesty, that insincerity characteristic of philosophic discussion. . . . Now the moment the complicity of the personal factor in our philosophic valuations is recognized, is recognized fully, frankly, and generally, that moment a new era in philosophy will begin. . . . So long as we ignore this factor, its deeds will be largely evil, not because *it* is evil, but because, flourishing in the dark, it is without responsibility and without check. The only way to control it is by recognizing it" (pp. 326-7).

These are very wise words. In spite of the risk, I propose to take the advice, and set down, as far as I can, the personal motives which make me like or dislike different aspects of behaviorism and instrumentalism, *i. e.*, motives which would make me *wish* them to be true or false.

I have a strong bias in favor of the view, urged by James and most American realists, that the mental and the physical are merely different arrangements of the same stuff, because this (like every other application of Occam's razor) gives opportunities for those logical constructions in which I take pleasure. I tried (in my *External World*) to show how the particulars that (in my view) make up the stuff of the world are capable of a two-fold classification, one as physical things, the other as biographies or monads, or parts of monads. Such logical constructions I find enjoyable. Desire for enjoyment of this sort is a creative bias in my philosophy—*i. e.*, what Kant (less self-consciously) would call a regulative idea of reason. The same bias makes me like behaviorism, since it would enable me to define a belief as a certain series of acts. An act inspired by two beliefs would be a member of the two series which would be the respective beliefs. In this definition I find, further, a good-natured malicious pleasure in thinking that even the theories conceived by those who hate mathematical logic can be taken over and stated in such terms as will make them repulsive to their own parents. I recognize that this is a shameful motive, but it does not

cease to operate on that account. All these motives combine to make
me like behaviorism and neutral monism, and to search for reasons
in their favor.

My bias as regards instrumentalism and pragmatism is quite
different. Often (though not in Professor Dewey) pragmatism is
connected with what I regard as theological superstition, and with
the habit of accepting beliefs because they are pleasant. Some
ascetic instinct makes me desire that a portion, at least, of my beliefs
should be of the nature of a hair shirt; and, as is natural to an
ascetic, I incline to condemn the will-to-believers as voluptuaries.
But these feelings are not roused in me by the pragmatism which is
advocated in this book: on the contrary, the very genuine scientific
temper in the book appeals to me. Nevertheless there is a profound instinct in me which is repelled by instrumentalism: the in-
instinct of contemplation, and of escape from one's own personality.

Professor Dewey has nothing but contempt for the conception of
knowledge as contemplation. He is full of that democratic philan-
thropy which makes him impatient of what seems to him a form of
selfish idleness. He speaks of

"that other great rupture of continuity which analytic realism would maintain:
that between the world and the knower as something outside of it, engaged in
an otiose contemplative survey of it. I can understand the social conditions
which generated this conception of an aloof knower. I can see how it pro-
tected the growth of responsible inquiry which takes effect in change of the environment, by cultivating a sense of the innocuousness of knowing, and thus
lulling to sleep the animosity of those who, being in control, had no desire to
permit reflection which had practical import . . ." (pp. 72–3).
and so on, and so on.

Will the present amusing inappropriateness of these remarks to
the case of one at least among analytic realists suggest to Professor
Dewey that perhaps he has somewhat misunderstood the ideal of
contemplation? It is not essential to this ideal that contemplation
should remain without effect on action. But those to whom contemplative knowledge appears a valuable ideal find in the practise of it
the same kind of thing that some have found in religion: they find
something that, besides being valuable on its own account, seems
capable of purifying and elevating practise, making its aims larger
and more generous, its disappointments less crushing, and its triumphs less intoxicating. In order to have these effects, contemplation must be for its own sake, not for the sake of the effects: for it
is the very contrast between action and pure contemplation that
gives rise to the effects. William James in his *Psychology* urges (if
I remember right) that when a man has been enjoying music he
should show how he has benefited by being kind to his aunt; but

the man who could not appreciate music apart from its effect on conduct would never be enough stirred by it to have his conduct improved, and would be just as unkind to his aunt after a concert as at other times. The habit of making everything subservient to practise is one which takes the color out of life, and removes most of the incentives to practise of a really noble kind.

Escape from one's own personality is something which has been desired by the mystics of all ages, and in one way or another by all in whom ardent imagination has been a dominant force. It is, of course, a matter of degree: complete escape is impossible, but some degree of escape is possible, and knowledge is one of the gateways into the world of freedom. Instrumentalism does its best to shut this gateway. The world which it allows us to know is man-made, like the scenery on the Underground: there are bricks and platforms and trains and lights and advertisements, but the sun and stars, the rain and the dew and the sea, are no longer there—sometimes we seem to catch a glimpse of them, but that is a mistake, we only see a picture made by some human being as an advertisement. It is a safe and comfortable world: we know how the trains will move, since we laid down the rails for them. If you find it a little dull, you are suffering from the "genteel tradition," you belong to an "upper" class given to a detached and parasitic life (p. 72). I have now expressed my bias as regards the view that we are not free to know anything but what our own hands have fashioned.

III. The External World as a Problem

I come now to the defense of certain views of my own against the criticisms of Professor Dewey, especially as contained in the eleventh essay, on "The Existence of the World as a Logical Problem."

A great deal of what is said in this essay depends upon the misunderstanding as to the sense in which I use "data," which we have already discussed. For example, on p. 290 ff., I am criticized for taking as "really known" (when we observe a table from different points of view) a set of facts which are complicated, involving series and logical correlations. Now such criticism all rests upon the supposition that what is "really known" is intended to be something which is believed at an earlier time than what is (if possible) to be proved by its means. This is not how I conceive the problem. I find myself, when I begin reflecting on the external world, full of hitherto unquestioned assumptions, for many of which I quickly realize that I have as yet no adequate reason. The question then arises: what sort of reason could I hope to discover? What, apart from argument and inference, shall I find surviving a critical scrutiny? And what inferences will then be possible? I give the name "data" or rather "hard data" to all that survives the most severe critical scrutiny of which I am capable, excluding what, *after the scrutiny*, is only arrived at by argument and inference. There is always much argument and inference in reaching the epistemological premisses of any part of our knowledge, but when we have completed the logical articulation of our knowledge the arguments by which we reached the premisses fall away.

The chief thing that I wish to make clear is that, in discussing the world as a logical problem, I am dealing in a scientific spirit with a genuine scientific question, in fact a question of physics. Professor Dewey, almost wilfully as it seems, refuses to perceive the question I am discussing, and points out the irrelevance of what I say to all sorts of other questions. It is perfectly clear that, starting from a common-sense basis, what a physicist believes himself to know is based partly upon observation and partly upon inference. It is also clear that what we *think* we observe is usually much more than what, after closer attention and more analysis, we find we really did observe—because habitual inferences become unintentionally mixed up with what was actually observed. Thus the conception of a "datum" becomes, as it were, a limiting conception of what we may call scientific common-sense. The more skilled an observer has become, the more what he thinks he has observed will approximate to what I should call a "datum." In all this, we are proceeding along ordinary scientific lines. And the utility of such analytic data for inference is fully recognized by Professor Dewey. But he is continually misled by the recurrent belief that I must be speaking about beliefs that are early in time, either in the history of the individual or in that of the race. However, I have said enough already on this aspect of the question.

A phrase about "our own" data leads to the question: "Who are the 'we,' and what does 'own' mean?" (p. 282 n). The answer to this is that it is quite unnecessary to have any idea what these terms mean. The problem with which I am concerned is this: Enumerate particulars in the world and facts about the world as long as you can; reject what you feel to be doubtful; eliminate what you see to be inferred. There then remains a residuum, which we may call "data." The outsider may define this residuum as "your" data—but to you they are not *defined* in their totality, they are merely enumerated: they are a certain collection of particulars and facts, and they are the total store from which, at the moment, you can draw your knowledge of the world. Then the question arises: what inferences are justified by this store of particulars and facts? This is a perfectly genuine problem. It is no use to find fault with me on the ground that my problem is not some other, which is more interesting to Professor Dewey, and which I am supposed to be intending to attack in a muddle-headed way. And it is no use to shut one's eyes to my problem on the ground that it may be inconvenient. Every philosophy has been invented to solve some one problem, and is incapable of dealing with many others; hence every philosophy is compelled to be blind to all problems except its own. It is time that philosophers learned more toleration of each other's problems.

Some of Professor Dewey's criticisms are so easily answered that I feel he must have found my views extraordinarily distasteful or he would never have made objections with so little cogency. Take, *e. g.*, the contention that it is a mistake to call color "visual" or sound "auditory" until we know that they are connected with eye and ear respectively. The answer is, that, quite apart from physiology, objects which (as we say) are "seen" have a common quality which enables us to distinguish them from objects "heard." We do not need to experiment by shutting the eyes and stopping the ears in order to find out whether the sense-datum of the moment is "visual" or "auditory:" we know this by its intrinsic quality. When I speak of "visual sense-data," I mean colors and shapes, and it is not the least necessary to know that it is through the eye that I become acquainted with them. Another very feeble argument is the objection (p. 285 *n*) to my calling certain things "self-evident" on the ground that a thing can not offer evidence for itself. This is not what is meant by "self-evident." What is meant is "known otherwise than by inference." Professor Dewey's contention almost suggests a quibble à la Plato to prove that no man can be self-taught, because we can only teach what we know and learn what we do not know, and therefore it is impossible that teacher and learner should be one and the same. But this is not the type of argument that Professor Dewey would wish to be caught using.

Another source of confusion in Professor Dewey's arguments is that he is apparently unaware of the distinction that I draw between the universal "red" and particulars which are instances of it.[5] I dare say this distinction may be mistaken, but it is in any case an essential part of my theory, and I can not be refuted by arguments which ignore it. This applies particularly to the paragraph on p. 288 beginning, "If anything is an eternal essence, it is surely such a thing as color taken by itself, as by definition it must be taken in the statement of the question by Mr. Russell. Anything

[5] See "On the Relations of Universals and Particulars," *Proc. Arist. Soc.*, 1911–1912.

more simple, timeless, and absolute than a red can hardly be thought of.'' And at the end of the same paragraph another even larger question is raised, namely that of the temporal position of a simple particular. In the case which I am supposing, we are told, ''we are dealing in the case of the colored surface with an ultimate, simple datum. It can have no implications beyond itself, no concealed dependencies. How then can its existence, even if its perception be but momentary, raise a question of 'other times' at all?'' (p. 289). One might retort simply by a *tu quoque:* tell us, one might say, what is your way of reaching other times? One might reply that it is of the very essence of my theory that the datum is usually *not* simple—that it is a fact, and facts are not simple (statements both noted by Professor Dewey, but supposed to constitute an inconsistency). One might point out that Professor Dewey, repeatedly, shows that he has failed to take account of the analysis of the time-order suggested both in Chapter IV of the book he is discussing and in the *Monist* for 1915—an analysis which, right or wrong, demands discussion in this connection. But the chief thing to point out is that, in the problem in question, we are up against the very question of causality and knowledge of the future, which, so far as I can discover, Professor Dewey has never faced.

After a description of the kind of world which I accept as datum, the essay proceeds (p. 292): ''How this differs from the external world of common sense I am totally unable to see. It may not be a very big external world, but having begged a small external world, I do not see why one should be too squeamish about extending it over the edges.'' Now there are several points to be made in reply to this criticism: (1) as to what I mean by an ''external'' world; (2) in what sense the world I start from is ''begged''; and (3) how this world that I start from differs from that of common sense.

1. The word ''external'' is perhaps an unfortunate one to have chosen, and the word ''inferred'' would have been better. Professor Dewey does not admit that we can be said to ''know'' what I call sense-data; according to him they simply occur. But this point, though he makes much of it, seems to me to make very little difference as regards our present question. He admits (pp. 259–260) that perceptions are the source of our knowledge of the world, and that is enough for my purposes. I am quite willing to concede, for the sake of argument, that perceptions are not cases of cognition; indeed my desire to accept neutral monism if possible gives me a bias in that direction. I see objections which I think he has not shown how to meet, but I am not at all sure that they can not be met. However that may be, Professor Dewey and I are at one in

regarding perceptions as affording data, *i. e.*, as giving the basis for our knowledge of the world. This is enough for the present; the question of the cognitive status of perceptions need not concern us.

Now it is a plain fact that what I see and hear has some relation to my knowledge which is not possessed by information obtained through historical or geographical reading. This is admitted, implicitly, by Professor Dewey in the passage just referred to. The words used for describing the difference are immaterial. When the difference is first noticed, it is vague and blurred, as is usually the case with newly cognized differences. Reflection tends to show that, as the difference comes to be drawn with more skill, less and less appears on the same side as what is seen and heard, and more and more appears on the same side as what we learn through reading. Nevertheless, if I am not mistaken, even the most rigid scrutiny will leave, on the same side with what is seen or heard, certain things remembered (with the fact that they are past), various observed relations (in part rather complicated), and some *a priori* knowledge— whether all of it logical or not, I do not know.

All this group of particulars and facts constitute what I call "data." They make up the world which I am intending to contrast with the "external" world. I do not wish spatial notions to obtrude: the world that I call "external" is so called only in this sense that it lies outside the group of data—"outside" in the logical sense. The problem that I wish to discuss is: "Can we make any valid inferences from data to non-data in the empirical world?" In the mathematical world we know that we can. Starting with a few numbers, we can infer other numbers *ad lib*. In the physical world, science and common sense believe that similar inferences are possible. Are they justified? If so, why? If we can not at present decide the question, can we see any way by which it *might* be decided? These problems are genuine, and no useful purpose is served by trying to evade them.

2. To say that I have "begged" a small external world is to miss the point. I have accepted it as datum, because that is the sort of world that, speaking empirically, seems to me, rightly or wrongly, to be given. Professor Dewey does not argue that this is not the case; he merely contends that it is not the world that is "given" in a different sense, *i. e.*, as I understand, given to babies, which is irrelevant. The "given" world that I am speaking of is that which is "given" to the most educated person to be found in the matter of physical observation and the distinguishing of observation from inference. If I have wrongly described the "given" world (in this sense), I am ready to amend the description. It makes very little difference to my problem what is the *detail* of the

description of the given world. If Professor Dewey will offer me an alternative (provided he will remember that it is not the *historical* primitive that I want), I make little doubt that the bulk of my argument will be able to adapt itself with little alteration. I have not "begged" my small external world any more than Columbus begged the West Indies; I have merely chronicled what I observe. I can not prove that it is there except by pointing to it, any more than Columbus could. But if others do not see what I point to, that does not prove that *I* do not observe it. There is no reason why what one person can observe should be also open to the observation of another. Nevertheless, to chronicle what one observes is not the same thing as to "beg" a world.

3. As to how my initial world of data differs from the world of common sense, there are various ways: (*a*) by extrusion of the notion of *substance*, since I do not consider a physical thing, such as a table, to be a datum at all, and I do consider that it is a series of classes of particulars, not a single particular. (I am not speaking of the fact that the table has physical parts: what I say would be equally true of an atom or electron, according to the theory). (*b*) Among *data* we can only include the existence of a particular during the time when it is a datum: its existence or non-existence before and after that time, if knowable at all, can only be known by inference. The things that Professor Dewey says on this subject (pp. 286–290) are only explicable to me by supposing that, when I speak of "inference to other times," he thinks that I mean inference to the existence of other times, whereas I mean inference to the existence-of-something-described at a time when something else is known to be existing. *E. g.*, I look out of the window and see, as we say, a tree; I look back to my book and see print. Can I know whether what I saw when I looked out of the window, or anything in any way correlated with it, exists while I am looking at my book? My world of data does not include anything which gives an answer to this, whether affirmative or negative; an answer will not be possible unless there are valid inferences from particulars at certain times to (described) particulars at certain other times. (*c*) In particular, my world of data does not include anything of other people except their outward show. In these and other ways it is very fragmentary as compared with the world of common sense.

Professor Dewey takes advantage (*e. g.*, p. 295) of occasions when, for the sake of brevity, I have adopted the language of common sense. To avoid this altogether would hardly be possible without adopting the language of mathematical logic. But there are hardly a dozen philosophers living who will take the trouble to read anything written in that language. And so long as one uses language they will condescend to read, one is condemned to the vaguenesses, inaccuracies and ambiguities which keep philosophy alive.

There is much that, if space permitted, I should have wished to say on the subject of *time*. Meanwhile, I will conclude with the hope that the reader will perceive the reality of the problem which concerns me. There is a passage in the Essay we have been considering which seems to show why Professor Dewey and I have such difficulty in understanding one another. He says (p. 299): "No one can deny that inference from one thing to another is itself an empirical event, and that just as soon as such inference occurs, even in the simplest form of anticipation and prevision, a world exists like in kind to that of the adult." Certainly no one denies that inference is an empirical event. What is being examined is not its *occurrence*, but its *validity*. The above passage seems to suggest that if I infer a world, there is a world. Yet I am not the Creator. Not all my inferences and expectations could prevent the world from coming to an end to-night, if so it were to happen. I trace in the above quotation, as in much of what pragmatists write, that instinctive belief in the omnipotence of Man and the creative power of his beliefs which is perhaps natural in a young, growing, and prosperous country, where men's problems have been simpler than in Europe and usually soluble by energy alone. Dr. Schiller says that the external world was first discovered by a low marine animal whom he calls "Grumps," who swallowed a bit of rock that disagreed with him, and argued that he would not have given himself such a pain, and therefore there must be an external world. One is tempted to think that, at the time when Professor Dewey wrote, many people in the newer countries had not yet made the disagreeable experience which Grumps made. Meanwhile, whatever accusations pragmatists may bring, I shall continue to protest that it was not I who made the world.

BERTRAND RUSSELL

BOOK REVIEWS

The Quest for Certainty: A Study of the Relation of Knowledge and Action. JOHN DEWEY. (Gifford Lectures, 1929.) New York: Minton, Balch and Co. 1929. Pp. 318.

It is not necessary to characterize a book which we shall all read, but one can not lay down Professor Dewey's Gifford Lectures without yielding to the temptation. This is a completer and better-rounded statement of the author's point of view than any which has preceded it, and on some points it is a clearer one. It is also a contribution to literature. It begins, one feels, where the author himself begins; the directing intent is laid down in the opening pages; and it moves forward with uninterrupted sweep to that which, one is persuaded, constitutes the personal goal of his thinking. The concluding chapter especially is impressive; it contains passages which will always be quoted.

In its simplest terms, the theme is not new, but is that in which the West has always announced itself as against the East; the modern world against the ancient: Man may not reach the goal of his quest for security by any flight to another world—neither to that other world of the religious mystic, nor to that realm of transcendent ideas and eternal values which is its philosophical counterpart. Salvation is through work; through experimental effort, intelligently directed to an actual human future.

The development of this theme is, of course, peculiarly Professor

Dewey's own. Man must recognize his continuity with nature, and he must read that continuity both ways. Nature in general is not a completed and independent reality prior to his action. Nor are the objectives of his quest legitimately or safely determined in complete abstraction from that experience in which environment is met and moulded. The world is not a "block-universe" and finished; its growing reality is in part for us to create. But the sense of this is not conveyed in the simple and bold terms of a Jamesian "absolute chance" and "will to believe," which either did or did not appeal to the reader's prior inclination; it comes by way of an examination of the relation between knowledge and action, and of the nature of "the valuable" as the object of an activity which, though intelligently directed, is never cast in final form or loses its character as experimental and hypothetical.

The persistent fallacy of epistemology has been the conception that the norm of knowledge is some antecedent reality. In their opposite ways, both rationalists and sensational empiricists are in error by their common assumption that reflection—thought involving inference—is reproductive, and that ideas are tested by some comparison with an object which has prior existence. For rationalism, this object is a reality already informed by transcendent and constitutive reason. For sensational empiricism, sensory qualities as merely given are the antecedent models with which ideas must agree if they are to be sound or "proved." But objects are not finalities which "call for thought only in the way of definition, classification, subsumption in syllogisms, etc." [1] Sense qualities are something *to be* known; they set the problem to be solved instead of supplying the answer which knowledge seeks. The model of true knowledge is to be found in the experimental investigations of science. The principal traits of such inquiry are three: "The first is the obvious one that all experimentation involves *overt* doing, the making of definite changes in the environment or in our relation to it. The second is that experiment is not a random activity, but is directed by ideas which have to meet the conditions set by the need of the problem inducing the active inquiry. The third and concluding feature, in which the other two receive their full measure of meaning, is that the outcome of the directed activity is the construction of a new empirical situation in which objects are differently related to one another, and such that the *consequences* of directed operations form the objects that have the property of being *known.*" [2] The concepts which direct such experimental inquiry comprise or prescribe a set of operations by which the presence of the character conceived is tested. [3] Thus

[1] P. 99; see also p. 112.
[2] Pp. 86–87.
[3] See p. 111.

"ideas have an empirical origin and status. But it is that of acts performed . . . not reception of sensations forced on us from without."[4] As directly given, objects are not the terminus and test of knowledge, but the occasion of it; experimental procedure reduces them to the status of data. "This resolution is required because the objects in their first mode of experience are perplexing, obscure, fragmentary; in some way they fail to answer a need. Given data which locate the nature of the problem, there is evoked the thought of the operation which, if put into execution, may eventuate in a situation in which the trouble or doubt which evoked inquiry will be resolved."[5] "Ideas that are plans of action or operations to be performed are integral factors in actions which change the face of the world. . . . A genuine idealism and one compatible with science will emerge as soon as philosophy accepts the teaching of science that ideas are statements not of what is or has been but of acts to be performed."[6] "Henceforth the quest for certainty becomes the search for methods of control; . . . theoretical certitude is assimilated to practical certainty; to *security,* trustworthiness of instrumental operations."[7]

The important consequences of this theory of knowledge, for Professor Dewey's further thesis, is suggested by the last two quotations. Knowledge here takes its place in a world which is in part its own creation. A knower, as such, is a doer, not a passive spectator of a ready-made world. The terms in which reality is defined, for our cognition, are terms into which our own activity, directed by this knowing, has already entered. Knowing is prediction of the result of our own intelligently directed ways of acting—if I do thus and so, the result will be such and such. "If we persist in the traditional conception, according to which the thing to be known is something which exists prior to and wholly apart from the act of knowing, then discovery of the fact that the act of observation, necessary to existential knowing, modifies that pre-existent something, is proof that the act of knowing gets in its own way. If knowing is a form of doing and is judged like other modes by its eventual issue, this tragic conclusion is not forced upon us."[8]

In the pages from which these excerpts are taken, the principles set down are illuminated and enforced by consideration of physical science, past and present, which constitutes an analysis and critique of scientific procedure which is worth reading quite apart from its

[4] P. 112.
[5] P. 123.
[6] P. 138.
[7] P. 128.
[8] P. 205; the context is especially concerned with certain implications of physical relativity.

bearing on the issue. In the omission of this here, much which gives significance and support to the conclusions must inevitably fail to be suggested.

With the main theses of this conception—the continuity of knowing and acting, the function of empirical concepts as prescription of operations to be performed, the significance of knowing as prediction of a future into which our action enters—the present writer is so fully in accord as to have no comment save applause. And I believe that nothing which a just theory of knowledge can contribute to other problems, theoretical and practical, is more important than this realization that reality can not be an alien and imposed somewhat, or a net of tight-bound circumstances in which we are caught, because the only reality there can be for us is one delimited in concepts of the results of our own ways of acting.

Yet I conceive that the proponents of the various "spectator" theories of knowledge may feel aggrieved by this account. If it is difficult to deny what Professor Dewey positively says, it is nevertheless possible to feel that something has been left unsaid which is important. In particular, it may be remarked that the author is preoccupied with the forward-looking function of knowledge to the neglect of its backward-looking ground or premises. It seems evident that Professor Dewey dislikes abstractions, and views with suspicion any attempt to separate factors or interrelated problems. Always his emphasis is upon the living integrality of process. Tradition conceptions, by contrast, have often formulated their problems and found their solutions by just such abstraction and separation of factors. One such problem—historically it overshadows and colors all the others—is this question of the ground, basis, validity of knowledge: How do we know? How is science possible? What justifies our cognitive assurance? To this question, we can not return the answer, "The dénouement of future experience will tell us," because the future is what we never catch up with. If knowledge is knowledge only as it directs action into the future it predicts, and this future is the test of its validity, then no knowledge is assured until it is dead and its function has ceased. Knowledge, on these terms, will be foresight—and the only assured foresight will be hindsight. Nor is it possible to escape the point by the observation that knowledge is hypothetical. "Hypothetical" is here ambiguous: if what is meant is that the *content* of knowledge is a *hypothetical proposition*—"If I should do thus and so, the results would be such and such"—then it is to be observed that it is not the hypothesis of this proposition which wants assurance; it is the judgment as a whole, and particularly the prediction contained in its consequent clause, whose ground and validity are in question. The only sense of "hypothetical" which is pertinent to the present issue is that of "tentative" or "probable." But if what is meant is that empirical knowledge is probable, then the question merely recurs in another form: What makes it probable? What justifies the judgment as a knowledge of probabilities?

By his predominant interest in the *function* of knowledge, Professor Dewey almost identifies knowing with *finding out;* [9] traditional theories mostly exhibit an opposite preoccupation and insist that the discussion of knowledge properly refers to the cognitive state which follows upon finding out, not that which leads up to it. If reference is taken to such experimental processes as characterize scientific investigation, it may be urged that the knowledge which directs and controls the experiment should not be confused with the knowledge which results from it. An experimenter already knows something, and in the light of this tries to find out something else. If he succeeds, he then knows two things (perhaps connected), what he knew before and what the experiment has just revealed. But the first of these items of knowledge is presumably independent of the experimental findings; it relates to something antecedently determined. And the second item becomes knowledge only when the experiment is concluded and its result, therefore, acquires the status of antecedent fact.

If I read Professor Dewey correctly, he would object to such analysis as artificial, because he would take the typical situation in knowing, and especially in scientific experiment, to be one in which activity is guided by an hypothesis tentatively held, which the result of this experimental activity will confirm or falsify. The guiding idea is itself prediction of consequences to be reached by certain operations it prescribes. But does this manner of reading the cognitive situation abrogate the distinction between the *ground* of knowledge and the *content* of knowledge as matters requiring separate examination? Let us accept, as typical of cognition, the case of hypothesis and experimental verification. Let us further agree that the significance of the hypothesis is the prediction of certain results to be reached by operations it prescribes. At the initiation of the experiment, when the hypothesis exercises its instrumental function of prescribing operations, is this hypothesis knowledge? The answer, in the typical case, will be that it has a certain probability. If the experiment confirms it, it will then have a higher probability (or perhaps certainty). But the question, "Why is it probable (or certain)?" will, at either moment, have to be answered, not in the light of what is, for that moment, future, but of what is present and

---

9 For example, "Taking what is already known or pointing to it is no more a case of knowledge than taking a chisel out of a tool-box is the making of a tool" (p. 188).

past. The content of the hypothesis—its prediction of a result of action—relates to the future; and we may agree that the significance of cognition generally lies in such leading and in such prediction. But at every moment, the validity of it as knowledge depends upon the past.

So far as I can see, there is nothing here which would deny to knowledge its significance as an instrument of action, nor the author's further point that reality as an object of knowledge is something into which our own activity enters as a partial determinant. Because these points relate to the *content* and *function* of knowledge: the content of a cognition may be the prediction of the future and of a future as conditioned by action, although the just ground of such prediction, or warrant for our knowledge, is something antecedent. However, if we grant that a practical belief has a just ground only in the light of what is past, we then make connection with traditional issues in their traditional form. Warranted beliefs, hypotheses justifiably held, are possible only if something learned from the past is pertinent to the future. The possibility of knowledge argues some continuing stability which extends through past and future both. It is such transtemporal stabilities, or the basis of them in reality, which constitute the object of the traditional quest for certainty. The elevation of such transtemporalities to the status of the transcendent, as eternal objects of a constitutive reason, or even their abstraction from that temporal process in which human action may make a difference, is—we may agree with Professor Dewey—an illicit procedure and the source of further errors. But in some terms or other, some such background, in the more-than-particular, will be required for empirical beliefs if the problem of their validity is to be solved.

Moreover, the presentations of sense-experience must exercise some other function than that of setting problems if empirical knowledge is to be possible. That presentation which is the occasion of the cognitive process must serve as clue to, or a sign of, what our practical belief predicts as the eventuation of a certain mode of action. Acts do not produce their empirical consequences regardless of the situation into which they enter. What that situation is, we must rely upon such given data of sense to disclose, even though they portray it only in fragmentary and inconclusive fashion. They constitute such ground as we may have that, in this circumstance or on this occasion, a particular mode of action will yield a predictable result. Furthermore, such ground of our prediction must reflect some generalization—that on such occasions as this, a particular act will result thus and so—and the only possible basis of this generalization is something prior, even though the generalization be a tentative one, subject to correction in the light of further experience. It can only be thus corrected when such further experience has itself become antecedent fact.

I do not suppose that there is anything here set down (unless in detail) with which Professor Dewey would disagree, since this does little more than emphasize the obvious: that if knowledge is to be other than a random leap in the dark, a belief must have some ground or warrant; and that what is future to it can not, in the nature of the case, provide such warrant. But perhaps these trivialities justify the observation that knowing has its retrospective as well as its prospective significance. Its content as prediction and its function as guide to action look toward the future; its warrant, or validity as belief, looks back to something prior. We may suspect that one reason for Professor Dewey's preponderant, and almost exclusive, emphasis upon the forward-looking aspect of content and instrumental function, is that the traditional problems of validity do not greatly interest him. In any case, nothing which might be here at issue touches the point—important for the sequel—that the reality we know is conditioned by our action, not something preformed, and contemplated by a passive spectator.

The other outstanding thesis of this theory of knowledge, which is carried forward to the consideration of further problems, is that the end of knowledge is not in knowing but is in doing; the subservience of the cognitive activity to further interests, which are to have authority over it. This may seem to be merely the definitive intent of "instrumentalism"; but that word has two quite different meanings. Plato, for example, is an instrumentalist in the sense of holding that the essence of a thing is the "good" of it. The axe is defined in terms of its cutting function. And no empirical axe is fully real just because no lump of metal ideally subserves that function. The bridle is an instrument for controlling a horse without injuring his mouth; and it is a transcendent idea because no such thing can be more than approximated to. Plato as much as Professor Dewey takes the correct apprehension of an axe to lie in a concept of which it might be said that it prescribes certain operations and forecasts their result. And for Plato likewise it is true that, in the case of particular empirical axes, this forecast is hypothetical and probable only. But for Plato it is the intellectual apprehension of this essence which is the aim of the cognitive process; the advance of knowledge is toward better and more precise concepts. For Professor Dewey, this advance is to be tested by a better accomplishment of the world's work; "Ideas are worthless except as they pass into actions which rearrange and reconstruct in some way, be it little or large, the world in which we live. To magnify thought and ideas for their own sake apart from what they do . . . is to reject the idealism which involves responsibility."[10] Thus the two points of view are in agreement that the good of the axe is in the woodpile, and that a just concept must so take it; Plato and Professor Dewey are both instrumentalists in holding a functional theory of the concept. But Professor Dewey would also maintain that the good of *knowing* or understanding the axe is in the woodpile, and thus is an instrumentalist in a further sense. It is this transfer of "the seat of intellectual authority"[11] to the arts of practical guidance and control, which is the underlying thesis of the book.

The issue here revealed becomes poignant whenever the interests of precision and finality of conception run counter to the practical applicability of knowledge and direct scientific endeavor away from those complex and unprecise affairs which are proximate to human interests. The subversive results of holding intellectual apprehension to be an end in itself are numerous and subtle. The hypostatization of Platonic ideas, and the consequent other-worldliness and contempt for the practical, is only an extreme example. It likewise leads to disrespect for sensibly observed material in science,[12] to a turning away from change to the changeless,[13] to relegation of the problematic and the individual to the "subjective,"[14] and to the elevation of abstract "standardized" things, such as the entities of physical science, to the position of a higher, more fundamental kind of reality.[15] It also results in an invidious designation of the abstract disciplines as more truly "science," in contrast to those departments of knowledge more directly pertinent to concrete and involved human affairs. Hence as a further effect, the social sciences may be misled, through an attempt to be more "scientific," to give over the effort at instrumentally valuable formulations in favor of empty abstractions and sterile classifications.[16] It may even, through the false dichotomy of intellectual and practical, result in false ideals of education; in "devotion to training in technical and mechanical skills on one hand and to laying in a store of abstract information on the other"—both in contrast to the "development of intelligence as a method of action."[17]

The real nature and legitimate intent of abstract scientific procedures is clearly set forth. Such remoteness from the concrete is necessary for "arriving at statements which hold for all expe-

10 P. 138.
11 Chapter heading of Ch. VII.
12 See p. 88.
13 See p. 84.
14 See p. 233.
15 See pp. 237 ff.
16 See pp. 199, 220 ff.
17 P. 252.

riences and observers under all possible varying circumstances."[18] The operations and relations implicit in our dealings with the concrete become explicit and generalized and are then symbolically dealt with. "All that was required for the development of mathematics as a science and for the growth of a logic of ideas, that is, of implications of operations with respect to one another, was that some men should appear upon the scene who were interested in the operations on their own account, as operations, and not as means to specified particular uses."[19] The relative perfection of conclusions is connected with the strict limitation of problems. "Artificial simplification or abstraction is a necessary precondition of securing ability to deal with affairs which are complex, in which there are many more variables and where strict isolation destroys the special characteristics of the subject-matter. . . . [But] objection comes in, and comes in with warranted force, when the results of an abstractive operation are given a standing which belongs only to the total situation from which they have been selected."[20] "The abstractions of mathematics and physics represent the common denominators in all things experienceable. . . . Erected into complete statements of reality as such, they become hallucinatory obsessions."[21] To make a transcript of this rational structure of nature in mathematical formulæ "gives great delight to those who have the required ability. But it *does* nothing; it makes no difference in nature."[22]

The underlying issue here is not so much metaphysical as ethical; or it is metaphysical because it is first ethical. Ontological subordination of the "abstract" to the "concrete" is the corollary of the ethical principle that the (intellectual) activity which leads to abstract objects should not *terminate* in them, but should be instrumental to something further and practical. It is the counterpart of the repudiation of the ancient ideal of contemplative insight in favor of absorption in the world's work. The assignment of exclusive or preëminent reality to the entities of exact science, as against those of every-day experience, is certainly a metaphysical blunder, and merits the vigorous criticism here accorded it. But surely the "common denominators of all experience" have their own kind of reality; they are not fictions. And in view of the author's earlier point, that real objects in general are the termini of intelligently directed activity, it becomes evident that "concreteness" does not connote mere givenness, but implies some sort of intellectual delimitation, abstraction, or construction. Otherwise we should conclude

[18] P. 218.
[19] P. 156.
[20] P. 217.
[21] P. 218.
[22] P. 211.

in favor of the exclusive reality of sensations. This being so, it does not appear in what sense the metaphysical preëminence of every-day objects over the scientific is more warranted than its opposite. Perhaps the author does not intend to assign such preëminence. In any case, the ethical thesis of instrumentalism should stand on its own feet.

With respect to this ethical issue, probably we shall all agree that Professor Dewey's emphasis upon practical doing falls in the right place, though some may feel that his enthusiasm for the strenuous life leads him to overstate the case, and smacks of rigorism. To "make a difference in nature" is not the whole end of man. Perhaps he will allow us moral holidays, for the celebration of scientific insight as an end in itself.

A further motive for emphasis upon the desirable continuity of science and practical affairs becomes evident in the ensuing chapters: it is to the end that something of the method learned in science may be carried over to the problems of concrete human ends. "The problem of restoring integration and coöperation between man's beliefs about the world in which he lives and his beliefs about the values and purposes that should direct his conduct is the deepest problem of modern life. It is the problem of any philosophy which is not isolated from that life." [23] As a result of the lack of continuity with natural science, beliefs about values are "pretty much in the position in which beliefs about nature were before the scientific revolution. There is either a basic distrust of the capacity of experience to develope its own regulative standards, and an appeal to what philosophers call eternal values, in order to ensure regulation of belief and action; or there is an acceptance of enjoyments actually empirically experienced irrespective of the method or operation by which they are brought into existence." [24] What is needed is an extension of the experimental method to the construction of human good. This would mean, on the one hand, the repudiation of transcendent "values," known by reason or divinely revealed, and, in consequence, of that subjectivism which throws the emphasis upon change in ourselves instead of the world in which we live. Standards would no longer be accepted as something antecedent and fixed; "All tenets and creeds about good and goods, would be recognized to be hypotheses." [25] The more exacting test of consequences would be substituted for fixed general rules.[26] On the other hand, the experimental method will deny any final significance to the mere fact of casual desire or given enjoyment. "The fact that something is desired only

[23] P. 255.
[24] P. 256.
[25] P. 277.
[26] See p. 278.

raises the *question* of its desirability." [27] "A *feeling* of good or excellence is as far removed from goodness in fact as a feeling that objects are intellectually thus and so is removed from their being actually so." [28]

"Where will regulation come from if we surrender traditionally prized values as our directive standards? Very largely from the findings of the natural sciences" [29]—when the effects of the separation of knowledge from action have been removed. "Judgments about values are judgments about the conditions and the results of experienced objects; judgments about that which should regulate the formation of our desires, affections and enjoyments." [30]

Many readers will, I think, find this part of Professor Dewey's doctrine puzzling to a degree in which the rest is not. The sense in which "experience can develop its own regulative standards" is not clear. It is to be observed, of course, that "experience" does not here mean something merely given; for Professor Dewey, the experiencer and his attitudes and acts are in the experience. Further, we shall all admit that what is good has to be learned; that in part the achievement of the valuable must come through our own more just evaluations, and that this learning is not a process of merely rational reflection, but is empirical, including observation of the consequences of acts and of the connections of things. But is it not the case that we must ourselves bring to experience the ultimate criterion and touchstone of the good; that otherwise experience could no more teach us what is good than it can teach the blind man what things are red? Experience—and experience alone—can teach us what is good, if by that we mean, what situations, things, events are good; that is, only the wisdom of experience can show us where goodness is to be found. Hence if we mean by "ideals" such concrete aims as democracy or wealth or the comity of nations, then experience must develop its own ideals—though whether it can be *trusted to* is, perhaps, another matter. But can experience determine the nature, essence, criteria of goodness? Before one embarks upon the practical and empirical problem of realizing the valuable or constructing the good, is it not essential that one should be able to recognize it when disclosed; that one should know, not what objects or what concrete situations, but what quality of life—whether pleasure or self-mastery, activity in accordance with virtue or the intellectual love of God—it is which is to be realized or constructed? Toward this problem, we can hardly take hypothetical attitudes, leaving the just answer for the social and historical process to deter-

[27] P. 260.
[28] P. 265.
[29] P. 273.
[30] P. 265.

mine, because the question whether human history is progress or decadence will depend upon it.

Professor Dewey has, I think, declined to separate these two questions; of the essence or criteria of the good and of its locus in experience and reality. And by so doing, he omits the former altogether. It is precisely this problem of the nature or definition of the good, to which traditional theories have been principally directed. Hence no issue is really joined. In spite of this, however, it seems to me that Professor Dewey's strictures upon traditional conceptions are wholly just and that the corrective which he urges is most salutary. With respect to the second problem, of concretely realizing the good, traditional doctrines have almost universally done one or other of two things: either they have, broadly speaking, assumed that moral science is concluded with the delimitation of the *summum bonum;* or they have proceeded as if he who apprehends this nature of the good can forthwith produce it or find it, with no more equipment than mother-wit provides. As examination of their "illustrations" will show, they go straight from basic principle to the most intricate and difficult of personal and social problems, with no intermediaries. This is as if one could proceed from the definition of "beauty" to the production of a symphony or to the criticism of Renaissance architecture. Quite clearly, either in or added to the traditional type of value-theory and ethics, there is needed just that continuity with a humanized science, just that learning of the connections and consequences of things, and just that experimental method and attitude of mind, in behalf of which Professor Dewey speaks. This is just that connection between an understanding of the world we live in and our beliefs about our purposes and values, which might bridge the present chasm between theoretical apprehension and the art of the good life. This is the goal of the quest for certainty and security.

With respect to values, there is a third question which philosophy has sought to answer: So far as these transcend man's power to achieve, how do they stand related to things in general? There is something which bears upon this in the concluding chapter of the book. But that chapter will be omitted here. Perhaps it is a matter peculiarly between Professor Dewey and his readers. I should not wish to underscore any part of it by quotation, or to mar it by marginal annotations.   C. I. LEWIS.

HARVARD UNIVERSITY.

THE JOURNAL OF PHILOSOPHY

PROPOSITIONS, WARRANTED ASSERTIBILITY, AND TRUTH

I PROPOSE in what follows to restate some features of the theories I have previously advanced on the topics mentioned above. I shall shape this restatement on the basis of ascriptions and criticisms of my views found in Mr. Russell's *An Inquiry into Truth and Meaning*. I am in full agreement with his statement that "there is an important difference between his views and mine, which will not be elicited unless we can understand each other."[1] Indeed, I think the statement might read "We can not understand each other unless important differences between us are brought out and borne in mind." I shall then put my emphasis upon what I take to be such differences, especially in relation to the nature of propositions; operations; the respective force of antecedents and consequences; tests or "verifiers"; and experience, the latter being, perhaps, the most important of all differences because it probably underlies the others. I shall draw contrasts which, in the interest of mutual understanding, need to be drawn for the purpose of making my own views clearer than I have managed previously to do. In drawing them I shall be compelled to ascribe certain views to Mr. Russell, without, I hope, attributing to him views he does not in fact hold.

I

Mr. Russell refers to my theory as one which "substitutes 'warranted assertibility' for truth."[2] Under certain conditions, I should have no cause to object to this reference. But the conditions are absent; and it is possible that this view of "substitution" as distinct from and even opposed to *definition,* plays an important rôle in generating what I take to be misconceptions of my theory in some important specific matters. Hence, I begin by saying that my analysis of "warranted assertibility" is offered as a *definition* of the nature of knowledge in the honorific sense according to which only *true* beliefs are knowledge. The place at which there is pertinency in the idea of "substitution" has to do with *words.* As I

1 *Op. cit.,* p. 401.

2 *Op. cit.,* p. 362. This interpretation is repeated on p. 401, using the words "should take the place of" instead of "substitutes."

wrote in my *Logic: The Theory of Inquiry*, "What has been said helps explain why the term "warranted assertibility" is preferred to the terms *belief* and *knowledge*. It is free from the ambiguity of the latter terms." [3] But there is involved the extended analysis, given later, of the nature of assertion and of warrant.

This point might be in itself of no especial importance. But it is important in its bearing upon interpretation of other things which I have said and which are commented upon by Mr. Russell. For example, Mr. Russell says "One important difference between us arises, I think, from the fact that Dr. Dewey is mainly concerned with theories and hypotheses, whereas I am mainly concerned with assertions about particular matters of fact." [4] My position is that something of the order of a theory or hypothesis, a meaning entertained as a *possible significance* in some actual case, is demanded, if there is to be *warranted* assertibility in the case of a particular matter of fact. This position undoubtedly gives an importance to ideas (theories, hypotheses) they do not have upon Mr. Russell's view. But it is not a position that can be put in opposition to assertions about matters of particular fact, since, in terms of my view, it states the *conditions* under which we reach warranted assertibility about particular matters of fact.[5]

There is nothing peculiarly "pragmatic" about this part of my view, which holds that the presence of an *idea*—defined as a possible significance of an existent something—is required for any assertion entitled to rank as knowledge or as true; the insistence, however, that the "presence" be by way of an existential operation demarcates it from most other such theories. I may indicate some of my reasons for taking this position by mentioning some difficulties in the contrasting view of Mr. Russell that there are propositions known in virtue of their own immediate direct presence, as in the case of "There is red," or, as Mr. Russell prefers to say, "Redness-here."

(i) I do not understand how "here" has a self-contained and self-assured meaning. It seems to me that it is void of any trace

---

[3] *Logic*, p. 9. Perhaps in the interest of clearness, the word "term" should have been italicized. The ambiguities in question are discussed in previous pages. In the case of *belief*, the main ambiguity is between it as a state of mind and as *what* is believed—subject-matter. In the case of *knowledge*, it concerns the difference between knowledge as an outcome of "competent and controlled inquiry" and knowledge supposed to "have a meaning of its own apart from connection with, and reference to, inquiry."

[4] *Op. cit.*, p. 408.

[5] As will appear later, the matter is inherently connected with the proper interpretation of *consequences* on my theory, and also with the very fundamental matter of *operations*, which Mr. Russell only barely alludes to.

of meaning save as discriminated from *there,* while *there* seems to me to be plural; a matter of manifold *theres.* These discriminations involve, I believe, determinations going beyond anything directly given or capable of being directly present. I would even say, with no attempt here to justify the saying, that a theory involving determination or definition of what is called "Space" is involved in the allegedly simple "redness here." Indeed, I would add that since any adequate statement of the matter of particular fact referred to is "redness-here-now," a scientific theory of *space-time* is involved in a fully warranted assertion about "redness-here-now."

(ii) If I understand Mr. Russell aright, he holds that the ultimacy and purity of basic propositions is connected with (possibly is guaranteed by) the fact that subject-matters like "redness-here" are of the nature of perceptual experiences, in which perceptual material is reduced to a direct *sensible* presence, or a *sensum.* For example, he writes: "We can, however, in theory, distinguish two cases in relation to a judgment such as 'that is red'; one, when it is caused by what it asserts, and the other, when words or images enter into its causation. In the former case, it must be true; in the latter it may be false." However, Mr. Russell goes on to ask: "What can be meant when we say a 'percept' causes a word or sentence? On the face of it, we have to suppose a considerable process in the brain, connecting visual centres with motor centres; the causation, therefore, is by no means direct." [6] It would, then, seem as if upon Mr. Russell's own view a quite elaborate physiological theory intervenes in any given case as condition of assurance that "redness-here" is a true assertion. And I hope it will not appear unduly finicky if I add that a theory regarding causation also seems to be intimately involved.

Putting the matter on somewhat simpler and perhaps less debatable ground, I would inquire whether what is designated by such words as "sensible presence" and "sensa" is inherently involved in Mr. Russell's view. It would seem as if some such reference were necessary in order to discriminate *"redness-here"* from such propositions as *"this ribbon is red,"* and possibly from such propositions as *"hippogriff-here."* If reference to a sensum *is* required, then it would seem as if there must also be reference to the bodily sensory apparatus in virtue of whose mediation a given quality is determined to be a *sensum.* It hardly seems probable to me that such knowledge is any part of the datum as directly "here"; indeed, it seems highly probable that there was a long period in history when human beings did not institute connection between colors

[6] *Op. cit.,* p. 200.

and visual apparatus, or between sounds and auditory apparatus; or at least that such connection as was made was inferred from what happened when men shut their eyes and stopped up their ears.

The probability that the belief in certain qualities as "sensible" is an inferential matter is increased by the fact that Mr. Russell himself makes no reference to the presence of the bodily *motor* element which is assuredly involved in "redness-here";—an omission of considerable importance for the difference between our views, as will appear later. In view of such considerations as these, any view which holds that all complex propositions depend for their status *as knowledge* upon prior atomic propositions, of the nature described by Mr. Russell, seems to me the most adequate foundation yet provided for complete scepticism.

The position which I take, namely, that all knowledge, or warranted assertion, depends upon inquiry and that inquiry is, truistically, connected with what is questionable (and questioned) involves a sceptical element, or what Peirce called "fallibilism." But it also provides for *probability*, and for determination of degrees of probability in rejecting all intrinsically dogmatic statements, where "dogmatic" applies to *any* statement asserted to possess inherent self-evident truth. That the only alternative to ascribing to some propositions self-sufficient, self-possessed, and self-evident truth is a theory which finds the test and mark of truth in *consequences* of some sort is, I hope, an acceptable view. At all events, it is a position to be kept in mind in assessing my views.

II

In an earlier passage Mr. Russell ascribes certain views to "instrumentalists" and points out certain errors which undoubtedly (and rather obviously) exist in those views—as *he* conceives and states them. My name and especial view are not mentioned in this earlier passage. But, aside from the fact that I have called my view of propositions "instrumental" (in the particular technical sense in which I define propositions), comment on the passage may assist in clarifying what my views genuinely are. The passage reads:

There are some schools of philosophy—notably the Hegelians and the instrumentalists—which deny the distinction between data and inference altogether. They maintain that in all our knowledge there is an inferential element, that knowledge is an organic whole, and that the test of truth is coherence rather than conformity with "fact." I do not deny an element of truth in this view, but I think that, if taken as a whole truth, it renders the part played by perception in knowledge inexplicable. It is surely obvious that every perceptive experience, if I choose to notice it, affords me either new knowledge which I could not previously have inferred, or, at least, as in the case of eclipses, greater certainty than I could have previously obtained by means of inference. To this the instrumentalist replies that any statement of the new knowledge obtained from perception is always an interpretation based upon accepted theories, and may need subsequent correction if these theories turn out to be unsuitable.[7]

I begin with the ascription to instrumentalists of the idea that "in all our knowledge, there is an inferential element." This statement is, from the standpoint of my view, ambiguous; in one of its meanings, it is incorrect. It is necessary, then, to make a distinction. If it means (as it is apparently intended to mean) that an element due to inference appears in *propria persona*, so to speak, it is incorrect. For according to my view (if I may take it as a sample of the instrumentalists' view), while to infer something is necessary if a warranted assertion is to be arrived at, this inferred somewhat never appears *as such* in the latter; that is, in knowledge. The inferred material has to be checked and tested. The means of testing, required to give an inferential element any claim whatsoever to be *knowledge* instead of conjecture, are the data provided by observation—and *only* by observation. Moreover, as is stated frequently in my *Logic: The Theory of Inquiry*, it is necessary that data (provided by observation) be *new*, or different from those which first suggested the inferential element, if they are to have any value with respect to attaining knowledge. It is important that they be had under as many different conditions as possible so that data due to *differential* origins may supplement one another. The necessity of both the distinction and the coöperation of inferential and observational subject-matters is, on my theory, the product of an analysis of scientific inquiry; this necessity is, as will be shown in more detail later, the heart of my whole theory that knowledge is warranted assertion.

It should now be clear that the instrumentalist would not dream of making the kind of "reply" attributed to him. Instead of holding that *"accepted* theories" are always the basis for interpretation of what is newly obtained in perceptual experience, he has not been behind others in pointing out that such a mode of interpretation is a common and serious source of wrong conclusions; of dogmatism and of consequent arrest of advance in knowledge. In my *Logic*, I have explicitly pointed out that one chief reason why the introduction of experimental methods meant such a great, such

---

[7] *Op. cit.*, p. 154. To clear the ground for discussion of the views advanced in the passage quoted in the text, and as a means of shortening my comments, I append a few categorical statements, which can be substantiated by many references to "instrumentalist" writings. Instrumentalists do *not* believe that "knowledge is an organic whole"; in fact, the idea is meaningless upon their view. They do *not* believe the test of truth is coherence; in the operational sense, stated later in this paper, they hold a correspondence view.

a revolutionary, change in natural science, is that they provide data which are new not only in detail but in *kind*. Hence their introduction compelled new kinds of inference to new kinds of subject-matters, and the formation of new types of theories—in addition to providing more exact means of testing old theories. Upon the basis of the view ascribed to instrumentalists, I should suppose it would have been simpler and more effective to point out the contradiction involved in holding, on one side, that the instrumentalist has no way of discovering "need for further correction" in accepted theories, while holding, on the other side, that all accepted theories are, or may be, "unsuitable." Is there not flat contradiction between the idea that "any statement of new knowledge obtained by perception is always an interpretation based upon accepted theories," and the view that it may need subsequent correction if these theories prove "unsuitable"? How in the world, upon the ground of the first part of the supposed "reply" of the instrumentalist, could any theory once "accepted" ever be shown to be unsuitable?

I am obliged, unfortunately, to form a certain hypothesis as to how and why, in view of the numerous and oft-repeated statements in my *Logic* of the *necessity* for distinguishing between inferential elements and observational data (necessary since otherwise there is no approach to warranted assertibility), it could occur to anyone that I denied the distinction. The best guess I can make is that my statements about the necessity of hard data, due to experimental observation and freed from all inferential constituents, were not taken seriously because it was supposed that upon my theory these data themselves represent, or present, *cases of knowledge*, so that there must be on my theory an inferential element also in them. Whether or not this is the source of the alleged denial thought up by Mr. Russell, it may be used to indicate a highly significant difference between our two views. For Mr. Russell holds, if I understand him, that propositions about these data are in some cases instances of knowledge, and indeed that such cases provide, as basic propositions, the models upon which a theory of truth should be formed. In my view, they are not cases of *knowledge*, although propositional formulation of them is a *necessary* (but not sufficient) condition of knowledge.

I can understand that my actual view may seem even more objectionable to a critic than the one that has been wrongly ascribed to me. None the less, in the interest of understanding and as a ground of pertinent criticism, it is indispensable that this position, and what it involves, be recognized as fundamental in my theory. It brings me to what is meant, in my theory, by the instrumental character of a proposition. I shall, then, postpone consideration of the ascription to me of the view that propositions are true if they are instruments or tools of successful action till I have stated just what, on my theory, a proposition is. The view imputed to me is that "Inquiry uses 'assertions' as its tools, and assertions are 'warranted' insofar as they produce the desired result."[8] I put in contrast with this conception the following statement of my view:

Judgment may be identified as the settled outcome of inquiry. It is concerned with the concluding objects that emerge from inquiry in their status of being *conclusive*. Judgment in this sense is distinguished from *propositions*. The content of the latter is intermediate and representative and is carried by symbols; while judgment, as finally made, has *direct* existential import. The terms *affirmation* and *assertion* are employed in current speech interchangeably. But there is a difference, which should have linguistic recognition, between the logical status of intermediate subject-matters that are taken for use in connection *with what they lead to as means*, and subject-matter which has been prepared to be final. I shall use *assertion* to designate the latter logical status and *affirmation* to name the former. . . . However, the important matter is not the words, but the logical properties characteristic of different subject-matters.[9]

Propositions, then, on this view, are what are affirmed but not asserted. They are means, instrumentalities, since they are the operational agencies by which *beliefs* that have adequate grounds for acceptance, are reached as *end* of inquiry. As I have intimated, this view may seem even more objectionable than is the one attributed to me, i.e., the one which is not mine. But in any case the difference between the instrumentality of a *proposition* as means of attaining a grounded *belief* and the instrumentality of a *belief* as means of reaching certain "desired results," should be fairly obvious, independently of acceptance or rejection of my view.

Unless a critic is willing to entertain, in however hypothetical a fashion, the view (i) that *knowledge* (in its honorific sense) is in every case connected with inquiry; (ii) that the conclusion or end of inquiry has to be demarcated from the intermediate means by which inquiry goes forward to a warranted or justified conclusion; that (iii) the intermediate means are formulated in discourse, i.e., as propositions, and that as means they have the properties appropriate to means (viz., relevancy and efficacy—including economy), I know of no way to make my view intelligible. If the view

---

[8] *Op. cit.*, pp. 401–402.

[9] *Logic: The Theory of Inquiry*, p. 120 (not all italics in original). The word "logical," as it occurs in this passage, is, of course, to be understood in the sense given that term in previous chapters of the volume; a signification that is determined by connection with operations of inquiry which are undertaken because of the existence of a problem, and which are controlled by the conditions of that problem—since the "goal" is to resolve the problem which evokes inquiry.

is entertained, even in the most speculative conjectural fashion, it will, I think, be clear that according to it, truth and falsity are properties only of that subject-matter which is the *end*, the close, of the inquiry by means of which it is reached. The distinction between true and false conclusions is determined by the character of the operational procedures through which propositions about data and propositions about inferential elements (meanings, ideas, hypotheses) are instituted. At all events, I can not imagine that one who says that such things as hammers, looms, chemical processes like dyeing, reduction of ores, when used as means, are marked by properties of fitness and efficacy (and the opposite) rather than by the properties of truth-falsity, will be thought to be saying anything that is not commonplace.

IV

My view of the nature of propositions, as distinct from that held by Mr. Russell, may be further illustrated by commenting upon the passage in which, referring to my view concerning changes in the matter of hypotheses during the course of inquiry, he writes: "I should say that inquiry begins, as a rule, with an assertion that is vague and complex, but replaces it, when it can, by a number of separate assertions each of which is less vague and less complex than the original assertion." [10] I remark in passing that previous observations of this kind by Mr. Russell were what led me so to misapprehend his views as to impute to him the assumption "that *propositions* are the subject-matter of inquiry"; an impression, which, if it were not for his present explicit disclaimer, would be strengthened by reading, "When we embark upon an inquiry we assume that *the propositions about which we are enquiring* are either true or false." [11] Without repeating the ascription repudiated by Mr. Russell, I would say that upon my view "propositions are *not* that about which we are inquiring," and that as far as we do find it necessary or advisable to inquire about them (as is almost bound to happen in the course of an inquiry), it is not their truth and falsity about which we inquire, but the relevancy and efficacy of their subject-matter with respect to the problem in hand. I also remark, in passing, that Mr. Russell's statement appears to surrender the strict two-value theory of propositions in admitting that they may have the properties of being vague-definite; complex-simple. I suppose, however, that Mr. Russell's reply would be that on his view these latter qualities are derivative; that the first proposition is vague and complex because it is a mixture of some (pos-

10 *Op. cit.*, p. 403.
11 *Op. cit.*, p. 361. My italics.

sibly) true and some (possibly) false propositions. While dialectically this reply covers the case, it does not seem to agree with what happens in any actual case of analysis of a proposition into simpler and more definite ones. For this analysis always involves modification or transformation of the terms (meanings) found in the original proposition, and not its division into some true and some false propositions that from the start were its constituents although in a mixture.

Coming to the main point at issue, I hold that the first propositions we make as means of resolving a problem of any marked degree of difficulty are indeed likely to be too vague and coarse to be effective, just as in the story of invention of other instrumentalities, the first forms are relatively clumsy, uneconomical, and ineffective. They have then, as means, to be replaced by others which are more effective. Propositions are vague when, for example, they do not delimit the problem sufficiently to indicate what kind of a solution is relevant. It is hardly necessary to say that when we don't know the conditions constituting a problem we are trying to solve, our efforts at solution at best will be fumbling and are likely to be wild. Data serve as tests of any idea or hypothesis that suggests itself, and in this capacity also their definiteness is required. But, upon my view, the degree and the quality of definiteness and of simplicity, or elementariness, required, are determined by the problem that evokes and controls inquiry. However the case may stand in epistemology (as a problem based upon a prior assumption that knowledge is and must be a relation between a knowing subject and an object), upon the basis of a view that takes knowing (inquiry) as it finds it, the idea that simplicity and elementariness are *inherent* properties of propositions (apart from their place and function in inquiry), has no meaning. If I understand Mr. Russell's view, his test for the simple and definite nature of a proposition applies indifferently to all propositions and hence has no indicative or probative force with respect to any proposition in particular.

Accepting, then, Mr. Russell's statement that his "problem has been, throughout, the relation between events and propositions," and regretting that I ascribed to him the view that "propositions are the subject-matter of inquiry," I would point out what seems to be a certain indeterminateness in his view of the relation between events and propositions, and the consequent need of introducing a distinction: *viz.,* the distinction between the problem of the relation of events and propositions *in general,* and the problem of the relation of a *particular* proposition to the *particular* event to which it purports to refer. I can understand that Mr. Russell holds that certain propositions, of a specified kind, are such direct effects of certain events, and of nothing else, that they "must be true." But this view does not, as I see the matter, answer the question of how we know that *in a given case* this direct relationship actually exists. It does not seem to me that his theory gets beyond specifying the kind of case *in general* in which the relation between an event, as causal antecedent, and a proposition, as effect, is such as to confer upon instances of the latter the property of being true. But I can not see that we get anywhere until we have means of telling *which* propositions in particular *are* instances of the kind in question.

In the case, previously cited, of *redness-here,* Mr. Russell asserts, as I understand him, that it is true when it is caused by a simple, atomic event. But how do we know in a given case whether it is so caused? Or if he holds that it *must* be true because it *is* caused by such an event, which is then its sufficient verifier, I am compelled to ask how such is known to be the case. These comments are intended to indicate both that I hold a "correspondence" theory of truth, and the sense in which I hold it;—a sense which seems to me free from a fundamental difficulty that Mr. Russell's view of truth can not get over or around. The event *to be* known is that which operates, on his view, as cause of the proposition while it is also its verifier; although the proposition is the sole means of knowing the event! Such a view, like any strictly epistemological view, seems to me to assume a mysterious and unverifiable doctrine of pre-established harmony. How an event can be (i) what-is-to-be-known, and hence by description is unknown, and (ii) what is capable of being *known* only through the medium of a proposition, which, in turn (iii) in order to be a case of knowledge or be true, must correspond to the to-be-known, is to me *the* epistemological miracle. For the doctrine states that a proposition is true when it conforms to that which is not known save through itself.

In contrast with this view, my own view takes correspondence in the operational sense it bears in all cases except the unique epistemological case of an alleged relation between a "subject" and an "object"; the meaning, namely, of *answering,* as a key answers to conditions imposed by a lock, or as two correspondents "answer" each other; or, in general, as a reply is an adequate answer to a question or a criticism—; as, in short, a *solution* answers the requirements of a *problem.* On this view, both partners in "correspondence" are open and above board, instead of one of them being forever out of experience and the other in it by way of a "percept" or whatever. Wondering at how something in experience could be asserted to correspond to something by definition outside experience, which it is, upon the basis of epistemological doctrine, the sole means of "knowing," is what originally made me suspicious of the whole epistemological industry.[12]

In the sense of correspondence as operational and behavioral (the meaning which has definite parallels in ordinary experience), I hold that my *type* of theory is the only one entitled to be called a correspondence theory of truth.

V

I should be happy to believe that what has been said is sufficiently definite and clear as to the nature and function of "consequences," so that it is not necessary to say anything more on the subject. But there are criticisms of Mr. Russell's that I might seem to be evading were I to say nothing specifically about them. He asserts that he has several times asked me what the goal of inquiry is upon my theory, and has seen no answer to the question.[13] There seems to be some reason for inferring that this matter is connected with the belief that I am engaged in *substituting* something else for "truth," so that truth, as he interprets my position, not being the goal, I am bound to provide some other goal. A person turning to the Index of my *Logic: The Theory of Inquiry* will find the following heading: "Assertibility, warranted, as end of inquiry." Some fourteen passages of the text are referred to. Unless there is difference which escapes me between "end" and "goal," the following passage would seem to give the answer which Mr. Russell has missed:

Moreover, inference, even in its connection with test, is not logically final and complete. The heart of the entire theory developed in this work is that

[12] In noting that my view of truth involves dependence upon consequences (as his depends upon antecedents, not, however, themselves in experience), and in noting that a causal law is involved, Mr. Russell concludes: "These causal laws, if they are to serve their purpose, must be 'true' in the very sense that Dr. Dewey would abolish" (*op. cit.*, p. 408). It hardly seems unreasonable on my part to expect that my general theory of truth be applied to particular cases, that of the truth of causal laws included. If it was unreasonable to *expect* that it would be so understood, I am glad to take this opportunity to say that such is the case. I do not hold in this case a view I have elsewhere "abolished." I *apply* the general view I advance elsewhere. There are few matters with respect to which there has been as much experience and as much testing as in the matter of the connection of means and consequences, since that connection is involved in all the details of every occupation, art, and undertaking. That warranted assertibility is a matter of probability in the case of causal connections is a trait it shares with other instances of warranted assertibility; while, apparently, Mr. Russell would deny the name of knowledge, in its fullest sense, to anything that is not certain to the point of infallibility, or which does not ultimately rest upon some absolute certainty.

[13] *Op. cit.*, p. 404.

the resolution of an indeterminate situation is the end, in the sense in which "end" means *end-in-view* and in the sense in which it means *close*.[14]

The implication of the passage, if not in its isolation then in its context, is that inquiry begins in an *indeterminate* situation, and not only begins in it but is controlled by its specific qualitative nature.[15] Inquiry, as the set of operations by which the situation is resolved (settled, or rendered determinate) has to discover and formulate the conditions that describe the problem in hand. For *they* are the conditions to be "satisfied" and the determinants of "success." Since these conditions are existential, they can be determined only by observational operations; the operational character of observation being clearly exhibited in the experimental character of all scientific determination of data. (Upon a nonscientific level of inquiry, it is exhibited in the fact that we *look* and see; *listen* and hear; or, in general terms, that a motor-muscular, as well as sensory, factor is involved in any perceptual experience.) The conditions discovered, accordingly, in and by operational observation, constitute the *conditions of the problem* with which further inquiry is engaged; for data, on this view, are always data of some specific problem and hence are not given readymade to an inquiry but are determined in and by it. (The point previously stated, that propositions about data are not cases of knowledge but means of attaining it, is so obviously an integral part of this view that I say nothing further about it in this connection.) As the problem progressively assumes definite shape by means of repeated acts of observation, possible solutions suggest themselves. These possible solutions are, truistically (in terms of the theory), *possible* meanings of the data determined in observation. The process of reasoning is an elaboration of them. When they are checked by reference to observed materials, they constitute the subject-matter of *inferential* propositions. The latter are means of attaining the goal of knowledge as warranted assertion, not instances or examples of knowledge. They are also operational in nature since they institute new experimental observations whose subject-matter provides both tests for old hypotheses and starting-points for new ones or at least for modifying solutions previously entertained. And so on until a determinate situation is instituted.

---

[14] *Logic: The Theory of Inquiry*, pp. 157–158.

[15] *Logic*, p. 105. "It is a unique doubtfulness" that not only evokes the particular inquiry, but as explicitly stated "exercises control" over it. To avoid needless misunderstanding, I quote also the following passage: "No situation which is *completely* indeterminate can possibly be converted into a problem having definite constituents" (*Ibid.*, p. 108).

If this condensed statement is taken in its own terms and not by first interpreting its meaning in terms of some theory it doesn't logically permit, I think it will render unnecessary further comment on the notion Mr. Russell has ascribed to me: the notion, namely, that "a belief is warranted, if as a tool, it is useful in some activity, i.e., if it is a cause of satisfaction of desire," and that "the only essential result of successful inquiry is successful action." [16]

In the interest of mutual understanding, I shall now make some comments on a passage which, if I interpret it aright, sets forth the nature of Mr. Russell's wrong idea of my view, and which also, by implication, suggests the nature of the genuine difference between our views:

> If there are such occurrences as "believings," which seems undeniable, the question is: Can they be divided into two classes, the "true" and the "false"? Or, if not, can they be so analyzed that their constituents can be divided into these two classes? If either of these questions is answered in the affirmative, is the distinction between "true" and "false" to be found in the success or failure of the effects of believings, or is it to be found in some other relation which they may have to relevant occurrences?" [17]

On the basis of other passages, such as have been quoted, I am warranted in supposing that there is ascribed to me the view that "the distinction between 'true' and 'false' is to be found in the success or failure of the effects of believings." After what I have already said, I hope it suffices to point out that the question of truth-falsity is *not*, on my view, a matter of the effects of *believing*, for my whole theory is determined by the attempt to state what conditions and operations of inquiry *warrant* a "believing," or justify its assertion as true; that propositions, as such, are so far from being cases of believings that they are means of attaining a warranted believing, their worth as means being determined by their pertinency and efficacy in "satisfying" conditions that are rigorously set by the problem they are employed to resolve.

At this stage of the present discussion, I am, however, more interested in the passage quoted as an indication of the difference between us than as a manifestation of the nature of Mr. Russell's wrong understanding of my view.[18] I believe most decidedly that

[16] *Op. cit.*, pp. 404, 405.

[17] *Op. cit.*, p. 405.

[18] I venture to remark that the words "wrong" and "right" as they appear in the text are used intentionally instead of the words "false" and "true"; for, according to my view, understanding and misunderstanding, conception and misconception, taking and mis-taking, are matters of propositions, which are not final or complete in themselves but are used as means to an end—the resolution of a problem; while it is to this resolution, as *conclusion* of inquiry, that the adjectives "true" and "false" apply.

the distinction between "true" and "false" is to be found in the relation which *propositions,* as means of inquiry, "have to relevant occurrences." The difference between us concerns, as I see the matter in the light of Mr. Russell's explanation, the question of *what* occurrences *are* the relevant ones. And I hope it is unnecessary to repeat by this time that the relevant occurrences on my theory are those existential consequences which, in virtue of operations existentially performed, satisfy (meet, fulfill) conditions set by occurrences that constitute a problem. These considerations bring me to my final point.

VI

In an earlier writing, a passage of which is cited by Mr. Russell, I stated my conclusion that Mr. Russell's interpretation of my view in terms of satisfaction of personal desire, of success in activities performed in order to satisfy desires, etc., was due to failure to note the importance in my theory of the existence of indeterminate or problematic situations as not only the source of, but as the control of, inquiry. A part of what I there wrote reads as follows:

> Mr. Russell proceeds first by converting a doubtful *situation* into a personal doubt. . . . Then by changing doubt into private discomfort, truth is identified [upon my view] with removal of this discomfort . . . [but] "Satisfaction" is satisfaction of the conditions prescribed by the problem.

In the same connection reference is made to a sentence in the Preface in which I stated, in view of previous misunderstandings of my position, that consequences are only to be accepted as tests of validity *"provided* these consequences are operationally instituted." [19]

Mr. Russell has made two comments with reference to these two explicitly stated conditions which govern the meaning and function of consequences. One of them concerns the reference to the consequences being "operationally instituted." Unfortunately for the cause of mutual understanding, it consists of but one sentence to the effect that its "meaning remains to me somewhat obscure." Comment upon the other qualification, namely, upon the necessity of "doubtful" problematic, etc., being taken to be characteristic of the "objective" situation and not of a person or "subject," is, fortunately, more extended:

> Dr. Dewey *seems* to write as if a doubtful situation could exist without a personal doubter. I cannot think that he means this; he cannot intend to say,

[19] The original passage of mine is found in Vol. I of the *Library of Living Philosophers,* p. 571. It is also stated as one of the conditions, that it is necessary that consequences be "such as to resolve the specific problem evoking the operations." Quoted on p. 571 of the *Library* from p. iv, of the Preface of my *Logic.*

for example, that there were doubtful situations in astronomical and geological epochs before there was life. The only way in which I can interpret what he says is to suppose that, for him, a "doubtful situation" is one which arouses doubt, not only in some one individual, but in any normal man, or in any man anxious to achieve a certain result, or in any scientifically trained observer engaged in investigating the situation. *Some* purpose, i.e., *some* desire, is involved in the idea of a doubtful situation.[20]

When the term "doubtful situation" is taken in the meaning it possesses in the context of my general theory of experience, I *do* mean to say that it can exist without a personal doubter; and, moreover, that "personal states of doubt that are not evoked by, and are not relative to, some existential situation are pathological; when they are extreme they constitute the mania of doubting. . . . The habit of disposing of the doubtful as if it belonged only to *us* rather than to the existential situation in which we are caught and implicated is an inheritance from subjectivistic psychology."[21] This position is so intimately and fundamentally bound up with my whole theory of "experience" as behavioral (though not "behavioristic" in the technical sense that the word has assumed), as interactivity of organism and environment, that I should have to go into a restatement of what I have said at great length elsewhere if I tried to justify what is affirmed in the passage quoted. I confine myself here to one point. The *problematic* nature of situations is definitely stated to have its source and prototype in the condition of imbalance or disequilibration that recurs rhythmically in the interactivity of organism and environment;—a condition exemplified in hunger, not as a "feeling" but as a form of organic behavior such as is manifested, for example, in bodily restlessness and bodily acts of search for food. Since I can not take the space to restate the view of experience of which the position regarding the existential nature of the indeterminate or problematic situation is one aspect (one, however, which is logically involved in and demanded by it), I confine myself to brief comments intended to make clearer, if possible, differences between my position and that of Mr. Russell. (i) All experiences are interactivities of an organism and an environment; a doubtful or problematic situation is, of course, no exception. But the energies of an organism involved in the particular interactivity that constitutes, or *is*, the problematic situation, are those involved in an ordinary course of living. They are *not* those of doubting. Doubt can, as I have said, be legitimately imputed to the organism only in a *secondary* or derived manner. (ii) "Every such interaction is a temporal process, not

20 *Op. cit.*, p. 407.
21 *Logic*, p. 106.

a momentary, cross-sectional occurrence. The situation in which it occurs is indeterminate, therefore, with respect to its *issue*. . . . Even were existential conditions unqualifiedly determinate in and of themselves, they are indeterminate [are such in certain instances] in *significance:* that is, in what they import and portend in their interaction with the organism.''[22] The passage should throw light upon the sense in which an existential organism is existentially implicated or involved in a situation as interacting with environing conditions. According to my view, the sole way in which a ''normal person'' figures is that such a person investigates only in the actual presence of a problem. (iii) All that is necessary upon my view is that an astronomical or geological epoch be an actual constituent of some experienced problematic situation. I am not, logically speaking, obliged to indulge in any cosmological speculation about those epochs, because, on my theory, any proposition about them is of the nature of what A. F. Bentley, in well-chosen terms, calls *''extrapolation,''* under certain conditions, be it understood, perfectly legitimate, but nevertheless an extrapolation.[23]

As far as cosmological speculation on the indeterminate situations in astronomical and geological epochs is relevant to my theory (or my theory to it), *any* view which holds that man is a part of nature, not outside it, will hold that this fact of being part of nature qualifies his ''experience'' throughout. Hence that view will certainly hold that indeterminancy in human experience, once experience is taken in the objective sense of interacting behavior and not as a private conceit added on to something totally alien to it, is evidence of some corresponding indeterminateness in the processes of nature within which man exists (acts) and out of which he arose. Of course, one who holds, as Mr. Russell seems to do, to the doctrine of the existence of an independent subject as the cause of the ''doubtfulness'' or ''problematic quality'' of situations will take the view he has expressed, thus confirming my opinion that the difference between us has its basic source in different views of the nature of experience, which in turn is correlated with our different conceptions of the connection existing between man and the rest of the world. Mr. Russell has not envisaged the possibility of there being another generic theory of experience, as an alternative

[22] *Logic,* pp. 106–107.

[23] *Behavior, Knowledge and Fact* (1935), Section XIX, ''Experience and Fact,'' especially, pp. 172–179. The passage should be read in connection with section XXVII, ''Behavioral Space-Time.'' I am glad to refer anyone interested in that part of my view that has to do with prehuman and pre-organic events to Mr. Bentley's statement, without, however, intending to make him responsible for what I have said on any other point.

to the pre-Darwinian conceptions of Hegel, on the one hand, and of Mill, on the other.

The qualification in my theory relating to the necessity of consequences being "operationally instituted" is, of course, an intimate constituent of my whole theory of inquiry. I do not wonder that Mr. Russell finds the particular passage he cites "somewhat obscure," if he takes it in isolation from its central position in my whole theory of experience, inquiry, and knowledge. I cite one passage that indicates the intrinsic connection existing between this part of my theory and the point just mentioned—that concerning the place of indeterminate situations in inquiry. "Situations that are disturbed and troubled, confused or obscure, cannot be straightened out, cleared up and put in order, by manipulations of our personal states of mind." [24] This is the negative aspect of the position that operations of an existential sort, operations which are actions, doing something and accomplishing something (a changed state of interactivity in short), are the only means of producing consequences that have any bearing upon warranted assertibility.

In concluding this part of my discussion, I indulge in the statement of some things that puzzle me, things connected, moreover, not just with Mr. Russell's view, but with views that are widely held. (i) I am puzzled by the fact that persons who are systematically engaged with inquiry into questions, into problems (as philosophers certainly are), are so incurious about the existence and nature of problems. (ii) If a "subject" is one end-term in a relation of which objects (events) are the other end-term, and if doubt is simply a state of a subject, why isn't knowledge also simply and only a state of mind of a subject? And (iii) the puzzling thing already mentioned: How can anybody look at *both* an object (event) and a proposition about it so as to determine whether the two "correspond"? And if one can look directly at the event *in propria persona,* why have a duplicate proposition (idea or percept, according to some theories) about it unless, perhaps, as a convenience in communication with others?

I do not wish to conclude without saying that I have tried to conduct my discussion in the spirit indicated by Mr. Russell, avoiding all misunderstanding as far as I can, and viewing the issues involved as uncontroversially as is consistent with trying to make my own views clear. In this process I am aware of the acute bearing of his remark that "it is because the difference goes deep that it is difficult to find words which both sides can accept as a fair statement of the issue." In view of the depth of the difference, I can hardly hope to have succeeded completely in overcoming this

[24] *Logic,* p. 106.

difficulty. But at least I have been more concerned to make my own position intelligible than to refute Mr. Russell's view, so that the controversial remarks I have made have their source in the belief that definite contrasts are an important, perhaps indispensable, means of making any view sharp in outline and definite in content.

I add that I am grateful to Mr. Russell for devoting so much space to my views and for thus giving me an opportunity to restate them. If the space I have taken in this reply seems out of proportion to the space given to questioning my view in Mr. Russell's book, it is because of my belief of the importance of that book. For I believe that he has reduced, with his great skill in analysis, a position that is widely held to its ultimate constituents, and that this accomplishment eliminates much that has been vague and confused in the current view. In particular, I believe that the position he has taken regarding the causal relation between an event and a proposition is the first successful effort to set forth a clear interpretation of what "correspondence" *must* mean in current realistic epistemologies. Statement in terms of a causal relation between an event and a proposition gets rid, in my opinion, of much useless material that encumbers the ordinary statement made about the "epistemological" relation. That I also believe his accomplishment of this work discloses the fundamental defect in the epistemological—as contrasted with the experiential-behavioral—account of correspondence will be clear to the reader. But at least the issue is that much clarified, and it is taken into a wider field than that of a difference between Mr. Russell's views and mine.

JOHN DEWEY.

COLUMBIA UNIVERSITY.

THE JOURNAL OF PHILOSOPHY

A SEARCH FOR FIRM NAMES

A YEAR or so ago we decided that the time had come to undertake a postponed task: the attempt to fix a set of leading words capable of firm use in the discussion of "knowings" and "existings" in that specialized region of research called the theory of knowledge. The undertaking proved to be of the kind that grows. Firm words for our own use had to be based on well-founded observation. Such observation had to be sound enough, and well enough labeled, so that it could be used with definiteness, not only between ourselves, but also in intercourse with other workers, including even those who might be at far extremes from us in their manners of interpretation and construction. It is clear, we think, that without some agreement such as this as to the simpler fact-names, no progress of the kind the modern world knows as scientific will be probable; and, further, that so long as man, the organism, is viewed naturalistically within the cosmos, research of the scientific type into his "knowings" is a worth-while objective. The results of our inquiry will be reported in perhaps half a dozen papers, some individually signed, and some over our joint names, depending on the extent to which problems and investigations have become specialized or combined as we proceed. We shall examine such words as fact, existence, event; designation, experience, agency; situation, object, subject-matter; interaction, transaction; definition, description, specification, characterization; signal, sign, symbol; centering, of course, on those regions of application in which phrasings in the vaguely allusive form of "subject" and "object" conventionally appear.

The paper now offered, the first of the group, arose from the accumulation of many illustrations, which we first segregated, and then advanced to introductory position because we found them to be yielding a startling diagnosis of linguistic disease, not only in the general epistemological field, where every one would anticipate it, but also in the specialized logical field, which ought to be reasonably immune. This diagnosis furnishes the strongest evidence of the need of the type of terminological inquiry we are engaged in, whether at our hands and from our manner of approach, or at the hands and under the differing approach of others. We are in full agreement as to the general development of the present paper, and as to the demonstration of the extent of the evil in the logics, its roots, and the steps that should be taken for its cure. The single signature attached, is, as was indicated above, little more than a mark of the division of labor.

It should be plain enough that the discussions in the first paper, as well as in those that are to follow, are not primarily for the purpose of criticising individual logicians. In view of the competence of the writers who are discussed, the confusions and inconsistencies which are found can be attributed only to something defective in the underlying assumptions which influence their approach. The nature of these underlying defects will, we trust, become evident as we proceed; and we hope that the specific criticisms we are compelled to make in order to exhibit the difficulty will be taken as directed solely to that end.

JOHN DEWEY
ARTHUR F. BENTLEY

THE JOURNAL OF PHILOSOPHY

A TERMINOLOGY FOR KNOWINGS AND KNOWNS [1]

SCIENCE uses its technical names efficiently. Such names serve to mark off certain portions of the scientific subject-matter as provisionally acceptable, thereby freeing the worker's attention for closer consideration of other portions that remain problematic. The efficiency lies in the ability given the worker to hold such names steady—to know what he properly names with them—first at different stages of his own procedure, and then in interchange with his associates.

Theories of knowledge provide their investigators with no such dependable aids. The traditional namings they employ have primitive cultural origins and the supplemental "terms" they evolve have frequently no ascertainable application as names at all.

We believe that the time has come when a few leading names for knowings and knowns can be established and put to use. We believe further that this should be undertaken upon a scientific basis, where by "scientific" we understand very simply "factual inquiry," in which the knowing man is accepted as a factual component of the factual cosmos, as he is elsewhere in modern research. We know of no other basis upon which to anticipate dependable results—more particularly since the past history of "epistemology" is filled with danger-signs.

What we advocate is in very simple statement a passage from loose to firm namings. Some purported names do little more than indicate fields of inquiry—some, even, do hardly that. Others specify with a high degree of firmness. The word "knowledge," as a name, is a loose name. We do not employ it in the titles of our papers and we shall not use it in any significant way as we proceed. It is often a convenience, and it is probably not objectionable—at least it may be kept from being dangerous—where there is no stress upon its accurate application, and no great probability that a reader will assume that there is; at any rate we shall thus occasionally risk it. We shall rate it as No. 1 on a list of

---

[1] This article is the second of a series (announced in Volume XLII, 1945, pp. 5–6) on "A Search for Firm Names"; the first appeared in Volume XLII (1945), pp. 6–27, 39–51, under the title "On a Certain Vagueness in Logic."

"vague words" [2] which we shall call attention to and add to from time to time in footnotes. Only through prolonged factual inquiry, of which little has as yet been undertaken, can the word "knowledge" be given determinable status with respect to such questions as: (1) the range of its application to human or animal behaviors; (2) the types of its distribution between knowers, knowns, and presumptive intermediaries; (3) the possible localizations implied for knowledges as present in space and time. In place of examining such a vague generality as the word "knowledge" offers, we shall speak of and concern ourselves directly with knowings and knowns—and, moreover, in each instance with those particular forms of knowings and knowns in which we may hope for reasonably definite identifications.

I

The conditions which namings such as we seek must satisfy, positively and negatively, include the following:

1. The names are to be based on observations such as are accessible to and attainable by everybody. This condition treats as negligible to knowledge any report of purported observation which the reporter avows to be radically and exclusively private.

2. The status of observation and the use of reports upon it is to be tentative, postulational, hypothetical.[3] This condition excludes all purported materials and all alleged fixed principles which are offered as providing original and necessary "foundations" for either the knowings or the knowns.

3. The aim of the observation and naming adopted is to promote further observation which in turn advances to similar use under similar aim. This condition excludes all namings which are asserted to give, or which claim to be, finished reports on "reality."

The above conditions amount to saying that the names we need have to do with knowings and knowns in and by means of continuous operation and test, in work in which any knowing or known establishes itself or fails to establish itself solely through continued search and research, and never on the ground of any

---

[2] Even the words "vague," "firm," and "loose," as we at this stage are able to use them, are loosely used. We undertake development definitely and deliberately within an atmosphere—one might perhaps better call it a swamp—of vague language. We reject the alternative—the initial dependence on some schematism of verbal impactions—and propose to destroy the authoritarian claims of such impactions by means of distinctions later to be introduced, including particularly that between specification and definition.

[3] The postulations we are using, their origin and status, will be discussed in a following paper. See also Dewey, *Logic*, Chap. I, and Bentley, "Postulation for Behavioral Inquiry," this JOURNAL, Vol. XXXVI (1939), pp. 405–413.

alleged outside "foundation," "premise," "axiom," or *ipse dixit* assertion. In line with this attitude we do not assert that the conditions stated above are "true"; we are not even arguing in their behalf. We advance them as the conditions we hold should be satisfied by the kind of names that are needed if we are to advance knowledge of knowledge. Our procedure, then, does not stand in the way of inquiry into knowledge by other workers on the basis either of established creeds or tenets, or of alternative hypotheses; we but state the ground upon which we ourselves wish to work, in the belief that others are prepared to coöperate. The postulates and methods we wish to use are, we believe, akin to those of the sciences which have so greatly advanced knowledge in other fields.

The difficulties in our way are serious, but we believe these difficulties have their chief source in the control exercised over men by traditional phrasings originating when observation was relatively primitive and lacked the many important materials which now are easily available. Cultural conditions (such as ethnological research reveals) favored in earlier days the introduction of factors which have now been shown to be irrelevant to the operations of inquiry and to stand in the way of the formation of a straightforward theory of knowledge—straightforward in the sense of setting forth conclusions reached through inquiry into knowledge as itself fact.

The basic postulate of our procedure is that knowings are observable facts in the same sense exactly as are the subject-matters which are known. A glance at any collection of books and periodicals discloses the immense number of subject-matters that have been studied and the various grades of their establishment in the outcome. No great argument is required to warrant the statement that this wide field of knowledge (possessed of varying depths in its different portions) can be studied not only in terms of things [4] known, but also in terms of the knowings.

In the previous paper instances were pointed out among prominent contemporary logicians of an extraordinary confusion arising from an uncritical use in logic, as theory of knowledge, of forms of primitive observation, sometimes to the utter neglect of the fuller and keener observation now available, and in other cases producing such a mixture of two incompatible types of observation as inevitably wrecks achievement. It was affirmed in

---

[4] "Thing" is another of our vague words. It is in good standing and useful where vague general reference is all that is intended, and where no stress of the types suggested by "object," "entity," or "phenomenon" enters. In such situations only should it be used.

that paper that further advance will require complete abandonment of the customary isolation of the word from the man speaking, and likewise also of the word from the thing spoken of or named. In effect and often overtly words are dealt with in the logics as if they were a new and third kind of fact lying between man as speaker and things as spoken of. The net result is to erect a new barrier in human behavior between the things which are involved and the operating organisms. While the logical writers in question have professedly departed from the earlier epistemological theories framed in terms of a mind basic as subject and an external world as object, competent analysis shows that the surviving separation which their writings exhibit is the ghost of the seventeenth-century epistemological separation of knowing subject and object known, as that in turn was the ghost of the medieval separation of a "spiritual" soul from a "material" nature and body.

The importance we allot to the introduction of firm names is very quickly felt when one begins to make observation of knowledge as a going fact of behavioral activity. Observation not only separates but also brings together in combination in a single sweep matters which at other times have been treated as isolated and hence as requiring to be forced into organization ("synthesized" is the traditional word) by some outside agency. The seeing of language with all of its speakings and writings as man-himself-in-action-dealing-with-things is observation of the combining type. Meaningful conveyance is, of course, included, as itself of the very texture of language. The full event is before us thus in durational spread. The observation is no longer in terms of "isolates" requiring to be "synthesized." Such procedure is common enough in all science. The extension as observation in our case is that we make it cover the speaker or knower along with the spoken of or known as one common durational event. Here primary speaking is as observable as is a bird in flight. The inclusion of books and periodicals as a case of observable man-in-action is no different in kind from the observation of the steel girders of a bridge connecting the mining and smelting of ores with the operations of a steel mill, and with the building of bridges in turn out of the products. For that matter it is no different from observation extended enough to take in not just a bird while in flight but bird-nest building, egg-laying, and hatching. Observation of this general type sees man-in-action not as something radically set over against an environing world, nor yet as merely acting "in" a world, but as action *of* and *by* the world in which the man belongs as an integral constituent.

To see an event filling a certain duration of time as a description across a full duration rather than as composed of an addition or other kind of combination of separate, instantaneous, or short-span events, is another aspect of such observation. Procedure of this type was continuously used by Peirce, though he had no favorable opportunity for developing it, and was basic to him from the time when in one of his earliest papers he stressed that all thought is in signs and requires a time.[5] The "immediate" or "neutral" experience of William James was definitely an effort at such a form of direct observation in the field of knowings. Dewey's development in use of interaction and transaction, and in presentation of experience as neither subjective nor objective, but as a method or system of organization, is strongly of this form; his psychological studies have made special contributions in this line, and in his *Logic, The Theory of Inquiry* (1938), following upon his logical essays of 1903 and 1916, he has developed the processes of inquiry in a situational setting. Bentley's *Process of Government* in 1908 developed political description in a manner approaching what we would here call "transactional," and his later analysis of mathematics as language, his situational treatment of behavior, and his factual development of behavioral space-time, belong in this line of research.[6]

[5] *Collected Papers*, 5.251: "The only cases of thought which we can find are of thought in signs"; 5.253: "To say that thought can not happen in an instant but requires a time is but another way of saying that every thought must be interpreted in another, or that all thought is in signs." See also comment in our preceding paper, p. 8. For a survey of Peirce's development (the citations being to his *Collected Papers*) see: "Questions Concerning Certain Faculties Claimed for Man" (1868), 5.213 to 5.263; "How to Make our Ideas Clear" (1878), 5.388 to 5.410; "A Pragmatic Interpretation of the Logical Subject" (1902), 2.328 to 2.331; "The Ethics of Terminology" (1903), 2.219 to 2.226. On his use of leading principles; see 3.154 to 3.171 and 5.365 to 5.369; on the open field of inquiry, 5.376n; on truth, 5.407, 5.565; on the social status of logic and knowledge, 2.220, 2.654, 5.311, 5.316, 5.331, 5.354, 5.421, 5.444, 6.610, 2.661; on the duplex nature of "experience," 1.321, 5.51, 5.284, 5.613.

[6] For James's development, see his essays in *Mind* in the early eighteen-eighties; Chapter X on "Self" in the *Principles of Psychology*, 1890; the epilogue to the *Briefer Course*, 1893; and *Essays in Radical Empiricism*, 1912. For Dewey, see *Studies in Logical Theory*, 1903; *How We Think*, 1910 (revised, 1933); *Essays in Experimental Logic*, 1916; *Experience and Nature*, 1925; *Logic, the Theory of Inquiry*, 1938; three psychological papers (all reprinted in *Philosophy and Civilization*, 1931) as follows: "The Reflex Arc Concept in Psychology," 1896—reprinted as "The Unit of Behavior"; "The Naturalistic Theory of Perception by the Senses," 1925; "Conduct and Experience," 1930. See also "Context and Thought," *University of California Publications in Philosophy*, 1931; "How is Mind to be Known?", this JOURNAL, Vol. XXXIX (1942), pp. 29–35; and "By Nature and by Art,"

If there should be difficulty in understanding this use of the word "observation," the difficulty illustrates the point previously made about the introduction of material from an incompetent source. The current philosophical notion of observation is derived from a psychology of "consciousness" (or some version of the "mental" as an isolate), and it endeavors to reduce what is observed either to some single sensory quality or to some other "content" of such short time-span as to have no connections except what may be provided through inference as an operation outside of observation. As against such a method of obtaining a description of observation, the procedure we adopt reports and describes observation on the same basis that the worker in knowledge—astronomer, physicist, psychologist, etc.—employs when he makes use of a test observation in arriving at the conclusions to be accepted as known. We proceed upon the postulate that *knowing* is always and everywhere the inseparable correlate of *the known*— that the two are twin aspects of common fact.

II

"Fact" is a name of central position in the material we propose to use in forming a terminology. If there are such things as Facts, and if they are of such importance that they have a vital status in questions of knowledge, then in any theory of knowings and knowns we should be able to characterize fact—we should be able to say, that is, that we know what we are talking about when we use the word as something which is definitely identifiable in the range of observation and firm naming.[7] The primary con-

this JOURNAL, Vol. XLI (1944), pp. 281–292. For Bentley, see *The Process of Government,* 1908; *Relativity in Man and Society,* 1926; *Linguistic Analysis of Mathematics,* 1932; *Behavior, Knowledge, Fact,* 1935; also three papers on situational treatment of behavior, this JOURNAL, Vol. XXXVI (1939), pp. 169–181, 309–323, 405–413; "The Factual Space and Time of Behavior," this JOURNAL (1941), pp. 477–485; "The Human Skin: Philosophy's Last Line of Defense," *Philosophy of Science,* Vol. 8 (1941), pp. 1–19; "Observable Behaviors," *Psychological Review,* Vol. 47 (1940), pp. 230–253; "The Behavioral Superfice," *Psychological Review,* Vol. 48 (1941), pp. 39–59; "The Jamesian Datum," *Journal of Psychology,* Vol. 16, (1942), pp. 35–79.

7 The wretched status of the word "fact" with respect to its "knowing" and its "known" (and in other respects as well) was illustrated in our preceding paper, pp. 48–49. Use of quotation marks to indicate that "a name" is under consideration rather than "the named" is common, and some logicians have attempted to make a pillar of construction out of it. We have exhibited the unreliability of this in the preceding articles. Solely as a matter of passing convenience we shall follow the custom at times, and also at times capitalize a word to indicate that "the named" and not the "name" is intended. The procedure is both vague and linguistic, and so may be classified along with the "vague words" one must ever keep a sharp eye upon.

sideration in fulfilling the desired condition with respect to Fact is that the activity by which it is identified and the *what* that is identified are both required, and are required in such a way that each is taken along with the other, and in no sense as separable. Our terminology is involved in fact, and equally "fact" is involved in our terminology. This repeats in effect the statement that knowledge requires and includes both knowings and knowns. Anything named "fact" is such both with respect to the knowing operation and with respect to that which is known.[8] We establish for our use with respect to both fact and knowledge that we have no "something known" and no "something identified" apart from its know*ing* and identify*ing*, and that we have no know*ing* and identify*ing* apart from the somewhats and somethings that are being known and identified. Again we do not put forth this statement as a truth about "reality," but as the only position which we find it possible to take on the ground of that reference to the observed which we regard as an essential condition of our inquiry. The statement is one about ourselves observed in action in the world. From the standpoint of what is observable it is of the same straightforward kind as is the statement that when chopping occurs something is chopped, and that when seeing takes place something is seen. We select the name "fact" because we believe that it carries and suggests this "double-barrelled" sense (to borrow a word from William James), while such words as "object" and "entity" have acquired from traditional philosophical use the signification of something set over against the doing or acting. That Fact is literally or etymologically *something done or made* has also the advantage of suggesting that the knowing and identifying, as ways of acting, are as much ways of doing, of making (just as much "behaviors," we may say), as are chopping wood, singing songs, seeing sights, or making hay.

For the purpose of facilitating further inquiry what has been said will be restated in negative terms. We shall *not* proceed as if we were concerned with "existent things" or "objects" entirely apart from men, nor with men entirely apart from things. Accordingly, we do not have on our hands the problem of forcing them into some kind of organization or connection. We shall proceed by taking for granted human organisms developed, living, carrying on, of and in the cosmos. They are there in such system that their operations and transactions can be viewed directly—including those which constitute knowings. When they

---

[8] It may be well to repeat here what has already been said. In making the above statement we are not attempting to legislate concerning the proper use of a word, but are stating the procedure we are adopting.

are so viewed, knowings and knowns come before us as differentiated within the factual cosmos, not as if they were there provided in advance so that out of them cosmos—system—fact—knowledge—have to be produced. Fact, language, knowledge have on this procedure cosmic status; they are not taken as if they existed originally in irreconcilably hostile camps. And this again is but to say that we have to do with knowings, both as to materials and workmanship, in the sense of ordinary science.[9]

The reader will note (that is, observe, give heed to) the superiority of our position with respect to observation over that of the older epistemological constructions. Who would assert that he can properly and in a worth-while manner *observe* a "mind" *in addition to* the organism which is engaged in the transactions pertinent to it in an observable world? The fact that attempted affirmative answers result in construing observation as private introspection is sufficient evidence of departure from procedures having scientific standing.[10] And the assertion or belief that things as "objects" outside of and apart from human operations are observed or are observable has comparable absurdity when carefully guarded statement is demanded of it. Observation is operation; it is human operation. If attributed to a "mind" it itself becomes unobservable. If surveyed in an observable world —in what we call cosmos or nature—the object observed is as much a part of the operation as is the observing organism.

This statement about observation, in name and fact, is necessary to avoid misinterpretation. It is not "observation," however, to which we are here giving inquiry; we shall not even attempt to make the word "firm" at a later stage. In the range in which we shall work—the seeking of sound names for processes involving naming—observation is always involved and such observation in this range is in fusion with name-application, so that neither takes place except in and through the other, whatever further applications of the word "observation" (comparable to applications of "naming" and of "knowing") may in widened inquiries be required.

[9] It is practically impossible to guard against every form of misapprehension arising from prevalent currency of language-attitudes holding over from a relatively pre-scientific period. There are probably readers who will translate what has been said about knowings-knowns into terms of epistemological idealism. Such a translation misses the main point—namely, that man and his doings and transactions have to be viewed as facts within the natural cosmos.

[10] "Conceptions derived from . . . anything that is so occult as not to be open to public inspection and verification (such as the purely psychical, for example) are excluded," Dewey, *Logic*, p. 19.

If we have succeeded in making clear our position with respect to the type of names for which we are in search, it will be also clear that this type of name comes in clusters. "Fact" will for us be a central name with other names clustering around it. If "observation" should be taken as central, it in its turn could be made firm only in orientation to its companionate cluster. In any case much serious coöperative inquiry is involved. In no case can we hope to succeed by first setting up separated names and then putting them in pigeonholes or bundling them together with wire provided from without. Names are, indeed, to be differentiated from one another, but the differentiation takes place with respect to one another in clusters; and the same thing holds for clusters that are differentiated from each other. This procedure has its well-established precedents in scientific procedure. The genera and species of botany and zoology are excellent examples—provided they are taken as determinations in process and not as taxonomic rigidities.[11]

III

In certain important respects we have placed limitations on the range of our inquiry, and on the methods we use. The purpose is to increase the efficiency of what we do. These decisions have been made only after much experimentation in manners of organization and presentation. The main points should be kept steadily in mind as we now stress them.

As already said, we do not propose to issue any flat decrees as to the names others should adopt. Moreover, at the start we shall in some cases not even declare our permanent choices, but instead will deliberately introduce provisional "second-string" names. For this we have two sound reasons. First our task requires us to locate the regions (some now very largely ignored) which are most in need of firm observation. Second, we must draw upon a dictionary stock of words which have multiple, and often confusedly tangled, applications. We run the risk that the name first introduced may, on these accounts, become involved in misapprehensions on the reader's part, sufficient to ruin it for the future. Hence the value of attempting to establish the regions to be named

[11] Other defects in the language we must use, in addition to the tendency towards prematurely stiffened namings, offer continuous interference with communication such as we must attempt. Our language is not at present grammatically adapted to the statements we have to make. Especially is this true with respect to the prepositions which *in toto* we must list among the "vague words" against which we have given warning. Mention of special dangers will be made as occasion arises. We do the best we can, and discussion should never turn on some particular man's personal rendering of some particular preposition in some particular passage.

by provisional namings in the hope that we will secure stepping stones to better concentration of procedure at the end.

We do not propose in this inquiry to cover the entire range of "knowledge," that is, the entire range of life and behavior to which the word "knowledge" at one time or another and in one way or another can be applied. We have already listed "knowledge" as a vague word and said that we shall specify "knowings" and "knowns" for our attention. "Knowledge" will remain throughout our entire treatment a word referring roughly to the general field within which we select subject-matters for closer examination. But even for the words "knowings" and "knowns" the range of common application runs all the way from infusoria approaching food to mathematicians operating with their most recondite dimensions. We shall confine ourselves to a central region: that of identifications under namings, of knowing-by-naming, of "specified existence," if one will. Time will take care of the passage of inquiry across the border regions from naming-knowing to the simpler and to the more complex forms.

We shall regard these naming-knowings directly as a form of knowings. *Take this statement literally as it is written.* It means that we do not regard namings as instrumental or in some other sense ancillary to something else called knowings (or knowledge). We do not split a corporeal naming from a presumptively non-corporeal or "mental" knowing; neither do we permit a mentaloid "brain" to make pretenses as substitute for a "mind" and thus maintain a split between knowings and namings. This is postulation on our part. But surely what we found in the logics under the separation of spoken word from speaking man would be enough to justify any postulate that offered hope of relief. The acceptance of this postulate, even strictly during working hours, may be difficult. We do not expect assent at the start, and we do not here argue the case. We expect to display the value in further action.

In general we shall postpone discussion of many intricately inter-related problems that suggest themselves as we go along. To the more important of these we shall devote special short papers when opportunity offers. This seems the only course practicable if we are not to wander so widely at times that objectives will be lost to view. Above all we assert and continue to assert—and it might be well if we could repeat it on every page—that our procedure is solely by hypothesis.

IV

Thus far we have been discussing the conditions under which a search for firm names for knowings and knowns must be carried on. In summary our procedure is to be as follows: Working under hypothesis we concentrate upon a special region of knowings and knowns; we seek to spotlight aspects of that region that today are but dimly observed; we suggest tentative namings; through the development of these names in a cluster we hope advance can be made towards construction under dependable naming in the future.

1. *Fact, Event, Designation.* We start with the cosmos of knowledge—with nature as known and as in process of being better known—ourselves and our knowings included. We name this cosmos *fact,* with all its aspects—all its knowings and all its knowns—included. We do *not* introduce, either by hypothesis or by dogma, knowers and knowns as prerequisites to fact. Instead we observe both knowers and knowns as factual, as cosmic; and never—either of them—as extra-cosmic accessories.

We specialize our studies upon the region of naming-knowings, of knowings through namings, wherein we identify two great factual aspects to be examined. We name these *event* and *designation.* The application of the word "fact" may perhaps in the end need to be extended beyond the behavioral processes of event-designation. We shall note the locus of such contingent extension, leave the way open for the future, and proceed to cultivate the garden of our choice, namely, the characteristic Fact that we have before us.

Upon these namings the following comments will, for the present, suffice:

(*a*) In Fact-Event-Designation we do not have a three-fold organization, nor a two-fold; we have instead one system.

(*b*) Given the language and knowledge we now possess, the use of the word "fact" imposes upon its users the necessity of selection and acceptance. This manifest status is recognized terminologically through our adoption of the name "designation."

(*c*) The word "aspect" as here used is not stressed as information-giving. It must be taken to register—register, and nothing more—the duplex, aspectual observation and report that is required, if we are to characterize Fact at all. The word "phase" may be expected to become available for comparable application when, under the development of the word "aspect," we are sufficiently advanced to consider time-alternations and rhythms of event and of designation in knowledge process.[12]

(*d*) "Event" involves in normal use the extensional and the

---

[12] "Aspect" and "phase" may stand, therefore, as somewhat superior to the "vague words" against which we give warning, though not as yet presenting positive information in our field.

durational. "Designation" for our purposes must likewise be so taken. The Designation we postulate and discuss is not of the nature of *a* sound or *a* mark applied *as* a name *to* an event. Instead of this it is the action, the activity, the behavioral action and activity, of naming, through which Event appears in our knowledge as Fact.

(*e*) We expect the word "fact" to be able to maintain itself for terminological purposes, and we shall give reasons for this in a succeeding paper, though still retaining freedom to alter it. As for the words "event" and "designation," their use here is provisional, and replacement is more probable. Should we, for example, now adopt such words as "existence" and "name," then, as the case stands at this stage, both words would carry with them to most readers many implications false to our intentions —the latter even more than the former; understanding of our procedure would then become distorted and ineffective.

(*f*) "Fact," in our use, is to be taken with a range of reference as extensive as is allotted to any other name for cosmos, universe, or nature, where the context shows that knowledge, not poesy, is concerned. It is to be taken with its pasts and its futures, its growings-out-of and its growings-into, its transitions of report from poorer to richer, and from less to more. It is to be taken with as much solidity and substantiality as nature, universe, or world, by any name whatsoever. It is to be taken, however, with the understanding that instead of gratuitous insertion of an unknown something as foundation for the factually known, what we are taking is the knowledge in full—the knowings-knowns as they come: namely, both in one, and without appeal to cosmic tortoise to hold up cosmic elephant to hold up cosmic pillar to hold up the factual cosmos of our consideration.

(*g*) To a myopic and short-time view Event and Designation appear as separates. The appearance does no harm if it is held where it belongs within narrow ranges of inquiry. For a general account of knowings and knowns the wider envisionment is required.

(*h*) Overlapping Fact, as we are postulating it within the range of namings, are, on one side, perceptions, manipulations, habituations, and other adaptations; and, on the other side, symbolic-knowledge procedures such as those of mathematics. We shall be taking these into account as events-designated, even though for the present we are not inquiring into them with respect to possible designatory, quasi-designatory, or otherwise fact-presenting functions of their own along the evolutionary line. Our terminology will in no way be such as to restrict consideration of them, but rather to further it, when such consideration becomes practicable.

(i) If Designations, as we postulate them for our inquiry, are factually durational-extensional, then these Designations, as designat*ings*, *are* themselves Events. Similarly, the Events as designational, *are* Designations. It is not the subject-matter before us, but the available language forms that make this latter statement difficult. The two uses of "are" in the sentences "Events are Designations" and "Designations are Events" differ greatly, each "are" representing one of the aspects within [13] the broader presentation of Fact. To recognize events as designated while refusing to call them designations in the activity sense, would be a limitation that would maintain a radical split between naming and named at the very time that their connective framework was being acknowledged. Our position is emphatic upon this point. It is clear enough that in the older sense events are not designations; it should be equally clear and definite that in our procedure and terminology they are designational—designation—or (with due caution in pluralizing) Designations. To control the two uses of the word "are" in the two forms of statement, and to maintain the observation and report that Designations are Events, while also Events are Designations—this is the main strain our procedure will place upon the reader. Proceeding under hypothesis (and without habituation to hypothesis there will be no advance at all) this should not be too severe a requirement for one who recognizes the complexity of the situation and has an active interest in clearing it up.

(j) Most generally, Fact, in our terminology, is not limited to what any one man knows, nor to what is known to any one human grouping, nor to any one span of time such as our own day and age. On the designatory side in our project of research it has the full range and spread which, as we said above, it has on the event side, with all the futures and the pasts, the betters and the poorers, comprised as they come. In our belief the Newtonian era has settled the status of fact definitely in this way for our generation of research, at the least. First, Newtonian mechanics rose in the shelter of its glorified absolutes to credal strength. Then at the hands of Faraday, Clerk-Maxwell, and Einstein, it lost its absolutes, lost its credal claims, and emerged chastened and improved. ᵀ gained thus the high rating of a magnificent approximation as compared with its earlier trivial self-rating as eternal certainty. The coming years—fifty, or a thousand, whatever it takes—remain quite free for change; any intelligent voice

[13] A vague word, be it observed.

will say this—the trouble is to get ears to hear. Our new assurance is better than the old assurance. The full knowledge—knowing and the known—event and designation—go forward together. Eventuation is observed. Accept this in principle, and not merely as a casual comment on an accidental happening—you then have before you what our terminology recognizes when it places Fact-in-growth as sound enough base for research with no need to bother over minuscular mentals or crepuscular reals alleged to be responsible for it.

2. *Circularity.* When we said above that designations are events and events designations, we adopted *circularity*—procedure in a circle—openly, explicitly, emphatically. Several ways of pretending to avoid such circularity are well known. Perhaps at one end everything is made tweedledum, and perhaps at the other everything is made tweedledee, or perhaps in between little tweedledums and little tweedledees, companionable but infertile, essential to each other but untouchable by each other, are reported all along the line. We have nothing to apologize for in the circularity which we choose in preference to the old talk-ways. We observe world-being-known-to-man-in-it; we report the observation; we proceed to inquire into it, circularity or no circularity. This is all there is to it. And the circularity is not merely round the circle in one direction; the course is both ways round at once in full mutual function.

3. *The Differentiations That Follow.* Given fact, observed aspectually as Event and as Designation, our next indicated task is to develop further terminological organization for the two aspects separately. We shall undertake this shortly and leave the matter there so far as the present preliminary outline is concerned. But to aid us we shall require firm statement as to certain tools to be used in the process. We must, that is, be able to name certain procedures so definitely that they will not be confounded with current procedures on a different basis. Events will be differentiated with respect to a certain range of plasticity that is comparable in a general way to the physical differentiations of gaseous, liquid, and solid. For these we shall use the names, Situation, Occurrence, and Object. As for Designation, we shall organize it in an evolutionary scheme of behavioral sign processes of which it is one form, the names we apply being: Sign, Signal, Name, and Symbol. The preliminary steps we find it necessary to take before presenting these differentiations are: first, steady maintenance of a distinction of the various branches of scientific inquiry with respect to selected subject-matters of research rather than in terms of materials assumed to be waiting for research in ad-

vance; second, a firm use of the word "specification" to designate the type of naming to be employed as contrasted with the myriad verbal processes that go by the name of "definition"; third, the establishment of our right to selective observational control of specific situations within subject-matters by a competent distinction of *trans*-actions from *inter*-actions.

4. *Sciences as Subject-Matters.* The broad division of regions of scientific research commonly recognized today is that into the physical, the biological, and the psychological. However, mathematics, where inquiry attains maximum precision, lacks any generally accepted form of organization with these sciences; and sociology, where maximum imprecision is found, also fails of a distinctive manner of incorporation.[14] Fortunately this scheme of division is gradually losing its rigidities. A generation or two ago physics stood aloof from chemistry; today it has constructively incorporated it. In the biological range today, the most vivid and distinctive member is physiology; yet the name "biology" covers many gross adaptational studies not employing the physiological techniques; in addition the name "biology" assuredly covers everything that is psychological, unless perchance some "psyche" is involved that is "non"- or "ultra"-human. The word "psychological" itself is a hold-over from an earlier era, in which such a material series as "*the* physical," "*the* vital," and "*the* psychic" was still believed in and taken to offer three different realms of substance presented as raw material by Nature or by God for our perpetual puzzlement. If we have to establish knowings and knowns in a single system of Fact, we certainly must be free from addiction to a presumptive universe compounded out of three basically different kinds of materials. Better said, however, it is our present freedom from such material enthrallment, attained for us by the general advance of scientific research, that at long last has made us able to see all knowings and knowns by hypothesis as in one system.

Within Fact we shall recognize the distinctions of the scientific field as those of subject-matters, and not as those of materials,[15] unless, indeed, one speaks of materials only in the sense that

[14] We shall deal with the very important subject of mathematics elsewhere. Sociological inquiries, with the exception of anthropology, are hardly far enough advanced to justify any use of them as subject-matters in our present inquiry.

[15] An extended consideration of many phases of this issue and approaches to its treatment is given by Coleman R. Griffith in his *Principles of Systematic Psychology,* University of Illinois Press, 1943. Compare the section on "The Scientific Use of Participles and Nouns," pp. 489–497, and various passages indexed under "Science."

their differences themselves arise in and are vouched for solely by the technical procedures that are available in the given stages of inquiry. Terminologically, we shall distinguish *physical, physiological,* and *behavioral* [16] regions of science. We shall accept the word "biological" under our postulation as covering unquestionably both physiological and behavioral inquiries, but we find the range of its current applications much too broad to be safe for the purposes of the present distinctive terminology. The technical differentiation in research of physiological procedures from behavioral is of the greatest import in the state of inquiry today, and this would be pushed down out of sight by any heavy stress on the word "biological," which, as we have said, we emphatically believe *must* cover them both. We wish most strongly to stress that physical, physiological, and behavioral inquiries in the present state of knowledge represent three great distinctive lines of technique; while any one of them may be brought to the aid of any other, nevertheless direct positive extension of statement from the firm technical formulations of one into the information-stating requirements of another can not be significantly made as knowledge today stands. Physical formulation does not directly yield heredity, let the genes prove all they may; nor does physiological formulation directly yield word-meanings, sentences, and mathematical formulas. To complete the circle, behavioral process, while producing physical science, can not directly in its own procedure yield report on the embodied physical event. This circularity, once again, is in the knowledge—in the knowings and the knowns—not in any easy-going choice we are free and competent to make in the hope that we can cleave to it, evidence or no evidence.

5. *Specification.* The word "definition" covers precise symbolic statements in mathematics; it covers procedures under Aristotelian logic; it covers all the collections of word-uses, old and new, which the dictionaries assemble, and many still more

---

[16] Our use of the word "behavioral" has no "behavioristic" implications. We are no more behavioristic than mentalistic, disavowing as we do, under hypothesis, "isms" and "istics" of all types. The word "behavior" is in frequent use by astronomers, physicists, physiologists, and ecologists, as well as by psychologists and sociologists. Applied in the earlier days of its history to human conduct it has drifted along to other uses, pausing for a time among animal-students, and having had much hopeful abuse by mechanistic enthusiasts. It rightfully belongs, however, we believe, where we are placing it. Such a word as "conduct" has many more specialized implications than has "behavior" and would not serve at all well to supply the name for a great division of research. We shall be open for any substitutes as work proceeds, but thus far have failed to find a more efficient or safer word to use. In such a matter as this, long-term considerations are much more important than are the verbal fashions of a decade or two.

casual linguistic procedures. The word "definition" must manifestly be straightened out, if any sound presentation of knowings and knowns is to be secured. We have fair reason to believe that most of the difficulty in what is called the "logic of mathematics" is due to an endeavor to force consolidation of two types of human behavior, both labeled "definition," though one stresses heavily while the other diverges from the use of namings, without preliminary inquiry into the simpler facts of the life linguistic. In our terminology we shall assign the word *definition* to the region of mathematical and syntactical consistency; while for the lesser specimens of "dictionary definition" we shall employ the name *characterization*. In our own work in these papers we shall attempt no "definition" whatever in the formal sense we assign the word. We shall at times not succeed in getting beyond preliminary characterization. Our aim in the project, however, is to advance towards accuracy in naming such as science ever increasingly achieves. Such accuracy in naming we shall call *specification*. Consider what the word "heat" stood for in physics before Rumford and Joule, and what it tells us in physical specification today. Consider the changes the word "atom" has undergone in the past generation. Modern chemical terminology is a highly specialized form of specification of operations undertaken. The best illustration for our purposes is probably, however, the terminology of genera and species. In the days when animals were theological specialities of creation, the naming level was that of characterization. After demonstration had been given that species had natural origins, scientific specification as we understand it developed. We still find it, of course, straining at times towards taxonomic rigidities, but over against this we find it forever rejuvenating itself by free inquiry up even to the risk of its own obliteration. Abandonment of the older magic of name-to-reality correspondence is one of the marks of specification. Another will be observed when specification has been clearly differentiated from symbolic definition. In both its aspects of Event and Designation we find Fact spread in "spectrum-like" form. We use "specification" to mark this scientific characteristic of efficient naming. Peirce's stress on the "precept that is more serviceable than a definition" involved the attitude we are here indicating. Specification operates everywhere in that field of inquiry covered by affirmation and assertion, proposition and judgment, in Dewey's *Logic*, as inquiry. The defects we exhibited in the traditional logics [17] were due to their lack of attention to specification; at no

---

[17] "On a Certain Vagueness in Logic," this JOURNAL, Vol. XLII (1945), pp. 5–27; 39–51. The Peirce citation is used on p. 8.

point in our examination did we make our criticisms rest on issues of consistency in definition.

6. *Transaction.* We have established Fact as involving both Designation and designated Event. We have inspected inquiry into Fact in terms of subject-matters determinable under the techniques of inquiry, and not in terms of materials presented from without.[18] Both treatments make selection under hypothesis a dominant phase of procedure. But selection under hypothesis affects all observation. We shall take this into account terminologically by contrasting events reported in interactions with events reported as transactions. A special paper will follow later dealing with this issue central to our procedure: the right, namely, to open our eyes to see. Here we can only touch broadly upon it. Prescientific procedure largely regarded "things" as possessing powers of their own, under, or in, which they acted. Galileo is the scientist whose name is most strongly identified with the change to modern procedure. We may take the word *"action"* as a most general characterization for events where their durational process is being stressed. Where the older approach had most commonly seen *self-action* in "the facts," the newer approach gained organization under Newton as a system of interaction, marked especially by the third "law of motion," namely, that action and reaction are equal and opposite. The classical mechanics is such a system of interaction involving particles, boundaries, and laws of effects. But before it was developed—before, apparently, it could develop—a different type of observation was made that was basic to it, and that we may call transactional. This may be seen in Galileo's report on inertia, appearing in the Newtonian formulation as the first "law of motion," namely, that any motion uninterfered with will continue in a straight line. This set up a motion, directly, factually, as event.[19] The field of knowings and knowns in which we are working requires transactional observation, and this is what we are giving it, and what our terminology is designed to deal with. The epistemologies, logics, psychologies, and sociologies today are still largely on a self-actional basis. In psychology a number of tentative efforts are being made towards an *interactional* presentation, with balanced

[18] Again a very vaguely used word.

[19] In the psychological range the comparable fundamental laboratory experiments of import for our purposes are those of Max Wertheimer upon the direct visual observability of motions. *See* "Experimentelle Studien über das Sehen von Bewegungen," *Zeitschrift für Psychologie*, Vol. 61 (1912), pp. 161–265. In a much weakened form his results are used in the type of psychology known as "Gestalt," but in principle they still await constructive development.

components. Our position is that the traditional language currently used about knowings and knowns (and most other language about behaviors, as well) shatters the subject-matter into fragments in advance of inquiry and thus destroys instead of furthering comprehensive observation for it. We hold that observation must be set free, and that, to advance this aim, a postulatory appraisal of the main historical patterns of observation should be made, and identifying namings provided for them. Our own procedure, not as more real or more generally valid than any other, but as the one that at this stage is needed in the field in which we work, is the *transactional*, in which is asserted the right to see together, extensionally and durationally, much that conventionally is talked of as if composed of irreconcilable separates. In the same spirit in which physicists perforce use both particle and wave presentations we here employ both interactional and transactional observation.[20] Important specialized studies belong in this field in which the organism is made central to attention. This is always legitimate in all forms of inquiry within a transactional setting, so long as it is deliberately undertaken and not confusedly, or with "self-actional" implications. As place-holders in this region of nomenclature we shall provisionally set down *behavior-agent* and *behavior-object*. They represent specialized interactional treatments within the wider transactional presentation, where commonly organisms or persons or actors are uncertainly named on the one side and environments are named in variegated forms on the other.

7. *Situation, Occurrence, Object.* We may now proceed to distinguish Situation, Occurrence, and Object as forms of Event. Event is durational-extensional; it is that which "takes place," that which is inspected as "a taking place." These names do not provide a "classification," unless classification is understood as a focusing of attention within subject-matters rather than as an arrangement of materials. The word "situation" is used with increasing frequency today, but so waveringly that the more it is used the worse its own status seems to become. We insist that in simple honesty it stand *either* for the environment to an object

---

[20] The word "field" is a strong candidate for use in the transactional region. For the present, however, it is impracticable. It has not been fully clarified as yet for physics, and the way it has been employed in psychological and social studies has been impressionistic and often unscrupulous. It must remain, therefore, on our list of vague words, candidates for improvement. When the physical status of the word is settled—and Einstein and his immediate associates have long concentrated on this problem—then if the terminology can be transferred to behavioral inquiry, we shall know how to make the transfer with integrity.

(interactionally), *or* for the full situation including whatever object may be selectively specified within it (transactionally), and that there be no wavering. We shall establish our own use for the word *situation* in this latter form. When an event is of the type that is readily observable in transition within the ordinary spans of human discrimination of temporal and spatial changes, we shall call it *occurrence*. The ordinary use of "event" in daily life is close to this, and if we generalize the application of the word, as we have provisionally done, to cover situation and object as well as occurrence, then we require a substitute in the more limited place. Occurrence fairly fills the vacancy. *Object* [21] is chosen as the clearly indicated name for stabilized, enduring situations, for occurrences which need so long a span of time, or perhaps so minute a space-change, that the space and time changes are not themselves within the scope of ordinary, everyday perceptual attention. Thus any one of the three words, Situation, Occurrence, Object, may, if focusing of attention shifts, spread over the range of the others, all being equally held as Event. We have here a fair illustration of what we have previously called a word-cluster. The Parthenon is an object to a visitor, and has so been for all the centuries since its construction. It is nevertheless an occurrence across some thousands of years. While for certain purposes of inquiry it may be marked off as object-in-environment, for thoroughgoing investigation it must be seized as situation, as to which the object-specification is at best one phase or feature. There is here no issue of reality, no absolute yes or no to assert, but only free determination under inquiry.

8. *Sign, Signal, Name, Symbol.* Turning to Designation, our immediate problem is not that of distinguishing the variety of *its* forms. Specification, the form most immediately concerning us, has already been noted. What we have to do instead is to place designation itself as one among a series of behavioral events. Circularity is again here strikingly involved. Our treatment must be in terms of Event as much as in terms of Designation, with full convertibility of the two. The event is behavioral. Designation as behavioral event can be viewed as one stage in the range of behavioral evolution from the sensitive reactions of protozoa to the most complex symbolic procedures of mathematics. In this phase of the inquiry we shall alter the naming. Viewing

---

[21] "The name *objects* will be reserved for subject-matter so far as it has been produced and ordered in settled form by means of inquiry; proleptically, objects are the *objectives* of inquiry." Dewey, *Logic, the Theory of Inquiry*, p. 119. For "situation" see *ibid.*, pp. 66 ff. The word "occurrence" is, as has been indicated, provisionally placed.

the behavioral event, we shall name it directly Name instead of replacing "name" by "designation" as seemed necessary for provisional practical reasons on the obverse side of the inquiry. At a later stage we shall undertake to establish the characteristic behavioral process as *sign,* a process not found in either physical or physiological techniques of inquiry. We shall thus understand the name "sign" to be used so as to cover the entire range of behavioral activity. There are many stages or levels of behaviors, but for the greater part of our needs a three-level differentiation will furnish gross guidance. The lower level, including perceptions, manipulations, habituations, adaptations, etc., we shall name *signal* (adapting the word from Pavlov's frequent usage). Where organized language is employed as sign, we shall speak of *name.* In mathematical regions (for reasons fully to be discussed later) we shall speak of *symbol.* Signal, Name, and Symbol will be the three differentiations of Sign, where "sign" indicates most broadly the "cognitive" or "knowledge-like" aspects of behavior in a long ascending series. Vital to this construction, even though no development for the moment may be offered, is the following statement: The name "Sign" and the names adjusted to it *shall all be understood transactionally,* which in this particular case is to say that they do not name items or characteristics of organisms alone, nor do they name items or characteristics of environments alone, but in every case *activity* that occurs as *of both together.*

V

By the use of Sign-Signal-Name-Symbol we indicate the locus for the knowing-naming process and for other behavioral processes within cosmos. By the use of Fact-Event-Designation we specify the process of event-determination through which cosmos is presented as itself a locus for such loci. The two types of terminology set forth different phases of a common process. They can be so held if we insist upon freedom for transactional observation in cases in which ancient word-forms have fractured fact, and if we lose fear of circularity. It is our task in later papers to develop this terminology and to test it in situations that arise.

For the present our terminological guide-posts, provisionally sketched, are as follows:

SUGGESTED EXPERIMENTAL NAMING

Fact: Our cosmos as it is before us progressingly in knowings through namings.

Event: "Fact" named as taking place.

Designation: Naming as taking place in "fact."

Physical,
Physiological,
Behavioral: } Differentiations of the techniques of inquiry, marking off subject-matters as sciences under development, and not constricted to conform to primitive pre-views of "materials" of "reality."

Characterization: Linguistic procedure preliminary to developed specification, including much "dictionary-definition."

Specification: Accuracy of designation along the free lines through which modern sciences have developed.

Definition: Symbolic procedure linguistically evolved, not directly employing designatory tests.

Action (Activity): Event stressed with respect to temporal change.

Self-Action: Pre-scientific presentation in terms of presumptively independent "actors," "souls," "minds," "selves," "powers," or "forces," taken as activating events.

Interaction: Presentation of particles or other objects organized as operating upon one another.

Transaction: Functional observation of full system, actively necessary to inquiry at some stages, held in reserve at other stages, frequently requiring the breaking down of older verbal impactions of naming.

Behavior-Agency: Behavioral organic action, interactionally inspected within transaction; agency in the sense of *re*-agent rather than of act*or*.

Behavior-Object: Environmental specialization of object with respect to agent within behavioral transaction.

Situation: Event as subject-matter of inquiry, always transactionally viewed as the full subject-matter; never to be taken as detachable "environment" over against object.

Occurrence: Event designated as in process under transitions such as are most readily identifiable in everyday human-size contacts.

Object: Event in its more firmly stabilized forms—never, however, as in final fixations—always available as subject-matter under transfer to situational inspection, should need arise as inquiry progresses.

Signs: Characteristic adaptational behavior of organism-environment; the "cognitive" in its broadest reaches when viewed transactionally (and not as organic or environmental specialty).

Signal: Transactional sign in the perceptive-manipulative ranges.

Name: Specialized development of sign among hominidae; apparently not reaching the full designational stage (excepting, perhaps, on blocked evolutional lines) until *homo sapiens*.

Symbol: A later linguistic development of sign, forfeiting specific designatory applications to gain heightened efficiency in other ways.

We regard the following as common-sense observation upon the manner of discourse about knowledge which we find current around us.

The knowledge of knowledge itself that we possess today is weak knowledge—perhaps as weak as any we have; it stands greatly in need of de-sentimentalized research.

Fact is notoriously two-faced. It is cosmos as noted by a speck of cosmos. Competent appraisal takes this into account.

What is beyond Fact—beyond the knowing and the known—is not worth bothering about in any inquiry undertaken into knowings and knowns.

Science thrives within limits such as these, and it is our best knowledge. Specification thrives in, and requires, such limits; why should not then also inquiry and specification for the knowings and the knowns themselves?

Knowings are behaviors. Neither inquiry into knowings nor inquiry into behaviors can expect satisfactory results unless the other goes with it hand in hand.[22]

JOHN DEWEY
ARTHUR F. BENTLEY

[22] Attention is called in summary to the "vague words" which at times one is compelled to use. "Knowledge," "thing," "field," "within," and "without" have been so characterized in text or footnotes; also all prepositions and the use of "quotes" to distinguish names from the named; and even the words "vague" and "firm" as we find them in use today. "Aspect" and "phase" have been indicated as vague for our purposes today, but as having definite possibilities of development as we proceed. It will be noticed that the word "experience" has not been used in the present text. No matter what efforts have heretofore been made to apply it definitely, it has been given conflicting renderings by readers who among them, one may almost say, have persisted in forcing vagueness upon it. We shall discuss it along with other abused words at a later place.

Section IV

METAPHYSICS AND AESTHETICS

The Journal of Philosophy

Psychology and Scientific Methods

THE SUBJECT–MATTER OF METAPHYSICAL INQUIRY

A NUMBER of biologists holding to the adequacy of the mechanistic conception in biology have of late expressed views not unlike those clearly and succinctly set forth in the following quotation: "If we consider the organism simply as a system forming a part of external nature, we find no evidence that it possesses properties that may not eventually be satisfactorily analyzed by the methods of physico-chemical science; but we admit also that those peculiarities of ultimate constitution which have in the course of evolution led to the appearance of living beings in nature are such that we can not well deny the possibility or even legitimacy of applying a vitalistic or even biocentric conception to the cosmic process as a whole."[1]

The problems connected with the organism as a part of external nature are referred to in the context of the quotation as scientific problems; those connected with the peculiarities of ultimate constitution as metaphysical. The context also shows that ultimate constitution is conceived in a temporal sense. Metaphysical questions are said to be those having to do with "ultimate origins." Such questions lie quite beyond the application of scientific method. "Why it [nature] exhibits certain apparently innate potentialities and modes of action which have caused it to evolve in a certain way is a question which really lies beyond the sphere of natural science." These "apparently innate potentialities and modes of action" which have caused nature as a whole to evolve in the direction of living beings are identified with "ultimate peculiarities"; and it is with reference to them that the biocentric idea has a possible legitimate application. The argument implies that when we insist upon the adequacy of the physico-chemical explanation of living organisms, we are led, in view of the continuity of evolution of organisms from non-living things, to recognize that the world out of which life developed "held latent or potential within itself the possibility of life." In considering such a

---

[1] Professor Ralph S. Lillie, *Science*, Vol. 40, page 846. See also the references given in the article, which is entitled "The Philosophy of Biology–Vitalism *vs.* Mechanism."

world and the nature of the potentiality which caused it to evolve living beings, we are forced, however, beyond the limits of scientific inquiry. We pass the boundary which separates it from metaphysics.

Thus is raised the question as to the nature of metaphysical inquiry. I wish to suggest that while one may accept as a preliminary demarcation of metaphysics from science the more "ultimate traits" with which the former deals, it is not necessary to identify these ultimate traits with temporally original traits—that, in fact, there are good reasons why we should not do so. We may also mark off the metaphysical subject-matter by reference to certain irreducible traits found in any and every subject of scientific inquiry. With reference to the theme of evolution of living beings, the distinctive trait of metaphysical reflection would not then be its attempt to discover some temporally original feature which caused the development, but the irreducible traits of a world in which at least some changes take on an evolutionary form. A world where some changes proceed in the direction of the appearance of living and thinking creatures is a striking sort of a world. While science would trace the conditions of their occurrence in detail, connecting them in their variety with their antecedents, metaphysics would raise the question of the sort of world which *has* such an evolution, not the question of the sort of world which causes it. For the latter type of question appears either to bring us to an *impasse* or else to break up into just the questions which constitute scientific inquiry.

Any intelligible question as to causation seems to be a wholly scientific question. Starting from any given existence, be it a big thing like a solar system or a small thing like a rise of temperature, we may ask how it came about. We account for the change by linking up the thing in question with other specific existences acting in determinate ways—ways which collectively are termed physico-chemical. When we have traced back a present existence to the earlier existences with which it is connected, we may ask a like question about the occurrence of the earlier things, viewed as changes from something still earlier. And so on indefinitely; although, of course, we meet practical limits in our ability to push such questions beyond a certain indefinite point. Hence it may be said that a question about ultimate origin or ultimate causation is either a meaningless question, or else the words are used in a relative sense to designate the point in the past at which a particular inquiry breaks off. Thus we might inquire as to the "ultimate" origin of the French language. This would take us back to certain definite antecedent existences, such as persons speaking the Latin tongue, others speaking barbarian tongues; the contact of these peoples in war, commerce, political administration, education, etc. But the term "ultimate" has meaning only in relation to the particular existence in question: French speech. We are landed in another historic set of existences, having their own specific antecedents. The case is not otherwise if we ask for the ultimate origin of human speech in general. The inquiry takes us back to animal cries, gestures, etc., certain conditions of intercourse, etc. The question is, how one set of specific existences gradually passed into another. No one would think of referring to latent qualities of the Latin speech as the cause of the evolution of French; one tries to discover actual and overt features which, *interacting* with other equally specific existences, brought about this particular change. If we are likely to fall into a different mode of speech with reference to human language in general, it is because we are more ignorant of the specific circumstances under which the transition from animal cries to articulate speech with a meaning took place. Upon analysis, reference to some immanent law or cause which forced the evolution will be found to be a lazy cloak for our ignorance of the specific facts needed in order to deal successfully with the question.

Suppose we generalize the situation still more. We may ask for the ultimate origin of the entire present state of things. Taken *en masse*, such a question is meaningless. Taken in detail, it means that we may apply the same procedure distributively to each and any of the things which now exist. In each case we may trace its history to an earlier state of things. But in each case, *its* history is what we trace, and the history always lands us at some state of things in the past, regarding which the same question might be asked. That scientific inquiry does not itself deal with any question of ultimate origins, except in the purely relative sense already indicated, is, of course, recognized. But it also seems to follow from what has been said that scientific inquiry does not generate, or leave over, such a question for some other discipline, such as metaphysics, to deal with. The contrary conception with respect to the doctrine of evolution is to be explained, I think, by the fact that theology used to have the idea of ultimate origin in connection with creation, and that at a certain juncture it was natural to regard the theory of evolution as a substitute or rival of the theological idea of creation.

If all questions of causation and origin are specific scientific questions, is there any place left for metaphysical inquiry at all? If its theme can not be ultimate origin and causation, is metaphysics anything but a kind of pseudo-science whose illusory character is now to be recognized? This question takes us to the matter of whether there are ultimate, that is, irreducible, traits of the very existences with which scientific reflection is concerned. In all such investigations as those referred to above we find at least such traits as the following: Specifically diverse existences, interaction, change. Such traits are found in any material which is the subject-matter of inquiry in the natural science. They are found equally and indifferently whether a subject-matter in question be dated 1915 or ten million years B.C. Accordingly, they would seem to deserve the name of ultimate, or irreducible, traits. As such they may be made the object of a kind of inquiry differing from that which deals with the genesis of a particular group of existences, a kind of inquiry to which the name metaphysical may be given.[2]

It may well seem as if the fact that the subject-matter of science is always a plurality of diverse interacting and changing existences were too obvious and commonplace to invite or reward investigation. Into this point I shall not go, beyond pointing out, in connection with the present theme, that certain negative advantages in the economizing of intellectual effort would at least accrue from the study. Bare recognition of the fact just stated would wean men from the futility of concern with ultimate origins and laws of causation with which the "universe" is supposed to have been endowed at the outset. For it would reveal that, whatever the date of the subject-matter which may be successfully reflected upon, we have the same situation that we have at present: diversity, specificality, change. These traits have to be begged or taken in any case. If we face this fact without squeamishness we shall be saved from the recurrent attempts to reduce heterogeneity to homogeneity, diversity to sheer uniformity, quality to quantity, and so on. That considerations of quantity and mathematical order are indispensable to the successful prosecution of researches into particular occurrences is a

---

[2] The name at least has the sanction of the historical designation given to Aristotle's consideration of existence as existence. But it should be noted that we also find in Aristotle the seeds (which, moreover, have at places developed into flourishing growths in his own philosophy) of the conception of metaphysics rejected above. For he expressly gives the more general traits of existence the eulogistic title "divine" and identifies his first philosophy with theology, and so makes this kind of inquiry "superior" to all others, because it deals with the "highest of existing things." While he did not himself seek for this higher or supreme real in time, but rather located it, in its fullness of reality, just beyond space, this identification of existence as such with the divine led to such an identification the moment theology became supremely interested in "creation." But unless one approaches the study of the most general traits of the matter of scientific inquiry with theological presuppositions, there is, of course, no ground for the application to them of eulogistic predicates. There is no ground for thinking that they are any better or any worse, any higher or any lower, than other traits, or that any peculiar dignity attaches to a study of them.

precious fact. It exhibits certain irreducible traits *of* the irreducible traits we have mentioned, but it does not replace them. When it tries to do so it cuts the ground out from under its own feet.

Let me emphasize this point by comment on a further quotation. "If we assume constancy of the elementary natural processes, and constancy in the modes of connection between them—as exact observation forces us to do—there seems no avoiding the conclusion that—given an undifferentiated universe at the start—only one course of evolution can ever have been possible. Laplace long ago perceived this consequence of the mechanistic view of nature, and the inevitability of this conclusion has never been seriously disputed by scientific men. Nevertheless, this is a very strange result, and to many has seemed a *reductio ad absurdum* of the scientific view as applied to the whole of nature."

Note that the inevitable conclusion as to the predetermined course of evolution and the apparent incredibility of the conclusion both depend upon the premise "given an undifferentiated universe at the start." Now this is precisely a premise which a scientific view can not admit, for science deals with any particular existence only by tracing its occurrence to a plurality of prior changing interacting things. Any Laplacean formula would, in any case, be a formula for the structure of *some* existence *in* the world, not for the world as a "whole." The scientific grounds which make it impossible to take the world *en masse* at the present time and to give a comprehensive formula for it in its entirety apply even more strongly, if possible, to some earlier state of affairs. For such a formula can be reached only by tracing back a specific present phenomenon to its specific antecedents.

A curious illusion exists as to formulæ for the ancient states of nature. It is frequently assumed that they denote not merely some absolute original (which is impossible), but also one from which later events unroll in a mathematically predetermined fashion. We seem to be passing in a one-sided way from the earlier to the later. The illusion vanishes when we ask where the formula came from. How was it obtained? Evidently, by beginning with some present existence and tracing its earlier course, till at some time (relevant to the object of the inquiry) we stop and condense the main features of the course into a formula for the structure of the state of things at the date where we stop. Instead of really deducing or deriving the course of subsequent events from an original state, we are simply taking out of a formula the traits which we have put into it on the basis of knowledge of subsequent events. Let the present state be anything you please, as different as may be from what is actually found, and it will still be true that we could (theoretically) construct a comprehensive formula for its earlier estate. In short, as a matter of fact, a Laplacean formula merely summarizes what the actual course of events has been with respect to some selected features. How then can it be said to describe an original state of nature in virtue of which just such and such things have necessarily happened? A statement that the world is thus and so can not be tortured into a statement of how and why it must be as it is. The account of how a thing came to be as it is always starts and comes back to the fact that it *is* thus and so. How then can this fact be derived according to some law of predestination from the consideration of its own prior history? For, I repeat, this history is *its* history.[3]

This discussion, however, oversimplifies matters. It overlooks the extent to which inference as to a prior state of affairs is dependent upon the diversity and complexity of what is now observed. We should be in a hard case in trying to fix upon the structure of the Latin language if our sole datum were, say, the French language. As matter of fact, in considering the growth of the French tongue we have other Romance languages to fall back upon. Above all, we have independent evidence as to the characteristics of Latin speech. If we had not, we should be reasoning in a circle. Science is rightly suspicious of accounts of things in terms of a hypothesis for whose existence nothing can be alleged save that if it existed it would or might account for something which is actually found. Independent evidence of the existence of such an object is required. This consideration has an interesting application to the question in hand. It brings out clearly the absurdity involved in supposing that any formula, of the Laplacean type, about some earlier state of existence, however comprehensive, is comprehensive enough to cover the whole scope of existence of that earlier time.

Let us suppose the formula to be descriptive of a primitive state of the solar system. Not only must it start from and be framed in terms of what *now* exists, but the present datum must be larger than the existing solar system if we are to escape reasoning in a circle. In such cosmological constructions, astronomers and geologists rely upon observation of what is going on outside of the solar system. Without such data, the inquiry would be hopelessly crippled. The stellar field now presents, presumably, systems in all stages of formation. Is there any reason for supposing that a like state of affairs did not present itself at any and every prior time? Whatever for-

[3] Compare Woodbridge, ''Evolution,'' *Philosophical Review*, Vol. 21, page 137.

mula is arrived at for the beginning of our present solar system describes, therefore, only one structure existing amid a vaster complex. A state of things adequately and inclusively described by the formula would be, by conception, a state of things in which nothing could happen. To get change we have to assume other structures which interact with it, existences not covered by the formula.

As a matter of fact, the conception of a solar system seems to have exercised an hypnotic influence upon Newton's successors. The gathering together of sun, planets and their satellites, etc., into a system which might be treated as an individual having its own history was a wonderful achievement, and it impressed men's imaginations. It served for the time as a kind of symbol of the "universe." But as compared with the entire stellar field, the solar system is, after all, only a "right little, tight little island." Yet unless its complex context be ignored the idea of "an undifferentiated universe" which, by some immanent potential force, determined everything which has happened since, could hardly arise.[4] That the French language did not evolve out of Latin because of some immanent causality in the latter we have already noted. It is equally true that the contact and interaction of those speaking Latin with those speaking barbaric tongues were not due to the fact that they spoke Latin, but to independent variables. Internal diversity is as much a necessity as something externally heterogeneous.[5]

The consideration throws light, I think, upon the meaning of potentiality with reference to any state of things. We never apply the term except where there *is* change or a process of becoming. But we have an unfortunate tendency to conceive a fixed state of affairs and then appeal to a latent or potential something or other to effect change. But in reality the term refers to a characteristic of change. Anything changing might be said to exhibit potentiality with respect to two facts: first, that the change exhibits (in connection with interaction with new elements in its surroundings) qualities it did not show till it was exposed to them and, secondly, that the changes in which these qualities are shown run a certain course. To say that an apple has the potentiality of decay does not mean that it has latent or im-

---

[4] One who turns to Spencer's chapter on the "Instability of the Homogeneous" will perceive that his proof of its instability consists in showing that it was really already heterogeneous.

[5] Some contemporary metaphysical theories attempt to start from pure "simple" entities and then refer change exclusively to "complexes." This overlooks the fact that without internal diversification in the alleged simple entity, a complex entity would no more exhibit change than a simple one. The history of the doctrine of atoms is instinctive. Such a metaphysics transgresses the conditions of intelligent inquiry in exactly the same way as the metaphysics of ultimate origins.

plicit within it a causal principle which will some time inevitably display itself in producing decay, but that its existing changes (in interaction with its surroundings) will take the form of decay, *if* they are exposed or subjected to certain conditions not now operating upon them. Potentiality thus signifies a certain limitation of present powers, due to the limited number of conditions with which they are in interaction plus the fact of the manifestation of new powers under different conditions. To generalize the idea, we have to add the fact that the very changes now going on have a tendency to expose the thing in question to these different conditions which will call out new modes of behavior, in other words, further changes of a different kind. Potentiality thus implies not merely diversity, but a progressively increasing diversification of a specific thing in a particular direction. So far is it from denoting a causal force immanent within a homogeneous something and leading it to change.

We may say then that an earlier condition of our earth was potential with life and mind. But this means that it was changing in a certain way and direction. Starting where we must start, with the present, the fact or organization shows that the world is of a certain kind. In spots, it *has* organization. Reference to the evolution of this organization out of an earlier world in which *such* organization was not found, means something about that earlier condition—it means that it was characterized by a change having direction—that is, in the direction of vital and intelligent organization. I do not see that this justifies the conclusion that that earlier world was biocentric or vitalistic or psychic. Yet two conclusions seem to follow. One is negative. The fact that it is possible and desirable to state the processes of an organized being in chemico-physical terms does not eliminate, but rather takes for granted whatever peculiar features living beings have. It does not imply that the distinguishing features of living and thinking beings are to be explained away by resolution into the features found in non-living things. It is the *occurrence* of these pecular features which is stated in physicochemical terms. And, as we have already seen, the attempt to give an account of any occurrence involves the genuine and irreducible existence of the thing dealt with. A statement of the mechanism of vital and thinking creatures is a statement of *their* mechanism; an account of their production is an account of *their* production. To give such an account does not prove whether the existence in question is a good thing or a bad thing, but it proves nothing at all if it puts in doubt the specific existence of the subject-matter investigated.

The positive point is that the evolution of living and thinking beings out of a state of things in which life and thought were not found is a fact which must be recognized in any metaphysical inquiry into the irreducible traits of the world. For evolution appears to be just one of the irreducible traits. In other words, it is a fact to be reckoned with in considering the traits of diversity, interaction, and change which have been enumerated as among the traits taken for granted in all scientific subject-matter. If everything which is, is a changing thing, the evolution of life and mind indicates the nature of the changes of physico-chemical things and therefore something about those things. It indicates that as purely physical, they are still limited in their interactions; and that as they are brought into more and complex interactions they exhibit capacities not to be found in an exclusively mechanical world. To say, accordingly, that the existence of vital, intellectual, and social organization makes impossible a purely mechanistic metaphysics is to say something which the situation calls for. But it does not signify that the world "as a whole" is vital or sentient or intelligent. It is a remark of the same order as the statement that one is not adequately acquainted with water or iron until he has found it operating under a variety of different conditions, and hence a scientific doctrine which regards iron as essentially hard or water as essentially liquid is inadequate. Without a doctrine of evolution we might be able to say, not that matter *caused* life, but that matter under certain conditions of highly complicated and intensified interaction is living. With the doctrine of evolution, we can add to this statement that the interactions and changes of matter are themselves of a kind to bring about that complex and intensified interaction which is life. The doctrine of evolution implies that this holds good of any matter, irrespective of its date, for it is not the matter of 1915, as caused by matter that has now ceased to be, which lives. The matter which was active ten million years ago now lives: this is a feature of the matter of ten million years ago.

I am, however, getting beyond my main point. I am not concerned to develop a metaphysics; but simply to indicate one way of conceiving the problem of metaphysical inquiry as distinct from that of the special sciences, a way which settles upon the more ultimate traits of the world as defining its subject-matter, but which frees these traits from confusion with ultimate origins and ultimate ends— that is, from questions of creation and eschatology. The chief significance of evolution with reference to such an inquiry seems to be to indicate that while metaphysics takes the world irrespective of any particular time, yet time itself, or genuine change in a specific direction, is itself one of the ultimate traits of the world irrespective of date.   JOHN DEWEY.

COLUMBIA UNIVERSITY.

The Journal of Philosophy

THE CHIEF TYPES OF MOTIVATION TO PHILOSOPHIC REFLECTION

THIS essay lays no claim to profundity of thought. I am simply presenting here familiar ideas in a somewhat novel form which I have found personally illuminating and highly suggestive in that it furnishes a means of placing certain attitudes which are making a great stir and raising a lot of dust in contemporary philosophy. For to be able to distinguish in the density of this dust those particles which are centripetal and permanent from those which are centrifugal and transient is absolutely essential to every student who is more interested in what the truth is in philosophy than he is in defending the characteristic tenets of a particular school. And to reach such a distinction one way, and in my judgment a way than which none is more excellent, is to make an objective classification and analysis of the chief types of motivation behind the various bits of philosophical dust contributing to this density. But before proceeding with the discussion, a word of explanation and of caution must needs be prefaced.

That all human motivation is highly complicated and curiously mixed is a fundamental and generally accepted truth. The noblest deed may be, and often is, the consequence of a chain of motives some of the links of which are prosaic and commonplace, if not even sordid. Nor need one be a student of criminology to know that many a hideous crime is the result of an entanglement of motives some of which are really praiseworthy. The good and the bad acts which men do are both made out of the same stuff. They flow forth from that common fountain-head of mental life—the undifferentiated emotional, instinctive, and sensational congery which constitutes what, for want of a better name, may be called the momentary active self.

This well-known fact puts a special limitation on any attempt to isolate and analyze the motivation which leads a particular human being to devote himself to the life of philosophic reflection. Indeed the problem here is even more insoluble than in the case of a single act, for the life of philosophic reflection is a highly involved set of activities comprising many single acts. And if it is difficult to unravel the complicated motivation behind a single act, it is *a fortiori* far more difficult to separate out the diverse elements entering into the motivating process which sustains through the years the career of a philosopher. In fact it must be frankly admitted that the greatness of the difficulty makes the task practically impossible so far as any individual philosopher is concerned. And since every philosopher knows full well that he does not sufficiently understand himself to trace out in detail the thread of motivation which sustains him in that life, he could hardly be so presumptuous as to claim to be able to analyze that which is behind the reflective activity of another. Instead of men choosing philosophy it seems rather that philosophy is a great over-individual which chooses certain human beings to voice its message and to articulate its insights. That these men are motivated in their philosophizing we can not question, but we must also admit that the motivation is too living and intricate for anyone to analyze sufficiently well to be able to say: " This man was motivated by this and that man by that." The truth is that the motivation of every real philosopher is compounded out of both this and that, and the more human and genuine the philosopher the more labyrinthine his motivation.

Nevertheless, every student of the history of philosophy must recognize the existence of distinct types of motivation, even though it is impossible to say that any particular thinker was guided by one rather than or to the exclusion of any other. This paper is concerned with these dominant types of motivation. Various sayings of philosophers are used to illustrate these several types, but I wish expressly to repudiate in advance the charge that I impute to any philosopher, and particularly to those from whom I quote, one of these types of motivation to the exclusion of the others. I hold that certain types of motivation are characteristic of certain kinds of philosophy, but I deny that originators, adherents, or protagonists of these kinds of philosophy are necessarily restricted as individual philosophers to the type of motivation which dominates their brand of philosophy. It is to be hoped that in this respect at least every philosopher is bigger than the particular *ism* which he may choose to defend.

The chief types of motivation which I find it worth while to distinguish are: (1) the *hedonic,* (2) the *theological,* (3) the *sociological,* and (4) the *scientific.* I shall discuss these in this order.

I

A great philosospher, one for whom I have a high personal regard and who is quite generally profoundly respected for his intellectual ability, once said to me that he could not accept any of the existing systems of philosophy (we were talking especially of Idealism), because to do so would mean that the gates of all further speculation would be closed, philosophizing would resolve itself into rethinking what other men have already thought, and consequently *there would be no fun in it.* This suggests what I mean by the hedonic motivation. It is philosophizing for the fun there is in it or building up a speculative system in order to have something interesting to do. From this point of view a philosophical *Weltanschauung* is an imposing toy, constructed by the human intellect to satisfy a kind of play instinct or fun-loving disposition. And naturally there is more fun in fabricating your own toy than in playing with one some one else has constructed. Just as many find enjoyment playing a parlor or an outdoor game, so the philosopher, having fallen in love with dialectical subtleties, finds an unadulterated mental pleasure in playing the one-man game of juggling intellectual abstractions.

Professor Royce gave fitting and beautiful expression to this type of motivation when, concerning the joy that philosophical students take in the reflective life, he wrote: "Let me admit frankly: it is indeed the joy, if you like, of playing cat and mouse with your dearest other self. It is even somewhat like the joy, if so you choose to declare, which infants take in that primitive form of hide and seek that is suited to their months. 'Where is my truth, my life, my faith, my temperament?' says the philosopher. And if, some volumes further on in the exposition of his system, he says, 'Oh! *there* it is,' the healthy babies will be on his side in declaring that such reflections are not wholly without their rational value. But why do I thus apparently degrade speculation by deliberately comparing it with a game? Because, I answer, in one sense, all consciousness is a game, a series of longings and of reflections which it is easy to call superfluous if witnessed from without. The justification of consciousness is the having of it. And this magnificent play of the spirit with itself, this infantile love of renewing its own wealth ever anew through deliberate loss, through seeking, and through joyous recognition, what is this, indeed, but the pastime of the divine life itself."[1]

For a Schopenhauerian temperament this type of motivation will inevitably take on a more sombre hue. In fact it seems to be able to fructify equally well in an extreme and shallow optimism or in a thoroughgoing and dismal pessimism. Whether one holds philosophizing to be a form of pleasure among many, no one of which is more ultimate than another, or the only vocation capable of producing a durable satisfaction, or whether he holds the world to be wholly

---

[1] *Spirit of Modern Philosophy*, p. 21.

and radically evil and philosophy a kind of negative good in that it may alleviate to a certain extent the awful misery of existence, or whether he holds some view in between these extremes, in any case this type of motivation is active. It underlies Epicureanism and Stoicism and some forms of Skepticism. Wherever and whenever men turn to philosophy as a kind of mental paradise or city of refuge situated within the domains of a veritable hell this type of motivation is in evidence.

In *Paradise Lost* there is an excellent illustration of the extreme pessimistic form of this type of motivation. Milton is describing the various occupations of the devils in the nether regions during the interim while Satan is absent on his journey to earth to beguile man. And it is with genuine respect that he writes of a certain group of imps who turned to philosophizing in order to mitigate their torments:

> Others apart sat on a hill retired,
> In thoughts more elevate, and reasoned high
> Of providence, foreknowledge, will and fate;
> Fixed fate, free will, foreknowledge absolute,
> And found no end, in wandering mazes lost.
> Of good and evil much they argued then,
> Of happiness and final misery,
> Passion and apathy, and glory and shame,
> Vain wisdom all, and false philosophy.
> Yet with a pleasing sorcery, could charm
> Pain for awhile, or anguish, and excite
> Fallacious hope, or arm the obdured breast
> With stubborn patience, as with triple steel.

Is there not here a fairly accurate poetic description of the hedonic motivation to philosophic reflection? Nor is it so very far from this to the ideas expressed in Mr. Russell's much-quoted and justly praised *Free Man's Worship*. Only for Mr. Russell men are in much the same position as the Miltonian devils. Confronted with the indubitable scientific knowledge that mankind is foredoomed to destruction, individually and collectively, thinking men may yet find freedom, and therewith a certain grim resignation in the contemplation of the awful impending catastrophe. Even though he knows with absolute certainty that physical processes are at work which will utterly efface from the universe, not only all man's manifold works, but man himself as a spectator of the cosmic drama, nevertheless, in philosophy the individual thinker may find a light that will illumine his little day. Substitute for the devils of Milton, Mr. Russell's free men, and the poet's account of the motivation to philosophic reflection in hell may be transferred back to earth. For it goes without saying that Milton took it from the earth originally.

Yet the fact that the devil philosophers and free men are hedonically motivated should not be taken as a complete disparagement of this type of motivation. For there is a sense in which every philosopher is a devil philosopher as well as a free man. Some of the noblest and keenest thinkers in philosophy's Hall of Fame entered through this portal. For as much as philosophy offers to men an interesting and pleasurable form of intellectual activity, one which is capable of calling forth the very best in human nature, and in philosophizing men can somehow find a balm for sorrow, an assuagement for grief, a relief, however momentary, from torment, yes, thanks to the fact that there is fun in philosophizing, every true philosopher can and should rejoice that the subject he loves is not wholly devoid of practical value.

And yet he whose quest for metaphysical truth is impelled by this type of motivation must be forever on his guard. Here lurk the subtle dangers against which Bacon warned in his famous idols. Actuated by this motive we may build a neat system which is not in accord with reality, because, forsooth, an ordered and systematic world is more pleasing than a chaotic one. Or, sharing Mr. Russell's preference for a philosophy which has something of the character of a hair shirt, perhaps we may be in danger of making the world out to be a great deal worse than it actually is. How often have the speculations of philosophers been condemned as arbitrary constructions, fantastic play or dream-worlds, *idola theatri!* And if too frequently the charge has been true, it has sometimes been due to the fact that certain systems are the fruits of an excessive hedonic motivation. And I, for one, am glad that Professor Royce corrected his too great emphasis on philosophy as play with the statement: " I confess to you that, although I myself often take a certain personal delight in the mere subtleties of speculation, although I also enjoy at times that miserliness which makes the professional student hoard up the jewels of reflection for the sake of gloating over their mere hardness and glitter, I find always that when I come to think of the thing fairly, there is after all no beauty in a metaphysical system, which does not spring from its value as a record of spiritual experience." [2] The hedonic motivation is peripheral and anthropocentric. It will not, because it can not, take one into the heart of reality. It stands condemned for its insufficiency and for sacrificing philosophy on the altar of pleasure.

II

Philosophy presupposes a relatively high state of civilization. It can not come into existence until a people has first developed a lit-

---

[2] *Loc. cit.*, p. 23.

erature, a legal code, and a religious liturgy and dogma. This means that it follows, both logically and temporally, the development of social, moral, and religious customs and manners, creeds and beliefs. Because men are necessarily deeply rooted in a highly cultured environment before they begin philosophic reflection, all the ideas which are characteristic of that environment have entered into the making of the mind of the thinker long before he becomes a thinker in the technical sense of philosophy.

Now in many minds it is precisely the religious ideas peculiar to the civilization in question which exercise the dominant rôle during the years preceding the rise of reflective self-analysis and speculative thought. And to begin with beliefs about religion which are dogmatically and uncritically accepted as eternal truths and then to indulge in the kind of arbitrary speculation which will harmonize and substantiate these beliefs, without first subjecting the beliefs themselves to critical analysis, is what I mean by being theologically motivated to philosophic reflection. There are numerous illustrations of this type of motivation in the history of philosophy. The stock illustration is Mediæval Scholasticism, but Neo-Scholasticism and much Protestant Christian Philosophy is permeated by the same type of motivation. Accepting the religious ideas current in your own environment as unassailable truths and working out a philosophical doctrine or system which will justify them is philosophizing prompted by this theological type of motivation, be the thinker Mohammedan or Confucian, Jew or Christian, Catholic or Protestant.

I hasten to add, however, that this does not mean that every theistic philosophy is theologically motivated. This is a radically mistaken inference which is too frequently put forth as a basic truism. A theistic philosophy is not theologically motivated when it is the result and an expression of a thinker's deepest and sincerest thought about the problems of philosophy and represents his acutest insight into the nature of things. It is only theologically motivated when it is adopted at the very beginning of reflection as a dogmatic assumption. Professor Royce, as Dr. Santayana has remarked, was a " person with no very distinctive Christian belief."[3] Nevertheless, he reached a philosophical position which he deliberately called theistic, and which would generally be regarded as true to the spirit of Christian philosophy. And yet Professor Royce could hardly be charged with being theologically motivated.

Nor does this mean, as is too often implied, that every theologically motivated system of thought or philosophic creed is theistic or even friendly to religion. There are negative as well as positive religious beliefs. There are highly intellectual environments in the

[3] *Winds of Doctrine*, p. 189.

modern world in which philosophic minds are germinating that are through and through anti-religious. There is an atheistic as well as a theistic dogma. Whoever philosophizes in order to disprove a religious conception of the world is just as much theologically motivated as he who philosophizes in order to establish such an interpretation. "Religion is a dangerous superstition which ought to be stamped out," are the words of a young graduate student in philosophy, and the idea which they express is dear to the heart of more than one contemporary philosopher. Of course, Nietzsche has become a classic example of a philosopher motivated from the beginning and throughout his career by an ineradicable and insane prejudice against all forms of religion, and especially of the Christian religion. Always for him the alternative with which the philosopher is confronted is *Christus oder Antichristus?* He says somewhere that he first became interested in Schopenhauer's philosophy because he was told that Schopenhauer was an enemy of religion. Here is the negative type of theological motivation at work. And it is always at work in the thinking of those philosophers who regard it as the unique task and bounden duty of philosophy to uproot religion. Haeckel is another conspicuous example.

What, now, is to be thought of the theological type of motivation? It is logically dependent upon the hedonic type and consequently shares its weaknesses. If the religious beliefs of men are not philosophically defensible, human happiness is impossible, therefore philosophy must by all means justify them—so argue those who are motivated by the positive form of theological motivation. If the religious beliefs of men are justifiable, human happiness is impossible, therefore it is the business of philosophy to make away with these absurd superstitions—so argue those who are motivated by the negative form of theological motivation. And the cynic might make a perfect simple destructive dilemma. If human happiness is possible, either religious beliefs must be proven true or they must be proven false, but they can neither be proven true nor false, ergo human happiness is impossible. Admit that the cynic is right and the theological type of motivation resolves into the negative hedonic type. Thus, either in its positive or negative form, the hedonic type of motivation is really the tap-root of the theological type. Consequently, the latter is just as anthropocentric and peripheral as the former. It, too, sacrifices philosophy on the altar of personal satisfaction.

Moreover, it is a contradiction for a philosopher to withhold any of his beliefs from the crucible of rigorous thought. The belief that there is a God, and all other religious beliefs, must be thrown in with all the rest of the equipage of naïve realism. But so also must the belief that there is no God. Anti-religious or naturalistic dogmatism is just as reprehensible as religious dogmatism, just as intolerant and dangerous, too. The ideal of a philosopher is to start *de novo,* without a prejudice to nurse or an axe to grind.

And yet the theological type of motivation has its good fruits. Here, too, is one of the fairest and most attractive of the approaches to philosophy. Many a student has made his way into the profoundest depths of metaphysical truth because of a burning desire to establish on an impregnable foundation his religious insights. And, on the other hand, philosophy could ill afford to loose the stimulus of its Nietzsches. Whoever condemns without ado the theological type of motivation proves himself ignorant of its potential power to create new and valuable philosophical interpretations. But while no true philosopher can afford to ignore the thought-systems which theologically motivated thinkers have given to the world I think there is a more excellent entrance into the domain of philosophy.

III

However, before taking up this more excellent type of motivation, it is first necessary to deal with another which is in danger of being considered identical with it. This is the sociological type of motivation. In dealing with it I will attempt to show wherein lies the falsity of its pretension of being equivalent to the scientific type.

There is a theory abroad that our whole social structure is a product of a haphazard and irrational growth, and is therefore *ipso facto* radically wrong. Owing to the fact that science (which is assumed to be a synonym for rationality) is a comparatively new development, or, at least, has only in our day reached its full fruition in a science of society, little or no rationality is supposed to have been at work in the processes which produced the various institutions and ideals, customs and laws which constitute the very essence of our modern civilization. Consequently, the real business of modern men, who, just because they are modern, must be alive to the existing chaotic social and industrial and international situation, is to create, on the foundation of modern physical and chemical science and under the immediate direction of modern social and political science, a rational social order to supplant the existing irrational order. The present order is held to be all out of joint because it is based on the principle: " Every man for himself and the devil take the hindermost." Let us apply our scientific knowledge to the task of making a better world, based on the principle of satisfying the largest possible number of desires or interests.

> The world is out of joint. O cursed spite
> That ever I was born to set it right,

Shakespeare has Hamlet say, but, admitting the truth of the premise, many men today would say: O blessed privilege that modern man was born to set it right. And since the sick world is to be healed by an application to it of the poultice of modern scientific knowledge, which presumably is the only remedy capable of drawing out the rottenness and corruption, this type of thought does a prodigious amount of talking about science and scientific method. So much, indeed, that a novice could easily be deceived into thinking that it must be a scientifically motivated philosophy.

Now whoever accepts this current theory as an indubitable truism, and indulges in philosophic reflection for the express purpose of constructing a philosophy which will support it, is sociologically motivated. That it is not really scientifically motivated is shown by the fact that it says that the old problems which arose when men philosophized from a *disinterested* desire to know what the world actually is—the problem of the one and the many, of change and permanence, of mechanism and teleology, of form and matter, *et cetera*—are all obsolete. It holds that any philosophy built up in the attempt to answer such questions thereby proves its inadequacy and antiquatedness. In other words, this type of philosophy does not concern itself with that eternal, non-human reality with which man is in contact in sense perception, because for it, *à la* Berkeley and Hume, there is no non-sensuous reality. Human experience, capitalized and italicized into *Experience*, is the only reality which man need acknowledge. Let us all, then, contribute what we can to the integration of this great social whole, *Experience*, until it becomes what scientifically trained thinkers want it to be. And to conciliate the religiously minded, let us call it God, the only true God because an ever-working, ever-growing, humanity-made God. Guided by this ideal we shall make a far, far better world and a far, far better God than men have ever known. So, also, shall we loose ourselves and our enslaved brethren from the encasing and galling fetters of traditional dogmas, philosophical and religious, including the nonsensical and absurd dictum that God is the same yesterday, today, and forever.

> Is true freedom but to break
> Fetters for our own dear sake,
> And with leathern hearts forget
> That we owe mankind a debt?
> No! true freedom is to share
> All the chains our brothers wear,
> And with hand and heart to be
> Earnest to make others free.

Singing this noble war-song, philosophers are to march triumphantly forward in the vanguard of a mighty and motley host to occupy the Promised Land, flowing with milk and honey scientifically bottled and extracted.

This type of motivation occurs frequently in *Positivism* and *Pragmatism*. Well known to all is the rôle it played in the philosophy of Auguste Comte. It comes to expression repeatedly in the social and ethical writings of Herbert Spencer. James's lectures on *Pragmatism* culminated in his famous doctrine of *meliorism*, the doctrine that man can make a better world. Nor is it to be marvelled at that James's own modest statement of the meaning of making a better world should have been greatly extended, as Pragmatism developed, until for many contemporary pragmatists philosophy itself has become wholly subjected to the position of an instrument in social reform. Hear Professor Dewey! " This essay may, then, be looked upon as an attempt to forward the emancipation of philosophy from too intimate and exclusive attachment to traditional problems. It is not in intent a criticism of various solutions that have been offered, but raises a question *as to the genuineness, under the present conditions of science and social life, of the problems.*" [4]

Could any better proof of the existence of a sociological type of motivation to philosophic reflection be offered than this saying of the most distinguished living representative of the pragmatic movement? As if new social problems could destroy the pertinence of the perennial problems of philosophy!

Who does not rejoice over the progress made in modern social and political science? Who does not freely admit that there are glaring imperfections in the present social order? Who does not sympathize with the helpless poor, the suffering widows, the homeless orphans, the aged and infirm, the nameless and numberless starving refugees inhabiting the earth today? But why should all this cause anyone to surrender himself to the vain hope that in this temporal sweep of events a stage may be reached, through the instrumentality of human manipulation of the vast cosmic mechanism, in which there will no longer be any poor, sorrowing, and suffering mortals, and that when such a stage is reached it can be permanently sustained and continually bettered (!) by the intellectual activity of the new humanity which is constantly being born to enjoy it? Here, surely, is a philosophy of life which no deeply profound philosopher could ever hold. To adopt it is to admit that the real world is past finding out and to withdraw clamoringly into a realm of fantastic dreams. Dr. Santayana has said that theologically motiva-

---

[4] *Creative Intelligence*, p. 5. Article entitled "A Recovery of Philosophy." It is significant that the italics are not mine but Professor Dewey's.

ted philosophy is " in the region of dramatic system-making and myth to which probabilities are irrelevant." But he recognizes that it is no whit more so than a sociologically motivated philosophy such as Pragmatism. Concerning both, he says: " If one man says the moon is sister to the sun, and another says that she is his daughter, the question is not which notion is more probable, but whether either of them is at all expressive. The so-called evidences are devised afterwards, when faith and imagination have prejudged the issue." [5]

I can not follow Santayana in putting these two types of philosophy on the same level. I have charged the hedonic and the theological types of motivation with being peripheral. I maintain that the sociological type is worse than peripheral because it deliberately turns its back on the great metaphysical problems as though they were non-existent, and by so doing it takes those who follow it away from reality into a jungle of fancies. The hedonic and the theological types of motivation are philosophically fruitful but the sociological is well-nigh barren. So far as I know it has never produced a really great piece of philosophical literature. James admitted in the preface of his *Pragmatism* that the views in it had already been superseded in his own thinking by a view called *Radical Empiricism,* a fact which Professor Perry's introduction to the posthumous collection of essays published under this title makes still clearer. Radical empiricism was the progenitor of Neo-Realism, a thoroughly scientific philosophy. Pragmatism, a sociologically motivated philosophy, was ephemeral in the mind of its greatest founder, the one who did more than anyone else to popularize and give it vogue. This is a prophecy of what will happen to the movement in the development of philosophy as a whole. For any philosophy dominated by a sociological motivation bears the image of death stamped upon it. All finite social orders are but spray on the infinite ocean of reality. This much we should learn from Spinoza. Man's highest prerogative is not the power to make a better world, but the capacity to know the real world, the reality of which he shares.

IV

I said above that a disinterested desire to know what the world is originally brought to light the great problems of philosophy. And this purely disinterested desire to penetrate to the inmost essence of reality I call the scientific motivation to philosophic reflection because the same motivation actuates a theoretical scientist in carying on his special experimental investigations. Every student of philosophy knows that science and philosophy originally arose together and that the special sciences only gradually split off from

[5] *Winds of Doctrine,* p. 210.

philosophy as human knowledge increased. Consequently, philosophy is rightly named "The Mother of the Sciences." Whatever the differences between philosophy and science (and differences there certainly are), this fact that both arose together proves that the proper motivation to philosophic reflection is the same as the motivation to science. And that is simply a disinterested and insatiable desire to know all there is to be known.

Plato and Aristotle both understood this. After enumerating to Theaetetus some of the most abstruse and technical questions of philosophy, questions the genuineness of which, under the present conditions of social life, Professor Dewey presumably doubts, Plato has Socrates say:

" I suspect that you have thought of these questions before now."

" Yes, Socrates, and I am amazed when I think of them; by the Gods I am! and I want to know what on earth they mean; and there are times when my head quite swims with the contemplation of them."

" I see, my dear Theaetetus, that Theodorus had a true insight into your nature when he said that you were a philosopher, for wonder is the feeling of a philosopher, and philosophy begins in wonder." [6]

And Aristotle probably had this passage in mind when he wrote: " It was owing to wonder that men began to philosophize in earlier times just as it is today, wondering at first about the problems that lie close at hand, and then little by little advancing to the greater perplexities. . . . But one who is perplexed and filled with wonder feels himself to be in ignorance. . . . And so if men philosophized in order to escape ignorance it is evident that they pursued wisdom just for the sake of knowing, not for the sake of any advantage it might bring. This is shown too by the course of events. For it was only after practically all things that are necessary for the comfort and convenience of life had been provided that this kind of knowledge began to be sought. Clearly then we pursue this knowledge for the sake of no extraneous use to which it may be put." [7]

Now it must be admitted that the satisfying of this desire to know just for the sake of knowing carries with it a high degree of pleasurable experience. Consequently, it is very easy to confuse the scientific type of motivation with the hedonic. But we are here confronted with the famous paradox of hedonism. If we desire to know for the sake of the pleasure it gives we are not likely to get

[6] Plato's *Dialogues.* Jowett's translation, Vol. IV, p. 210.

[7] *Met.*, I, 2, 982 b 12. Translation from Bakewell's *Sourcebook in Ancient Philosophy*, p. 217.

the real pleasure accompanying the cognitive experience. It is only when we desire to know just for the sake of knowing that we can reasonably expect the desire to be satisfied. For any ulterior motive whatsoever is apt to get in the way of the fact, so that instead of knowing what reality is, as a matter of fact we only take it to be what it pleases us for it to be. And this criticism is applicable even to such a saying as Paulsen's: " The ultimate motive impelling men to meditate upon the nature of the universe will always be the desire to reach some conclusion concerning the meaning, the source and the goal of their own lives. The origin and end of all philosophy is consequently to be sought in ethics." [8] Knowledge for the sake of knowledge is the only adequate and worthy motivation to philosophic reflection and this is the scientific motivation. The philosopher is one who, like Theaetetus, wants to know what on earth the answers to philosophical questions are. He is one whose head at times quite swims with the contemplation of such questions. But this does not mean that he deliberately contemplates such questions for the sake of getting mentally drunk. It is because he is simply built that way. As long as man is man, burning by nature with insatiable curiosity, there will be individuals who will devote themselves to philosophy even though they find there no special pleasure or relief from pain, even though theological dogmas lose completely their appeal, even though trying to make a better world seems utterly futile. As long as the actual world looms awful and mysterious above the mind of man, philosophy will nobly flourish. For, being by nature intelligent, man can not rest until his mind has pierced the veil.

There are only two types of philosophy that are through and through scientifically motivated—*Absolute Idealism* and *Realism*. They have persisted in various nuances from Parmenides and Plato on the one hand and Heracleitus, Leucippus and Democritus on the other hand, to the distinguished absolute idealists and realists of our day. And if realism is frequently enticed by the hedonic and absolute idealism by the theological, and if both may sometimes be caught lying with the sociological type of motivation, nevertheless, each, when it comes to itself, will return to the great saying of Dr. Bosanquet: " It is not the business of philosophy to praise the universe or to exalt the satisfactions of goodness," [9] with its, in my judgment, equally great implication: It is the business of philosophy to sound the depths of the infinite ocean of reality on which man's little bark is tossed. 		DANIEL SOMMER ROBINSON.

MIAMI UNIVERSITY.

[8] *System of Ethics*, Eng. trans., p. 3.
[9] *Value and Density of the Individual*, p. 327.

TRADITION, METAPHYSICS, AND MORALS

IN his recent article on "The Chief Types of Motivation to Philosophic Reflection,"[1] Professor Robinson holds me up as a conspicuous example of the type in which "philosophy itself has become wholly subjected to the position of an instrument in social reform." The evidence cited in support of this classification is the following quotation from an essay of mine entitled "The Recovery of Philosophy": "This may, then, be looked upon as an attempt to forward the emancipation of philosophy from too intimate and exclusive attachment to traditional problems. It is not in intent a criticism of various solutions that have been offered, but raises a question *as to the genuineness, under the present conditions of science and social life, of the problems.*" To the quotation, Dr. Robinson adds the remarks: "Could any better proof of the existence of a sociological type of motivation to philosophic reflection be offered than this saying . . .? As if new social problems could destroy the pertinence of the perennial problems of philosophy!" (*Op. cit.*, p. 38.)

The adjective "perennial" appears to beg the question; new problems will hardly destroy perennial ones. But the text says "traditional." I have sometimes wondered if some thinkers might not be confusing the eternal or, at least, the perennial with the traditional; I was hardly prepared, however, for such a frank avowal of the identification. The text, moreover, qualifies the hypothesis offered concerning the bearing of present conditions upon tradi-

[1] This JOURNAL, Vol. XX, No. 2, pp. 29–42.

331

tional problems. It does not propose the abandonment of the latter; it tries to ease the transition by speaking of a process of emancipation from "too intimate and exclusive attachment" to them. But Dr. Robinson will have nought to do with taking advantage of the easement thus provided. The weaning process appears in his paraphrase as destruction. Again the text refers to present conditions of *science* as casting doubt upon traditional problems. But since Dr. Robinson is set upon offering the reader an example of a sociological type of motivation, reference to science disappears. And while the text speaks of social conditions, the paraphrase reads social problems—a change the more significant because the entire context of Dr. Robinson's discussion assumes that the sociological motivation is wholly concerned with remedying and reforming present ills, while the phrase "social conditions" implies that social *advances* may have put traditional problems in a different light. Finally the human term "social" is narrowed down to the professional term "sociological."

The omissions and changes suggest the famous philological derivation of Middletown from Moses. Cut off "oses" and add "iddletown" and you have it. I do not imply that the changes and omissions were made intentionally. On the contrary; perhaps they will not appear significant to Dr. Robinson even when they are pointed out. But if a philosopher writing in behalf of a disinterested scientific motivation is unwilling to perform the humble task of sounding the meaning of a passage which he quotes, what are the prospects that his philosophy will be able "to sound the depths of the infinite ocean of reality on which man's little bark is tossed"? (P. 41.)

The point at issue is not a personal one; [2] it concerns the relation of philosophy and metaphysics to morals in its broadest sense. This is itself one of the oldest and perhaps one of the questions of most distinctively perennial interest. It would appear that if any problem were worthy of disinterested inquiry into subject-matter in which indications of subject-matter shall supply the conclusion,

[2] In its personal aspect, however, I may point out that the very page from which Dr. Robinson quotes contains such a statement as this: "The limited object of my discussion will, doubtless, give an exaggerated impression of my conviction as to the artificiality of much recent philosophizing." And further qualifications are that a historic mode of approach would with a less limited object in view bring out the fact that some questions that are "now discussed mainly because they have been discussed" were genuine in their own setting. And it is also stated that "it would be a grateful task to dwell upon the precious contributions made by philosophic systems which as a whole are impossible" upon their "fertile and ample ideas." ("Recovery of Philosophy," pp. 5–6.) The reader can judge for himself the justice of the antithesis between "disinterestedness" and a Philistinish "sociological motivation."

it is precisely this problem. But note the paradox. Dr. Robinson, upholding the claims of disinterested scientific inquiry against those whom he conceives to cast aspersions upon it, settles the question by reference not to subject-matter but to "motivation"! His criterion is a moral one, and according to many moralists, a narrow one from even the moral point of view.

Here is a paradoxical inversion that is worthy of serious reflection. I will not go the extreme of saying that it suggests that aversion to recognition of the implication of moral issues in philosophy and metaphysics gives evidence of a desire to protect from examination a certain type of morals, a certain preconception as to the nature of what is ultimately good. But it is evident on its face that certain moral preconceptions are taken for granted without critical examination when an attempt is made to decide an issue by appeal to motivations. Says Dr. Robinson: "Knowledge for the sake of knowledge is the only *adequate and worthy* motivation to philosophic reflection and this is the scientific motivation" (p. 41, italics mine). This may turn out to be true. But true or false, nothing can disguise the fact that it is a moral judgment, while the very conception of disinterested scientific inquiry requires that truth or falsity be settled by examination of subject-matter, not by imputation of motives. As it stands we have Dr. Robinson's own moral *ipse dixit* for its truth. And this once more in an article devoted to ruling morals out of philosophy! Disinterested, I take it, is a moral term relating to the spirit in which alone inquiry can be successfully prosecuted. But as used by Dr. Robinson it implies that moral inquiry can not itself be disinterestedly pursued, and that only inquiry which sets out with the unshaken conviction that only "knowledge for the sake of knowledge" is "worthy" is disinterested. One would suppose that the *results* in and of knowledge might be left to adjudge the question as to what knowledge actually is. Why assume that those who reach the conclusion that "knowledge for the sake of knowledge" denotes knowledge functioning in life must already have set out with a particular moral warp and bias? There is just one way of settling the validity of the conclusion: by an examination of the argument and following whither it leads. But Dr. Robinson has an easier way, that of assigning motives. And this, let it be repeated once more, in a discussion which aims to protect philosophy from moral infection!

If I now return to the context of the passage quoted, it is not for personal reasons, but for the sake of a brief consideration of the issue of the relation of metaphysics to morals as an objective, "disinterested" issue. No one can take exception to the listing of metaphysical questions furnished by Dr. Robinson: "the problem of the one and the many, of change and permanence, of mechanism and teleology, of form and matter, *etc.*'' (p. 37). The sociological type of motivation declares, so he says, that these questions are all ''obsolete.'' Since I am held up as the conspicuous living representative of this school, there is a plain implication that the ''obsoleteness'' of *these* questions is the same thing as the ''non-genuineness'' of traditional problems to which I referred in the passage quoted. On p. 40, the implication is made explicit, with a qualification to the effect that such questions are the ones whose genuineness I ''presumably'' doubt.

The one passage which Dr. Robinson quotes from me occurs on p. 5 of my essay. Pages 6–52 following are a discussion of just the traditional problems which it is conceived may be profitably regarded as not genuine under present conditions of science and social life. An inquiry would presumably not have to be so very disinterested to be aware that these pages are the place to look for light on the matter of just what questions I did have in mind. If Dr. Robinson was too bored with them to read them, I sympathize rather than blame. But in that case, why refer to me at all? Any one who consults these pages will perceive that there is in them no reference to the type of metaphysical problems to which Dr. Robinson refers, which he represents me as regarding as obsolete and not genuine. The traditional problems therein discussed are wholly the *psychological and epistemological* questions that, arising in the seventeenth century, were formulated in the eighteenth and dominated so largely nineteenth-century thought.

So far the discussion seems to be devoted simply to setting myself right personally. But the intent is impersonal. It is conceivable that emancipation from *these* problems of a tradition that developed no longer ago than the seventeenth century may be a helpful and indeed indispensable condition of ''recovery'' of the more objective metaphysical questions mentioned by Dr. Robinson. The psycho-epistemological tradition that inherits from the eighteenth century may be precisely one of the chief causes of the obscuration of the older and more objective questions of which the Greeks were aware. There are those beside unworthy pragmatists who entertain this belief.

Pages 53–58 of the essay on ''Recovery of Philosophy'' do, however, contain a critical reference to one tradition that goes back to Greek thought, a tradition which it is intimated the present condition of *science* should emancipate us from: *viz.*, the identification of philosophy with knowledge of *the* real object, that is, of reality which is regarded as superior in degree and kind to the realities of everyday life and natural science. Two things should here be noted. First, this identification in the end is accountable for the *solution* which classic Greek thought gave to the metaphysical problems, a solution which leaned to the side of the one, the permanent, the form, and against the equal claims of the many, the changing, and matter. Even though the problems are perennial in interest, a recognition of the genuineness of the Greek problems surely does not commit us in advance to an acceptance of classic Greek conclusions. The other point is that whenever we have the distinction of higher and lower reality, superior and inferior being, we have a moral distinction, a distinction of better and worse. The traits of existence as an object of *metaphysical* inquiry are not (till we bring in moral considerations) concerned with questions of higher and lower grades or ranks of being. Plato taught that non-being in some sense *is*, even though he ranked it lower morally than being (which according to him in some sense is not). Accordingly, in criticizing this particular tradition as not genuine "under the present conditions of science" one is questioning an element in the *moral* tradition. And a moral inquiry should, it would seem, be allowed at least to submit to inquiry moral elements in the philosophic tradition, even if it must keep hands off the metaphysical elements.

And this brings us to the gist of the question. If emancipation from recent psycho-epistemological traditions should turn out to serve as a means of return to disinterested inquiry to questions concerning the nature of things, there arises an important problem: How are metaphysical distinctions related to moral distinctions and issues? This is a question not of motivation, but of subject-matter. If those are wrong who hold that a disinterested historic inquiry will show that the Greek classical metaphysics erred in its metaphysical conclusions precisely of a *moral* bias in favor of the one, the unchanging, and formal as against the many, change, and material, they can hardly be shown to be wrong by an imputation of motives, but only by an examination of pertinent subject-matter. If they are wrong in holding, aside from the historical question, that metaphysical distinctions are intimately connected with moral distinctions and issues, that, too, is a question not to be disposed of by alleging motives, but by an examination of subject-matter and by following whither it leads.

It is the importance of the question, not a particular solution of it, which is asserted. But when Dr. Robinson declares that "sociological" interest has never produced a great piece of philosophical literature (p. 39), I beg to refer him to the *Republic* and *Laws* of Plato. One who follows Plato laggardly and from afar may cite, when it comes to appeal to authority, Plato as authority for the conviction that the Good is the central metaphysical concept and fact, and may remind anyone concerned that if anyone ever made philosophy an instrument of political reform and organization, it is this same Plato. It would require a fervor of "sociological" motivation in philosophy hardly to be found to-day to suggest that "philosophers should be kings," and to assert that till they are kings social ills and discords will not be remedied. Again, since Dr. Robinson cites Royce with respect, others who also hold him in respect may quote from the same writing from which Dr. Robinson quotes: "Philosophy . . . has it origin and value in an attempt to give a reasonable account of our own personal attitude toward the more serious business of life. You philosophize when you reflect critically upon what you are actually doing in your world. What you are doing is, of course, in the first place, living."[3] A consideration of the infinite ocean of reality hardly becomes of necessity biased when we include the bark, however frail and however fluctuating it may be, as a significant part of the ocean, and include within our disinterested inquiry a sense of the bearing of the inquiry upon the course and direction of the tossing bark of humanity.

JOHN DEWEY.

COLUMBIA UNIVERSITY.

[3] Royce, *Spirit of Modern Philosophy*, pp. 1, 2.

The Journal of Philosophy

EVENTS AND THE FUTURE

IT is quite possible to use the word "event" as a fundamental term in science and yet carry over into the meaning of the term implications which belong to an order of scientific conceptions which "event" is employed to replace, and which are incompatible with satisfying the conditions which "event" is selected to meet. An illustration of this fact, and of the philosophical consequences of it is found in Broad's *Scientific Thought*. Following Whitehead, Broad points out that "there are many types of objects whose characteristic qualities need a certain minimum of duration to inhere in." For example, if nothing is a mind which does not have memory, a long enough duration to permit memory is clearly necessary to the existence of a mind. Again, "suppose that a certain sort of atom consisted of a nucleus and an electron rotating about it at a certain characteristic speed. Such an atom would need at least the duration of one complete rotation to display its characteristic properties. . . . If the duration of one complete rotation be sliced up into adjacent successive parts, *the contents of the parts will differ in quality from the contents of the whole.*" [1]

I quote the passage because it gives an indispensable character of anything which may be termed an event: namely, a qualitative variation of parts with respect to the whole which requires duration in which to display itself. If we assume only qualitative homogeneity in a mind, we shall not have memory, and hence by definition not a mind. For the later portion of the total duration, even if *otherwise* exactly like the earlier, must, if there be memory, differ from it by recalling the previous state, and hence can not be a mere unchanged persistence of the earlier.

Unfortunately, however, Mr. Broad at once goes on to show that he does *not* regard qualitative variation to be involved in the definition of an event. He says "there may well be objects which are temporally homogeneous. This would mean that, however you divide up their *history*, the contents of the slices are the same as each other and as the whole quality. . . . Now science regards the *ultimate* scientific objects as being spatio-temporally homogeneous. And it assumes that these ultimate scientific objects never begin or end.

[1] Broad, *Scientific Thought*, p. 403, italics not in original.

Thus the ultimate scientific objects are regarded as *eternal* in the sense of existing throughout all time. The only ultimate scientific changes are the groupings and regroupings of such objects according to a single set of fundamental laws.'' [2]

Now I am not concerned here to try to show that there are no such *objects*. Mr. Broad says that he does not know whether the assumption that there are such objects is true or not, and I shall not profess to know that it is false. But one can assert on purely formal grounds that such objects are not events, nor parts of events. Eternal objects have no ''history,'' much less a history which can be ''divided.'' And if it is stated that such objects are the ''temporally homogeneous'' slabs out of which events or histories are composed, it is not evident how the union or co-adjacence of the timeless can give rise to time, nor how the qualitatively homogeneous can pass into the qualitatively heterogeneous; nor, to generalize, how ''eternal objects'' subject to a ''single set of fundamental laws'' can permit of *regroupings*, nor what conceivable meaning can attach to the phrase ''ultimate scientific *changes*.'' The argument is not helped out by saying that the ultimate objects are eternal in the sense of ''existing throughout all time.'' For unless there are changes and changes such that eternal objects can be put in correspondence with them, on the basis of which correspondence eternal objects may be said to have duration, there is no time for them to exist ''throughout.'' There is also no sense in terming them *temporally* homogeneous. Their homogeneity with respect to temporality is utter irrelevancy to it. In short, the only logical significance which can be attached to the passage cited is one which makes ''objects'' logically prior to events, while it also sets serious barriers, to put it mildly, in the way of deriving events from objects as defined. While nominally much is made of events, the emphasis turns out Pickwickian. [3]

The bearing of the implication that (i) there are adjacent slabs of time which (ii) are qualitatively homogeneous with one another, appears in Broad's explicit discussion of time and the future, in an earlier part of the book, namely, Chapter Two. There he says that by event he is going to signify ''anything which endures at all, no matter how long it lasts or whether it be *qualitatively alike or*

[2] *Ibid.*, p. 403, italics mine.

[3] Contrast with Whitehead's: ''Objects are entities recognized as appertaining to events,'' *Principles of Natural Knowledge*, 81. There was, of course, no obligation upon Broad to follow Whitehead, but the thought of the latter so hangs together that it is not possible to borrow his conception of events, and then place ''*recognita*'' or objects behind and under events, without getting into precisely such difficulties as the above.

qualitatively different in adjacent stages in its history."[4] Here we have an express statement that there may be stages of history which are qualitatively like each other. It is my purpose to show that this assumption determines the results at which he arrives with respect to time, especially as regards futurity. Assuming that the definition means just what it says, and that by qualitative likeness he intends identity, and not merely close similarity—which, of course, admits heterogeneity—there appears to be no basis whatever for the idea of "adjacent stages." Bare persistence is not history and it has no stages; the moment they are referred to as stages qualitative change is introduced. Stages mean differences. A persistent "duration" without change may be alleged to be part of a history when enclosed in a larger whole in which there is qualitative variation, but it can not be itself a history. And without a history what is meant by imputing endurance to the thing called "event"? But where there are adjacent stages, every such stage is an event, or history, and hence it has stages, which are events. Or, every event comprises events and is itself comprised in an event.[5]

The only other way in which we can intelligibly speak of adjacent stages in what persists as qualitatively the same is in relation to some *other* event. If we have taken genuine stages of difference in M and have assigned a certain date of beginning and end to each of these, then we may compare M as to these stages with N, and assign an identical duration (or some part of it) to N, and, by setting up a one-to-one correspondence between it and the stages of M, apportion it, in spite of its homogeneity. That we do thus divide into stages things which do not themselves exhibit *perceptible* differences is a well-known fact. But to say that a, in spite of qualitative identity, is a temporal stage of N, is to assert that it can be put in one-to-one correspondence with α, which is a qualitative variation of M, standing in turn in specified relation to β, γ, δ, . . . other qualitative variations of M.

Given the conception of an event as something internally unchanged, it is clear that the beginning of an event, and the occurrence of a qualitative variation in an event (if there be any distinction between these two things), is something other than an event. So Mr. Broad quite logically says that qualitative changes "involve the coming into existence of an event," and that such a change, which he calls a *becoming*, is of such a peculiar character that it is misleading to term it a change. "When we say that a thing changes in quality, or that an event changes in pastness, we are talking of events that exist both before and after the moment at which the change takes

---

[4] *Op. cit.*, p. 54; italics not in original text.

[5] Whitehead, *The Principles of Natural Knowledge*, p. 61, 77.

place. But when an event becomes, it *comes into existence;* and it was not anything at all until it had become" (p. 68, italics in original text). From this it follows logically that past and present events exist, since they *have* become; future events do not exist at all, since they have not become. Thus it follows from his conception of the intrinsically homogeneous character of an event that the future occupies a status existentially which is radically different from that of past and present events. The "future is simply nothing at all" (p. 70). "A present event is defined as one which is succeeded by nothing;" "there is no such thing as ceasing to exist; what has become exists henceforth forever" (p. 68 and p. 69). Thus the sum total of existence is always increasing; something becomes; when this event is past, a fresh slice of existence has been added to the total history of the world.

The distinction between "event" and "becoming" follows logically from his definition of event. Events become but they are not becomings. What is given us by Broad is thus a lot of unchanging things, termed, nevertheless, events, with abrupt insertions of changes; time in the usual sense would appear to proceed by jerks or interruptions. How this view is adjusted to any notion of causal continuity does not here concern us. The point is that it is indispensable to Broad's argument to speak of events as *that which* come into existence. But if an event *is* a becoming, it is not intelligible to speak of the eventing of an event; or the becoming of a becoming. And an event is a becoming if as an event it involves qualitative variation or heterogeneity throughout itself. A distinction between event and becoming can be drawn only if an event is conceived as a solid homogeneous slab throughout, that is, is conceived of as *not* an event or a history. Broad carries over into his nominal use of the term "event" considerations pertinent to modes of thought which attach to what we may call the "pre-event" era of scientific history.

The bearing upon "time" and the future should be fairly evident. If existences are histories or events in the sense of becomings, then past-present-future are on the same level, because all are phases of any event or becoming. Any becoming is from, to, through. Its fromness, or out-of-ness, is *its* pastness; its towardness or intrinsic direction, it *its* futurity; that through which the becoming passes is *its* presentness. No becoming can be perceived or thought of except as out of something into something, and this involves a series of transitions which, taken distributively, belong both to the "out-of" and the "into," or form a "through." The present has thus nothing privileged about it; it is as legitimate to speak of the present century or the present geological age as of the present "moment." The present is defined in relation to an "out-of" and by a future or "into," as truly as the past by the present.

Since without change into, there is no becoming or event, futurity is comprised directly in any and every event which can be said to be present, or, better, be said to *have* a phase of presentness.

On this basis it is mere fiction that we know pastness and futurity only by means of inference from presentness. Any experience of anything in being an experience of a becoming or event contains within itself qualities which are named pastness, presence, and futurity. To recall a specific past event or to foresee or predict a future specific event requires inference, but in the same sense it demands inference to make a determinately specific judgment about anything said to be present. Psychologically, expectancy stands on the same level as memory; in the same sense in which the latter can be said to refer directly to the past, the former can be said to refer directly to the future. In fact, it is questionable whether psychologically the attitude of expectancy is not more usually co-present with observations of what is going on than that of recall. It is even possible that we so commonly ignore it just because it is so omnipresent that there is no need to make it an object of explicit attention.

Mr. Broad gives what seems to me a correct account of *judgments* about the future, but to make a false use of his analysis. It is true that we can not refer intellectually to *a* future event, if the future is dissevered from the present, for then it does not exist for us to refer to. But when he says that it is not true that a judgment involving the future can "mean anything that begins with the statement: 'There is an event' (p. 76), he says something gratuitously unnecessary. The judgment involving the future is: "There is a going-on or a becoming such that it has a specified directional movement." To make the judgment about the future explicit is not to refer to a non-existent; it is to infer the further becoming of what is going-on. "It will probably rain tomorrow" asserts a quality of toward-whichness characteristic of what is happening to-day defined in terms of yesterdays. In its completeness it is a judgment regarding some out-of-which-through-which-into-which.

When Mr. Broad says that any judgment that professes to be about the future seems to "involve two peculiar and not further analyzable kinds of assertion," one of which "asserts that further events *will* become" (italics mine), and the other that so-and-so "*will* characterize some of the events which *will* become" (italics mine), he simply restores under the name of "will" what he officially denies under the name of futurity.[6] "Will be" and the future tense are

[6] *Op. cit.*, pp. 76–77.

equivalents and both go back to an "it-is-going-to," where the going-to characterizes what *is*. "Will become" is equivalent to futurity, precisely because it does not refer to some *other* event wholly disconnected from the present, but to an event or becoming which is going-on. Hence the "was," the "is," when temporally limited to a phase of the going-on, and the "will be" all stand on the same level with respect to judgment. All of them as judgments are equally susceptible of error, but that is because all involve inference. For to say that every event, or going-on, has a phase of pastness, presentness, and futurity is not to say that *what* has been, is, and will be, is immediately self-revealing, or that it can be determined without an intellectual or mediating factor.

To save space I have written somewhat dogmatically. But the argument is hypothetical. It contrasts what follows *if* an event is a becoming or involves qualitative changes throughout, with what follows if something nominally termed an event is defined so as to exclude internal heterogeneity. In my opinion, Mr. Broad first nominally introduces duration into his "events" and then takes pains to eliminate all temporality from them. Having done that, he is obliged to re-introduce time by a succession of arbitrarily assumed interruptions or jerks, called becomings.

JOHN DEWEY.

COLUMBIA UNIVERSITY.

The Journal of Philosophy

DEWEY'S NATURALISTIC METAPHYSICS

READERS of this Journal are doubtless studying, or have studied, Professor Dewey's recent book on *Experience and Nature,* certainly the weightiest and most incisive account he has given of his philosophy. In reviewing it, I may therefore be excused from attempting to sum up his chief contentions in his own language, considering especially that his language, as he himself says, is the chief or only obstacle to understanding him. Nor would the fairest paraphrase of his conclusions do him justice. Without the many pointed allusions and incidental insights that humanize his pages, without his constant appeals to the economy of the working mind, many of his positions would remain paradoxes, and it would be impossible to discover the scrupulous fidelity to facts, seen at a certain angle, which dictates his words, even when they seem most unintelligible. Here is a remarkable rereading of things with a new and difficult kind of sincerity, a near-sighted sincerity comparable in philosophy to that of contemporary painters in their painful studies. The intellect here, like the fancy there, arrests its dogmatic vision and stops short at some relational term which was invisible because it is only a vehicle in natural seeing. No wonder that these near elements, abstracted and focused in themselves, have a queer look. For my part, I am entirely persuaded of the genuineness and depth of Dewey's views, within the limits of his method and taken as he means them. He is, fortunately, not without an active band of followers who will be able to interpret and elaborate them in his own spirit. I am hardly in their case, and all I can hope to accomplish is to fix the place and character of this doctrine in relation to the points of view which I instinctively take or which seem to me, on reflection, to be most comprehensive. And I will append such conclusions as I may provisionally reach on this subject to a phrase by which Dewey himself characterizes his system: *Naturalistic Metaphysics.* In what sense is this system naturalistic? In what sense is it metaphysical? How comes it that these two characters (which to me seem contradictory) can be united in this philosophy?

Naturalism is a primary system, or rather it is not a special system at all, but the spontaneous and inevitable body of beliefs involved in animal life, beliefs of which the various philosophical systems are either extensions (a supernatural environment, itself natural in its own way, being added to nature) or interpretations (as in Aristotle and Spinoza) or denials (as in idealism). Children are interested in their bodies, with which they identify themselves; they are interested in animals, adequate playmates for them, to be bullied with a pleasing risk and a touch of wonder. They are interested later in mechanical contrivances and in physical feats and adventures. This boyish universe is indefinitely extensible on its own plane; it may have heaven around it and fairyland in its interstices; it covers the whole field of possible material action to its uttermost reaches. It is the world of naturalism. On this material framework it is easy to hang all the immaterial objects, such as words, feelings, and ideas, which may be eventually distinguished in human experience. We are not compelled in naturalism, or even in materialism, to ignore immaterial things; the point is that any immaterial things which are recognized shall be regarded as names, aspects, functions, or concomitant products of those physical things among which action goes on. A naturalist may distinguish his own person or self, provided he identifies himself with his body and does not assign to his soul any fortunes, powers, or actions save those of which his body is the seat and organ. He may recognize other spirits, human, animal, or divine, provided they are all proper to natural organisms figuring in the world of action, and are the natural moral transcript, like his own feelings, of physical life in that region. Naturalism may, accordingly, find room for every sort of psychology, poetry, logic, and theology, if only they are content with their natural places. Naturalism will break down, however, so soon as words, ideas, or spirits are taken to be substantial on their own account, and powers at work prior to the existence of their organs, or independent of them. Now it is precisely such disembodied powers and immaterial functions prior to matter that are called metaphysical. Transcendentalism is not metaphysical if it remains a mere method, because then it might express the natural fact that any animal mind is its own center and must awake in order to know anything: it becomes metaphysical when this mind is said to be absolute, single, and without material conditions. To admit anything metaphysical in this sense is evidently to abandon naturalism.

It would be hard to find a philosopher in whom naturalism, so conceived, was more inveterate than in Dewey. He is very severe against the imagination, and even the intellect, of mankind for having created figments which usurp the place and authority of the mundane sphere in which daily action goes on. The typical philosopher's fallacy, in his eyes, has been the habit of hypostatizing the conclusions to which reflection may lead, and depicting them to be prior realities—the fallacy of dogmatism. These conclusions are in reality nothing but suggestions or, as Dewey calls them, "meanings" surrounding the passing experience in which, at some juncture, a person is immersed. They may be excellent in an instrumental capacity, if by their help instinctive action can be enlarged or adjusted more accurately to absent facts; but it would be sheer idolatry to regard them as realities or powers deeper than obvious objects, producing these objects and afterwards somehow revealing themselves, just as they are, to the thoughts of metaphysicians. Here is a rude blow dealt at dogma of every sort: God, matter, Platonic ideas, active spirits, and creative logics all seem to totter on their thrones; and if the blow could be effective, the endless battle of metaphysics would have to end for lack of combatants.

Meantime there is another motive that drives Dewey to naturalism: he is the devoted spokesman of the spirit of enterprise, of experiment, of modern industry. To him, rather than to William James, might be applied the saying of the French pragmatist, Georges Sorel, that his philosophy is calculated to justify all the assumptions of American society. William James was a psychologist of the individual, preoccupied with the varieties of the human imagination and with the possible destinies of the spirit in other worlds. He was too spontaneous and rare a person to be a good mirror of any broad general movement; his Americanism, like that of Emerson, was his own and within him, and perhaps more representative of America in the past than in the future. In Dewey, on the contrary, as in current science and ethics, there is a pervasive quasi-Hegelian tendency to dissolve the individual into his social functions, as well as everything substantial or actual into something relative or transitional. For him events, situations, and histories hold all facts and all persons in solution. The master-burden of his philosophy, which lends it its national character, is a profound sympathy with the enterprise of life in all lay directions, in its technical and moral complexity, and especially in its American form, where individual initiative, although still demanded and prized, is quickly subjected to overwhelming democratic control. This, if I am not mistaken, is the heart of Dewey's pragmatism, that it is the pragmatism of the people, dumb and instinctive in them, and struggling in him to a labored but radical expression. His pragmatism is not inspired by any wish to supply a new argument to support some old speculative dogma. Nor is he interested, like Nietzsche and Vaihinger, in a heroic pessimism, desperately living as if postulates were true which it knows to be false. He is not interested in speculation at all, balks at it, and would avoid it if he could; his inspiration is sheer fidelity to the task in hand and sympathy with the movement afoot: a deliberate and happy participation in the attitude of the American people, with its omnivorous human interests and its simplicity of purpose.

Now the philosophy by which Americans live, in contrast to the philosophies which they profess, is naturalistic. In profession they may be Fundamentalists, Catholics, or idealists, because American opinion is largely pre-American; but in their hearts and lives they are all pragmatists, and they prove it even by the spirit in which they maintain those other traditional allegiances, not out of rapt speculative sympathy, but because such allegiance seems an insurance against moral dissolution, guaranteeing social cohesion and practical success. Their real philosophy is the philosophy of enterprise. Now enterprise moves in the infinitely extensible boyish world of feats and discoveries—in the world of naturalism. The practical arts, as Dewey says, assume a mechanical unity and constancy established in the universe. Otherwise discoveries made to-day would not count to-morrow, inventions could not be patented, the best-laid plans might go astray, all work might be wasted, and the methods of experts could not be adjusted more and more accurately to their tasks. This postulated mechanical system must evidently include the hands and brain of the worker, which are intertwined inextricably with the work done. It must also include his mind, if his mind is to be of any practical account and to make any difference in his work. Hence the implicit American philosophy, which it is Dewey's privilege to make explicit, involves behaviorism. This doctrine is new and amazing if taken to deny the existence of thought; but on its positive side, in so far as it puts all efficient processes on one level, it has been an implication of naturalism from time immemorial. For a naturalist nothing can be substantial or efficacious in thought except its organs and instruments, such as brains, training, words, and books. Actual thought, being invisible and imponderable, eludes this sort of chase. It has always been rather ignored by materialists; but it remained for American optimists to turn their scorn of useless thought into a glad denial of its existence. This negative implication of behaviorism follows also from the commonsense view that mind and body act upon each other alternately; for when this view is carried out with empirical rigor, it corrects the speculative confusion which first suggested it. What it called mind turns out never to have been anything but a habit in matter, a way people have of acting, speaking, and writing. The actuality of spirit, mystically momentary, does not fall within the purview of this empirical inventory any more than the realm of truth, invisibly eternal. Men of affairs, who can easily tell a clever man from a fool, are behaviorists by instinct; but they may scout their own conviction when it is proposed to them by philosophers in paradoxical language. The business intellect, by the time it comes to theorizing, is a little tired. It will either trust a first impression, and bluff it out, or else it will allow comfortable traditional assurances in these hazy regions to relieve it of responsibility.

Is Dewey a behaviorist? On the positive side of the theory, he certainly is; and it is only when we interpret what he says about ideas, meanings, knowledge, or truth behavioristically, that the sense and the force of it begin to appear. Often, indeed, he seems to jump the barrier, and to become a behaviorist in the negative sense also, denying the existence of thought: because it would be to deny its existence if we reduced it to its material manifestations. At least at one point, however, the existence of thought in its actuality and spiritual concentration is admitted plainly. Not, indeed, on the ground which to most philosophers would seem obvious and final, namely, that people sometimes do actually feel and think. This consideration might seem to Dewey irrelevant, because actual feeling and thinking are accounted for initially, on his view, by the absolute existence of the specious or conventional world: they do not need to be introduced again among its details. An impersonal transcendental spectator, though never mentioned, is always assumed; and the spectacle of nature unrolled before him may be, and strictly speaking must be, wholly observable and material. There can not be any actual mind in experience except the experience itself. The consideration which nevertheless leads Dewey to graft something consciously actual and spiritual upon the natural world is of quite another sort. Essentially, I suspect, it flows from his choice of "events" to be his metaphysical elements (of which more presently); incidentally it is attached to the sympathetic study which he has made of Aristotle. Events, he thinks, have natural "endings," "culminations," or "consummations." They are not arbitrary sections made in the flux of nature, as if by geometrical planes passed across the current of a river. They are natural waves, pulsations of being, each of which, without any interruption in its material inheritance and fertility, forms a unit of a higher order. These units (if I may express the matter in my own language) fall sometimes into the realm of truth, when they are simply observable patterns or rhythms, and sometimes into the realm of spirit, as in animal perception or intent, when the complex tensions of bodily or social life generate a single sound, an actual pang, or a vivid idea. Mind at such moments possesses a hypostatic spiritual existence, over and above the whole behaviorist or pragmatic ground-work of mind: it has become conscious, or as Aristotle would say, has reached its second entelechy and become intellect in act. This hypostatic spiritual existence Dewey seems to recognize at least in esthetic contemplation; but evidently every actual feeling or idea, however engrossed in action or however abstractly intellectual, is in the same case. Such an admission, if taken to heart, would have leavened this whole philosophy; but Dewey makes it grudgingly, and hastens to cover it up. For instance, when he comes upon the phrase "Knowledge of acquaintance," a phrase intended to express just such instant innocent immediate perusal of essence, he refuses to understand it as it was meant, and says that acquaintance implies recognition and recognition familiarity; on the ground, I suppose, that people are called "acquaintances" when they bow to one another: and we are left with an uncomfortable suspicion that it is impossible to inspect anything for the first time. In another place we are told that consummations are themselves fruitful and ends are also means. Yes, but in what sense? Of course, no earthly flame is so pure as to leave no ashes, and the highest wave sinks presently into the trough of the sea; but this is true only of the substance engaged, which, having reached a culmination here, continues in its course; and the habit which it then acquired may, within limits, repeat the happy achievement, and propagate the light. One torch by material contact may kindle another torch; and if the torches are similar and the wind steady, the flames, too, may be similar and even continuous; but if anyone says that the visible splendor of one moment helps to produce that of another, he does not seem ever to have seen the light. It will therefore be safer to proceed as if the realm of actual spirit had not been broached at this point, and as if the culminations recognized were only runs or nodes discoverable in nature, as in the cycle of reproduction or in sentences in discourse. The behaviorist landscape will then not be split by any spiritual lightning, and naturalism will seem to be established in its most unqualified form. Yet in this case how comes it that Dewey has a metaphysics of his own, that cosmology is absent from his system, and that every natural fact becomes in his hands so strangely unseizable and perplexing?

This question, which is the crux of the whole system, may be answered, I think, in a single phrase: *the dominance of the foreground*. In nature there is no foreground or background, no here, no now, no moral cathedra, no centre so really central as to reduce all other things to mere margins and mere perspectives. A foreground is by definition relative to some chosen point of view, to the station assumed in the midst of nature by some creature tethered by fortune to a particular time and place. If such a foreground becomes dominant in a philosophy naturalism is abandoned. Some local perspective or some casual interest is set up in the place of universal nature or behind it, or before it, so that all the rest of nature is reputed to be intrinsically remote or dubious or merely ideal. This dominance of the foreground has always been the source of metaphysics; and the metaphysics has varied according as the foreground has been occupied by language or fancy or logic or sceptical self-consciousness or religious rapture or moral ambition. Now the dominance of the foreground is in all Dewey's traditions: it is the soul of transcendentalism and also of empiricism; it is the soul of moralism and of that kind of religion which summons the universe to vindicate human notions of justice or to subserve the interests of mankind or of some special nation or civilization. In America the dominance of the foreground is further emphasized by the prevalent absorption in business life and in home affections, and by a general feeling that anything ancient, foreign, or theoretical can not be of much consequence.[1] Pragmatism may be regarded as a synthesis of all these ways of making the foreground dominant: the most close-reefed of philosophical craft, most tightly hugging appearance, use, and relevance to practice today and here, least drawn by the lure of speculative distances. Nor would Dewey, I am sure, or any other pragmatist, ever be a naturalist instinctively or on the wings of speculative insight, like the old Ionians or the Stoics or Spinoza, or like those many mystics, Indian, Jewish, or Mohammedan, who, heartily despising the foreground, have fallen in love with the greatness of nature and have sunk speechless before the infinite. The pragmatist becomes, or seems to become, a naturalist only by accident, when as in the present age and in America the dominant foreground is monopolized by material activity; because material activity, as we have seen, involves naturalistic assumptions, and has been the teacher and the proof of naturalism since the beginning of time. But elsewhere and at other periods experience is free to offer different perspectives into which the faithful pragmatist will be drawn with equal zeal; and then pragmatic metaphysics would cease to be nat-

---

[1] I can imagine the spontaneous pragmatism of some President of a State University, if obliged to defend the study of Sanskrit before a committee of Senators. "You have been told," he would say, "that Sanskrit is a dead language. Not at all: Sanskrit is Professor Smith's Department, and growing. The cost is trifling, and several of our sister universities are making it a fresh requirement for the Ph.D. in classics. That, Gentlemen, is what Sanskrit *is*."

uralistic and become, perhaps, theological. Naturalism in Dewey is accordingly an assumption imposed by the character of the prevalent arts; and as he is aware that he is a naturalist only to that extent and on that ground, his naturalism is half-hearted and short-winded. It is the specious kind of naturalism possible also to such idealists as Emerson, Schelling, or any Hegelian of the Left, who may scrupulously limit their survey, in its range of objects, to nature and to recorded history, and yet in their attitude may remain romantic, transcendental, piously receiving as absolute the inspiration dominating moral life in their day and country. The idealists, being self-conscious, regarded this natural scene as a landscape painted by spirit; Dewey, to whom self-consciousness is anathema, regards it as a landscape that paints itself; but it is still something phenomenal, all above board. Immediacy, which was an epistemological category, has become a physical one: natural events are conceived to be compounded of such qualities as appear to human observers, as if the character and emergence of these qualities had nothing to do with the existence, position, and organs of those observers. Nature is accordingly simply experience deployed, thoroughly specious and pictorial in texture. Its parts are not (what they are in practice and for living animal faith) substances presenting accidental appearances. They are appearances integrally woven into a panorama entirely relative to human discourse. Naturalism could not be more romantic: nature here is not a world but a story.

We have seen that the foreground, by its dominance, determines whether the empirical philosopher shall be provisionally a naturalist or shall try being something else. What now, looked at more narrowly, is the character of this foreground? Its name is Experience; but lest we should misunderstand this ambiguous word, it is necessary to keep in mind that in this system experience is impersonal. It is not, as a literary psychologist might suppose, a man's feelings and ideas forming a life-long soliloquy, his impressions of travel in this world. Nor is it, as a biologist might expect, such contact of sensitive animals with their environment as adapts them to it and teaches them to remember it. No: experience is here taken in a transcendental, or rather in a moral, sense, as something romantically absolute and practically coercive. There exists a social medium, the notorious scene of all happenings and discoveries, the sum of those current adventures in which anybody might participate. Experience is deputed to include everything to which experience might testify: it is the locus of public facts. It is therefore identical with nature, to the extent and in the aspects in which nature is disclosed to man. Death, for instance, should be set down as a fact of experience. This would not be possible if experience were something personal, unless indeed death was only a transition to another life. For so long as a man's sensations and thoughts continue, he is not dead, and when dead he has no more thoughts or sensations. But is such actual death, we may ask, the death that Dewey can have in mind? The only death open to experience is the death of others (here is a neat proof of immortality for those who like it); and death, for the pragmatist, simply *is* burial. To suppose that a train of thoughts and feelings going on in a man invisibly might at last come to an end, would be to place the fact of death in a sphere which Dewey does not recognize, namely, in the realm of truth; for it would simply be true that the man's thoughts had ceased, although neither he nor anybody else could find that fact in experience. For other people it would remain a fact assumed and credited, for him it would be a destiny that overtook him. Yet Experience, as Dewey understands it, must include such undiscoverable objects of common belief, and such a real, though unobserved, order of events. The dominant foreground which he calls Experience is accordingly filled and bounded not so much by experience as by convention. It is the social world.

How conventional this foreground is will appear even more clearly if we note the elements which are said to compose it. These are events, histories, situations, affairs. The words "affairs" and "situations," in their intentional vagueness, express very well the ethical nerve of this philosophy; for it is essentially a moral attitude or a lay religion. Life is a practical predicament; both necessity and duty compel us to do something about it, and also to think something about it, so as to know what to do. This is the categorical imperative of existence; and according to the Protestant tradition (diametrically opposed to the Indian) the spirit, in heeding its intrinsic vocation, is not alienated from earthly affairs, but on the contrary pledges itself anew to prosecute them with fidelity. Conscience and nature here exercise their suasion concurrently, since conscience merely repeats the summons to enter a field of responsibility—nature —formed by the deposit of its past labors. The most homely business, like the widest policies, may be thus transfused with a direct metaphysical inspiration; and although Dewey avoids all inflated eloquence on this theme, it is clear that his philosophy of Experience is a transcendental moralism. The other two terms, however, "events" and "histories," point to the flux of matter, although this is still gathered up and subdivided under units of discourse. "Event" is now a favorite word among philosophers who are addressed to the study of nature, but bring with them an empirical logic; and it well expresses that conjunction. An event does not involve a spectator, and does involve an environment on the same plane as the event: so far events belong directly to the flux of nature. At the same time an event is a change, and all the dialectic of change applies to the conception. Are events the crises between existence characterized in one way and existence characterized in another way? Or are events the intervals between such crises? But if these intervals, each having a somewhat different quality, were taken separately, they would not lodge in a common space or time; there would be no crises between them, no change, and (as I think would appear in the end) they themselves would have no existence. If events are to be successive, and fragments of the flux of nature, they must be changes in an abiding medium. In other words, an event, in its natural being, is a mode of substance, the transit of an essence. Moreover, natural events would have to be microscopic, because intervals containing no internal crisis, however long or even eternal they might seem sentimentally, could not be measured and would count as instants. This corollary is well fitted to remind us that nature laughs at our dialectic and goes on living in her own way. Her flux, like the flow of a river, is far more substantial than volatile, all sleepy continuity, derivation, persistence, and monotony. The most ordinary form of change in her—perhaps the only fundamental form—is motion; and it would be highly artificial to call the parts of a motion events where there are no crises and no intervals. Even night and day, unless we choose a particular point on the earth's surface for our station, are not events, since both are perpetual. It is apparently only on higher levels, genetically secondary, that nature produces events, where movement becomes rhythmical, and a culmination is followed by a breakdown and a repetition, as in animal birth and death. These secondary rhythms naturally attract the attention of a human observer, whose units of perception are all impressionistic and pictorial; he selects events from the vast continuities of nature because they go with rhythms in his own organism, with which his intuitions—the only vital culminations—are conjoined. Hence the empirical impression that nature is a series of events, although if they were mere events they could not be parts of nature, but only essences succeeding one another before vacant attention or in discourse; in other words, we should be in the mock world of psychologism.

The superficial level proper to empirical events becomes even more obvious if instead of calling them events we call them histories. The parts of nature seem events when we ignore their substance and their essence and consider only their position; anything actual is an event only, so to speak, at its margins, where it ceases to be itself. But before the parts of nature can seem to be histories, we must impose on them dramatic unities fetched from a far more derivative sphere. Histories are moral units, framed by tracing the thread of some special interest through the maze of things, units impossible to discriminate before the existence of passions and language. As there is a literary psychology which represents the mind as a mass of nameable pictures and describable sentiments, so there is a romantic metaphysics which hypostatizes history and puts it in the place of nature. "Histories" bring us back into the moral foreground where we found "situations" and "affairs." The same predicaments of daily life are viewed now in a temporal perspective, rather than as they beset us at any one moment.

That the foreground of human life is necessarily moral and practical (it is so even for artists) and that a philosophy which limits itself to clarifying moral perspectives may be a very great philosophy, has been known to the judicious since the days of Socrates. Why could not Dewey have worked out his shrewd moral and intellectual economy within the frame of naturalism, which he knows is postulated by practice, and so have brought clearness and space into the picture, without interposing any metaphysics? Because it is an axiom with him that nothing but the immediate is real. This axiom, far from being self-evident, is not even clear: for everything is "real" in some sense, and there is much doubt as to what sort of being is immediate. At first the axiom produced psychological idealism, because the proudly discoursing minds of philosophers took for granted that the immediate for each man could be only his own thoughts. Later it has been urged (and, I think, truly) that the immediate is rather any object—whether sensible or intelligible makes no difference—found lying in its own specious medium; so that immediatism is not so much subjective as closely attentive and mystically objective. Be it noted, however, that this admitted objectivity of real things remains internal to the immediate sphere: they must never be supposed to possess an alleged substantial existence beyond experience. This experience is no longer subjective, but it is still transcendental, absolute, and groundless; indeed it has ceased to seem subjective only because it seems unconditioned; and in order to get to the bottom and to the substance of anything, we must still ask with Emerson, What is this *to me*, or with William James, What is this *experienced as*. As Dewey puts it, these facts of experience simply *are* or *are had*, and there is nothing more to say about them. Such evidence flooding immediate experience I just now called mystical, using the epithet advisedly; because in this direct possession of being there is no division of subject and object, but rapt identification of some term, intuition of some essence. Such is sheer pleasure or pain, when no source or object is assigned to it; such is esthetic contemplation; such is pure thinking, the flash of intellectual light. This mystical paradise is indefinitely extensible, like life, and far be it from me to speak evil of it; it is there only that the innocent spirit is at home. But how should pragmatism, which is nothing if not prehensile, take root in this Eden? I am afraid pragmatism is the serpent; for there is a forbidden tree in the midst, the tree of Belief in the Eventual, the fruit of which is Care; and it is evident that our first parents must have partaken of it copiously; perhaps they fed on nothing else. Now when immediate experience is crossed by Care it suffers the most terrible illusion, for it supposes that the eventual about which it is troubled is controllable by the immediate, as by wishes, omens, or high thoughts; in other words, that the essences given in the immediate exist, generate their own presence, and may persist and rearrange themselves and so generate the future. But this is sheer superstition and trust in magic; the philosophy not of experience but of inexperience. The immediate, whether a paradise or a hell, is always specious; it is peopled by specters which, if taken for existing and working things, are illusions; and although they are real enough, in that they have definite character and actual presence, as a dream or a pain has, their reality ends there; they are unsubstantial, volatile, leaving no ashes, and their existence, even when they appear, is imputed to them by a hidden agency, the demon of Care, and lies wholly in being perceived. Thus immediate experience of things, far from being fundamental in nature, is only the dream which accompanies our action, as the other dreams accompany our sleep; and every naturalist knows that this waking dream is dependent for its existence, quality, intensity, and duration on obscure processes in the living body, in its interplay with its environment; processes which go back, through seeds, to the first beginnings of life on earth. Immediate experience is a consummation; and this not in esthetic contemplation alone, but just as much in birth-pangs or the excitement of battle. All its episodes, intermittent and wildly modulated, like the sound of wind in a forest, are bound together and rendered relevant to one another only by their material causes and instruments. So tenuous is immediate experience that the behaviorist can ignore it altogether, without inconvenience, substituting everywhere objects of conventional belief in their infinite material plane. The immediate is, indeed, recognized and prized only by mystics, and Dewey himself is assured of possessing it only by virtue of his social and ethical mysticism, by which the whole complex theater of contemporary action seems to him to be given immediately: whereas to others of us (who are perhaps mystical at other points) this world of practice seems foreign, absent from our better moments, approachable even at the time of action only by animal faith and blind presumption, and compacted, when we consider its normal texture, out of human conventions, many of them variable and foolish. A pragmatist who was not an ethical or social mystic, might explore that world scientifically, as a physician, politician, or engineer, and remain throughout a pure behaviorist or materialist, without noticing immediate experience at all, or once distinguishing what was given from what was assumed or asserted. But to the mystic, if he is interested in that world, it all comes forward into the immediate; it becomes indubitable, but at the same time vague; actual experience sucks in the world in which conventional experience, if left to dogmatize, would have supposed it was going on; and a luminous cloud of immediacy envelops everything and arrests the eye, in every direction, on a painted perspective; for if any object becomes immediate, whatever it may be, it becomes visionary. That same spiritual actuality which Dewey, in passing, scarcely recognized at the top of animal life, he now comes upon from within, and without observing its natural locus, lays at the basis of the universe. The universe, in his system, thereby appears inverted, the accidental order of discovery being everywhere substituted for the natural order of genesis; and this with grave consequences, since it is not so easy for the universe as for an individual to stand on its head.[2]

Consider, for instance, the empirical status of the past. The only past that ever *is* or *is had* is a specious past, the fading survival of it in the present. Now the form which things wear in the foreground, according to this philosophy, is their *real* form; and the meaning

[2] A curious reversal of the terms "natural" and "ideal" comes about as we assume that the immediate is substantial or that it is visionary. Suppose I say that "everything ideal emanates from something natural." Dewey agrees, understanding that everything remote emanates from something immediate. But what I meant was that everything immediate— sensation, for instance, or love—emanates from something biological. Not, however, (and this is another verbal snare) from the concepts of biological science, essences immediately present to the thoughts of biologists, but from the largely unknown or humanly unknowable process of animal life. I suppose we should not call some of our ideas scientific if they did not trace the movement of nature more accurately and reliably than do our random sensations or dramatic myths; they are therefore presumably truer in regard to those distributive aspects of nature which they select. But science is a part of human discourse, and necessarily poetical, like language. If literal truth were necessary (which is not the case in practice in respect to nature) it would be found only, perhaps, in literature—in the reproduction of discourse by discourse.

which such immediate facts may assume hangs on their use in executing some living purpose. What follows in regard to past time? That the survival or memory of it comprises all its reality, and that all the meaning of it lies in its possible relevance to actual interests. A memory may serve as a model or condition in shaping some further enterprise, or may be identified with a habit acquired by training, as when we have learned a foreign language and are ready to speak it. Past experience is accordingly real only by virtue of its vital inclusion in some present undertaking, and yesterday is *really* but a term perhaps useful in the preparation of tomorrow. The past, too, must work if it would live, and we may speak without irony of "the futurity of yesterday" in so far as yesterday has any pragmatic reality.

This result is consistent with the general principle of empirical criticism by which we are forbidden to regard God, truth, or the material cosmos as anything but home vistas. When this principle is applied to such overwhelming outer realities, it lightens the burden of those who hate external compulsions or supports; they can henceforth believe they are living in a moral universe that changes as they change, with no sky lowering over them save a portable canopy which they carry with them on their travels. But now this pleasant principle threatens the march of experience itself: for if my ancestors have no past existence save by working in me now, what becomes of my present being, if ever I cease to work in my descendants? Does experience today draw its whole existence from their future memories? Evidently this can not be the doctrine proposed; and yet if it be once admitted that all the events in time are equally real and equally central, then at every point there is a by-gone past, intrinsically perfectly substantial and self-existent; a past which such memories or continuations as may be integral to life at this later moment need continue only very partially, or need recover only schematically, if at all. In that case, if I ever find it convenient to forget my ancestors, or if my descendants find it advantageous to forget me, this fact might somewhat dash their vanity or mine if we should hear of it, but can not touch our substantial existence or the truth of our lives. Grant this, and at once the whole universe is on its feet again; and all that strange pragmatic reduction of yesterday to tomorrow, of Sanskrit to the study of Sanskrit, of truth to the value of discovering some truth, and of matter to some human notion of matter, turns out to have been a needless equivocation, by which the perspectives of life, avowedly relative, have been treated as absolute, and the dominance of the foreground has been turned from a biological accident into a metaphysical principle. And this quite wantonly: because practice, far from suggesting such a reduction, precludes it, and requires every honest workman to admit the democratic equality of the past and the future with the present, and to regard the inner processes of matter with respect and not with transcendental arrogance. The living convictions of the pragmatist himself are those involved in action, and therefore naturalistic in the dogmatic sense; action involves belief, belief judgment, and judgment dogma; so that the transcendental metaphysics and the practical naturalism of the pragmatist are in sharp contradiction, both in logic and in spirit. The one expresses his speculative egotism, the other his animal faith.

Of course, it is not Dewey nor the pragmatic school that is to blame for this equivocation; it is a general heirloom, and has infected all that criticism of scholastic dogma on which modern philosophy is founded. By expressing this critical principle more thoroughly, the pragmatists have hoped to clear the air, and perhaps ultimately may help to do so. Although I am myself a dogmatic naturalist, I think that the station assumed by Dewey, like the transcendental station generally, is always legitimate. Just as the spirit has a right to soliloquize, and to regard existence as a strange dream, so any society or nation or living interest has a right to treat the world as its field of action, and to recast the human mind, as far as possible, so as to adapt it exclusively to that public function. That is what all great religions have tried to do, and what Sparta and Carthage would have done if they had produced philosophers. Why should not America attempt it? Reason is free to change its logic, as language to change its grammar; and the critic of the life of reason may then distinguish, as far as his penetration goes, how much in any such logic or grammar is expressive of material circumstances, how much is exuberant rhetoric, how much local, and how much human. Of course, at every step such criticism rests on naturalistic dogmas; we could not understand any phase of human imagination, or even discover it, unless we found it growing in the common world of geography and commerce. In this world fiction arises, and to this world it refers. In so far as criticism can trace back the most fantastic ideas—mythology, for instance—to their natural origin, it should enlighten our sympathies, since we should all have lived in the society of those images, if we had had the same surroundings and passions; and if in their turn the ideas prevalent in our own day can be traced back to the material conditions that bred them, our judgment should be enlightened also. Controversy, when naturalism is granted, can yield to interpretation, reconciling the critical mind to convention, justifying moral diversity, and carrying the sap of life to every top-most intellectual flower. All positive transcendental insights, whether empirical, national, or moral, can thus be honored (and disinfected) by the baldest naturalism, remaining itself international, Bohemian, and animal. The luminous fog of immediacy has a place in nature; it is a meteorological and optical effect, and often a blessing. But why should immediacy be thought to be absolute or a criterion of reality? The great error of dogmatists, in hypostatizing their conclusions into alleged preëxistent facts, did not lie in believing that facts of some kind preëxisted; the error lay only in framing an inadequate view of those facts and regarding it as adequate. God and matter are not any or all the definitions which philosophers may give of them: they are the realities confronted in action, the mysterious but momentous background, which philosophers and other men mean to describe by their definitions or myths or sensible images. To hypostatize these human symbols, and identify them with matter or with God, is idolatry: but the remedy for idolatry is not iconoclasm, because the senses, too, or the heart or the pragmatic intellect, can breed only symbols. The remedy is rather to employ the symbols pragmatically, with detachment and humor, trusting in the steady dispensations of the substance beyond.

GEORGE SANTAYANA.

The Journal of Philosophy

"HALF-HEARTED NATURALISM"

THE ambiguity of philosophic terms and of the conceptions for which the words stand is indicated by the way in which Mr. Thilly cites, approvingly, Mr. Santayana's characterization of my mode of thinking as half-hearted naturalism.[1] To Mr. Santayana, naturalism is a desirable thing; the shortwindedness of my devotion to it is matter for adverse criticism.[2] To Mr. Thilly, my half-heartedness is the saving clause; it intimates an idealistic strain which in spite of myself gives a redeeming touch to what would otherwise be, I suppose, sheer mechanistic materialism. There is no word in the history of thought which carries more varied meanings than "nature"; naturalism shares in its diverse significations.

I am not equipped with capacities which fit one for the office of a lexicographical autocrat, and I shall make no attempt to tell what naturalism must or should signify. But I may take advantage of the opportunity to say what empirical naturalism, or naturalistic empiricism, means to me. I can not hope to offer anything new, or anything which I have not said many times already. But perhaps by concentrating on this one point I may make the tenor of my thinking clearer, and incidentally throw some light on why it appears, from two opposed ends of the philosophic gamut, to be half-hearted.

"In nature," says Santayana, "there is no foreground or background, no here, no now, no moral cathedra, no center so really central as to reduce all other things to mere margins and perspectives" (p. 678). The statement is dogmatic; I do not say this in reproach; Mr. Santayana professes himself a dogmatic naturalist, and everyone, in my conception, must be dogmatic at some point in order to get anywhere with other matters. But even a dogmatist may be asked the grounds for his assertion, not, indeed, in the sense of what proof he has to offer, but in the sense of what is presupposed in the assertion, from what platform of beliefs it is propounded. I

---

[1] Thilly, *The Philosophical Review*, Vol. XXXV, p. 532, in an article entitled "Contemporary American Philosophy." Santayana, this JOURNAL, Vol. XXII, p. 680, in an article entitled "Dewey's Naturalistic Metaphysics." All further quotations of Santayana are from this article.

[2] *Ibid.*: "I am myself a dogmatic naturalist," p. 687.

can not think that Santayana supposes that it is self-evident to others or to himself that nature is of the sort mentioned. The sweep and import of the statement is the more striking in that Santayana professes to operate without any metaphysics and is confident that a whole-hearted naturalism is inarticulate, a kneeling, before the unknowable and an adjuration of all that is human.[3] Since knowledge of nature is not the ground for Santayana's statements as to its character, their ground, I take it, is negative and antithetic; the traits denied are those which are characteristic of human life, of the scene as it figures in human activities. Since they are found where man is, they are not, it would seem, attributable to anything but man; nature, whatever else it is or is not, is just something which does not have these traits. In short, his presupposition is a break between nature and man; man in the sense of anything more than a physically extended body, man as institutions, culture, "experience." The former is real, substantial; the latter specious, deceptive, since it has centers and perspectives.

To me, then, Santayana's naturalism appears as broken-backed as mine to him seems short-winded. It is in virtue of what I call naturalism that such a gulf as Mr. Santayana puts between nature and man—social or conventional man, if you will—appears incredible, unnatural and, if I am rightly informed as to the history of culture, reminiscent of supernatural beliefs. To me human affairs, associative and personal, are projections, continuations, complications, of the nature which exists in the physical and pre-human world. There is no gulf, no two spheres of existence, no "bifurcation." For this reason, there are in nature both foregrounds and backgrounds, heres and theres, centers and perspectives, foci and margins. If there were not, the story and scene of man would involve a complete break with nature, the insertion of unaccountable and unnatural conditions and factors. To any one who takes seriously the notion of thoroughgoing continuity, the idea of existence in space and time without heres and nows, without perspectival arrangements, is not only incredible, but is a hang-over of an intellectual convention which developed and flourished in physics at a particular stage of history. It is not pragmatism nor any particular philosophical view which has rendered this conception questionable, but the progress of natural science. One who believes in continuity may argue that, since human experience exhibits such traits as Santayana denies to nature, the latter *must* contain their prototypes.

---

3 "A naturalist instinctively, . . . who, heartily despising the foreground, has fallen in love with the greatness of nature and has sunk speechless before the infinite" (p. 679).

The new physics finds them necessary to describe the physical world in its own terms.[4]

There are many occasional statements in Mr. Santayana's expositions which indicate that his agnosticism is not as complete in detail as it is in formal official statement. In discussing specific matters he often suggests that he shares the belief of the ordinary man that human experience, adequately safeguarded by a normal organism and a proper equipment of apparatus and technique, may afford dependable indications of the nature of things that underlie it; that we do not merely fall back on an "animal faith" that there is some adorable substance behind, but that we come to reasonable terms with its constituents and relations. If one generalizes this position, then the main features of human life (culture, experience, history—or whatever name may be preferred) are indicative of outstanding features of nature itself—of centers and perspectives, contingencies and fulfillments, crises and intervals, histories, uniformities, and particularizations. This is the extent and method of my "metaphysics":—the large and constant features of human sufferings, enjoyments, trials, failures and successes together with the institutions of art, science, technology, politics, and religion which mark them, communicate genuine features of the world within which man lives. The method differs no whit from that of any investigator who, by making certain observations and experiments, and by utilizing the existing body of ideas available for calculation and interpretation, concludes that he really succeeds in finding out something about some limited aspect of nature. If there is any novelty in *Experience and Nature,* it is not, I should say, this "metaphysics" which is that of the common man, but lies in the use made of the method to understand a group of special problems which have troubled philosophy.

Experience thus conceived is obviously opposed to the usage of the word in the English psychological tradition, a divergence which I was at some pains to point out in criticizing the latter. I consider myself justified, however, in departing widely from the strain of Locke and Hume and James Mill, because I believe that I am only reverting, with some critical purification, to the implications of its

4 The use of the terms "events" and "affairs" in *Experience and Nature,* which Mr. Santayana finds redolent of a submergence of real "nature" in an all-absorbing human moralism, was dictated by the fact that physical science is now compelled, on its own behalf, to employ, if not these words, at least these ideas. On the philosophical side, it is dictated by the fact that the metaphysics, adhered to as far as I can make out by Santayana, which treats nature as a single substance whose parts and changes as such are illusory, is a flight of metaphysics which is beyond me, and which appears to be a survival of a rationalistic spiritualism which he officially repudiates.

everyday untechnical meaning. Experience, thus conceived, constitutes, in Santayana's happy phrase, a foreground. But it is the foreground *of* nature. If I differ from Santayana as to this latter point, the difference lies in that he thinks of the foreground as a screen which conceals the background; to me it conducts our thought to the background. Apparently he conceives of the foreground as lying between human intuition and experience and the background; to me human experiencing is the foreground, nature's own. He also may think that the background alone is nature to the exclusion of the foreground; I am not sure. But I am sure that the foreground is itself a portion of nature, an integral portion, and that nature is not just the dark abysmal unknown postulated by a religious faith in animality, especially since on such a view animality itself becomes a matter of faith.

Holding these views, the reader may dimly imagine the shock I felt when I read that it is axiomatic with me that "nothing but the immediate is real" (p. 683).[5] A large portion of Mr. Santayana's article is a dialectic development of the consequences of such a belief, and naturally a destructive one. Since he thinks the view is mine I can only be grateful to him that he did not devote his skillful dialectic to showing that the whole of *Experience and Nature* is a mass of contradictions; the doctrines of "instrumentalism" with its assertion of recurrent identities in nature and of efficacious connections among natural existences, and of knowledge as always mediate and relational, evidently contradict the belief that only the immediate is real. But perhaps lack of interest in my discussion of specific topics on the part of Mr. Santayana saved me from that fate. I repeat, then, that I hold that everything which is experienced *has* immediacy, and that I also hold that every natural existence, in its own unique and brutal particularity of existence,

---

[5] Lest silence be taken to imply assent, I state specifically that the positions taken by me are as distant as may be from those attributed to me by Santayana on pp. 685–686. If I held them I should admit his argument against them to be conclusive, but they are as unreal to me as they are to him. As he says, "practice precludes" any such beliefs, and while I am not as much of a pragmatist—or at least not the kind of pragmatist—as I am sometimes alleged to be, I am not so witless as to try to unite respect for practice with a belief in the exclusive absoluteness of immediacy. He says: "The dominance of the foreground, avowedly relative, has been turned from a biological accident into a metaphysical principle (p. 686). But since I do not regard the foreground as an accident and since I also do not regard the mid-distant biological as an accident with regard to the physical, my "metaphysical principle" is that the related foreground may be taken as a method for determining the traits of the background. Treating the foreground as an "accident" illustrates what to me is *un*natural in Santayana's notions. In lieu of many references which might be made to *Experience and Nature,* I content myself with one, p. 262.

also *has* immediacy, so that the immediacy which characterizes things experienced is not specious, being neither an unnatural irruption nor a supernatural imposition. To *have* traits, however, is not to *be* them, certainly not in any exclusive sense; and a considerable part of my discussion of special topics is an attempt to show that characteristic traits of the subjects dealt with are to be accounted for as "intersections" or "interpenetrations" (I could think of no better words) of the immediate and the nexional or mediatory, just as my criticism of various philosophical theories rests on showing that they have isolated one phase at the expense of the other. That I do not think the immediacy which matters of experience have is specious or nonnatural, I freely admit, for a nature that had no immediacy would not even exist, and the precious word "substance" would then turn out to be a synonym for that other word "essence." But perhaps such a naturalism as this is *too* whole-hearted to be acceptable.

Mr. Santayana says: "Suppose I say that 'everything ideal emanates from something natural.' Dewey agrees, understanding that everything remote emanates from something immediate. But what I meant was that everything immediate—sensation, for example—emanates from something biological" (p. 685, foot-note). This statement of what I believe is a specific case of the assumption that I hold that only the immediate is real and that the foreground is a foreground of nothing. So I repeat that while "consciousness" is foreground in a preëminent sense, experience is much more than consciousness and reaches down into the background as that reaches up into experience. I agree that the ideal "emanates" from the biological; I have been even criticized by other critics as if I held it to be a mere gaseous emanation from the biological. In reality I think that the ideal, sensation, for example, is as real as the biological from which it emanates, and, expressing a higher meed of the interaction of things than does the biological without sensation, is in so far I will not say more real, but a fuller reality. Nor do I believe that sensation *is* immediate, though it *has* immediacy. It bears within itself connections; it carries something of the remote conditions which call it into existence; otherwise it could never serve as a sign nor have cognitive value. And lest this disclaimer should be interpreted in the sense which Santayana points out in the context, namely, to mean that the *concept* of sensation is derived from biological concepts as terms in discourse, I add that I mean the derivation from the biological of the ideal in a literal existential sense. When Mr. Santayana goes on to say that it emanates from "the largely unknown or humanly unknowable process of animal life," there is indicated, perhaps, a difference. That the biological process and its history of eventuating (*pace* Santayana, for the suggestion of "history" and "event") in sensation is largely *unknown*, is only too evident. But to my mind this ignorance is not because experience interposes a veil, but because experience has not been sufficiently probed for its indications. To Mr. Santayana, if I understand him—and perhaps I do not any better than he does me—experience is such that "humanly unknowable" is his proper phrase. But in that case, why refer to the underlying conditions as biological? Or is it merely that all discourse, since experiential, is specious and conventional, and that one phrase is as good as another over against the abysm of unknowable Substance, God, Matter?

Santayana finds traces of my actual position, in as far as it is identical with his in the matter of the biological basis and substantiation of the ideal, in my implicit behaviorism. But Mr. Santayana always makes it as difficult as possible for anyone to agree with him, and so he criticizes behaviorism as a peculiarly "American" form of externalism. The real gravamen appears to be that Santayana thinks that the behavioristic account of thought in connection with animal functions is bound to deny mind itself. There are psychologists who call themselves behavioristic who doubtless do precisely this thing. Santayana thinks that I must be either a behaviorist in this sense or a speculative egotist, and that my empiricism compels me, in spite of tendencies in the former direction, to become the latter. But the main thesis of *Experience and Nature* is that human experience is intelligent (including, of course, misintelligent) and emotional behavior. In other words, I have tried to bring together on a naturalistic basis the mind and matter that Santayana keeps worlds apart. The attempt, I know, is unusual; perhaps it is doomed to frustration, but I should not want that matter prejudged on the basis of my own ineptness. The trial is bound to be made again, and again, and I hope with increasing success. That success is impossible, given Santayana's premises, I am quite aware. But why not change the premises? My dependence upon the social or conventional medium may be too great, but my faith in it does not extend to believing that the last word on matter and mind has been said by it.

Mr. Santayana says that the foreground as conceived by me is a social world, a social medium. This he terms, somewhat invidiously, I think, convention. But, accepting the word "convention," I state what I have already implied, that "convention" is not conventional, or specious, but is the interaction of natural things when that interaction becomes communication. A "sign" may be conventional, as when a sound or a mark on a piece of paper—themselves physical existences—symbolizes other things; but *being* a sign, the sign-function, has its roots in natural existences; human association is the fruit of those roots. I can understand Santayana's idea that the social medium is conventional in a prejudicial sense only as another illustration of that structural dislocation of non-human and human existence which I have called a broken-backed naturalism.

One of the basic contradictions which Santayana might readily have pointed out in my conclusions, if I really hold that only the immediate is real, concerns the social. He says that I have a "tendency to dissolve the individual into his social functions" (p. 675), which, put in logical language, signifies that I resolve the immediate into the mediate. But since I find in human life, from its biological roots to its ideal flowers and fruits, things both individual and associational—each word being adjectival—I hold that nature has both an irreducible brute unique "itselfness" in everything which exists and also a connection of each thing (which is just what *it* is) with other things such that without them it "can neither be nor be conceived." And as far as I can follow the findings of physics, that conclusion is confirmed by the results of the examination of physical existence itself. Since experience is both individualized and associational and since experience is continuous with nature as background, as a naturalist I find nature is also both. In citing Mr. Santayana's denial that nature has here, now, and perspective, I found myself in stating my own view compelled to use the plural form: —heres, nows, perspectives. I would not draw an inference from the mere use of a word, but Santayana's use of the singular form is suggestive that he thinks experience is something sole and private, and so thinking attributes a similar view to others who use the term. It *is* absurd to confer upon nature a single here, now, and perspective, and if that were the only alternative, I should agree with Mr. Santayana in his denial. But there are an indefinite multitude of heres, nows, and perspectives. As many as there are existences. To swallow them up in one all-embracing substance is, moreover, to make the latter unknowable; it is the logical premise of a complete agnosticism. But such an embrace also makes substance inconceivable, for it leaves nothing for it to absorb or substantiate. Moreover, the things which have heres and nows all interact with one another; they form a world of intercourse and association, though not of that communication which is a fuller exhibition of their connections with one another. If, perchance, I have exaggerated by my manner of speech the associated aspects of experience, it is because the traditional theory of experience dominated by a false psychology (as the traditional view of nature which Santayana reflects is dominated by a false physics) has ignored and denied that phase, assuming, as Mr. Santayana appears to do, a sole and lonely here and now.

It is not my purpose to criticize Mr. Santayana's philosophy, but to make an evidently much-needed statement of what I hold in distinction from what is imputed to me. This intention moves me even when I go on to say that I find two movements and two positions in Santayana which are juxtaposed, but which never touch. In his concrete treatments of any special topic when a matter of controversy to which traditional school labels are attached is in abeyance, he seems genuinely naturalistic; the things of experience are treated not as specious and conventional, but as genuine, even though one-sided and perverse, extensions of the nature of which physics and chemistry and biology are scientific statements. But he has a number of pigeonholes into which every philosophy must go with its appropriate, fixed, and absolute tag attached:—his own philosophy when it becomes self-conscious as well as those of others. When he lets himself go in any body of subject-matter, free from the influence of traditional and professorial labels, I not only learn much from him, but I flatter myself that I am for the most part in agreement with him. But when he deals with a system of thought and finds it necessary to differentiate his own system from it, his naturalism reduces itself to a vague gesture of adoring faith in some all-comprehensive unknowable in contrast with which all human life— barring this one gesture—is specious and illusory. Only in this way can I explain the fact that while I find myself in so much agreement with him he is in such profound disagreement with me. The case seems to resemble that of the Irishman who said the two men looked very much alike, especially one of them. Barring that feature of Mr. Santayana's thought to which exception has been taken, I am happy to be that one.

JOHN DEWEY.

COLUMBIA UNIVERSITY.

THE JOURNAL OF PHILOSOPHY

CRITIQUE OF NATURALISM

NATURALISM is not a new name in philosophy. And like some other words, it may have changed its meaning. Does it mean the same for the 1944 school of naturalism as it meant in James Ward's *Naturalism and Agnosticism*, first edition 1899? Or even in Pratt's *Naturalism* of 1939? Probably not. But the important meaning for us today is the one given it by the 1944 group who so dub their world-view. Their use of the term is now the influential one. For they have emerged in force from the welter of revolts against idealism and dualism in the early 1900's and they form a definite school or type in the philosophic arena. They are full of zeal and energy for the gospel they proclaim as the one thing needful to bring philosophy down out of the clouds (or up out of the bogs). As we should expect, their membership is largely of the younger, more progressive thinkers. Fifteen disciples—or leaders—have lately issued a symposium, *Naturalism and the Human Spirit* [1] (the get-together spirit of our time launches reforms in symposia). In virtue, then, of the vigor and influence of this young school, we take them as the proper exponents of naturalism's meaning. What is that meaning?

To judge it fairly, the obvious course is to read out their written words. Now in the case of an old school, which has had centuries to reflect on what its words might imply or suggest, those words will probably commit their users to just about what the school means to stand for, no more and no less. In the case of a younger school, a school which has but recently come to self-consciousness, this is less likely to be so. A young school believes that it is stressing a new perspective on the world, or perhaps an old perspective whose value it is the first to realize. It sees in this perspective a way out of the age-long deadlocks of philosophy, a way that will ensure established results on which all philosophers will agree. To emphasize the importance of its discovery, it is likely to coin some new term or phrase for that discovery, or at least to use some old one in a new sense. So we find the names

---

[1] New York, Columbia University Press, 1944. Quotations will be from this book unless otherwise stated. See Editor's Note, page 384 (Eds.).

"phenomenology," "logical empiricism"; and so we find the naturalist of today appropriating the old words "nature" and "scientific method" to his novel uses. But of course "nature," being an old word, has had many meanings: which of these, if any, does he keep, or what new meanings does he bring in? And the like of "scientific method," though to a lesser degree, the phrase being more modern. A plant bedded in bad soil we uproot and put in better ground, but we are likely to bring some of the old dirt unnoticed with the roots. Might this be true of these two favorite terms of the naturalist? Perhaps the reformers are so eager to leave the old beds that they don't notice how much of the dirt they have brought along. Not seldom in the history of philosophy have seemingly novel ideas been found to be old ones under a new name. As Costello prudently remarks, "We must take care lest our suppressed illusions come back to plague us in altered guise, like grinning fiends from out the Freudian deep" (p. 296). And Pratt had said of his book *Naturalism*:[2] "My little book I consider a defense of Naturalism against its most dangerous enemies, the majority of whom are usually found in the ranks of the 'naturalists.'" What then do the symposiasts we are to examine *really* stand for? As we all know, they *say* they stand for the study of nature by scientific method. But what do they mean by nature and by scientific method? To what does their usage of these words commit them?

I now give point to the inquiry by a specific accusation. Namely, their usage of said words in the contexts of the book shows them to be materialists. Their naturalism is just materialism over again under a softer name. They claim to have superseded that perennial type of metaphysic; I believe they slip back into the same old rut. True, they are careful to *define* materialism in such a way as not to be accused of it; but to all intents and purposes they stand for the same sort of thing that materialists have always stood for. Thus they do not, as they claim to do, settle the old conflict between idealism and materialism (or for that matter, between scholasticism and process-metaphysic); they perpetuate the conflict by taking sides.

The accusation is at least suggested by what Hook, one of the group, had already said of materialism: "Its differences with idealism were . . . over the massive issue . . . of naturalism and supernaturalism."[3] Certainly materialism and naturalism are alike in their *horror supernaturae*. Certainly some of these naturalists have inveighed mightily against both the idealist and the

---

[2] New Haven, Yale University Press, 1939. Preface, pp. ix–x.
[3] This JOURNAL, Vol. XLI (1944), p. 546.

Thomist traditions, defenders of non-material being. But of course this only gives ground for suspicion. And the naturalists have most emphatically denied that they are materialists. Attend then to the way in which they deny it.

The protagonist Dewey says "he [the naturalist] is aware that since 'matter' and 'materialism' acquired their significance in contrast with something called 'spirit' and 'spiritualism,' the fact that naturalism has no place for the latter also deprives the former epithets of all significance in philosophy" (p. 3). That is, the naturalist considers "matter" to be, shall we say, a real entity *only* in contrast with spirit or mind taken as another and a *separate* entity. And by this token naturalism, discarding such opposed entities, is on a higher plane, above the opposition between materialism and idealism, dualism and monism, etc.

Now let us at once admit that naturalism is not materialism in the sense of believing in matter as a fixed being, a mindless bit of solid stuff, which would be meaningless unless there were, or appeared to be, minds to be contrasted with it. But we are not talking of materialism in that sense. I spoke of materialism "to all intents and purposes"; I was speaking in instrumentalist terms. Surely the naturalists are just the ones who ought to conceive the issue in such terms. What then *should* we mean by materialism? To answer the question, note this: what makes materialism *vs.* idealism a significant issue for us men is the question: are the states and events we call conscious or mental or spiritual *wholly* at the beck and call of the states and processes we call physical? If they are, you are going to order your life in a very different way from the way you would order it if they are not. Materialism, the only sort of materialism that *matters*, declares they are. As Donald Williams, a confessed materialist, puts it: "in the entire universe, including the knowing mind itself, there is nothing which could not be destroyed (or repaired) by a spatio-temporal redistribution of its components." [4] And Williams argues for materialism thus: "Even the idealist or the dualist, when he actually wants to understand or control something, makes use of the spatio-temporal schema." [5] For it is understanding and consequent control of goods that we men want; and once more, surely the naturalist of all people should admit this, for his instrumental philosophy seeks above all things the means of controlling nature for the securing of man's highest values. So the real issue is: can the states or processes we call mental or spiritual exercise a control over those we call physical, to some

[4] *Philosophical Review*, Vol. LIII (1944), p. 418.
[5] *Ibid.*, p. 438.

degree independent of any spatio-temporal redistributions; or, if we really understood what is going on when minds seem to control bodies, should we see that the spatio-temporal redistributions are the sole factors? To accept the latter is to be a materialist. Other definitions ignore the issue. A genuine materialism will, of course, admit that as things are now, when we understand so little of the electrical and radiant energies that govern the nervous system, we have to use the rough-and-ready method of influencing our fellows by communicating ideas (through physical means only, be it noted). But he will insist that an idea is but a potential or tentative muscular response, and the only way to be sure it will work out into the proper deed is to know with precise scientific knowledge the physical laws that rule the behavior of the organism. For after all, what matters about matter is what matter does: what it does *to* us and what we can make it do *for* us. James the starter of pragmatism saw this, but it has been forgotten. So, when I accuse the naturalists of materialism, I mean a working materialism, a philosophy that goes beyond pure theory to set up a way of life. And I say that their program and method leads to or implies that in the last analysis all processes in the known universe, mental, spiritual, vital, or what not, are wholly at the beck and call of the processes we have agreed to call physical, and therefore the only reliable way of control over nature—and over other men—is secured by knowledge of spatio-temporal distributions. That is the only materialism that counts, that has bearing on human life and the prospects of man's future.

You may, as a materialist, believe in graded levels—inorganic, plant, animal, man, none of which can be wholly described in terms of the levels below it. You may define thought as some queer synthesis of sensa, which synthesis is not itself a sensum (so, for instance, R. W. Sellars). On the other hand, you may believe each level can be fully defined in terms of a lower level. In either case you may remain a materialist. The crucial point is whether the *behavior* of the higher (mental) level can be *predicted* and therefore *controlled* surely and accurately from a knowledge of the lower. It is power that counts, it is power that the naturalist hopes by his scientific method to gain: power to ensure the arrival of things on the higher level by proper "redistribution" of things on the lower. The question of logical reducibility is beside the point. What does it amount to, whether the beautiful contrast of red and black is reducible to the natures of the red and the black or whether the relation is irreducible to its terms—so long as we can *get* the relation by placing the colors side by side?

We find the naturalistic textbook of Randall and Buchler [6] laying great stress on the fallacy of reductionism, committed as they say by materialism. But the point is irrelevant, merely verbal. In fact, a nest of verbal conflicts has grown around the pivotal point at issue—as Williams has shown in the paper above mentioned (pp. 424 ff.). Is the materialist a nominalist or realist in metaphysics, a subjectivist or realist or objective relativist in epistemology; can he substitute the term "experience" for the terms "mind" and "body" alike, etc., etc.? It is surprising enough that the new naturalists haven't taken their own instrumentalism seriously here. In particular note what Hook says in his discussion with Sellars about materialism.[7] Hook finds materialism wrong because "the form or shape of matter is not material, the organization of material particles is not another particle, a relation between events is not an event." Well, on that showing there never lived a materialist. Even Democritus would not have said that the velocity of an atom was an atom. A Frenchman isn't a Frenchman, for his hair is black! So the naturalist escapes the *name* of materialism by identifying materialism with one side of some irrelevant issue and denying that side. They all seem to sense bad odor in the name. But when it comes to the real test, to what should be their own test, the consequences of their program and platform, I say they are materialists. And now to draw the evidence from what they have written.

Dewey, the acknowledged leader, says: "the naturalist is one who has respect for the conclusion[s] of natural science" (p. 2). This statement, we suppose, is not meant to be a final definition; only an indicator. It raises questions. How much does the term "natural science" include? Does it include introspective psychology? Here the outsider reflects that the natural sciences which have given well established results, genuine conclusions, are those that deal with physical facts only: physics, chemistry, astronomy, biology, geology. Even these have some undecided points, as all know; but so far as there are decisive conclusions, they are conclusions about facts, processes, laws, which *so far as treated in those sciences have only physical traits*. Take the case of anthropology. This science gives unquestionable results when it tells us what Indians, Negritos, etc., actually do in the body: they meet, they bow, they chant, burn sticks, carve bowls, and so on. When it comes to the question, what their ceremonies mean to us or to them, indecision comes in. The like with soci-

---

[6] John H. Randall, Jr., and Justus Buchler, *Philosophy: an Introduction.* New York, Barnes and Noble, 1942.

[7] This JOURNAL, Vol. XLI (1944), p. 546.

ology, political science, history, and introspective psychology. These sciences haven't got sure conclusions in what we call the mental aspect, that aspect which makes them interesting and valuable to mankind. Like the philosophies, they differ among themselves. Ergo, physical sciences, any sciences so far as they are physical, are the only ones whose conclusions the naturalist should respect. Physical nature is the only nature accessible to sure, or reasonably sure, knowledge about the world. Whatever is to be explained, then, must be explained in physical terms; no other kind of explanation is properly verifiable. True, the naturalists don't want to be dogmatic; they wouldn't say "no other kind could ever possibly be justified." But ought they not to say "from all the evidence we have so far had in regard to the sciences, the physical sciences seem to be the sole purveyors of established truth"? I submit, this is the obvious suggestion from the words of Dewey, even if it is not strictly what he meant.

But doubtless he meant something more. We know well that for him and for the other naturalists it is not so much the conclusions of science that they stress, as the method. That is for them all-important, the *sine qua non,* the one thing needful. Randall, summing up at the end of the book, says that naturalism is "an attitude and temper: it is essentially a philosophic method and a program" (p. 374). And how often has Dewey urged that we apply scientific *method*—experiment, verification—to our social and moral problems: "application of scientific methods of inquiry in the field of human social subject matter" (p. 3). So let us now turn about from conclusion to method, treating naturalism as a method rather than a body of results. What then does the naturalist's adoration of scientific method commit him to affirm about the world?

For surely one's method indicates his view of the thing investigated. Men don't shoot forth methods *in vacuo;* method is not independent of subject-matter. We don't use the same method to persuade a child as a man; we use a telescope to see stars, not to dissect the seeds of a plant. If a certain method is advocated, the advocate divulges his view of the probable nature of the facts to be studied. No mere methodology: a method envisages, however tentatively, a metaphysic.

Now, I don't know of any standard analysis of scientific method in the naturalist camp. We take for granted experiment and verification by observation; but that leaves us rather in the air. Does the mystic verify the Divine being by direct observation? Can the introspective psychologist experiment with private minds? To find the answer to such specific questions, all we can do is to pick out statements from the present volume, hoping not to misrepresent the writers' meaning. Most of those that I have found are pretty general and vague, while the more definite point decidedly towards materialism. Thus Lamprecht says "in this essay 'naturalism' means a philosophical position, empirical in method, that regards everything that exists or occurs to be conditioned in its existence or occurrence by causal factors within one all-encompassing system of nature" (p. 18). This throws little light on the meaning of the method; "empirical" is claimed by introspective and behaviorist psychologists alike, and explaining by causal factors is common property—except so far as physics now employs chance. Nor can we learn anything about the method from the phrase "all-encompassing system of nature"; does it include only the physical world? Or does it include whatever one might think he has good reason for believing real— e.g., Deity, angels, etc.? More on that question later, when we ask what "nature" means; just now the method only. Hook also mentions method: he defines naturalism as "the wholehearted acceptance of scientific method as the only reliable way of reaching truths about the world of nature, society, and man" (p. 45). Elsewhere Hook says, "There have been many varieties of thought that have gone by the name of materialism and naturalism in the history of philosophy. . . . What is common to them is not a theory of stuff or the constitution of matter or a theory of knowledge or a system of ontology, but the belief that valid knowledge is knowledge warranted by scientific method and the confidence that the application of scientific method (not necessarily the methods and techniques of physics as a special discipline) to all fields of experience, will enlarge our understanding or increase our control." [8] This sounds as if there may be good scientific method in such fields as sociology, politics, or ethics. But alas! it doesn't tell us what that method is. Come to another statement. Edel says: "Reliance on scientific method, together with an appreciation of the primacy of matter and the pervasiveness of change, I take to be the central points of naturalism as a philosophical outlook" (p. 65). "Primacy of matter" sounds materialistic but the context leaves one in doubt whether "matter" may mean only "subject-matter." Anyway, we are not told what scientific method is. Dewey makes a less indefinite pronouncement when he speaks of "scientific method, which after all is but systematic, extensive, and carefully controlled use of alert and unprejudiced observation and experimentation in collecting, arranging, and testing evidence" (p. 12). But we want to know, for instance,

[8] This JOURNAL, Vol. XLI (1944), p. 549.

whether or not introspection is good evidence and how evidence is tested. Miss Lavine in fact seems to regard scientific method as a variable affair. She says "surely the growth of the fields of history of science, social anthropology, [etc.] . . . have already cast the gravest suspicion upon the notion of an unconditioned scientific method" (p. 207). To this writer, if I understand her, scientific method is a type of response to the social needs of the day, and as those needs vary from one generation to another, so scientific method may be expected to vary. If that is so, we can hardly look for a cut-and-dried definition of it as the one perennial deliverer of mankind from philosophic bungling—even though the naturalists all feel it to be such. Let us then look only for what the school takes it to mean for the present. After all, that is enough for our purpose. Nagel makes a more definite statement: "perhaps the sole bond uniting all varieties of naturalists is that temper of mind which seeks to understand the flux of events in terms of the behaviors of identifiable bodies" (p. 211). And, of course, this is meat to the materialist, for we presume that Nagel is talking about scientific method. From even so thorough an analyst as Dennes, on the other hand, we get no certain note. He says: "There is for naturalism no knowledge except that of the type ordinarily called scientific. But such knowledge cannot be said to be restricted by its method to any limited field . . . to the exclusion, let us say, of the processes called history, and the fine arts. For whether the question is about forces 'within the atom' or . . . Beethoven's Second Rasumowski Quartette . . . there is no serious way to approach controlled hypotheses . . . except by inspection of the relevant evidence and by inductive inference from it" (quoted with approval by Randall, p. 359). If he would only tell us of what sort is the relevant evidence—whether, for instance, we can trust introspective reports or must use behaviorist methods! It is most unfortunate that these naturalist writings have many passages like this one. Dennes says also, speaking of naturalism's respect for scientific method and rejection of the supernatural, "Its spirit is in these respects very close to the spirit of traditional and more specifically materialistic naturalism. . . . But contemporary naturalism recognizes much more clearly than did the tradition from which it stems that its distinction from other philosophical positions lies in the postulates and procedures which it criticizes and rejects rather than in any positive tenets of its own about the cosmos" (quoted by Randall, p. 359). Yes, we know how it rejects the supernatural. But what positively does it do with the natural? We see plainly that it doesn't want to be called materialist. We see also that when it says something specific and positive about its method, it *actually* looks toward the kind of procedure found in the *purely physical* sciences. Take this statement by Dewey in regard to observation: "the nature of observation . . . is rarely discussed in its own terms—the terms, that is, of the procedures employed by inquirers in astronomical observatories; in chemical, physical, and biological laboratories; in the examinations conducted by physicians; and in what is done in field excursions of botanists and zoölogists" (p. 4). Note that the sciences mentioned are concerned *only* with physical subject-matter. And so we are not surprised when Larrabee says of naturalism in America, "Far more important than any theory has been the practical materialism of Thomas Jefferson's conviction that 'the business of life is with matter' " (p. 320).

But probably the best test of what scientific method means will be found in the naturalist's treatment of mind and consciousness: a specific problem and at the same time a central one. Turn then to what Krikorian says in his contribution, "A Naturalistic View of Mind." Here we find very definite commitments. Many passages might be quoted; we select a few that show a frank behaviorism. "The naturalistic approach to mind is the experimental approach. This means that mind must be analyzed as behavior, since behavior is the only aspect of mind which is open to experimental examination" (p. 252). "Mind may be defined as control of behavior by anticipation" (p. 252). "The futuristic reference of mind, however, need not be interpreted primarily in introspective terms" (p. 254). "Anticipatory response may have its introspective aspect, yet *introspection itself, as will be shown, may be behavioristically described*" (p. 254, italics mine). Of thought he says: "McDougall demands a psychic entity . . . to perform the activity of reasoning. But why postulate an unverifiable psychic entity for this activity? As Lloyd Morgan puts it, 'May not the relating activity, so called, be just as reasonably assigned to the physiological process in the cortex and the organization as a whole?' " (pp. 257–258). Again, referring to McDougall: "But for a naturalist the analysis of conation does not demand 'purely psychical facts.' Conation . . . has a bodily basis. Conative action as behavior is open to investigation" (p. 259). Again: "Desires are not unobservable entities in some inaccessible realm; they are a certain type of observable behavior. . . . The degree of one's hunger may be verified by the amount of food one eats; the degree of weariness may be determined by the number of hours one sleeps; and the degree of one's pain may be determined by the amount of anodyne one takes" (p. 268). Of mind as an individual personal unit: "Structurally the unity is the biological organism; behaviorally the unity is the integrated action" (p. 269).

Mind is one big bone of contention between idealist and materialist. The naturalist claims to have risen above the quarrel, to a plane where idealism and materialism alike disappear. Has he? His maxim is scientific method. Scientific method demands experiment and observation confirmable by fellow men. Mental states or processes, just in so far as they are not physical, not "behavior," are not open to such observation. He says they are "inaccessible." But of course they are accessible to their owner; it is only to fellow men, to the public, that they are inaccessible. Scientific method thus means, to the naturalist, that observation of the non-public has no sense nor meaning. Publicity is the test; the private and hidden is ruled out of court. And the only publicly observable things are the physical things. Thus the naturalist, when he investigates what men call *mental* affairs, has to *treat* them as bodily or physical affairs. And that is what materialism really amounts to; a working, not a merely verbal, materialism. When, then, it comes to a specific issue, to the issue fought over through the ages between idealist or spiritualist or dualist and materialist, he definitely takes sides with the materialist. That is the commitment to which "scientific method" forces him. So much for the naturalist's usage of that term.

Turn now to the other word, so central to his creed, the word "nature." What does he mean by it? We may best take up the question in two aspects: what nature as he understands it is not, what it definitely excludes, and what it is, what it includes. We begin with the negative aspect: what nature is not.

Well, to be sure, nature is not the supernatural. What then is meant by supernatural? What are typical instances of the supernatural? Says Hook, "The existence of God, immortality, disembodied spirits, cosmic purpose and design, as these have been customarily interpreted by the great institutional religions, are denied by naturalists for the same generic reasons that they deny the existence of fairies, elves, and leprechauns" (p. 45). As the next paragraph begins, "I do not see that anything is gained by blinking the fact that the naturalist denies the existence of supernatural powers" (p. 45), we may fairly presume that "supernatural" would be applied by him to the terms "God," etc., above mentioned. Randall in his summary says, "There is no room for any Supernatural in naturalism—no supernatural or transcendental God and no personal survival after death" (p. 358). So far the objects of Christianity or other religion; but the list is longer. It includes also certain alleged moral principles. Dewey speaks of "the professedly nonsupernatural philosopher who is antinaturalist" and "never ceases to dwell upon . . . the morally seductive character of natural impulse and desire"; also "the doctrine that the truly moral factors in human relations are superimposed from a spiritual non-natural source and authority" (p. 2). These instances probably illustrate the supernatural, since Dewey calls the thinkers "professedly" non-supernatural, as if they were *really* supernaturalists. He goes on: "in addition to frank supernaturalism there are philosophers who claim to rest their extra- (if not super-) naturalism upon a higher faculty of Reason or Intuition, not upon a special divine revelation. While I am personally convinced that their philosophy can be understood only as a historical heritage from frank supernaturalism . . ." (p. 2; we need quote no further). If I mistake not, Kant, Fichte, and Hegel would illustrate the last set. So we must add to the religious group the moral intuitionists and the rationalist idealists. Dewey seems to regard all three as enemies of naturalism; probably so would Hook. What then characterizes these enemies, making them so hostile? "Antinaturalism," says Dewey, "has operated to prevent the application of scientific methods of inquiry in the field of human social subject matter" (p. 3). There lies its poison: the exclusion of scientific method. It would seem to be precisely that exclusion which characterizes supernaturalism or antinaturalism. I find in the present volume no more positive identification than this. Result so far: naturalism stands for scientific method; whatever rules out scientific method—that is the supernatural. We are back where we were. "Nature" means that which is open to scientific method. Scientific method is all we have got.

So far only the negative aspect of "nature." But surely the term must have some positive distinctive trait. Surely naturalism is more than the vicious-circle imperative—"investigate by scientific method that which can be investigated by scientific method." Do the right because it is right to do the right! What *is* right? How can we identify the things that make up nature, that we may investigate them and consign the rest to oblivion?

Randall says, "There is no 'realm' to which the methods for dealing with Nature cannot be extended. This insistence on the universal and unrestricted application of 'scientific method' is a theme pervading every one of these essays" (p. 358). And he had already said, "naturalism, in the sense in which it is maintained in this volume, can be defined negatively as the refusal to take 'nature' or 'the natural' as a term of distinction. . . . For present-day naturalists 'Nature' serves rather as the all-inclusive category, corresponding to the role played by 'Being' in Greek thought, or by 'Reality' for the idealists. In this sense, as Mr. Dennes recognizes, naturalism, in becoming all-inclusive, ceases to be a distinctive 'ism.' It regards as 'natural' whatever man encounters in whatever way—Nature, as Mr. Costello puts it, is a collective name for 'quite a mess of miscellaneous stuff' " (pp. 357-358). But now consider: "whatever man encounters in *whatever* way" would include "fairies, elves, and leprechauns," immortal souls, Thomistic hierarchies of angels, the Perfect First Cause of the universe, just as much as the social trends of the present age or the law of inverse squares in electrical forces. Does naturalism make any choice between these? Randall is well aware of the danger of being too inclusive, and goes on to say: "But while naturalism . . . holds that everything encountered by men has some natural status in Nature, this does not mean that naturalism can absorb all the philosophic theories of what man encounters and in that sense cease to be a distinctive position" (p. 358). "Naturalism thus merges in the generic activity of philosophy as critical interpretation—the examination of the status of all these varieties of 'stuff' in Nature. . . . Positively, naturalism can be defined as the continuity of analysis—as the application of what all the contributors call 'scientific methods' to the critical interpretation and analysis of every field" (p. 358). Shall we put it this way then: Nature means everything; apply scientific method to everything and you will find out what is sham and what is reality, what is genuine value and what is shoddy. Supernature in the sense of that to which we can't apply scientific method, simply is not. That, I think, is Randall's meaning when he says that naturalism does not absorb all the *philosophical theories* of what man encounters. Some of those theories, the supernaturalist ones, are decidedly wrong, and must be thrown out. There *is* nothing supernatural. To requote: "There is no room for any Supernatural in naturalism—no supernatural or transcendental God and no personal survival after death" (p. 358). And, I take it, the reason why he says this is that as naturalist he believes those two concepts named *have been* investigated and scientific method has found no way of testing, no opening for itself. Thus once more the term "nature" gets whatever definite meaning it has from its working partner, scientific method. The situation is ironically close to the Thomist's matter-form couple: nature the passive matter for investigation gets its specific character by the operation of the active principle or form, the said method. Ironical but not irenical alas! For the naturalist takes the Thomist to be his worst enemy.

Just scientific method then—that is all we can put our hands on. The method itself determines what is fit to be investigated, what is hopeless of investigation. The creed has no longer two articles: nature and method. It has only one: method. Nature, like the scholastic primary matter, is mere potentiality, something that may be subjected to scientific method. And this interpretation is confirmed by a statement made in Randall and Buchler's decidedly naturalistic textbook: "Naturalism excludes what is not scientifically investigable, and calls the domain of possible investigation 'nature' " (p. 183).

Can this one-point interpretation be right? I submit additional evidence. A reader, following the book from the start, soon begins to wonder why the above terms are not carefully defined, especially by *this* young group, usually so insistent on scientific precision. He continues puzzled till he reaches page 121, Schneider's article, a deliberate attempt to define the term "nature." What then does the reader find? Schneider, after dismissing two possible definitions which do not here concern us, proposes a third which he is minded to adopt: nature in the sense of the essence of a thing, in contrast with what is accidental to it. Thus we say—my example only—the nature of man is to think, but whether he thinks about the moon or the table is more or less accidental. This sounds like the Aristotelian-Thomist view, and in fact Schneider says, "I am consciously reverting to this ancient ontology, because I think I see the blunders of its corrupted, medieval guise and the folly of its modern repudiation" (p. 125) (extremes again meet). But for us now the important point is: he takes a thing's nature to mean what it normally is, what it ought to be. A man is what he ought to be when he is true to the human nature he embodies. Nature, says Schneider, "is normative. The real is the genuine. Similarly, 'to be true to one's nature' is not a foolish phrase, though it is redundant. To be one's natural self is to be true, healthy, sound, reliable" (p. 124). "Nature is a norm, but neither a statistical norm nor an ideal" (p. 125). "Natural love is not average love but normal, healthy love" (*ibid.*). " 'Natural' means more than probable" (*ibid.*). ". . . it is possible to identify a normal or healthy organism without calculating averages. A normal automobile is a working machine" (pp. 125–126). "That is natural which works" (p. 126). And finally, though he admits that the view is liable to caricature, he says, "I prefer it to the idealist's identification of the real with the ideal, to the orthodox naturalist's belief that all things are equally natural, and to the orthodox empiricist's belief that the probable is natural" (*ibid.*). Thus, unlike the others of this group, he has proposed a specific meaning for "nature" akin to an old "supernaturalist" meaning and in his own words to be preferred "to the orthodox naturalist's belief that all things are equally natural" (*ibid.*). Is this a serious break with the view of "nature" which we got from Randall's words? Randall says of Schneider's view: "Mr. Schneider's suggestive proposal to revive the traditional normative usage of 'nature' and 'the natural' . . . has much to recommend it. . . . Whether Mr. Schneider would go so far as to advocate 'Nature (loud cheers!)' is left unanswered. But as he admits, this normative usage is hardly established in present-day naturalistic thinking, and aside from his paper none of the essays in this volume even suggests it. Some, like Mr. Costello's, seem definitely hostile to the idea" (p. 357, footnote). I think we should heed these words. They throw a definite light on the indefinite meaning of "nature." When one of the group proposes a positive distinctive concept, it is found in Randall's eminently judicious summary to be somewhat at outs with the general understanding of the term. What then is left for us but to see "nature" as just and only any material awaiting approval or condemnation at the hands of scientific method? In sum then, scientific method is the be-all and end-all (or begin-all) of present-day naturalism, the one thing needful, the solver of the great deadlocks of past philosophy, the guarantee of fertile discoveries in the future. As Randall affirms, naturalism "now possesses in great detail a knowledge of the structures or ways of behaving of things, and the elaborate set of techniques and standards of inquiry and verification that constitute the scientific enterprise, the most potent instrument the wit of man has yet devised for analysis and control" (p. 374). The sentence is an apotheosis of science; for the "great detail" of our "knowledge of the structures," etc., has been contributed by the natural sciences, not by philosophy. Let us then stress the second part: "the elaborate set of techniques . . . the scientific enterprise, the most potent instrument," and so on.

True enough, this seems to have been denied elsewhere, by Randall or by the co-author Buchler of the textbook mentioned above. Defining the naturalist's attitude toward scientific method, that book says "nor does it elevate scientific method to the status of a universal panacea. The reason is, first, that it accepts non-cognitive experience as well as cognitive—art and religion besides science—as contributing to a world-perspective" (p. 227). But I find this assertion merely verbal. When it comes to the point of testing some alleged religious or artistic insight—for, of course, these would not be accepted uncritically—the test will follow behavioristic methods. Is that picture over there really beautiful?

You say yes. I happen to doubt that you really feel it so. I apply suitable physical apparatus to your glandular and muscular responses and find that they are not the responses characteristic of a man's appreciation of beauty. You have deceived yourself. Your supposed artistic insight or experience isn't there. In fact the scientific, the behaviorist method gives the only possible way of being sure that a person *has* an artistic or religious experience. We can't take his word for it: that is a report about something merely private, outside the realm of verifiable truth. If only Randall and Buchler had named some particular artistic or religious contribution to a world-perspective, which they would credit as true beyond a reasonable doubt, needing no scientific confirmation! I have grave doubt that they could. At any rate the writers of *our* symposium have definitely and decidedly elevated scientific method "to the status of a universal panacea." They must; there isn't anything else in their kit-bag.

So let us rest with this account of naturalism's creed. And now return to the charge: the creed drives one into materialism. The reason—to repeat—is this. Whatever else scientific method means, it means that verification involves public confirmation, publicity, the witness of other men. The merely private is the unverifiable. Now, frankly, the only group of phenomena that is open to the witness of many is the physical group. The behaviorists in psychology have seen this: as C. L. Hull remarks, they don't argue and try to persuade as philosophers do, but simply record facts, physical facts wherein there is no disagreement. And Krikorian the naturalist has seen it, as we have quoted above. Not all the naturalists do see it; but I can find no escape from it in their creed. Even if, as perhaps a last resort, they admit the need of social witness but insist that there is a non-physical or inner aspect in the events we call mental—if they admit that all reality must be embodied but declare that the embodiment isn't the whole of it—even then they can't prove their claim by scientific method unless they can get this inner aspect socially confirmed—which means publicly exhibited, as a physical fact. The well-known societarian emphasis of our naturalists is right in line with their veneration for scientific method. Both drive straight into materialism, the doctrine that all verified truth is of physical events and properties alone.

If they have demonstrated beyond reasonable doubt that the scientific is the only permissible method, they have to the same degree demonstrated that materialism is the only true metaphysic. If they have only assumed the validity of the method as the most promising yet found, then they have only assumed the truth of materialism as the most probable metaphysic. In either case, so far as they are philosophers at all, they are materialists in the working sense of the term. And since there do persist today other types of philosophy which deny the all-sufficiency of scientific method—to wit, Thomism, idealism, mind-body dualism, mysticism, and so on—the naturalists are once more back on the partisan level. Whether right or wrong, they actually renounce the synthetic attitude which Dewey's words seemed to imply.

Now for a personal "Concluding Unscientific Postscript."

If you naturalists believe you have done something positive other than a gesture of welcome to a materialist metaphysic, I address you as follows. And please note that I raise no objection to the instrumentalism that guides you, or to your doctrine of the ubiquity of process. On the contrary, your instrumentalism and your process-perspective seem to me indispensable contributions to philosophy. And what I say is said from the instrumental point of view.

For, on that platform, the merit of a method is to be tested by its results. You have given no new results in philosophy; you point only to the results gotten by the physical sciences. If you think philosophy is anything besides these sciences, you should, on your own showing, if you want us to believe your method is right, experiment with it to see if it gives knowledge *in addition* to what they give: something more than physics, to wit, metaphysics. Not one of you has even tried for this. You have, of course, an implicit metaphysic; every methodist has. But you are apparently afraid to bring it into the open and defend it. That being so, all you can do, as far as we outsiders are concerned, is to ask us to suspend judgment. Your own creed tells you not to believe anything till it is experimentally confirmed. How can you expect us to believe you have the right method for *philosophy* until you show us that it succeeds in giving us objective truth comparable with that of the sciences, truth on which the philosophic experts agree? Will you then be content if the rest of us say: yes, you may have a promising method for philosophy, but we can't make any decision about it till you have used it to give new and specific information about reality? I fear you will not— I fear that you claim to have proved the rightness of your method in philosophy beforehand; an *a priori* claim you should be the last to make.

You may reply: but scientific method *has* been tested, it *has* given proved results, and no other known method has; so by all that's likely we ought to use it in philosophy. What a circle! Scientific method has succeeded with physical things. Granted. So, you say, try it on non-physical things—values, thoughts, angels, immortal souls, and so on. You find it won't apply to them—so they aren't real. As if to say: here is something we are going to apply to all reality, so what it doesn't apply to we shall simply call unreality. Or do you fall back on agreement? The physical sciences are the only ones that give universally accepted results? Of course, if agreement is our only aim, we had better stick to the easier problems of the material world. But are you sure there isn't any reality, any black cat in that dark room of the super-natural? *You* may feel sure, but as far as agreement goes, the majority of philosophers, even in our scientific age, are against you. That doesn't lessen your conviction, does it? Apparently agreement doesn't matter so much. And, after all, as the majority *are* against you—not the majority of an uneducated rabble either —doesn't that suggest that you search out some other way of getting agreement than the scientific way? For of course we all want agreement, but we don't want it at too heavy a cost—at the cost of many views that seem to have shown a survival value for man. By all that's likely, if you are going to appeal to that, your exclusive emphasis on scientific method will only prolong dissension in philosophy. Certainly you can't claim to have proved its right-ness for a survey of "whatever man encounters in whatever way."

On the other hand you may deny to philosophy any objective truth peculiar to itself, comparable to the scientific results. You may decide that philosophy is nothing but methodology of science. If so, there will be very little for you as philosophers to do in writing and teaching; the scientists know their own methods better than you do and you should become a physicist or biologist or other particular scientist in order to have weight as a methodolo-gist. If I understand Dewey, he would have philosophers go into sociology or social ethics, in the naturalistic way—that way would be the greatest hope for the future of humankind. But as to teach-ing philosophy in our universities, in a separate Department, you might continue for a few years until you have got the fundamentals of scientific method pretty well cleared up—but after that what? You might give courses in the history of philosophy to show how false most of the systems are—not a very inspiring educational program. About all you could be is a watchdog of science, barking away any supernaturalist suggestions, or as Sellars has put it "a hanger-on of the various sciences with the courtier-like office of clapping hands." [9] But surely your students, if they heed your teaching, will not themselves go into philosophy; they will apply

[9] This JOURNAL, Vol. XLI (1944), p. 693.

scientific method in some science or other. For what mind of sizable proportions would wish to devote his life to denouncing the unscientific?

But whatever you do, the fact remains—one more of the ironies of poor human nature—that you instrumental naturalists, insisting that all truth must be experimentally tested, have performed no experiments of your own, unless perhaps Dewey's experiments in education. And as to the results of these, opinion is today as divided as it is between idealism and materialism, between Thomism and pragmatism, or any other of philosophy's fighting couples.

The naturalist reform of philosophy rightly urges us to accept only what is established by rigid scientific method, *in the domain of things to which that method is applicable.* But there may be truth available to other methods; through the centuries the majority of philosophers have thought so, and still think so. Such truth may pertain to the hidden private mind of man, to the supernatural, even to certain irrational factors in the world. In ruling it out by an exclusive emphasis on scientific method, naturalism has left us just where we were before, in the arena of partisan conflict. It has contributed nothing new to the cause of philosophic unity or of established truth.

W. H. SHELDON

YALE UNIVERSITY

EDITOR'S NOTE:

The above article reviews the anthology: *Naturalism and the Human Spirit*, edited by Yervant H. Krikorian and published by Columbia University Press in 1944, with articles by: John Dewey, Sterling Lamprecht, Sidney Hook, Abraham Edel, Eliseo Vivas, Herbert Schneider, George Boas, Edward W. Strong, Thelma Z. Lavine, Ernest Nagel, Krikorian, William R. Dennes, Harry Todd Costello, Harold A. Larrabee, and John Herman Randall, Jr.

The Editors

VOLUME XLII, No. 19 SEPTEMBER 13, 1945

COMMENTS AND CRITICISM

ARE NATURALISTS MATERIALISTS?

Professor Sheldon's critique [1] of contemporary naturalism as professed in the volume *Naturalism and the Human Spirit* consists of one central "accusation": naturalism is materialism pure and simple. This charge is supported by his further claim that since the scientific method naturalists espouse for acquiring reliable knowledge of nature is incapable of yielding knowledge of the mental or spiritual, "nature" for the naturalists is definitionally limited to "physical nature." He therefore concludes that instead of being a philosophy which can settle age-old conflicts between materialism and idealism, naturalism is no more than a partisan standpoint, and contributes no new philosophical synthesis. Whether or not contemporary naturalists have broken new ground in philosophy is too large a theme for a brief discussion, and is in any case a historical question. But the other issues raised by Mr. Sheldon serve as a challenge to naturalists to make their views clearer on a number of points and to remove some obvious misunderstandings concerning the positions they hold. It is to these tasks that the present discussion is devoted.

I

According to Mr. Sheldon, the "real issue" between materialism and other philosophies is the following: "Can the states or processes we call mental or spiritual exercise a control over those we call physical, to some degree independent of any spatio-temporal redistributions; or, if we really understood what is going on when minds seem to control bodies, should we see that the spatio-temporal redistributions are the sole factors?" (pp. 255–256). The issue so conceived is held to be an intensely practical one. For if one answers the second question in the affirmative

---

[1] W. H. Sheldon, "Critique of Naturalism," this JOURNAL, Vol. XLII (1945), pp. 253–270. All page references will be to this article.

"you are going to order your life in a very different way from the way you would order it if they are not. . . . When I accuse the naturalists of materialism, I mean a working materialism, a philosophy that goes beyond pure theory to set up a way of life." As Mr. Sheldon sees the issue, the program and method of the naturalists

leads to or implies that in the last analysis all processes in the known universe, mental, spiritual, vital, or what not, are wholly at the beck and call of the processes we have agreed to call physical, and therefore the only reliable way of control over nature—and over other men—is secured by knowledge of spatio-temporal distributions. That is the only materialism that counts, that has bearing on human life and the prospects of man's future.

You may, as a materialist, believe in graded levels—inorganic, animal, man, none of which can be wholly described in terms of the levels below it. . . . On the other hand, you may believe each level can be fully defined in terms of a lower level. In either case you may remain a materialist. The crucial point is whether the *behavior* of the higher (mental) level can be *predicted* and therefore *controlled* surely and accurately from a knowledge of the lower. It is power that counts, it is power that the naturalist hopes by his scientific method to gain: power to ensure the arrival of things on the higher level by proper "redistribution" of things on the lower. The question of logical reducibility is beside the point. . . . [P. 256.]

It appears at first blush that the issue thus raised is a genuinely factual one which can be settled by appeal to empirical evidence. For the issue seems to be concerned simply with the most effective way in which things and their qualities can be brought into, maintained in, and ushered out of existence. One is a materialist, on Mr. Sheldon's showing, if one believes that power is acquired by learning how to manipulate embodied things, if one attempts to guide the destinies of men and their affairs by redistributing spatio-temporal objects. Everyone who pursues a vocation in this world whether as engineer or physician, sociologist or educator, statesman or farmer, is perforce a materialist. One is a materialist even when one tries to influence one's fellows by communicating ideas to them, for, as Mr. Sheldon notes, such a method of influencing them employs physical means: verbal and written speech, the arts, and other symbolic structures. Apparently, therefore, only those can call themselves non-materialists who maintain that causal efficacy resides in some disembodied consciousness, unexpressed wishes, silent prayers, angelic or magical powers, and the like. A non-materialist, on this conception, is one who regards minds as substances, capable of existing independently of spatio-temporal things, but logically incapable of being adjectival or adverbial of such things. A materialist, on the other hand, is one who believes there is no evidence for the existence of minds so described, and who in addition finds insuperable difficulties in supposing that a mind so conceived can enter into causal relations with anything else. If this is indeed the difference between a materialist and one who is not, then the naturalists whom Mr. Sheldon accuses of materialism are glad to find themselves in his company—for in his *practical* commitments (the only ones that really count, according to himself) if not his theoretical ones, he is certainly a materialist. In any event, the evidence for materialism so construed is overwhelming; and naturalists will cheerfully admit his accusation of themselves as materialists not as a criticism but as an acknowledgment of their sanity.

Nevertheless, it is unlikely that so innocuous an interpretation of Mr. Sheldon's critique can be faithful to his intent. For though he insists that the issue he is raising is a highly practical one, and though he dismisses as so much irrelevant subtlety various types of materialism which naturalists and others have carefully distinguished, his intent is presumably to tax naturalists with a view in which they themselves "sense bad odor" (p. 257).

What is this view? Unfortunately, Mr. Sheldon nowhere makes it explicit. He accuses naturalists of excluding from nature everything but the physical, and of adopting a method of inquiry which deprives them of any knowledge of the mental. Indeed, he formulates the issue between materialism and idealism in terms of a sharp contrast between the physical and the mental. But he is not very helpful in making clear what are the marks which set off one of these kinds from the other. He does, to be sure, suggest that the physical is simply that which is capable of spatio-temporal distribution and redistribution; and since the mental is for him an exclusive disjunct to the physical, he also suggests by implication that the mental is that which is not capable of such distribution. However, these suggestions are hardly sufficient for the purpose at hand. Are such properties and processes as temperature, potential energy, solubility, electrical resistance, viscosity, osmosis, digestion, reproduction, physical in Mr. Sheldon's system of categories? Since they are all properties or powers or activities of things having spatio-temporal dimensions, the answer is presumably in the affirmative. Nevertheless, though they characterize things having spatial dimensions, none of the items mentioned has itself a spatial dimension; thus, temperature has no volume, solubility no shape, digestion no area, and so on. And if a property is to be regarded as physical provided that it qualifies something having a spatio-temporal dimension, why are not pains, emotions, feelings, apprehensions of meanings, all subsumable under the physical? For to the best of our knowledge such "mental" states and events occur only as characteristics of spatio-temporal bodies—

even though, like potential energy or viscosity, they do not themselves possess a spatial dimension. Accordingly, Mr. Sheldon formulates no clear criterion in terms of which the physical can be sharply demarcated from the mental; and he has therefore not provided sufficient hints as to what the doctrine is which he finds naturalists holding. A distinction between two types of materialist doctrine therefore appears to be in order.

According to one type of materialism, the mental is simply identical with, or is "nothing but," the physical. It is of this type that Mr. Sheldon is thinking when he declares that a genuine materialist "will insist that an idea is but a potential or tentative muscular response" (p. 256). This view can be stated with some precision in approximately the following manner. Let us call those terms "physical terms" which are commonly employed in the various physical sciences of nature; this class of expressions will then include such words and phrases as "weight," "length," "molecule," "electric charge," "osmotic pressure," and so on. And let us call those terms "psychological terms" of which no use is made in the physical sciences, but which are customarily employed in describing "mental" states; this class of expressions will contain such phrases as "pain," "fear," "feeling of beauty," "sense of guilt," and the like. Materialism of the type now under consideration may then be taken to maintain that every psychological term is *synonymous with,* or has *the same meaning* as, some expression or combination of expressions belonging to the class of physical terms. Proponents of this view, if any, can be imagined to argue somewhat as follows: Modern science has shown that the color *red* appears only when a complicated electro-magnetic process also occurs; accordingly, the word "red" has the same *meaning* as the phrase "electro-magnetic vibration having a wave-length of approximately 7100 Angstroms." (This latter phrase is unduly simple. It requires to be complicated by including into it other terms denoting physical, chemical, and physiological states of organic bodies. But the point of the illustration is not affected by the oversimplification.) And those professing this view must be taken to claim that analogous synonyms can be specified for the distinctive psychological terms such as "pain" and "feeling of beauty."

When the consequences of this view (frequently given the label "reductive materialism") are strictly drawn, statements such as "I am in pain" must be regarded as *logically entailing* statements of the form "My body is in such and such a physico-chemico-physiological state." Whether any competent thinker has ever held such a view in the specific form here outlined is doubtful, though Democritus, Hobbes, and some contemporary behaviorists are often interpreted to assert something not very dissimilar to it. Those who do hold it maintain often that the obvious differences between a color and an electro-magnetic vibration, or between a felt pain and a physiological condition of an organism, are "illusory" and not "real," since only physical processes and events (i.e., those describable exclusively with the help of physical terms) have the dignity of reality. But whatever may be said for reductive materialism—and very little can be said in its favor—it can be categorically asserted that it is *not* a view which is professed, either tacitly or explicitly, by the naturalists whom Mr. Sheldon is criticizing. If "materialism" means reductive materialism, then those naturalists are not materialists.

But there is a second and different type of materialism, though it is sometimes confused with the preceding one. It maintains that the occurrence of a mental event is contingent upon the occurrence of certain complex physico-chemico-physiological events and structures—so that no pains, no emotions, no experiences of beauty or holiness would exist unless bodies appropriately organized were also present. On the other hand, it does not maintain that the specific quality called "pain," for example, is "nothing but" a concourse of physical particles ordered in specified ways. It does not assert that "an idea is but a potential or tentative muscular response." It does not declare that the word "pain," to use the technique of exposition of the preceding paragraphs, is synonymous with some such phrase as "passage of an electric current in a nerve fiber." It does assert that the relation between the occurrence of pains and the occurrence of physiological processes is a contingent or "causal" one, not an analytical or logical one. Many proponents of this view entertain the hope that it will be possible some day to specify the necessary and sufficient *conditions* for the occurrence of mental states and events in terms of the distributions, behaviors, and relations of a special class of factors currently regarded as fundamental in physical science—for example, in terms of the subatomic particles and structures of contemporary physics. Sharing such a hope is not a *sine qua non* for this type of materialism, and in any case whether the hope is realizable can not be settled dialectically but only by the future development of the sciences. However, whether a materialist of this type entertains such a hope or not, he does not claim but denies that propositions dealing with mental events (i.e., those employing psychological terms) are *logically deducible* from propositions dealing exclusively with physical ones (i.e., those containing only physical terms).

The question of the truth of materialism of this type can be decided only on the basis of empirical evidence alone. Many of the details of the dependence of mental upon physical processes are far from being known. Nevertheless, that there is such a dependence can not reasonably be doubted in the light of the evidence already accumulated. A system of philosophy built on a conception of mind incompatible with this evidence is therefore nothing if not wilful and undisciplined speculation. Accordingly, if "materialism" signifies a view something like the one just outlined, Mr. Sheldon is not mistaken in his accusation of naturalists as materialists. And if the issue between materialists and idealists can be settled only by adopting a notion of mind which denies that minds are adjectival and adverbial of bodies, then he is also right in declaring that naturalists have done nothing to settle it. Nor would they wish to resolve an age-old conflict on those terms.

It is relevant to ask now whether naturalists believe the mental to be "wholly at the beck and call" of the physical, and how they would reply to Mr. Sheldon's query whether "the states or processes we call mental or spiritual exercise a control over those we call physical, to some degree independent of any spatio-temporal redistributions." Two things should be noted. First, there is a certain sting in Mr. Sheldon's metaphors which must be removed in order not to prejudice discussion. To speak of the mental as being "wholly at the beck and call" of the physical suggests a degrading status for the mental, a slavish helplessness, which outrages our sense of fact. Physical processes, on any but a magical view of things, do not beckon or call—only human beings do. If there is a suggestion here that the properties of organized matter on any level *must* be read back into matter organized on any other level, then as already indicated naturalists do not subscribe to such notions of the *physical*. Second, if the point of these questions rests on a conception of minds as substantial but ethereal entities, capable nevertheless of controlling or being controlled by physical substances, naturalists will dismiss the questions as not addressed to themselves: they simply do not subscribe to such notions of the *mental*. On the other hand, if these views of the physical and mental are not assumed by the questions, there remains very little for the naturalists to say in reply—as will immediately appear.

For suppose a chemist were asked whether he believed that the properties of water are at "the beck and call" of hydrogen and oxygen atoms, or whether he thought that water "controlled" the behaviors and properties of its constituents. Would he not reply that the questions are meaningful only on the assumption that the properties of water are not only *distinguishable* from those of its constituents taken singly or in isolation from each other, but are also *substantially distinct* from the properties of hydrogen and oxygen atoms when these are related in the way in which water molecules are organized? On the other hand, the chemist would certainly maintain that the existence of water and its properties is contingent upon the combined presence of certain elements interrelated in definite ways. But he would call attention to the fact that when these elements are so related, a distinctive mode of behavior is exhibited by the structured unity into which they enter. Nevertheless, this structured object is not an *additional* thing which, in manifesting its properties, controls from some external vantage point the behavior of its organized parts. The structured object in behaving the way it does behave under given circumstances is simply manifesting the behavior of its constituents *as* related in that structure under those circumstances. To be sure, the occurrence of those properties we associate with water may be controlled by "redistributing" spatio-temporal things—provided always that the combination of the atomic constituents of water can be effected practically. But in undergoing such redistributions the constituents themselves come to behave in precisely the manner in which their relations to one another within a structured molecule of water requires them to behave: their behavior is not *imposed* upon them from without.

The naturalist proceeds in an essentially no different manner in giving his account of the status of minds. Like the chemist in reference to the properties of water, he maintains that the states and events called mental exist only when certain organizations of physical things also occur. And also like the chemist, he holds that the qualities and behaviors displayed by physical things when they are properly organized—the qualities and behaviors called mental or spiritual—are not exhibited by those things unless they are so organized. But these qualities and behaviors of organized wholes are not additional things which are *substantially* distinct from the properties and behaviors of spatio-temporal objects in their organized unity. Accordingly, naturalists most emphatically acknowledge that men are capable of thought, feeling, and emotion, and that in consequence of these powers (whose existence is contingent upon the organization of human bodies) men can engage in actions that bodies not so organized are unable to perform. In particular, human beings are capable of rational inquiry, and in the light of their findings they are able to "redistribute" spatio-temporal things so as to ensure the arrival and departure of many events both physical and mental. They achieve these things, however, not as disembodied minds, but as distinctively organized bodies. To the naturalist, at any rate, there is no more mystery in the fact that certain kinds of bodies are able to think and act rationally than in the fact that cogs and springs arranged in definite ways can record the passage of time or that hydrogen and oxygen atoms ordered in other ways display the properties of water. "Things are what they are, and their consequences will be what they will be; why then should we desire to be deceived?"

II

Mr. Sheldon claims that in adopting scientific method as the way for securing reliable knowledge, naturalists seriously restrict the class of things concerning which they can acquire knowledge. As naturalism envisages the nature of this method, according to him, the method is applicable only to things which are physical or "public," and not to states and events which are mental or "private." How valid is this claim? Are naturalists precluded by their choice of method from ever discovering anything about things divine or angelic if the universe contains them? And, in particular, must a naturalist if he is serious in his adoption of scientific method rule out of court the "private" data of introspective observation?

A preliminary distinction between two meanings of "scientific method" will help clear the way for the naturalist's reply. For the name is often used interchangeably both for a set of general canons with the help of which evidence is to be gathered and evaluated, and for a set of specialized techniques associated with various instruments each of which is appropriate only for a limited subject-matter. Mr. Sheldon draws part of his support for his conclusions concerning the scope of scientific method from this double sense of the name. He contends that methods are not produced *in vacuo*, and are not independent of subject-matter. "No mere methodology," he declares; "a method envisages, however tentatively, a metaphysic" (p. 258). And he cites in illustration the telescope, which is an excellent instrument for studying the stars, but is hardly suited for dissecting the seeds of plants. No one, surely, will think of denying the truth of this last observation. However, it does not therefore follow that the logical canons involved in testing the validity of propositions in astronomy are different from the logical canons employed in biology; for the fact that a telescope is the suitable technical means for exploring stars but not seeds is not incompatible with the claim that a common set of principles are adequate for appraising evidence in all the physical domains which encompass these subject-matters. Nor does it follow that because principles of evidence are competent to guide inquiries into physical subject-matter, they are not so competent for inquiries into psychological subject-matter. In any event, however, it is scientific method as the use of a set of general canons of inquiry, not as a class of special techniques, which is professed by naturalists as the reasonable way for securing reliable knowledge. And although Mr. Sheldon complains that naturalists have supplied no standard analysis of scientific method (p. 258), it surely can be no secret to him that the writings of many naturalists are in fact preoccupied with just such general principles of evidence.

But Mr. Sheldon's chief complaint is addressed to the naturalists' account of the nature of the verificatory process. The naturalists maintain that "reliable knowledge is publicly verifiable." Do they not therefore exclude the very possibility of knowledge concerning matters that are not "public" but are "private"? "Does the mystic verify the Divine being by direct observation?" asks Mr. Sheldon. "Can the introspective psychologist experiment with private minds?" (p. 258). If, however, what is thus private is excluded from the domain of application of scientific method, is not the naturalist forever compelled to remain in the domain of the physical?

The following remarks may serve to clarify the naturalist's position on this matter.

(*a*) In maintaining that scientific method is the most reliable method for achieving knowledge, the naturalist means what he says. He recommends that method for acquiring *knowledge,* for achieving *warranted assertions,* but not for acquiring esthetic or emotional experiences. He does not wish to deny that men have mystic experiences of what they call the Divine, that they enjoy pleasures and suffer pains, or that they have visions of beauty. He *does* deny that *having* such experiences constitutes knowledge, though he also affirms that such "mental states" can become *objects* of knowledge. Accordingly, while he insists that the world may be encountered in other ways than through knowledge and admits that scientific method possesses no valid claim to be the sole avenue for such encounters, he also insists that not every encounter with the world is a case of knowledge. Indeed, for many naturalists, the experience of scientific method is instrumental to the enrichment of other modes of experience. This point is elementary but fundamental. It completely destroys the vicious circle in which Mr. Sheldon has attempted to trap the naturalist—the circle according to which nature for the naturalist is what is open to scientific method, while scientific method is simply the method recommended for approaching nature (p. 263). What is viciously circular in maintaining that if anything is to be *known* (in whatever other manner it may be *experienced*), reliable knowledge of it is acquired through the use of scientific method? For things can be encountered without first having to be known, and scientific method can be described and employed without everything in nature having first to be experienced. It no more follows from this that everything in nature is known or can be experienced only as a mode of knowledge, than it follows that since every assertion about anything whatsoever is *statable,* every thing has already been stated or exists only as a possible statement.

(*b*) Though Mr. Sheldon sometimes appears to suggest that the observable alone is confirmable or verifiable, the naturalist maintains that the meanings of these terms do not coincide. Mr. Sheldon declares:

> Scientific method demands experiment and observation confirmable by fellow men. Mental states or processes, just in so far as they are not physical, not "behavior," are not open to such observation. He says they are "inaccessible." But of course they are accessible to their owner; it is only to fellow men, to the public, that they are inaccessible. Scientific method thus means, to the naturalist, that observation of the non-public has no sense or meaning. Publicity is the test; the private and hidden is ruled out of court. . . . [P. 262.]

The crux of this argument resides in the transition from the statement that mental states are not open to observation by one's fellow men, to the conclusion that therefore the private and the hidden are ruled out of court by the naturalist. But this is a *non-sequitur.* For let us grant, at least for the sake of the argument, that A's mental states can not be observed by his fellow men. Let us even accept the much stronger claim that statements like "B can not experience A's feelings" are *analytically* true, so that it is *logically impossible* for B to experience A's feelings. Does it follow that B can not publicly verify that A does experience some feeling, of pain, for example? That it does not follow will be evident from applying Mr. Sheldon's argument to the supposition that a subatomic interchange of energies is taking place in accordance with the specifications of modern physical theory. No one will claim that such subatomic events are literally observable, at least by human investigators. Nevertheless, though those events are not observable, propositions about them are certainly confirmable or verifiable—and in fact publicly verifiable by observations on the behaviors of macroscopic objects. Evidently, therefore, there may be states and events which are not observable, even though propositions about them are publicly verifiable.

(c) Nevertheless, so Mr. Sheldon urges, if the naturalist is consistent he can not rely on scientific method to yield reliable knowledge of the mental *qua* mental or "private." He can not use this method to assure himself that he has an abdominal pain, for example, unless a surgeon first exhibits and publicly verifies the existence of an inflamed appendix.

But the imputation of such views to the naturalist is a caricature of the latter's position. The latter does maintain, to be sure, that A's feelings of pain have their physical and physiological causes. Since, however, the naturalist is not a reductive materialist, he does not maintain that the painful quality experienced by A is "nothing but" the physical and physiological *conditions* upon which its occurrence depends. He will therefore not assert that the dentist who notes a cavity in A's tooth experiences A's pain; on the contrary, he will insist that A's body is uniquely favored with respect to the pains A suffers—a circumstance which he attributes to the distinctive physiological events that are transpiring in A. Accordingly, the naturalist will recognize that the proposition that A is experiencing a pain is verifiable in two ways: directly by A, in virtue of the privileged position in which A's body occurs; and indirectly by everyone (including A) who is in a position to observe processes causally connected with the felt pain.

However, and this is the essential point, the fact that A can directly verify the proposition that he is in pain, without having to consult a surgeon or dentist, does not make the proposition any the less *publicly verifiable*. For the surgeon or dentist can also verify it, not, to be sure, by sharing A's qualitative experience, but in other ways: by asking A, for example, or by noting the condition of A's body. In brief, therefore, to maintain that propositions about the occurrence of pains and other mental states are publicly verifi*able*, does not mean that they must always be verifi*ed* indirectly; and, conversely, to acknowledge that propositions about mental states have not been indirectly verifi*ed* is not incompatible with the thesis that they are publicly verifi*able*.

(d) The point involved is important enough to deserve some amplification. It is well known that the temperature of a body can be determined in several alternative ways: for example, with the aid of an ordinary mercury thermometer or of a thermo-couple. In the one case, changes in temperature are registered by variations in the volume of the mercury, in the other by variations in the electric current flowing through a galvanometer. The instruments thus exhibit two quite disparate qualitative alterations: for the thermometer is not equipped to register the effects of thermoelectric forces, while the thermo-couple lacks the necessary structure to record thermal expansions. It is evident, therefore, that the qualities and behaviors displayed by each instrument are a consequence of its specific mode of construction and of the special position it occupies in a system of physical transactions. Nevertheless, in spite of the qualitative differences between them, each instrument can be satisfactorily employed for ascertaining temperature variations—at any rate within specifiable limits of such variations. It is well to note, incidentally, that in recording the temperature of some other body, an instrument is at the same time indicating its own temperature. Moreover, if the instruments are both in working connection with some other body so that they serve to measure the latter's temperature, it is possible to use the behavior of either instrument in order to predict certain aspects of the behavior of the other, and thus to determine the temperature of the other. Were the instruments blessed with the powers of consciousness (let us permit ourselves this fancy), the thermometer would experience a unique quality when it was recording the temperature of some body—a quality or state which would be "private" to the thermometer and incommunicable to the thermo-couple. Nevertheless, even though the thermo-couple would be unable, because of its own distinctive mode of organization and unique physical position, to experience the qualities exhibited by the thermometer, it would not be precluded from recording (and thus "verifying") the temperature both of the third body and of the thermometer itself.

Consider now the bearing of this physical illustration upon the issue raised by Mr. Sheldon. *A* can not *experience B*'s mental states, any more than the thermometer can exhibit (or experience) the distinctive qualitative behaviors of the thermo-couple, and for the same reasons. But *A* can *know* that *B* is undergoing some specified experience, just as the thermometer can be employed to measure the temperature of the thermo-couple. The distinction between the public and the private, upon which Mr. Sheldon builds his case against the naturalist, thus consists—so far as questions of *knowledge* are involved—in the differences between the causal relations of two distinct or differently organized bodies.

(*e*) In thus admitting as publicly verifiable all the facts designated by Mr. Sheldon as "mental," naturalists do not, of course, thereby commit themselves to the various propositions for which such data are often cited as evidence. Thus, naturalists do not as a matter of principle, deny that mystics have had ecstatic visions of what they call the Divine, any more than they deny that men experience pains; for they believe that the occurrence of such visions and experiences has been publicly verified. On the other hand, recognizing as warranted the proposition that such *events* do occur does not, by itself, decide what further propositions are confirmed by those occurrences. Indeed, this question can not be decided in general, and requires detailed investigation for each proposition considered. The point is that there is surely a difference between admitting as true the proposition that someone has undergone the experience he calls "experience of the Divine," and admitting as therefore true the proposition which affirms the existence of a Deity—just as there is a difference between acknowledging a pain and attributing it to a heart lesion. In either case, the proposition mentioned last requires the confirmation of independent evidence if it is to be counted as a validly established one. The testimony of a mystic is *testimony*, but is not necessarily *evidence* for the proposition the mystic asserts—though it may be evidence for some *other* proposition—no more than a patient's report about his pains is necessarily evidence for the truth of his belief that he is suffering from a fatal disease. If naturalists disagree with those who assert the existence of gods and angels, they do not do so because they rule out of court the testimony of all witnesses, but because the testimony does not stand up under critical scrutiny. The *horror supernaturae* with which Mr. Sheldon not unjustly charges the naturalists is therefore not a capricious rejection on their part of well-established beliefs: it is a consequence of their refusal to accept propositions, like the belief in ghosts, for which the available evidence is overwhelmingly negative.

(f) One final point requires some attention, for it is briefly hinted at by Mr. Sheldon and is often given central prominence in discussions such as the present one. The point concerns the alleged greater certainty of some propositions than others, and in particular the greater certainty of propositions about introspective observations than of propositions about other matters.

Mr. Sheldon raises the issue in connection with a behaviorist attempt to establish the fact that someone is undergoing an experience of the beautiful. He believes that if a naturalist, faithful to scientific method, wishes to be sure that someone is having such an experience, he must apply physical apparatus to the glandular and muscular responses of the person in question. For the naturalist, according to Mr. Sheldon, can not take the person's word for it: "that is a report about something private, outside the realm of verifiable truth" (p. 267). But it should be clear at this stage of the present discussion that Mr. Sheldon would have a point only if the naturalist were a reductive materialist: that is, if the naturalist were to maintain that a feeling of beauty is "nothing but" a glandular and muscular response. However, since the imputation of such a view to the naturalist is a mistaken one, why should the latter proceed in the fashion suggested by Mr. Sheldon? For a man's glandular and muscular responses are no more identical with his feelings of beauty than are his oral reports that he is having them. An oral report may be more reliable evidence for the occurrence of such feelings than is the reaction of some brass instrument—especially since, as in the present instance, we possess little accurate knowledge concerning the glandular and muscular conditions for the occurrence of such feelings. To be sure, the naturalist will not deny himself the use of physical apparatus if such instruments do provide decisive evidence on disputed matters and if people are suspected of prevarication concerning their feelings—witness, for example, the occasional reliance on "lie detectors." But such instruments do not supply *inherently* more reliable evidence simply because they are physical; whether they do in fact supply such evidence is something that must be settled by detailed inquiry.

But does a naturalist, it is sometimes asked, believe himself justified in accepting a proposition about his "private" experiences, if that proposition is not confirmable by others? Does not a naturalist have to maintain, if he holds reliable knowledge to be publicly verifiable knowledge, that such a proposition as "I now have a bad headache" which he might utter is not made certain simply by the pain he is feeling, but must be confirmed by others before it can be regarded as well-established? In brief, must not a naturalist declare *all* propositions to be unwarranted, unless they are verifiable by other than introspective evidence? In answering these questions in the affirmative, so one criticism runs, the naturalist is adopting a dogmatic and arbitrary criterion for warranted knowledge, a criterion in conflict with common sense as well as with the practice of many competent psychologists.

However, a distinction previously introduced must be repeated here. The naturalist takes seriously his characterization of reliable knowledge as publicly verif*able* knowledge. Accordingly, the proposition "I now have a bad headache," if it constitutes a piece of knowledge, must be confirm*able* by others as well as by the person making it. But it by no means follows from this that the proposition must actually be confirm*ed* by others if the person making it is to be justified in accepting it as true. Just how much confirmatory evidence must be available for a given proposition before it can be accepted as warranted can not be specified once for all. But undoubtedly there are cases (as in the instance of the proposition about the headache) in which a minimum of evidence (i.e., the felt pain) suffices to warrant its acceptance by the person asserting the proposition—so that any additional evidence will be, for him, supererogatory. But the possibility here considered is not unique to propositions about matters of introspective observation. A chemist who observes that a piece of blue litmus paper turns red when immersed in a liquid, will assert that the paper is indeed red and conclude that the liquid is acid. He will normally regard it a waste of time to search for further evidence to support either of the propositions he is asserting, even though other evidence could be found for them.

On the other hand, the naturalist—like disciplined common sense and the experienced introspective psychologist—is sensitive to the dangers and limitations of "pure" introspection. He knows, for example, that introspection alone can not discover the causes (nor, for that matter, the precise locations) of the pains he feels; for statements asserting the mere *existence* of qualities do not provide theoretical knowledge of the *relations* in which those qualities stand to other things. Even the fact that the felt quality of a pain is "private" is not established by introspective methods alone; this fact, like the fact that certain pains are associated with contemporaneous physico-chemical changes in teeth and nerve fibres and can therefore be controlled by "redistributing" spatio-temporal things, can be ascertained only by overt experiment involving manipulation of "public" things. Theoretical knowledge of pains thus opens up fresh directions for human activity and new types of experience—possibilities which remain unrealized as long as attention is directed simply to the sheer *occurrence* of painful qualities. Assured knowledge of the nature of pains, however, is not the product of mere introspective study. In any event, the annals of physics as well as of medicine and psychology have made clear to the naturalist the serious errors into which men fall when they accept introspective observations without further experimental controls. It is needless to belabor this point—even the text-books are full of illustrations for it. As eminent psychologists have themselves noted, introspective observation is not radically different from any other kind of observation. Whether one employs one's body or some recording instrument for making qualitative discriminations, one must in either case take great care in interpreting its reports and drawing conclusions from them. Moreover, the psychological and social sciences would be denuded of nearly everything of interest if the propositions they asserted were exclusively confined to matters that are capable of direct observation or acquaintance, and if those sciences did not attempt systematically to *relate* the qualities and events immediately apprehended with things and events not so experienced. The dichotomy so insistently and frequently introduced between the "inner" and "outer," between the "private" and "public," therefore seems to many naturalists as little more than a relic from a conception of the mind as a substantial, autonomous agent, operating mysteriously in a body which is not its natural home. Neither this conception nor the dichotomy serve to further the progress of either philosophy or science.

Indeed, this conception of mind has tragic consequences for the human values which Mr. Sheldon wishes to defend against what he believes is the threat of scientific method. For it flies in the face of mountains of evidence concerning the place of man in nature, and leaves human values unanchored to any solid ground in experience. It is not the philosophy of naturalism which imperils human values but Mr. Sheldon's dualism. By ruling out as irrelevant investigation into the natural causes and consequences of the value commitments men make, it deprives human choice of effective status, opens the door wide to irresponsible intuitions, and dehumanizes the control of nature and society which scientific understanding makes possible. In spite of Mr. Sheldon's deprecating remarks about the uncertain conclusions which anthropology, social psychology, psychiatry, and the other social sciences have been able to reach concerning the "mental aspect" of human activities (pp. 257–258), no one familiar with the history of these disciplines will question the claim that our assured knowledge and our control of these matters has increased as a consequence of introducing into those domains the method of modern science. Is there any competent evidence for believing that the continued use of this method will retard the advance of such knowledge and control rather than promote it? What viable alternative to this method does Mr. Sheldon propose that has not already been tried and discredited? What good reason can he offer for entrusting the maintenance and the realization of human goods to a historically provincial dualism between the mental and the physical—a dualism which the progress of science has made increasingly dubious? It is this doctrine from which Mr. Sheldon's critique of naturalism derives, and not the philosophy attacked by him, which requires a responsible defense.

JOHN DEWEY
SIDNEY HOOK
ERNEST NAGEL

COLUMBIA UNIVERSITY AND
NEW YORK UNIVERSITY

Time and Its Mysteries. Series II. Four Lectures given on the James Arthur Foundation, New York University, by DANIEL WEBSTER HERING, WILLIAM FRANCIS GRAY SWANN, JOHN DEWEY, and ARTHUR H. COMPTON. New York: New York University Press. London: Humphrey Milford. Oxford University Press. 1940. viii + 137 pp. $2.00.

The present volume contains the annual lectures delivered on the James Arthur Foundation during the years 1936 to 1939. The addresses by the three physicists ("The Time Concept and Time Sense among Cultured and Uncultured Peoples" by the late Professor Hering, "What is Time?" by Dr. Swann, and "Time and the Growth of Physics" by Professor Compton) deal with the development of chronometry and with significant innovations in both technology and physical theory arising from refinements in the measurement of time. Although these essays are informative, they are not free from dubious history (as when Professor Compton credits Galileo with the experiment of dropping balls from the tower of Pisa) or from the perversity of offering mystification and paradox as enlightenment (as when Dr. Swann discusses relativity).

Professor Dewey's address on "Time and Individuality" deals with more general themes. His thesis is that development is the mark of individuality and that "temporal seriality is the very essence of the human individual." Moreover, in opposition to the view that sequential change is foreign to the nature of inanimate things, he maintains that "the principle of a developing career applies to all things in nature." Two corollaries are drawn from this metaphysical conclusion. The first is that progress is not inevitable, but is contingent on the efforts of men to control change in a given direction; consequently, the ground of democratic ideas and practices must be a faith in the potentialities of individuals. The second is that art complements science in being a manifestation of individuality as creative of the future; hence, since "the free individuality which is the source of art is also the final source of creative development in time," the regimentation of artists is treason to the better future which such regimentation would serve.

Professor Dewey's essay is provocative, but his argument is puzzling. He rests his case concerning the universal validity of the "principle of a developing career" on two main contentions. The first is that "scientific objects" are purely relational, so that the method of physical science is concerned with the measurement of change and "not with individuals as such"; the second is that it is becoming clear that in physics "statements of what actually occurs are statistical in character as distinct from so-called dynamical laws that are abstract in character, and disguised definitions." Professor Dewey seems to me correct in his characterization of scientific objects. But is it really the case that the methods of the natural sciences are not concerned with "individuals as such"? Do we not have reliable physical knowledge concerning such manifest individuals as the sun, the earth, and even individual human beings? The second contention appears to me even more dubious. I will not stop to argue the question whether the theories and laws of mechanics, classical thermodynamics, relativity theory, and a good part of optics and electrodynamics are in fact statistical laws, and if not whether they are disguised definitions. I do not think that the answer is affirmative in either case. The crucial question is whether, even if the statements of physics are statistical in character, it follows that development characterizes all things in nature. It does not seem to me that this consequence can be validly drawn; for there is no contradiction in using both a statistical and a non-statistical ("dynamic") theory for the same subject-matter, as is evident from the fact that both statistical mechanics and thermodynamics can be employed in the domain of thermal phenomena.

Professor Dewey also appeals to the Heisenberg indeterminacy relation as evidence for the fact that "the individual is a temporal career whose future can not be *logically* deduced from its past," so that "for physical individuals time is not simply a measure of predetermined changes in mutual positions, but is something that enters into their being." Waiving the question whether the proposed interpretation of the Heisenberg principle is adequate, it is amusing to find Professor Dewey denying that science is concerned with the intrinsic natures of things while at the same time he makes statements which do just that. Moreover, while the predictions of science are only probable, as Professor Dewey rightly maintains, this fact is not a specific outcome of the Heisenberg principle; for it is justifiable to assert that fact even for the classical dynamical theories, so long as those theories have an empirical content and are not "disguised definitions." It is not clear, therefore, what relevance the Heisenberg principle has for Professor Dewey's argument.

Professor Dewey maintains that a thing's potentialities are not fixed and intrinsic to it, but depend on the consequences of its interactions with other things. It is somewhat strange, however, to find him also maintaining that the validity of this doctrine is essentially related to a view which regards the "spatial rearrangement of what existed previously" as in some sense an inferior manifestation of development than a "qualitatively new" happening. For since we can not tell what the character of physical theories will be like after another hundred years of research, this seems like giving needless hostages to the future. But what I find really strange, in the light of Professor Dewey's main thesis, is to have him declare that an individual can lose his individuality by becoming imprisoned in routine, that "our behavior becomes predictable because it is but an external rearrangement of what went before," and that the human problem is the control of change in a given direction. Since this problem, if it is to be solved, presumably involves making predictions concerning the future on the strength of past behaviors, these various doctrines do not seem to me compatible. I do not think, therefore, that the metaphysical underpinning Professor Dewey supplies for his democratic faith is an adequate or, for that matter, a needful structure. And I think that in attempting to supply it in the manner of the present essay he has not been faithful to his own best teachings.

ERNEST NAGEL.

COLUMBIA UNIVERSITY.

The Journal of Philosophy

DEWEY'S ESTHETIC THEORY. I

The Earlier Theory

THE esthetic problem is a crucial philosophical problem. It has not always been so treated; it has too often been a hasty addendum to a system or a corroboration, plausible or fanciful, of a general philosophical position. Failure to do better by an experience that pervades and enlivens ordinary experience and that is perhaps the most arresting of special experiences has left a gap in philosophical theory, and has deprived life at this point of the support of thought. When the poets, moved by the beauty of nature, have sung of

> that blessed mood,
> In which the burden of the mystery,
> In which the heavy and the weary weight,
> Of all this unintelligible world is lightened,

they have challenged the philosophers not to neglect what it is that is revealed in "the mighty world of eye and ear." Though Keats' conviction that "Beauty is truth, truth, beauty" offers us a riddle rather than a problem, still it is not one of those riddles that should "tease us out of thought"; it should stimulate thought. As "a wild surmise" it has agitated but not provoked thought. Has Dewey readjusted the too usual philosophical attitude toward esthetic experience? Has he turned a direct and persistent, not an indirect and casual, attention to "the language of the sense"? Yes and no. Yes—when he eagerly explores art and follows the steps of the artist to see what he is about. No—when in a traditional fashion he absorbs it in his metaphysical conclusions. Like many others he then reduces the data of the esthetic problem to conformity with an already formed general view of life. Zealous on behalf of recent forms of art he does not employ the method of reducing art to another form of life, but the more "honorific" transformation of all life that is life into art, of all experience that is *"an* experience" into art. Art enthusiasts have often praised art in just this fashion; life, they have said time and again, should perfect itself in the spirit of art, life should itself be a work of art. Dewey has his own version of art and the perfect life. But whether art merely serves the rest of life or becomes all that is best in life, the data of the esthetic problem are destroyed, not elicited and interpreted. Art is denied special character. When Dewey concerns himself specifically with art, with what is added to "ordinary" life by a work of art, he contributes immensely to esthetic theory. The poetic quotations at the beginning of the paragraph were not there as introductory decorative matter. They point the way to what Dewey has done, for he has shown how sense developed, integrated, becomes the meaningful experience that is esthetic experience. Especially in two chapters in *Art as Experience* [1]—"The Common Substance of the Arts" and "The Varied Substance of the Arts"—he so interprets "the language of the sense" that he tells us the language it speaks.

The esthetic theory made out of his general point of view (what might be called his metaphysics of art) is reached thus: the transformation of means into end increases value in life and thus reveals the ideal value,—the *amalgamation* of means and end: in art there is to be found this ideal transformation, and thus art is an example of perfection and is moreover that which all forms of life become when perfect. The other theory, fully developed in *Art as Experience,* is based on a search through life and through art for what happens when sense experience, what is present to eye and ear, takes on increasing importance. Why, he asks, is it not a miracle but comprehensible that great artists can make the sensuous world in its way all important? The two theories do not conflict for they have little to do with each other. With great skill he occasionally incorporates the first verbally into his argument for the other.

An earlier work, *Experience and Nature,* [2] in chapters not directly concerned with art, frequently refers to the esthetic problem and gives hints as to a possible solution. There seemed to be a promise of an account of art that would give it special character— despite Dewey's besetting fear that to distinguish from is to separate from the rest of life. But when the special topic of art is reached in Chapter IX, certain red herrings get across the trail,— social injustice, class distinctions, the ever lurking honorific or invidious intentions of apparently innocent conceptual distinctions. In defence of the oneness of life, which he finds always challenged, with amazing dialectical skill he makes the different into the identical. He reiterates his conviction that art is not distinctive except as perhaps it provides an especially transparent and persuasive illustration of what *everything* good essentially is, of what *all* human activity achieves, of what *all* life ought to be. He attacks society past and present—it has prevented the good life; and all thought by subtle devices has deceived us as to the nature of the good life,—

[1] John Dewey: *Art as Experience.* New York: Minton, Balch & Co. 1934.

[2] *Experience and Nature,* New York: W. W. Norton & Co., Inc. 1929. All references throughout the first part of this article, "The Earlier Theory," are to this work.

at times self-deceived and again disingenuous and malign. The argument builds up a splendid eulogy of a better state of affairs. It develops an ethics and urges a social reform. But under the honors thrust upon it art is buried.

The argument takes this course. We should discard the customary general distinction between the arts, practice, practical activity, and speculative or theoretic activity as false to fact and the source of invidious distinctions. Dewey is true to the implications of pragmatism in finding in such intellectual distinctions a motive, and he pays heed to one strain in modern psychology in disclosing that the motive wears a disguise. The Greeks saw the difference between practical and intellectual activities as one of degrees of worth, labor a necessity of our needs, of the partial and humble aspects of our nature, thought the assertion of our power to envisage the universal. In practice we acknowledge dependence and incompleteness; in theory we display our freedom, lay hold on perfection; wherefore the Greeks looked down upon practice, the arts, and honored science, theory. The one is the drudgery of life, the other the highest form of enjoyment. The simple and absolute antithesis here expressed is rather a melodramatic than a realistic rendering of the Greek attitude. At any rate it provides for Dewey a properly social impetus toward a theory of art,—the theory that art occurs in the coalescence of the two aspects of life. Modern thought does not bestow its honors so unhesitatingly as did the Greeks. Consistently with their whole manner of life they could place contemplation, the self-sufficient mood of thought, above production, the labor that is servant to our needs. But we honor labor; modern thought demands more of man than passive enjoyment and its demands are not exactions merely but a new form of praise. In that contemplation is merely passive and production active, only the latter creates, has the *power* that we admire. The general contrast between production of changes in the world and mere inspection before and after change is present in the special region of art; by the modern sense of values it is the artist who produces that is honored, not the man of taste who merely enjoys or possesses. Furthermore, when distinctions are made among works of art, the modern tendency is to applaud the new, the novel, the additional. The vagaries of merely capricious impulse might, Dewey thinks, give us pause; they may and should persuade us to a profounder insight and lead us to see in the work of art the drawing together of the novel and the routine, the fusion of "the basic uniformities of nature" with "the wonder of the new and the grace of the gratuitous."

To recapitulate: practise and thought offer a contrast that led the Greeks to prefer thought to practise but that leads us to prefer practise to thought. In art there is that which destroys the basis of both preferences. Reflection on what we value in art should make us dispute both the Greek and our own choice. In art thought and practise blend.

Thought, intelligence, science is the intentional direction of natural events to meanings capable of immediate possession and enjoyment; this direction—which is operative art—is itself a natural event in which nature otherwise partial and incomplete comes fully to itself; so that objects of conscious experience when reflectively chosen, form the "end" of nature. The doings and sufferings that form experience are, in the degree in which experience is intelligent or charged with meanings, a union of the precarious, novel, irregular with the settled, assured, and uniform. . . . Wherever there is art the contingent and ongoing no longer work at cross purposes with the formal and recurrent but commingle in harmony. [*Experience and Nature*, pp. 358–359.]

What is true of all properly conscious experience—that in it "the instrumental and the final, meanings that are signs and clues and meanings that are immediately possessed, suffered and enjoyed, come together in one"—is "preëminently true of art." Though another notion lurks beneath, art here develops "meaning" in what it presents and thus raises the value of experience. Taken simply this is what Plato half thought when he saw beauty as perhaps embodiment of Idea; and is what Hegel has said. In the account of art as a creative activity, overcoming dualities to compound the novel with the familiar, the "ongoing" with the formed, it is closely related to Nietzsche. These resemblances are, of course, far-fetched if "meaning" retains for Dewey a plainly instrumental function, but whether or not it always in this connection does is ambiguous. Dewey acknowledges that the special virtues of art have been "truly declared" by certain systems of esthetic theory to be "a union of necessity and freedom, a harmony of the many and one, a reconciliation of the sensuous and the ideal"; but that the understanding of art was thus increased need not be acknowledged, for these systems were "without empirical basis and import in their words." Thus Dewey formally phrases his impression that the philosophers with whom he may seem to agree did not sufficiently know what they were talking about. It might be conceded that they did not bring their thought so to bear on art and esthetic experience as to make it clearly enough reveal, certainly not to modern eyes, what is happening there; and that especially in parts of *Art as Experience* Dewey moves closer to the actual scene. His is a fresh realization and a differently argued proof. Such statements as the following have a new ring.

Art is solvent union of the generic, recurrent, ordered, established phase of nature with its phase that is incomplete, going on, and hence still uncertain, contingent, novel, particular. . . . Of any artistic act and product it may be said both that it is inevitable in its rightness, that nothing in it can be altered without altering all, and that its occurrence is spontaneous, unexpected, fresh, unpredictable. The presence in art, whether as an act or a product, of proportion, economy, order, symmetry, composition, is such a commonplace that it does not need to be dwelt upon. But equally necessary is unexpected combination, and the consequent revelation of possibilities hitherto unrealized. . . . The "magic" of poetry—and pregnant experience has poetic quality—is precisely the revelation of meaning in the old effected by its presentation through the new. It radiates the light that never was on land and sea but that is henceforth an abiding illumination of objects. Music in its immediate occurrence is the most various and etherial of the arts, but in its conditions and structure the most mechanical. [*Loc. cit.*, pp. 359–360.]

There is no need, Dewey thinks, to apologize for these commonplaces, till "their evidential significance for a theory of nature's nature" is commonly recognized.

In *Experience and Nature* Dewey is distracted from the emerging possibilities of sense as the medium of meanings by his theory of means-end amalgamation, by what he conceives to be the method of art and an ideal of method—a method that is perfect in that it relates means and end absolutely and so guarantees not merely eventual success but success all along the way. Value is a kind of transcendent efficacy. This strand in Dewey's thought has been criticized often enough, but it can not be omitted from a discussion of his esthetic theory. It is art viewed as an amalgamation of means and end that supports his conviction that art is the ideal of life, is any experience that is what experience ought to be, is what all life must become. He turns from art as art to art as social improvement, as the social millennium. Reviewing the conceptions that have emerged from his analysis of art he sees their wider and entrancing possibilities; these conceptions are those of labor and contemplation, of effort and enjoyment, of uniformities and novelties; plainly art has a far wider than its special meaning. The argument must expand beyond the apparent range of the topic. Dewey's phrasing here characterizes with unintentional accuracy the nature of this argument: he writes, "the theme *has insensibly passed over* into that of the relation of means and consequence, process and product, the instrumental and the consummatory. Any activity that is simultaneously both, rather than in alternation and displacement, is art" (italics not in text). The substance of what follows becomes primarily moral admonition and ethical theory: all life *ought* to consist of activities simultaneously instrumental and consummatory, what *is* so is therein good, what is rather one than the other is thereby bad. The Greeks had perhaps greater intellectual consistency and an easier conscience when, feeling free to do so, they commended and preferred the life of contemplative enjoyment. We "know better," but do not put our knowledge frankly into effect. We seek comfort for the consequent inconsistencies in our thought or for its violation in our practise—placate the toiler and our democratic consciences—by the plea of necessity and the convention of eulogistic question-begging epithets. Impatient with our toleration of toil that is far from enjoyable, Dewey asks us not to obscure the issue by calling such toil useful and necessary. "We optimistically call much of our labors in home, factory, laboratory, and study useful and let it go at that, thinking that by calling them useful we have somehow justified and explained their occurrence." The only permissible form of usefulness is that which serves human needs. What is the use of shoes if the toiler in the factory lives a "narrowed, embittered, and crippled life"? The human need for "possession and appreciation of the meaning of things" is "ignored and unsatisfied in the traditional notion of the useful."

Our classificatory use of the conception of some arts as merely instrumental so as to dispose of a large part of human activity is no solving definition; it rather conveys an immense and urgent problem. [*Loc. cit.*, pp. 362–363.]

The question is how to dispose of the distinction on which it rests so that all activities shall be consummatory—or still better at once consummatory and instrumental. Art is the answer. Art in the proper sense transcends the obstructing distinctions,—centrally that between means and end; in it "meanings that are signs and clues and meanings that are immediately possessed, suffered, and enjoyed, come together in one." That all life may be immediately enjoyable, all life should be art for in art all means are parts of the end and an end is a means to a further end. This is the condition of continuous immediate enjoyment and of increasing enjoyments. Only wicked or stupid habits of thought preserving unreal distinctions prevent this consummation, prevent perfection. The feasibility of perfection all turns on conceiving the processes of which the work of art is the outcome as its ingredients, and therefore as equally with it enjoyable. An alternate talent for the perfect life is the power to love the processes toward a desired result equally with it once we know their relation to it. Now it is true that many of the experiences that lead into an appreciation or into the production of a work of art are retained in one's experience of it, are ingredients in the culminating experience, but many are preparatory only however well we recognize their relation to the outcome. But for the hoped-for result they would not be undertaken at all. I doubt if the life of the artist has fewer of these recalcitrant processes than that of others. Its necessary toils are often willingly undergone and so irradiated by their end, but they are not, as Dewey would have it, all loved. It's a strange insistence on absolute acceptability all along any route. The proof of its possibility is simply that of arbitrary definition;

Dewey bluntly refuses to call means, means, unless they are also ends, or indeed to call ends, ends, unless they are also means to further ends. (All other means are "pseudo-means.") But that is to obliterate the distinction on which rests the movement of his argument and from which also arises the motivation of the practical situation in which he is interested. For let the means become ends and, as has happened, instead of only thereby being means they may cease to be means and beguile us from the end they were to have served; a task that serves a desired end may indeed not merely reconcile us to it, it may even come to have too great an attraction of its own. Some means have no such dangerous attractiveness. Our study of French irregular verbs is a price we willingly pay for our enjoyment of French literature, but we do not think it a part of what we are paying for. The work of art, for Dewey the ideal illustration of the amalgamation of means and ends, does not contain as ingredients, or parts, the preceding technical processes. In a manner of speaking, yes, perhaps, but seriously speaking, no. If Dewey refers only to the preceding imaginative experiences that are present in it, assent is easy, but such a limitation of his meaning ignores his demand that *all* instrumental activities shall be ingredients in their end and equally with it acceptable.

Dewey seems to feel that the formula, the amalgamation of means and end, by defining a perfect state of affairs makes it attainable. When we know that means are never means except as they take on the desirability of their end, we will see that pseudo-means, not being means, are futile, and we will no longer permit toil and drudgery. A work of art amalgamates means and end, it proves the possibility of the ideal, and presents a suggestive and stimulating image of perfection. If we pay heed to it life will become what it ought to be, all life will be the life of art. Not raising the question of the general application of the means-end formula to the nature and conditions of human effort, one asks, is an amalgamation of the instrumental and the consummatory or even a relatively close approach to it present in the life of art? Does "every process of free art prove that the difference between means and end is analytical, formal, not material and chronological"? The artist would hardly agree that all his efforts are literally parts of his goal (except as he agrees to play the game of speaking in that way). Dewey would retort in the terms of his definition of art—only that can be called art in which the means and the end do coalesce.

In the following passage *meaning* is evidently nothing more than a reference to means or to ends. A work of art "means" for the spectator primarily past processes, for the artist primarily future results.

What has been said enables us to redefine the distinction drawn between the artistic, as objectively productive, and the esthetic [the artistic he uses to refer to the experience of the artist, the esthetic to the enjoyment of art by men in general.] Both involve a perception of meanings in which the instrumental and the consummatory peculiarly intersect. In esthetic perceptions an object interpenetrated with meanings is given; it may be taken for granted; it invites and awaits the act of appropriative enjoyment. In the esthetic object tendencies are sensed as brought to fruition; in it is embodied a means-consequence relationship, as the past work of his hands was surveyed by the Lord and pronounced good. . . . Artistic sense on the other hand grasps tendencies as possibilities; the invitation of these possibilities to perception is more urgent and compelling than that of the given already achieved. While the means-consequence relationship is directly sensed, felt, in both appreciation and artistic production, in the former the scale descends on the side of the attained; in the latter there predominates the invitation of an existent consummation to bring into existence further perceptions. [*Loc. cit.*, pp. 374–375.]

Conversely any activity in which "meaning" transforms means into ends is art.

Thinking is preëminently an art; knowledge and propositions which are the products of thinking, are works of art, as much so as statuary and symphonies, [for]every successive stage of thinking is a conclusion in which the meaning of what has produced it is condensed; and it is no sooner stated than it is a light radiating to other things—unless it be a fog that obscures them. The antecedents of a conclusion are as causal and existential as those of a building. They are not logical or dialectical, or an affair of ideas. . . . Scientific method or the art of constructing true perceptions is ascertained in the course of experience to occupy a privileged position in undertaking other arts. But this unique position only places it the more securely as an art; it does not set its product, knowledge, apart from other works of art. [*Loc. cit.*, pp. 378–379.]

Meaning as defined above is a recognition of tendencies fulfilled or a recognition of the means toward further ends. As a symbol of successful desire whatever is so viewed is always to be embraced. Causal conditions do not impose themselves on us as necessary means, for they *are* means only when they "mean" their ends, when they are "freely used because of perceived connection with chosen consequences." The "freely" surely begs the question. Taken simply it means that we choose the causal conditions freely in the sense of deliberately, as recognized means to a chosen end; if we want the end we must needs take these means. Such a choice is however free just because compelled by our free choice of the end; the means are not in themselves a free choice. Life is full of distasteful means realized and chosen exactly as such; but for their "meaning" they would not be chosen in any sense, and our hope about them is not that they shall become ingredients in the end, but rather that they shall leave no after-taste. The necessary means *may* have their own appeal, or they *may* borrow appeal from their ends. But Dewey's optimism puts a strain on even the most well-disposed toward life. It promises if not exactly a new heaven—it has marked if obscured similarities with others—certainly a new earth. All our ends we may, he thinks, pursue under idyllic conditions, for we can love the route toward them as much as we love the goal. "To entertain, choose, and accomplish anything as an end or consequence is to be committed to a like love and care for whatever events and acts are its means." [3] Though in many cases this may be happily so, yet it varies with temperament and with brute fact.

When Dewey faces social injustice he must believe that toil is unnecessary, that drudgery must be not merely reduced and shared but eliminated. He is strangely compelled by his hatred of unjustly distributed labor to undertake to disprove the necessity for any form of toil. Had his account of the work of art, into which skill, and paint, and tones, etc., enter, as he puts it, as ingredients, faced the plain facts of how they come so to enter, the process of art would serve less well as a sample of absolute acceptability, of the coalescence of the instrumental and the consummatory. What he calls elements, in the whole that is the final work of art, have been made so by past and present effort on the part of artist and spectator; and the artist's attempt to master his material, to conceive his subject, our attempts to get what the artist presents, are often toilsome and are often accompanied by fear that they may lead nowhere—or to some worse place. We may well wish to do away with the gap between means and ends, or always to possess guaranteed means, but in the first desire, we ask for Arcadia where not only the weary but everyone else can only be at rest, and in the second we demand only mechanical perfection. In the attempt to make "meaning" "perfectly" productive, he has made it "perfectly" mechanical. The perfect amalgamation of means and end destroys the active and desiring being in whose interest it has been invoked.

Throughout Dewey puts forward meaning as a value peculiarly present in art. In the means-end theory meaning has efficiency value, is a reference of means to their ends, and of ends to their means. But in many of his descriptions of its presence in a work of art, descriptions which retain the instrumental-consummatory value theory, it has an additional character; it is the presence in the work of art of preceding processes but it is also the presence of "character" and "distinction." In the following quotation the first version of meaning is stated, the second added: "consequences belong integrally to the conditions which produce them, *and* the latter possess *character and distinction*" [4] (italics not in text). It

3 *Loc. cit.*, pp. 366–367.
4 *Loc. cit.*, p. 371.

is on the notions of "character" and "distinction," the defined in perception, that Dewey builds what seems to me the important and brilliant account of the nature of art that gives *Art as Experience* much greater interest than his attempts to prove that esthetic value is pragmatic, indeed superpragmatic, value. In the following statement the values of meaning as imaginative grasp and as instrumental efficacy are both recognized, the latter as conditioning the former: "*It is marked out in perception, distinguished by* the efficacy of the conditions which have entered into it"[5] (italics not in text). In the following there is the suggestion that meaning realized is as such a value: "When appetite is perceived in its meanings . . . we live on the human plane, responding to things *in* their meanings."[6] In the following passage meanings are fruitions and also liberators of subsequent action, but even as instruments of further action what they fruitfully create is "more meanings and more perceptions."

To be conscious of meanings or to have an idea, marks a fruition, an enjoyed or suffered arrest of the flux of events. But there are all kinds of ways of perceiving meanings, all kinds of ideas. Meaning may be determined in terms of consequences hastily snatched at and torn loose from their connections; then is prevented the formation of wider and more enduring ideas. Or, we may be aware of meanings, may achieve ideas, that unite wide and enduring scope with richness of distinctions. The latter sort of consciousness is more than a passing and superficial consummation or end; it takes up into itself meanings covering stretches of existence wrought into consistency. It marks the conclusion of long continued endeavor, of patient and indefatigable search and test. The idea is, in short, art and a work of art. As a work of art, it directly liberates subsequent action and makes it more fruitful in a creation of more meanings and more perceptions. [*Loc. cit.*, p. 371.]

Dewey has a habit of incorporating into a challenging statement something that blunts our objections if it does not exactly silence them. As in the above, meaning is important instrumentally *but* as instrumental toward more meaning and more perceptions, so in the following the means in the work of art are ends, *but* "in their present stage of realization." "The brick, stone, wood and mortar are means only as the end-in-view is actually incarnate in them, in forming them. Literally, they *are* the end in view in its present stage of realization."[7] In the phrases "in forming them," "in their present stage of realization," we have implications that deliberate action is what we know it as,—effort toward no guaranteed end, by means that are not part of the end. When Dewey views means as really ends, he moves us into a world in which our state of bliss would be that of Browning's duchess who "liked whate'er she looked

---

[5] *Loc. cit.*, p. 371.
[6] *Loc. cit.*, pp. 370–371.
[7] *Loc. cit.*, pp. 373–374.

at, and her looks went everywhere.'' In such a world it is not so much that effort may cease as that effort is quite out of place. But at moments Dewey can forget this version of perfection and fully acknowledge that there are present even in a work of art the usual conditions of human effort; in the creation of a work of art "the integration is progressive and experimental, not momentarily accomplished. Thus every creative effort is temporal, subject to risk and deflection.''[8] Contrast with the statement previously quoted: "Every process of free art proves that the difference between means and end is analytic, formal, not material and chronological.''[9]

Whenever he relaxes his hold on the notion of art as reconciliation of the instrumental and the consummatory, the question for Dewey becomes not what formula shall transform life into art, but just what art does to life when it enters into it. The means-end formula haunts the background of the argument, but the concern is to discover, to lay hold on and display the substance of art, to find a way through the treacherous terminology of esthetic theory to a specific theory of art. His conviction remains the same: any degree or form of distinction between means and end is to be done away with—but its connection with the esthetic theory developed is formal. Present verbally the old words stand in a new light. Art perfects life, it makes for life; experience that is *an* experience always has the qualities of art. Even in these ambiguous statements we glimpse for art freedom from the rigid means-end test. In his contributions to the journal of the Barnes Foundation and in *Art as Experience,* Dewey examines art with an enthusiasm and a discernment that should put new life into esthetic discussion. On some of the perennial issues of art theory and of art criticism (substance and form, art and morality, art and propaganda), he speaks with a mastery of the nature of the underlying confusions of thought and with a lucidity that should make it possible to bury these long-dead bones of contention.[10]

E. A. SHEARER.

SMITH COLLEGE.

[8] *Loc. cit.,* p. 376.
[9] *Loc. cit.,* p. 374.
[10] To be continued in next issue, No. 24.

VOL. XXXII, No. 24   NOVEMBER 21, 1935

DEWEY'S ESTHETIC THEORY. II[1]

THE PRESENT THEORY

IN *Art as Experience* Dewey's present esthetic theory comes to full expression. There are effective side attacks, adding impetus to the main argument, on all the obscurantist tenets that have gathered round such central issues as substance and form, art and morality,—in its modern dress, art and propaganda. When in full swing the argument is a direct and confident account of art as that in which sensuous experience grows into its full possibilities. The determination that art shall not break away from the rest of life animates the early illustrations of life as art when life is fully itself, and some of the statements on the naturalistic basis of art. Art soon becomes important enough to make unnecessary all such precautions.

The naturalistic basis of art is one of the topics fully developed in *Art as Experience* and the chief theme in the papers in the *Journal of the Barnes Foundation*. At times a conventionally natural-

---

[1] Continued from preceding issue, No. 23.

istic interpretation, invoking familiar analogies between bodily activities and esthetic experience, it becomes, especially in the careful descriptions and analyses of *Art as Experience*, an erection on the biological basis of the human superstructure—or rather an account of how bodily experiences develop their full possibilities. A naturalistic statement of the usual type is in a paper in the *Journal of the Barnes Foundation*, Vol. II, No. 2:

> From the psychological standpoint, this integration in pictures means that a correlative integration is effected in the total set of organic responses; eye-activities arouse allied muscular activities which in turn not merely harmonize with and support eye activities, but which in turn evoke further experiences of light and color, and so on. Moreover as in every adequate union of sensory and motor actions, the background of visceral, circulatory, respiratory functions is also consonantly called into action. In other words integration in the object permits and secures a corresponding integration in organic activities. Hence, the peculiar well-being and rest in excitation, vitality in peace, which is characteristic of aesthetic enjoyment. In pictures that may happen to obtain celebrity for a time, some factor is overaccentuated—so while vision is captured and impressed for the moment, the final reaction is partial and one-sided, a fatiguing demand is made upon some organic activities which are not duly nourished and reinforced by the others. Thus it is not too much to say that the statement of an objective criterion of value in paintings set forth for the first time by Mr. Barnes will make possible in time an adequate psychological, even physiological, analysis of aesthetic responses in spectators, so that the appreciation of paintings will no longer be a matter of private, absolute tastes. . . . Only when an organism shares in the ordered relations of its environment does it secure the stability essential to living. And when the participation comes after a phase of disruption and conflict, it bears within itself the germs of a consummation akin to the esthetic. [Pp. 7–8.]

These broad parallels between bodily performances and esthetic experiences are vague and fanciful, the biological terminology may produce the illusion of "scientific" evidence. They do little more than remind us of the relationship between body and mind, which is not in dispute; the nature of the relationship is too much in dispute to be the ready source of esthetic data. Esthetic theory has seized many opportunities to consort with physical science; understanding of art does not seem, however, to have profited much from the many biological excursions that have been made in its interest. To assert a correspondence between bodily integration, tension, equilibrium, rhythm, and these as present in a work of art, is to allege one does not know exactly what. Even when as often the analogies relied upon are brilliantly and subtly enforced, that they reveal underlying identities or interpretative parallels can be conceded only as a play of fancy. Balance, tension, strain, relaxation, symmetry, integration, unity are neutral concepts that acquire special meanings in each of their many fields of application. The unity, the tension of a drama, is not the unity, the tension of an organism. There is no such serious denial as Dewey attacks that life has continuity, is all of a piece, that these concepts are generally applicable and generally applied is a mark of the unity of Life; they serve as preliminary descriptions at all levels of experience. It is, however, what they come to mean in particular applications that interprets and defines the differences within the unity of Life.

Such passages as the following play upon the more general analogies that have been a frequent substitute for philosophy of art:

Indeed it may be questioned whether any scientific system extant, save perhaps those of mathematics, equal artistic structure in integrity, subtlety and scope, while the latter are evidently more readily and vividly understood and are the source of a more widespread and direct satisfaction. Probably a time will come when it will be universally recognized that the differences between coherent logical schemes and artistic structure in poetry, music and the plastic arts are technical and specialized rather than deepseated. [*Journal of the Barnes Foundation*, Vol. II, No. 2, pp. 5–6.]

This is in the temper of the many discourses on the poetry of mathematics and the mathematics of poetry.

Variants on the theme recur throughout *Art as Experience;* it fades out whenever Dewey deals directly with poetry, music, and the plastic arts. Starting and ending with "sense," with seeing and hearing, he interprets its language. He discloses how there comes into life meaning, definition, distinction, individuality. He describes these not as built upon sense or as symbolized by sense, but as present in fully operative sense.

Since there has been little done in what Dewey here accomplishes, and since his account of the meaning of sense almost compels understanding and assent, much quotation will be necessary. Anything short of the full text is a poor substitute. What he makes evident is how sensations gather to themselves, condense upon themselves, an increasing meaning. In ordinary experience the qualitative and varyingly intense and rich character of sense, of sound and sight, is esthetic in character, if not in the high degree that we connect with art, or with experience that is highly imaginative though unrecorded in art. By extension of the range of reference of sensation, references found in sense and not through sense, by the consequent possibilities of organization, there is built the world of the higher imagination, the world of individual things enjoyed as such,—a world that depends on the imaginative power at work in each of us, and that is extended by every new artistic creation. The varied meanings of the word "sense" suggest, Dewey thinks, what our past experience accumulates within sense experience.

"Sense" covers a wide range of contents; the sensory, the sensational, the sensitive, the sensible, and the sentimental, along with the sensuous. It includes almost everything from bare physical and emotional shock to *sense itself*

—that is *the meaning of things* present in immediate experience. Each term refers to some real phase and aspect of the life of an organic creature as life occurs through sense organs. But *sense, as meaning so directly embodied in experience as to be its own illuminated meaning*, is the only signification that expresses the function of sense organs when they are carried to full realization. [P. 22. Italics not in text.][2]

It is thus that the varied wonder and splendor of this world are made actual for man in the qualities he realizes. The meaning of things present in immediate experience is not to be had in a glance or in mere recognition.

When a flash of lightning illumines a dark landscape, there is a momentary recognition of objects. But the recognition is not itself a mere point in time. It is the focal culmination of long, slow processes of maturation. . . . Mere recognitions occur only when we are occupied with something else than the object or person recognized. It marks either an interruption or else an attempt to use what is recognized as a means for something else. To see, to perceive is more than to recognize. It does not identify something present in terms of a past disconnected with it. The past is carried into the present so as to expand and deepen the content of the latter. . . . Identification nods and passes on. Or it defines a passing moment in isolation, it marks a dead spot in experience that is merely filled in. The extent to which the process of living in any day or hour is reduced to labelling situations, events, and objects as ''so-and-so'' marks the cessation of a life that is a conscious experience. Continuities realized in an individual, discrete form are the essence of the latter. [Pp. 23–24.]

There are similar passages in Schopenhauer, and also in Croce when he is not read through the dust of a controversial version of idealism or with pre-judgment as to the meaning of his terms. It is the generalization of the impatience of artists and critics with the demand for or the praise of recognizability; they have been taken as saying that to see is not to recognize when for the most part they have been insisting that ''to see, to perceive, is more than to recognize.'' Bergson can be quoted to the same effect:

When we distinguish one man from another—it is not the individuality itself that the eye grasps, i.e., an entirely original harmony of forms and colors, but only one or two features that will make practical recognition easier. [Henri Bergson: *Laughter*, tr. by C. Brereton and F. Rothwell, p. 152.]

Or an extravagant passage to the same effect in Croce:

We do not intuitively possess more even of our intimate friend, who is with us every day and at all hours, than at most certain traits of physiognomy which enable us to distinguish him from others. [Benedetto Croce: *Æsthetic*, tr. by Douglas Ainslie, 2nd Ed., p. 10.]

The power of sense to evolve and to pool in each separate sense its general resources, to absorb meanings, is asserted briefly in the

[2] The page references throughout the remainder of this article are to *Art as Experience*, unless otherwise indicated.

following passages from the second chapter of *Art as Experience;* the richly developed proof comes much later in the book.

Art itself is the best proof of the existence of a realized and therefore realizable union of material and ideal. . . . There is no limit to the capacity of immediate sensuous experience to absorb into itself meanings and values that in and of themselves—that is in the abstract—would be designated ''ideal'' and ''spiritual.'' . . . One can discriminate rock from flimsy tissue paper by the surface alone, so completely have the resistances of touch and the solidities due to stresses of the entire muscular system been embodied in vision. The process does not stop with the incarnation of other sensory qualities that give depth of meaning to surface. Nothing that a man has ever reached by the highest flight of thought or penetrated by any probing insight is inherently such that it may not become the heart and core of sense. [Pp. 27, 29.]

Compare Croce, who has not, however, as has Dewey, seen how significant for esthetic theory is the embodiment in one sense of the qualities of other senses.

The belief that a picture yields only visual impressions is a curious illusion. The bloom on a cheek, the warmth of a youthful body, the sweetness and freshness of a fruit, the edge of a sharp knife, are not these, too, impressions obtainable from a picture? Are they visual? What would a picture mean to an imaginary man, lacking all or many of his senses, who should in an instant acquire the organ of sight along? [*Ibid.*, p. 18.]

The chapter in *Art and Experience* quoted from in the above paragraph is named, in reference to the famous passage from Keats, ''The Live Creature and 'etherial things.' '' It is perhaps Dewey's most stirring account of the vivifying incorporation of ''nature'' in esthetic experience, of the passage from ''sense'' as ''bare physical and emotional shock'' to ''sense itself, that is the meaning of things present in immediate experience.'' It is an exhilarating chapter in the feeling it gives of the potential values of life; for even if all forms of illuminated sense experience do not, as Dewey's illustrations might at times make us think, show us the delightful, yet heightened realization of the character and quality even of that in life which is not good in itself, is in itself a good. The sordid, the ugly, the tragic, effectively imaged in sense, may, Schopenhauer to the contrary, make the painfulness of life more seriously painful, but they make it life; anything imaginatively realized may be the source, to use Dewey's phrase of this chapter, of ''an experience that is *an* experience.''

How the sensuous matter of esthetic experience is wrought into the individualized objects that populate the world of imagination is most fully demonstrated in the central chapters of *Art as Experience,* the chapters on the common substance and on the special substance of the arts. In these chapters Dewey discusses the significance of the medium. He uses the term to designate the sense material of art as it is distributed among the various arts, to each art its own. Or rather, he puts it thus—an art is an art in its devotion to a special form of sense experience. Artists in the different fields of art concentrate on the special sense organ of their field, such as that of seeing or hearing, and by concentration make operative its full energies and possibilities. Within sense experience, "dumb" in its germinal state, man develops distinctions and character, meaning and expressiveness. Ordinary experience employs "sense" with such indifference as to which of the various senses or sense qualities is attended to that no *one* develops its full possibilities. In music the medium is sound as such, the full range of the sense of hearing; in other fields it is certain sense qualities, in painting, color, in architecture, to which sculpture is akin, "the (relatively) raw materials of nature and of the fundamental modes of natural energy" (this hardly provides a single sense or sense quality as the directly expressive medium). But whatever may be the chosen sensuous material of each of the arts, the artist can so concentrate on it as his image forming his expressive medium as to focus in it a unified and complete experience.

In ordinary perception we depend upon contribution from a variety of sources for our understanding of the meaning of what we are undergoing. The artistic use of a medium signifies that irrelevant aids are excluded and one sense quality is concentratedly and intensely used to do the work usually done loosely with the aid of many. [P. 201.]

Whether sensuous qualities are used as mediums casually or artistically what they convey is the meaning of experience otherwise merely lived. The theory at this point is a modern rendering of Hegel's interpretation of the purgation function of art, by which it brings home to the mind and imagination of man *what* he does actually feel: "by this means is brought before a man's intelligence what otherwise he merely *is*." Emotional discharge for Dewey is a necessary but not a sufficient condition of expression; "self-expression" and expression are not to be confused.

There are storms of passion that break through barriers and that sweep away whatever intervenes between a person and something he would destroy. There is activity, but not, from the standpoint of the one acting, expression . . . the enraged being is only raging, quite a different thing from *expressing* rage. . . . What is sometimes called an act of self-expression might better be termed one of self-exposure. . . . Our appetites know themselves when they are reflected in the mirror of art, and as they know themselves they are transfigured. [Pp. 61, 62, 77.]

Man does not express either himself or anything else in emotional displays or as his various tendencies pass immediately into or are obstructed in action. He expresses when, facing himself or anything else that inhabits the sensuous world, as everything does, he can find in the sense qualities definition, meaning, ''not just in the sense of physical outline but in the sense of expressing that quality which is one with the character of an object.'' Thus he expresses what would otherwise merely be. The artist can carry far forward the expressive powers of sense, for concentrating on his medium he can make it speak for itself more fully, and for all the senses.

In any ordinary visual perception we see by means of light; we distinguish by means of reflected and refracted colors: that is a truism. But in ordinary perceptions, this medium of color is mixed, adulterated. While we see, we also hear; we feel pressures, and heat or cold. In a painting, color renders the scene without these alloys and impurities. They are part of the dross that is squeezed out and left behind in an act of intensified expression. The medium becomes color alone, and since color must now carry the qualities of movement, touch, sound, etc., that are present physically on their own account in ordinary vision, the expressiveness and energy of color are enhanced. . . . [Again:] In art, the seeing or hearing that is dispersed and mixed in ordinary perceptions is concentrated until the peculiar office of the special medium operates with full energy, free from distraction. . . . Colors *are* the paintings; tones are the music. . . . Esthetic effects belong intrinsically to their medium; when another medium is substituted, we have a stunt rather than an object of art. . . . By temperament, perhaps by inclination and aspiration, we are all artists—up to a certain point. What is lacking is that which marks the artist in execution. For the artist has the power to seize upon a special kind of material and convert it into an authentic medium of expression. The rest of us require many channels and a mass of material to give expression to what we should like to say. Then the variety of agencies employed get in the way of one another and render expression turbid, while the sheer bulk of material employed makes it confused and awkward. The artist sticks to his chosen organ and its corresponding material, and thus the idea singly and concentratedly felt in terms of the medium comes through pure and clear. He plays the game intensely because strictly. . . . The true artist sees and feels in terms of his medium and the one who has learned to perceive esthetically emulates the operation. [Pp. 195–196, 197, 200.]

Thus is explained that happy absorption, so enviable to the layman, of the musician in sounds, of the artist in sights. Naturally sensitive to and confident in his special medium, the artist heightens, intensifies, enriches its significance. Used alone each sense is compelled toward its full possibilities; in ordinary life it falls far short of its full expressiveness, for leaning on the other senses it takes part in a relatively chaotic and dull expression; only in concentrated attention can it work its special and its full effects.

Dewey illustrates sense expressiveness chiefly from music, painting, and architecture. Literature might seem to deny that the special medium of the artist is a chosen sense or chosen sense quality, for it works with *all* the senses if especially with those of the eye and the ear. Is the answer that the poet has an inclusive genius which permits him the paradox of a distributed concentration? An easier answer is that his medium is *words,* but this would deny that an artist works in sensuous material not in conventional symbols; words are a method of summoning media, not in themselves a sensuous medium, except, importantly, as sounds—and words are not simply sounds. The poet's special skill with words may be his "technique," comparable to the painter's skill with paint or the musician's command of his instrument. It is in what we can do with words that, as Croce remarks, we all possess some measure of the necessary instrument of art,—technique. In his most direct account of literature as the development of a sense medium, Dewey conceives of its medium as sounds,—sounds that reverberate with their history. Words are like dice weighted as they fall upon our ears by the history of their use.

> Sounds, which are directly or as symbolized in print the medium [of literature] are not sounds as such, as in music, but sounds that have been subjected to transforming art before literature deals with them. Only exclamations and interjections retain their native aspect as sounds. The art of literature thus works with loaded dice; its material is charged with meanings they have absorbed through immemorial time. [P. 239.]

Besides the special powers that each art possesses in its special medium, each possesses the common substances of space and time. As necessarily present in all experience these will be present in art. Art manipulates space and time for its purposes, each art as it especially can. Beyond its power to make expressive the space and time it directly presents, art has a special power over space and time, in its here and now it can bring to a focus all space and all time. Dewey recalls our familiar experience that in some way in a work of art we lay hold on all there is. The following passage is one of many that evoke and characterize this over-tone of all important esthetic experience:

> We are accustomed to think of physical objects as having bounded edges; things like rocks, chairs, books, houses, trade, and science, with its efforts at precise measurement, have confirmed the belief. Then we unconsciously carry over this belief in the bounded character of all objects of experience, (a belief founded ultimately in the practical exigencies of our dealings with things) into our conception of experience itself. We suppose the experience has the same definite limits as the things with which it is concerned. But any experience, the most ordinary, has an indefinite total setting. Things, objects, are only focal points of a here and now in a whole that stretches out indefinitely . . . any experience becomes mystical in the degree in which the sense, the feeling, of the unlimited envelope becomes intense—as it may do in experience of an object of art. . . . Whether the scope of vision be vast or minute, we experience it as a part of a larger whole and inclusive whole, a part that now focuses our experience. . . . This sense of an including whole implicit in ordinary experience is rendered intense within the frame of a painting or poem. [Pp. 193–194.]

The analysis of the space and time material explicitly and centrally present in the work of art, the variety of treatment of time and volume by which the arts extend their range of expressiveness, Dewey works out in such detail that to do justice to it needs close study of the text. It is an amazingly subtle and vivid account of the expressive values of time and space, each on its own, and of the strange manner in which either of them may express the distinctive qualities of the other. Certain central statements will give a little of the substance and some of the quality of his thought.

In painting space certainly relates; it helps constitute form. But it is directly felt, sensed, as quality also. If it were not, a picture would be so full of holes as to disorganize perceptual experience. [P. 206.]

Has there ever been a more arresting reference to the necessary substance of all things—distinctive quality, to the substantial results of the "shaping spirit of imagination?" To continue the quotation:

Psychologists, until William James taught better, were accustomed to find only temporal quality in sounds, and some of them made even this a matter of intellectual relationship instead of a quality as distinctive as any other trait of sound. James showed that sounds were spatially voluminous as well—a fact which every musician had practically employed and exhibited whether he had theoretically formulated it or not. . . . Near and far, close and distant, are qualities of pregnant, often tragic import—that is, as they are experienced, not just stated by measurement in science. . . . In experience they are infinitely diversified and cannot be described, while in works of art they are *expressed*. For art is a selection of what is significant, with a rejection by the very same impulse of what is irrelevant, and thereby the significant is compressed and intensified. [Pp. 206–209.]

(Note the distinction between art and experience—art is not here simply a perfect experience.)

Without the arts, the experience of volumes, masses, figures, distances and directions of qualitative change would have remained rudimentary, something dimly apprehended and hardly capable of articulate communication. [P. 208.]

In this general connection he comments astutely on the difficulties for the artist of the overcrowded and overswift space and time conditions of modern life.

The bustle and ado of modern life render nicety of placing the feature most difficult for artists to achieve. Tempo is too rapid and incidents too crowded to permit of decisiveness—a defect found in architecture, drama, and fiction alike. The very profusion of materials and the mechanical force of activities get in the way of effective distribution. There is more of vehemence than of the intensity that is constituted by emphasis. [P. 212.]

On the general principles of the expressiveness of space and time he shows how especially certain recent paintings have got the better of the submergence of the distinctive in the haste and confusion of modern life.

As the artist, additionally to the common values of space and time, extracts from his medium its special values, he further creates out of the chaotic, the "brute flux of existence," realized occupants of space and time; he brings before us the nature of things, persons, events, indeed he gives them their nature. The materials of his medium are infinitely amenable, the artist constantly breaks down what had been thought to be stubbornly resistant, and so extends the bounds of expression. "The abiding struggle of art is thus to convert materials that are stammering or dumb in ordinary experience into eloquent media" (p. 229). Life thus takes on character. "Words attempt to convey the *nature* of things and events. Indeed it is through language that these have a nature over and above a brute flux of existence. That they can convey character, nature, not in abstract conceptual form, but as exhibited and operating in individuals is made evident in the novel and drama" (p. 243). Each medium elicits distinctions, character, in terms of its special energy, but no limitations can be assigned to the possibilities of any medium for art may break down barriers that had been supposed inherent.

Color does something characteristic in experience and sound something else; sounds of instruments something different from the sound of the human voice . . . the exact limits of the efficacy of any medium cannot be determined by any *a priori* rule. . . . The work of art exploits *its* medium to the uttermost—bearing in mind that material is not medium save when used as an organ of expression. [Pp. 226, 228.]

What each can do awaits the artistic event. The latter part of the chapter on the varied substance of the arts records many of the triumphs of each of the arts in its handling of its special medium.

The individuated, the characteristic, can be communicated, is the communicable. Submerged in the brute flux of existence we can not know nor tell what we are, what anything is. But in art we face things, and can face them in common.

It enables us to share vividly and deeply in meanings to which we had been dumb, or for which we had but the ear that permits what is said to pass through in transit to overt action. For communication is not announcing things, even if they are said with the emphasis of great sonority. . . . In being communicated, the conveyance of meaning gives body and definiteness to the experience of the one who utters as well as that of those who listen. [P. 244.]

Art is thus that which for Dewey can never claim too high a value; it is not merely the condition of, but the very fact of, human association in its pure form.

Men associate in many ways. But the only form of association that is truly human, and not a gregarious gathering for warmth and protection, or a mere device for efficiency in outer action, is the participation in meanings and goods that is effected by communication. The expressions that constitute art are communication in its pure and undefiled form. Art breaks through barriers that divide human beings, which are impermeable in ordinary association. [P. 244.]

A principle at work within art, the principle first signalized by Aristotle, is that of unity, that of integration. It is in the nature of the individual, the distinctive, to have unity. In high imaginative achievement, accumulated gains mutually contributory, part to part and as between part and whole, reach a pure completeness and inclusiveness. Life by its very nature creatively absorbs past into present; the imagination deliberately weaves and blends and fuses into wholes greater than those of the natural assimilations of life. In part sense absorbs that by which it grows through the play of lifelong associations; in part it is wrought by imaginative efforts into the shapes and forms within which it is transformed, within which it is the stuff of the quality and character of the world,—of life lived imaginatively, not merely suffered and endured. Here as elsewhere to integrate, to unify, is a creative method; for the artist as for the scientist, as for the man of action, new wholes are formed by the integration of the thereby augmented parts. How imaginative synthesis thus operates Dewey makes evident in some of the passages already quoted. He never loses hold of his conviction that art creates distinctive quality; it is as its distinctive quality pervades a work of art that it has for him the final, the authentic artistic unity. This is its animating spirit, the soul of which all structural processes are the body.

There is no name to be given it. As it enlivens and animates, it is the spirit of the work of art. It is its reality, when we feel the work of art to be real on its own account and not as a realistic exhibition. It is the idiom in which the particular work is composed and expressed, that which stamps it with individuality. It is the background which is more than spatial because it enters into and qualifies everything in the focus, everything distinguished as a part and member. [P. 193.]

The unity of a work of art is the pervasive presence in all its parts of the special quality, the distinctive character by which a work of art is such. Moreover, as we have seen, it is in the power of certain imaginative moments to have an almost literal universality, to condense within themselves the widest ranges of experiences. The most rare and serious of these moments focuses within itself all space and all time. We have here a familiar form of esthetic mysticism which may be taken as unintelligible or, as Dewey presents it, as explication of the furthest possibilities of concentrated experience. For him the unity of life is a central thesis. In his mood of finding life simply the same throughout he sees the unity of art as only more fully unity than unity elsewhere. But when he foregoes responsibility for all of life and devotes his attention to art, then it appears that imaginative synthesis produces not the concentration of fact in theory, not the amalgamation of means and ends, but integration to the end of art—individualism. Imaginative distinction and synthesis of parts brings about the felt presence of the same quality in all of them. Though like Croce he hesitates to help himself to the word which is "the mother of all confusions"—intuition —he must use it to designate the manner in which the imagination appropriates its objects, that sense of the whole in the part, of the whole sensed as such, by which it brings to us qualitative unity.

Not only must this quality be in all "parts," but it can only be felt, that is, immediately experienced. I am not trying to describe it, for it cannot be described nor even be *specifically* pointed at—since whatever is specified in a work of art is one of *its* differentiations. I am only trying to call attention to something that everyone can realize is present in his experience of work of art, but that is *so* thoroughly and pervasively present that it is taken for granted. "Intuition" has been used by philosophers to designate many things —some of which are suspicious characters. But the penetrating character that runs through all the parts of a work of art can only be emotionally "intuited." The different elements and specific qualities of a work of art blend and fuse in a way which physical things can not emulate. This fusion is the felt presence of the same qualitative unity in all of them. "Parts" are discriminated, not intuited. But without the intuited enveloping quality, parts are external to one another and mechanically related. . . . This is the qualitative "background" which is defined and made definitely conscious in particular objects and specified properties and qualities. . . . A work of art elicits and accentuates this quality of being a whole and of belonging to the larger, all-inclusive whole which is the universe in which we live. . . . This is the explanation of that feeling of exquisite intelligibility and clarity we have in the presence of an object that is experienced with esthetic intensity. [Pp. 192–195.]

Immediacy here is not bare immediacy; it holds in its hands the gains of the past and takes into itself the distant. It brings all that it can make relevant—and nothing can be merely denied relevance—into the character of the moment. This is not a matter of amalgamated means and end, of overleapt process, but of accumulated and cumulative achievement. It is that power by which sense can hold present before us what it has gathered within it through the past and present efforts of the imagination. At fortunate moments I can see and hear sounds and sights for all I can make them worth,—in so far as I have looked and listened in the past and in so far as in the present moment, I put all my energies in the service of eye and ear.

Early in *Art as Experience* Dewey makes shrewd use of a certain colloquialism to drive home his point that art is what all life should be. From the dreary stretches of ordinary life there may stand out a more lively experience; we exclaim "that's an experience that *was* an experience." Or we realize of an experience that it is "*an* experience." Thus we imply that it is only under certain conditions that experience is really experience—fully occurent, not abortive. These Dewey holds are the good moments of life. This notion of an experience that is *an* experience, proposed early in *Art as Experience,* he harks back to when he wishes to reassure himself that all life is art when life is fully itself, when life is good. The moments of life that we can grasp, can shape imaginatively, are the good moments in life. We can agree with Dewey that such moments have value, esthetic value, but we can not agree that they are therefore *the* good moments of life. These are moments that have form; we can live in them or recall them with satisfaction, for they are definite, individuated, not vague, characterless. An experience of this sort is good because imaginable, it can be realized not merely passively endured. And this will be so even when it is also a moment that calls for endurance. We can readily appreciate the character of such bad moments in life, *that* is the virtue of experiences that *are* experiences. It is our appreciation of their character that is good, not their character. This might be proposed as one of the possible elements of good in things evil, definitely evil. These are not dead spots in life, they have the distinctive quality of fully conscious life. That the imagination can lay hold on what it presents is surely the sufficient defense of tragic art, cutting beneath all attempts to distil from tragedy hedonistic values or those of warning or resignation.

Dewey's argument that experience that has form is good experience has undue force because one of the conditions of distinctive character—unity—has tended to be taken in esthetic theory and elsewhere as a value in itself, and also as peculiarly an artistic value. But unity, integration, structure are constructive within the "bad" and are, moreover, neutral as to the kind of values they bestow. Distinguished and related parts may produce and heighten any value,—the values of thought and action as well as of expression. Dewey himself shows how structure, unity, works within all experience. But his fear of disruption in life and the legend that unity, form, is peculiarly esthetic, supports his conviction that an experience that has unity is an esthetic experience, and that all such experiences therefore are in some general sense good. Whenever life has the distinct character that enables us to realize it imaginatively it is, he argues, good. What of a distinctive and vividly bitter experience? It is easy enough to get its flavor. It is good to get its character, but it is not good to get it. Failure to make this distinction is what prolongs the hedonistic view of art in simple or in sophisticated form. The most "knowing" face with artistic equanimity portraits of the ugly, paintings of the dismal,—tragedy, but they see them as overlaid with rich and rare esthetic pleasures. Dewey does not so beg the hedonistic question, but finding it good to lay hold imaginatively on life, he would take this as an opportunity for his always urgent perfectionism and account life thus vivified good. The confusion works from the other direction with those who would wish us to let the imagination dwell only on those forms of life that we would call good, would approve of, or would choose to experience. We can agree with Dewey that it is good for life to have character; when not a welter of meaningless detail, when it has coherent emphasis, life has the tang of quality; we may choose to be released even into disaster from the nameless miseries of monotony, of boredom. Something particularized—release from something we know not what—the moments in life that have, as it were naturally, the significant structure, the emphasis on the relevant with which the artist provides the work of art, are esthetically good. It is not that such moments are the best moments of life, but that they have esthetic value, and that is always a value, however absent other forms of value. How art increases the distinctive, the qualitative, in life (as it may whether life is "good" or "bad") is what Dewey demonstrates; art assists us to trace the various features of life and to know them for what they are. To quote the concluding sentence of Chapter III in *Art as Experience:*

An object is peculiarly and dominantly esthetic, yielding the enjoyment characteristic of esthetic perception, when the factors that determine anything which can be called *an* experience are lifted high above the threshold of perception and are made manifest for their own sake.

Dewey carries forward the interpretation of art that extends from Aristotle and, with an increasingly defined emphasis on the creative character of the imagination, through Hegel, Schopenhauer, and Nietzsche to Croce and Bergson. For all these thinkers art shapes fluid experience into form and helps us to realize it in its individual character; it makes what follows after follow on, what lies together hang together, and so gives character to scene and situation. That Dewey is in a tradition and helps to define that tradition is so much the better, for theory of art has often been too casual, too spontaneous, has lacked the force of a persistent development, and has led us down too many alluring blind alleys. His magnificent contribution is his unqualified acceptance of the sensuous material of art. He is unhampered by any inclination to lead us through it to something better. Others have told us that art helps us to see *by* sense or *through* sense; Dewey tells what art makes us see *in* sense. For him the naturalistic basis is not something to make the best of, but something to make the most of. Moreover, he so displays how sense develops its meaning as to seem to catch life as it comes into being, and to lay bare the creating process of its range of quality, of expressive character. His esthetic theory has many facets, and if the light from one at times obscures that from another, he illuminates the possibilities of sense with a steady light. He sets aside the trivial theories that would make art pleasure, or play, or wish fulfillment, as well as the equally trivial elevations of art into another world. For him art makes life better, but it does not make something better than life. Out of sense it builds "the mighty world of eye and ear."

E. A. SHEARER.

SMITH COLLEGE.

THE JOURNAL OF PHILOSOPHY

ART AS COGNITIVE EXPERIENCE

"THERE is no test that so surely reveals the one-sidedness of a philosophy as its treatment of art and esthetic experience."[1] The statement is John Dewey's; one might express a very common view by adding, "ironically enough," for no criticism is oftener made of Dewey's philosophy than that it is one-sided: so much does it tout the practical, the pragmatic, the scientific, the on-going, the utilitarian, the instrumental, that there is a shameful and, alas, characteristic neglect of "the last things," the ends, what is good in itself, culminations, conclusions, the forever joys, the beautiful things. In short, it would be said that by John Dewey's test John Dewey flunks.

No one could seriously deny that Dewey's great and abiding concern was with the problem of generalizing the processes of scientific investigation for the purposes of social intelligence, but only the superficial reader of his works could accuse him of lacking interest in matters of art and aesthetics. In *Experience and Nature*, in *Philosophy and Civilization*, there are important and extended discussions of aesthetic problems. In nearly everything he ever wrote appear passages dealing with the arts. And of course there is *Art As Experience*, certainly one of the half dozen central works in the huge Dewey corpus and one of the great books in twentieth-century aesthetics. Among recent philosophers of the first magnitude, indeed, only Santayana exceeds Dewey in attention paid aesthetic problems.

I

There are today at least two live questions—both of them very ancient indeed—concerning cognition and the arts. One is the question whether critical judgments of works of art are ever significantly meaningful and if so by what criteria they can be known to be true or false. The second is the question whether in any important sense and to any considerable extent the aesthetic experience has cognitive components, whether we learn from the arts, whether—as it has from of old been put—the artist is entertainer and pleaser merely, or something more too: teacher, clarifier, even

---

[1] *Art As Experience* (hereafter AAE), p. 274. *Experience and Nature* will be abbreviated E&N; *Philosophy and Civilization*, P&C.

revelator. It is this latter question or, more properly, cluster of questions, I wish here to raise again, and look to John Dewey for whatever help his writings can afford in making out an answer.

The matter would scarcely be worth bothering about if Dewey's treatment of the problems were as pat, as cavalier, as neatly simple and all-disposing as it must be supposed to be when, as so often happens, Dewey is lumped with the crasser positivists, the simpler-minded of the semanticists, and the hairy-eared worshippers of Scientism. Indeed Dewey's position is very difficult to understand and to state, partly because, no doubt, it is not altogether clear, unambiguous, and free from contradiction, but partly because the problems are so complex as scarcely to admit of off-hand solutions.

Choose to put the question, "Is art a form of *knowledge?*" or "Is the value of aesthetic experience some kind of *truth* value?" and Dewey says "No" to you. For in his system and indeed in the pragmatic tradition generally, "knowledge" and "truth" get defined within a context whose ruling assumption is that the truth-seeker and knowledge-provider *par excellence* is the experimental scientist. Like Plato, Dewey became deeply involved in the distinction between true opinion and knowledge. Dewey does not spend much time in concern with "successful working" itself; he is little interested in the nature of keys and solutions in isolation, in what just happens to correspond or work out. But he is fascinated with the problem of capturing the essence of those means which dependably *lead* to workings and solutions. This it is that gives him his definitions. Knowledge is the sort of help for solving problems you gain by conducting your investigation in this and this manner: consider Newton. Truth is what you gain a right to assert by proceeding with your inquiry in this and this fashion: observe Darwin. Ask about what a man may just happen to "know" or about the "truths" that may dwell with him unawares, and you are likely to be answered, perhaps even a little impatiently, "Oh, all right, if you want to use the words that way, but. . . ." And then we're right back: for a concrete from which to abstract a good sound meaning for "truth" and "knowledge," consider the methods of the scientist.

With this in mind it is easy to understand the kind of answer made to Suzanne Langer when she tried to establish a symbolic mode coördinate with the one employed by the empirical scientist, another way of getting truth, a way, for instance, used by the musician. The answer is, in effect: "Why all this concern to justify art by torturing the words 'knowledge' and 'truth' so that they might be made applicable to the aesthetic domain? What an exaggeration of the importance of these values; as if there were not plenty of other ways of justifying art!''[2]   The reply is in the spirit of Dewey.

Given this much, there are those who want to dispose of the matter with admirable neatness, for instance by saying that we can divide off the cognitive from the emotive, and *everybody* knows that art works are expressive of emotion, and so on.   Now this, I want to say, is not Dewey's line at all. Perhaps it will not be utterly misleading to put it this way: Dewey chooses to appropriate "truth" and "knowledge" for use in describing a certain problem-solving procedure exemplified by the empirical sciences, but he does not thereby give away the whole cognitive show.   No, there remains for art a function far more complex, far more important, far more closely related to man's quest for a satisfying, understanding relation to his social and material world than is assigned it by a philosophy which rushes to the emotive-cognitive bifurcation.   Dewey does not take that tone of condescension toward the artist or the lover of art which says, almost: Now do quit thinking of art as saying anything, as having meaning, as affording insight; art is simply—but, don't you see, this is very much indeed—entertainment.

Dewey's presumed negative to certain bald questions about art as truth and knowledge must now be qualified by the addition that those are not quite the right questions, or that at least they are not put in the proper way.   Ask if art has, frequently and importantly, a meaning, and ideational content, a thoughtful basis, a communicative function, and the answer is a decisive and vigorous "Yes."   This needs to be made out in some detail.

In a general way, the aesthetic experience is an arrival, a culmination, a consummation; whereas inquiry is a departure, a struggle, a search.   But just about here the ice gets very thin: we must not, Dewey repeatedly warns, harden this into a full-fledged distinction between means and ends, intrinsic and extrinsic values.   The ways and means of science have their elegancies and their delights, and art is not just for itself, but has its instrumentality, its usefulness.

There are of course the obvious senses in which an architectural work has its utilitarian function and in which any work of art as a physical object is an instrument for the evocation of a richly qualitative experience in the prepared beholder.   But in addition art at its best consists of acts

---

2 See Ernest Nagel's review of *Philosophy in a New Key*, this JOURNAL, Vol. XL (1943), pp. 323–329.

that directly refresh and enlarge the spirit and that are instrumental to the production of new objects and dispositions which are in turn productive of further refinements and replenishments. Frequently moralists make the acts *they* find excellent or virtuous wholly final, and treat art and affection as mere means. Estheticians reverse the performance, and see in good *acts* means to an ulterior external happiness, while esthetic appreciation is called a good in itself, or that strange thing an end in itself. But on both sides it is true that in being preëminently fructifying the things designated means are immediate satisfactions. They are their own excuse for being just because they are charged with an office in quickening apprehension, enlarging the horizon of vision, refining discrimination, creating standards of appreciation which are confirmed and deepened by further experiences. It would almost seem when their non-instrumental character is insisted upon as if what was meant were an indefinitely expansive and radiating instrumental efficacy. [E&N, pp. 365–366.]

Art must not be called useless, then, but neither can it properly be said to be thoughtless, extra-logical, or meaningless.

We are aware that thinking consists in ordering a variety of meanings so that they move to a conclusion that all support and in which all are summed up and conserved. What we perhaps are less cognizant of is that this organization of energies to move cumulatively to a terminal whole in which the values of all means and media are incorporated is the essence of fine art. [AAE, p. 172.]

Only the psychology that has separated things which in reality belong together holds that scientists and philosophers think while poets and painters follow their feelings. In both, and to the same extent in the degree in which they are of comparable rank, there is emotionalized thinking, and there are feelings whose substance consists of appreciated meanings of ideas. . . . Thinking directly in terms of colors, tones, images, is a different operation technically from thinking in words (i.e., presumably, scientific symbols). But only superstition will hold that, because the meaning of paintings and symphonies cannot be translated into words, or that of poetry into prose, therefore thought is monopolized by the latter. If all meanings could be adequately expressed by words, the arts of painting and music would not exist. [AAE, pp. 73–74.]

Construction that is artistic is as much a case of genuine thought as that expressed in scientific and philosophical matters, and so is all genuine esthetic appreciation of art, since the latter must in some way, to be vital, retrace the course of the creative process. [P&C, p. 116.]

Dewey regrets the restrictive quality of logical theory as damaging both to logic and to that which comes to be denigrated as extra-logical.

. . . The neglect of qualitative objects and considerations leaves thought in certain subjects without any logical status and control. In esthetic matters, in morals and politics, the effect of this neglect is either to deny (implicitly at least) that they have logical foundation or else, in order to bring them under received logical categories, to evacuate them of their distinctive meaning. . . . [P&C, p. 95.]

So far from being non-logical, a work of art is, in its exhibition of the unifying pervasiveness of a quality, a virtually perfect instance of that coherence which is or should be the major concern of logic.[3] It is perfectly proper, Dewey tells us, to speak not only of the logic of the work of art as a product, but of the logic of art as a process, creative and appreciative.[4]

It is only a blinding prejudice that keeps us supposing that ideas, intellectual ideas if you like, are not qualitatively felt. "Certain trains of ideas . . . are beautiful or elegant." "Different ideas have their different 'feels', their immediate qualitative aspects, just as much as anything else" (AAE, p. 120).

Dewey here, of course, is suggesting the aesthetic characteristic of intellectual experience, the other side of his point about the logic of the artistic; but it is important to notice at the same time what an important place *felt* ideas have in poetry. T. S. Eliot distinguishes poets according to this capacity.

Tennyson and Browning are poets, and they think; but they do not feel their thought as immediately as the odour of a rose. A thought to Donne was an experience; it modified his sensibility.[5]

When it comes to art as *meaningful* experience, not the most heavy-handed thumper of the poetic tub ever outdid Dewey in words of praise and recommendation. Art's chief usefulness lies in its catering to the "characteristic human need . . . for possession and appreciation of the meanings of things . . ." (E&N, p. 362). "The 'magic' of poetry . . . is precisely the revelation of meaning in the old effected by its presentation through the new" (E&N, p. 360). To be fully conscious of meanings, to have full perception, thoroughly to appreciate a situation—these are the very defining characteristics of that fruition experience which is called art. But what is this *meaning* that is assigned such an important function in art works? Briefly, things are meaningful, in Dewey's usage, when they hang together, cohere, exhibit internal and external relations. Things lack meaning just to the extent that they are isolated, unrelated, unintegrated:

> Things fall apart; the centre cannot hold;
> Mere anarchy is loosed upon the world. . . .

A chief job of the teacher is to promote awareness of *meanings* in this sense, not merely the meanings of words, but the meanings of experiences.

3 P&C, pp. 98–99.
4 P&C, pp. 102–103.
5 *Collected Essays*, "The Metaphysical Poets," p. 247.

It is the nature of an experience to have implications which go far beyond what is at first consciously noted in it. Bringing these connections or implications to consciousness enhances the meaning of the experience.[6]

But this is an important and often noticed characteristic of prized works of art, that they are inexhaustible, that new connections and implications forever open up within them and between them and other aspects of life. Thus the experience that gets called "art" is the vividly and richly unified experience, the one in which parts are distinguishable but not separable; it is the kind of experience which most impressively exhibits the quality of meaningfulness.

It must be said that this ascription of meaning to art does not entail a complete breakdown of the distinction between art and science, though Dewey is sometimes guilty of employing so much vigor in his attack on a conventionalized distinction as to overlook differentiating characteristics. Science employs its symbols for purposes of direction and largely withdraws from the concrete embodiment of the qualitative fruition which is the destination. *This kind* of meaning art works do not possess in any predominant degree. But if the characterization of art as without meaning is intended to isolate the aesthetic from all other modes of experiencing—that is, to deny to art any important role of symbolizing, signifying, representing, describing, interpreting—then the charge needs to be refuted. In fact the unique quality of art may be said to be "that of clarifying and concentrating meanings contained in scattered and weakened ways in the material of other experiences" (AAE, p. 84). The assignment of *quality* and *sensuousness* to art and of *meaning* and *ideas* to science and logic will perhaps do no harm so long as it is kept firmly in mind that the distinction is "secondary and methodological" (AAE, p. 259).

By clarifying and concentrating and embodying meanings, art is an important means of communication between art and man. This is not to side with Tolstoy against Véron, to be a "communicationist" instead of an "expressionist." The intent of the artist is not the point. In expressing himself the artist uses a medium—it is not too much to say a language—and thus makes accessible to others a new-formed (not merely a new-fangled) experience. This is communication.[7]

Communication is the process of creating participation, of making common what has been isolated and singular. . . . Men associate in many ways. But

[6] *Democracy and Education*, p. 255. See also E&N, p. 371. On art as perception seee AAE, pp. 176, 243.

[7] AAE, pp. 106, 104.

the only form of association that is truly human . . . is the participation in meanings and goods that is effected by communication. The expressions that constitute art are communication in its pure and undefiled form. [AAE, p. 244.]

Art, in being "the most universal form of language, . . . is the most universal and freest form of communication" (AAE, p. 270). We are all to some extent devitalized, immobilized, isolated persons. We "search for the great community" and are lost. For battering at the stupid walls which hem us in no instrument does so well as art. "The function of art has always been to break through the crust of conventionalized and routine consciousness." [8]

Art, Dewey has written, is a great educator,[9] a freshener, an explorer of possibility,[10] a mode of prediction not found in charts.[11] It has the closest affinity with intelligence [12]; in Dewey's system, that is the supreme compliment. And yet we do well to shy away from "intellectualistic" theories of aesthetics. Too much are they prone to set art up in rivalry to science, to reveal thus their hatred and misunderstanding of the whole scientific enterprise: hence the bad name "scientism." Too much are they likely to damage the aesthetic experience itself by encouraging a "message-hunting" spirit. And too much are they likely to isolate one strand of the aesthetic in forgetfulness of the rest.[13] But neither is Dewey an "emotivist." [14] Nor a "positivist" insofar as that term suggests a reduction of art to the "pleasuring of an idle moment" (AAE, p. 348).

Very often indeed disputes about the relation of Art to Truth do little more than to expose attitudes in opposition, two cheering sections. One says into its megaphones: Art *is* Truth! From Art alone, true Knowledge. And, in all the din, what comes out is: Hurray for Art. Go! Go! Go! Then from across the way, the words are: Art has nothing to do with cognition. This turns out to be: Hold that line!

Dewey, I have tried to say, chooses to restrict the words "truth" and "knowledge" to scientific-type inquiry. One may question the wisdom of this restriction but cannot properly infer from it any attitude of opposition or condescension to art or artist.

---

8 *The Public and Its Problems*, p. 183.

9 P&C, p. 125; AAE, p. 347.

10 AAE, p. 242. On this topic see also Dorothy Walsh, "The Cognitive Content of Art," *Philosophical Review*, Vol. LII (Sept. 1943), pp. 433–451.

11 AAE, pp. 348–349.

12 AAE, pp. 38, 172, 44; E&N, p. 378; P&C, p. 120.

13 AAE, p. 290.

14 AAE, chapter IV.

Quite to the contrary, it is perhaps no bad summary to say of Dewey, what cannot be said of all exponents of a "scientific" kind of philosophy, that he takes art seriously.

JAMES L. JARRETT

UNIVERSITY OF UTAH

Section V

MIND, MEANING, AND LOGIC

VOL. XI. No. 19. SEPTEMBER 10, 1914

THE JOURNAL OF PHILOSOPHY
PSYCHOLOGY AND SCIENTIFIC METHODS

PSYCHOLOGICAL DOCTRINE AND PHILOSOPHICAL TEACHING[1]

ABSTRACT methodology has long seemed to me the dreariest field among all the territories, waste and fertile, occupied by philosophy. That philosophy—which, in the last analysis, means some philosopher—should, by means of a general philosophical position, attempt to catalogue the various provinces in the domain of learning, to set forth their respective boundaries, to locate their capital cities and fix their proper jurisdictions, appears to me an undertaking more likely to reveal the limitations of the philosopher's experience, interests, and intelligence than to throw light upon the subject. In discussing the relations of philosophy and psychology, I therefore disavow any attempt to pass upon what psychology must be or ought to be; I am content that psychology should be whatever competent investigators in that field *make* it to be in the successful pursuit of their inquiries. But a teacher and student of philosophy is within his scope when he reflects upon what philosophy in its own past has done in fixing the standpoints, ruling conceptions, and procedures of present psychology, and in raising questions as to the after-effects of this influence—its bearing, namely, upon present philosophical study and teaching.

From this point of view, I say without more ado that, so far as I can observe, the larger part of the time and energy of teachers of philosophy is taken up in the discussion of problems which owe their existence—at least in the way in which they are currently formulated—to the influence of psychology. In its dominant conceptions and professed methods, this psychology is a survival of a philosophy which is daily becoming more incredible and more irrelevant to our present intellectual and social situation. Grant that philosophy has no more to do, intrinsically, with psychology than it has with any other positive science, the fact remains that philosophy is neither taught nor studied, neither written nor read, by discarnate logical essences, but by human beings whose intellectual interests, problems, and attitudes,

---

[1] A paper prepared for the joint discussion of the American Philosophical and Psychological Associations, on the Standpoint and Method of Psychology, New Haven, December 30, 1913.

to say nothing of their vocabulary, are determined by what they already know or think they know in cognate fields. Let a man be as persuaded as you please that the relation between psychology and philosophy is lacking in any peculiar intimacy, and yet let him believe that psychology has for its subject-matter a field antithetical to that of the physical sciences, and his problems are henceforth the problems of adjusting the two opposed subject-matters: the problems of how one such field can know or be truly known by another; of the bearing of the principles of substantiality and causality within and between the two fields. Or let him be persuaded that the antithesis is an unreal one, and yet let his students come to him with beliefs about consciousness and internal observation, the existence of sensations, images, and emotions as states of pure consciousness, the independence of the organs of action in both observation and movement from "consciousness" (since the organs are physical), and he will still be obliged to discuss the type of epistemological and metaphysical problems that inevitably follow from such beliefs. The beliefs do not cease to operate as intellectual habits because one gravely hangs the sign "philosophy" over the shop whence one dispenses one's philosophical wares.

More specifically: The student of philosophy comes to his philosophical work with a firmly established belief in the existence of two distinct realms of existence, one purely physical and the other purely psychical. The belief is established not as speculative, not as a part of or incident to the philosophy he is about to study, but because he has already studied two *sciences*. For every science at once assumes and guarantees the genuineness of its own appropriate subject-matter. *That* much of naïve realism even the later study of epistemology hardly succeeds in displacing.

Given this established "scientific" background, it does not require much reflection to effect a recognition of problems of peculiar difficulty. To formulate and deal with these difficulties, then, becomes the chief work of philosophical teaching and writing. If it is asked what are the nature and scope of these difficulties, the simplest way of answering is to point to the whole industry of "epistemology." There are many ways of formulating them with technical specificality, no one of which, however, is likely, within the limits of space I can afford, to receive general assent, even as a bare statement of difficulties. But I venture upon the following: The physical world is, by received conception, something with which we become acquainted by external observation and active experiment. But the true nature of perception and action, as means of knowing, is to be got at only by introspection, for they are, by received theory, purely mental or psychical. The organ, the instrument, and the method of knowing the external world thus fall within the internal world; it is psychology that tells us about them in telling us about sensations, images, and the various associated complexes that form the psychical apparatus of knowing. But now how can these psychical states, these phenomena of consciousness, get outside of themselves and even know that there is a "real" or "external" world at all, much less whether what is known in any particular case is the "real" object, or is a real object modified by a mental contribution or a mental translation, or whether the sensation or image, as the only object immediately "known," is not itself the real object? And yet since sense-perception, observation of things, and reflective inquiry about these things, are among the data that psychological introspection studies, how can it study them unless there are such things to study? In this simple dialectic situation one may find implicit the endless circle of *epistemological* realism and idealism in their many varieties. And, one may also search not in vain for traces of attempts to solve these same problems in philosophies that professedly are purely empirical and pragmatic.

Let me attempt, in the interests of clearness, another statement that is not quite so formal. The student of philosophy comes to his work having already learned that there is a separate psychic realm; that it is composed of its unique entities; that these are connected and compounded by their own unique principles, thereby building up their own characteristic systematizations; that the psychic entities are by nature in constant flux, transient and transitory, antithetical to abiding spatial things; that they are purely private; that they are open to internal inspection and to that only; that they constitute the whole scope of the "immediately" given and hence the things that are directly—non-inferentially—"known," and thus supply the sole certainties and the grounds of all other beliefs and knowings; that in spite of their transient and surface character, these psychic entities somehow form the self or ego, which, in turn, is identical with the mind or knower. The summary of the whole matter is that with states of consciousness and with them alone to be and to appear, to appear and to be certain, to be truly known, are equivalents.

Can any one, I ask, ponder these conceptions and not admit that they contain in germ (and in actively flourishing germ) the substance of the questions most acutely discussed in contemporary philosophy? If such be the case, then the statement that philosophy has no more connection with psychology than with any other science, expresses not a fact, but a revolution to be accomplished, a task to be undertaken. One has, I think, either to admit that his philosophizing is infected with psychology beyond all cure, or else challenge the prevailing conceptions about the province, scope, and procedure of psychology itself.

One who has already denied to himself the right to undertake in the name of philosophy the revision and reinterpretation of the work of a special science may well seem to be precluded from making any such challenge. In setting forth such a self-denying ordinance, I also made, however, the statement that a philosopher is within his scope when he looks in a science for survivals of past philosophies and reflects upon their worth in the light of subsequent advance in science and art. The right to undertake *such* a critical revision can be queried only by those who measure the worth of a philosophical problem by the number of centuries in which it has been unsuccessfully discussed.

There is, then, at least *prima-facie* ground for holding that the orthodox psychological tradition has not arisen within the actual pursuit of specific inquiries into matters of fact, but within the philosophies of Locke and Descartes, modified perhaps in some regards by the philosophy of Kant. With all due respect to the scientific findings of any group of inquiries, I can not find it in my heart to extend this disposition of acquiescence to the first tentative escapes from medieval science. I have not the time or the disposition herewith to prove that the notion of psychic states immediately given, forming the sole incontrovertible basis of "knowledge,"—*i. e.,* certainty—and having their own laws and systematizations, was bequeathed by seventeenth-century philosophy to psychology, instead of originating independently within psychology. That is another story, and yet a story whose materials are easily accessible to all. My present purpose is the more restricted one of pointing out that in so far as there are grounds for thinking that the traditional presuppositions of psychology were wished upon it by philosophy when it was as yet too immature to defend itself, a philosopher is within his own jurisdiction in submitting them to critical examination.

The prospects for success in such a critical undertaking are increased, if I mistake not, by the present situation within the science of psychology as that is actually carried on. On the one hand, there are many developments (as in clinical psychology, in animal, educational, and social psychology) that decline to lend themselves to the traditional rubrics; on the other hand, a certain discrepancy between the researches actually carried on by experimentalists and the language in which alone it is supposed to be proper to formulate them is worrying an increasing number of psychologists, and is increasingly seeming to impose upon them the restrictions of an irritating and cumbersome artificiality. If one went over the full output of the laboratories of the last five years, how much of that output would seem to call, on its own behalf and in its own specific terms, for formulation in the Cartesian-Lockean terms? Supposing the slate were cleared of historic traditions, what would be the natural way of stating the object, method, and results of the inquiries? When psychologists themselves are breaking away, in at least a considerable portion of their undertakings, from *exclusive* preoccupation with their inherited apparatus, the philosopher is not called upon to assume the whole burden of piety.

As a specific illustration, one may point to the change that will come over the spirit and tenor of philosophic discussion if the activities and methods of behaviorist psychologists grow at the expense of the introspectionist school. The change could hardly fail to be radical, as soon as there was a generation of teachers and students trained in the behaviorist point of view. It would be radical because the change effected would not be an affair of different ways of dealing with old problems, but of relegation of the problems to the attic in which are kept the relics of former intellectual bad taste.

Even a well-wisher (from the philosophic side), to the behaviorist movement must, however, express a certain fear and a certain hope. To sum them up in a single statement, it is possible to interpret the notion of "behavior" in a way that reflects interests and ideas that are appropriate only to the context of the type of psychology against which the behaviorist movement is professedly a protest. The limitation of behavior, for example, to the activities of the nervous system seems to me to express a by-product of the older problem of the relations of mind and body which, in turn, was an outcome of the notion of the mental (or psychical) as constituting a distinct realm of existence. Behavior, taken in its own terms and not as translated into the terms of some theoretical preconception, would seem to be as wide as the doings and sufferings of a human being. The distinction between routine and whimsical and intelligent—or aimful—behavior would seem to describe a genuine distinction in ways of behaving. To throw overboard "consciousness" as a realm of existences immediately given as private and open only to private inspection (or introspection) is one thing; to deny, on the basis of a behavior of the nervous system, the genuineness of the difference between conscious (or deliberate) behavior and impulsive and routine behavior is another thing. The obliteration of the conscious in its adjectival sense (as a quality of some types of response) because it is not discoverable by inspection of the operation of neurones or muscles seems to be the product of ways of thinking congenial only to a separation of physical and purposive action. And this separation would surely not arise if one *began* with behavior, for the separation implies an ascription of independent existence to the mental, on the basis of which alone some acts may be termed purely physical.

There is certainly every reason to think that the behavior of the nervous system is an important element in human behavior; there is reason to think that it is the crucial element in the mechanism of human behavior. But unless we start with behavior as more than physical, as meaning the sum total of life-attitudes and responses of a living being, and take these attitudes and responses at their face value, we shall never be able to discover the existence and importance of the nervous system as the mechanism of behavior. There must be genuine functions of which it is the operative mechanism, if it is to be identified as a mechanism.

Perhaps one example will make clearer what I am driving at. The psychology of immediately given conscious existence was compelled to treat meanings as simply aggregates of elementary states of consciousness, whose existence and aggregation as conscious things are open to immediate introspection. The behaviorist, in reaction from the artificiality and inadequacy of such a view, looks for some fact of ostensible, overt movement, that may be identified with thought, *i. e.*, meaning-functions. Quite naturally he fastens upon physical changes in the vocal apparatus. These movements open to objective detection and registration *are* what the other school had termed thought—consciousness as meanings, concepts, judgments, reasonings, or whatever. For my own part, I do not doubt that vocalization, including overt laryngeal changes, furnishes the mechanism of the greater part (possibly the whole) of thought-behavior. But to say that we can tell what speech or meaningful behavior *is* by examining this mechanism is putting the cart before the horse; the fact of speech behavior must be given as a primary fact before we can identify any particular set of structures as concerned in its exercise. The behavior standpoint means, unless it is sheared down in behalf of some unexpressed preconception, that speech is just what men *do* when they communicate with others or with themselves. Knowing the apparatus through which this doing is carried on, we doubtless know more about it than we should otherwise know; by this discovery we bring the doing under better control. But to say that physical movements, when the concrete empirical qualities of language are eliminated, *are* language is to begin by mutilating the facts. Exactly the same considerations apply to purposive behavior—that is, conscious behavior, the event from which ''consciousness'' is derived by making an adjective into a noun. Purposive behavior exists and is given as a fact of behavior; not as a psychical thing to be got at by introspection, nor as physical movement to be got at by physical instruments. It *is* and it *exists* as movements having specific qualities characteristic of them. We may distinguish between the movement and the quality, and thereby make a distinction between the physical and the mental. The distinction may serve to bring the performance of the function under greater control. But to ascribe independent complete existence to the movement, to say that *is* deliberate behavior, behavior having meaningful or conscious quality, is a fallacy of precisely the same kind as ascribing complete and independent existence to purpose as a merely psychical state. And it is a fallacy that flourishes only in an atmosphere already created by the belief in "consciousness"—just as the latter belief could hardly have arisen save in an atmosphere where all concrete behavior, all achievable action, was regarded as degraded and insignificant in comparison with religious contemplation that related men to a truly spiritual world, which was wholly extra-worldly, supernatural, and hence wholly nonphysical.

I am only suggesting a continuation of the same line of thought when I say that in so far as behaviorists tend to ignore the social qualities of behavior, they are perpetuating exactly the tradition against which they are nominally protesting. To conceive behavior exclusively in terms of the changes going on within an organism physically separate in space from other organisms is to continue that conception of mind which Professor Perry has well termed "subcutaneous." This conception is appropriate to the theory of the existence of a field or stream of consciousness that is private by its very nature; it is the essence of such a theory. But when one breaks loose from such a theory he is authorized to take behavior as he finds it; if he finds attitudes and responses toward others which can not be located under the skin, they still have the full claim to recognition.

The teacher of philosophy has, therefore, at the present time a deep concern with the way in which psychology is developing. In the degree in which he feels that current philosophy is entangled in epistemological questions that are artificial and that divert energy away from the logical and social fields in which the really vital opportunities for philosophy now lie, he will welcome every sign of the truning away by psychologists from subjective immediatism; every sign of a disposition to take a more objective, public, and out-door attitude. The future of the teaching of philosophy for the next generation seems to be intimately bound up with the crisis psychology is passing through. Anything that tends to make psychology a theory of human nature as it concretely exists and of human life as it is actually lived can be only an instrument of emancipation of philosophy.

JOHN DEWEY.

COLUMBIA UNIVERSITY.

THE JOURNAL OF PHILOSOPHY
PSYCHOLOGY AND SCIENTIFIC METHODS

CONCERNING ALLEGED IMMEDIATE KNOWLEDGE OF MIND

IN his suggestive book entitled *The Problem of Conduct*, Professor Taylor discusses mistakes as to one's own motives. He says, "It is a commonplace of ethics that the human heart is so utterly deceitful that we are constantly being deluded not only as to the motives of our fellows, but even as to our own. What more common, for instance, than the discovery that an action we believed ourselves to have performed from motives of magnanimity was really prompted by a desire to make ourselves a reputation?" In such cases "we have at first sight a puzzling psychological problem. . . . Surely, it may be argued, there can be no such thing as an unconscious motive; an emotion is, from the very nature of the case, just what it is at the time felt to be, nothing more and nothing less." In short, accepting the idea that motives are states of consciousness or feelings which are just what they are as states of consciousness, how is error possible as to what they are?

Professor Taylor imagines a case in which the influence of an emotion prompts a person to confer a benefit upon a fellow at some cost to himself, which he takes for an act of generosity. Later on, the same person finds himself *not* strongly prompted to perform a similar act under circumstances such that there is no chance for the beneficence being known. If the man is frank with himself, he will admit that his motive on the first occasion was not the feeling of pure generosity which he had supposed it to be. But how was error possible, the emotion being "just what it was felt as being; an unfelt emotion being a *contradictio in adjecto*"? The solution is that the "mistake came not in estimating the emotion, but in apprehending the circumstances necessary for its production."[1]

Students of ethical theory ought to be grateful to Professor Taylor for raising so definitely a question usually slurred over. I think his proposed solution makes the best of a bad job if one accepts his psychological premises, which are not so much his as the

---

[1] See Taylor, *Problem of Conduct*, pp. 98–99.

truisms of an introspective psychology; for ethical theory as to the nature of motives has been profoundly affected—in common with most other branches of ethical theorizing—by the terminology and notions of introspectionist psychology with its assumption of ideas, feelings, as just states of consciousness, whose nature is identical with their happening. We all recognize that meaning or nature is not all one with occurrence in the case of physical happenings, that it is something to be searched out with exceeding pains, utilizing all the knowledge we command. No one expects that the nature of infantile paralysis or of fire or gold will be open to the most careful *direct* inspection. One has, however, only to read Descartes to see that at the same time when this notion was first gaining ground as to physical existences, it was insisted that mental events, especially facts of something called consciousness, carry their whole character in their bare face or presence, so that about them immediate certainty remains not only possible, but inevitable. Clearly Mr. Taylor's difficulty is due to a translation of this doctrine into the ethical doctrine of motives. That motives are feelings (emotions, sentiments) and that feelings are of such a sort that they are known to be just as and what they are in their occurrence is of the essence of this translation.

Does not the conflict of this ethical rendering with the fact of difficulty in ascertaining one's own motive give good ground for questioning the psychological assumption on which it rests? Is Professor Taylor's solution successful? Just what does it imply? Its apparent implication is that we were not wrong in thinking we were animated by a motive or feeling of generosity. Our mistake was only in supposing that this emotion would be aroused by certain conditions, those of distress of another, when as matter of fact it is aroused by distress plus opportunity for the act to secure the attention of others. This, I say, is the apparent implication. For otherwise the feeling was not one of generosity at all, but only of love of notice or of praise. Then there was a mistake about the feeling itself —which is said to be a contradiction in terms.

But in escaping one difficulty is not a greater one raised? Can the feeling be said to be generosity when it can be excited only if the act it prompts is an object of favorable regard on the part of others? Is not this the most extreme ethical subjectivism, equaled, if equaled at all in history, only by the doctrine ascribed to Protagoras in the Platonic *Theœtetus?* Is it not the same as saying that if a man "feels" that his motive in committing what others would describe as an act of malicious revenge is one of lofty justice, all debate is closed? Such was his motive. The other alternative is that the "feeling as barely felt" has *no* character or nature; that to conceive it *as* generosity (or *as* love of praise) is identical with referring it to conditions of production and to the consequences which follow from it, a reference which is as difficult and as exposed to error as in the case of physical events.

I am questioning in short whether the distinction upon which Mr. Taylor relies, between "estimating an emotion" and "apprehending the circumstances necessary for its origin," is anything more than verbal. I do not see how any emotion can be estimated *except* in terms of its objective conditions or its objective consequences, preferably both. Is not to "feel" a feeling *as* generosity or greed or fear or anger all one with ascribing to it certain conditions of origin and of outcome? Before we raise the question as to whether I can be wrong about my own attitude, we must then consider the question as to whether we can be *either* right or wrong about it unless we view it in connection with the circumstances which evoke it and the consequences which flow from it.

For my own part, then, I can see no meaning in "estimating" an attitude of my own to be anger excepting that it is an attitude produced by an insult or an unexpected injury, and which leads, if unchecked, to certain violently destructive acts. (This, of course, is a very gross identification, quite too gross to be of scientific value, and is used only for purposes of illustration.) Unless this position can be successfully denied, there is a dangerous ambiguity in saying "an emotion is from the very nature of the case what it is at the time felt to be." It may mean the tautology that the *event* is just what it is, irrespective of whether or not we know or characterize it. Then it stands on exactly the level as any natural occurrence of which no notice is taken. Or it may mean that as matter of fact we take it—judge it, class it—to be such and such, whether it *is* so or not, just exactly as we take a certain moving twig to be a snake in spite of the fact that it *is* a twig. Only by compounding into one these two different facts—both facts, but different facts—does, I am persuaded, the notion arise that there states of consciousness or feelings exist which wear their hearts on their sleeves, so much so that the sleeve is the heart, and *vice versa.*

In other words, we come to exactly the position taken by Dr. Singer in criticizing a current assumption. "Did we start with an immediate fact of consciousness and construct a world? Then let us now begin with the world and construct a fact of consciousness." And again, "It takes all the science in the world to make out whether A is in love or whether B sees red."[2] And the context makes it clear that this holds even when A or B is one's self.

2 This JOURNAL, Vol. IX., pp. 16, 17.

One has, of course, only to extend this line of reasoning to be in the middle of the discussion of introspectionist *versus* behaviorist psychology. Says Watson, "One must believe that two hundred years from now, unless the introspection method is discarded, psychology will be still divided on the question as to whether auditory sensations have the quality of 'extension,' whether intensity is an attribute which can be applied to color, whether there is a difference in 'texture' between image and sensation; and upon many hundreds of others of like character."[3] And why not, if the meaning which any one of these questions may have is really a matter of the *connection* of one event with certain other events, events which either constitute the circumstances of its production or which are its results? To decide upon these connections is a matter of observation, but of observation of exactly the same sort as is used in arriving at a conclusion as to the nature of, say, typhoid fever, an observation which, instead of staring at what is directly present with the hope that the stare, if sufficiently intent, will disembowel the object, uses all the resources of what is already known about other things to uncover a specific connection between events. I am quite sure that some of the objections to behaviorism, at least in its general sense, would disappear if it were recognized by its critics that behavior is not an isolated thing—a muscle twitching—but concerns the connection of an organic event with circumstances necessary to its production and with other events which follow from it. It would then be clear, I think, that we do not first have a certain feeling or state of mind or consciousness complete in itself, generosity, fear, anger, or whatever, but that there is a certain (instinctive) reactive attitude which *when viewed* in its connections, in its relation to the situation in which it occurs and the specific consequences which flow from it, may be called emotion or sentiment or feeling of, say, generosity. I have employed the word "viewed" which might be thought to imply "consciousness," and I have admitted that a certain complex reference of an attitude to other things may properly be called a feeling or sentiment. This probably appears like a surrender of behaviorism. But I would point out that nothing more is here involved than is stated by Watson when he says: "The separate observation of 'states of consciousness' is, on this assumption, no more a part of the task of the psychologist than of the physicist. We might call this the return to a non-reflective and naïve use of consciousness. In this sense consciousness may be said to be the instrument or tool with which all scientists work."[4] That is to

[3] *Behavior,* p. 8.
[4] *Ibid.,* p. 27.

say, I am merely assuming that an *observation* takes place, and that its aim is to *understand*. When (or if) the psychologist wishes to observe and understand observation and understanding, he must take for his object a certain event studied in its context of other events—its specific stimulus and specific consequences. It may well be true that at present there are no methods by which one can determine at what points in the animal scale observation (in the sense defined) and understanding take place,[5] but the query as to their first manifestation would not be an inherently impossible, a meaningless one. "One can assume either the presence or absence of consciousness anywhere in the phylogenetic scale without affecting the problems of behavior one jot or one tittle." This is certainly true if we start with the introspectionist's conception of "consciousness." But if we start with observation and understanding as they are *used* in daily life and by the scientist, then of course the case stands differently. The problem is when and where a specific or differential type of behavior presents itself.

Now I take it that the observations of daily life differ from those of the laboratory chiefly in the coarseness or grossness of the former, due to lack of control of detailed conditions. This is not a reason for discarding the former; it is an argument for making them, as rapidly as possible, more refined and accurate. But men would never have arrived at a minute anatomy of man or of the nervous system if they had not started from the gross observation of these things. In fact, the objects of gross observation always persist as limiting conditions which give point and meaning to specific determinations. Just so I think the coarser observations of the non-laboratory psychologist about, say, observation and understanding as they display themselves in human life, may set very important problems to future experimentalists, suggest hypotheses and even determine the limits within which experiments may be fruitfully carried on. To be more specific, I take the recent discussion of "consciousness" by Bode.[6] I am not concerned about names. It makes little difference if such a discussion be called philosophy and the name psychology be reserved for laboratory findings. (I use the word "laboratory" loosely to mean all findings under conditions of great artificial control.) But it makes a good deal of difference whether the inquiry is intellectually legitimate, that is, whether it deals with genuine subject-matter. It may make a real scientific difference, in other words, whether the things called observation and understanding are identifiable with a type of behavior which con-

---

[5] Watson, *Ibid.*, p. 4.
[6] In the volume entitled *Creative Intelligence.*

trasts with merely impulsive and routine human behavior in that future things, things not yet having happened, operate as part of the stimulus in a present response: Bode's hypothesis roughly stated. For in time this identification may define the limits of an inquiry into behavior carried on under conditions of refined control. Meantime, the coarser observations into human conduct may serve to keep alive the sense that the naïve sense of "consciousness," that in which it is a tool of layman, physicist, and psychologist alike, is itself capable of being understood from a behavioristic point of view. And this also is a matter of scientific import. For it protects experimental behaviorists from a charge of wilfully denying the existence of certain facts (facts like those of observation and understanding as used by all scientific men) merely because their technique is not yet developed to the point of dealing with them. To recognize that the behavioristic principle can make a place for them is important. For science is, after all, carried on by men, and a seeming denial that such facts do exist and do come under the behavioristic principle is sure to keep alive in the minds of some a futile introspectionist method, by setting to one side a realm of facts to which (so it is thought) it *must* be applied since the behavioristic method confessedly does not apply.

However, this may not seem to justify the use of the words "feeling" and "sentiment," or the recognition of any distinctively *conscious* attitude. This may appear like a relapse into the "state of consciousness," psychology proving that one's behaviorism is hardly, after all, skin deep. So I conclude with pointing out in what sense such a term as sentiment may be applied to a specific type of angry behavior. Obviously *not* in the sense in which Taylor —in common with the usual tradition—uses the word, to indicate something which is, *per se* in its original self-enclosure, generosity or anger or whatever. In their *first* sense, such terms must denote strictly a way of reacting to particular stimuli, not anything which may be called a "feeling." But suppose that one of these behavioristic attitudes is connected with what precedes and issues from it in the way of behavior. Then a new fact may come into existence, or the old fact gain a new quality. To tell a child who is quite innocent of any feeling or sentiment, who is merely grabbing for something to put in his mouth, that he is selfish or greedy is to requalify a mode of response in this way. It is a way of telling him that he is *going* to act in a certain way and that his action when complete is *going* to call out a certain unfavorable attitude on the part of others. Now suppose the child carries over this way of observing and understanding his immediate attitude into his own attitude—

that is to say, next time as soon as he begins to react in this way he also acts to observe his act in its context of origin and consequence. Now this supervening of a new attitude toward a more primary attitude may constitute the old attitude into a motive or spring of action which in current terminology is an impulse or sentiment or feeling.

My suggestions or theses are, then, threefold. Negatively, there is no more reason for supposing that personal events have a nature or meaning which is one with their happening, and hence open to immediate infallible inspection, than is the case with impersonal events. In each case the event only sets a problem to knowledge, namely, the discovery of its connections. Secondly, it is desirable and possible that we should observe and understand observation and understanding and allied phenomena themselves. Such a study would be a study of "consciousness" in the naïve sense mentioned. Thirdly, such a study, with a recognition of "consciousness" in this sense, is quite compatible with a behavioristic standpoint, whether or no the technique exists at a given time for its successful accomplishment.

JOHN DEWEY.

COLUMBIA UNIVERSITY.

The Journal of Philosophy

KNOWLEDGE AND SPEECH REACTION

A NEW conception that is thorough-going always simplifies. In fact it usually originates when a prevailing point of view has got overloaded, cumbrous and involved. The notion of behavior is already having a simplifying and reducing effect upon epistemology and in my opinion is only beginning its career. But a new point of view also tends to oversimplify, to neglect, ignore and thereby in effect to deny. It is one thing, for example, to deny qualities, meanings, feelings, consciousness, *etc.*, as they have been defined by prior theories, especially by modern psychology with its helplessly subjective and private metaphysics. It is another thing to deny the facts which common sense and common speech independently of any theory call by these names. Personally, I believe that the identification of knowing and thinking with speech is wholly in the right direction. But, with one marked exception, I have not seen any analysis of speech which appears adequate or which does not lay itself open to the charge of omitting and virtually denying obvious facts.[1]

1. When it is asserted that speech as thought is a reaction, the question at once arises: What is its stimulus? The easy and simple reply is wrong. We are likely to say that speech is a reaction to a thing sensibly present, that, for example, I say "this is a knife" because a knife is sensibly present as a stimulus to speech. The behaviorist, of all persons, can not afford to give this account of the stimulus to speech. For if he does, he subjects himself to a final retort. The sensible presence of the knife is, then, already a case of knowledge, and speech instead of constituting knowledge merely voices, utters or reduplicates a knowledge already there in full existence. If the stimulus is not a thing sensibly present, neither is it merely some prior complete act or piece of behavior which causes contractions in the vocal organs. The utterances of a talking-machine

[1] The exception is the remarkably clear and comprehensive paper by Mead, in this JOURNAL, Vol. XIX, No. 6, on "A Behavioristic Account of the Significant Symbol."

are induced by an internal mechanism but they are not speech or knowledge; neither is a hiccough or groan or sigh, although it is caused in the vocal musculature by prior organic conditions.

There is a difference between the concept of stimulus-reaction and that of cause-effect. The former includes, of course, the latter, but it adds something. It has, in addition, the property of an adaptation, or maladaptation, which is effected. But adaptation alone is not enough to differentiate stimulus and response in the case of speech. A sigh may relieve suffering and in so far be adaptive. Seeing as an act may be part of the stimulus to saying "that is a knife," but it can not be the entire stimulus. For seeing as a complete stimulus gives rise to the response of reaching and taking or withdrawing, not of speech. What has to be accounted for is the postponement of the complete overt reaction, and its conversion into an intermediate vocal reaction. There must be some break in the seeing-reaching sequence, some obstacle to its occurrence, to induce a diversion from the hand to the voice. There must be a defective or hesitant connection between seeing and handling which is somehow made good and whole by speech. Hence the stimulus to speech can not be identified, *per simpliciter*, with its object. The latter is its consequence, not its antecedent.

2. Before fully developing the implications of this point we must turn to another phase of speech reaction. Not every speech reaction, even when genuine and not a mere vocalization, is a cognitive statement even by implication. Story-telling need not purport to state "facts" or "truths"; its interest may be increased by *vraisemblance*, but this trait serves a dramatic or imaginative end, not an intellectual one. A reader of Shakespeare may become a student of the sources upon which Shakespeare drew, and make speech reactions to this study. Then the reaction is cognitive. But he need not do so; he may be content to confine his speech reaction to a dramatic production. Again the reader may become interested in whether Shakespeare meant to represent Hamlet as mad; then his reaction is a judgment. But he may be satisfied merely to use speech as a means of re-creating a Hamlet either sane or mad; as a mode of story-telling or drama it makes no difference. There is no outside criterion till we go outside of mere story-telling. The play's the thing and it has no object of knowledge.

These remarks are intended to call attention to the need of discovering some differential trait of those speech reactions which do constitute knowledge. A story or play is there, and the re-enacting of it in a speech mode is purely additive. It makes another piece of behavior, but this new mode of behavior does not react back into the play or story or its conditions. It is complete on its own account. A play of Shakespeare may mean a hundred different things to a hundred different audiences or a hundred different persons in the same audience, and the diversity of the hundred speech reactions evoked is no matter. The speech reactions need have no connection with what Shakespeare himself meant in his reaction, beyond being caused by the latter. But a judgment or thought about what Shakespeare himself meant does not have any such self-sufficing independence. It has to link up with something outside itself. It has to be a reaction not merely to the play as a provocative cause, but has to be a response which somehow fits into or answers to the play as stimulus. Our problem is to name that distinctive feature of a speech reaction which confers upon it the quality of response, reply, answer; of supplying something lacking without it.

We thus return to our prior analysis. The statement "this is a knife" is cognitive because it is more than a mere evocation of a prior piece of behavior. It serves to supplement or complete a behavior which is incomplete or broken without it. As response it is reaction in another sense than when we say in physics: action and reaction are equal and in opposite direction. Some physical reactions are quite independent of that action to which they are reactions except in a casual sense. But a response in statement is intimately connected with that to which it answers. It is not merely to it or away from it, but is back *into* it: that is, it continues, develops, directs something defective without it. Without speech reaction the action which causes it is blind trial or error; with it, or rather through it, the evoking action becomes purposive, that is, continuous, cumulative. To be more specific the response "this is a knife" is produced by reactions of seeing and incipient reactions of reaching, touching, handling, which are up to the point of speech reaction fumbling, choked and conflicting. Speech reaction unifies them into the attitude of unhesitant readiness to seize and cut. It integrates or coordinates behavior tendencies which without it are uncertain and more or less antagonistic. This trait is the differentia of judgment from speech reaction in the form of story telling and vicarious dramatic reproduction. Unless we acknowledge and emphasize this trait, the behavioristic theory falls an easy victim to the contention that language merely echoes or puts into verbal form an apprehension that is complete without it. The dilemma is unescapable. Either the speech reaction does something to what calls it out, modifying it and giving it a behavior characteristic which it otherwise does not have, or it is mere utterance of what already exists apart from it.

This fact throws light upon the oversimplification referred to at the outset. It is easy to overlook the modifying, re-directive and integrative function of speech as a response. Then only one side of it is recognized, that of its being *caused* by a prior action. The result is an identification of stimulus and object of knowledge which not merely goes contrary to facts but which undermines the behavioristic statement. For since the stimulus as cause is there when the reaction takes place, the object must also be there, if stimulus and object are simply identified. Then, cognitively speaking, speech is a futile echoing, however useful it may be as a practical device for fixing attention or supplying a convenient memorandum for recollection.

Mr. Mursell, in his recent interesting article,[2] seems to me to illustrate the oversimplification in question and also its consequences. Speaking of perceptual judgments—speech reactions which state perceptions—he says they are "those judgments where the stimulus of the speech reaction is that to which the judgment has reference. I see a colored patch and respond by saying 'that is red.' I see my desk light burning and the muscles of my vocal organs are innervated to make the assertion 'the light is burning.'" So far the account is inconclusive with respect to our problem. No one would deny that speech reaction has reference to its stimulus or that an act of seeing is at least part of its stimulus. But the passage continues as follows: "In such cases the relation between the judgment and *its object* seems sufficiently clear. The object is the *cause* of the judgment, the causal nexus taking an intricate path through the nervous ganglia." (Italics mine.) Here the nature of the reference is unambiguously stated. Stimulus is cause, and as cause it is also the object of judgment.

If the stimulus is not simply a tendency to see, that is, an innervation of the optical apparatus, but is a seeing of "desk-light-burning," the non-behaviorist can adequately retort that seeing the light and the desk and their respective positions is already a case of knowing or judgment, so that speech is merely an addition, supernumerary for judgment though doubtless of practical and social utility. The case stands otherwise if the stimulus is an obstructed or incomplete act of vision, and speech serves to release, to direct and clinch it. In the latter case, the patch would *not* be known as red, say, or the light as the light of a lamp on the desk until the speech reaction definitely determined a stimulus. There is nothing paradoxical in this conception. We constantly react to light by using it, without knowing or naming it—without an explicit distinction and identification, and we very well know in dealing with novelties how names clear up and fix otherwise confusing and confused situations. Be-

2 This JOURNAL, Vol. XIX, p. 187, "Truth as Correspondence."

havioristically, above all, we must conceive that speech response is not something final and isolated, but that it operates in turn as condition of some more effective and adequate adjustment. While practically this function may be often performed in a direction *away* from its cause, as when we call out to a person in danger to look out, without stopping to tell him why he should look out, intellectually its office is turned *toward* the cause to modify it. And the *object of judgment* is thus not the cause simply; it is the consequence, the modification effected in its cause by the speech reaction. The speech response is retroactive as it were; not that it can modify anything which has passed out of existence, but it influences a contemporary act of vision and a tendency to reach or handle so as to give them a directed unity which they would not otherwise achieve save at the termination of a period of trial and error.

3. The analysis is still oversimplified. Speaking is connected with an ear and auditory apparatus, and their neuro-muscular and intra-organic connections. It is contrary to fact to identify a speech reaction with simply the innervation of the vocal organs. This gives no differentia of speech from a sigh, or grunt, or ejaculation due to respiratory reactions to pain. A speech reaction is the innervation-of-vocal-apparatus-as-stimulus-to-the-responses-of-other-organs-through-the-auditory-apparatus. It involves the auditor and his characteristic reaction to speech heard. Often and primarily the auditor is another organism whose behavior is required to complete the speech reaction, this behavior being the objective aimed at in the speech reaction.[3]

When the speech reaction consists in a "silent" innervation the principle is the same. It is then addressed to our own ear and the total connections thereof. Instead of making a command, or giving warning or advice to another agent for him to react to, we address it to ourself as a further re-agent. The agent issuing the stimulus and the one receiving it form two agents or persons or behavior systems. Failure expressly to note the implication of the auditor and his further behavior in a speech reaction is, I think, chiefly responsible for the common belief that there is something arbitrary, conceived in the interest of upholding a behavioristic theory at all cost, in identifying thought with speech. For when speech is confined to mere vocal innervations, the heart of knowledge is clearly not there. But neither is the heart of speech. Introduce connection with the responsive adjustments of the audience, and the forced paradox disappears. We have, as Mr. Mead has shown, the conditions for meaning.

[3] This is the point which is brought out so effectively in the article by Mead already referred to.

A speech reaction is a direction to subsequent behavior: Look and see; listen and hear; jump, turn to the left—remarks addressed to another who is in connection with ourselves, a partaker in the same behavior system, and then to ourselves, as a further re-agent, when there is no other person present.

Commands, optatives and subjunctives are the primary modes of speech reaction; the indicative or expositive mood is an amplification. For example, even a treatise by a mathematician or chemist is a guide to the undertaking of certain behavior reactions—a series of acts which when executed will result in seeing the things which the author has responded to with certain statements. It follows that the *object* of a speech reaction is the concordant responses which it sets up. Antecedent stimuli are a part of this object but are not the complete object of knowledge; the latter involves the further determinations which antecedent stimuli undergo by means of behavior evoked by speech. The object of knowledge or speech is the ultimate *consent* of the coördinated responses of speaker and hearer; the object of *affirmation* is the *con*firmation of co-adapted behavior. Its object is that future complex coördination of serial acts into a single behavior-system which would not exist without it. One's responses are co-adapted to the auditor's and the auditor's to one's own. Certain consequences follow.

1. The first is the refutation of solipsism. Not only can two persons know the same object, but a single personal reaction *can not* know an identical object. As a single and singular being I may make a primary non-cognitive reaction to a stimulus. I may shiver when the ear is stimulated in a certain way. But when I say, "that is the noise of a saw" the statement is addressed to the responses of an auditor in such a way as to demand a concordant reaction. He listens and looks, and says, "no, that is the sound of an axle of a wheel." Then I have to look, to respond with further behavior. The speech reaction is not complete till a concordant response is established. In other words, speech is conversation; it involves a duality of experiences or views. A single presence or view does not constitute judgment or statement. This particular manner of putting the fact may be unusual but there is nothing strikingly novel in the conception. Cognition involves recognition, acknowledgment, a contrast and connection of two different times or places of experience by means of which a distinctive identification is set up. A single act can not, as singular, establish the identification required to characterize an event as an object. There must be recurrence in a slightly different context. This is a thing that requires a response like that made before, or which will exact a

like response in the future, or of some other re-agent in the present. And without the sameness or correspondence of the responses of the two times or places, there is literally, contra-diction. An object of knowledge must consistently cover or comprehend responses to at least two distinct stimuli.

2. This conclusion has a direct bearing upon the nature of the correspondence which defines truth. The correspondence is found in the inclusion in a single contemporary behavior system of diverse behavior reactions. No correspondence can be conclusively established between a present response and a past one in their separation, or between a present one and a future one in their separateness. There must be one harmonious behavior function which includes the elements of both. Mr. Mursell in the article referred to makes correspondence retroactive. He says:[4] "When I assert that Cæsar crossed the Rubicon, I am reproducing the original reaction made by observers two thousand years ago, who saw him splash through the stream and found in the sight a stimulus to the response 'He has crossed the Rubicon.'" This account involves the mistake pointed out in the case of the statement "this is red color." It assumes that the object is known and also truly known prior to the speech reaction. How do I know that some former observer made the speech reaction ascribed to him? This ascription is the point at issue, and the account quoted merely begs the question. A correct statement of the data that Mr. Mursell recognizes would be: "I say that an observer two thousand years ago said that Cæsar has crossed the Rubicon; then I reproduce that saying on my own account. Then I say that the two sayings agree or correspond." Undoubtedly they do. But at no point have I got beyond my own sayings. The correspondence is merely between a saying of my own about what some one else said with another saying of my own. There is only a new kind of solipsism, that of private speech. In this historical case, I clearly can not direct my remark to a man long since dead and secure concordant behavior response from him. But I do address myself to others and say that if they will look at historic records, including those of a subsequent course of events, their responses will correspond to mine—or that the different reactions will all enter into a single complex behavior system.

Another illustration of Mr. Mursell's brings out the same points. He says: "Suppose I say Napoleon's tomb is in Paris. Let us assume that I read the words somewhere. Pushing back along the chain of recorded responses of which the printed symbols that I

[4] P. 187.

saw are the last, I come finally to the place where the original observer, who started the whole series, stood. I am directed to a particular locus, and there I receive a stimulus that issues in the response, 'Yes, Napoleon's tomb is in Paris.' And this it is which constitutes the truth of the judgment. . . . The chain of recorded responses always directs us to some specific locus.''[5] The last statement must be unqualifiedly admitted. But what and where is the locus? If it is merely past—and not a stimulus-response continuing into the present—then I can only state that ''I say that an original observer said that the tomb is in Paris.'' In short, as I push back along the chain, I finally come after all only to my own saying about what another said. If I go to Paris then indeed I come upon quite another saying which is congruous with my prior saying that the tomb is in Paris, but in this case the object is not one of a retroactive response. Or, I may respond without going to Paris in such a way as to call out reactions from other persons who make the same deliverance—that the tomb is in Paris. Here also the object is the attained co-adaptations in behavior.

Supposing we take a judgment about an event in the geological ages preceding the existence of human beings or any organisms possessed of speech reactions. In such instances, it is clear that there can be no question of correspondence with the speech reaction of a contemporary observer. By description the retroactive correspondence of sayings is ruled out. Yet no one doubts that there are some judgments about this ancient state of affairs which are truer than others. How can this be possible, since there can be no question of reproducing the judgment of an observer? If we say that what we now judge is what a contemporary observer would have said if he had been present, we are clearly begging the question. Nor could a contemporary observer have made as accurate and comprehensive a judgment in some respects as we can make, since we can also judge what occurred at a given period in the light of what happened afterwards. Clearly our speech reaction is to observations of present perceptions of data, rocks, fossils, *etc.* The other auditor and speaker to whom the statements are addressed are other possible observers of these and similar data. The ulterior ''object'' is the concordant, mutually reinforcing behavior system, including, of course, the speech responses. Sciousness in this, as in other cases, is con-sciousness. And this equating is not a mere figure of speech; it gives the original meaning of the word.

Summing up, we may say that there are three types of response which it is necessary to distinguish. First, there is direct organic response-of-the-autonomic-and-sensori-central-motor-systems-to

5 *Op. cit.*, p. 188.

stimuli. These stimuli are not, for and in the reaction, objects. Their connection with response is causal rather than cognitional. The reaction is physico-chemical, though it may terminate in a spatial or molar change. Neither the stimulus nor the response is an object of knowledge, though it may become part of an *object-to-be-known*. If the stimulus were adequate or complete, complete adaptative response or use would take place. Being incomplete, it is a challenge to a further response which will give it determinate character. Thereby the to-be-known becomes an object of knowledge; it becomes an answer instead of a query.

Secondly, the speech response occupies an intermediate position. By clinching, fixing its stimulus, it releases further modes of response. Saying that the colored patch is red enables us to take it as the thing we have been hunting for, or to react to it as a definite warning of danger. The prior activities form part of the subject-matter of the thing thus known. But they are *not* the object known. The object known is the coördination of the prior behavior with the consequent behavior which is effected by the medium of speech. Till the assumption is banished that stimulus to knowing and object of knowledge are the same thing, the analysis of knowledge and truth will be confused. Thirdly, the eventual coördination of behavior involves the response of a further re-agent, namely, the auditor, whether another organism or one's own. This coördination of the activity of speaker and hearer forms the ulterior object of knowledge. As a co-ordination or co-adaptation of at least two respondents, it constitutes that correspondence which we call knowledge or truth. Correspondence of past and present responses can be determined only by means of a further response which includes both of them within itself in a unified way. The theory explains the relation of truth to consistency as well as to correspondence. The different responses must consist, cohere, together. Consistency gets an objective, non-mentalistic meaning when it is understood to mean capacity for integration of different responses in a single more comprehensive behavior.

We may conclude by suggesting a possible explanation of the oversimplification of the behavioristic account of speech which has been pointed out. Introspective psychology of necessity broke up the subject-matter of psychology into a number of *disjecta membra,* of disjoined fragments treated as independent self-sufficing wholes. I say "of necessity" because the connecting links of these fragments are found in a context of environmental conditions and organic behavior of which the introspectionist can not be aware. Now behaviorism has too often confined itself to finding behavioristic counterparts of the same material and topics with which introspective psychology has dealt.[6] Consequently actual and concrete behavior has been broken up into a number of disjoined pieces instead of being analyzed freely on its own account. Thus certain errors of introspective psychology have been reduplicated in the very behavioristic psychology which is a protest against introspectionism.

JOHN DEWEY.

COLUMBIA UNIVERSITY.

[6] The case is quite analogous with the situation described by Mr. Kantor with reference to the nervous system. See his article in this JOURNAL, Vol. XIX, p. 38, on "The Nervous System, Psychological Fact or Fiction?" As Mr. Kantor states, too often "the nervous system is taken to be the tangible counterpart of the intangible psychic." Similarly, certain modes of behaviors have been treated as objective substitutes for prior subjective entities and processes.

The Journal of Philosophy

SOME MEANINGS OF MEANING IN DEWEY'S
EXPERIENCE AND NATURE

MEANING is plural. So it is with the meaning of meaning. It would be an injustice to the empirical spirit of Dewey to presuppose, at the very outset of our inquiry, that his interpretation of the nature of meaning (or rather, of meanings) is a singular and stable affair. No, we must expect uncertainty and fluctuation. After all, the important thing, as Dewey says, in any critical undertaking, is richness of meaning rather than truth (especially if we add the adjective "fixed" to this last). So we will at least begin by adopting Dewey's spirit. We will accept the denotative method and simply point to this and that meaning of meaning as they happen or precisely as they are presented to us in *Experience and Nature*. We will treat all his meanings of meaning as equal, since they are all immediately "had" by the casual reader. If this leads us to an evaluation within Dewey's own use we will admit it only reluctantly.

Perhaps the first character to impress us is that meaning is restricted, it is not to be referred to all reality (or, more precisely, it occurs within nature). There is, it seems, a world (or a level) of meaningless natural or physical events to which meanings are added. Dewey tells us that events "acquire" meanings. "A directly enjoyed thing adds to itself meaning . . ." (p. 167), ". . . events come to possess characters . . ." (p. 174), ". . . universals, relations, meanings, are of and about existences, not their exhaustive ingredients. The same existential events are capable of an infinite number of meanings" (p. 319). He speaks of "converting physical and brute relationships into connections of meanings," for on the merely animal level that which procures satisfaction is not yet an object or "thing-with-meanings" (p. 370). All this seems perfectly clear as well as important, for it marks off Dewey's position from that of idealism. But, empirically enough, Dewey does not leave us here. He feels constrained to point out that natural events themselves are relational, are cases of interaction, are not only sources of later "added" meanings, but are themselves vague, immediate, non-articulated meanings. But more of this in the sequel.

Delving further into meaning as restricted and as only a part of nature we find other characteristics. We are told that meaning is restricted to social communication and social communication is restricted to linguistic behavior. Language gives rise to socially shared activity, to participation, and this *is* meaning. Thus Dewey tells us that language "created the realm of meanings" (p. 168). "Meanings do not come into being without language, and language implies two selves involved in a conjoint or shared undertaking" (p. 299). "Language is a natural function of human association; and its consequences react upon other events, physical and human, giving them meaning or significance" (p. 173). Now this, again, is definite enough, but, true to the empirical spirit, Dewey does not stick to it in any hard and fast dialectical fashion. On occasion, Dewey is not loath to extend the sphere of meaning to the non-human and the non-social, to physical interactions preceding the rise of language and communication, to qualities in their non-communicable and indefinable immediateness. "Meanings are objective because they are modes of natural interaction; such an interaction, although primarily between organic beings, also includes things and energies external to living creatures" (p. 190). "Apart from language, from imputed and inferred meaning, we continually engage in an immense multitude of immediate organic selections. . . . We are not aware of the qualities of many or most of these acts; we do not objectively distinguish and identify them. Yet they exist as feeling qualities, and have an enormous effect upon our behavior. . . . They give us our *sense* of rightness and wrongness, of what to select and emphasize and follow up, and what to drop, slur over and ignore, among the multitude of inchoate meanings that are presenting themselves. They give us premonitions of approach to acceptable meanings, and warnings of getting off the track. Formulated discourse is mainly but a selected statement of what we wish to retain among all these incipient starts, following ups and breakings off" (pp. 299, 300). Here we at least seem to have meaning antecedent to language and discourse and the social participation based in such.

But we must hasten on with our description of the meanings of meaning. Another important interpretation is that meanings refer simply to consequences, the future, possibilities, what is to come. "What a physical event immediately is, and what it *can* do or its relationship are distinct and incommensurable. But when an event has meaning, its potential consequences become its integral and funded feature. When the potential consequences are important and repeated, they form the very nature and essence of a thing. . . . Since potential consequences also *mark* the thing itself, and form its nature, the event thus marked becomes an object of contemplation;

as meaning, future consequences already belong to the thing" (p. 182). But Dewey even goes further at times and identifies meaning with awareness of consequences. "Commonsense has no great occasion to distinguish between bare events and objects; objects being events-with-meanings. . . . Events have effects or consequences anyway; and since meaning is awareness of these consequences before they actually occur, reflective inquiry which converts an event into an object is the same thing as finding out a meaning which the event already possesses by imputation" (p. 324). If we waive the question as to whether consequences must be anticipated, we again seem to have a perfectly definite interpretation of meaning. The meaning of anything (or better, of any event) lies in its future, in that which succeeds it. But we are not left here. We are also told that meaning refers to the present and the past. To dwell a moment on the latter we need only to point out Dewey's emphasis on conditions, antecedents, causes, and their rôle in meaning to make this clear. "The proposition that the perception of a horse is valid and that a centaur is fanciful or hallucinatory, does not denote that these are two modes of awareness, differing intrinsically from each other. It denotes something with respect to causation, namely, that while both have their adequate antecedents, the specific causal conditions are ascertained to be different in the two cases. Hence it denotes something with respect to consequences, namely, that action upon the respective meanings will bring to light (to apparency or awareness) such different kinds of consequences that we should use the two meanings in very different ways. . . . Since conditions in the two cases *are* different, they operate differently" (p. 322). This example, though recognizing the place of "conditions" (i.e., prior conditions) as well as consequences in meaning, might seem to reduce the former to the latter. This can hardly be said of the following, however: "The union of past and future with the present manifest in every awareness of meanings is a mystery only when consciousness is gratuitously divided from nature and when nature is denied temporal and historic quality. When consciousness is connected with nature, the mystery becomes a luminous revelation of the operative interpenetration in nature of the efficient and the fulfilling" (pp. 352, 353). That is, we seem here to be told to look for meaning in total "histories," in immanent temporal wholes rather than in the future or consequential alone.

An interpretation closely connected with the last is that meanings are tools. On this basis any method or means of attaining desired consequences would be a meaning. Language, being one of the most widespread and delicately varied of tools, would consequently be a chief form of meaning. "As to be a tool, or to be used as means for consequences, is to have and to endow with meaning, language, being the tool of tools, is the cherishing mother of all significance" (p. 186). Yet we are told that meanings are both instruments and *also* immediate ends, fulfillings. Hence we are led to wonder whether their distinguishing characteristic is that they are tools. "Communication is uniquely instrumental and uniquely final. It is instrumental as liberating us from the otherwise overwhelming pressure of events and enabling us to live in a world of things that have meaning. It is final as a sharing in the objects and arts precious to a community, a sharing whereby meanings are enhanced, deepened and solidified in the sense of communion" (pp. 204, 205).

And this brings us to another distinction that Dewey emphasizes, namely, that between meaning as reference and meaning as immediate sense. By meaning as reference Dewey seems to mean a situation where the symbol and the symbolized, the sign and the thing signified, are quite external and where meaning is directly appreciated as a reference to some character outside that which means or refers. Dewey sometimes calls this cognitive or intellectual meaning. On the other hand, "sense" refers to meaning directly given, where there has been no analysis into sign and the signified. We have even here a reference, a relation, an interdependence, but it is of elements in a whole rather than of two wholes looked upon as quite external to each other. There is reference, but not awareness of reference as such. Dewey sometimes speaks as though "signification" or meaning as cognitive reference were due to a problem and its solution, whereas "sense" or immediate meaning does not. The following may serve to present his distinction: "The qualities of situations in which organisms and surrounding conditions interact, when discriminated, make sense. Sense is distinct from feeling, for it has a recognized reference; it is the qualitative characteristic of something, not just a submerged unidentified quality or tone. Sense is also different from signification. The latter involves use of a quality as a sign or index of something else, as when the red of a light signifies danger, and the need of bringing a moving locomotive to a stop. The sense of a thing, on the other hand, is an immediate and immanent meaning; it is meaning which is itself felt or directly had. When we are baffled by perplexing conditions, and finally hit upon a clew, and everything falls into place, the whole thing suddenly, as we say, 'makes sense.' In such a situation, the clew has signification in virtue of being an indication, a guide to interpretation. But the meaning of the *whole* situation as apprehended is sense" (pp. 260, 261).

But we are not done with our denotative duties even yet. We

must not close this empirical survey until we have pointed out one more character or type of meaning, one which really brings us back to the beginning of our list. Meaning is simply one form of inter-action—namely, interaction between an organism (Dewey does not always say human, but we may perhaps assume the adjective) and an extra-organic environment. "The qualities [direct meanings—in this case, sensations] never were 'in' the organism; they always were qualities of interactions in which both extra-organic things and organisms partake. When named, they enable identification and discrimination of things to take place as means in a further course of inclusive interaction. Hence they are as much qualities of the things engaged as of the organism" (p. 259). Thus we can readily see that meaning has its prerequisites and that it is a restricted sort in a larger world of events. "Organic and psycho-physical activi-ties with their qualities are conditions which have to come into ex-istence before mind, the presence and operation of meanings, ideas, is possible. They supply the mind with its footing and connection in nature; they provide meanings with their existential stuff" (p. 290).

The reader is by now very exacerbated. Why such a collection of quotations? And, further, do you mean to imply that all these meanings of meaning you think you have distinguished are mutually exclusive? But patience. The empirical method is to blame for all this. I have been trying merely to describe, to point out. Who am I that I should lay down *a priori* rules as to the significance we shall place on Dewey's words? I have tried to let them speak for themselves. If they are somewhat incoherent and diversified on the one hand and if they suggest a possible unification and reduction on the other, we must solve our problem by appeal to some other procedure—the denotative one has tried and has failed to point out what we want. So it is with fear and trembling and only because of the importunate demands of my reader that I venture forth on somewhat of an evaluation and criticism. Dewey's interpretations of meaning have now been "had." They present a mixture of stability and uncertainty—a problem. Intelligence awakes and de-mands a (possible) solution.

II

First of all let us put thrifty miserliness aside, let us cast many of the different meanings overboard. We will have plenty of labor making port with only a few and even those in emaciated form. And of those left, let us first of all consider meaning as consequent to language and a matter of the social sharing of action to which language gives rise.

No one would be so foolish as to deny that language does help in community of action (although there certainly may be community of action without language), nor that language is always and intimately bound up with meaning. But what bothers me is: Is meaning to be *restricted* to language and the shared activity to which it gives rise? In the first place, it does not seem quite legitimate to restrict meaning to socially shared activity. The non-active, the active but not socially shared would seem to be characters of the real world. Are they simply meaningless? And even in distinctly shared activities, are there not always non-shared and non-communicated features, and are these forthwith to be relegated to the realm of the meaningless? Is there any meaning which gets completely and exhaustively shared with other people? Is not every communication maimed and partial if not in some measure downright false when compared with the meaning which one is trying to communicate? Dewey maintains that there is a distinction between non-shared and shared activity. Yet this distinction must be meaningless, for if it had meaning it would be included entirely in one of the pair distinguished. In short, he can not legitimately say anything about the non-shared, for saying would be a sharing and thus would destroy the very nature of the non-shared (if we can talk about the nature of that which is meaningless). But perhaps Mr. Dewey would tell us that all this dialectical quibbling is foolish. There is such an ''event'' as non-shared activity and it has meaning not only after it has become an object involving a social sharing, but before; i.e., a meaning can be a merely *potential* sharing. Well and good, then, our objection is admitted.

Let us turn to the language side of it. Can meaning be restricted to linguistic behavior? First, to take an empirical and personal case: I have always liked sailing, but have never taken the time to verse myself in nautical terminology. I remember once when the tack of the mainsheet was not drawn tightly enough, with the consequence that there were diagonal wrinkles from the foot to the luff for quite a ways up. I saw those wrinkles and I appreciated what the trouble was, but I did not know the names for the portions of the sail involved. When I tried to express myself I discovered how difficult it was and how many circumlocutions were necessary in order to put my meaning in words. I had no terminology directly applicable to the portions of the sail I wished to designate. The meaning of those wrinkles likely involved much incipient or imaginal linguistic behavior on my part. But the unique *point at stake* not only involved more than language (and thus transcended language); it could not be turned over into language without torture and a good deal of pointing. And I am inclined to think that the situation would have meant something to me even though I had not desired to communicate to someone else concerning it. The illustration may not be worth much. But there are other characters in experience than what we mean by language. If this were not so it would be nonsense to restrict meaning to language. Now are these other characters meaningless? Probably Dewey would answer: No, but their meaning lies in their linguistic usage, which, of course, changes them. We are in the same predicament as before. If meanings transcend language, then language is not the exhaustive nature of meaning. But if they do not, then we are forced to admit either that there is no reality other than language, or that there is meaningless reality. Dewey, I think, would accept this latter alternative and call such meaningless reality, "existence." But I am still so dense that I can not understand why the contrast between language and the non-linguistic (or meaning and existence) is meaningless.

The point I have been trying to make is a simple one. If you *restrict* meaning to the linguistic and to the socially shared you can only do so by asserting the reality of the non-linguistic and the non-shared. Now to claim or to imply reality would seem to involve, whether explicitly or implicitly, the attribution of some sort of character or nature. To say that this realm of bare existence or the meaningless is simply "had" does not get out of the difficulty. For had-ness is a case of meaning. Mere immediate presence, givenness, hypostatized particularity, are all meanings, natures. In short, the limitation of meaning is itself a meaning, and the exclusion of meaning from any portion of reality means something. But more of this anon.

Let us turn to the identification of meaning with the future, with consequences. This interpretation has peculiar force. Although we do not need explicitly to distinguish and separate that which means and that which is meant in order to have meaning (as Dewey admits), yet whenever we are challenged to think of our meaning we do discover these two elements, and such a discovery involves a temporal process. Now inasmuch as we ordinarily go, in this process, from that which means to that which is meant, and inasmuch as we usually identify meaning with the meant, it seems quite natural to say that the meaning of anything is its future, or the later elements in the series of events.[1] Now this at first sight seems to do well enough even when we mean the non-future; when, for example, the

---

[1] I shall not discuss specifically the notion that meaning is a tool or means. It often is. But again we have a restriction which will not strictly hold up. Dewey recognizes this in saying that culminations are meanings. I might also suggest that Dewey's non-teleological series (his natural events, causes-effects, termini, etc.) are also cases of meaning. The argument is the same.

thing meant is past. For must we not reproduce this past situation in order to mean it, and thus is not what is meant the reproduction which, in relation to our symbol, is future? But we have a "nigger in the wood-pile." It is quite true that we may mean a future reproduction and even that we never can refer to a past (or to any temporal situation) without also involving a reference to a future. But how can we distinguish a reproduction from that which is not such? A reproduction, however much of the future it involves, *also* refers to a past and is what it is because it is not merely future. In short, meanings often (I personally believe always) bear a reference to that which is past, and however indirect you make that reference you will have to deal with it sometime.

But I hear protests. What I mean, says Dewey, is not that the past is meaningless and that we never refer to it, but that it only has significance in so far as it makes a difference in the future, in so far as it modifies consequences. But Dewey has already admitted that every difference of antecedence makes a difference of consequence. Now it may be that the most important thing in a given meaning centers around the future, but this is far from saying that the meaning is the future or merely in the future. Rather, we must recognize that some meanings at least (and I believe every meaning) involve a temporal unity of both past and future (and I may add, present). It is the same problem as before. Do you mean anything by restricting meaning to the future? If you do, then you have a meaning outside the realm to which meaning is restricted. Perhaps past differences are explored because of consequential differences. But they are still in some sense past and their importance for the future does not reduce them to the future, nor does it give us a merely one-way dependence.

I wish to evaluate briefly one other use (or perhaps I had better here say possible use) of meaning for Dewey. This one is perhaps the most inclusive of all, but it is one which Dewey does not himself definitely speak of as the nature of meaning. I refer to the so-called denotative or pointing method itself. We are told that in the last analysis we can designate what we mean only by pointing to it. This certainly is a matter of reference, is, in fact, an attempt to give us reference in its lowest and most irreducible form. But just what is designated by this pointing?

We will pass by the question of the relation of pointing to language, whether it antedates language, is included within language, or is the more inclusive, language being merely an elaboration. But this much seems clear, Dewey feels that in pointing we have got at the heart of reference (and thus of meaning). It is meaning at its simplest. Yet even here we have complexity. There seems to be on the one hand a pointing and on the other something pointed to. Let us consider the former. I think the analogy of the pointed finger is very definitely in Dewey's mind. Is the finger necessary for the pointing? Or, more generally, can you have a pointing unless you have that which is pointed? Must you not have a starting point (as well as terminus)? Dewey does not say, but we may answer for him. Yes, pointing is always *from* as well as *to,* it is directional, selective. It is always a case of a limited perspective having its footing in a relatively definite location—in a part, not in the indiscriminate whole of reality.

So far, I'm inclined to think Dewey would agree, although this is a mere guess. But how about that which is pointed to? Here Dewey will perhaps speak for himself a little more definitely. These things meant or denoted appear to be immediate experiences which we simply have or enjoy. I confess I do not know what sort of thing this "simply having" is. It becomes especially difficult to decipher when we are told that it has relations, occurs in a continuum with other experiences, is qualitative, and on occasion is even allowed to possess meaning. To say that it is just what it is and we have got to take it as such (because it is ineffable) may lead to hard words, but is scarcely a help to one who, gropingly, is really trying to understand. Perhaps there is something the matter with my introspective powers, but somehow I can not seem to locate any absolutely ineffable immediates in my own experience, though I am sure there is a taste of ineffability flavoring *all* of them (as I tried to say when I questioned whether any experience or meaning is completely communicable). I wonder if simply pointing at them would not destroy some of the absoluteness of their ineffability? But let us not stray too far from the issue. If I get Dewey straight, what he is trying to say about whatever it is that is pointed to is that it remains itself somehow independent of the pointing. That which is denoted exists not only apart from its being denoted, but even as a denoted something it is still the same as it was before entering that relation. Even while being pointed to it is still independent of the pointing. I do not think I am mistaken as to Dewey's position here. For if pointing modified the thing pointed to, then we could never point out, exactly, the original experience just as it was "had" (as Dewey insists).

So even in meaning as denotation we come back to the same story. Namely, we find that meaning is a restricted sphere that finds itself in a larger environment. The same simple question arises. Must not the distinction between these two itself have meaning? Can one designate in *any* fashion that which is absolutely independent of all designation?

But I hear an objection. I am told I have not distinguished between two standpoints, namely, between that of observing a mere existence and the mere existence itself, or between an experience for a spectator or in memory and that experience as it is directly "had." I am perfectly willing to admit the distinction, but I hasten to add that it means something. And I also feel inclined to believe that, because it is a distinction, it must involve an identity. If the non-observed experience or immediate existence is to be anything but an absolutely unknowable, empty somewhat (nay, even here we are ascribing some sort of nature to it), if it is to be admitted as anything at all, it must possess some relative identity, at least, with the designated, observed, meaningful experience from which it is distinguished. Dewey would seem to recognize this when he assumes that you can later designate an experience which originally was simply "had." But we can not assert a (relative) identity where there is no common character in any sense. (And we might well ask if we have not got meaning wherever there is a common character running through differences.) The realm of existence can not be *merely* different from the realm of observed and designated experience. There may very well be a difference of emphasis in the nature of existence and in the nature of meaning, but this would lead us to say that they are simply two aspects of every experience and of all reality. Neither can be absolutely independent of the other. There is no realm of existence from which all meaning can be excluded.

All this appears to be merely negative. It has opposed Dewey's stand. Yet we can not leave without a positive statement. I sincerely believe there is significance and value in Dewey's contention that meaning is restricted. And so, starting from the empirical, we have been led to the critical, and now (horror of horrors!) we are going to plunge into the dogmatical. Well, take it or leave it. Nevertheless, I am going to present, very crudely, an outline of my own doctrine of meaning.

III

I want to start with a hint from Dewey, from a distinction he makes within the realm of meaning. "There is thus an obvious difference between mind and consciousness; meaning and an idea. Mind denotes the whole system of meanings as they are embodied in the workings of organic life; consciousness in a being with language denotes awareness or perception of actual events, whether past, contemporary, or future, *in* their meanings, the having of actual ideas. The greater part of mind is only implicit in any conscious act or state; the field of mind—of operative meanings—is enormously wider than that of consciousness. Mind is contextual and persistent; consciousness is focal and transitive" (p. 303). This distinction between the contextual and the focal which with Dewey is a relatively insignificant distinction between two kinds of meaning, I intend to make central in the very meaning of meaning. My thesis is simply this: that which means (the symbol) is always a focal aspect of a larger contextual whole which is its meaning (in the sense of that which is meant or is symbolized).

We have seen how meaning can not be completely confined within any limited portion of reality. Yet I think Dewey is right in his feeling that, whatever be its limits, meaning does in its nature involve a partiality. What Dewey failed to do was to appreciate how *both* these elements are bound up in meaning; he failed to grasp the relation of the meaning in the sense of the symbol or that which refers to the meaning in the sense of the meant. We always mean (refer to) some identity in difference or whole. But we are always satisfied with a relatively few features of that whole, providing we feel that they somehow give us the core.

Take definitions. They give us meanings in the sense that they give us essential elements. These essential elements are sufficient, ordinarily, for our dealings with the vastly more complex whole of which (so far as our definition is good) they are the focal features. Take the definition of book. We would probably agree on including printed pages bound together having a certain minimum size and perhaps possessing outside covers. But the total thing meant ultimately by book carries us step by step into an overwhelming contextual whole involving all sorts and kinds of books, innumerable concrete details reaching out in every direction.

Take words. The main difficulty here in applying our view is that the symbols we find in language, once we analyze them, seem so arbitrary. Their naturalness is simply a matter of familiarity growing out of social custom. Think of the word "cat." Any other sound or combination of sounds would seemingly fit in with that four-legged creature which the word symbolizes. But the point is that, for us, this particular sound has become a real part of the total whole involved. The symbol is not a self-contained whole external to and set over against another self-contained whole which is its meaning. No, the symbol is a true part of the meaning and ordinarily is about all of the meaning we get hold of except for the sense that there *is* more and that, were we challenged, we could go to and explore this larger whole in some detail. So when we are talking about a cat (whether in particular or in general) the main thing we have is the sound or sight of the word, plus a greater or less fringe of shifting imagery. But we are always sure that there is a more, and that what we have is a part of it, although a vicarious part truly functioning for the whole. Thus words (and symbols in general) are peculiarly treated as the whole meaning, while yet they are recognized to refer beyond themselves. Their reference is not a pointing to something external, but is their own vicarious partiality. But this analysis is not to be restricted to language. In fact it is the very arbitrariness of symbols in language which lends false color to the notion that the meaning (that which refers) and the meant are separate and external. Here is a sailor. He is out in a storm at night. He hears above the roar a whine, a shriek, a crack. He can not see, but he knows what has happened aloft. Those sounds mean, just as truly as any language, that a sail has been blown out of its bolt ropes. Clearly the sign or symbol is here not external to the signified. Or take another case. A man walking through a forest hears a groan. It is not simply so much noise, it has a startling meaning in that lonely place. A doctor understands the meaning of every slightest change in the breathing of his patient suffering from pneumonia. A smile means gladness, a drooping face and tear-stained cheek mean sorrow. Need I go on? Is it not clear that in each of these the symbol is truly an aspect which brings a larger whole to a focus? The symbol is that part of the whole thing meant which passes muster for the whole, with which the whole is peculiarly identified.

In every case of meaning concrete details in the nature of that which is meant are implied, but ignored. Now by existence, I think, we always in some sense mean a total, detailed context in all its concreteness. But, of course, we never get this, we can only approximate. Thus we never can completely go from a symbol to its full meaning (that which is meant), to the total existence to which it refers. Yet wherever we stop we feel the element of arbitrariness in the cessation. We are always in the realm of meaning because every whole we experience indicates and bears with it a larger context. What happens then to existence? Sometimes it is made an unknowable somewhat outside all experience. Sometimes it becomes synonymous with the mere fact of detailedness wherever found. This latter is the most popular to-day. Differences are put on their own, and thus existence often comes to be equated with mere particularity and our result is a specificism.

I think we come nearer the mark, however, when we realize that meaning and existence are relative terms. Existence refers to the fact of differentiation within any whole. Meaning refers to the fact that every whole is more peculiarly involved in and dependent upon some of these different features than others and thus that these parts, in thus summing up and focalizing the whole, can ''represent'' the whole. But they could not do so were they all. They are both sufficient and insufficient. Their sufficiency is due to their value and centrality, their vicarious nature. Their insufficiency is due to their larger setting upon which they depend and whose nature they bear, but do not exhaust.

Thus Dewey is right when he treats meaning as restricted, but he is also wrong. For he does not realize that it is a restriction which enlarges. He fails to recognize the identity which all meaning presents—the identity of the partial and the complete.

EVERETT W. HALL.

LAWRENCE COLLEGE.

VOL. XXV, No. 13. JUNE 21, 1928.

MEANING AND EXISTENCE

IN their *Meaning of Meaning,* Ogden and Richards relate the following incident quoted from a book entitled *Among Congo Cannibals,* written by J. H. Weeks: "I remember on one occasion wanting the word for Table. There were five or six boys standing around, and tapping the table with my forefinger, I asked, 'What is this?' One boy said it was a *dodela,* another that it was an *etanda,* another stated that it was *bokali,* a fourth that it was *elamba,* and the fifth said it was *meza.*" It turned out afterwards that "one boy thought we wanted the word for tapping; another understood that we were seeking the word for the material of which the table was made; another had the idea that we required the word for hardness; another thought we wished for a name for that which covered the table; and the last, not being able, perhaps, to think of anything else, gave us the word, *meza,* table—the very word we were seeking."[1]

The incident appears to me relevant to the first part of the recent article by Professor Hall.[2] In it, following what he takes to be the denotative method that I recommend and try to use in *Experience and Nature,* he selects a number of passages in which I am dealing with meanings, and implies that the selection is equivalent to the "pointing" required by the empirical denotative method. I can not complain that he has dealt severely with them or me, or that he relies upon any merely verbal analysis. But he seems to ignore the fact that "pointing" is not so simple and direct an affair as pointing a finger—or tapping on a table. In *Experience and Nature,* the words "showing" and "finding" are usually added in explanation

[1] *The Meaning of Meaning,* p. 174.
[2] "Some Meanings of Meaning in Dewey's *Experience and Nature,*" this JOURNAL, Vol. XXV (1928), pp. 169–181.

of "pointing," while this is described, for example, as follows: "Index to a starting point and road which if taken may lead to a direct and ineffable presence."[3] The implication is that any idea, reasoning, theory, hypothesis, is an indication to a road to be taken so that its value is that of stating a method to be used, the value being tested by its capacity to terminate in the situation required. Hence—as the above incident shows—the "denotative empirical method" is not an affair of pointing directly to things (things being inclusive of passages in a book), but of having such ideas as point and lead by use as methods to some directly experienced situation. Hence regard for context is indispensable. Moreover, since the parties in question failed to understand one another because they did not share in a common situation—in one of communication—the anecdote may be taken to illustrate the need of a shared situation whenever the understanding of ideas and symbols enters into question. Hence I make the following comments in the hope that what I say may serve to indicate a road that will lead to and terminate in the *situations* that are designated by the symbol "meaning," and aid in instituting a shared situation and so promote understanding.

I

Reference to Mr. Hall's text shows that he finds diversity and possibly inconsistency in at least five types of cases in which I refer to meanings. Some of the cases overlap, so I shall state them all before proceeding to deal with any of them. First, there are quotations to support the statement that I hold meaning to be *restricted* to communication and that in turn to linguistic behavior.[4] In conflict with this view are quoted statements by me which indicate to Mr. Hall that I accept "meaning" antecedent to language and discourse and the social participation based upon them. The second set of quotations concerns the temporal relations of the occurrence of meanings, and seems to indicate that after officially restricting meaning to a future reference, the facts compel me also to introduce "immanent temporal wholes." The third point concerns an apparent inconsistency between the instrumental and the final or consummatory character of meanings. The fourth set of quotations concerns meaning as "referential" and as "immanent." The fifth, as he points out, brings us back to the first point: there are quota-

[3] *Experience and Nature,* p. 86. The word "ineffable" occasions difficulty. The idea might be expressed by saying "presence in a non-symbolic way." Something can be said *about* a situation so present or "had," but it can not possibly be duplicated by any possible number or combination of symbols.

[4] The term " restriction " is not only used by him on p. 170, but is repeated several times with emphasis in his own discussion in the second part of the article.

tions that are taken by Mr. Hall to indicate that I at some times assert that meanings arise in direct interaction of the human organism with a physical environment, apart from any social mediation, or the function of "communication."

Let me state first that my general position is correctly stated by Hall in his second paragraph; namely, I hold that events "acquire meanings" or that "meaning occurs within nature."

1a. *Restriction to Communication.*—Coming to his first point, the assertion I make is that events "acquire" meaning through the fact of communication, which is an observably empirical fact in some phases of human intercourse. But being begotten is quite a different affair from subsequent development. There is not a word quoted by Mr. Hall to indicate that this further growth is "restricted" to conditions of *origin*. To say (as I do say in a passage cited) that "meanings do not *come into being* without language" is neither to say, nor to imply, that conditions of origin are identical with those of all subsequent status. Not only that, but a phrase in a sentence cited says explicitly that "its [languages's] consequences react upon other events physical and human, giving them meaning or significance." What is more important than this particular indication of the arbitrary character of Mr. Hall's imputation to me of restriction of meaning to linguistic behavior is the fact that the text of *Experience and Nature* devotes considerable space to showing that after communication has been instituted, its pattern is extended to all sorts of acts and things, so that they become signs of other things. There is nothing original in the idea of "language of nature"; such contribution as I have made to the idea consists simply in finding the locus of the *origin* of the voice and message of natural things in human communication.[5] What has led Mr. Hall wrong in this particular case of his use of the denotative method is failure to recognize the context of discussion of *origin*, so that in consequence he gives an illegitimate extension of passages that concern genesis to all further developments and functions.

1b. *Qualities and Meanings.*—The notion that, after I have found the origin of meaning in that interaction of natural events that constitutes the distinctive trait of human social life, I attribute meaning to events antecedent to any communication, contains an analogous misconception. (This statement applies to the latter part of the paragraph on p. 170 and also to the entire point made on p. 173.)

---

[5] The bearing of this point affects Mr. Hall's discussion in the second part of his article, since that is based upon imputing to me quite arbitrarily the "restriction" mentioned. Take for illustration his example from sailing (on p. 174). It is wholly compatible with my position that wrinkles, etc., in sails should convey to us messages that a particular speech terminology is inadequate to set forth.

I certainly hold that there are natural "prerequisites" of the origin of meaning in communication. Among these indispensable preconditions are the immediate qualities called, in psychological terminology, "feelings"; these are, as I have said, the existential basis and "stuff" of meanings. It is only by imputing to me the position that these qualities or feelings are themselves meanings that he can attribute to me inconsistency. That such qualities or feelings exist prior to, and independent of, any language function—even in the widest sense of sign-function—and that they guide behavior in all kinds of subtle ways, I distinctly hold. But I explicitly deny that they are meanings. Mr. Hall may hold they *are* meanings, and he may be able to give such reasons for so holding as to entitle him to the belief. But he is hardly entitled to imply or assert that I hold such a view, and then find inconsistency in my views.[6]

2. *The Temporal Question.*—That events acquire meaning by having their potential consequences identified with them as their properties (as in the case of practically anything designated by a common noun) I certainly hold. I also hold that when it is a question of *critical* search for *valid* meaning, namely, for that meaning we are *entitled* to treat as the genuine meaning of the events in question, we are obliged to have recourse to antecedent conditions. For when a question arises as to what the consequences *really* are, we must take into account a course of events and sometimes a long one.

3. *Instrumental and Final.*—The right determination of meanings thus involves the consideration of "total histories" or "immanent temporal wholes," for while the meaning of existences is constituted by expected or potential consequences, the nature of these consequences can be properly decided only in connection with such larger histories. When such a history is explicitly taken into consideration, the distinction of instrumental and final meanings is made or comes into view. That there are some things which have their meaning determined by use in attaining or accomplishing other things or that are tools, and that some meanings are deliberately determined as means of reaching other meanings, I do not suppose is questioned by any one.

Instrumental meanings also, and obviously, imply as their ulterior goal some meaning *to* which they are instrumental, or a meaning that is final, fulfilling, consummatory. On the basis of any empirical method, there are no meanings which are always and inherently instrumental or final; this is a matter of their status and rôle

---

[6] On p. 173, after quoting from me a statement about qualities, he inserts in brackets after the word "qualities," the phrase "direct meanings—in this case sensations." It is easy to convict any one of inconsistency by attributing to him conceptions which one holds one's self, but which the one criticized repudiates.

in some actual situation. Hence the need for taking a situation as a " total history." Antecedent events as such, or "efficient" events as preparatory conditions, define an instrumental meaning; the last or closing events taken in their meaning with respect to events that have preceded have final meaning. Each is correlative with the other with respect to the temporal course as a whole. A further reason why the relation of meanings in this phase to a " total history " is made much of is the fact that philosophical literature is so filled with instances of sharp separation of instrumental and final. It became necessary in criticism of such views to point out that *any* event, however instrumental, may also be fulfilling with respect to what antecedes; while, since the event with the final meaning is involved in an ongoing course of events, it has in this phase instrumental value. Instead of an inadvertent inconsistency, the reference to " total histories " is thus an integral and consistent part of the entire hypothesis.

4. *Referential and Immanent.*—There is an undoubted ambiguity in the word "meaning" as it is currently used. We say something means something else in the sense of signifying it, being a sign of it. This is equivalent to taking one thing as evidence for something else, a ground for inference to the other thing, as when we say smoke means fire—that is, where smoke is observed, fire is inferred. But events are also clothed with meaning on their own behalf; thus something is directly taken to be " smoke " in the instance just cited; the character of being smoke belongs to the event as it is observed—although in some other case "smoke" might be a character signified or inferred. The words "referential" and "immanent" are used to designate the two uses, so as to avoid the ambiguity that resides in the word as it is ordinarily employed.

Since it will be admitted, I take it, that I did not originate the ambiguity, but found it in the current use of "meaning," the question that arises concerns only the relationship of the two meanings to other phases of my entire hypothesis regarding meaning. (1) The recognition of the two kinds is consistent with the theory of origin in communication; sounds first gain meaning as signs when used to stand for something besides themselves; while in consequence of such repeated use, the things stood for come to be the "immanent" meaning of the sounds in question. (This is the case with the illustration of "cat" used by Mr. Hall on p. 179.) According to my hypothesis, immanent meanings exist in consequence of the repeated successful outcome of referential or evidential meanings. (2) As to the temporal matter, the thing signified in the case of an event as sign is something that is experienced in consequence of an act based upon taking an existence as sign or evidence; it is subsequent or future in the course of experience. But critical testing of the validity of such a meaning involves recourse to larger temporal wholes. (3) Thus the fulfilling or consummatory meaning of a referential case becomes the immanent meaning, the directly taken-for-granted meaning, of subsequent situations. Thus, as far as I can make out, there is no inconsistency in the various parts of the whole theory; they hang together, imply and support one another.

II

The foregoing is meant to cover the first section of Mr. Hall's article, in which he cites various passages of mine; by anticipation it covers also certain portions of his second section as well. There is, however, a point of considerable importance in his second section that has not been touched upon.[7] If I grasp the point of his criticism, it may be put baldly as follows: My treatment has no way of distinguishing events without meaning from others having meaning except as I attribute to the former some nature or character, and thus assign meaning to them. The distinction implies a connecting identity; that identity is itself one of meaning. It is, accordingly, argued that the distinction I have drawn is in reality one between partial, imperfect meaning and a fuller and more inclusive meaning, not between that without meaning and that with meaning. His third section, as I understand it, develops this idea positively. I shall, then, deal with this argument in both its critical or negative aspect and its positive form.

For a reason that will presently appear the portion of his argument based upon a logical analysis of my position will have to be dealt with briefly. That when I think of anything or when anything enters into discourse it in so far acquires meaning, there can be no doubt. And, of course, when events-without-meaning are referred to, that very fact brings them within the field of thought and discourse, and in so far confers meaning upon them, if only the meaning of being without meaning. One could go further: to refer to anything as an *event* is in so far to ascribe character or nature and hence a meaning to it. Of all this, there is no doubt. But to use these considerations as evidence that things have meaning prior to, and independently of, entering into thought or discourse is another matter. Such an argument converts a predicament of dis-

---

[7] I do not wish to leave the impression that I suppose that there are no laxities or inconsistencies in the treatment of meaning in *Experience and Nature*. There is one such case (but I think only one) in the passages cited by Mr. Hall, and I accept responsibility for that as far as it may have misled Mr. Hall. The exception is the use of the phrase ''*sense* of rightness'' in the passage quoted by him on p. 170. There is an undoubted shift here from ''qualities'' (or ''feelings'') to qualities with meaning, or ''sense.''

course into a trait of existence—a somewhat unconvincing procedure. The fact that if one supposes, by way of hypothetical premiss, that there are existences without meaning, they would nevertheless acquire some meaning in virtue of entering into discourse—and in my conception this is precisely what happens—deprives this argument of probative value. It is akin to the argument once used by idealists when they said that the realist's assertion that there are things not related to mind presupposes that things are related to mind.

The positive argument, as I understand it, comes to the following: What signifies, being a symbol, is meaning; what is signified is also meaning, but a larger and more inclusive meaning. Symbol and symbolized are thus related as a partial and a complete meaning; although we rarely if ever attain to the complete meaning, there is always a sense that it is there, and that we might go to it and explore it in at least some greater detail. "The symbol is not a self-contained whole external to and set over against another self-contained whole which is its meaning. No, the symbol is a true part of the meaning" (p. 179). "The meaning (that which refers) and the meant" are not "separate and external." For example, a sailor in a storm hears a whine, a roar, a crack. "These sounds means that a sail has been blown out of its bolt ropes. Clearly the sign or symbol is here not external to the signified" (p. 180).

Let me restate the matter in terms of my own hypothesis. There are two possible cases, those of "referential" and "immanent" meaning. In the former, there is an event that has the meaning of indicating, signifying, being a sign or evidence of something else. This case would be exemplified if the sailor were inexperienced or were a landlubber. He would hear the shriek and crack, and would think it signified something, but he would have to *infer*—use the noise as a symbol—and do something to find out what it signified. If, however, the sailor is experienced, the consequences of his prior-tested and verified inferences enter directly into the object of perception; the noise will *be*, to him, a sail blown out of its bolt ropes. This sort of thing is what is intended by the phrase "immanent meaning,"—precisely the same sort of thing happened in the case of the supposititious landlubber when he identified an event as a noise, a cracking noise, etc. In such cases there is no distinction of something as sign and something else as thing signified; there is a total situation "had," having its direct meaning-content. Upon my hypothesis, however, there are no "immanent meanings" except in consequence of the results of prior referential or reflective (inferential) meanings. And the event in its immanent meaning also enters into some other situation with reference to a part of which it serves as a sign—in the referential sense. For example, just as the landlubber in hearing the peculiar noise would ask what it signifies, the sailor will ask, on "knowing" that the sail is blown out, What next? Or, what shall I do about it?

Returning to Mr. Hall's account, the following difference between it and mine is evident. According to him, the sound *is* intrinsically a meaning. According to me, the sound is something which is used or taken as a sign, and hence "meaning" is here a name for the *relation* between it and something else—the relation being the function or office of serving as a sign of something else. The related is identified and demarcated by the operation of inference. In the same way, the thing signified is not meaning unqualifiedly; it is something *having* meaning; something indicated and taken as satisfying the requirements of the thing or events having the signifying rôle. Of course, the signifying event is not self-contained; if it were it would not signify; the very meaning of being a signifying event is that it stands in the *relation* of indicating. And when the inference is completed, there is a "whole," a situation in which the distinction between signifying and signified no longer holds; for the completion of the inference is found in a situation which is directly "had"—the situation "we go to" and then go from.

In taking the symbol and the thing symbolized as themselves "meanings" in their own right and behalf, and not because of the relation they enter into—that of inference,—Mr. Hall to my mind unwittingly begs the entire issue. Thus he says "the *symbol* is not a self-contained whole, but is a true part of the meaning." But the question at issue is already decided when a thing is termed a "symbol"—to term it a symbol is, of course, to assign meaning to it. The real issue concerns the conditions under which a thing *becomes* a symbol—or at least concerns the question whether they *are* symbols inherently or become symbols in their use as signs or evidence in inference. Consider the following sentence of Mr. Hall's: "It is the arbitrariness of symbols in language which lends false color to the notion that meaning (that which refers) and the meant are separate and external" (p. 180). To call *that which* means meaning and *that which* is meant meaning is simply, I submit, to beg the issue. His statement is open to the obvious reply that he has taken advantage of an elliptical use of language. "Meaning" as "that which refers" is a short expression for some existence that stands as a sign or as ground for inferring something else. "The meant" is a short expression for something in its capacity of being intended or signified in the reference. Mr. Hall's view is that which signifies is intrinsically a meaning, and that it means a meaning. My view is that a *thing* signifies another *thing* in being employed as an evidential sign, and that in this *relation* both acquire meaning. Even in case Mr. Hall's view is right and mine is wrong, the case can not be settled by taking advantage of the ambiguity involved in an elliptic use of language. Then, in the case of "cat" that has come to have immanent meaning and of the sail-blown-out-of-bolt-ropes, we have by my theory the funded immanent result of the successful issue of prior referential or reflective relations. It is necessary, as was pointed out earlier, not to be misled by the ambiguity in the ordinary uses of the word "meaning," and so shift without warning from one sense to the other.

This discussion is not supposed to prove my position or disprove Mr. Hall's. It is intended to make clear the distinction between them, and to make explicit the assumptions on the basis of which Mr. Hall reaches the conclusion that "existence" is itself but a partial meaning within a larger whole of meaning. To my mind his argument is an able and ingenious restatement of the idealistic position as conveyed, for example, in Royce's distinction of external and internal meanings. The topic of meaning is certainly one of the most important in contemporary philosophical discussion, and while I regret that my article is necessarily so controversial, I wish to express my appreciation of the genial temper and acuteness of Mr. Hall's article, and my gratitude to him for giving me the opportunity to restate some points in my own hypothesis in their relations to one another.

JOHN DEWEY.

COLUMBIA UNIVERSITY.

VOL. 1. No. 3.   FEBRUARY 4, 1904

THE JOURNAL OF PHILOSOPHY

PSYCHOLOGY AND SCIENTIFIC METHODS

NOTES UPON LOGICAL TOPICS

I. A CLASSIFICATION OF CONTEMPORARY TENDENCIES[1]

IT is an interesting example of the irony of history that it was Kant who remarked, about a century and a quarter ago, that since Aristotle logical theory has neither lost nor gained an inch—that it appeared complete and settled. To-day the greatest difficulty students of logic have to contend with is the variety of independent and specialized points of view, a variety so great that it is almost impossible for any one person to be at home in all of them, independently of the diversity of opinion found in any one of them. A rough attempt to catalogue these various points of view and tendencies, even when undertaken by one quite ignorant in some of the fields, may be of use at least in defining some problems which are pressing in the further development of logic. Accordingly, a rough scheduling of tendencies follows.

1. *Formal Logic.*—The logic of scholastic tradition. It was, of course, formal logic which Kant, wrongly ascribing to Aristotle, regarded as finished and settled. But Kant's very insistence upon the purely formal character of thinking as such—his insistence that pure logic has nothing to do with any of the objects or contents of knowledge, being confined to analytic consistency with reference to identity and non-contradiction, was one of the chief forces in calling out by reaction other conceptions of logic.[2] The more rigorously one carries out the program of excluding from logical theory all reference to truth, belief and the evidential value of data, the more

---

[1] I am glad to take advantage of the foundation of a publication of this type to record notes which are too informal to justify publication in more finished shape, and yet which, as notes of a student, may be of some use to other students of the same subject.

[2] See, for example, how Hamilton and Mansel, who followed Kant in applying logic to formal laws of thinking, evoked the reaction of Mill on the one side, and of T. H. Green on the other. Mill, 'An Examination of Sir William Hamilton's Philosophy,' 1865, and T. H. Green, 'Works,' Vol. II., 'Logic of the Formal Logicians.' (Lectures delivered in 1874–5.)

apparent the emptiness of such logic becomes, and the more the mind seeks for some other conception of thought to serve as a basis for logic of another type.

2. *Empirical Logic.*—Hence it was inevitable that when the rationalistic school went to seed in its doctrine of a purely empty thinking process, empiricism strove to build up a constructive logic of 'experience' as a source and guarantee of practical and scientific truths. John Stuart Mill was, of course, explicit in teaching that true logic is concerned with adequacy of evidence and proof, with the validating and discrediting of belief—with, in a word, all the processes which have to do with the consideration of any truth which is not self-evident. Rarely has any piece of intellectual work met so fully the need which called it out, and imposed itself so overmasteringly upon its generation, as did the logic of Mill. The empiricist, since Mill, repeats by his actions, if not by his words, what Kant said of Aristotle, that logic is henceforth complete and settled.[3]

The tendency of current textbooks to incorporate within themselves both the formal and the empirical logics, as if they simply amicably divided the field between them, is a good illustration of the capacities of the human mind. The assumption that thought has a deductive and an inductive process, which work by different laws, and that the formal, syllogistic logic adequately describes the deductive function, while the empirical logic as adequately represents the inductive, furnishes as striking an instance as one could find of the catholic willingness of the human mind to accommodate itself even to diammetrically opposite assumptions provided that will save the trouble of systematic, reconstructive thinking.

3. *Real Logic.*—I use this term not as assuming that this sort of logical theory is 'real,' while others are artificial, but as a phrase, in the absence of any commonly recognized designation, with which to refer to those tendencies which give thought itself a content, and which reach their limit in the assumption that truth itself is just the perfected content of thought. The irony of history, to which I alluded at the outset, is, of course, the fact that it was Kant's transcendental logic which brought to an end the settled and fixed condition he attributed to logic. His so-called transcendental logic was nothing more nor less than an attempt to show the positive part played by thought in the determination of any experience which is capable of having attributed to itself the distinctions of truth and falsity.

[3] Nevertheless, the work of John Venn, 'Principles of Empirical or Inductive Logic,' London, 1889, is such an independent rendering of Mill as to be worthy of more attention than it receives in the current Teutophile philosophy.

Under this head come all who have been positively influenced by the Kantian theory of judgment as involving an objective synthesis, possible only through certain thought functions. It is a term, therefore, which has to be applied largely by way of contrast. It includes almost all those who do not believe in the purely formal notion of thought, and yet are unwilling to accept empiricism. It names certain tendencies rather than any very homogeneous or defined body of thought. To take some of the best known writers, the names of Bradley, Bosanquet, Lotze, Sigwart and Wundt would all appear here, much as they differ from one another.

These three captions refer to movements that are sufficiently well defined to be termed schools of logical thought. They represent, that is to say, intellectual standpoints which have become sufficiently conscious of themselves to get formulation, and to be aware of their incompatibilities with one another. The tendencies that I am about to schedule are rather just tendencies. They are forces at work rather than schools of doctrine. Consequently, they are not necessarily incompatible either with one another or in all respects with the three tendencies just mentioned.

4. Attempts to reform the traditional syllogistic and inductive logics so as to bring them into greater accord with 'common sense' and with the methods and results of scientific inquiry. Such attempts, in the main, start from the accepted terminology of logical theory and try to free it from those connotations which attach to it in virtue of either the scholastic or the empirical standpoints; and to show how, without accepting any particular philosophical standpoint, logical conceptions must be interpreted in order to meet the working logic of practical life, and of scientific investigation and verification. To my mind the best representative of this tendency is Professor Alfred Sidgwick, and as I hope to devote one of my later notes specially to his reformatory work, I shall say nothing more about it here.

5. *Mathematical Logic.*—Under this head two tendencies are to be noted. One is the disposition to interpret and to construct logic as mathematics, and the other to build up the system of mathematical science as itself the adequate representative of logic. Most systems of symbolic logic illustrate the former. By the latter I mean the work which has been done primarily by mathematicians as mathematicians under the conception that mathematical science is in no sense limited by the concept of quantity, but has to do with all reasoning which may be exhibited in necessary form or that deals with necessary conclusions. I am not enough of a mathematician to characterize this movement closely, but I am sure I am not far out of the way in referring to the work of Benj. Pierce, and of the recent

Italian school of Peano as typical examples. I suppose this strictly logical tendency has been much more influential in building up the hyperspace geometry and the modern theory of numbers than the layman recognizes. In our present condition of specialization it is somewhat difficult for one and the same person to be well posted on the more general and philosophical aspects of logical theory, and at the same time to be at home in the recent development of scientific mathematics. I am inclined to believe that a person who should be properly equipped on both sides, and who was also at home in recent psychology, could render the logic of reasoning a very great service. Professor Royce has already given us some tantalizing specimens of what is possible in this direction.[4]

Among those who are interested in logic from the mathematical side there seems to be a further division of tendency. One school seems explicitly or implicitly to hold by the traditional formal logic, and to be engaged in making it more rigorous by the use of symbols, thus carrying out the program of more strict formalism, eliminating ambiguities arising from context and putting the formulæ of logic into a more compact and sequential form.

But, on the other hand, Mr. C. S. Peirce (if I interpret him aright) believes that one of the chief advantages of the mathematical, or symbolic statement is that logic may transcend thereby the limitations of mere formalism and become a potent instrumentality in developing a system which has inherent reference to the pursuit of truth and the validation of belief.

6. *Psychological Logic.*—Without in any way prejudging in advance the question as to whether logic and psychology are independent disciplines which can be brought into contact with each other only at the risk of corruption to both, one may note the fact that there is a renaissance of interest in the psychology of the reflective processes. This psychological development is giving at once such a novel and such a significant interpretation of the nature of thought in general, and of its various phenomena in particular, that it is hard to see how it can continue without in time affecting somewhat profoundly the consideration of strictly logical problems. If, for example, psychologists should come to a pretty definite consensus that thinking is originally conditioned by inhibited and, therefore, postponed action, it would seem as if such a view could not fail to modify the details of logical theory. Professor James's identification of

[4] I refer especially to parts IV. and V. of the second chapter of his ' World and the Individual,' Second Series, and to his presidential address upon ' Recent Logical Inquiries,' *The Psychological Review,* Vol. IX., p. 105. I do not include his supplementary essay in the first volume of his ' World and the Individual,' because he has (unfortunately, it seems to me) given his interpretation an ontological rather than a logical turn.

abstraction with a selective function, taking place on the basis of interest, which runs through all psychical processes whatsoever, and his theory of the teleological nature of conception, if accepted in psychology, can hardly fail to carry with them some kind of moral for logic. And, to take an instance that is seemingly somewhat more remote from logic proper, his conception of the stream of consciousness as involving a rhythm of substantive and transitive sort, and of carrying with it necessarily a certain relationship between the more or less definite (or, what is the same thing, the more or less vague) must be either true or false in psychology—and if true in psychology must modify in some way or other the conception of thought that obtains in logic.

7. *Logic in Connection with Comparative and General Grammar.* —It goes without saying that logic in its beginnings, logic at the hands of Plato and Aristotle, went along with and was largely dependent upon an analysis of the sentential structures in which thought is embodied. Logic more than repaid what it borrowed from its analysis of language fixing the categories of grammar and language study for many centuries. The science of language had practically no independent existence, but was a mode of phrasing the recognized distinctions of classic logical theory. But, as every one knows, within the last hundred years the study of language has entered upon an independent development of its own, and has now practically shaken itself free from the incubus of its externally imposed categories, which in turn originated from a more superficial study of linguistic phenomena. The time has about come, I think, when logic may again borrow from the extensive and profound analysis of language in as significant and important a way as the logic of Aristotle borrowed from the narrow and obvious language data at command.

Up to the present those who have attempted to make the connections between general grammar and logic have, for the most part, been already committed to a certain psychology. I do not wish to be ungrateful to the services rendered by Steinthal and his followers, but it seems to me, nevertheless, true that their efforts have been very much compromised (and this is true also in some degree, I should say, of Wundt) by the attempt to fit the results of philology into the *cadres* of a preexistent psychology, the Herbartian. The situation will be more promising in the degree in which students of language, working freely with their own data, and using psychology only as a working tool, make their own logical renderings and translations. It would not be difficult to gather from modern grammarians of the comparative and historical schools, a large body of data of great significance for the logical theory of propositions and terms—that is, of judgment and ideas.

8. *Logic and Scientific Methods.*—Of course, the status of scientific method has always had reflex influence upon logic; but in the main this has taken effect in the past through the efforts of those who were already logicians in utilizing the methods of experimental science in connection with the building up of their own systems. Without ignoring the tremendous fluctuation that has come to logic from such endeavors, we may expect, I think, still more fertilization when scientific men undertake an independent statement of the logical bearings of their own modes of procedure. We clearly are entering upon this stage of development. It is necessary only to refer to such names as Poincaré, Boltzmann and Mach.

JOHN DEWEY.

THE UNIVERSITY OF CHICAGO.

The Journal of Philosophy

INTUITION, CONSISTENCY, AND THE EXCLUDED MIDDLE

I

THE existence of mathematical activity has been ever a visible sign of faith to those who believe in things unseen. Yet agreement upon the subject-matter of mathematics and the metaphysical locus of that subject-matter never has been complete even among the experts. That the fundamental issues involved can not be regarded as settled is evident from the publication of two recent books.[1] Fraenkel's *Mengenlehre* in the famous "yellow series" now appears in an enlarged edition. Most of the expansion since the second edition is occasioned by the contemporary controversy on the foundations of mathematics, a controversy in which eminent mathematicians both living and dead are represented on every front. Although Fraenkel's book is primarily a textbook, occupied with the logical foundation of the theory of classes rather than with its technical application to function theory, it merits attention from philosophers interested in testing their conclusions in none too well-known domains. It is a model of lucidity and impartiality in statement, and even for the initiate there is a wealth of information marshalled in an expert manner. The almost exhaustive bibliographical appendix is a valuable aid to students of the subject.

The need for distinguishing symbols from the subject-matter to which they point is very pressing at a time when in logic, mathematics, and physics they are so often confounded. However indispensable symbols may be as safeguards and resting places for inference, it is not themselves they symbolize. Hilbert's characterization of mathematics as a play with meaningless marks according to fixed rules can not be an adequate statement of what mathematics is. For even as pawns in a game the marks are not *merely* marks or physical objects, since each represents the class of all marks in some sense like it. Even on such a crude behavioristic theory of mathematics Hilbert's marks have a symbolic rôle. A book on mathematical existence is therefore an urgent need. Unfortunately,

---

[1] The first section of this paper is a review of *Mathematische Existenz*, Oskar Becker. Halle a.d.S.: Max Niemeyer. 1927. Pp. viii + 369; and *Einleitung in die Mengenlehre*, Adolf Fraenkel. Dritte Auflage. Berlin: Julius Springer. 1928. Pp. 424. The last two sections are an attempt to raise and dispose of two issues suggested by them.

Becker's book is not likely to supply it; and indeed his inquiry is not directed to the subject-matter which the mathematician studies, but to the "mathematizing activity" of the mathematician. Becker does take his departure from the current opposition between consistency (Hilbert) and constructibility (Brouwer) as criteria of mathematical existence, but it is for the supposed light it sheds on human capacity that the miscellany of mathematical, historical, and psychological illustrations is exhibited. Most of the material is irrelevant, however interesting the historical studies may be in other connections. The book has six sections, of which only the last is devoted explicitly to the problem the author sets for himself; and only a part of this is analysis and statement rather than history.

It is, of course, futile to quarrel with an author for what he has not done. But what shall one say to a book on music, for example, which, instead of examining the physical and social conditions that make for its production, or of elaborating its technique, or inquiring perhaps into its place in a rational life, studied some supposedly special musical faculty of man functioning in isolation from his physical and social milieu? Would it not be relevant to ask whether the difficulties encountered in such a study are not consequent upon a misconception of the proposed problem? Becker's approach to mathematics is just such an approach. Mathematics is concerned, according to him, not with certain invariants in the physical world, nor with the logical elaboration of their transformation, nor with a technique of measurement, but with acts of the individual consciousness. It is inevitable that the applicability of mathematics to nature becomes a problem, and that a god must be invoked to solve it (pp. 324 ff.); but it is a problem only on the assumed premises. It is not the allocation of mathematical structure, not the ontological status of its entities, that is Becker's theme. He asks, rather, what is the meaning of mathematics as a type of human activity, what are the "life tendencies" at the bottom of it, and what significance do the "consistency-constructibility" interpretations of mathematical existence have for human destiny?

Becker's answer is given in terms of the *Weltanschauung* borrowed from Husserl and Heidegger. An understanding of human existence is a prerequisite for an understanding of existence in general, and it is only in terms of the former that the world is intelligible (p. 185). (This is the analogue to the phenomenological dogma that only of what is immanent to pure consciousness can we be indubitably certain.) The issue between Brouwer and Hilbert is resolved as the issue between such an anthropomorphic postulate and a realism which declares man an insignificant creature in a universe with fixed structure. The palm of victory is therefore awarded to Brouwer, although there is never an attempt to establish that postulate or to show that the alternatives in this disjunction are exhaustive. The fundamental quality of human life is asserted to be a concern (Sorge) about its own activity and destiny. So the search for proofs of consistency is interpreted as a concern for perpetuating unchecked the deductive process, and a desire to escape inquiry into the (tragic) nature of the objects deduced. But "noesis is ontologically prior to noema," and deduction requires that the syntheses of consciousness involved be really completable, that the intent of consciousness be fulfilled in the intuition of essence; the foundation of mathematics must lie not in the orderly process of the universe, but in the capacities of man (p. 196). Man's career is temporal, the living moment is doomed to pass away irrevocably, and it is in the certainty of his own death that the individual is alleged to grasp the essence of his own existence. There are two kinds of time. "Historical time" is real and non-measurable; in this, the life and death of the individual is a unique, non-recurrent event. "Natural time" is abstract and measurable; in this, repetition of similars is the rule. Only historical time is creative, although the creativeness of its unique moments is compensated by the fact that they must perish. Those series in mathematics which are incomplete and growing (wherein each term requires separate determination) are exemplifications of historical time, and true analogues of the destiny of man. Yet the task of mathematics is to "subdue" such growing sequences and exhibit their terms as recurrent instances of some law. Similarly, the individual man in his attempt to transcend his own unique actuality, turns to reason to predict the future and exhibit his own moment as a recurrent term in an eternal series. Mathematical existence must be understood in terms of this constant interplay of historical with natural time, an interplay which is the image of man's conquest of death through his prediction of the future.

One can not help feeling that a method which defines Jonah as that which the whale swallowed, can tell us next to nothing distinctive about Jonah, if the whale swallowed anything else. An interpretation of mathematics as the correlate of the activity of consciousness not unjustly raises suspicions that the vehicle of Becker's suggestive insights is a myth, and that we are given much more a pycho-analysis of the mathematician than an analysis of his subject-matter. A study of method is often a cure for unchecked fancy; therefore a statement of the principles which Becker professes may throw light, not only upon his position, but upon some of the issues in the mathematical *Grundlegungstreit*.

The cardinal principle of Becker, as well as of his master Husserl, is this: "Every genuine phenomenon must reveal its own essence to whoever apprehends it in an immediate grasp or intuition" (p. 309). Such an intuition lays hold with indubitable certainty of those entities, and only those, which are immanent to "pure consciousness" (a type of ideal continuity, present to all conscious beings, to which matters of sense are transcendent). Logic is the science of *a priori* forms known independently of the empirical sciences, but competent nevertheless to legislate and evaluate their methods. Logical principles must in the last analysis be self-evidently true, since the demand that all mediate knowledge receive certification can have meaning only if we are capable of recognizing some principles as self-evident. Every step of a mediate proof must be apodictically necessary, a necessity grasped in a primary intuition. A new "eidetic" science—a science of essence—is thus declared possible, a science which is, moreover, independent of all experimental procedure. Each essence must be known intuitively, independently of other essences, so that the new eidetic science is a kind of positivism transplanted from the realm of sense to that of intelligibles. Indeed, Husserl is not unwilling to call himself a positivist, if among the indubitable simples there be included such essences as "$a + 1 = 1 + a$" or "a proposition is not colored." It is the heart of the doctrine, and can not be overemphasized, that only what is "this-side" of consciousness is absolutely certain, and that of empirical objects we can not have that luminous knowledge which is beyond every doubt. One is not surprised to find that empirical uniformities are declared by Becker to be fundamentally unintelligible.[2]

II

Intuition as a special intellectual capacity is a well-worn word, and in philosophic and scientific doctrines has meant many things. The array of data alleged to be intuitively known is impressive; among them have been sensations, inner states, essences, God, logical principles, the past, values, principles of mechanics, and the freedom of the will. But probably no defender of intuition in any of its forms, whether it be taken as sensory apprehension or as intellectual

---

2 "Wesensgesetze gelten unverbrüchlich, sie gehen den empirischen Gesetzen 'voran,' sie sind a priori. Sie bilden den festen Rahmen innerhalb dessen sich die empirischen Gesetze mit einer gewissen Freiheit entfalten können, den sie aber nicht überschreiten können. Die Wesensgesetze machen das aus, was an einer Erscheinung begreiflich ist. Blosse empirische Gesetze sind grundsätzlich unbegreiflich wenn wir uns auch so an sie gewöhnen, dass sie nicht mehr als wunderbar empfinden und für selbstverständlich halten; in eigentlichen Sinne sind sie das nie." *Jahrbuch f. Philos. u. phänom. Forschung*, Bd. 6, p. 400. Husserl's own detailed exposition of his method is found in the first volume of the *Logische Untersuchungen* as well as in the initial volume of the *Jahrbuch*.

affirmation, will indorse all these items as self-evident. And indeed the doctrine of indubitably given truths, revived with such disastrous consequences by Descartes, has been fighting a losing battle with the demands of a discursive reason for verification and experiment.

The development of mathematics in the second half of the last century was successful in showing up as unwarranted the doctrine that a sensory, spatial intuition was necessary for the pursuit of the science as a deductive one. Carefully formulated rules of procedure replaced uncontrolled intuitive methods, so that the validity of the theorems was made to depend upon conformity to those formulations, and not upon an appeal to a vague self-evidence. The fruitful character of the rigor thus introduced in well known.[3] Nevertheless, although sensory intuition is no longer regarded as a method of proof, there is still a striking insistence in most schools of mathematicians who have reflected upon their science, that intuition in some form is indispensable for its foundation. For it is recognized that however hypothetical the force of mathematical theorems may be, the connection between premise and conclusion can not be a hypothetical connection; and therefore the validation of mathematics is not complete until those principles of inference are validated. It is with this certification of the general principles of procedure that the current controversy is concerned.

Now, whether mathematics is made to rest upon a pure intuition of the integers in connection with the intuition of time (Brouwer), or whether its foundation is discovered in some immediate knowledge of concrete marks (Hilbert), or whether with Russell and Husserl we assert "luminously self-evident" logical principles; in every case an appeal to self-evidence or immediate knowledge is a begging of the question, if that self-evidence is taken as a guarantee that the intuited data are both adequate to support the mathematical structure and self-consistent to permit its further development. Mathematics is more than the structure of its symbolism, for example, and if the latter is truly to symbolize, the reference and adequacy of sign to signified matter must be carefully and laboriously worked out, not taken for granted as self-evident. If we remember how sad has been the history of philosophies and sciences which have worked on the premise that self-evidence is something with which we begin, we may hesitate to endorse an attempted foundation of any discipline upon such a basis, even if

---

[3] The complete success of the logistic movement has not yet been attained. Even if one neglects the protests of men like Hölder, Poincaré, and Hilbert that there is an irreducible alogical moment present in their science, the well-known difficulties with the multiplicative axiom or the axiom of reducibility must be a warning to the over-confident.

no alternative method presents itself. The price that has been usually paid for an intuitive foundation of knowledge has been the sharp separation, on the one hand of physical and mental activities which involve trial and error and demand constant verification as the conditions of certainty and consistency, from the immediate grasp of first principles on the other. A philosophy which sanctions the *a priori* in its usual forms leaves the connection between material and formal logic unexplained, and too often makes a confusing puzzle of both the applicability and application of logic to existence. That puzzle becomes obviously absurd if the intuited data are declared to be metaphysical simples, whether atoms of sensation, atomic propositions, or simple ideas, each self-contained, each a diminutive absolute; and it is inevitable that on such views belief in a causal nexus should be nothing less than superstition.

Now what is the evidence for self-evident principle? what guarantee have we that alleged self-evidence is really such? There are two types of argument offered, the psychological and the logical. The psychological argument, very crudely stated, is this: With respect to some propositions we have a feeling of affirmation which makes belief in those propositions inevitable, and the index of our feeling may be taken as a sign that "it must be so." But, like Peter's idea of Paul, it too often turns out that the feeling is evidence more for the habits of the inquirer than a guide to the connection of ideas or things,—whether the feeling of affirmation takes the form of the inconceivability of the opposite or whether it is the apprehension of a clear idea. Since the discovery of geometries alternative to that of Euclid, for example, we can hardly claim self-evidence for our supposed sensory intuitions of spatial relations; and all the Nelsons who continue those claims reveal themselves as pathetic dictators to the tides of scientific progress. And even Husserl has introduced important corrections into his phenomenological analyses.[4]

The logical argument is very simple, but powerful: Any reason we may offer for a statement may itself be challenged, and we are thus compelled, on pain of an infinite regress, to acknowledge some general principle immediately grasped. If there is no *first* term in the series which constitutes our knowledge at which we can stop to say "This is so and so," then nowhere in the series is such an affirmation possible. But the force of this argument is due, partly, to a confusion between logical priority and temporal antecedence; partly, as Peirce has shown, to a misapprehension of the nature of

---

[4] Cf. Nelson, "Bemerkungen über die nichteuklidische Geometrie," in *Abhandl. d. Fries'schen Schule*, N. F. Bd. I. and N. Hartmann *Metaphysik der Erkenntnis*, p. 488 ff.

a continuous series; and partly, to a lack of recognition of the difference between the immediate quality of our thought as an event and its relational or inferential character as knowledge. The position [5] here taken suggests the following: Action is temporally prior to thought, so that adjustments to the environment may be made without a knowledge of the principles involved. Such adjustments are tentative, subject to error, and the formulation of the principles involved is quite as experimental as the adjustments. Reason is thus a late arrival in the career of an organism, and the activity of the organism is fixed by its own habits as well as by the habits of the environing world. When those habits become formulated as principles, the characters of objects may be re-arranged and redefined, not in the order of our observation of them, but in terms of such principles as will permit the inclusion of some characters in others. Conclusions are determined by premises in accordance with general habits of thought which have emerged as successful in producing reliable knowledge. The general principles of logic, considered as habits of thought, express and reflect the habits of that which is not affected by thought but which exercises compulsion upon thought. Consequently, these general rules are not something one can take on or off at will; they are not certified by intuition; they are rather the residue of a sifting process in which *operation* with those principles to obtain knowledge which must on occasions stand the test of action, is the only guarantee we possess of their efficacy and compatibility. It is therefore not impossible that some of our most cherished rules may yet break down, and that the most rigorous proof yet devised may turn out to be leaky.[6] If we are more certain of the laws of logic than of any other principles, it is not because they reveal themselves in an epiphany, but because all our operations upon things, all our discourse and communication, give them credence and support. "The controlling force in reasoning is not reason, but instinct and circumstance," remarks Santayana; and it was an excellent Hegelian insight which, recognizing the dual rôles of mediacy and immediacy in knowledge, found ready-made solutions and technical expertness the end products of long reflection, however familiarly or immediately they may present themselves. Self-evidence is a character that belongs to propositions at the *end*, not at the beginning of our knowledge.

[5] It is evident that it is taken bodily from Peirce.

[6] The history of mathematics testifies to the fact that not even the domain of the queen of the sciences is exempt from error. There is a vigorous endorsement of the view here taken in Bocher, "The Fundamental Conceptions and Methods of Mathematics," in the *Congress of Arts and Sciences*, Vol. I, p. 459. Cf. also N. Wiener, "Is Mathematical Certainty Absolute?" this JOURNAL, Vol. XII, p. 568.

It may be urged that one is involved in a vicious circle in trying to validate general laws of logic, since one must already use them in that process. But all that is really at issue is whether one may use a special instance to prove a general argument. To think is as much a natural event as to eat, and one may do either without using consciously the general principles involved. One may ask significantly what are the conditions for valid inference, even though in raising the problem one is, it is hoped, thinking validly. It is only Scholasticus who would enter the water only after he has learned how to swim.

This rejection of intuition as a certification of truth, whether of things or principles, has its moral for some of the issues at stake in a philosophy of mathematics. The desideratum in mathematics is that the process of deduction should never lead to contradiction. The classical method of demonstrating the self-consistency of any branch of the science is to show that it is *as* consistent as some other branch (usually arithmetic or logic), by exhibiting numbers and arithmetical relations, for example, which will satisfy the mooted axioms. But is arithmetic itself self-consistent? The answer usually given has been an appeal to an intuition of integers, or to constructs from logical simples intuitively founded, or to empirical objects "satisfying" them. But, really, appeal to intuition is question-begging, whether that intuition consists in the exhibition of logical constructs or empirical objects, *unless* these are already verified as capable of bearing the weight thrust upon them. In every case of an exhibition of entities as satisfying theorems, there is a prior question which must be settled: Do these entities have the character which we suppose them to have, are they really such that these properties may be significantly attributed to them? We may believe that no physical object is self-contradictory, either because consistency is an attribute of properties in a logical system (and therefore objects taken as brute existences are neither consistent nor self-contradictory); or because when a thoroughgoing analysis of objects is carried through, self-contradictory attributes never appear in the same context. The first interpretation of our belief can be of no assistance in our present task. It is therefore not the mere exhibition, as such, which shows axioms to be consistent, but the extended operation with them in various contexts that accomplishes this.[7] Contradiction can not subsist between actions, objects,

[7] In this respect no priority can be given to physical objects over ideas or logical constructs. The demand that empirical objects be the ultimate exhibited elements is, moreover, a program and not an accomplishment. How is one to demonstrate the consistency of the rules of the differential calculus by exhibition of empirical objects?

or propositions *as such;* they must first be taken into a system of meanings or relations.

What guarantee have we, therefore, that axioms adopted do not involve a self-contradiction? The point of this paper is that there is no absolute guarantee. If we feel more certain about some part of our knowledge than of others, it is because it has stood the test of centuries of use. The recent discoveries of "antinomies" in mathematics should make us cautious about the unrestricted application of so-called universal principles. The history of logic is witness to the development of our knowledge of logical doctrines— the logic of relations is a late growth as an explicit formulation; and the new formulation of valid leading principles, e.g., theory of types, is a slow process.

Hilbert's heroic attempt to find criteria of absolute consistency, even if his program can be completed,[8] has not quite the significance he seems to attribute to it, and not much is won by calling "meta-mathematical" those principles which are in dispute. One may indeed take certain elementary combinations of signs as ultimate data, but only in the sense that one takes scale readings or sense data to be ultimate discriminated elements in a science. It must not be forgotten, however, that there is a long process of inference involved in reducing a complex problem to such easily manipulable and observable items. If those inferences are taken for granted, it is only because of their efficacy in other contexts.

In denying the claims of intellectual intuition to be the tribunal of truth, one is not compelled to embrace a sensationalistic empiricism which identifies thought with sense perception. Thought moves on a plane different from the clash of atoms or the stimulation of nerve endings. But at least to one reader of the *Theaetetus,* if Plato's refutation of sensationalism masquerading as knowledge is complete, his arguments are equally cogent against a positivism of essence.

III

Brouwer's attack upon the actual infinite, and his association of the series of integers with time, led him to deny the principle of excluded middle when applied to certain sequences of numbers. Two types of infinite sequences are recognized: (1) the so-called determinate series, e.g., the series of integers ordered according to magnitude, wherein the occurrence of any integer is fixed and exhibited by the principle of order; (2) and the so-called growing series for which the occurrence of any integer is not exhibited by the law of the series, but reference to some temporal, extra-serial process is involved.[9]

8 Cf. the remarks of Fraenkel, p. 377 ff.
9 Cf. Fraenkel, pp. 226 ff.

Suppose we take as the meaning of a certain property P of an integer n greater than 16 the following: satisfying the relation "$2^n + 1$ is prime," and ask "Are there numbers n such that n has the property P?" If we can find such a particular number n, we answer yes; if we give a proof that the possession of P for an n leads to a contradiction, we answer no; if we succeed in doing neither, we affirm nevertheless that although at the time we can not decide between the yes or no, these alternatives are significant and exhaustive, and that in some sense of "are," there either are or are not such numbers. Now, Brouwer believes we must recognize for this last case a third alternative, namely, that no genuine disjunction is involved; and that the question must be left open, because prior to the actual exhibition of a number having P, the class of such numbers may be the null class for which predication is nonsense. But only an examination of all the integers could decide such a question; and since an infinite series can not be examined *seriatim*, the principle of excluded middle must be rejected for series where no rule is given whereby that examination could be accomplished in a finite number of steps. When mathematical existence is interpreted to mean actually exhibited, or constructible from a set or exhibited elements, there is no contradiction between the two statements: "There exist numbers having P, as is shown by the particular number n" and "an integer can never have P as is shown by the nature of integers." Since upon Brouwer's principles the denial of a universal theorem demands the existence (as interpreted by him) of numbers satisfying the contradictory predicate, obversion is not in general possible, and the *tertium non datur* is always valid only for finite collections.

Becker transforms these difficulties with "any" and "there is." to suit his thesis already sketched. According to him, for growing sequences, the negative judgment "There is no n having P" has no meaning, since the series of numbers which are *actually* examined for P, is growing in time, the growth depending upon the activity of the mathematician; of such a growing collection we can not say whether a number having P will appear in it or not.

There is really a twofold problem raised by the denial of the *tertium non datur:* (1) The first is as to the meaning to be attributed to "there is," and to negation. (2) The second is as to the alleged indetermination of a growing series.

(1) It must be admitted that if the existential import of propositions is so interpreted that "there is" is to mean exhibition or construction, no inference is legitimate from a universal proposition not implying such existence to a proposition which does. "If x is a man, then x is mortal for every value of x," does not, on the

usual interpretation of this proposition, permit the inference to the existence of some men, or even to a quantitatively determinate class of x's. Therefore, in order that a pair of affirmative and negative propositions should be contradictories, the negation of such a universal must be so interpreted as not to require the existence of any men, even though the universal does imply that if any men exist every collection of them must be free from immortals. Formally, the denial of a proposition "p," is "not p" or "p is false." Consequently, a formulation of the principle of excluded middle which runs thus: "In an infinite series of numbers either all numbers have the property P, or there is a number in the series which is not P," is *not* the formulation of a complete disjunction when "there is" means given or exhibited or constructed; and a denial of this incorrect formulation of the principle is not the denial of the principle itself. On the other hand, if, for example, "there is" asserts existence in the same sense as the universal asserts the existence of its subject, the above disjunction is complete, and there is no reason to deny the *tertium non datur*. All this is well known and it is sufficient to ward off attack on the principle from this direction.[10]

Of course, we are seldom content with a merely formal denial of a proposition, but wish to "break into" the proposition in order to affirm something of the subject which contradicts the former affirmation. This is possible only where the subject-matter has been previously analyzed; and the predicates are contradictory only if the subject is taken in a determinate context. To be square and to be circular are exclusive characters, although a body (triangular prism) may possess both—but not in the same connection. Consequently, every case of disjunction is conditional upon the context (temporal, spatial, etc.) in which the subject is found, and conditioned by the necessity that the subject be such that the predicate may be significantly attributed to it.

(2) On the ground that the future is incomplete and our knowledge of it vague, it is often asserted that logic breaks down in trying to deal with it; for a contingent subject-matter a proposition is not either true or false, since it may be undetermined in its truth value. Becker makes the more drastic claim that certain series of integers possess this same contingent character. Suppose we take the series of numbers of the form $x = 2^n + 1$ for increasing values of n, and define another series K such that if x is prime the number 1 is assigned to K; if composite, the number 2. The series K then has this appearance: 1, 1, 2, 1, 2, . . . If we ask whether, after the sixteenth place, the number 1 is contained in K, Becker maintains

---

[10] Cf. Burkamp, "Die Krisis des Satzes vom ausgeschlossenen. Dritten," in *Beitr. z. Philos. d. deutschen Idealismus*. Vol. 4.

that we not only can not answer either "yes" or "no," but not even "yes or no." His reason is that our knowledge of primes of this form does not extend beyond $n = 16$, and therefore the occurrence of 1 in K is contingent upon our determining the prime or composite character of x when n is greater than 16. K is thus a "growing" series with respect to the property of containing 1. The use to which Becker puts this observation has already been indicated.

It must be admitted that propositions about the future are not categorically true or false. The proposition "In 1930 Hoover will be the President of the United States is a proposition of this kind. But even an "incomplete whole" may be the subject of predication, on the assumption of certain permanences throughout the totality whenever completed. Therefore the proposition "In 1930 Hoover will either be President of the United States, or he will not be President" is true,' *if* Hoover is still alive in 1930 and *if* the condition of the world at that time will be such that to be President or not will still be significant. It is possible, therefore, to enumerate exhaustive (though very general) properties about the future, if that future is not altogether independent of the character of the present, or of any particular time—a condition which indeed is the condition for intelligible discourse about it.

Becker himself admits (p. 9) that even his growing series, although allegedly indeterminate with respect to some properties, are fully determinate with respect to others: the above series of numbers x is determinate with respect to the property "congruent 1 mod 4." It only remains to ask what is the nature of the indetermination which Becker affirms of the series K.

To locate indetermination in a number series is not a happy choice, and is inevitably confusing. To impute indetermination to the future means not only (if it means that at all) that our knowledge is incomplete; it means also that not all the possibilities of events will be made actual, and that the realization of possibilities is contingent upon all sorts of things. The indetermination which may be attributed to number series can hardly have the same sense as this. If we begin a series S arbitrarily thus: 1, 5, 2, . . . , then any proposition made about the numbers not yet written down is indeterminate in some respects, though not in all; the terms of the sequence will be, at least, numerals, although we do not know in what order the individual numerals will appear. To be numerals the terms must possess certain characters independent of the order in which they appear in this particular sequence. However, in the series K, even this indetermination disappears. The occurrence of a 1 is no longer arbitrary but is completely determined by the prime or composite character of x, even though the chain of determination may be altogether unobvious. The physical operation of *writing down* 1 or 2 is, of course, dependent on our knowledge or ignorance; it is also dependent on many other contingencies. Since the contingency due to our knowledge in this case would vanish if the theory of numbers were complete, on Becker's view, the contingency of a subject-matter is identical with the partial character of our knowledge. The danger is very great, therefore, that if with him we take series such as K as models of real change, the characteristic incompleteness of the flux of events will be overlooked, and that the contingency of nature will be regarded as a human makeshift.

ERNEST NAGEL.

NEW YORK CITY.

The Journal of Philosophy

THE SPHERE OF APPLICATION OF THE EXCLUDED MIDDLE

I WISH to raise the question of the kind of subject-matter to which the formal principles of logic are legitimately applicable, centering the discussion for the most part about the principle of excluded middle. Naturally I should not raise the question unless I had in mind a certain idea about the matter. If—as I believe—the principles, since they are purely formal, are applicable only to formal or non-existential subject-matter, confusion is bound to result when they are directly applied as criteria or rules in a philosophy of physical or existential affairs.

I take it there is general acknowledgment that a radical difference is found between universal and particular propositions. The latter alone are existential in import, the former being hypothetical or of the "if-then" type. To secure their existential application, there must be an independent particular proposition asserting the existence of something having the properties denoted by the "if" clause. The principle of excluded middle is assuredly, along with those of identity and contradiction, the content of a universal proposition; indeed, those who set most store by them insist that they are the most universal of all propositions. It would then follow without argument that they are hypothetical or of the "if-then" type, and in themselves imply nothing about applicability to existences. To be applicable to existence there must be independent propositions of a matter-of-fact kind, supported by empirical or matter-of-fact evidence, that things as they exist have the properties which meet the conditions set forth in the universal propositions.

The proposition, that A is either B or non-B, is in itself completely indifferent to the question whether anything exists having the properties designated by A and B. It is a complete fallacy to argue from the "A" of a formal and universal proposition to an "A" which stands for something existent. The two are as unlike as the formal and the material, the "essential" and the existential. But the universals of Aristotle were taken to be existential wholes inclusive of particulars. In spite, then, of the general present recognition of the difference in kind between universal and particular propositions, the Aristotelian conception that the principle of excluded middle applies directly to all existences is retained. Formal characters are thus given material meaning and the troublesome question of the relation of the logical to the ontological or existent is begged wholesale at the outset.

So much for the source of an ambiguity and confusion and the consequent need of raising the question of the legitimate application of the principle of excluded middle. The significant question is whether there are material or matter-of-fact grounds for assigning to actual existences the properties which are designated in the formal propositions. This is a question as to the nature of actual existences. This is obviously too large a question to go into here. But that things have the formal properties that characterize ideas that are employed in reasoning about them and that are necessary for consistent reasoning is in any event an unjustified assumption, and the steady trend of our knowledge of actual existence is one that renders the assumption increasingly incredible.[1]

I shall confine further discussion to two points bearing on this incredibility. One concerns the contingency connected with particularity of existences and events, and the other the fact that existences change and are in transition. The first point may be conveniently introduced by a reference to a sentence in a recent article by Mr. Nagel—with most of which I am in hearty sympathy.[2] "It must be admitted," he says, "that propositions about the future are not categorically true or false."—in other words, that the principle of excluded middle does not apply. But he seemingly qualifies the force of this admission, for he goes on to say that it is possible "to enumerate exhaustive (though very general) properties about the future if that future is not altogether independent of the past." I wonder if Mr. Nagel would not admit that the word "exhaustive" is unfortunate in this context. It may hold in some sense which Mr. Nagel had in mind. But, taken literally, an exhaustive enumeration would remove all contingency from the future and would make, in theory at least, the future in question so determinate as to be of the fixed nature required for the application of the principle of excluded middle. This interpretation, however, would seem to be excluded by the phrase in parenthesis, namely, "very general." For it can hardly be meant that any number of general propositions could exhaustively determine a particular event.

They could not do so even if we had infinite time in which to make the enumeration. For the properties enumerated would still be conditional, and the uniqueness of the occurrence of the event would still escape statement. There are only two theories as far as I can see upon which this conclusion would not follow. One is logical

---

[1] Those who object to the use of the term "ideas" may substitute the terms "essences" or "universals" without its making any difference in the argument.

[2] "Intuition, Consistency, and Excluded Middle," this JOURNAL, Vol. XXVI, the quotation being from p. 488.

atomism, or the notion that each genuine ultimate existence is wholly simple. In this case, a single proposition would exhaust each ultimate existence. The other alternative is that every particular existence represents in fact an intersection of universals. Both of these theories, however, seem to be dialectic products of the assumption that logical and formal principles have a direct material and ontological application, rather than conclusions from empirical evidence.

The supposition that the uniqueness of an existence can be propositionally and symbolically conveyed by adding a statement of date and place to the enumeration of general properties affords no way out. This device is effectively used in physical science. But the "space" and "time" of physics denote properties in respect to which existences are most generally *comparable* with one another—or are *not* unique. To the wise this fact is a warning that physics is not concerned with the individuality of existences.

The admission that the principle of excluded middle does not directly apply to future existences carries with it the admission that it does not apply to present and past existences. This statement will be challenged, at least as far as the past is concerned; for it may be contended that the past is over and its subject-matter all in and hence determinately fixed. The rejoinder that the past was once a future of something else may seem to be a mere dialectic evasion, since it is *now* past. But, as Mr. Nagel says, the assertion that the future is wholly independent of the present is fatal to all intelligent discourse about existences having temporal quality. The belief that the past is merely past, that it is all ended and over with, rests upon precisely such an assumption of independence of present and future. The past, if taken to be complete in itself, is arbitrarily sheared off from *its* future, which extends to our present and its future. The fixation of a past for purposes of inquiry and reasoning is legitimate, and to this fixation in an idea (or "essence") formal principles apply. But to assume that the actual event has the same properties as has the subject-matter by means of which we reason about it, is to make precisely the same conversion of the logical into the existential, the formal into the material, which is at issue.

Up to this point, the argument has nominally turned about an admission regarding propositions about the future. Many persons will refuse to allow that admission and hence will deny the validity of the argument that has been made. It may be well, then, to point out that the force of the argument does not depend upon the special issue regarding propositions about the future. It depends upon the fact that no number of propositions can exhaustively determine any concrete existence—except upon the assumption of one or other of the two theories previously referred to. The "A" and "B" of the law of excluded middle are always conceptual (or subsistential) in character and the "A" and "B" of an existential proposition are identical only in outward symbolization. The gap between conception (or essence) and existence remains.

Mathematical reasoning, by use of the principle of contradiction, justifiably reaches the conclusion that the value of Pi can not be stated in any finite enumeration. But the conclusion has no existential applicability until it is shown, by empirical evidence, that there are existences which have the exact properties of the mathematical circle, diameter and circumference. And I suppose it would be generally admitted that there is no existent circle in the mathematical sense—although existent figures have characteristics that make mathematical conclusions methodologically valuable in our intellectual dealings with them. But this is a very different matter from direct carrying over of logical forms to them.

The implication of the argument is not that things "contradict" one another. It is that contradiction is a purely logical category and is not false but nonsensical or meaningless when applied to things. The counterpart of this fact is that "identity" in the sense in which it figures in formal logic is also irrelevant to existence. Things and events *conflict* with one another and with themselves although our thinking about them must be self-consistent. There is a device often employed for reducing the fact of conflicting qualities—properties that are *physically* opposed—to logical consistency. It is said that all that is necessary in order to make the law of excluded middle directly applicable to things is to discriminate relations. Water may be both cold and not-cold at the same time, but not in the same relation. Specify the nexus and all difficulty disappears, and so with an object which is blue in one aspect and not in another, etc. But this argument points in the direction of our conclusion. For the abstracted relation is purely conceptual—or subsistential and universal—in character. It does not exist by itself in *rerum natura*. It is a way of thinking the existence for the purpose of thinking. The more we discriminate different relations, the more it follows that the existence in question actually possesses opposed—although not *logically* contradictory—properties and the law of excluded middle is not directly applicable to it. Otherwise a relation or universal is hypostatized into an independent existence.

These considerations lead insensibly to the other point. Existences have temporal quality. They are in change or in transition, in movement from one state characterized by certain traits to another. The door, it is said, must be either open or not-open, where "the door" is taken to denote an actual existence. But the statement overlooks two facts. In the first place the door may be opening or shutting, that is, in process from one state to another. The other fact is that there is no existent door which is one hundred per cent. shut. It is shut *enough* for certain practical purposes, but it is also open—there are cracks. The difficulties encountered in a laboratory experiment in securing, say, airtightness are significantly illustrative. They indicate the ideational and ideal character of "open" and "not-open." The ideal is applicable to existence *indirectly* as setting a limit to which to work, but this is a radically different matter from direct application of the principle of excluded middle. "Heat" as a concept or essence is not "cold" or non-heat. As concepts each should have self-identical and mutually exclusive meaning. But an *existence* may be changing from hot to cold or *vice versa*. It is not so much false as meaningless—nonsensical—to assert that it *is* either hot or not-hot, for what it *is* is a *change* from hot to cold.

This property may in turn be fixed in an idea and put in exclusive formal opposition to a state of non-change. But again in this operation we have passed from the sphere of existences to that of ideas about existence. We have passed from conditions of existence to conditions of effective inquiry about existence. The formal properties of the latter operation are important, but their importance is no justification for equating the formal and material, the logical and the ontological. We can not combine in a coherent scheme the metaphysics underlying the Aristotelian logic with the metaphysics implied in our present scientific knowledge of natural existences.

In spite of the positive character of many assertions that have been made, my prime intent is to raise a question. The question of the status of contradiction and excluded middle is a phase of a larger question. The basic issue concerns the relation of the logical and the ontological, the formal and the material or existential, and it can not be intelligibly discussed apart from that issue. Meantime to argue from mathematics to existence is simply to beg this fundamental issue.

JOHN DEWEY.

COLUMBIA UNIVERSITY.

CAN LOGIC BE DIVORCED FROM ONTOLOGY?

PREOCCUPATION with methodology has often led to the denial of an intimate connection between method used and the irreducible traits of subject-matter explored. This paper is a protest against such a diremption. The position taken and the arguments used are not new, and both have been learned, in part at least, from Professor Dewey's own writings. The only reason for saying here what follows, is because in his article on the excluded middle he seems to leave open the possibility of an affirmative answer to the question in the title.

I

Professor Dewey himself subordinates the particular question of the sphere of application of the principle of excluded middle to the fundamental issue of the relation of the logical and the ontological, the formal and the existential. There seems, therefore, to be no doubt in his own mind that logical and ontological characters are discoverable in experience, and that some evidence can be produced to decide in favor of the logical or ontological order of disputed traits. Unfortunately, nowhere in his paper does Professor Dewey suggest what that distinction is. It is clear, of course, that if no criteria of ontological traits are offered, the issue raised by him becomes indeterminate.

One must turn to Professor Dewey's other writings in order to fix the problem. In the first place, he claims for himself both a metaphysics and a logic. His metaphysics is a description of the generic traits of existence. His logic is a formulation of the method of such thinking which eventuates in an intentional reorganization of experience. Secondly, those are the generic factors, which are irreducible traits in every subject-matter of scientific inquiry. He declares that "qualitative individuality and constant relations, contingency and need, movement and arrest, are common traits of all existence." Thirdly, it is of the essence of Professor Dewey's doctrine that while we do define the general criteria of ontological traits as those which are pervasive and inescapable, yet these traits carry no tag which would permit their identification apart from a reflective inquiry. Ontological characters, like other characters, become objects of knowledge only as *conclusions* of an inferential process. Finally, on Professor Dewey's theory of knowledge, the fixed and secure objects of knowledge represent the transformations, produced by the thinking process for purposes of control and continuity, of the antecedent existences given to a non-cognitive experience.

It seems to follow, therefore, that objects of knowledge possess some traits which belong to them in virtue of the reflective context within which they occur, and that such traits can not be attributed directly (that is, outside of this context) to an antecedent existence. These specifically logical traits can be recognized as such, presumably, by comparing the qualities of objects of knowledge with objects of direct experience. But if the nature of existence is discovered, not by some prior definition of what it is, but by an experimental inquiry, the outcome of that inquiry must in some sense be identified with independent features of existence. When light falls on a metal plate and an electric current flows in consequence, the quantitative relation between intensity or frequency of light and strength of current, which is established by inquiry, is an independent factor in the domain surveyed. If the traits of objects found in an inferential process are *merely* logical traits, then no ontological characters of objects can be discovered *within* a reflective inquiry. And if metaphysical traits are not found within a reflective context, the only occasion when they could be noted would be in those non-reflective experiences of enjoying and possessing to which Professor Dewey has so eloquently called attention. Hence if ontological traits do not emerge in a reflective inquiry, Professor Dewey can not properly be said to know them, even if he may experience them in other ways. Over and above the logical traits of objects of knowledge, ontological characters must be present as well, if the generic traits of existence are to be known and not only possessed or enjoyed. Professor Dewey seems to ask, therefore, not whether ontological traits are something additional to logical traits, but whether ontological traits can be identified, at least in part, with the logical traits.

The question naturally arises how Professor Dewey comes to have a metaphysics. How does he *know* that specificity, interaction, change, characterize all existence, and that these distinctions are not merely logical, made for purposes of getting along in this world, but characters of an independent existence? Why does he impute the features presented in human experience to a nature embracing, but containing more than, that experience? It is submitted here that if logical traits are cut off from ontological traits, so that the former have no prototype in the latter, Professor Dewey's belief that the precarious and stable are exhibited, not only in the human foreground, but as outstanding features of nature throughout, is untenable. For the single argument which he advances against those critics who deny to nature, independent of experience, the characters disclosed in human experience, is one drawn from continuity. And it is not difficult to see that it is the only argument which he is entitled to use. "One who believes in continuity may argue that, since human experience exhibits such traits, nature *must* contain their prototypes." "For this reason, there are in nature both foregrounds and backgrounds, heres and theres, centers and perspectives, foci and margins" (this JOURNAL, Vol. XXIV, p. 58). If this argument for these characters is as conclusive to Professor Dewey as it is to the writer, it seems necessary to suppose that while there may be other ontological traits besides the logical, nature must contain the prototype of the logical as well.

There is no way of comparing the traits of nature manifested in experience with traits of nature existing in that background which is not experience. There is no way of discovering, by using reflection, that nature does not possess the characters she is discovered to possess *in* reflection. If, to use Professor Dewey's figure, objects of knowledge are the finished tools obtained by transforming crude ore, then it is the finished tools which are known. That nature does possess non-logical characters is a fact to which our common-day experience testifies. Such characters are real; but not more real than characters which reflection discovers and notes. Their ontological status is the same. One has as little reason to expect to discover logical characters outside of an intellectual or knowledge situation, as one would have to expect to discover a sensible quality in a non-sensory way.

For one who is committed to a whole-hearted naturalism, the continuity between logic and metaphysics can not be broken. The logical method we use is a method developed in the successful operation upon the things of existence—things which in their physical dimension exercise brute compulsion upon us, and which are discovered to stand to each other in relations approachable by intellect. By the very principle of continuity, the method must be more than mere method, even if the function of that method is the human one of making more secure the eventuation and enjoyment of immediate qualities. The method must in some sense reflect or refract orders of things which are knowable orders; orders which are never completely known, but which become known only if antecedent existence is transformed and modified. For we know things in the sense that we know the *relations* between them. To know the latter we must manipulate and change the former. Is there any reason to believe that in getting knowledge we ever determine what the latter must be?

One need not believe that it is the inherent properties of the ultimately real that are disclosed in knowledge; one may agree that it is the correlations of changes which is the goal of inquiry, and that such correlations are hypothetical, to be tested by consequences rather than by antecedents. One may say with Professor Dewey that the objects of thought are the objects of the thought of reality from the point of view of the most highly generalized aspect of nature as a system of interconnected changes; one may insist with him that the sole meaning of the relations thought is to be found in all the *possible* experienceable consequences which they entail. But it nevertheless remains true that such relations are discovered as an integral factor in nature, and that however hypothetical some of them may be, in some cases no alternatives to our believing in them are obtainable. Principles which every one must have who knows anything about existence, Aristotle remarked, are not hypotheses. And it is Professor Dewey who reminds us that "nature has both an irreducible brute unique 'itselfness' in everything which exists and also a connection of each thing (which is just what *it* is) with other things such that without them it 'can neither be nor be conceived' " (*loc. cit.*, p. 63).

II

To show that there must be a connection between logic and ontology is easier than to exhibit that connection in detail. Not more than a gesture in that direction is attempted here. But first certain reservations must be made.

It is granted that a non-ontological interpretation of logic can be sustained by confining the distinctly logical to the symbolic or psychologic mechanism involved in getting things thought and said. If the "laws of thought" are taken to define the use of words like "is" and "not," or to describe supposed facts of psychology, then obviously they do not refer to generic traits of existence. The only contention that is here advanced, is that such interpretations do not do full justice to the operative rôle of the laws. Secondly, the laws may be understood as methodological resolutions we make to ourselves in conducting inquiries. Just as the choice of geometry is a matter of some convention and can not be proved false by experiment, so the laws of logic, it is claimed, are our postulates for organizing our experience, are the rules of our method, and not the laws of nature. But one can very well agree with what this theory affirms, without affirming what the theory denies. For the laws of logic are unique in that they turn up in every conceivable inquiry, and in that no alternative postulates have ever been successfully applied; one suspects, therefore, that they represent factors invariant in *every* subject-matter.

Finally, it is not denied that logic is concerned primarily with the way of getting knowledge, with our second intentions of things, with things as objects of reflective thought. Logical principles are concerned with the mutual relations of propositions, not with the mutual relations of things: and propositions bear to each other relations incomparable in some respects with the relations between things. Consequently, a fundamental meaning which must be assigned to the principle of contradiction is that a proposition can not be both true and false; and to the principle of excluded middle, that a proposition must be either true or false. Nevertheless, from a reading of these principles which makes them declare something about propositions, we are led to metaphysical readings:

uniquely determined subjects can not both have and not have the same character; existence is determinately what it is; determinate existence excludes certain characters, and a determinate subject must either possess or not possess a given attribute; the characters which things possess fix the relations between propositions about them. It is true that propositions, and not things, contradict each other. But the ground of contradiction is to be found not in the propositions, but in the nature of the things which the propositions say. The saying of things is not the things said; and yet the saying conveys what the things are. If the principle of excluded middle does not tell which of two attributes or relations a thing must have, it does tell us that, given an attribute or relation, a thing either has or has not got it.

It may be objected that in limiting the discussion to determinate being, the question of the relation between logic and ontology has been begged at the outset. Logical distinctions, it is here admitted, are applicable to determinate subject-matter only. But it is also maintained that in so far as there is *complete* indetermination or chaos, *nothing* can be said. Chance is a metaphysical character, while at the same time absolute chaos or pure contingency is as much a limiting concept as pure form. Even the contingent, on this view, possesses an aspect of the determinate, just as the existential determinate possesses an aspect of the precarious. But is determinateness, it may be asked, a "direct" property of things, or is it discoverable only in non-existential subject-matter?

Professor Dewey seems to believe the existence of transitions indicates that determination is non-existential. When it is said that the existent door must be either open or not-open, he points to the fact that the door may be opening or shutting, and that no existent door is one-hundred percent. shut. "Open" and "shut" are therefore ideal in nature, setting limits toward which one may work in existential affairs. But one may well ask whether this dilemma is not due to a failure to define operationally and denotatively the ideas used. "Shut" may indeed be a universal whose instances are qualitatively dissimilar, so that the meaning of "shut" in different contexts is different. But fix one context, make explicit by pointing to a set of operations or conditions what it is to be shut, and the moving door meets or does not meet these conditions. It is because "shut" is first conceived in terms of an unexpressed ideal rather than in terms of empirical procedure, that the apparent inapplicability of the excluded middle is plausible. So two events are said to be simultaneous, not intrinsically, but by reference to the explicit operations which define simultaneity. Two events may be judged differently with respect to simultaneity, as a door may be judged differently as to its being shut—but not when the characters defined are first fixed operationally. If "door" can be defined existentially and not in terms of intrinsic characters, may not "shut" be defined in the same unambiguous way?

It is perfectly true that only thinking can be said to be self-consistent, however much that consistency is conditioned by the nature of things. Thinking is a selective process, and the principle of excluded middle is applicable only if we discriminate relations. Professor Dewey concludes that to abstract relations is "a way of thinking existence for the purpose of thinking," and that it is hypostatizing relations into independent existences if we suppose logical principles to be directly applicable to existence. But does it follow that because a universal does not exist by itself, it does not exist at all apart from the abstractive process? Does it follow, because isolation and abstraction are distinctive intellectual operations, that the objects of thought are not intrinsic factors in nature? Does Professor Dewey deny, because, to be effective, thought must approach nature piecemeal, that nature inherently has heres and nows, centers and perspectives? The systematic character which some things possess is reflected in our discourse and thought in a way which includes the accent of our speech and the habits of our thought; but it is not that accent and habit which endow things with system.

When Professor Dewey distinguishes between universal and particular propositions in terms of existential import, he leaves himself open to considerable misunderstanding. In the first place, the reading he gives is not the sole interpretation they can carry. But secondly, if, with Professor Dewey, we insist on an operational interpretation of ideas, we may well ask what is the meaning to be given to the protasis of the hypothetical universal. "Reduced pressure lowers boiling point," is a hypothetical proposition, since it does not say that there is low pressure, but states what its consequences are. At the very least, however, it does describe some categoric features of certain physical behavior. But it also supposes, that while there may not actually be low pressure, low pressure is intelligible in terms of the operations between existing things. Hence, while matter-of-fact evidence is required for the application of hypotheticals to particular existents, the reference to existence is never excluded from the universal, and is in fact doubly made. The existence of subject-matter in general can not be questioned if meanings require existential operations.

Predications about the future, as well as about the past and present, require that some relations which are and have been exemplified in existence will continue to be significant. In general, this is a hypothesis which in particular cases is often proved wrong. But were it always wrong, it would be difficult to see how the future can be subject for discourse at all, or how the present, when it has become the past of such a future, can be thought and investigated. Hence a future completely different from the present is as little intelligible as a past so dissimilar. But in entertaining significant predications about the future, alternatives for which the excluded middle holds, the contingency of future occurrences is not denied. "A sea-fight must either take place to-morrow or not, but it is not necessary that it should take place to-morrow, neither is it necessary that it should not take place, yet it is necessary that it either should or should not take place to-morrow."

It is difficult to know what kind of material evidence Professor Dewey would regard as conclusive for assigning to actual existences the formal properties in question. But very recently a book has been published in which some reasons for such identification are given by means of an analysis of the formal properties of machines. The analysis occurs on pages 161 to 163. The name of the book is *The Quest for Certainty*.

ERNEST NAGEL.

NEW YORK CITY.

VOL. XXVII, No. 7.   MARCH 27, 1930

THE APPLICABILITY OF LOGIC TO EXISTENCE

TOWARD the close of an article in this JOURNAL, I remarked that "in spite of the positive character of many assertions that have been made, my prime intent is to raise a question. . . . The basic issue concerns the relation of the logical and the ontological, the formal and the material or existential."[1] The article by Mr. Nagel "Can Logic be Divorced from Ontology?"[2] is welcome for two reasons. In the first place, I am convinced that differences of view on this question are fundamental to many other differences among philosophers, and to such an extent that the nature of these differences can be adequately understood only as the underlying difference from which they proceed is made explicit. Next to actual agreement nothing is more clarifying in philosophic discussion than the location of the source of disagreement. So I hope the article of Mr. Nagel will be the first of a number dealing with this issue.

In the second place, Mr. Nagel's contribution has made me aware

[1] Vol. XXVI, p. 705.
[2] Vol. XXVI, pp. 705–712.

that there was considerable ambiguity of statement in my previous article, so that I did not make my conception of the issue clear, and gave occasion to stumbling on the part of intelligent readers. So I am glad of the opportunity to restate my view of the nature of the problem—which I was more concerned to raise than, in that article, to try to solve. So let me first say that the question of the *relation* of the logical and the existential was intended to be taken in a positive, not a negative, sense. That is, I should answer the question put in the title of Mr. Nagel's article in the negative; I do not think that logic can be divorced from ontology. I agree that logical characters can not be "cut off " from existential (p. 707); that the "ground" of the logical must be found in the ontological (p. 710); that "method must in some sense reflect or refract orders of things that are knowable orders"; that "the continuity between logic and metaphysics can not be broken" (p. 708); and, generally, that "there must be a connection between logic and metaphysics" (p. 709). But these agreements only raise the questions: In what sense? What kind of a continuity is there? What sort of connection holds? There are other relations besides the literal identity or "equating" which I denied. And about Mr. Nagel's answers to these questions I am still in some doubt.

There seem to be two reasons for failure to get the meaning of my previous article. For one of them I am directly responsible. The usual meaning of "apply" is "to bring to bear practically," to use or administer. I employed expressions which contradicted my actual meaning, since my positive point is that logical characters can be employed or brought to bear practically upon other existences, while my negative point is that they do not inherently characterize other existences in such a way as to afford premises on which existential inferences may be directly based. My actual meaning is perhaps expressed in the following sentence: "The significant question is whether there are material or matter-of-fact grounds for *assigning* to actual existences the properties which are designated in the formal propositions" of identity, excluded middle, and contradiction.[3] The principle of contradiction is directly assignable to Pi as a logical or mathematical (symbolic) object, so that, as I pointed out, it justifies a direct conclusion—namely, the non-finite character of enumeration of its value. What I was denying was that it had *that* kind of applicability to physical existence, though I had no intention to deny that the mathematical object could be used, or be applicable, in *dealings* with such existence. Rather, the opposite.

The other ground of misapprehension is perhaps that while my

[3] P. 702; italics not in text.

discussion was limited to the three formal "laws," identity, contradiction, and excluded middle (with the emphasis on the latter), Mr. Nagel discusses for the most part the general question. It is true that I said that "the question of the status of contradiction and excluded middle is a phase of a larger question" (p. 705), but confusion may arise when what was said of an included phase is carried over too directly to the larger issue which I refrained from discussing. However, as I have already said, it is the larger issue in which I am most interested, and so I welcome Mr. Nagel's discussion.

I

He makes some statements that are in line with what I had in mind, however ambiguously I may have expressed my meaning. Thus he says (p. 709) that "logical relations are concerned with the mutual relations of propositions, not with the mutual relations of things," and that "only thinking can be said to be self-consistent, however much that consistency is conditioned by things" (p. 711), and that logic is concerned primarily with "our second intentions of things, with things as objects of reflective thought" (p. 709). Such statements are in strict harmony with my thought. On the other hand, I should not dream of denying either that valid objects of thought are *conditioned* by prior existence or that they are *indirectly* applicable to them by means of operations, themselves existential, which are integral elements in the *complete* object of thought. Without assuming either agreement or disagreement, I shall now proceed to a discussion of issues in the light of some specific points raised by Mr. Nagel.

I begin with the point that lies nearest to the specific content of my original article—the discussion of excluded middle. In reference to the application of the principle of excluded middle to a door as shut or not-shut, he says, "Fix one content, make explicit by pointing to a set of operations of conditions what it is to be shut, and the moving door does or does not meet those conditions" (p. 710). Precisely. Fixing context, defining a set of operations, is just the work of thought. Upon *its* product, then, the excluded middle can be directly brought to bear. This was my point. And as I explicitly pointed out, the resulting definition—the reflectively defined object—is of use or avail in *dealing* with actual existence. What was denied was that *apart* from this work of reflection in fixing content and defining meaning, the properties designated by the excluded middle characterize existence. Mr. Nagel has given a valuable explicit statement of what I called "the ideational and ideal character of 'open' and 'shut'" (p. 705). Instead of the difficulty being due to "failure to define operationally" the ideas used, the reverse is true. This operational definition is precisely what constitutes the object of thought, and its *absence* from *prior* existence is just why the properties of excluded middle do not characterize, and may not be assigned to, the strictly existential door. Exactly the same point may be made about "low pressure" (p. 711). Mr. Nagel says "while there may not *actually be* low pressure, low pressure is *intelligible* [4] in terms of the operations between existing things." Precisely. I should not desire a better illustration of my meaning.

In the same connection belongs Mr. Nagel's reference to the determinateness of existence. Here he has, unless I err, unwittingly taken advantage of an ambiguity in the term "determinate." When he says "existence is determinately what it is" (p. 710), he is referring to existence as it is apart from connection with the reflectively determined object. The statement, of course, is true, but it has no bearing upon the relation of contingency to excluded middle. For a contingent or indeterminate thing is "determinately what it is," namely, indeterminate. There is no denying that determination in this sense is existential. But such determinateness is a different sort of thing from the determinateness of objects of thought due to fixing a context and defining operations. What I was objecting to—and Mr. Nagel appears to be committed to the same objection—is the direct carrying over of *such* determination to prior existence.

The same considerations apply to the bearing of the excluded middle upon future events. I did not dream of denying that the contingent has elements of definite characteristics, nor that predictions rest upon elements of continuity of existence between present, past, and future. When Mr. Nagel says (p. 712): "A sea fight must either take place tomorrow or not, but it is not necessary that it should take place, neither is it necessary that it should not take place, yet it is necessary that it either should or should not take place," he is pointing out the difference that holds between necessity as directly characterizing existence and necessity characterizing the object of thought. It is the disjunction, the "either-or," that is necessary. Does Mr. Nagel hold that this disjunction inherently characterizes existence, or does he hold that an object of thought which is disjunctively defined may then be brought to bear, through operations, upon existence?

II

I turn now to the more general consideration. Mr. Nagel points out quite correctly that I have a metaphysics in the sense of attrib-

[4] Italics not in text.

uting certain generic characters to Nature as existent. He points out with equal correctness that as *objects of knowledge* these properties are reflectively arrived at. He then raises the question of the ground or criterion for distinguishing between logical and ontological characters, since both are the results of reflective inquiry involving inference [5] (p. 706).

In general the answer is simple. The distinction is made on the grounds of experience. Reflective inquiries themselves exist and are *had* in direct experience as other things are had. They are then capable of being made the objects of reflective inquiry. When so inquired into, their distinctive properties are ascertained. Thus the criterion does not differ from that used in distinguishing the properties of a cat from those of a dog. If reflective inquiry were not primarily itself an existence, its distinguishing properties could not be empirically determined. If it is such an existence, we can investigate it. Whether its properties are distinctively different from those found in other things is, of course, itself a matter to be decided by comparing the results of the various inquiries. But the present question concerns simply the criterion of distinction, so that it is not necessary to go into that matter here. It may be pertinent, however, to note that in each case the existential assignment of properties, whether to the existence of inquiry or to other existence, is dependent upon the actual performance or execution of indicated operations, the conclusion remaining propositional, or symbolic, short of such application—short of being brought "practically to bear." Does Mr. Nagel hold, for example, that implicatory relations as such characterize existences apart from reflection just as spatial and temporal qualities so characterize them? Discussion of this question would help define the issue.

III

The previous remarks suggest the answer to the question as to the "ontological status" of logical or intellectual properties, though they do not directly define it. If one takes into account the existence of reflection, then, of course, there is no argument. It is truistic that with respect to this existence, its characteristic properties are ontological—they exist. But this does not settle the question whether they exist apart from reflection, which would be the case were reflection merely a psychological or (better put) pedagogical

[5] I am not sure of the exact implications of Mr. Nagel's own discussion of this point, so I confine myself to the question of the criterion. The source of my inability to understand is his seeming implication (on pp. 706–07) that it follows from what I said that objects of reflection should have *only* logical traits.

process leading to the direct apprehension of things as antecedently possessed of logical properties. It does not settle the question as to whether they are ontological in the sense of being generic metaphysical characters similar to those of contingency, perspectives, heres and nows to which Mr. Nagel refers.

While I deny that they are such genetic antecedent properties, I do not deny that existence, apart from reflection, *conditions* reflection as an existence, nor that the latter has a temporal continuity with prior existences. The union of stability and precariousness is, as I have tried to show elsewhere, a condition of the occurrence of thought, whose ulterior function is, accordingly, to give to other existences a stability or determination they would not possess without it. My position may perhaps be made clearer by a distinction between the potential and the actual. To use a barbarous locution, I hold that existence apart from that of reflection is logi*cible*, but not logi*cized*. Similarly, certain stuffs in nature are ed*ible* but not eat*en* until certain operations of organisms supervene. These operations produce distinctive additive consequences. Through them, qualities and relations previously potential become actualized.

I am at a loss to see why my reference to the formal properties of machines (p. 712) should have seemed incompatible with the position taken in my article. Machines are machines, works of art brought into existence by operations that effect a re-disposition of prior existences. The redisposition that constitutes the machines renders new functions and uses possible; the traits that form the structure on which these functions and uses depend provide characteristic formal properties. But the fallacy of transferring these properties to the material on which machines operate is just the fallacy I was engaged in pointing out.

A loom as a reflectively constructed machine is applied, that is, "practically brought to bear," upon yarn—itself, by the way, a manufactured product. In this operation yarn becomes cloth marked by a pattern. This product has an ontological, that is, existential status. But it does not follow from this fact that the formal properties of the machine characterize inherently either the yarn or the cloth. The analogy to my mind with identity, excluded middle, contradiction, as general characters of the objects that are products of the art of reflection is complete and reasonably obvious. These characters are then applicable, useful, in dealing with other existences through operations they symbolically or intellectually define.

JOHN DEWEY.

COLUMBIA UNIVERSITY.

THE JOURNAL OF PHILOSOPHY

CHARACTERISTICS AND CHARACTERS: KINDS AND CLASSES

THE terms "when" and "conditions" are ambiguous in their logical force, the latter being determined only by the context. Sometimes their import is existential or temporo-spatial; sometimes it is strictly logical. When it is asked, "when will the sun rise to-morrow?" "when" as it appears in the question has an evident temporal reference. The when which introduced the clause "when it is asked," is equivalent to if, meaning whenever or if ever such a question is asked. Of itself it does not imply that such a question is asked. An independent proposition is required in order to determine existential applicability. The same ambiguity is attached to conditions. Sometimes it means circumstances which are temporo-spatial, frequently causal conditions, although not always such. But when it is affirmed "If he comes, I shall leave," the antecedent or protasis is a logical condition of the apodosis or consequent. In any hypothetical proposition, the antecedent if clause, is a condition of the consequent, or then clause, in a purely logical, non-existential sense.

In the instances cited, the context takes care of the meaning and there is no danger of confusion in logical theory. Such, however, is not always the case. It is the purpose of this article to deal with some significant instances of confusion in theory. By way of anticipation, I refer to the fact that, since the time of Mill, the terms "quality" and "attribute" are frequently used interchangeably, although the former designates something existential and the latter names a logical form; linguistically, the first is "concrete" and the second is "abstract." Any quality has temporo-spatial import; attributes appear only in if-then propositions. In the terms of the following discussion, the logical force of a quality in a proposition is to serve as a trait or characteristic by means of which we distinguish some observed existential object or event. In "blood is red," red is taken to be a trait or characteristic which in conjunction with other qualities enables us to distinguish a thing as blood. When we say "characteristic trait" we mean precisely that a specified quality is such as to serve as a diagnostic mark, an evidential sign, of the presence of an object of a specified kind. If, on the other hand, we have a *definition* of what it is *to be* blood, independently of the occurrence of any particular case at a given time and place, the proposition is of the *if-then* type, and the definition is in terms of a relation of attributes or *characters*.

In certain cases, the danger of confusion in logical theory is already generally recognized, although I am far from sure that the implications involved are steadily maintained. The term "all" is an example. In one sense, it means a *collection*, which is existential. For example, in the proposition "All the oranges in this box are guaranteed to be first-grade and sound," *all* has a collective force, and is capable of being stated as a definite sum through enumeration of objects as units. The same is true of *all* in the propositions "The following named persons are all that were saved from the wreck." Such a proposition as "All men are mortal" is, however, thoroughly ambiguous. In one meaning, it has an existential force: it affirms "Every human being who has ever existed, now exists, or will exist in the future has died or will die." It is as existential in import as are those cited above about oranges and about men saved from a wreck. It differs, however, in that the existent things to which it refers are non-enumerated and are incapable of enumeration; incapable of it because of the nature of the subject-matter, not simply because of human incapacity.[1]

The proposition "All men are mortal" may, however, have a meaning that is of a different logical type from that just given. It may mean "*If* anything whatever is human, *then* that thing is mortal." Such a proposition does not affirm that any man exists; to have existential application it must be supplemented by another proposition that human beings exist. It states a relation, taken to be necessary, between the characters or attributes *being* human and *being* mortal.

The connection of this excursion with the problem concerning the names "characteristics" and "characters" is evident. The *if-then* proposition just cited states a relation between *being* human and *being* mortal; it does not state a relation between the *fact* of life and the *fact* of death. It would be equally valid (or invalid) if no human being ever lived. For what it states is that what is *defined* as mortal is necessarily related to that which is *defined* as human. In short, it states a relation between certain meanings or certain conceptions, not between specified existential facts. To contents having this logical place and force I give the name *characters*. Take now the proposition "All men now living will die at

---

[1] I pass over at this point logical problems of whether propositions of the latter type are about *collections*. The problem, however, is not a verbal one, but is one from which consequences of fundamental logical importance follow.

some time in the future.'' It states a connection between observable existences, not between matters to which the term ''being such-and-such'' may be applied. It does not say that one proposition *implies* another because of the nature or character of their defined meanings, but says that from something about an actual existence something else of an existential nature may be *inferred*. It affirms that certain observed qualities of a thing or event are diagnostic marks or evidential signs of something not now observed, but which has nevertheless existence somewhere in the space-time world. It is to such qualities that I am giving the name *characteristics*. The definition of what it is to be human is a proposition of a radically different type; it is a proposition of the *if-then* nature. The constituent terms of such a proposition I call *characters*. Since the difference in question is between propositions of existential (and contingent) import and those of non-existential and necessary or universal import, the point at issue is not a verbal one. If the particular names given are objected to, some other words must be found if we are to avoid basic confusion in logical theory. The difference is intimately connected with that which exists between *inference* and *implication*.

In language, the difference in question is expressed by ''concrete'' and abstract words. It is the difference expressed linguistically by red and redness, by heavy and weight, by hot and heat, by just and justice, by a man and humanness. While certain verbal endings, such as *-ity, -ness* and *-tion* are characteristic of abstract words, the English language gives no sure indication in its verbal forms of the force of a word. When we say ''The leaves are turning color,'' we are referring to an existential quality. But there is no word ''colority'' or ''colorness'' in common use. Yet in physical science, ''color'' stands for a definition; it formulates a relation of characters of the nature of periodic vibrations to other characters of radiation and absorption—vibration, absorption and radiation being abstract nouns. There is the same difference between what is defined in this formula and color as a quality that there is between the T of physics and hot and cold as existential qualities. Definitions of relations between characters affirm functional relations between variables independently of whether the variables exist. In the case of T, for example, there is defined a variation in, say, the size of a mercury column in constant correlation with variation in molecular motion. The concrete quality, hot or cold, does not appear in the formula; color as a quality does not appear in the scientific definition of color as colority. We use also certain mathematical terms in a dual and ambiguous way. In mathematical *science*, triangle means triangular*ity*, a relation of angular and linear characters. When we say an existential figure is triangular, we are speaking of an existential characteristic as something which satisfies the conditions prescribed by the definition. Yet we often speak of the relation of characters, designated by colority or triangularity, as derived from the concrete cases by *abstraction* in a sense where "abstraction" means an emphatic selection of a certain quality to the deliberate neglect of all other qualities. In this view of the origin of the "abstract" and universal, there is found the ultimate source of the confusion with which I am dealing. I am not concerned here with the nature of abstraction beyond pointing out that *if* abstraction be defined as the selection of one quality and the ignoring of other qualities, then it can not give rise to a universal, such as whiteness or colority, the T of physics, or to any *scientific* conception, law, or principle. If, on the other hand, abstraction be conceived as the operation by which universals are reached, then it involves a passage from existential quality to something of a different logical order; we may dwell on a single quality as long and as hard as we please, and a concrete quality it still remains; white, not whiteness. The scientific conception of colority or whiteness was never arrived at on any amount of direct inspection and comparison of existential qualities, nor was the mathematical conception of triangularity directly extracted from things of triangular shape. The things doubtless *suggested,* under certain conditions, certain conceptual formulæ. But that which is universal can not be logically grounded in what is existential, although psychologically and historically the latter may be a circumstantial occasion of its formation.

In distinguishing between characteristics and characters as differences of logical form, we also have the key to the logical difference between description, propositions that state things are so-and-so, and definitions, which affirm a relation being such-and-such characters.

Unfortunately, however, the word "definition" is equivocal in its popular usage. Aside from meaning the statement of a necessary relation of characters or attributes, it is often used to designate the operation of discrimination and identification of a thing as one of a certain kind, or as an equivalent of *distinguishing.* We can describe or distinguish an eclipse of the moon by setting forth a certain conjunction of observed traits; namely, its disappearance from view when the earth comes between it and the sun. But a definition of an eclipse is of a radically different form. It is given in an *if-then,* non-existential, form. If the term "all" appears, it means whenever, if-ever, certain characters are taken, then certain other characters are necessarily involved.

I now turn to a specific case of logical theory in which the confusion discussed is found. Mill says, quite correctly of course, that when we affirm "snow is white, milk is white, linen is white" we do not mean that these things *are* a color, but that they *have* a color. Then, however, he proceeds to say that "whiteness is the name of the color exclusively."[2] This statement merely ignores the difference between "is" and "has" as two logical forms, one non-existential, the other existential. The difference between white and whiteness is said to be simply that between a quality referred to a thing and the quality taken in isolation; this mode of conception is not confined to Mill. But *whiteness* does not designate a color at all; it designates a certain way of *being* colority. It is, in effect, a definition of the conditions that must be satisfied if *white* can be validly affirmed of any existential object. *Whiteness* is the functional correlation of the radiating-absorbing capacity of certain vibrations combined in certain proportions. There is the same sort of difference between it and *white* that there is between a definition of humor and a joke. The instance may seem trivial. But unless the difference of logical dimensions exemplified in it is borne in mind, the relation between the logical forms of the *observed* matter of the world and of scientific *conceptual* structures is lost, to the confusion of theory.

Mill preserved a strong sense for fact even when the fact contradicts his official doctrine. He raises the question whether abstract words are general or singular. He says some of them are clearly general, being names of a class of attributes. Color, he says, is general because it refers to whiteness, blueness, redness, etc. Whiteness is similarly general with respect to its different shades. The same thing is true of magnitude with respect to different degrees of magnitude, and of weight with reference to different degrees of heaviness. But such abstract terms as equality, squareness, etc., designate an attribute "that is one and does not admit of plurality." Perplexed by the apparent inconsistency, he concludes that "the best course would probably be to consider these names as neither general nor individual, and to place them in a class apart."[3] I think that slight reflection shows that Mill has here slipped over from definitions that are non-existential to characteristic traits of existential things. Heaviness is heaviness, magnitude is magnitude, just as much as equality is equality and squareness is squareness. The difference of degrees he speaks of are in fact difference in the *quality of concrete things*. His reasoning would lead to the conclusion that equality is also the name for a class of attributes, since *different-sized things* are equal to one another. With respect to magnitude, a large thing does not exemplify magnitude any more than does a small thing. A thing either *has* size or it does not. Things may vary from dirty

[2] *Logic*, Book I, Ch. 2, Sec. 4.
[3] *Ibid.*, Sec. 4.

white to pure white, but white*ness* does not permit of degrees. It is somewhat curious that he realizes the point in the case of *visibility*, although things are certainly marked by various degrees of visibility.

Mill's sense for fact is marked in his statement that it is better to regard such terms as equality, whiteness, visibility, as neither general nor singular, but put them in a class apart. Were the point here followed up and made explicit, it would be evident that general (generic, relating to a kind) has existential logical import while abstract terms, definitions of a relation of characters, do not. When this fact is recognized, it is seen that abstract terms, including weight and color (colority) are in a "class apart" because they are *universal*. Weight is neither heavy nor light, and magnitude defines size but *has* no size. The import of the reference to Mill is not confined to Mill. Contemporary logical writings are full of the confusion of the generic (general) and the universal, in spite of the common nominal recognition of the ambiguity of *all*.

The confusion in question is most obvious in the current habit of treating propositions about a singular as of the same type as *if-then* propositions, both being termed A propositions or universal affirmatives. Thus we have the conventional syllogism, "All men are mortal, Socrates is a man, therefore Socrates is mortal," as the stock example of an AAA syllogism. If the major is a universal proposition, it is of the *if-then* form: Whatever is human is mortal, or there is a necessary relation of the attributes (characters) *being* mortal and *being* human. The minor is an existential proposition, affirming that Socrates has the characteristics that satisfy the conditions prescribed by the definition of human. Thereby Socrates, although an individual, is determined to be one of a *kind;* otherwise, or as absolutely unique, nothing could be affirmed of him. Thus the major is truly universal and the minor is generic. The two propositions have different logical forms, since the affirmation that Socrates is one of a kind, because he has certain characteristics, is dependent upon an operation of *observation*.

Take the proposition "Professional runners have hypertrophied hearts." It is a strictly generic proposition, affirming a connection between the characteristics that identify and distinguish kinds of objects. Yet in current propositional logic, we find propositions of this form cited as universal propositions and assimilated to the form of mathematical propositions, or those of the *if-then* type. This assimilation is found in texts that in other connections affirm correctly that no universal implies a singular one. The universal proposition correlative to the generic one quoted would state a necessary relation between two conceptions or characters. Unless such a universal proposition can be established, the proposition cited would have to read "professional runners *may* have hypertrophied hearts"; that is, *some* runners have them. The difference between "all" and "some," when *all* is a true universal, is thus not one of *quantity* but of logical form. *Some* is quantitative but indeterminately so; it is made determinate in propositions that state the number of cases having the characteristic in question in numerical ratio to the total number of cases. Even if, in the case cited, the ratio were one hundred percent. the full statement would have to affirm that one hundred percent. *of those so far examined* are so-and-so. It could not mean that "all" are so-and-so without respect to the number examined unless a true universal proposition of a necessary relation of characters had been established.

Unfortunately, there is no strict and commonly accepted linguistic expression that differentiates *kinds* (a term of existential import), and the *if-then* contents that are determined in a universal proposition. We speak, and properly, of the various kinds of mankind; of the various species of the genus, *Ranunculus*. But we also call them, indifferently, *classes*. Then we speak of various classes of triangularity, e.g., scalene, right-angular, and equiangular, as if they were of the same logical form as the kinds or "classes" just mentioned. But in one case, the subject-matter is existential, and, in the other case, it is a matter of determination by definition. White, red, blue, etc., are *kinds* of color in the concrete. The propositions that such-and-such different rates of vibration in relation to absorption-radiation *define* what it means to *be* such-and-such a color (phase or mode of colority) is not a proposition about kinds. There are no kinds of triangularity; there are modes of *being* triangular determined by the definition of triangularity. The use of the terms "kinds" and "classes" as synonymous is so well established in taxonomic classifications, like those of botany and zoölogy, that there are great obstacles in the way of establishing a proper logical terminology. But recognition of the difference in logical form, just mentioned, is imperative. I suggest that the term "class" be restricted to the modes that are determined by definition, or an *if-then* proposition.

In any case logic must make a choice. There is a determined effort to assimilate all logical forms to those of mathematics. If this course be adhered to, then all reference to singular and generic propositions must be ruled out of logical theory. If the proposition "Socrates is mortal" is introduced it must then be recognized that "Socrates" and "mortal" are merely hypothetical values introduced in a propositional function and they have no existential reference. An examination of the conception of "inclusion" would have to be undertaken, and the radical ambiguity noted in its logical force as applied indifferently to membership in a kind and to being a mode determined by an *if-then* relation of characters. The difference is recognized when special cases are in question, but I have seen no case of recognition of its universal force in logical theory. I quote the following from a recent text as a recognition in a special case. "There are several theorems which are true when the terms are propositions, but false when they are classes. Thus if p implies q or r, then p implies q or p implies r, is a true theorem for propositions . . . . It is false when interpreted for classes. For example, it is false that if all English people are either men or women, then all English people are men or all English people are women."

The latter proposition, called in the quotation one about classes, is an existential proposition; it is about *kinds*. The theorem that is said to be about propositions is a true *if-then* or universal non-existential proposition. Were this difference in logical form recognized as the *reason* why what holds in one case does not hold in the other, it would affect much more than the particular case cited. For if propositions about kinds are admitted as genuine propositions in logical theory, then it must be recognized that not all logical forms can be assimilated to those of the mathematical type. Thus the other alternative in the choice referred to above is before us. The case stands: Either logical theory must eliminate all reference to singular and generic propositions, to inclusion (save as an instance or mode implied in a universal proposition) and to inference, or it must, in recognizing the latter as logical forms, move on to a coherent theory of their distinction from and relation to universal propositions.

Choice between the alternatives mentioned is, therefore, not to be made arbitrarily. If propositions about singulars, characteristics, and kinds, and propositions about universals, characters, and classes bear a necessary logical relationship to each other, then logical theory must recognize both types of propositions, and is under obligation to frame a coherent theory of their relation. The confusion of the two types, exemplified in constant use in current texts of generic and universal propositions as being of the same form, both begs the question at issue and obscures what is probably the most fundamental problem of logical theory. In what precedes I have several times referred to universal propositions as propositions that give the *warrant* for taking certain qualities in conjunction as valid evidential marks in inference. This position is not necessary to establishment of the difference in form between generic and universal propositions and between kinds and classes. It does imply, however, the doctrine that the two types of logical forms bear a necessary relation to one another. In a further paper I shall develop this phase of my position.

JOHN DEWEY.

COLUMBIA UNIVERSITY.

THE JOURNAL OF PHILOSOPHY

WHAT ARE UNIVERSALS?

I

IN a previous paper I dealt with the difference between characteristics and characters and the consequent difference between general and universal propositions, and between kinds and classes.[1] Characteristics were defined as the qualities of an existence that serve as the traits that enable it to be identified and distinguished as one of a kind. Characters form the content of an *if-then* proposition, a formula for defining *being* such-and-such. In this paper, I propose to discuss the nature of universals as that nature is determined by their identification with the content of *if-then* propositions. I shall begin by recurring to the equivocal meaning of *inclusion*. In one sense, it means being part of a collection or a member of a kind. Thus when it is said that "negroes are human beings" and that "Sambo is a negro," a kind of existence is first included in a superior kind, having other members, and then an individual thing is affirmed to be a member of the first kind. When it is said that triangles are plane figures, the linguistic form seems to be the same, but what is meant is that the definition of plane determines also the definition of triangularity. The latter is one of the modes or ways of *being* plane. Here *inclusion* designates falling within the scope of a definition: determined as one of the modes of the relation of characters that are fixed by the definition. Being plane has no meaning except as determined in the modes of being triangular, quadrangular, polygonal. "Human being" would still have a meaning if no negroes were known. Inclusion is here a matter of necessary relations of meaning, not of conjunction of observable facts.

The following illustration, taken from the Oxford Dictionary, may make the point clearer. "It is necessary to include in the *idea* of Labour all feelings of a disagreeable kind . . . connected with the employment of one's thought, or muscles, or both, in a particular occupation." Here is exemplified an instance of what is *necessary* in a *definition*, that which is an indispensable part of an *idea* or conception. Being a part of an idea is obviously different from being a part of an existential collection or a member of an existential

---

[1] This JOURNAL, Vol. XXXIII (1936), pp. 253–261.

kind. The statement says that the definition or conception of labor is necessarily incomplete and inadequate unless the character of being disagreeable is included or *comprehended.* It would be awkward linguistic expression that would say "Human beings comprehend negroes," while it would be a natural expression to say that the idea of humanity necessarily comprehends treating negroes as human. Similarly, when it is said that "Every good poet includes a critic," it is clear that what is meant is that being a poet implies being a critic; one character can not subsist without the other. The logical import is radically other than when it is said an item is included in a collection or a kind is embraced, enclosed, in another kind.

Suppose that instead of the term "inclusion" the term "in" be used. There is a legitimate sense in which the rules of chess, the definitions of king, queen, pawn, etc., are *in* the moves of the game. They determine what is valid. The game of chess is also *in* the kind of games denominated "indoor games." In the latter case, one of a kind is meant. In a certain sense, the law of the parallelogram of forces is *in* the course taken by a sailboat. It is a formula or rule by means of which the actual changes of direction and velocity of the sailboat may be determined. But there is no question of inclusion in a kind; there is no *kind* of parallelogram of forces of which the movement of a yacht may be said to be a member. There are many instances of the application of the principle or formula, namely, all the motions that may be resolved into a compound of forces operating in different directions. The exemplifications or modes of a principle may, I suggested in my former article, be termed a *class.* So far as any kind has at a given time a determinate number of members it may at that time be exhaustively divided. A class, in the sense defined, can not be *divided* because it has an indefinite range of possibilities of existential application.[2]

If universal propositions are of the nature of rules, formulæ, principles, laws, certain consequences are implied. I begin by saying that if only the Platonic theory of universals had been a logical theory, instead of an ontological one, it would be logically more correct than the Aristotelian. For the latter holds that form, the universal, is *in* existential singulars in some existential sense. The Platonic doctrine, interpreted logically, means that the universal is "in" them in the sense in which the rules of chess determine the value of the pieces. The supposition is, of course, contrary to historic fact. Plato regarded the universal, Beauty, as itself more beautiful than any actual thing, instead of treating it as the prin-

[2] Division and classification (as the latter is here defined) are not coördinates.

ciple by means of which, if it were ascertained, the characteristics might be determined in virtue of which any actual thing may be validly affirmed to be beautiful.

II

From the point of view of what has been said, every universal, like any rule, is a formulation of an operation to be performed. A universal does not claim to describe; description is in terms of the conjunction of qualities that enable us to discriminate and identify the kind of which a thing is. The universal "includes" the latter as a physician's prescription includes the medicines that are compounded by acting upon it when it is used as a direction of things to be done. Although C. S. Peirce did not employ the operational terminology, his account of the nature of "leading principles" is an anticipation of this conception of them. He starts from the fact that habits are active when we make inferences. At first we use these habits or are used by them without being aware of them. Gradually we become conscious of them on the basis of the consequences they yield. We then find that some of these habits in their recurrences produce consequences that are stable while others produce consequences that are unstable. The former as they are formulated become consciously guiding principles in drawing further inferences. We also learn that guiding principles may be arranged on the basis of their scope. The principle that a rotating disc of copper will come to rest when (if) placed between the poles of a magnet is confined in application to discs of copper. Other principles are found to be directive or guiding principles in all inferences that persist in stability, that are not overthrown by subsequent operations. They are not premises, but they guide the formation of all premises and conclusions.[3]

The point of view here expressed is clearly operational. Moreover, it implies that selection of directive principles and their validation and invalidation is controlled by the *consequences* the operations yield when they are performed. While, then, leading principles are derived from natural operations, proximately from biological habits and ultimately from the natural operations from which biological operations are derived, they are not *mere* formulations of physical and biological operations. They present natural operations modified and controlled by the consequences (in the way of

[3] I am paraphrasing material found in *Collected Papers*, III, 162–170, and V, 365–368. The guiding principles of the highest order of applicability constitute the subject-matter of logic. This highly important factor, however, does not concern my further discussion, although in another context it is of fundamental importance.

valid inferences) which they produce.[4] Every art and craft utilizes natural operations but it modifies them to suit the purposes it has in view, the objective consequences to be produced.

It is my conviction that Peirce has laid the basis for a valid logical theory of universals. It is the business of leading principles, as formulæ of operations, to guide us in the drawing of inferences. They accomplish this task by indicating what qualities of things are characteristic of the presence of a specified kind of object or event. In uncritical common sense, as that distinguished what is merely empirical, inferences are drawn on the basis of qualities of things, the qualities being selected for logically irrelevant reasons; such as their intensity, frequency of appearance, congeniality to our emotions, etc. The laws or principles of science state those operations by the consequences of which we can determine what qualities are evidential signs and what are not. An "empirical" law states a general fact; that is, the recurrent presence of a certain set of conjoined traits. But it does not get beyond the descriptive; it is circumstantial, resting upon the accumulation of spatio-temporal conditions in the sense in which conditions mean circumstances.[5] Such a description can not be exhaustive. But when we can establish a relation between one character of being such-and-such and another such-and-such character, we can direct experimental observation to determine whether the conditions are present that as characteristic traits, warrant an inference.[6]

The proposition, to recur to an illustration of the previous paper, that professional runners have hypertrophied hearts may state a "general fact," one confirmed by every case examined. But if an inherent relation between violent muscular action, forced respiration and excessive heart action be established, and if the relation of these characters can be further shown to be a mode determined by laws of physico-chemical action, then the general fact rests on something more than enumeration of circumstantial conditions. It be-

---

[4] Peirce repeatedly expresses his sympathy with scholastic realism as against nominalism and conceptualism. In so doing, he interprets the Universalia as natural operations, holding that the weakness of the other two theories arises from failure to note that *ways* of action are characteristic of nature. When the principles are repeatedly used as directive principles of operations, their consequences become more coherent and continuous; thereby existential material becomes more *reasonable*. Failure to note this latter point is the chief thing Peirce had against the pragmatism of James, both using test by consequences.

[5] See the previous paper, p. 253.

[6] Since technically, the inference is subject to the fallacy of affirming an antecedent because the consequent is affirmed, even the greatest number of different operations converging to a common point can never yield more than probability as regards a physical or existential law, as distinct from a dynamical law or definition.

comes, as we say, rational, not merely empirical. The related characters defined in the physico-chemical principles in question have an indefinitely wider range of application than simply to the case of runners and their hearts. The field of inference is indefinitely ex-- tended, as well as each case rendered more precise.

III

The following conclusions are implied in what has been said. (1) The problem of the relation of universals to individuals is a logical rather than an ontological one. For while the operations defined by universal propositions rest upon existential operations, they carry the latter over into the field of inference, with such modifications as fit them to be determinants of evidence. The problem is to institute just *those* operations (form just those conceptions, definitions, laws) whose consequences disclose the qualities of existence that are valid evidential characteristics. The formulation of a natural operation with reference to the accomplishment of this office introduces the former into a new distinctive context, and in this content the old problems of imitation, participation, immanent ontological residence, do not arise.

(2) Similarly, the problem of the relation of the possible to the actual takes on a logical form. A physical or existential operation, such as the blowing of the wind, the steering of a boat, is by description actual. The formulation, in which the relation of a conceptual antecedent to a conceptual consequent is set forth, has a meaning independent of a specified particular case. It has an indefinite number and variety of possible applications. This freedom from restriction to specified and specifiable cases, is the source of the notion that it is independent of *any and all* application, and thereby dwells in a realm of possibility cut off, save accidentally, from the actual. Since the universal is determined with reference to possible applicability, no such separation of realms exists.

(3) A Universal is *ideal.* It is such in the literal sense of being ideational. But it is also such in the sense of being normative or prescriptive. It is not only ideal in the sense of being non-physically existential (since it defines an operation *to be* performed, but also in the sense that it states conditions that the qualities of existence must satisfy and conform to if they are to be employed as evidential characteristics in inference. As already noted, ordinary empirical inferences are so grounded upon merely circumstantial evidence, the contingencies of spatio-temporal presentation and recurrence, that they are undirected, valid by accident rather than because of logical principles. If a necessary connection were shown between being black (blackness) and certain other characters, we

should have a prescription to perform just those operations of observation which would determine that black color as a quality in conjunction with other qualities is a sign from which the existence of a crow can be inferred; but only in this case.

(4) Universals, definitions, laws, are subject to revision. They are not merely hypothetical in linguistic form (*if-then* propositions) but what is more important they are, as prescribing operations, *working* hypotheses, and hence are subject to modification through the consequences to which they give rise. The revision of conceptions and principles is a constant phenomenon of scientific practice. I do not see how this fact can be harmonized with any conception of their nature save that they are themselves constituted *in reference* to the directive function they exercise. The notion that there is some universal in Being, whether existentially or subsistentially, which is eternal and immutable is only an awkward way of saying that if only inquiry proceeds long enough and with sufficient care some principle will finally emerge that may no longer need revision. The idea that the universals are already, in and of themselves, Eternal Objects, Essences, etc., and that by trial and error we finally hit upon the particular one which is applicable to particular cases is gratuitous. For in fact they are formed and reformed entirely upon the basis of their consequences in actual operation. The existence of error in their formulation needs no explanation other than is found in fact that we constantly *do* the wrong thing, perform the wrong operation, in all the affairs of life: i.e., we act in ways which produce other consequences than those intended. The history of the advance of science is the story of improvement in the instruments, the apparatus, etc., and the techniques of operations performed accompanying the improvement in mathematical symbolism; i.e., formulations.

IV

I conclude with a summary statement of how the theory advanced is related to traditional theories regarding universals. According to it, realism is correct in insisting upon universals and upon the fact that they enter in some way into the determination of known and knowable existences. But because of failure to note their operational character with reference to inferential inquiries, they are conceived by realism to be, so to say, static forms of Being in itself. Some contemporary forms of logical realism conceive of them as operations, namely, as the invariant operations of nature itself. But this improved version still treats the logical universal as merely a direct apprehension of natural operations, an immediate registration of them as it were. It thus fails to explain the adaptive modifications natural operations undergo in becoming universals, or in being used as directive principles in inferential inquiry, as well as the revision they are constantly subject to. In addition the theory rests upon an assumption that can not be verified, viz., that there are operations in nature that are strictly and exactly immutable and invariant. That there are operations in nature *sufficiently* stable to be depended upon is testified to by every art and science. But that they are absolutely invariant is both unproved and unprovable, since it is a matter of circumstantial fact where we must be content with an order of probability.

Nominalism is thus on the right track as far as it insists upon the necessity of *symbols*. For the transfer of an operation from existence to an *if-then* form is accomplished only by means of symbols. But nominalism has always been guilty of ignoring the operational basis and function of the symbols upon which it placed its sole emphasis, and in most cases in consequence it ignored their functional and prospective reference. They were treated as mere practical conveniences and conventions. In so doing, nominalism denies the necessity of universals in regulating inferences, and is also guilty of self-contradiction. For if all existences are individual and singular, then words are also. In this case, they are not symbols; they can not have the representative character of standing for a number of different particulars, much less have the capacity for standing for operations that can be performed in an indefinite possibility of cases.

Although conceptualism has probably been, in recent times, the most widely entertained of the three theories, it is the most incoherent of them all,—not because universals are not conceptual and ideal but because of a completely wrong theory of abstraction and the nature of conception. It takes advantage of the ambiguity of "in" and "inclusion" already mentioned. This fact is shown in the use made by conceptualism of the notion of the "common" element, an element said to be extracted by sheer inspection and comparison of singular cases. If it *is* common, then the position of realism is conceded. If "brownness" is just a name for the brown quality common to a number of things, then *brown* is not just a quality, but in being common to all the different things is a nature, character, or universal. I shall not argue here for what seems to me to be a fact, namely, that as qualities of things no two *browns* are of exactly the same quality, the *brown* of this table being only the brown of *this* table. It suffices here to say that abstraction is of the nature of a definition of what it is *to be* brown and that this definition, as I argued earlier, involves moving into an order that is other than that of qualities—in this particular case one of vibrations, absorption, and radiation. No amount of direct inspection and comparison of qualities will yield the needed conception or definition. What is common and constant is not the quality as quality but the logical function assigned it as an evidential sign of something else. Instead of being directly given for comparison and abstraction, the commonness in question is the *product* of operations that depend upon a universal or conception being already at command. We can not extract the common character of ''horsiness'' from horses until each singular has already been determined *to be* a horse, and this determination implies that, through the operative use of a universal, certain qualities have been warranted to be evidential characteristics of a certain kind of thing. Conceptualism escapes from logical realism only by assuming the very matter at issue in its reference to the ''common.''

At the close of the former article, it was said that the question of the subject-matter of logic—with especial reference to the question of whether or not it is strictly mathematical—depends upon the answer given to the question of whether there is a necessary relation between characters and characteristics, between generic and universal propositions. The present paper is, as far as it goes, an attempt to show that there is such an intrinsic relationship, the determination of characteristics and of evidential values in inference depending upon the use of universal propositions; while the latter in turn are framed and employed with express reference to their operative function in determination of evidential values. According to this conclusion, logic can be a coherent and unified theory only as it brings implication and inference into relation with each other. Otherwise, inference is either assimilated to implication, being treated as a defective case of it (as in many of the current doctrines of induction), or else it is ruled out of logic entirely. Another alternative is to recognize (as seems to be the case in logical positivism) inference alone and to treat logical and mathematical forms that determine implication relations as mere linguistic practical devices for handling empirical inferences, contributing nothing beyond practical convenience to the latter undertaking. The recognition of the correlative character of inference and implication liberates us from both of these one-sided positions.

JOHN DEWEY.

COLUMBIA UNIVERSITY

THE JOURNAL OF PHILOSOPHY

GENERAL PROPOSITIONS, KINDS, AND CLASSES

IN an earlier article I called attention to the fact that Mill stated that since abstract terms are sometimes singular and sometimes general, it might be better to put them in a "class apart." I argued that this class apart was that of universal *if-then* propositions; abstract terms being, when they have logical import, the content of such propositions. I stated that confusion has arisen in logical theory because such propositions are not definitely and consistently marked off from propositions that are general in the sense of *generic*, that is, referring to kinds, the latter being designated linguistically by common nouns instead of abstract nouns. I added that "contemporary logical writings are full of the confusion of the generic (general) and the universal, in spite of the common nominal recognition of the ambiguity of *all*." [1] I propose here to illustrate this last statement as a means of effecting recognition of a difference in logical form between two kinds of propositions both of which are termed *general*.[2]

The nature of classes is introduced by Miss Stebbing by means of an example, the class of scholars. It is said that "scholars are all the *individuals* who are learned, viz., a set of individuals distinguished from other sets of individuals in that *each* individual of the set possesses the property of being learned." [3] The set determined by a property or a conjunction of properties is said to constitute a class. Later, we find the statements "General propositions are about properties which *individual* objects may possess"; and "Every property determines a class, namely, the class consisting of the *objects* which possess the property." [4] I am not citing these passages to take objection to them. On the contrary, Miss

[1] This JOURNAL, Vol. XXXIII (1936), p. 258. The present article is a further development of certain logical principles advanced in the two earlier articles, "Characteristics and Characters," "What Are Universals?" published in this JOURNAL, Volume XXXIII (1936), pp. 253–261, pp. 281–288.

[2] I use L. C. Stebbing, *A Modern Introduction to Logic*, especially Ch. IX, on "Classes and Propositions" as representative of the current position and take her statements because of the clearness and explicitness with which the matter at issue is treated.

[3] *Op. cit.*, p. 140. The italics are not in the original text. The reason for introducing them appears in the sequel of the present discussion.

[4] *Op. cit.*, p. 144 and p. 142; the italics are still mine.

Stebbing brings out clearly the important fact that general propositions are directly about a relation of properties and indirectly about objects having these properties. Moreover, the text goes on to indicate the logical difference between A and E propositions on one side, and I and O propositions on the other. The former can be understood if we "understand what is meant by being an S and a P. Hence it is convenient to interpret them as not implying the existence of S."[5] I and O propositions, on the other hand, do imply (refer to, or postulate) existence.

There is, of course, no objection to be taken to these statements. But what one would expect to follow from them is that there is a basic logical difference between general propositions about properties, determining a kind of *objects* marked by these properties, and the *if-then* propositions that do not "imply" the existence of objects. What one naturally expects is that it would be affirmed that the former are necessarily of the I and O form and the latter alone of the A and E form. But this distinction between the two types of general propositions is not drawn. It would also seem to follow that a distinction should be made between the concept of *"classes"* as determined by propositions of the first form, and the logical concept of whatever it is that is determined by the *if-then* A and E universal propositions.[6]

Such, however, are not the conclusions drawn. Both types of propositions are treated as general propositions and that which is determined by propositions of the two forms is indiscriminately termed a class. As far as can be made out, the ground for the identification is as follows: The sound idea that generic propositions are directly concerned with properties which refer to the whole range of objects that may possess them, not to any given one thing among them, is gradually converted into the idea that such propositions have no inherent existential reference at all. This conclusion is thought to be supported by the further (undeniable) fact that in the case of some generic propositions, for example, those about centaurs, sea-serpents, etc., there are in point of fact no existences to which they can refer.

    [5] *Op. cit.*, p. 143. While the passage quoted refers to "convenience," it is stated on the next page that A and E propositions are of the *if-then* type and that such propositions do not imply existence.
    [6] Because of the association of the term "general" with *generic* and of these terms with *kinds*, I have suggested that the word "kinds" be used to designate that which is determined by general propositions of the first type, reserving the word "classes" for that which is determined by the universal propositions that do not have reference to objects as existences. But the important thing is not the words used, but recognition of the difference in logical form and the need for *some* linguistic designation of the difference.

1. As to the first point. It is truly said that "we can assert 'all men are mortal' although we are certainly not acquainted with *each* individual man." It is also said that "no *actual* man enters into the assertion since the assertion is true whether any *given* man is known or not," for "a property or characteristic is being considered in abstraction from the individual or individuals to which it may refer." [7]

Is there not a fallacy here? It is certainly true that the proposition, if valid at all, is valid irrespective of reference to any *given* man. But when *actual* and *given* are treated as equivalent, lack of reference to a given man may be treated as if it meant the absence of reference to any existent object at all. The earlier quotations make a proposition general in that it refers indifferently and equally to *each and every* object having specified properties. Is this absence of specific reference to one of a set rather than to other objects of the set equivalent to absence of reference to any object whatever? The author, like other contemporary writers on logic, is well aware of the ambiguity of "all." The bare sentence "All men are mortal" may be interpreted to mean that there is a relation between *being* human and *being* mortal. In that case, it is an *if-then* proposition, free from existential reference; it expresses a relation of abstract characters. It may also be interpreted to mean that each and every one of the set of objects that have the properties that distinguish men have also the property of dying or of subjection to death. The latter proposition is existential in reference, and, in spite of the presence of the word "all," is logically an *I* proposition. The fallacy may also be stated as follows.[8] It is one thing to make a proposition about characteristics or properties in *abstraction* from the existence of any *given* man. It is another thing to make a proposition *about* abstractions as such. Only by confusing these two senses of abstraction does the conclusion that is drawn follow. The term "any" suffers from the same ambiguity as the word "all." It may mean *each and everyone;* or it may mean *whatever* is determined by an *if-then* universal proposition, irrespective of existence.

2. The conception that general propositions as such, irrespective of the distinction that has been made between their two forms, lack existential reference is thought to be confirmed by consideration of null-classes. When "Indian popes" is given as an example of a null-

---

[7] All quotations are from p. 143; italics are mine.

[8] There is no logical *contradiction* involved if some man, say Melchizedek or Elijah, is found to exist who did not die. The fact would require a modification of the proposition "All men are mortal"; we should have to affirm that "All men, except some specified individuals, are mortal." But the *if-then* proposition affirms a *necessary* connection between abstract characters.

class, it is correctly stated that *"up to the present"* that class has no members. The temporal clause makes clear the existential reference of the proposition "there are no Indian popes"; or that there is no logical incompatibility between *being* a pope and *being* an Indian such that the E propositions "If a pope, then not an Indian," and "If an Indian, then not a pope" can be affirmed. Similarly with the proposition "There are no sea-serpents." The proposition means that no creatures of this kind have ever been observed; the proposition is existential in reference, although negatively so. But there is no logical contradiction in their existence; it simply happens, so to speak, that none have been found to exist, while there is a considerable, although not absolute, probability (if the contradiction in terms be allowed) that if one existed it would have been observed. As for the "null-class" of knighted scavengers, stranger things have happened than that a person of this kind should exist. An instance of a null-class of the other type is found in propositions about round-squares. Here is the logical contradiction between the abstract characters "squareness" and "circularity" that is affirmed. Similarly, the long succession of attempts to "square the circle" were logically put an end to only by the demonstration that *pi* is not a root of any rational algebraic equation. Thus argument from null-class propositions fails to support the conclusion that general propositions as such lack existential reference, since it holds in only one (the "universal") form of such generals.

The confusion dealt with is the more significant because Miss Stebbing takes special pains to point out that propositions about "membership" of an individual in a "class" (a kind in my terminology) are different in logical form from propositions that affirm the inclusion of a class in another class. It is repeatedly pointed out that a proposition that affirms, for example, that "Socrates is an Athenian" is of different form from such a proposition as "Athenians are Greeks." It is also pointed out that failure to recognize and mark this difference in form was a source of confusion and error in earlier logical theory.[9] For a proposition of the first form is about a singular object as such, while that about the relations of kinds deliberately avoids this restriction. In spite, however, of this acknowledged difference in logical form and force, the singular proposition is treated as if it could be derived by substitution or insertion from not only the generic proposition but also from the hypothetical universal. This phase of the confusion of logical theory is promoted by the use of abstract symbols—showing that their presence is no protection against systematic error. It is said "We can express 'men' by the propositional function '$\hat{x}$ is

9 See pp. 29, 40, 43, 60, 173, and 461.

human.' If for x in '$\hat{x}$ is human' we substitute the name of an individual who is human, we have a sentence expressing a true proposition."[10] For example, we can substitute Socrates for x in "$\hat{x}$ is human." This process may seem simple and straightforward. But what is the *warrant* for the affirmation that Socrates or any particular man is human? It does not follow from the propositional function in fact; and logically the idea that it does follow is forbidden by the valid distinction that has been drawn between a proposition of "class-membership" and a general proposition. A propositional function is everywhere recognized to be neither "true" nor "false"; while it requires observations of existential objects to determine the fact that a given object exists and that it has the characteristics designated by, say, human. The absence of existential reference found in the universal proposition holds *a fortiori* of propositional functions. If, however, the proposition is general in the sense of being one about a relation of kinds, the question of substitution stands on a somewhat different footing. If "all men are mortal" is affirmed, and we can determine the fact that Socrates existed and that he was a man, then we can conclude that he is mortal; that he will die or has died. But even in this case, the proposition is not one of mere substitutive subsumption. It still requires operations of independent observation to establish the existence and characteristics of Socrates. These observations are *directed* by the generic proposition. But the results of the observations test the validity of the generalization. Theoretically it is possible that Socrates might have the characteristic properties that identify him as a man and yet not have the trait of dying, even though the factual evidence against the possibility is of a very high order. In other words, the singular case might be such as to demand a revision of the generalization, just as the observations that warranted the proposition "This is black and is a swan" upset the generalization "All swans are white." If there were a universal proposition affirmed to the effect that there is a necessary relation between the abstract characters "humanity" (or "animality") and "mortality," then and only then would one be committed to the conclusion that Socrates is (necessarily) one who will die or has died. The logical reaction of the singular proposition back into the generic proposition disposes, once for all, of the conception of insertion or substitution.

It may be worth while to mention that Miss Stebbing definitely recognizes that the logical import of words like *a* and *an* does not of itself determine the propositional force of the sentence in which they appear.[11] Thus the sentence "An English poet was stabbed"

[10] *Op. cit.*, p. 142.
[11] *Op. cit.*, p. 79.

almost certainly refers to some singular human being, while "A poet is inspired" is most naturally interpreted to affirm a relation between the abstract characters *being* poetic and *being* inspired, thereby affording a criterion, say, for the difference between a poetaster and a "true" poet. It is now recognized on all hands that an analogous ambiguity attaches to "the." When we speak of "the river" or "the mountain" we usually mean to refer to a singular familiar object; when we speak of *the* atom we mean either a kind of thing as a whole or else the characters which define *being* atomic. The systematic recognition of these ambiguities also enforces recognition of the two different logical forms of general propositions.

One further instance of the confusion existing in logical theory will be given. It is stated that "A general proposition is an implicative proposition." [12] This statement certainly holds of general propositions of the *if-then* or universal form. If the proposition "All who are wise are trustworthy" means there is a necessary connection between the (abstract) characters "wisdom" and "trustworthiness," then other *if-then* propositions in which wisdom and trustworthiness are terms are implied. If the proposition is a factual generalization stating that as far as observation has gone, the singular existences who are wise have also been found to be trustworthy, it is difficult to see what *implications* the proposition has. *Inferences* may be drawn which are existential in reference, but they rest upon factual evidence, not upon the mere implicative force of the proposition. From the *I* proposition *Some Germans are poets* an inference may be drawn from the fact that a given man is a German poet to traits or characteristics other than that he is a German; namely, to *all* the properties that describe the kind, poets. The fact that he is a German poet does not, however, *imply* other propositions unless "implication" is so loosely construed as to be equivalent to the possibility of inference—in which case logical necessity is not included in the conception of implication. Leaving words aside, there is a difference between a conclusion that follows necessarily and demonstratively and one that is only probable, because resting ultimately on observed evidential data. This difference exists no matter how the words "inference" and "implication" are employed. We draw inferences from facts; the conditions and relations are then certainly of a different form from those of hypothetical propositions, whatever names be given to the two forms.

In the same context, "All squares are rectangles" is given as an example of a general proposition. "What is asserted is a connexion between two properties or characteristics. These characteristics are considered apart from the particular things which have the

[12] *Op. cit.*, p. 44.

characteristics."[13] I shall not repeat what has already been said about the ambiguity of the concept of abstraction and of being "considered apart from particulars." I wish to connect the statements with the doctrine that such propositions affirm "that one class is wholly (or partially) included in (or excluded from) another class." When the proposition is understood to affirm that objects that have the property which demarcates a *square* have also the property that demarcates a *rectangle*, no exception can be taken. Square *things* are rectangular things. But understood in this sense, it follows, in accordance with the (correct) position that such propositions are of the I form, that it is a proposition ultimately about observable existences. Passing over the question of whether there are in fact *any* objects that have the exact properties in question, I point out that its form is different from the universal proposition that there is a necessary relation between the (abstract) characters, "squareness" and "rectangularity," for the latter is a mathematical proposition, not one about objects.

The bearing of this upon the nature of inclusion (or exclusion) is as follows: The relation of a less extensive kind to a kind of wider extension is evidently one to which the idea of enclosure is properly applicable. The relation, since it is of *things* that are determined by properties, is suitably enough symbolized by means of a physical enclosure, like the familiar case of the circle wholly within a circle of greater diameter. Can the same thing be said of square*ness* and circular*ity* or is the logical meaning of *inclusion* very different in the latter case? Does *rectangularity* "include" *squareness* in any other sense than that mathematically a proposition about the former *implies* a determinate proposition about the latter? And if it is taken to *exclude*, say, triangularity or circularity, does "exclusion" here mean anything other than logical incompatibility? We are logically forbidden to affirm of triangularity as such what may be affirmed of rectangularity as such, although of course with reference to the character of being *plane* figures they both have common implications.[14] Rectangularity is a *wider* conception than that of squareness. But greater and less width of inclusiveness here means that a proposition about it has a wider range of implications. If the situation is expressed by symbolic diagrams, a scheme of brackets or braces is much more suitable than one of circles.

[13] *Op. cit.*, pp. 43–44.

[14] It is possible to draw an *actual* figure in such a way that it can not be determined, without a precision of instruments of measurement that it may be impossible to attain, whether it is *a* square or *a* rectangle. *If* it is one, then certain implicated propositions follow from the fact that the given figure *exemplifies* the character.

In an earlier article, I illustrated the point about the two meanings of inclusion by a quotation from Mill to the effect that the *idea* of labor contains or includes the *idea* of disagreeable feelings accompanying exercise of an occupation.[15] If this *definition* of labor be accepted, then the proposition that enjoyable work is labor is *precluded;* that is, it is ruled out by definition. Being a necessary constituent of a conception or definition would seem, then, to be very different from the fact that a smaller set of things is an existential part of a larger existential set. The point made is also connected with the current ambiguous use of the term "classes," as that term is employed indiscriminately to designate both types of "general" subject-matter—that which is existential in reference and that which is non-existential.

I conclude with a brief allusion to an objection that may be made. It may be said that my argument turns, at certain points, upon giving the term "objects" an unjustifiably narrow meaning, that of existences. The reply is simple. Admitting that the wider use of the term is proper, my argument emphasizes the necessity for discrimination in logical theory between existential objects and logical and mathematical objects.

JOHN DEWEY.

COLUMBIA UNIVERSITY.

---

[15] This JOURNAL, Vol. XXXIII (1936), p. 281.

THE JOURNAL OF PHILOSOPHY

A SYMPOSIUM OF REVIEWS OF JOHN DEWEY'S *LOGIC: THE THEORY OF INQUIRY* [1]

PROFESSOR DEWEY: LOGICIAN—ONTOLOGICIAN

IT was all but inevitable that the editors of this JOURNAL should have planned for the celebration of Professor Dewey's eightieth birthday by devoting an issue to a symposium on his recently published *Logic: The Theory of Inquiry.* As one of his many admirers, one who has been immeasurably indebted to him, I deem it a great honor to have been invited to take part.

Within a ten-year span that included the beginning of our century, many things were happening in the intellectual world, each of which at the time seemed as the arising of a little cloud out of the sea, like a man's hand; and there was no prophet to foretell what was to follow. In the realm of philosophy William James delivered an address before the Philosophical Union of the University of California on "Philosophical Conceptions and Practical Results." John Dewey contributed four essays to a volume of the Decennial Publications of the University of Chicago, entitled *Studies in Logical Theory.*[2] There followed other lectures and papers by these two philosophers, and a storm arose. The commotion has not yet subsided. On the contrary, what has come to be known as "Dewey's instrumentalism" is now accepted as a permanent feature of our philosophical climate.

That the acceptance has been gradual has been due in part to Mr. Dewey's own gradual development of his logical theory. In fact it was not till within the last year that we have had a systematic presentation of it, showing the articulation of its various elements. The completeness of this presentation is evidenced by the fact that all the important topics usually considered logical now find a place in the theory, a place determined by its ruling motif. This motif is that logic is the theory of inquiry, an inquiry

[1] *Logic: The Theory of Inquiry.* JOHN DEWEY. New York: Henry Holt and Company. 1938. viii + 546 pp. $3.00.

[2] In what follows, this volume will be referred to briefly as *Studies,* and *Logic: The Theory of Inquiry* as *Logic.* All page references without further identification will be to the latter volume.

into inquiry. A mere glance at the Index shows that nothing has been left out, and the organization of the material into a system has the appearance of having been accomplished by the motif itself. It would almost seem as if the author were not the author but an amanuensis taking dictation from the motif.

The participants in this symposium have been asked for "a considered examination of Mr. Dewey's contributions to logic," "an appraisal and criticism of the whole body of his work in that field." This is a large order, and to fill it would require a volume as large as the *Logic* itself. His contribution consists not only in a positive logical theory, but also in criticisms of other theories. Criticism and construction have gone on concurrently in all of his work, and this is as of course it should be. No theory worth its salt bombinates *in vacuo*. Every live theory lives in an environment of other theories; and in its reaction to its environment it appropriates and rejects. In its turn it becomes part of the environment of other theories, which severally appropriate and reject from among its offerings. By this token, Mr. Dewey's theory has been and is intensely vital. It would be blindness to what is going on in logic today not to see that Mr. Dewey is a large part of what he now meets there. Even those, if there be any, who will have none of him are to a great extent what they are because of what in him they repudiate. I am glad that I am not one of them; for, like Mr. Dewey, "I have learned most from writers with whose positions I have in the end been compelled to disagree" (p. iv). But perhaps I should not say "in the end." In the end there may be more agreement than disagreement. At any rate, when I now come to speak of some of his great contributions to logical theory, it will be seen that there is a very large measure of agreement: recognition of this greatness is in so far a test of agreement.

Mr. Dewey has been in the vanguard of those who have fought to dislodge from their position, once thought impregnable, the logicians of the school of Absolute Idealism. When he began to fight, even most of the youngsters in logic were in that camp, which now is not indeed abandoned, but it is at least considerably depleted. This is largely the result of Mr. Dewey's work.

Again, Mr. Dewey recognizes and has brought others to recognize that logic is all of a piece with ontology. I know that this word is to him as a red rag to a bull: he uses it as such in challenging *other* bulls. But this is perhaps because it has never occurred to him that the word can ever be used except in a malicious sense. Only those who have "perverse" views of what it is "to be" are for him "ontological." But he himself has very definite views as to the nature of *being*. He began to tell us something of these views in his paper, "The Postulate of Immediate Empiricism" (in this JOURNAL, Vol. II, 1905, pp. 393–399), and he gave us a fuller statement in his Carus Lectures. If "ontology" is employed in its etymological sense, these views are as ontological as Aristotle's. In calling them ontological I do not mean to disparage, I mean to praise. How can any logical theory be entirely satisfactory if it is not inextricably tied up with an ontology? In the natural sciences it is coming to be recognized that hard and fast partitions between this and that special science must be broken down—as they are actually breaking down—if we are to have any adequate special science. And so it should be in philosophy. A logical theory without an ontology as its identical twin is not even an adequate *logical* theory. And by this test, Mr. Dewey's logical theory passes muster as adequate, since his logic is, to use another metaphor, interwoven with his ontological experientialism as warp of its woof and woof of its warp.

Still another great contribution to logical theory is Mr. Dewey's insistence that all logical theories, including his own, are hypotheses, to be tested in the continuum of inquiry. The *a priori* has been abandoned in all other scientific studies: why should it be held fast in logic? Mr. Dewey assumes that inquiry is a continuous process which develops its own standards by continuous self-correction. Since logic is itself a continuous inquiry—inquiry into inquiry—it likewise is autonomous. I can not but marvel at the skill he has displayed in fitting the various elements found in the proximate subject-matter of logic, each into its place in the operation of inquiry *as a going concern*. He does not claim that this work is complete. He calls his treatise "introductory," and looks to others to develop what he has initiated, "a theory of logic that is in thorough accord with all the best authenticated methods of attaining knowledge" (p. v).

For these reasons and for others that lack of space prevents mentioning here, it is my "considered" judgment that Mr. Dewey's work in the field of logic has won for him a place among the world's great logicians.

However, the situation in which this work leaves me is, to some extent, "disturbed, troubled, ambiguous, confused, full of conflicting tendencies, obscure, etc." (p. 105). This situation is also "clearly objective" (*Studies*, p. 38). I can mention only one or two of its perplexities.

From start to finish Mr. Dewey has been iteratively emphatic in maintaining that "conversion of eventual functions into antecedent existence [is] *the* philosophic fallacy, whether it be performed in behalf of mathematical subsistences, esthetic essences, the purely physical order of nature, or God."[3] For the present I am interested in the "fallacy" only as it concerns "the purely physical order of nature," and it is with reference to this field alone that I wish to question Mr. Dewey's right to call such a conversion a fallacy.

Mr. Dewey himself in his *Logic* accepts the assertions of science as warranted, if they are made after the most careful use of existential and conceptual means (or "ideas") in conducting the inquiries that eventuate in these assertions: for him they are the best-warranted assertions obtainable up to date. But in almost every one, if not in every one, of these assertions, the content of the idea that is proved by the issue to have the eventual function of bringing about the settled outcome of the inquiry, is "converted into antecedent existence." For instance Einstein had the idea that the path of any light-ray that passes through the gravitational field of the sun is deflected during passage by a certain amount. This idea guided astronomers to the adoption of appropriate existential means for testing the idea, and the outcome of that test was the judgment that *existentially* the path of such light *is* so deflected. Not only the light that was actually used in making the photographs in the experiment, but all light-rays that have ever passed through that gravitational field and through similar fields, are now asserted by physicists to have been deflected during passage, in accordance with Einstein's idea. Again, Mr. Dewey says that "a geologist, on the ground of the traits of a rock here and now existent and here and now perceived, infers the *existence* of an animal of a certain species living so many hundreds of thousands of years ago" (p. 466. I have supplied the italics). If these are not instances of "conversion of eventual functions into antecedent existence," I must confess that I do not know what the quoted phrase means.

Of course no scientist, unless he be a pre-Jamesian psychologist, reads back his results into the "preliminary situation" *as it was then immediately experienced by him*. He reads them back into "the larger natural world," of which Mr. Dewey says that "of course [it] exists independently of the organism" (pp. 33–34).[4]

---

[3] *Experience and Nature*, p. 29. Cf. *Studies*, p. 37, *Essays in Experimental Logic*, pp. 121–122.

[4] Cf. *Experience and Nature*, pp. 43–44: "The visible is set in the invisible; and in the end what is unseen decides what happens in the seen; the tangible rests precariously upon the untouched and ungrasped."

If space permitted, I should like to discuss the question whether Mr. Dewey has a pet fallacy of his own, that of converting immediately experienced precariousness into a physical character of the world we live in (*op. cit.*, p. 45). I am not sure that he does, but the whole question is very perplexing.

If such reading back be a fallacy, why not call it the *scientist's* fallacy, rather than the psychologist's or the philosophic fallacy?

But how about "logical forms" as distinguished from "ideas" as "conceptual means"? I say "as distinguished" although I do not find in the work before us any very clearly drawn distinction; but whatever be the distinction, Mr. Dewey's thesis is that logical forms are not to be read back into antecedent reality, because "while inquiry into inquiry is the *causa cognoscendi* of logical forms, primary inquiry is itself *causa essendi* of the forms which inquiry into inquiry discloses" (p. 4). Now, if the contents of *ideas* may, after successful inquiry under controlled conditions, be asserted of antecedent existence, why may not *logical forms* also, after successful inquiry under controlled conditions, be thus asserted? Are we not here confronted with a choice of postulates? Mr. Dewey postulates that such logical forms as "kinds" and "universals" and causal relations and mathematical functions are only modes of operating upon subject-matter under investigation, and come into being only when inquiry is instituted. I prefer the postulate that the logical forms *that serve to resolve a problematic situation* serve that purpose because they are actually the forms of the subject-matter under investigation—not of course of the subject-matter as it was immediately experienced when inquiry started, but as successful inquiry shows the subject-matter to have been in "the larger natural world" within which it has its setting. Mr. Dewey regards such a position as untenable. Although he first presents his theory as a postulate, he ends by maintaining that his is "the proper interpretation" (p. 458), "the only view that provides a consistent logical interpretation" of at least some of the *"facts"* (pp. 453–454). I question this assertion; here I can not do more. However, I can say that I agree with Mr. Dewey that the imperative, as well as most promising, task for logic is to "develop a theory . . . that is in thorough accord with all the best authenticated methods of attaining knowledge," and I acclaim the work he has done to that end as an invaluable contribution to logical theory.

I congratulate him, but I congratulate the rest of us more, that at fourscore he gives promise of still many years of equally important work.

EVANDER BRADLEY McGILVARY.

UNIVERSITY OF WISCONSIN.

THE NEW LOGIC AND THE OLD

Professor Dewey says of his recent volume, *Logic: The Theory of Inquiry,* that it "is marked in particular" by application of the author's earlier ideas, here re-affirmed in principle, "to interpretation of the forms and formal relations that constitute the standard material of logical tradition." As a consequence of this interpretation, logical tradition is explicitly called in question with reference to its basal assumptions. This new challenge to the tradition seems to me essentially the same as that presented in the author's earlier writings. Several years ago I undertook to discuss the earlier formulation and to indicate the confusion involved in it.[1] The new formulation carries with it the same confusion, and I propose to devote the short space here available to an attempt once again to state the difficulty. I am sure either that the difficulty belongs to the author's own construction or that I fail to follow his statement at crucial points. Naturally, I am predisposed in favor of the first alternative; but if the latter states the case, my remarks may at least serve to show that the change of venue has not entirely succeeded in clarifying fundamental issues. In either case, the main purpose of the following remarks is constructive in respect of the author's own standpoint; and because of my agreement with so much of what is said my criticism, however mistaken, can hardly be quite external.

By authority of the chapter on "The Needed Reform of Logic," logical tradition is made to rest in the end on an assumption which is erroneous if the central thesis of the present volume is true. That assumption is said to be "the theory of antecedent subjects given ready-made to predication." And, as is emphasized in a footnote appended to this passage, "The underlying logical point at issue is not the *special* Aristotelian conception of substance, but the idea that *any* kind of subject, such as 'this' or a sense datum, can be given ready-made to predication."[2]

Now whatever may or may not be said about Aristotle's view of logic or the views of the modern formalists with reference to the point at issue, I should have supposed it to be historically certain that the tradition in logical theory commonly called idealistic does not rest on the assumption in question, but that it does rest on the negation of that assumption. If there is any one doctrine which may be said to be fundamental within that tradition, surely it is precisely the doctrine that the subject is everywhere given with a penumbral aspect; that the subject is given "ready-made" is even explicitly repudiated, and its repudiation is advocated as the beginning of philosophical wisdom.[3]

---

[1] Cf. the article, "On the Second Copernican Revolution in Philosophy," *The Philosophical Review*, Vol. XLI (1932), pp. 107–129.

[2] P. 91. The italics are the author's.

[3] In the volume, *The Idealistic Argument in Recent British and American*

If that part of logical tradition at least is not to be left standing unscathed, then something further is needed than proof that no subject is given ready-made to predication. What further is needed is the broader denial that subjects are in any sense whatever given to predication. Sometimes the author's central thesis is interpreted by him as if it entailed this stronger negation; this is the interpretation of it with which he usually goes gunning for "antecedent subjects." Generally, however, the central thesis is not thus taken; on the contrary, it is so construed as to reject this interpretation as entirely too "subjectivistic." But in this latter construction the author's position on the point at issue does not differ in principle from the idealistic tradition in logical theory. And all of this constitutes the main confusion of which I complain and in respect of which light is sorely needed if the logic of inquiry is to establish its claim to essential novelty in the history of logic.

The central theme of the new logic is stated as follows: "Logical forms accrue to subject-matter when the latter is subjected to controlled inquiry."[4] The development of this theme, however, runs in two contrary directions. In one direction, it reads as if it says that the matrix of logical forms is exclusively the procedure or on occasion even the technique of inquiry into subject-matter, which itself is not held to be in any degree determinant of these forms; in this direction, one is told that logical forms are formulations of "habits" of inquiry. In another direction, and generally, the thesis is read as if it says that subject-matter is itself efficacious in the determination of logical forms, that inquiry is a peculiar sort of procedure conditioned by the subject-matter inquired into; in this direction, one finds logical forms arising only in "inference" or "discourse" which is inquiry grounded in the structure of a "situation."

As has already been intimated, the first of these two readings is implicit in the criticisms of "antecedent subjects," which are denied on the ground that inquiry, within which alone logical forms emerge, is an operational technique and procedure by means of which the subject of predication is functionally "taken." In such passages as the following, however, the reading becomes tol-

Philosophy, I have considered the point in some detail with reference to Bradley, Bosanquet, and Royce. That Hegel's writings must be similarly interpreted I should hold to be even obvious. The first part of the analysis in the *Phenomenology*, for example, is avowedly designed to exhibit the instability of the "this" of sense experience which is throughout problematic; and the grandiose performance of the *Logic* undertakes to do the same with reference to the most "immediate" logical category.

4 P. 101.

erably explicit. "It can hardly be denied that there are habits of inference and that they may be formulated as rules or principles. If there are such habits as are necessary to conduct every successful inferential inquiry, then the formulations that express them will be logical principles of all inquiries." Or, again: "A generality is involved in every expectation as a case of a habit that institutes readiness to act (operate) in a specified way. . . . Explicit formulation in propositional form of the expectation, together with active use of the formulation as a means of controlling and checking further operations in the continuum of inquiry, confers upon the potentiality a definite logical form." Or, again: "We are brought to the conclusion that it is modes of *active response* [author's italics] which are the ground of generality of logical form, not the existential immediate qualities of that which is responded to." Other passages to the same effect might readily be found, but the tenor of them all is perhaps essentially caught up in the phrase, "habits of inference." [5]

If such passages are taken to mean what *prima facie* at least they say, namely, that logical forms and principles are formulations of habits of inference, and if further it be assumed that such habits do not differ in any important respects from habits like walking and clutching which are not ordinarily supposed to involve inference, then it certainly follows that the procedure of inquiry as a biologically conditioned habit is the matrix of logical forms. And since predication is everywhere but an instance of such a habit, it must be held not only that subjects are not in any sense given to predication, but also that the very notion of "antecedent subjects" to be given is without content and void.

Hereupon, to be sure, the entire logical tradition falls into ruin. For that tradition does unquestionably depend on the assumption that there are antecedent subjects and that these subjects are somehow given to predication. But it must not be overlooked that the interpretation of the central thesis of the new logic which thus undermines the tradition also undermines itself by rendering itself as "subjectivistic" as logic was ever conceived to be when formulated in "mentalistic" terms. On this reading of the logic of inquiry the primary difference between it and Hume's conception, for example, is a terminological one; in the former inference is identified with an "expectation" expressive of the behavior of the biological organism instead of, as with Hume, a "tendency to feign" grounded in the associational complex of the "psychical" mechanism. It is bio-centric instead of psycho-centric, but it remains a purely "personal" response.

[5] The passages quoted are from pages 13, 251–252.

Of course, this subjectivistic reading of the logic of inquiry is generally explicitly repudiated. Emphasis is usually placed on the stability of the habit of inference, its fruitage in consequences as an operational procedure; and the consequences are naturally drawn from the only source available, namely, the "situation." Thus subject-matter is made foundational within the continuum of inquiry and consequently in the determination of logical forms and principles. In short, the central thesis of the new logic is commonly given the second of the two readings above noted.

That this reading is the one officially accredited seems to me quite clear. Inquiry is defined as "the controlled or directed transformation of an indeterminate situation into one that is so determinate in its constituent distinctions and relations as to convert the elements of the original situation into a unified whole." [6] And a situation is said to be "*not* a single object or event or set of objects and events," but objects and events in "a contextual whole." [7] Thus objects and events, presumably in the good old-fashioned realistic sense in which they are simply what they are, become fundamental aspects of the continuum of inquiry; they are made determinative there. We do not form a "kind" of that group of persons who happen to be shoemakers and cross-eyed and bald, for example, because "such a set of conjoined traits is practically worthless for the *purpose of inference.*" [8] And it is thus worthless, because "inference is conditioned upon an existential connection which may be called *involvement.* The problems of inference have to do with discovery [*sic*] of *what* conditions are involved with one another and *how* they are involved." [9] Likewise, in the realm of abstract reasoning or "discourse" continuity is also conditioned by subject-matter; the only difference is that there the conditioning circumstance is "constituted by the *implicatory* relation." The continuum of inquiry, in short, is exhibited only in situations which are meet for inference or discourse, and these are situations within which the relations of involvement or implication obtain. Since these relations obtain only within some sort of subject-matter, all of this is equivalent to saying that subject-matter is everywhere in inquiry systemic and imperious. It is the condition of both inference and discourse, the condition of the emergence of logical forms which "accrue"

[6] Pp. 104–105.
[7] P. 66.
[8] P. 268; author's italics.
[9] P. 278; author's italics.

only to a certain sort of subject-matter, namely, that which is "inherently doubtful"[10] and amenable to controlled inquiry.

The traditional distinctions of subject, predicate, and copula fall within such situations. "Observed facts of the case in their dual function of bringing the problem to light and of providing evidential material with respect to its solution constitute what has traditionally been called the *subject*. The conceptual contents which anticipate a possible solution and which direct observational operations constitute what has traditionally been called the *predicate*. Their functional and operative correspondence with each other constitutes the *copula*."[11] But surely, if all of this be so, the subject is always there antecedent to predication and is always in some sense given to it. No doubt, the subject can not be a mere "this" given ready-made to predication; but "it is just what it existentially is" and there is "no incompatibility" between this fact and the further fact that "it is the needed evidential ground of a definite characterization."[12] Even if one should go the length of saying that the subject is actually generated by the predicate because it is "taken" by the latter in its directive function in respect of "observational operations," one would still have to admit that the total "situation" within which the subject-copula-predicate distinctions fall is somehow given to inquiry. And this is in fact admitted. "Apart from an inclusive situation which determines *in correspondence with each other* the material that constitutes the observed singular this and the kind of characterizing predicate applicable to it, predication is totally arbitrary and ungrounded. There must be some one *question* to which both the subject 'this' and the predicate (say, *Washington Monument*) are relevant. That question grows out of and is controlled by some total situation. Otherwise propositions made are pointless."[13] For "the operations that institute a 'this' as subject are always selective-restrictive of something from out of a larger field."[14]

With this, however, we are in principle back in the view of predication advocated long ago by the idealistic tradition in logical theory. Of course, there is a difference in terminology: what in the tradition is named "reality" or "the whole" or "a world"

10 "*We* are doubtful because the situation is inherently doubtful. . . . The habit of disposing of the doubtful as if it belonged only to *us* rather than to the existential situation in which we are caught and implicated is an inheritance from subjectivistic psychology" (pp. 105–106; author's italics).

11 Pp. 124–125.

12 P. 127.

13 P. 126; author's italics.

14 P. 127.

is here christened "the problematic situation" or "the continuum of inquiry" or "judgment" taken as "the settled outcome of inquiry . . . the concluding objects that emerge from inquiry in their status of being conclusive." [15] This difference in terminology is indeed indicative of a difference of conception and emphasis important in the end for philosophical construction. But so far at least as "the underlying logical point at issue" is concerned, there is no fundamental difference between the two theories. Both hold that something operationally involved in predication is in fact antecedent to it and is somehow given to it—namely, the broad subject-matter, whether called by the name *subject* or not, with reference to which the techniques and procedures of inference and discourse are oriented and are determinable.

Explicit acknowledgment of this essential identity between the logic of inquiry and that of the idealistic tradition would, of course, entail rejection of the claim to novelty made in behalf of the former. It would also call for revision of much that is said in criticism of "psychical" processes. But all of this is no sound reason why the acknowledgment should not be made. And, in any event, it is, and is at least tacitly admitted to be, the only alternative to reducing the new logic to relativistic terms, which are none the less "subjectivistic" because they are drawn from biology rather than from "mentalistic" psychology.

The conclusion of the preceding remarks is, indeed, a repetition in principle of the conclusion advocated in the earlier article referred to at the beginning. But there is nothing surprising about this, in view of the fact that the logical theory here under survey is avowedly grounded in the same epistemology with which that earlier discussion was concerned. The confusion as here stated is but a new formulation of the confusion there in question, upon which in the end it rests. Should it be supposed that the way out is to renounce any and every epistemological basis for logical theory, however, such a supposition would be only the inauguration of a new error. Any theory whatsoever of logical subject-matter inevitably presupposes some theory of epistemological subject-matter which is foundational: the predicament, if predicament it be, ought frankly to be recognized and accepted. In my opinion, not the least service rendered to the study of logic by Professor Dewey's very serviceable volume lies precisely in its emphasis on this relationship.[16] For in this emphasis it has called attention to the fundamental consideration, sometimes forgotten or

---

[15] P. 120; cf. the entire chapter on "The Construction of Judgment."

[16] In this statement I am, of course, referring to epistemology as the discipline concerned with the problem of knowledge.

even denied, that any serious treatment of "forms and formal relations" necessarily sets them within the context of some view of the basal facts of *meaning* and *relevancy* and that any thorough-going treatment of this subject-matter can not stop short of explicit recognition and defense of the accompanying context.

G. WATTS CUNNINGHAM.

CORNELL UNIVERSITY.

MEANING AND ACTION

To say anything new and important about Dewey's logic would be, I suspect, beyond my powers. I shall not attempt it but, instead, wish to offer here brief comment on one conception of his, which I take to be central for his logic and for his point of view in general, and which I believe to be both correct and important: the conception, namely, that meaning and action are essentially connected.

Dewey does not write by the method of theorem and corollary; and one does not find any single statement into which the full significance of this thesis has been compressed and from which all its implications can be drawn. But what is here in question is no platitude, to the effect that since humans are active beings their meanings are likely to reflect their interests and their practice. Nor does it merely serve to point an emphasis, characteristic of the theory in which it appears but setting it in opposition to no other which could plausibly be maintained. Rather, it is the distinctive conception, incompatible with most views, that the cognitive or meaning situation does not admit of bifurcation into an activity of the knower and a preformed object which is contemplated; that knowing or meaning is integral with other activities which shape the objects to which they are addressed; that meanings themselves serve to frame the situations of action into which they enter, and exercise an operational force upon what they serve to formulate. It is implied that an idea or a meaning, apart from some possible action and the reality in which it should eventuate, is a fictitious entity not found in human thinking. And conversely, it is implied that the objects of knowledge, without reference to meanings and the actions to which they may lead, are equally fictitious. From this conception there issues a sharp challenge to those views—comprising the greater number—which would portray the reality known as "antecedent" to the activity of knowing, and to "spectator" theories of knowledge which would represent the knower as a disinterested contemplator of a ready-made world which *qua* knower he does not affect.

So far from being a commonplace, this thesis, when fully

grasped, has something of the aspect of a hard saying. Almost it is as if Dewey had claimed that all meanings and all inquiry are subject to a kind of indeterminacy principle. Thought itself displaces or transforms that which it means or inquires about: but if it thus affects the object concerned, how can inquiry disclose what it sets out to reveal? One can not suppose that this thesis has met with that acquiescence which the relative absence of discussion would suggest. Its force has been insufficiently felt. This conception has not been generally accepted by philosophic readers; but it has been answered mainly by neglect.

Yet however contrary to prevailing views, or even paradoxical, this conception may be, the considerations which would enforce it are fairly obvious. That thinking, meaning, knowing are other than—as Dewey claims—activities performed at need, is *prima facie* implausible. But if they are thus instigated, an effect of them upon that to which they are directed is implied. That the activity of the knower is itself a part of the world-process and a factor in determining its events, could not easily be denied. But if it is such, then plainly the conception that objects of inquiry are merely given to a contemplative knower, must be fundamentally erroneous.

For example, empirical knowledge, on almost any view, will be admitted to have the aspect or the pervasive implication of prediction. Any report of empirical fact, and any generalization such as a law of natural science, leads either to categorical predictions of future events or to hypothetical predictions that such and such will take place under certain specifiable circumstances. And that the main if not the exclusive motive of science and empirical knowledge in general is found in the possibility of such predictions, will be denied by no one. Yet if the world-process were that kind of antecedently determined enchainment of events which it is often supposed that science must take it to be, in order that such prediction may be possible and valid, then precisely in being thus predictable reality must be inaccessible to and unalterable by any activity of the knower. In that case, what boots it to know this completely inevitable futurity? It requires no initiative on our part—cognitive or of any other sort—to "avoid the impossible and coöperate with the inevitable."

Such considerations might perhaps meet with the reply that our aim in knowing what is predetermined lies in something else; that we wish to know whether it will rain, not in order to affect the weather, but in order to know whether to carry an umbrella. But if this way of meeting the difficulty—suggested by the common-sense answer in our trivial example—were to be taken as a satisfactory kind of analysis of situations in which knowledge and action are involved, it would lead to difficulties which are serious if not insuperable. Because it would seem to assume that there are two sorts of futurities; those which are predetermined for our inquiry and about which alone unconditional predictions can be made—"It will rain"—and those which are not thus antecedently determined —"I shall get wet"—which depend on what we do in the light of this knowledge. The former class are inaccessible to our action; the latter are not cognitions of objective reality but matters of decision. By implication, the world-process must be viewed as divisible into those events which are unconditionally predictable and about which we can do nothing, and those our activity can affect but which are not the objects of any cognitive inquiry. Fully carried out, this would lead to the conclusion that knowledge —or at least knowledge as having implications for the future—is exclusively of the inevitable; but that this knowledge is of practical value exclusively for its bearing on what is unpredictable.

The point is not so much that one who should elevate the attitude suggested to the status of philosophical analysis would stand in danger of violating his own systematic presuppositions—though that is a fact. It is not consistently possible to carry out such a double-aspect view of the world: to think of it as if one could, *qua* knower, view it as made up of predetermined and unbreakable chains of events, with one's self outside and looking on; and then, having through such passive receptivity acquired knowledge, could step out of one's contemplative rôle and take a hand in shaping the future thus predicted. One can not in this fashion place the subject, who both knows and acts and whose knowing is integral with and for the sake of his acting, both in and out of the process of events to which his knowing and his acting are addressed. But I say that this is hardly the point: probably that "universal determinism" sometimes supposed to be an essential presupposition of science is not something to be judged false or true but merely a pedantic fable; such that even if admitted in words it could find no application to any actual situation in which a human investigator has a real purpose in prosecuting an inquiry.

The more important point is one which concerns the meaning of our predictions themselves—and so far as empirical knowledge is implicitly predictive, the meaning of what we know in general. Such meaning can not exclude but must include the significance of the knower's activity. Because the validity of a genuinely cognitive meaning must be capable of verification. That a substantive meaning applies or does not apply, that a proposition is true or false, must be capable of test. And what tests are pertinent, must be implicit in the meanings themselves. Whoever speaks of X but does not know how it could be determined whether a presented thing is X or not, means nothing by his term : whoever asserts P but could not specify how the truth or falsity of P should be determined, makes no genuinely meaningful statement. So much of the pragmatic conception of meaning is quite generally accepted, and could not well be denied; though hairs may be split in the interpretation of it.

The meaning of a prediction, or of a cognition implying predictions, must be found in some future possible experience or experiences which would confirm its truth. *But there are no such verifying or confirming experiences which can be predicted without reference to the activity of the subject.* There are no future experiences which, concretely enough specified, are inevitable. There could be no experience of ours genuinely foreseeable but such that literally we could do nothing about it. In fact, precisely the point of foreseeing what is called "inevitable"—and it is seldom the experience itself which is so called—is that at least we may blunt the poignant painfulness of what is anticipated, or sharpen and clarify its satisfying quality, by our foresight. And in the case of most predictable eventualities, we can do something more than merely to modify their character as experienced by going forward to meet them in an altered attitude.

Furthermore, there is no dichotomy between categorically predictable eventualities—"It will rain"—and hypothetical and avoidable ones—"I shall get wet." All verifications, all predictable confirming experiences belong in the second classification. The fact of rain is verifiable only by some manner of experiencing it; by getting wet, or by seeing it, or hearing it, or . . . . But we shall not get wet if we protect ourselves; and there would be some manner or another of avoiding any one of these verifying experiences. We might refuse altogether to put our statement to the test. Each such possible verification turns out, on examination, to be some eventuality which will accrue or not accrue according as we adopt or refuse to adopt some attitude or course of action. And beyond such future possible experiences which would verify it, "It will rain" means nothing. Put in general terms, the meaning of any "fixed" or "objective" fact which could be believed in or asserted has, as the final terms of its analysis, some set of hypothetical propositions, the hypotheses in which concern some mode of action. In this nature of our empirical meanings lies the connection between knowing and doing, and the explanation of the fact that knowledge of that reality which "is what it is independently of being known" has application to our practice.

There would not be space here for comment on the consequences of this point concerning meanings. And, obviously, my discussion has been inadequate to the point itself. It is the less necessary to elaborate these implications because so many of them have been made clear in Dewey's writings.

C. I. LEWIS.

HARVARD UNIVERSITY.

SOME LEADING PRINCIPLES OF PROFESSOR DEWEY'S LOGICAL THEORY

The conception of logic which Professor Dewey has been proposing since the turn of the century is by now so familiar that it would be pointless to restate it in detail in this review of his latest formulation of it. But no careful reader of this treatise, however faithfully he may have followed Professor Dewey's writings, can fail to be stirred by the energy with which it recaptures the splendid ideal of logic as an organon for the effective conduct of inquiry; nor can he help being impressed by the bold power with which it re-interprets, on the basis of the dominant idea of inquiry as a mediatory process with logical principles as its tools, the themes of traditional logic and epistemology and the diversely oriented analyses of contemporary thinkers. Professor Dewey's previous contributions to logical theory, scattered through a score of books, now fall into a more definite pattern than before, with the consequence that the grounds of his dissent from, as well as of his dependence upon, traditional and contemporary schools are made more evident.

On the other hand, this volume also makes clear that Professor Dewey has not ceased to look upon his logical theory as a hypothesis, the detailed confirmation of which would have to be supplied by others in the future. His attention remains focussed primarily on the larger context within which logical principles operate, and in which they obtain a significance as something more than elements in a self-contained mathematical system; and even in this most complete formulation of his theory, the various functions which the principles of formal logic have as tools of inquiry are sketched with only enough detail to supply suggestive programs for further exploration. In consequence, the book offers a general underlying conception of logic with which many students will enthusiastically concur, while at the same time leaving them puzzled at or at issue with many of its special analyses. Professor Dewey explicitly recognizes the programmatic character of his reconstruction of logical theory, and like Peirce whom he admires he regards claims to finality as blocking the road to inquiry; accordingly, his inquiry into inquiry must be taken to mark only the beginning of a large project of continued research.

Professor Dewey is a naturalist in philosophy, and he writes of logical forms and principles as would a naturalist in the familiar biological sense of the word. His treatise is a study of the morphology of inquiry, and it aims to exhibit, as a biologist might in connection with various forms and organs of life, the conditions under which logical forms occur and are developed, their specific functions, their dependence upon and their transformation of their environment, and their own interrelations on the basis of their contributions to the achievement of their objectives.

But Professor Dewey is not just a classificatory naturalist. His examination of logical principles is carried through in terms of an inclusive theory, according to which subject-matter acquires logical traits on being subjected to the differential physical transformations of inquiry; in consequence, logical principles are taken to formulate the empirically ascertained conditions which must be instituted if inquiry is to have a successful termination. This cardinal thesis has the force of a paradox, only as long as the methods and conclusions of inquiry are isolated from the contexts in which they operate and emerge by being examined solely on the basis of their finished formulations. The thesis is further clarified if it is noted that in Professor Dewey's usage the phrase "logical form" stands for the *way* in which selected features of a situation in which inquiry occurs *function* in it, while the phrase "logical principles" denotes a *mode of operation*—and not, as is sometimes the case among students of formal validity, for quasi-grammatical forms and rules. Just as plants and animals are studied to the best advantage only within their natural environment so that the distinguishing traits and uses of their various organs may be ascertained, so on Professor Dewey's view the specific techniques and principles of logic receive an adequate theoretical interpretation only by being exhibited in the rôles they play within the process of inquiry.

A variant of this general principle of contextual analysis controls all of Professor Dewey's writings: it requires that process and product be taken as correlative distinctions, so that neither can be understood or assigned a status in existence independently of the other. Thus, an effective use is made of this principle in Professor Dewey's discussion of ethical issues when he maintains that the character of means employed enters constitutively into the character of ends attained. Its special application to logical theory stipulates that the conclusions of inquiry must be construed in terms of the procedures used to establish them, and that objects of knowledge, conceived as products of inquiry, can not be assigned an existence antecedently to it.

This is not a suitable occasion for marshalling evidence for the principle as a sound precept of analysis; but in any case, the apparently paradoxical features of Professor Dewey's logical theory follow from his whole-hearted acceptance of it. Consider, for example, his well-known thesis that the objects of knowledge do not have an existence antecedent to inquiry. It depends on the manifestly empirical claim, which must be decided on matter-of-fact grounds, that inquiry involves a physical reconstitution of its environing situation before the latter can function as an object of knowledge. But if this claim is warranted, then it does follow with the help of the above principle that objects of knowledge can not be intelligibly assigned an existential status prior to and in independence of specific inquiries.

Professor Dewey's refusal to read the conclusions of science except in terms of the operations of inquiry, as well as his interpretation of logical principles as rules for the conduct of inquiry rather than as formulations of ontological invariants, have brought forth the accusation that his philosophy confounds questions of validity and logical order with questions of origin and development. There is perhaps only a hair-line which divides a sound application of the principle of contextual analysis from a commission of the genetic fallacy; but it does not seem to me that Professor Dewey has stumbled across it into forbidden territory. He has simply applied to matters of logic the sort of analysis prized highly in the sciences. Thus, competent students would dismiss as thoroughly incompetent any proposal to assign meanings to such propositions as that light is corpuscular or that space is curved which neglects the complicated symbolic transformations needed before such statements can be given existential reference or which fails to note the technological apparatus required in order to implement them with a physical sense. Refusal to heed such proposals illustrates not the genetic fallacy but scientific caution and wisdom. Professor Dewey's similar insistence that logical principles be construed in terms of the relatively stable use that is made of them in inquiry is likewise free from the fallacy; for his insistence arises from a refusal to conceive principles as if their sole identifiable habitat were textbooks and treatises, and from a conviction that it is their function in inquiry which exhibits their sole meaning and relevance. There is clearly a difference between confusing questions of origin and validity, and assigning a meaning and a degree of adequacy to propositions wholly on the basis of the circumstances of their use.

In this brief appraisal of Professor Dewey's *Logic* it is not possible to examine the details of his reconstruction of the theory of inquiry. There is one special point, however, which seems to me worth while raising. The central technical innovation of his theory is the interpretation of judgment as the settlement of an issue, so that a judgment involves the functional correlation of perceptual and conceptual material; and in elaborating this notion he introduces a set of parallel distinctions, of which the most important is the difference between generic and universal propositions. The intent of the parallel terms is to demarcate the rôles of perceptual and ideational material in inquiry, and Professor Dewey's explicit criticism of other writers on logic frequently takes the form that they have confounded them. Generic propositions, in brief, are said to have existential import referring to spatio-temporal connections between existents, and to be contingent even though warranted by inquiry; universal propositions express necessary relations between characters or possibilities, and may be valid even if no things exist with the required traits. For example, Professor Dewey declares that "All men are mortal" is generic, if it means that all men have died or will die; but that it is universal if it means that if anything is human then it is mortal—that is to say, if it asserts a necessary relation between the characters of being human and being mortal (pp. 256ff.).

The first point to observe about this distinction is that it can not be read off from the linguistic form of statements alone and that it refers to a difference of function in inquiry. Generic propositions are thus employed to identify and isolate perceptual material, and to prepare it as evidence for or against a proposed solution of the issue at hand; universals function as statements of possible operations and their consequences, to be instituted in the interest of solving the problem (p. 274). It is therefore confusing to have Professor Dewey himself offer certain propositions as categorically illustrating one or the other of these propositional forms, for example, the Newtonian formula for gravitation as a universal proposition. If the form of a proposition is its function, is he faithful to his general standpoint in citing such formulae, taken out of their specific contexts, as examples for his distinctions? Could not inquiries be found in which this formula helps to prepare existential material in order to identify it for the sake of other operations to be performed? But in the second place, the reader is left to wonder just what is the force of "necessary" in the account of universals as involving *necessary* relations between characters. Professor Dewey's statement of his distinction and his occasional illustrations of it invite the identification of generic propositions with what in current literature are called synthetic ones, and of universal propositions with analytic ones; and some of his readers have already succumbed to the temptation to interpret the distinction in such an unambiguous way. Such an identification, however, simply will not do, in spite of Professor Dewey's occasional references to universal propositions as definitory in nature (e.g., p. 272). For he explicitly declares that universals formulate possible modes of acting, so that the execution of the operation prescribed by the proposition also tests its force and relevance for solving the problem at hand. But no analytic proposition, in the contemporary technical sense, would be tested in the way frequently proposed by Professor Dewey for his universals (cf. p. 264). Moreover, he distinguishes between two sorts of universal propositions, one kind being exemplified by propositions of mathematical physics (e.g., Newton's law of gravitation), and the other by propositions of mathematics (e.g., two plus two equals four); and he recognizes that the former kind do not exhaust the possibilities, so that they may have to be abandoned under the stress of factual demands, while the latter are apparently free from such limitations (p. 398). This subsidiary distinction only aggravates the puzzle as to what is to be understood by the specification that universals assert necessary relations between characters. It follows that the whole basis of his distinction between them and generic propositions remains obscure, while at the same time the grounds for his criticism of those logicians whom he calls "formalists" are not obviously relevant. Could he not be persuaded to restate the matter with greater clarity and fullness?

In so far as I understand the distinction between generic and universal propositions, it does not seem to me to be a sharp one, though it calls attention to important stages in the continuum of inquiry. Certain propositions, suggested but not derived from empirical material, may be asserted with confidence because the conditions for warranted assertions have been approximated for them. These propositions do not enter integrally into the theoretical framework of science, and their correction or even total abandonment does not involve a radical recasting of that framework; such propositions, I am suggesting, may be Professor Dewey's generic ones. On the other hand, some propositions gradually acquire such a commanding position in the set of warranted assertions of the period (in terms of comprehensiveness and deductive power), that they reach the status of leading principles of empirical analysis and in large measure control the general direction of research in the science of which they are a part. These propositions are not easily challenged by the facts of experience, not because they have no significant alternatives, but because to challenge them would involve a fundamental overhauling of the theoretical systems of science; they thus function as assured procedural principles, no longer at the mercy of random experiments because suitable devices are provided for obviating apparent contradictions with experience without impairing their fruitfulness as guides to further inquiry. Such propositions seem to me to fall into Professor Dewey's first kind of universals. But the propositions of mathematics differ radically from those just mentioned. They are analytic, and though also instrumental in inquiry are instrumental in a different way. For their function is to make transitions in discourse, to facilitate calculations of various sorts, rather than to direct the analysis of empirical material or to formulate possible modes of action. The recognition of these distinctions seems to me fundamental for an adequate theory of inquiry; but while Professor Dewey does not overlook them, his discussions of them and of related topics do not constitute the most enlightening portions of his treatise.

In spite of its limitations as to details, no half-way sympathetic reader of this book can lay it down without the conviction that it offers a conception of logic which has its roots firmly attached to the procedures of science, and that its integral view of the subject ranks among the great visions of the day. Those who read it must acquire courage and inspiration to contribute their share toward completing the fundamental task which Professor Dewey has envisaged with such startling clarity and adequacy.

ERNEST NAGEL.

COLUMBIA UNIVERSITY.

Section VI

ETHICS AND SOCIAL PHILOSOPHY

The Journal of Philosophy
Psychology and Scientific Methods

THE LOGIC OF JUDGMENTS OF PRACTISE

I. Their Nature

IN introducing the discussion, I shall first say a word to avoid possible misunderstandings. It may be objected that such a term as practical judgment is misleading; that the term "practical judgment" is a misnomer, and a dangerous one, since all judgments by their very nature are intellectual or theoretical. Consequently, there is a danger that the term will lead us to treat as judgment and knowledge something which is not really knowledge at all and thus start us on the road which ends in mysticism or obscurantism. All this is admitted. I do not mean by practical judgment an alleged type of judgment having a different organ and source from other judgments. I mean simply a kind of judgment having a specific type of subject-matter. There are propositions relating to *agenda*— to things to do or be done, judgments of a situation as demanding action. There are, for example, propositions of the form: M.N. should do thus and so; it is better, wiser, more prudent, right, advisable, opportune, expedient, etc., to act thus and so. And this is the type of judgment I denote practical.

It may also be objected that this type of subject-matter is not distinctive; that there is no ground for marking it off from judgments of the form S is P, or mRn. I am willing, again, to admit that such may turn out to be the fact. But meanwhile there is a *prima-facie* difference which is worth considering, if only for the sake of reaching a conclusion as to whether or no there is involved a kind of subject-matter so distinctive as to imply a distinctive logical form. To assume in advance that the subject-matter of practical judgments *must* be reducible to the form of S P and mathematical propositions is assuredly quite as gratuitous as the contrary assumption. Moreover, current discussion exhibits not, indeed, a complete void, but a decided lacuna as to propositions of the type mentioned above. Mr. Russell has recently said that of the two parts of logic the first enumerates or inventories the different kinds or forms of propositions,[1] and it is noticeable that he does not even mention any of the above sort as a possible kind. Yet it is conceivable that omission of this type seriously compromises the success and efficacy of the exposition of other types.

Additional specimens of practical judgments may be given: He had better consult a physician; it would not be advisable for you to invest in those bonds; the United States should either modify its Monroe doctrine or else make more efficient military preparations; this is a good time to build a house; if I do that I shall be doing wrong; etc., etc. It seems silly to dwell upon the practical importance in our lives of judgments of this sort, but not wholly silly to say that their practical importance arouses curiosity and even suspicion as to their relative neglect in the discussion of the theory of logical forms. Regarding them, we may say:

1. Their subject-matter implies an incomplete situation. This incompleteness is not psychical. Something is "there," but what is there does not constitute the entire objective situation. *As* there, it requires something else. Only after this something else has been supplied will the given coincide with the full subject-matter. This consideration has an important bearing upon the conception of the indeterminate and contingent. It is sometimes assumed (both by adherents and opponents) that the validity of these notions entails that the *given* is itself indeterminate—which appears to be nonsense. The logical implication is that of a subject-matter as yet *unterminated,* unfinished or not wholly given. The implication is of future things.

2. Their subject-matter implies that the proposition is itself a factor in the completion of the situation, in carrying it forward to its conclusion. According as the judgment is that this or that should be done, the situation will, when completed, have this or that content. The proposition that it is well to do this is a proposition to treat the given in a certain way. Since the way of treating is established by the proposition, the proposition is *a* determining factor in the outcome. As a proposition about the supplementation of the given, it is a factor in the supplementation—and this not as an extraneous matter, something subsequent to the proposition, but as its own logical import or force. Here is found, *prima facie,* at least, a marked distinction of the practical proposition from descriptive and narrative propositions, from the familiar *S–P* propositions and from those of pure mathematics. The latter imply that the proposition does not enter into the constitution of the subject-matter of the proposition. There also is a distinction from another

1 "Scientific Method in Philosophy," page 57.

kind of contingent proposition, namely, that having the form: "he has started for your house;" "the house is still burning;" "it will probably rain." The unfinishedness of the given is stated in these propositions, but it is not implied that the statement is a factor in determining their completion.

3. The subject-matter implies that it makes a difference how the given is terminated: that one outcome is better than another, and that the proposition is to be a factor in securing (as far as may be) the better. In other words, there is something objectively at stake in the forming of the proposition. A right or wrong descriptive judgment (or any judgment confined to the given, whether temporal, spatial, or subsistent) does not affect its subject-matter; hence it does not either help or hinder. But a practical proposition affects the subject-matter for better or worse, for it is a judgment as to the condition (the thing to be done) of the existence of the complete subject-matter.[2]

4. A practical proposition is binary. It is a judgment that the given is to be treated in a specified way; it is also a judgment that the given admits of such treatment, that is, admits of a specified objective termination. This is to say that it is a judgment, at the same stroke, of end—the result to be brought about—and of means— of the given situation and the proposed act as conditions of the outcome. Ethical theories which take the matter of ends—as so many of them do—out of connection from determination of means, also take discussion of ends out of the region of judgment. If there be such ends, they have no intellectual status.

To judge that I should see a physician implies that the given elements of the situation should be completed in a specific way and also that they afford the conditions which make the proposed completion practicable. The proposition is of both resources and obstacles— intellectual determination of elements lying in the way of, say, proper vigor, and of the elements which can be utilized to get around or surmount these obstacles. The judgment regarding the need of a physician implies the existence of hindrances in the pursuit of the normal occupations of life, but it equally implies the existence of positive factors which may be set in motion to surmount the hindrances and reinstate normal pursuit.

It is worth while to call attention to the reciprocal character of the practical judgment in its bearing upon the statement of means.

---

[2] The neo-realists have shown a peculiar disinclination to discuss the nature of future consequences as terms of propositions. They certainly are not identical with the mental act of referring to them; they are "objective" to it. Do they, therefore, already subsist in some realm of subsistence? Or is subsistence simply a name for the fact of acts of thought having a reference?

From the side of the end, the reciprocal nature locates and condemns utopianism and romanticism: what is sometimes called idealism. From the side of means, it locates and condemns materialism and predeterminism: what is sometimes called mechanism. By materialism I mean the conception that the statement of the given contains and exhausts the entire subject-matter of the practical judgment: that the facts in their givenness are all "there is to it" so far as intelligence is concerned. The given is undoubtedly just what it is; it is determinate throughout. But it is the given of something to be done. The survey and inventory of present conditions (of facts) are not something complete in themselves; they exist for the sake of an intelligent determination of what is to be done, of what is required to complete the given. To conceive the given in any such way, then, as to imply that it negates in its given character the possibility of any doing, of any modification, is self-contradictory. As a part of a practical judgment, the discovery that a man is suffering from an illness is not a discovery that he must suffer, or that the subsequent course of events is determined by his illness; it is the indication of a needed and of a possible mode of action by which to restore health. Even the discovery that the illness is hopeless falls within this principle. It is an indication not to waste time and money on certain fruitless endeavors, to prepare affairs with respect to its continuance or death, etc. It is also an indication of search for conditions which will render similar cases in the future remediable, not hopeless. The whole case for the genuineness of practical judgments stands or falls with this principle. It is of course open to question. But decision as to its validity must rest upon empirical evidence. It can not be ruled out of court by a dialectic development of the implications of the judgment of what is already given or what has already happened. That is, its invalidity can not be deduced from an assertion that the character of the scientific judgment as a discovery and statement of what is forbids it. For this assertion is only to beg the question at issue. Unless the facts are complicated by the surreptitious introduction of some preconception the *prima-facie* empirical case is that the scientific judgment—the determinate diagnosis—favors instead of forbidding the possibility of change of the given. To overthrow this presumption means, I repeat, to discover specific evidence which makes it impossible. And in view of the immense body of empirical evidence showing that we add to control of what is given (which is the subject-matter of scientific judgment) by means of scientific judgment, the likelihood of any such discovery seems extremely slight.

These considerations throw light upon the proper meaning of

(practical) idealism and of mechanism. Idealism in action does not seem to be anything except an explicit recognition of just the implications we have been considering. It signifies a recognition that what is given is given *as* obstacles to one course of active development or completion and as resources for another course by which the movement directly blocked may be indirectly secured. It is not a blind instinct of hopefulness or that miscellaneous obscurantist emotionalism often called optimism, any more than it is utopianism. It is the recognition of the increased liberation and intelligent control of the course of events which are achieved through accurate discovery. Or, more specifically, it is this recognition operating as a ruling motive in extending the work of discovery and the utilization of its results.

"Mechanism" as a method of knowledge is the reciprocal recognition on the side of means. That is, it is the recognition of the import within the practical judgment, of the given, of fact, in its determinate character. The facts in their isolation, taken as complete in themselves, are not mechanistic. At most, they just are, and that is the end of them. They are mechanistic as indicating the mechanism, the means, of accomplishing the possibilities which they indicate. Apart from a forward look (the anticipation of the future movement of affairs) mechanism is a meaningless conception. There would be no sense in applying the conception to a finished world, to any scene which is simply and only done with. Propositions regarding a past world, just as past (not as furnishing the conditions of what is to be done) might be complete and accurate, but they would be of the nature of a complex catalogue. To introduce, in addition, the conception of mechanism is to introduce the implication of possibilities of future accomplishment.[3]

5. The judgment of what is to be done implies, as we have just seen, a statement of what the given facts of the situation are, taken

[3] I may refer in passing to the bearing of this upon a point in my recent paper (this JOURNAL, Vol. XII., page 337). Supposing the question to be that of some molten state of the earth in past geologic ages. Taken as the complete subject-matter of a proposition—or science—the facts discovered can not be regarded as causative of, or a mechanism of, the appearance of life. For by definition they form a closed system; to introduce reference to a future event is to deny the definition. Contrariwise, a statement of that past condition of the earth as a mechanism of the later emergence of life means that that past stage is taken not merely as past, but as in process of transition to its future, as in process of alteration in the direction of life. Change in this direction is quite as much an integral part of a complete statement of the early stage of the earth's history as is its molten, non-living state at a given date. A purely geologic statement may be quite accurate in its own universe of discourse and yet quite incomplete and hence inaccurate in another universe of discourse.

both as indications of the course to pursue and as furnishing the means to be employed in its pursuit. This statement demands accuracy. Completeness is not so much an additional requirement as it is a condition of accuracy. But it is important to note that accuracy depends fundamentally upon relevancy to the determination of what is to be done. Completeness does not mean exhaustiveness *per se,* but adequacy as respects decision as to end and its means. To include too much, or what is irrelevant, is a violation of the demand for accuracy quite as well as to leave out—to fail to discover—what is important.

Clear recognition of this fact will enable one to avoid certain dialectic confusions. It has been argued that a judgment of given existence, or fact, can not be hypothetical; that factuality and hypothetical character are contradictions in terms. They would be if the two terms were used in the same respect. But they are not. The hypothesis is that the facts which constitute the statement of the given are relevant and adequate for the purpose in hand—the determination of a possibility to be accomplished in action. The data may be as factual, as absolute as you please, and yet they in no way guarantee that they are the data of this particular judgment. Suppose the thing to be done is the formation of a prediction regarding the return of a comet. The prime difficulty is not in making observations, or with the mathematical calculations based upon them—difficult as these things may be. It is in being sure that we have taken as data the observations really implicated in the doing rightly of this particular thing: that we have not left out something which is relevant or included something which has nothing to do with the further movement of the comet. Darwin's hypothesis of natural selection does not stand or fall with the correctness of propositions regarding breeding. The facts of artificial selection may be as stated —in themselves there may be nothing hypothetical about them. But their bearing upon the origin of species *is* a hypothesis. Logically speaking, the factual proposition is a hypothetical proposition in that connection.

6. The bearing of this remark upon the nature of the truth of practical judgments (including the judgment of what is given) is obvious. Their truth or falsity is constituted by the issue. The determination of end-means which constitutes the content of the practical proposition is hypothetical until the course of action indicated has been tried. The event or issue of such action *is* the truth or falsity of the judgment. This is an immediate conclusion from the fact that only the issue gives the complete subject-matter. In

this case, at least, verification and truth completely coincide—unless there is some serious error in the prior analysis.

This completes my account, preliminary to a consideration of value-judgments. But the account suggests another and independent question with respect to which I shall make an excursus. How far is it possible and legitimate to extend or generalize the results reached to apply to given facts? That is to say, is it possible and legitimate to treat all scientific or descriptive statements of matters of fact as implying, indirectly if not directly, something to be done, future possibilities to be realized in action? The question as to legitimacy is altogether too complicated to be discussed as an appendage. But it can not be denied that there is a possibility of such application, nor that the possibility is worthy of careful examination. We may at least frame a hypothesis that all judgments of fact have reference to a determination of courses of action to be tried and the discovery of means for their attempted realization. In the sense already explained all propositions which state discoveries or ascertainments, all categorical propositions, would then be hypothetical, and their truth would coincide with their tested consequences effected by intelligent action.

This theory may be called pragmatism. But it is a type of pragmatism quite free from dependence upon a voluntaristic psychology. It is not complicated by reference to emotional satisfactions or the play of desires.

I am not arguing the point. But possibly critics of pragmatism might get a new light upon its meaning were they to set out with an analysis of ordinary practical judgments, and then proceed to consider the bearing of the results upon judgments of facts and essences. Mr. Bertrand Russell has remarked[4] that pragmatism originated as a theory about the truth of theories, but ignored the "truth of fact" upon which theories rest and by which they are tested. I am not concerned to question this statement so far as the context of the origin of pragmatism is concerned. Philosophy, at least, has been mainly a matter of theories; and Mr. James was conscientious enough to be troubled about the way in which the meaning of these theories is to be settled and the way in which they are to be tested. His pragmatism was in effect (as Mr. Russell recognizes) a statement of the need of applying to philosophic theories the same kinds of test used in the theories of the inductive sciences. But this does not preclude the application of a like method to dealing with so-called "truths of fact." Facts may be facts, and yet not be the facts *of* the inquiry in hand. In all scientific inquiry, however, to call them

[4] "Philosophical Essays," pages 104 and 105.

facts or data or truths of fact signifies that they are taken as the *relevant* facts of the inference to be made. *If* then (as this would seem to indicate) they are implicated, however indirectly, in a proposition about what is to be done (if only as to some inference to be made) they themselves are theoretical in logical quality. Accuracy of statement and correctness of reasoning would then be factors in truth, but so also would be verification. Truth is a triadic relation, but one of a different sort from that conceived by Mr. Russell.

II. JUDGMENTS OF VALUE

I

It is my purpose to apply the conclusions previously drawn as to the implications of practical judgment to the subject of judgments of value. First, however, I shall try to clear away some sources of misunderstanding. I am not concerned with the *nature* of value as that has recently been the object of controversy. For my purposes it makes no difference whether value is comprised within consciousness, independent of consciousness, or a relation between an object and some form of consciousness. I am going to deal with valuation, not with value.

Unfortunately, however, there is a deep-seated ambiguity which makes it difficult to dismiss the matter of value so summarily. The *experience* of a good and the *judgment* that something is a value of a certain kind and amount, have been almost inextricably confused. The confusion has a long history. It is found in medieval thought; it is revived by Descartes; recent psychology has given it a new career. The senses were regarded as modes of knowledge of greater or less adequacy, and the feelings were regarded as modes of sense, and hence as modes of cognitive apprehension. Descartes was interested in showing, for scientific purposes, that the senses are not organs of apprehending the qualities of bodies as such, but only of apprehending their relation to the well-being of the sentient organism. Sensations of pleasure and pain, along with those of hunger, thirst, etc., most easily lent themselves to this treatment; colors, tones, etc., could then be assimilated. Of them all he says: "These perceptions of sense have been placed within me by nature for the purpose of *signifying* what things are beneficial or harmful."[5] Thus he makes it possible to identify the real properties of bodies with their geometrical ones, without exposing himself to the inference that God (or nature) deceives us in the perception of color, sound, etc.

---

[5] "Sixth Meditation."

These perceptions are only intended to teach us what things to pursue and avoid, and as *such* apprehensions they are quite adequate. His identification of any and every experience of good with a judgment or cognitive apprehension is clear in the following words: "When we are given news the mind first judges of it and if it is good it rejoices."[6]

This is a survival of the scholastic psychology of the *vis æstimativa*. Lotze's theory that the emotions, as involving pleasure and pain, are organs of value-judgments, or, in more recent terminology, that they are cognitive appreciations of worth (corresponding to immediate apprehensions of sensory qualities) presents the same tradition in a new terminology.

As against all this, the present paper takes its stand with the position stated by Hume in the following words: "A passion is an original existence, or, if you will, modification of existence; and contains not any representative quality, which renders it a copy of any other existence or modification. "When I am angry I am actually possest with the passion, and in that emotion have no more a reference to any other object, than when I am thirsty, or sick, or more than five feet high.'"[7] In so doing, I may seem to some to be begging the question at issue. But such is surely the *prima-facie* fact of the matter. Only a prior dogma to the effect that every conscious experience *is, ipso facto,* a form of cognition leads to any obscuration of the fact, and the burden of proof is upon those who uphold the dogma.[8]

A farther word upon "appreciation" seems specially called for in view of the uncriticized currency of the doctrine that "appreciation" is a peculiar kind of knowledge, or cognitive revelation of reality: peculiar in having a distinct type of reality for its object and for its organ a peculiar mental condition differing from the intelligence of every-day knowledge and of science. Actually, there do not seem to be any grounds for regarding appreciation as anything but an intentionally enhanced or intensified experience of an object. Its

---

[6] Principles of Philosophy," page 90.

[7] "Treatise of Human Nature," Part III., Sec. iii.

[8] It is perhaps poor tactics on my part to complicate this matter with anything else. But it is evident that the "passions" and pains and pleasures may be *used* as evidences of something beyond themselves (as may the fact of being more than five feet high) and so get a representative or cognitive status. Is there not also a *prima-facie* presumption that all sensory qualities are of themselves bare existences or occurrences without cognitive pretensions, and that they have the latter only as signs or evidence of something else? Epistemological idealists or realists who admit the non-cognitive character of pleasure and pain would seem to be under special obligations carefully to consider the thesis of the non-cognitive nature of all sensory qualities as such.

opposite is not descriptive or explanatory knowledge, but *deprecia-tion*—a degraded realization of an object. A man may climb a mountain to get a better realization of a landscape; he may travel to Greece to get a realization of the Parthenon more full than that which he has had from pictures. Intelligence, knowledge, may be involved in the steps taken to get the enhanced experience, but that does not make the landscape or the Parthenon as fully savored a cognitive object. So the fullness of a musical experience may depend upon prior critical analysis, but that does not necessarily make the hearing of music a kind of non-analytic cognitive act. Either appreciation means just an intensified experience, or it means a kind of criticism, and then it falls within the sphere of ordinary judgment, differing in being applied to a work of art instead of to some other subject-matter. The same mode of analysis may be applied to the older but cognate term "intuition." The terms acquaintance and familiarity and recognition (acknowledgment) are full of like pitfalls of ambiguity.

By a value judgment, then, I mean simply a judgment having goods and bads for its subject-matter. Such being the case, it may well be asked: Why give it any special consideration? Why should logic, in addition to a theory of judgment, bother with value-judgments as a special class any more than with dog-judgments or granite-judgments? And my answer is there is no reason, save that value-judgments are a species of practical judgments (which present specific problems for consideration); and that the failure to observe this fact has resulted—so it seems to me—in much confusion, especially in moral theories about the judgment of good, right, and standards. And, I have no doubt, the same confusion has affected for evil the economic theory of valuation of commodities and services.

A practical judgment has been defined as a judgment of what to do, or what is to be done: a judgment respecting the future termination of an incomplete and in so far indeterminate situation. To say that judgments of value fall within this field is to say two things: One, that the judgment of value is never complete in itself, but always in behalf of determining what is to be done; the other, that judgments of value (as distinct from the direct experience of something as good) imply that value is not anything as yet given, but is something to-be-given by future action, itself conditioned upon (varying with) the judgment. Practical judgments do not primarily concern themselves with the question of the value of *objects*. They deal primarily with fixing upon the course of action demanded to carry an incomplete situation to its fulfilment. The adequate control of such judgments may, however, be facilitated by judgment of the worth of objects which enter as ends and means into the action contemplated. For example, my primary (and ultimate) judgment has to do, say, with buying a suit of clothes, whether to buy and, if so, what? The question is of better and worse with respect to alternative courses of action, not with respect to various objects. But the judgment will be a judgment (and not a chance reaction) in the degree in which it takes for its intervening subject-matter the value-status of various objects. What are the prices of given suits? What are their styles as respect to current fashion? How do their patterns compare? What about their durability? How about their respective adaptability to the chief wearing use I have in mind? Relative, or comparative, durability, cheapness, suitability, style, esthetic attractiveness constitute value traits. They are traits of objects not *per se,* but *as entering into a possible and foreseen completing of the situation.* Their value is their force in precisely this function. The decision of better and worse is the determination of their respective capacities and intensities *in this regard.* Apart from their status in this office, they have no traits of value in judgment. A determination of better value as found in some one suit is equivalent to (has the force of) a decision as to what it is better to do. It provides the lacking stimulus so that action occurs, or passes from its indeterminate-indecisive-state into decision.

Reference to the terms "subjective" and "objective" will, perhaps, raise a cloud of ambiguities. But for this very reason it may be worth while to point out the ambiguous nature of the term objective as applied to valuations. Objective may be identified, quite erroneously, with qualities existing outside of and independently of the situation in which a decision as to a future course of action has to be reached. Or, objective may denote the status of qualities of an object *in respect* to the situation to be completed through judgment. Independently of the situation requiring practical judgment, clothes already have a given price, durability, pattern, etc. These traits are not affected by the judgment. They exist; they are given. But as given they are not determinate values. They are not *objects of* valuation, but *data for* valuation. We may have to take pains to discover that these given qualities are, but their discovery is in order that there may be a judgment of value. Were they already definite values, the traits would not be estimated; they would be stimuli to direct response. If a man had already decided that cheapness constituted value, he would simply take the cheapest suit offered. What he judges is the value of cheapness, and this depends upon its weight or importance in the situation requiring action as compared with durability, style, adaptability, etc. Discovery of shoddy would not affect the *de facto* durability of the goods, but it would affect the value of cheapness—that is, the weight assigned that trait in influencing judgment—which it would not do, if cheapness already had a definite value. A value, in short, means a *consideration*, and a consideration does not mean merely an existence, but an existence having a certain claim upon the judgment to be formed. Value judged is not existential quality noted, but is the influence attached by judgment to a given existential quality in determining judgment.

The conclusion is not that value is subjective, but that it is practical. The situation in which judgment of value is required is not mental, much less fanciful. It is existential, but it exists *as* something whose good or value resides (first) in something to be attained in action and (secondly) whose value both as an idea and as existence depends upon judgment of what to do. Value is "objective," but it is such in an active or practical situation, not apart from it. To deny the possibility of such a view, is to reduce the objectivity of every tool and machine to the physical ingredients that compose it, and to treat a distinctive "plow" character as merely subjective. *Value-in-judgment* always has to do with something *as* tool or means, and instrumentality is an added (and selective) specification.

At the risk of whatever shock, this doctrine should be exposed in all its nakedness. To judge value is to engage in instituting a determinate value where none is given. It is not necessary that antecedently given values should be the data of the valuation; and where they are given data they are only terms in the determination of a not yet existing value. When a man is ill and after deliberation concludes that it be well to see a doctor, the doctor doubtless exists antecedently. But it is not the doctor who is judged to be the good of the situation, but the *seeing* of the doctor: a thing which, by description, exists only because of an act dependent upon a judgment. Nor is the health the man antecedently possessed (or which somebody has) the thing which he judges to be a value; the thing judged to be a value is the restoring of health—something by description not yet existing. The results flowing from his past health will doubtless influence him in reaching his judgment that it will be a good to have restored health, but they do not constitute the good which forms his subject-matter and object of his judgment. He may judge that they *were* good without judging that they are now good, for to be judged now good means to be judged to be the object of a course of action still to be undertaken. And to *judge* that they were good (as distinct from merely recalling certain benefits which accrued from health) is to judge that *if* the situation had required a reflective determination of a course of action one would have judged health an existence to be attained or preserved by action. These are undoubted dialectic difficulties which may be raised about judgments of this sort. For they imply the seeming paradox of a judgment whose proper subject-matter is its own determinate formation. But nothing is gained by obscuring the fact that such is the nature of the practical judgment of what is to be done: it is a judgment of what and how to judge —of the weight to be assigned to various factors in the determination of judgment. It is precisely this character which constitutes the necessity of the reference of the subject-matter of judgment beyond judgment: which makes it impossible for a practical judgment as judgment to have a self-contained meaning and truth. It would be interesting to inquire into the question whether this peculiarity may not throw light upon the nature of "consciousness," but into that field we can not go.

II

From what has been said, it immediately follows, of course, that a determinate value is instituted as a determination of what is to be done. Wherever a determinate good exists, there is an adequate stimulus to action and no judgment of what is to be done or of the value of an object is called for. It is frequently assumed, however, that valuation is a process of applying some fixed or determinate value to the various competing goods of a situation; that valuation implies a standard of value and consists in equating various goods with the standard as a supreme unquestioned value. This assumption requires examination. If it is sound, it deprives the position which has been taken of any validity. For it renders the practical judgment a matter of applying a value existing ready-made outside the valuation, instead of making—as we have done—the valuation a determination within the practical judgment. The argument would run this way: Every practical judgment depends upon a judgment of the value of the end to be attained; this end may be such only proximately, but that implies something else judged to be good, and so, logically, till we have arrived at the judgment of a supreme good, a final end or *summum bonum*. If this statement correctly describes the state of the case, there can be no doubt that a practical judgment depends upon a prior judgment of value; consequently, the hypothesis upon which we have been proceeding reverses the actual facts.

The first thing by way of critical comment is to point out the ambiguity in the term end. I should like to fall back upon what was said earlier about the thoroughly reciprocal character of means and end in the practical judgment. If this be admitted, it is also admitted that only by the judgment of means—of things having value in the carrying of an indeterminate situation to a completion—is the end determinately made out in judgment. But I fear I can not count upon this as granted. So I will point out that end may mean either the *de facto* limit to judgment, which by definition does not enter into judgment at all, or it may mean the last and completing object of judgment, the conception of that object in which a transitive incompletely given situation would come to rest. Of end in the first sense, it is to be said that it is not a value at all; of end in the second sense that it is identical with the finale of the kind of judgment we have just been discussing, so that as value it is determined in judgment, not a value employed to control the judgment. It may be asserted that in the illustration used some typical suit of clothes is the value which affords the standard of valuation of all the suits which are offered to the buyer; that he passes judgment on their value as compared with the standard suit as an end and supreme value. This statement brings out the ambiguity just referred to. The need of something to wear is the *stimulus* to the judgment of the value of suits offered, and possession of a suit puts an end *to* judgment. It is an end *of* judgment in the objective, not in the possessive sense, of the preposition "of"; it is not an end in the sense of aim, but in the sense of a terminating limit. When possession begins judgment has already ceased. And if argument *ad verucundiam* has any weight I may point out that this is the doctrine of Aristotle when he says we never deliberate about ends, but only about means. That is to say, in all deliberation (or practical judgment or inquiry) there is always something outside of judgment which fixes its beginning and end or terminus. And I would add that according to Aristotle, deliberation always ceases when we have come to the "first link in the chain of causes, which is last in the order of discovery," and this means "when we have traced back the chain of causes [means] to ourselves." In other words, the last end-in-view is always that which operates as the direct or immediate means of setting our own powers in operation. The end-in-view upon which judgment of action settles down is simply the adequate or complete means to the doing of something.

We do deliberate, however, about aims, about ends-in-view—a fact which shows their radically different nature from ends as limits to deliberation. The aim in the present instance is not the suit of clothes, but the *getting of a proper* suit. That is what is precisely estimated or valuated; and I think I may claim to have shown that the determination of this aim is identical with the determination of the value of a given suit through comparison of the values of cheapness, durability, style, pattern of different suits offered. Value is not determined by means of comparing the various suits with an ideal model, but by weighing the claims to the cheapness, durability, adaptability of various suits against one another—involving, of course, reference also to length of purse, suits already possessed, etc., and other specific elements in the situation which demands that something be done. The purchaser may, of course, have settled upon something which serves as a model before he goes to buy; but that only means that his judging has been done beforehand; the model does not then function in judgment, but simply in his act. And there is a consideration here involved of the utmost importance as to practical judgments of the moral type: The more completely the notion of the model is formed outside and irrespective of the specific conditions which the situation of action presents, the less intelligent is the act. Most men might have their ideals of the model changed somewhat in the face of the actual offering, even in the case of buying clothes. The man who is not accessible to such change in the case of moral situations has ceased to be a moral agent and become a reacting machine. In short, the standard of valuation is formed in the process of practical judgment or valuation. It is not something taken from outside and applied within it,—such application means there is no judgment.

It may, however, be contended that this does not justify the statement made to the effect that the limiting situation which occasions and cuts off judgment is not itself a value. Why, it will be asked, does a man buy a suit of clothes unless that is a value, or at least a proximate means to a further value? The answer is short and simple: Because he has to; because the situation in which he lives demands it. The answer probably seems too summary. But it may suggest that while a man lives, he never is called upon to judge whether he shall act, but simply *how* he shall act. A decision not to act is a decision to act in a certain way; it is never a judgment not to act, unqualifiedly. It is a judgment to do something else—to wait, for example. A judgment that the best thing to do is to retire from active life, to become a Simon Stylites, is a judgment to act in a certain way, conditioned upon the necessity that irrespective of judging a man will have to act somehow anyway. A decision to commit suicide is not a decision to be dead; it is a decision to perform a certain act. The act may depend upon reaching the conclusion that life is not worth living. But as a judgment, this is a conclusion to act in a way to terminate the possibility of further situations requiring judgment and action. And it does not imply that a judgment about the worth of life as a supreme value and standard underlies all judgments as to how to live. More specifically, it is not a judgment upon the value of life *per se,* but a judgment that one does not find at hand the means of making life worth while. As an act to be done, it still falls within and assumes life. As a judgment upon the value of life as such, it by definition evades the issue. No one ever influenced a person considering committing suicide by arguments concerning the value of life, but only by supplying conditions and means which made life worth living, in other words, by furnishing direct stimuli to living.

However, I fear that all this argument may only obscure a point obvious without argument, namely, that all deliberation upon what to do is concerned with the completion or determination of a situation in some respect incomplete and so indeterminate. But nevertheless every such situation is specific; it is not *merely* incomplete; on the contrary, the incompleteness is always *of* a specific situation. Hence this situation sets limits to the reflective process; what is judged has reference to it and that which limits never is judged in the particular situation in which it is limiting. Now we have in ordinary speech a word which expresses the nature of the conditions which limit the judgments of value. It is the word "invaluable." The word does not mean something of supreme value as compared with other things any more than it means something of zero value. It means something out of the scope of valuation—something out of the range of judgment; whatever is not and can not be in the situation at hand any part of the subject-matter of judgment and yet instigates and cuts short the judgment. Unfortunately for discussions, "to value" means two radically different things: to prize and appraise; to esteem and to estimate. I call them radically different because to prize names a practical, non-intellectual attitude, and to appraise names a judgment. That men love and hold things dear, that they cherish and care for some things, and neglect and contemn other things, is an undoubted fact. To call these things values is just to repeat that they are loved and cherished; it is not to give a reason for their being loved and cherished. To call them values and then import into them the traits of objects of valuation, or to import into values, meaning valuated objects, the traits which things possess as held dear is to confuse the theory of judgments of value past all remedy.

III

The statement that values are determined in the process of judgment of what to do (that is in situations where preference depends upon reflection upon the conditions and possibilities of a situation requiring action), will be met by the objection that our practical deliberations usually assume precedent specific values and also a certain order or grade among them. There is a sense in which I am not concerned to deny this. Our deliberate choices go on in situations more or less like those in which we have chosen previously.

When deliberation has reached a value, and action has confirmed or verified the conclusion, the result remains. In *that* situation one thing *is* better than another. Moreover, situations overlap. The m which is judged better than n in one situation is found worse than l in another, and so on; thus a certain order of precedence is established. And we have to broaden the field to cover the habitual order of reflective preferences in the community to which we belong. The valu-eds thus constituted present themselves as facts in subsequent situations. Moreover, the dominating objects of past valuations present themselves as standard values, by the same kind of operation.

But we have to note that such value standards are only presumptive. Their status depends, on one hand, upon the extent in which the present situation is like the past. In the progressive or a rapidly altering social life, the presumption of present value is weakened. And while it would be foolish not to avail oneself of the assistance in present valuations of the values established in other situations, we have to remember that habit operates to make us overlook differences and presume identity where it does not exist—to the misleading of judgment. On the other hand, the contributory worth of past determinations of value is dependent upon the extent in which they were made critically, and especially upon the extent in which the consequences brought about through acting upon them have been carefully noted. In other words, the presumptive force of a past value in present judgment depends upon the verification the prior estimate of it has received.

In any case, so far as judgment takes place at all (instead of the thought of a prior good operating as a direct stimulus to action) all valuation is in some degree a revaluation. Nietzsche would probably not have made so much of a sensation, but he would have been within the limits of wisdom, if he confined himself to the assertion that all judgment, in the degree in which it is critically intelligent, is a transvaluation of prior values. I can not escape recognition that any allusion to modification or transformation of an object through judgment will arouse partisan suspicion and hostility. To many it will appear to be a survival of an idealistic epistemology. But I am talking about practical judgments —judgments where the object of judgment is something to be done. I see but three alternatives. Either there are no such judgments—as judgments they are wholly illusory; or the future is bound to be but a repetition of the past, a reproduction of something eternally existent in some transcendent realm, which is the same thing logically;[9] or the object of a practical judgment is some change,

[9] Upholders of this view generally disguise the assumption of repetition by the notion that what is judged is progress in the direction of approximation

some alteration, to be brought about in the given, the nature of which change depends upon the judgment itself and yet constitutes the subject-matter of judgment. Unless the epistemological realist accepts one of the two first alternatives, he seems bound, in accepting the third, to admit that not merely do practical judgments as after effect make a difference in things (this he seems ready enough to accept about many propositions), but that the import and the validity of the judgments is a matter of the difference thus made. One may, of course, hold that this is just what marks the distinction of the practical judgment from the scientific judgment. But one who admits this fact as respects a practical judgment can no longer hold that it is fatal to the very idea of judgment to suppose that its proper object is some difference to be brought about in things and that the truth of the judgment is constituted by the differences actually made in consequences which issue.

But (to obviate misunderstanding) this does not mean that some psychic state or act makes the difference. The point is purely logical, and is twofold. In the first place, the subject-matter of the judgment is a change to be brought about; and in the second place this subject-matter does not become an *object* until the judgment has issued in act. It is the act which makes the difference, but nevertheless the act is but the complete object of judgment and the judgment is complete as a judgment only in the act. The anti-pragmatists have been asked (notably by Professor A. W. Moore) how they sharply distinguish between judgment—or knowledge—and act and yet freely admit and insist that knowledge makes a difference in action and hence in existence. This is the crux of the whole matter. And it is a logical question. It is not a query (as it seems to have been considered) as to how the mental can influence a physical thing like action—a variant of the old question of how the mind affects the body. On the contrary, the implication is that the relation of knowledge to action becomes a problem of the action of a mental (or logical) entity upon a physical one only when the logical import of judgment has been misconceived. The positive contention is that the realm of logical propositions presents in a realm of *possibility* the specific rearrangement of things which overt action presents in actuality. Hence the passage of a proposition into action is not a

to an eternal value. But as matter of fact, progress is never judged (as I have had repeated occasion to point out) by reference to a transcendent eternal value, but in reference to the success of the end-in-view in meeting the needs and conditions of the specific situation—a surrender of the doctrine in favor of the one set forth in the text. Logically, the notion of progress as approximation has no place. The thesis should read that we always try to repeat a given value, but always fail as a matter of fact. And constant failure is a queer name for progress.

miracle, but the realization of its own character—its own meaning as logical. I do not profess, of course, to have shown that such is the case for *all* propositions; that is a matter which I have not discussed. But in showing the tenability of the hypothesis that practical judgments are of that nature, I have at least ruled out any purely dialectic proof that the *nature* of knowledge as such forbids entertaining the hypothesis that the import—indirect if not direct— of all logical propositions is some difference to be brought about. The road is at least cleared for a more unprejudiced consideration of this hypothesis on its own merits.

JOHN DEWEY.

COLUMBIA UNIVERSITY.

The Journal of Philosophy
Psychology and Scientific Methods

DEWEY AND URBAN ON VALUE JUDGMENTS

THERE is an important class of theories according to which value is an object of judgment. This does not mean simply that values, like other things, may be and are judged; but that in this case, at least, the object is created by the act of being judged. Valuation is judgment, and to be valuated is to be valuable. It is possible to hold that all judgment is, in keeping with this view, either valuation, or to hold that valuation is a special kind of judgment. The latter or dualistic view of judgment is familiarly expressed in the antithesis between the "practical" and the "theoretical" reasons, or between "appreciation" and "description," or between "normative judgments" and "judgments of fact," or between *"Beurtheilung"* and *"Urtheilung."* [1] The former view is exemplified by Schiller's view that all judgments are "practical," [2] and by Rickert's view that judgment is essentially an act of acceptance or rejection.[3] Most dualistic views are only provisional, a stage in the reduction of all judgments to the type of valuation. This is broadly true of all those theories of judgment that appear in voluntaristic philosophies, such as pragmatism and Fichtean idealism. The practical version of judgment is first distinguished from a popular or traditional version of judgments of fact, after which the latter is corrected and reduced to the former.

Among the views which regard the practical or valuating judgments as constitutive of values, it is important to distinguish two classes, the humanistic and the absolutistic. The former construe judgment in an anthropological or psychological sense, the latter in a transcendent, metaphysical or "logical" sense. According to the views of the former class, values are created by the actual judgments of men, with all their relativity and variability; whereas according

[1] Windelband, *Präludien*, third edition, pp. 52–53.

[2] F. C. S. Schiller, "Are All Judgments 'Practical'?" this Journal, Vol. VII., p. 682.

[3] ". . . der eigentliche Kern des Urteils, das Bejahen und Verneinen, ein Billigen oder Missbilligen, ein Stellungnehmen zu einem Werte ist." H. Rickert, *Der Gegenstand der Erkenntniss* (1904), second edition, p. 108.

to views of the latter class, values are created only by some qualified, standard, or universal judgment which is somehow immanent or presupposed in the fallible judgments of finite minds.

To the former, or humanistic class, belongs the relatively crude view of Westermarck, and the more sophisticated and circumspect views that have recently been set forth by instrumentalists and pragmatists. Professor Dewey may be assumed to speak representatively if not authoritatively for this school. He presents the crux of the matter when he states that "practical judgments" imply "the seeming paradox of a judgment whose proper subject-matter is its own determinate formation." "To judge value," he says, "is to engage in instituting a determinate value where none is given." In other words, "the object of a practical judgment is some change, some alteration to be brought about in the given, the nature of which change depends upon the judgment itself and yet constitutes the subject-matter of (the?) judgment."[4] This means, I take it, that in this peculiar and "paradoxical" case value is both that which is judged, in other words the objective component of the judgment, and also a larger whole which embraces or involves the judgment. This is, to say the least, paradoxical, and could scarcely be regarded as a satisfactory disposition of the matter even though no other account of the facts should appear to be possible.

It is fair to state that Professor Dewey disclaims any intention of dealing with the nature of values. "I am going to deal with valuation," he says, "not with value."[5] It soon appears, however, that he regards "valuated objects" as the only values worth studying; and he continually speaks of values when he means valuated objects, as though the two expressions were interchangeable. Thus, for example, he speaks of value as "practical," "existent," "objective," and as a factor in "completing a situation," when the whole force of the argument depends on identifying value and valuated object. It is true also that he takes pains to distinguish two senses of "valuing." There is, on the one hand, the attitude of "prizing," or "esteeming," merely, which is a "practical, non-intellectual attitude"; and there is the attitude of "appraising or estimating," which implies a judgment. The two are commonly merged and confused in the conception of "appreciation."[6] But though he calls attention to the confusion and deprecates it, he does not, as we shall see, avoid it. And though he does not deny that the simpler emotional attitude defines values of a sort, he does at any rate clearly affirm that the judicial or intel-

[4] J. Dewey, "The Logic of Judgments of Practise," this JOURNAL, Vol. XII., pp. 516, 517, 521–522.

[5] *Ibid.*, p. 512.

[6] *Ibid.*, pp. 512–513, 520.

lectual attitude also determines values, and it is to these values that he confines attention in the present paper.

In examining the examples upon which Professor Dewey bases his contention, and which he thinks have been strangely neglected in the orthodox accounts of judgments, it is very important to bear the following general consideration in mind. *It is impossible to interpret any judgment merely from its verbal record.* What is judged in any given case depends upon what is intended at the time by the judging mind. A dozen different judgments may be expressed in the same linguistic form. This is peculiarly true of the very complicated judgments which the author cites. He would himself, I take it, be the last person to deny this; nevertheless his failure to specify in each case just what the judge may be supposed to mean by what he says, gives to his whole discussion an ambiguity which assists his argument, but does not clarify the issue. Take, for example, his favorite instance, the judgment ''I should consult a physician.'' This might mean: 'In view of the general practise of mankind, this is a case for medical advice.' One would be mistaken in this judgment provided one were misinformed as to the general rule of procedure, or provided one had exaggerated one's symptoms. There would be no reference, express or implied, to the probable outcome; and should the act prove fruitless, one's judgment would in no wise be proved at fault. Or this same linguistic form might mean: 'My state of health being such as it is, if I consult a physician I shall probably be cured.' In the case of such a judgment of probable outcome, while there is a future reference, the contingent event would still not affect the truth of the judgment. Though one should in the sequel not be cured, one's cure would still have been probable in view of the statistical evidence. Or one might mean: 'If I consult a physician I shall be cured.' Here again, although there is a hypothetical reference to a future event, the non-occurrence of that event would not disprove the judgment, in case I did not fulfil the condition and consult the physician. Or, finally, one might mean: 'Because I am going to consult a physician I shall recover my health.' This is evidently a complex judgment, one component of which does depend for its truth or error on a future contingency. It should be analyzed into two judgments, because either one of two independent facts would disprove it. If there should be no causal relation between consulting physicians and the recovery of health, I should be mistaken; or if I should not as a matter of historical fact recover my health, I should be mistaken, but on different grounds.

In other words, the identity of a judgment depends not on its verbal form, but on what it virtually appeals to for its disproof or verification. Every judgment has objective reference of two sorts, both of which are necessary as an act of judgment, independently of its being true or false. In the first place, it is "about" something, whose reality is not in question, and which serves as the locus of verification. In the second place, there is something judged. A judgment, in short, is like a promissory note, which has its date and place of maturity, and its amount. The first of these factors has usually been termed the "subject" of the judgment, because it is commonly named by the grammatical subject. If, however, we regard the judgment as an act of mind directed to some feature of its environment, it is more convenient to term this the "object" of the judgment. It must somehow be equally compatible with the fact which would prove the judgment, and with the fact which would disprove it. It may, perhaps, best be regarded as a constituent of both alternative facts. Thus, in judging that "the Emperor of Austria is dead," there is "the Emperor of Austria," in any case, as the common constituent of his being dead or alive. The object of the judgment is "the Emperor of Austria" in the sense that both the verifying fact and the discrediting fact would concern him. I am judging something *about* "the Emperor of Austria"; who constitutes, therefore, the quarter to which one must resort for evidence relevant to this particular judgment. Were there no such person, then the judgment would be no judgment; or it would be analyzable, as Mr. Russell has shown, into two judgments: "there is an Emperor of Austria," and "he is dead." I leave open the possibility that all judgments may ultimately be reducible to the form "there is so and so," or "this is so and so." In this case all judgments would be like a promissory note redeemable at any time or place. But if one were forced to this conclusion it would be owing to the very principle for which I am here contending, the principle, namely, that every judgment is about something whose existence is given or unquestionable.

But in every judgment there is not only what the judgment is about, but *what is judged about it*. Thus the judgments "the Emperor of Austria is dead," and "the Emperor of Austria is alive," are both about the same object, but in the one case one thing is judged about him, and in the other case something else. This we may term the "objective" of the judgment. It is that hypothetical state of the object which would verify the judgment, or fulfil the expectation which the judgment expresses. It is not a fact, simply, but a hypothetical fact. In other words, it is a component of the more complex fact of my judgment. It is that toward which my motor set or determining tendency is directed; but *only in the sense of being the direction of that set or tendency*. It is adverbial in character, a qualification or description of the judgment; in short, the way I judge.[7]

It is because, then, of such a virtual appeal to the same object, and such an identical expectation with reference to that object, that it is possible for two or more minds, or the same mind at different times, to judge the same. Thus the outcome of the present war is the object of many contemporary judgments. Some of these judgments are, furthermore, such that the victory of the Allies would fulfil the expectation that underlies them. In that case, though they be expressed by different minds, at different times, and in different languages and grammatical forms, they would be said to constitute the same judgment. Unless this sort of epistemological identity were possible, knowledge could have no history and no social status. It would not even be possible for a hypothesis to be verified, for it could not be the same hypothesis which was first entertained, and then held persistently in mind until the appropriate evidence should be forthcoming. It would not be possible for old judgments to be overthrown, or for one scientist's judgment to be confirmed by another's, because the same judgment could not be reconsidered or tested by different investigators.

Professor Dewey's failure to state precisely what constitutes the identity of a judgment and makes it just that judgment, gives to his whole discussion an elusiveness and fluidity that makes it almost impossible to criticize it. The critic must first formulate the view for himself, and since he can not certainly be sure of exhausting the possible meanings of an ambiguous text, he must always run the risk of missing the point. I shall endeavor to put that construction on the text which reflects its characteristic motive, and which at the same time sheds most light on our general problem of value.

Suppose a situation in which I suffer from ill-health and hope to recover through the agency of a physician. There are several items in this situation which must be distinguished. I suffer from ill-health and am aware that I dislike it. I desire recovery and am aware that I desire it. I believe that consulting a physician conduces to recovery. I adopt the course of consulting a physician, as a course conducive to my recovery. I believe that I am going to recover, and since in this case the object of belief and of desire coincide, I hope that I am going to recover. Subsequently, because of what I dislike,

---

[7] I can not here enter into a detailed analysis of this type of process. I am confident that it can be dealt with in behaviorist terms, provided we recognize that all behavior has to be described in terms of direction and goal, as is implied in the use of such terms as "set," "tendency," "*Aufgabe*," etc. The function of words requires the same sort of analysis. For a further discussion of these matters, *cf.* my articles on "The Truth-Problem," this JOURNAL, Vol. XIII., especially pp. 561 ff.

desire, and believe, I do consult the physician, and thereupon, in consequence of having consulted the physician, I recover. There are evidently many more or less independent components in this very complex process, some of them judgments, and some of them "non-intellectual" affective or motor attitudes which condition values. But there is no case so far as I can see of a value's being constituted by a judgment of it, or of value's being both cognized and created by the same mental act.

In so far as I dislike my present symptoms, they are evil. My judging that I dislike them does not make them evil, but simply refers to their being evil as a fact. It is like any perceptual judgment, except in respect of its peculiar degree of certainty.

In so far as I desire recovery, my future recovery is good. It is good relatively to my present desire, and its goodness would not be undone even though I should perish in the very moment of desire. This is the kind of value that attaches to all ideals, however quixotic, though they be "unrealized" or even unrealizable. That I should have dreamed a dream is sufficient to impart to the content of that dream a value that is quite independent of my rude awakening. Owing to this fact, which no theory of value can afford to disregard, it is evident that the realm of values exceeds that of existence. It is necessary to attach the predicate of value to "prospectives," possibilities, hypotheticals, or subsistents. That I should be aware that such is my desire introduces no new value, but merely makes me cognizant of the fact of my desire.

The belief that the consulting of physicians conduces to recovery is like any belief in a law or general rule. It is not peculiar to a practical or valuing situation, and it conforms to the ordinary and unparadoxical notion of judgment as referring to a given and independent state of things to which the judging mind appeals and defers.

The act of adopting the proposed plan as conducive to the desired result may seem to introduce something new, but that is only because it requires further analysis. We must distinguish the act of adoption from the judgment which justifies it. In so far as my adoption of the projected course of action implies that I give it preference or take a favorable attitude to it, it possesses value. Though doubtless weak in intensity, this is a case of what Professor Dewey calls "prizing" or "esteeming." It invests its object with value, but it does not judge or cognize value; though it might, of course, be accompanied by a reflective awareness of the attitude. The judgment as to the sequel does cause me to take the attitude. I do adopt the plan as one believed to conduce to a certain result; but that which in this case gives value to the plan is not its relation to the sequel, but the affective attitude to it which my judgment as to the sequel has led me to take. Or, it is because my judgment as to the sequel has caused me to take the attitude, that the plan possesses value. Though a judgment led me to the attitude which invests the plan with value, *that* value was not what I judged.

But does the mediating judgment in this case possess another value as its object? In a certain sense, yes. The judgment that the plan will bring the desired result, does attribute to the plan a transferred or indirect value. There is no objection, so far as I can see, to extending the realm of value to include things which, though not valued themselves, are instrumentally or causally related to things which are. But in this case it is evident that the transferred value in question is owing not to the *judgment* of its causal relation, but to the *fact* of that relation. The plan would not have this kind of instrumental value, unless the causal judgment were *true*. The existence of the judgment is not sufficient if the judgment is erroneous; and the plan would have the value in question even if there were no judgment. It follows that while the judgment is in this case in a certain sense a judgment of or about value, it does not create the value which it judges.

The attitude of hope is, as we have seen, a mixed attitude. It is desire qualified by belief. But its object possesses value by virtue of the component of desire. Beliefs as to the future, predictions or expectations, have nothing to do with value, except in so far as they are affectively tinged. Desiring recovery, that future contingency possesses value independently of the element of belief with which it is here associated. It would not be less valuable in the case of despair than it is in the case of hope. The expectation or prediction does undoubtedly refer for its verification to events that have not transpired at the moment of the judgment; but this is equally the case with scientific predictions in which one is not in the least emotionally concerned. Such verifying events must be awaited, but their futurity does not contradict their given or independent character. They are not the products of the judgment, but are facts to which the judgment is prepared to submit.

When the whole performance is consummated, as we suppose it to be, by my recovery of health, we have value in two new senses. In the first place, the state of health is good as having been antecedently desired. Its value is not determined by an act of judgment, but by what we call the "fulfilment of desire." The same state may also possess value, although this is not necessarily the case, as something now presently liked or enjoyed. Its value in this respect also would be independent of any act of judgment. In these two senses, as fulfilling and terminating desire, and as being the immediate object of feeling, an existence may be said to possess value. To judge value of this type would involve the additional act of reflective awareness of the desire as satisfied by the existence, or of the feeling as directed to it. While it might plausibly be maintained that such a reflective awareness invariably accompanies the affective attitudes in question, it is in any case a different and distinguishable thing, having a different object. The difference of object is the same difference that must be supposed to obtain in any case of introspection between a mental state and the observation of it.

Finally, we have to consider the fact that the outcome of the performance, the condition of health itself, was due to the antecedent judgments concerning it. In this case, we appear to have a judgment or a series of judgments which bring to pass their own object. I judged that I was going to recover my health, and then for my very judging of it, I do recover my health. How can my judgment have had its object, when that object still lay in the future, and when through its being causally dependent upon the judgment, it could not come into existence until after the judgment had had time to operate? We seem to have a judgment which is somehow antecedent to a part of itself. Here, as I understand it, is Professor Dewey's paradox.

But instead of allowing ourselves to be driven to a paradox, we should, I submit, insist upon such an account of the matter as shall avoid the paradox. We must deny that that future contingency which is the objective component of the judgment, and which is indispensable to the judgment's occurring at all, is *not* the same as that later event which may or may not occur, or which if it does occur is conditioned by the previous occurrence of the judgment. We must, in other words, supply enough entities to go round. This is entirely possible if we provide an *objective,* or *hypothetical,* or *possibility,* as the content of the antecedent judgment, and distinguish it from the later existence; precisely as we would distinguish the hypothetical payment or failure to pay which is defined by the face of the note as what would honor or dishonor it, from the actual conduct of the payer. These two objects must sustain a peculiar and intimate relation to one another, in that the latter must be the case that "satisfies" the former. It is even true, as we have seen, that the two must intersect, or possess some common constituent, which constitutes the judgment's "maturity," or locus of verification. In the example before us this common constituent comprises the time of the recovery vaguely marked as later than the consultation with the physician, and the particular individual whose health is in question. Health is *now due from this individual,* according to the terms of the judgment. These, and doubtless other factors as well, enter into both the objective and the historical occurrence, and without them neither the judgment nor the occurrence could exist. But even though the constituents of the objective and of the fact should coincide altogether, it would be necessary to attribute to them some difference of ontological status. I have proposed above that the objective should be regarded as a description of the behavior of the judging organism, a goal defined by its set or determining tendency. In some sense this sort of thing must be provided for, and however we provide for it, it must be entitatively distinguished from that actual occurrence or event which would realize it. An objective sustains two relations, one to the act of mind which intends it, the other to the existence which exemplifies or is, in the mathematical sense, a value of it. It may sustain the former relation before it sustains the latter, or even in cases when it does not sustain the latter at all.

In some such way as this the paradox may and must be avoided. We should then have a judgment not bringing about its own objective component, but bringing about the existence which exemplifies its objective component. And the value which is prospectively created by antecedent desire, and prospectively apprehended by the judgment which illuminates and guides that desire, would be different from that value which eventually comes to pass.

I submit, then, that the character of practical judgments requires no amendment of our ordinary notions of judgment. Judgments of value do not create that value-object which they judge; nor are they causes of their own component parts.

In a recent article,[8] Professor Urban professes, albeit darkly and dubiously, to be of one mind with Professor Dewey. I shall not attempt to determine whether two views, both of which unfortunately impress me as dark and dubious, are or are not identical. But since Professor Urban "thinks" they are "in agreement," I shall take his word for it and assume that the following remarks are not irrelevant.

Professor Urban comes out expressly for the doctrine that the "value-judgment" is to be distinguished from all "judgments of truth and fact."[9] Unlike most of the authorities he cites (including, I should suppose, Professor Dewey) Professor Urban is a dualist in respect of judgment. But what he means by the antithesis is far from clear. What is a "judgment of truth"? Is it a judgment which predicates truth of a proposition? That would surely be too occasional a form of judgment to constitute a type coordinate with valuation. It is more probable, since he links judgments of truth with judgments of fact, that he means to refer to judgments which *are* true or false. The antithesis would then be between judgments that are, and judgments that are not, either true or false. But since

[8] This JOURNAL, Vol. XIII., p. 673.
[9] *Ibid.,* p. 683.

it is customary to mean by judgment that act of cognition that is distinguished by the alternative of truth or falsity, valuation would appear to be a judgment that lacks the generic judgment character. Certainly the antithesis must remain hopelessly obscure until one has defined what one means by judgment in general, and has distinguished this cognitive form independently of the accident of truth or error. It would seem much more in accordance with usage to say that if valuation is neither true nor false, it is something other than judgment.

But let us consider some of the motives that have induced Professor Urban to set up his antithesis. In the first place, he points out that value attaches not to objects, but to objectives, that is, to complexes of the type "that x is ϕ."[10] But this is peculiar neither to value nor to judgment. Factuality certainly attaches to complexes of the same sort, as when we say, "It is a fact *that, etc.*" This would be regarded as a case of judgment, but not of value. On the other hand, that which is desired, hoped, feared, commanded, forbidden, or otherwise regarded in dozens of ways that constitute the commonest affective-motor attitudes, is also "that so and so shall be." In these cases we have values, but not judgments. It is undoubtedly true, as Meinong, Russell, and many others have recognized, that these attitudes require the admission of *Gegenstände* that are not objects or things in the ordinary sense. But they furnish no criterion by which to distinguish judgments of truth and fact from other judgments, nor valuing from non-valuing attitudes.[11]

In the second place, Professor Urban argues that there are certain *a priori* "propositions about value" (are these propositions truths or facts?) which are independent of the particular psychological facts about interests, and which are coordinate with the *a priori* propositions about being. Thus, he contends that all objects have either positive or negative value, and that of any two values one must be higher than the other. But it seems perfectly clear upon an examination of the argument, that these alleged *a priori* propositions are either applications of *a priori* propositions concerning being, or are obtained from the empirical character of interest. That every object must possess positive or negative value, can be regarded as *a priori* only in so far as it is derived from the law of excluded middle, negative value being regarded as the non-possession of value. To argue that all objects possess value requires an appeal to the

10 "That" is here used as a conjunction.

11 I find nothing seriously objectionable in Professor Urban's contention that "value is an objective" ("Value and Existence," this JOURNAL, Vol. XIII., p. 464); although I think its universality to be doubtful, and I think it undesirable to leave objectives as entitative finalities. But I do object to the supposition that this in the least argues for the uniqueness of "value judgments."

empirical character of interest. "All objects, as objects, are of interest either actually or potentially, and wherever there is interest there is value."[12] But how does Professor Urban know that all objects are as such capable of being objects of interest? If he knows it at all, which is doubtful, it is because of the actual ubiquity of interest as a modality of consciousness, or the psychological possibility of associating an attitude of interest with any other attitude by which a thing becomes an object.

The necessity of a value's being "higher or lower" than any other value is derived, if at all, either from the empirical fact that values have all-commensurable intensive magnitude, a contention that has often been disputed; or from the empirical fact that interest is always psychologically associated with preference, that is, from the fact that interests are always (?) so interconnected with other interests in one subject that the expression of one interest implies at least the momentary subordination of other interests. In other words, Professor Urban's generalizations about value are facts about value, which are either of the general logical sort common to all facts, or of a particular sort derived from the special peculiarities of that sort of psychophysical fact known as interest.

In the third place, Professor Urban insists that the conception of "ought," which he believes to be peculiar to value-judgments, is irreducible to the categories of being and non-being. "The value-judgment," he says, "is not 'A is as it ought to be,' but rather 'that A ought to be.' "[13] But Professor Urban must be aware that the difficulties, if any, attaching to this form of judgment, are not peculiar to value. What is required is a judgment that shall assert something only hypothetically or contingently existential. But that is the case with all judgments involving variables. Suppose that one says that "x is a man implies x is mortal." One does not assert that "there is a man," or that "this is a man." Nevertheless, one is judging either truly or falsely concerning a logical or implicational fact. One may express it, if one wishes, by saying, "if a case of man should occur, it would be mortal." And similarly with obligation. Some purpose requires or implies x. This can equally well be expressed as "x ought to occur," or as "if a occurs and is a value of x, then it is such as ought to occur." Similarly, "the comet ought to be visible in such and such a place at such and such a time," or "the key ought to be of such and such a shape"; meaning that the law of the comet's motion and the shape of the lock determine the conditions of visibility or fitness, whether or not these conditions are fulfilled by existence. Judgments of this sort are not peculiar

[12] *Ibid.*, p. 675.
[13] *Ibid.*, p. 687.

to value, nor are they distinguishable from judgments of truth and fact.

The *prospective* character of judgments of "ought" is even less calculated to prove what Professor Urban wants to prove. "It is the very nature of the value-judgment," he says, "that it apprehends, not something completely given, but rather something to be. Value is not a determination of being, but a direction of becoming."[14] It is incredible that Professor Urban should propose to restrict judgments of truth and fact to judgments concerning the completely given. The commonest of all scientific judgments are those concerning the future, the so-called judgments of prediction. And only less common than these are judgments asserting a direction of becoming, such, for example, as the generalization based on the second law of thermodynamics, or such laws as Spencer believed to determine cosmic evolution. The most familiar biological phenomena, such as growth and instinct, can not be judged at all except in such terms. Are such judgments, then, value-judgments? And are they not judgments of fact and truth?

Professor Urban accuses me of confusing "the qualities of an object on account of which it is valued with the value itself, the fact that it ought to be."[15] Now whether we prefer to use the substantive "value" to denote the object which is valuable, or the fact that it is valuable, is a matter of no importance. In any case, Professor Urban's essentially sane habits of mind prompt him here to identify value with the *fact* that a thing ought to be. A judgment of value would then be a judgment regarding such a fact. Like any other judgment, this would be true if the fact were as judged, and otherwise false. This leaves one quite in the dark as to the constituents of this particular kind of fact, whether, for example 'ought' is an intuited ultimate, not further definable, or whether, as I think, it consists in an implicative relation of interests. But at least it makes it perfectly clear that there is no differentia of value to be found in the analysis of judgment.

I still believe that the underlying cause of this whole muddle is a confusion of the essential act of judgment with the motor-affective attitudes with which it is psychologically associated. This is almost invariably betrayed by an author's fondness for such hybrids as "appreciation," "approval," "acknowledgment," *etc.* If one wishes to emphasize the fact that in our experiences of value, judgment, affection and will are intimately associated, well and good. But then let the essential character of judgment be first distinguished from its accidental associations. Fact, existence, truth, object, objective, are

14 *Ibid.*, p. 687.
15 *Ibid.*, p. 685.

terms belonging to the analysis of judgment as such. The structure and function of judgment can not be described without reference to them. Then, and then only, after one has discriminated judgment abstractly, can one safely venture into the perplexing field of the subjective and objective varieties of judgment. Then one may, if one wishes, collect and label a whole menagerie of judgments, not only value judgments, but verbal judgments, visual judgments, private judgments, public judgments, German judgments, American judgments, and German-American judgments,—with some guarantee that at least they are all judgments.

RALPH BARTON PERRY.

HARVARD UNIVERSITY.

The Journal of Philosophy
Psychology and Scientific Methods

THE OBJECTS OF VALUATION

IN an earlier number of this JOURNAL,[1] I presented a theory about valuation-judgments. In so doing, I intentionally put to one side the question of the nature of value. I did not wish to add further complication by introducing a subject about which so much difference of opinion already existed. It seemed to me that it was theoretically possible to distinguish the logical or formal aspect of valuation from the nature of value in the same way in which it is possible to distinguish the logical form of, say, a descriptive judgment from the particular subject-matter described, or an asymmetrical transitive relation from the question as to whether the relation concerns a spatial, temporal or numerical series. I still think this distinction of problems is logically sound, but intervening discussions have changed my mind about its availability at the present time. Consequently, I hope at a later time to take up a discussion of the nature of value itself. Just now I want, however, to take advantage of some of the recent discussions to show wherein I failed to make clear the primary point of my theory. I shall use selections from the articles of Mr. Perry[2] and Mr. Bush as texts upon which to hang certain comments.

Mr. Perry says: "Suppose a situation in which I suffer from ill-health and hope to recover through the agency of a physician. There are several items in this situation which must be distinguished. I suffer from ill-health, and am aware that I dislike it. I desire recovery and am aware that I desire it. I believe that consulting a physician conduces to recovery. I adopt the course of consulting a physician, as a course conducive to my recovery. . . . Subsequently, because of what I dislike, desire and believe, I do consult the physician, and, thereupon, in consequence of having consulted the physician, I recover. . . . But there is no case of a value's being constituted by a judgment of it."

[1] Vol. XII., pp. 512–523, since reprinted with some additions in my *Essays in Experimental Logic*, pp. 349–389.

[2] This JOURNAL, Vol. XIV., No. 7, Dewey and Urban on Valued Judgments, the quotation being from pp. 173–174.

Now on the basis of the particular situation described by Mr. Perry I quite agree. According to the terms of the illustration, there is already in determinate existence a negative value, ill-health, there is also a determinate positive value, recovery (which, of course, is none the less determined for knowledge because it does not as yet physically exist). In addition to these intrinsic, immediate, or independent values, as they are variously termed by different writers, there is also a determined instrumental, or dependent, value: seeing the physician is serviceable, useful, valuable, *for* the positive value of health. Nothing could be clearer or more satisfactory. The most that a deliberative judgment could effect under such circumstances would be to assist in bringing into *physical* existence a value already, as value, given. And only an extreme bungler could confuse the assistance given by judgment in bringing a value into existence with that given by judgment in determining a value as such.

Of that particular bungling performance I plead not guilty. It might be a purely verbal matter to say that I do not conceive that propositions *about* values already given *as* values are valuation judgments at all, whether they are about value as immediate or about value in the sense of useful, any more than I should wish to term a judgment about a pin a pin-judgment. In such a case as that stated above, there is nothing whatever to mark off any distinctive logical type of judgment. If we call such judgments valuation-judgments, they are on precisely the same logical level as any propositions about matters of established fact. I can not make it too emphatic that I started out, so far *as respects cases of this kind,* from precisely the point of view maintained by Mr. Perry.

But there remains a question of fact, a question which is not concerned with the proper linguistic use of the term valuation or value-judgment. Are there not situations in which, while a man dislikes ill-health, it is not, *under the specific circumstances,* the object of his supreme dislike, and where, moreover, he does not know *what* he should supremely dislike and supremely desire? Are there not situations wherein the adequate data for settling a determinate like and dislike *can not* be had until after an act which issues from a preliminary estimate or valuation as to what the good *will* be? This does not mean that health has not been a good in the past, or that it it is not a good "in general." It means that there may be a case in which an agent is genuinely uncertain whether to desire—or like— the recovery of health or to desire making a medical discovery at the cost of his own health. In such cases there is no good or value given to judgment; whether the good be recovery of health or loss-of-health-along-with-increase-of-reputation-and-a-medical-discovery-to-aid-others is genuinely unsettled. Now it was of this sort of situation and of this only that I contended that valuations aid in determining a new good; and contended that *such* valuations possess a distinctive logical character which the orthodox logics have passed over too lightly. Now either or both of these convictions may be wrong, but their error can hardly be shown until the prior question has been raised: Are there situations such that it is objectively uncertain what *their* good, value or end is—it being understood that their good *if* determinately given would be an intrinsic and immediate good? After this question has been dealt with, the question of the nature of the judgment of valuation (estimation or appraisal) involved in them will naturally follow.[3]

The passage from Mr. Bush is as follows:[4] "The city of Syracuse has a very beautiful institution. The state fair is held there every autumn, and on the evening of the last day there is a parade of all the city's children. The people of Syracuse regard this parade with an almost passionate affection. It seems natural to say that they value it supremely. Does value really attach to things like this or to the means used to bring them about? Of course, it is a verbal question, but it is a question that takes us to considerations where instrumentalism is no longer a sufficient point of view."

As in the case of the former quotation, I can only express my unqualified agreement—except that instrumentalism is not so much insufficient as grossly impertinent, irrelevant. It would be, as Mr. Bush intimates, a purely verbal matter to say that in such cases no valuing at all occurs. Yet such a verbal approach might be one way of getting at a fact, namely, that no valuing occurs in the sense of reflective comparison, an inquiry which involves deliberating, weighing one consideration against another. This might be a rhetorical

---

[3] It is possible, though I am not sure, that I might make my point in terms of Mr. Perry's own thinking by reference to his theory of the "objective" of judgments involving belief or commital. See this JOURNAL, Vol. XIII., pp. 569-573. It seems reasonable to suppose that there are cases of genuine doubt as to what the "objective" *should* be, as to what the purport or deliverance of an entertained belief *better* be. In such a case, if we employ reflection, if we make a judgment to decide upon an "objective" as a precondition of applying that "objective" in a further judgment, there is found, I fancy, a kind of judgment logically similar to that which I was dealing. When Mr. Perry in the same connection says that the "pragmatic theory is correct in emphasizing the formative, creative action of mind, and in likening the cognitive situation to the desiderative or volitional situation" (p. 572), and yet in a later article takes such pains to deny any formative action on the part of thought in constituting the object of a desiderative situation, I confess myself perplexed. I get the feeling that he has left his older opinion about the nature of valuation-judgment untouched by his revision of his theory of belief-judgment, and that if he applied his latter theory to the former topic it would inevitably result in a view of valuation not incompatible with that which I set forth.

[4] This JOURNAL, Vol. XV., No. 4, pp. 95-96.

way of getting at the fact that to the citizens the object is in-valuable, that is to say one whose worth is not subjected to critical questioning. The citizens value it "supremely" not in the sense that after considering and comparing any number of things they have arrived at a definitive scale in which the procession outweighs all other goods, but in the sense that they unreservedly, without any questioning, prize and cherish the institution.

So far there is, I take it, no difference of opinion between Mr. Bush and myself; he recognizes as explicitly as any one could desire that I expressly drew a distinction between the non-cognitive act of prizing, finding good or dear, and the cognitive act of valuation. But he goes on to ask whether in making this distinction "the word value does not become synonymous, in the instrumentalist presentation, with the word use." And if such be the case, why not, as Mr. Bush pertinently asks, drop the word value and confine one's self to the term use or valuable? And he goes on to interpret my position as meaning "value occurs when we face the question, What things or methods have the value of utility under the circumstances?"

Just here is where I entirely failed to make myself comprehensible to Mr. Bush. Just how far the obscurity of my exposition is the cause I can not well judge; if my exposition as a whole gave Mr. Bush this impression, I express my appreciation of his tenderness in dealing with an account which is complicated and prolix to no other end than to arrive at a result which can be stated in a few sentences and with which, as he says, no one would disagree. Possibly the term "instrumentalism" itself suggests that judgments are held to be about instruments or means; possibly calling a judgment of valuation a practical judgment suggests, in the current implications of the word practical, the same idea. If so, both suggestions are quite misleading. The instrumental theory of judgment does not mean that judgment is about instruments; it refers to the *function* of all judgment *qua* judgment, not to the subject-matter of some judgments. In any case, the emphasis was put not upon the instrumental, but upon the *experimental* character of valuations. It may well be that the primary linguistic connotation of the term "practical" is useful; unfortunately we have no unambiguous words in this connection. But I tried to make it clear that by "practical" I meant *what* is to be done, rather than *how* to accomplish something already given as a satisfactory end. Judgments about means, so far as they do not themselves enter into judgment about the constitution of an end or good,[5] are, I should say, technical rather than

---

[5] See *Essays in Experimental Logic*, pp. 340–344, and pp. 358–362 for cases in which valuation of means and of ends, respectively, are two ways of getting at the same thing.

practical; by which I mean that our important practical inquiries concern ends and goods.

This brings me, of course, to exactly the point which I made in discussing the passage from Mr. Perry. Sometimes every immediate or intrinsic good goes back on us. We do not confront any indubitable good. We are in the dark as to what we *should* regard with passionate esteem; we are beginning to suspect that something which we prized unquestioningly and directly in the past is no longer worth our while, because of some growth on our part or some change in conditions. Now in such a state of affairs we may of course trust to luck; we may wait for something to turn up which will afford a new unquestioned object to cherish and hold to. But sometimes we attempt to further by means of deliberation the production of such a good. We search in order to form an estimate of what would be the good of the situation if we could attain it. Add to these conditions the further condition that we can not be *sure* that we shall prize or like the thing in question until it has been brought into existence by an act following upon a judgment, and we have before us the kind of situation with which I was concerned. It frequently happens that, being in uncertainty, I conclude after consideration that the best thing that I can do is so and so—in short, that if I act so as to bring certain consequences into existence I *shall* like them or find them good. But when I act and the consequences follow, I do not relish them at all. Now this, I submit, is a very different sort of thing from discovering that I have made a mistake in my judgment as to the useful means of accomplishing something. It means that I have made a mistake in my valuation of an immediate good—that is of what, *when it is brought into existence,* will be an immediate good —or bad.

Let us return to the illustration of Mr. Bush. It is conceivable that some citizen of Syracuse who had habitually regarded the procession with passionate regard, might be led to question its worth. He might learn that a number of children had been made ill, or become seriously over-excited, or were becoming over-fond of display for sake of attracting attention to themselves. This would not alter what was past, his former liking, the fact that he *had* experienced an immediate, independent good. But it would lead him to a new act of valuation; he would seriously question whether he is henceforth to regard the parade with liking, hesitation or repugnance. He might attempt to use his judgment to come to a reasoned conclusion in the matter, and might then try to arrange so that the next parade would not involve these obnoxious features. Or he might attempt to arrange some other function giving the opportunity for an immediate realization of the beauty of congregated child-life. In any case, the result when it occurs will be an immediate good or bad—a matter of direct liking or the reverse. But, none the less, it will have been constituted, in part,[6] by the prior valuation—the prior reflective estimate of a non-instrumental good.

I should be glad to think that this explanation, if I have succeeded in making anything plain, would evoke an opinion that if this is what is meant, nobody will disagree. But I am not sanguine that such will be the case. For my view goes contrary to the classic view not only as to the logic of all judgments, but of moral and political conceptions. For the prevailing view is that goods, ends, "values" are all given, given in the sense of being completely there for knowledge, provided only we could get at them. Disputes in ethical and social theory have concerned themselves for the most part only with the question of *where* and *how* the goods are given: whether in experience, feeling, sensation, or in thought, intuition, reason; whether in the subject or in the object; whether in nature or in some transcendental realm. The important fact (provided it be a fact) that serious inquiries into conduct, individual and collective, must be concerned with an hypothetical and experimental effort to bring *new* goods into existence, an attempt made necessary by the slipping away of all given determinate goods, fails to secure recognition. I console with a belief that while my own inexpertness in statement is largely responsible for my failure to make myself understood, some of the difficulty lies with the immensely difficult transformation in methods of thinking about all social matters which the theory implies.

JOHN DEWEY.

COLUMBIA UNIVERSITY.

---

[6] I have never said that judgment is the *sole* determinant of a new object, but only that it serves to *re*construct or *re*organize, which implies another and independent variable.

IN DEFENSE OF A *WORTHLESS* THEORY OF VALUE

THERE are two objections which it seems to me important to register at once to Mr. Picard's recent article "Value and Worth"[1] supported as it is in part by Mr. Dewey's article "Valuation and Experimental Knowledge"[2] For the rest I may leave the theory to the criticism of others more competent to deal with it as a whole.

My first objection is that the distinction which Mr. Picard draws between worth and value, while it rests upon a perfectly clear (I should have said fully and currently acknowledged) difference, is not a distinction within the field of value; nor does the term *worth* seem to me a particularly appropriate designation to apply to what is admittedly not a value. The procedure is too much like choosing a more or less adequate definition of value; finding a case in which value is imputed but which the definition does not fit; and then ruling out the case as not being one of value precisely, but of something more or less like value, which for convenience we call worth. If, as a matter of fact, any sort of worth is really not a case of value, then it seems quite clear that it is also not a sort of worth. *Nonvaluable worth* is in English a plainly non-significant term, and thus even the terminology would be a serious blemish in Mr. Picard's theory—particularly serious in a field where terminology has been so fruitful of confusion and needless controversy.

But I have other fault to find than the use of questionably selected terms. What Mr. Picard calls worth he says appears on reflection, and he would say also, I suppose, that it was therefore the product of reflection, constituted by reflection. Now our acknowledgment of worth in any given case may very well be accounted for by the activity of reflection, may, that is, be the result of cognitive process; but what we thus come to acknowledge in cognition is, at least in those cases which Mr. Picard suggests, nothing more than a fact, and the acknowledgment can be put in the form of a judgment of fact. On reflection we come to see that such and such an act, such and such a thing, such and such a person, is or was or will be valuable—valuable, of course, to some one. And this some one is a conscious being, between whom and the valuable object, act, or person, there is, was, or will be that relation that we call a value-relation. If I acknowledge in reflection that an act is morally good or a picture esthetically good, my cognitive processes, as engaged in this acknowledgment, have nothing whatever to do with making the act good or the picture beautiful. The act is good or the picture

[1] This JOURNAL, Vol. XIX, No. 18, pp. 477–489.
[2] *The Philosophical Review*, Vol. XXXI, 4, pp. 325–351.

beautiful as it enters into relation with a subject to whom it gives satisfaction in contemplation—a whole society of subjects, perhaps, who agree in their tastes, moral or esthetic or even logical.[3]

To make the point plainer we may use the examples which Mr. Picard offers as sufficient evidence of the distinction he is mainly drawing, the distinction which he thinks has not been taken into account in value theory of the type which has been most rigorously expounded by Mr. Perry. In this sort of theory, says Mr. Picard, "intrinsic values defined as affective-volitional relations of interest are the same sort of entities as the intrinsic values which appear when we ask questions as to whether the worths are justified."[4] Such a theory "does not take into account the additional element of worth that may appear upon reflection," and the theory thus uncritically "identifies affective interest with interest that is wholly cognitive."[5] The answer to this criticism is simply that the reality of what appears is not added by the reflective cognition which discovers it, and secondly that a wholly cognitive interest is not interest at all, unless by cognitive interest Mr. Picard means an interest in the act or the object of cognition. And in either of these cases the interest had better be called motor-affective or affective-volitional. The purest of pure mathematicians may, I should suppose, unless he be a Kant, take delight in his cognitive processes or the objects of his cognition without the slightest danger to the rigor of his demonstrations or the validity of his discoveries.

Take the examples which Mr. Picard suggests: "I may like a certain picture that my newly acquired esthetic taste condemns."[6] It is plain here either that the taste has not been acquired,[7] or that taste simply means ability to perceive that the picture fulfills certain requirements. This is indeed purely a matter of judg-

---

[3] The essential disagreement that is cited so often to rule out the case of esthetic taste here is very largely a Philistine myth or a misunderstanding of the intensity of artists' interest in the particulars of their productions. Such intensity of interest in detail, and annoyance with differences of opinion about it, or at least with the expression of these differences of opinion, has led critics to find a disagreement in the fundamentals of taste that is not present. It is among genuine artists of larger mould, says Stark Young in a recent discussion of this subject, that a real communion of saints is likely to be realized. (*New Republic*, August 30, 1922.)

[4] This JOURNAL, Vol. XIX, No. 18, p. 482.

[5] *Ibid.*, p. 484.

[6] *Ibid.*, p. 484.

[7] This is Mr. Dewey's view in the article cited, p. 350: "We go through the act in deference to habit and social expectations, but at the bottom of our hearts we are aware that we are going through a supernumerary rite. The judgment is faked, not genuine. There is, accordingly, no ground for surprise in the fact that the judgment does not determine a motor-affecto attitude."

ment, and the judgment is one of fact, not one of value. But even if it is a correct judgment, the esthetic worth of the picture depends on the picture's conforming to the requirements, not on an observer's knowing that it does so conform. And this does not make the worth or value of the picture objective and independent, or constituted otherwise than in a subject-object relation. For the standard is of course the formula drawn up by some one in accordance with likings and dislikings, whether of the formulator himself or of some one whose likes and dislikes he was attempting to satisfy or to define. And conformity to the standard (an objective fact which any properly trained person may note) means being of such sort that, when the subject comes along whose likes the standard names, this subject will like the work of art, the picture. It will be for him immediately valuable. It will really suit his real taste. [8]

Mr. Picard's other example, that of disliking " good " music, seems to me to fall under the same analysis, but I should like to use it to comment upon Mr. Dewey's contribution to this phase of the subject. It is instrumental values in which Mr. Dewey's interest seems greatest, and with reference to which he has with great clarification of the issues renewed his arguments—arguments which would establish the status of a sort of values called into existence by an activity which he insists is logical as well as experimental, and which he names the judgment of evaluation. But for his theory he finds such apparently unaccountable cases of intrinsic value as this of the music, especially illuminating, and he uses them as confirming his analysis. [9] He says that in such cases, as in all valuation, we must first make the " proximate judgment " that " it is good—or better—to perform a certain act in order to make a complete ulterior judgment possible." [10] Now take the case where the complete ulterior judgment called for is that this particular " good " music, which at present I do not like, *is* good. This ulterior judgment is to be the record of a new affecto-motor attitude which is really mine, which I have really acquired. It is to be an actual part of my genuinely new taste; but the acquiring of the taste is itself the result of the " proximate judgment," whose object or content is an act I am to perform, and the "proximate judgment" will be of the valuation type just mentioned: " that it is good—or better—to

---

[8] People whose tastes are formed on models may gradually come to adopt a standard suited primarily to these others. But they thus come very often really to like what is in the "best taste." Their taste has been educated, genuinely acquired—and very good taste it may be. The training, however, is mostly one in perceptive discrimination, not, as Mr. Dewey would have it, in judgments of valuation.

[9] *Op. cit.*, pp. 350–351.

[10] *Ibid.*, p. 350.

perform a certain act in order to make a complete ulterior judgment possible.''

Mr. Dewey seems less interested than formerly to prove that this is a new or peculiar type of judgment from the point of view of logical theory; but he still insists on its being just that rational, logical process which makes the genuinely new event part of a rational experience. To any one who supposes reason itself as an existence to be natural and irrational like the rest of nature, it is not important that this specific act of valuation be called logical or even rational. It takes reflection upon activity of *any* sort to fit that activity into the Life of Reason, and evaluation, being an event, can hardly by a naturalist be considered as in itself logical. Discourse alone may have that characteristic. The issues are metaphysical, as all issues end by being, and as Mr. Dewey notes. But to take the example offered—the case of the music—what judgments and what acts ought to be performed? When I have reached the state of admitting the music to be good, and of wanting to have this judgment, not as what Mr. Dewey calls faked, but as a record of my own actual liking, what ''proximate judgment'' or series of judgments am I to make, whose object or objects are acts?

The following appears to be a fair account of what happens in such a case. I ask myself how I am to come to like good music, for I have already admitted that this music *is* good, albeit it falls at present unpleasantly on my ear. And I then say that I had better listen to more music, or that I had better study harmony, or I had better learn to play the violin; for these are acts through the performance of which people come to like good music. Which I do requires deliberation upon the circumstances; there is real doubt as to what I have time for, what ways are suited to my capacities, and so on; and this doubt becomes resolved only when I have arrived at the issue of this deliberation. The deliberation may have involved the use of all my mental powers, but it is only at the end of it that I make the judgment itself—the '' proximate judgment '' required. At this point in my activities, however, the value in question will not have been enstated. In fact, if it ever does become enstated—and this seems to me a very well authenticated empirical account of the facts—the making of the judgment will have been but one step in a long causal sequence, at the end of which there will occur a value situation, a situation caused by the judgment no more than by the various activities of eyes and ears and other organs, of violins and bows and perhaps of pianos and piano-movers; perhaps also of a very large number of other persons and things. There will occur at the end of all this a situation in which I as subject contemplate with pleasure and satisfaction, through my ears and by means of all the newly developed connections which these have established with previously inactive or uncoördinated cortical areas, the sounds of the music which fell on them before so unacceptably. And in the occurring of this relation the value of the music occurs; without this situation it does not. And what is more, unless this situation occurs, it can never with truth be said that I like the music; unless this *sort* of situation occurs with *some* subject, it can never be truly said that the music is good.

So that the last stage in the process, which is not judging, but is contemplating and liking, constitutes the value in a very different sense from that in which the value situation itself is constituted by the " proximate " valuation judgment, the judgment of practise that I had better listen to music or study music, or whatever it happened to be. It is admitted that the value situation would not have occurred without the judgment, that the judgment was one link in a causal chain leading to the situation; but the judgment no more constitutes it than the violin does, or the music that I hear in the course of my education, or any of the other links in any of the other causal chains involved. The judgment may have been made because I wanted to come to value good music, and it may have helped to put my mind in a condition which was necessary for it to be in before I could come to enjoy the training through which I finally came to enjoying good music. And this judgment is an example of the type of judgment that constantly occurs in the minds of rational beings. But I see no reason for saying that it ever constitutes either the enjoyment or the value. Not *this* value, Mr. Dewey would answer, but value of the special type that just this sort of judgment does constitute. But always I find that all of Mr. Dewey's values, in so far as they have any common elements or characteristics to justify grouping them under the term *value* at all, can be shown to be constituted in the motor-affective relation which constitutes immediate value. It is only the particular sort of entity that Mr. Picard has attempted to establish as worth that I am here attempting to deny as a form of value, or, if it is a form of value, to bring under an affecto-motor theory. Mr. Dewey seems in this case not to have helped Mr. Picard's position. The valuation judgment helps, as do a thousand other things and activities, to enstate the value, to bring me to the point, that is, of being able to do the actual valuing. But I can not see that a study of such judgments is particularly important for understanding values, or for learning to value justly. For it is clear that even evaluating in Mr. Dewey's sense is preferring, and preference springs as a genuine new experience out of previous experience, as all new things come out of old. To insist that, because a theory of value finds the preceding judgments all old at the time when the new valuing occurs, such a theory denies the reality of doubt or of possibilities, is like insisting that the distinguishing of the past as past denies that a really new, that is, *future,* future can or does issue from the past.

What Mr. Perry's type of value theory asserts is that values do occur, that they are genuinely new; and it would seem to me that they are satisfactory or unsatisfactory according as the subject's faculties are acute or not, and his training in specific fields thorough or not. It is not training in the field of a special sort of judgments called valuation judgments but a training in the field of scientific facts and in the principles and the peculiarities of the arts, that will make the act in which deliberation issues satisfactory. But this act will always be preference or liking; it will never be " intellectual, logical, cognitive," as Mr. Dewey would have it.[11] The object of all study and education is to achieve taste, the ability to like rightly and adequately in all the fields of our experience; but surely Hume's discussion of necessary connection is enough to convince us that it is only experience already had that establishes knowledge of matters of fact, such as the relation of taste to its formation in mental history. Mr. Dewey appears to be insisting *per contra* that we progress by an *a priori* logic, his process of logical evaluation as performed in judgments of practise, to our values. No one need doubt that even individual values are determined in their existence in the individual's history, part of which is his strictly intellectual, or even his logical, life; but the act in which value is constituted is an act of irrational preference. It is part of life and existence, not part of dialectic; our knowledge, therefore, of its actual connection with its preceding causes, judgmental or other, comes only with *post facto* reflection. Values are thus not constituted in judgment, albeit they *are* constituted only in a relation of which a mind that in most cases has done much judging is one term.

Criticism on this basis is, indeed, as Mr. Dewey says, a *post facto* account of irrational prejudice. But what else do we ask, since irrational prejudice is exactly human preference? In the case of morals what do we ever mean by Mr. Dewey's " should-be-liked " but that which men of knowledge and discernment *do* like in imagined ideals or in contemplated states, and which we feel sure, therefore, that all men would like were they sufficiently enlightened?

From the above discussion it appears that Mr. Dewey's theory

11 *Op. cit.,* p. 335.

offers a justification, albeit unsuccessful, for Mr. Picard's worths in the cases I have discussed. But it justifies them as a particular sort of values, and this is far from Mr. Picard's conception of them. For Mr. Picard makes worth entirely distinct from value, as being what judgment or cognition acknowledges in the absence of any constitutive affective interest; while Mr. Dewey says that " ' worth ' is the tribute paid by reason to value,"[22] which, I take it, means that in certain cases of value, value is acknowledged to be worth. And reflection on the matter, instead of revealing the confusion which Mr. Picard imputes to my own previous discussion, indicates rather the very real objection that I should have to making cognition responsible for the facts which it comes to recognize. The recognition of the fact that a particular value exists is, as Mr. Picard himself is at great pains to point out, not the setting up of that relation which constitutes value. It is, however, an acknowledgment that such a relation has been or is or will be or can be set up. And this acknowledgment is all that I find in these cases of " worth," which, so far as Mr. Picard illustrates them, are plainly enough either not values, or else values which are acknowledged, but not at the time of the acknowledgment felt. This acknowledgment is the sort that value-theorists are constantly making when they tell you, for example, that from the point of view of the organism value may occur when there is a center of activity to serve as the basis of an interest that is directed outward.[13] Surely Mr. Picard does not assert that his reflective acknowledgment of this fact about value constitutes a " worth " here, where the amœba, let us say, enters into a relation which is constitutive of an immediate value. The uncritical assumption to which he has called attention[14] is in my own case, at least, a reflective conclusion.

Further to justify this " uncritical " theory, let me indicate how it would deal with the criterion of formal structure which Mr. Picard has drawn up to make his distinction clear—to show, that is, that intrinsic worth is not constituted by the same sort of interest-relation as that which constitutes immediate value. The one relation—that of value—he calls dyadic; the other is triadic and constitutes worth. The dyadic relation is the one I am defending as being the only value relation, and I need not discuss it further. But Mr. Picard says that " a worth-relation has three terms: *individual,* the *object* or *act judged,* and the *object* or *act* to which the judged object is referred."[15] In the judgment of intrinsic worth the ref-

[12] *Op. cit.,* p. 351.
[13] *Cf.* Picard: *Values: Immediate and Contributory,* p. 42.
[14] This JOURNAL, Vol. XIX, No. 18, p. 482.
[15] This JOURNAL, Vol. XIX, No. 18, p. 488.

erence is made thus: A is worthy *on its own account*. This is the sort of worth that may appear only on reflection, the sort that is an additional worth over and above any immediate value, such value at times even being negative when the worth is present. The three terms, then, in the triadic relation are (1) the individual who does the judging, who acknowledges the fact that A is worthy, (2) the object judged, namely, A, and (3) the object to which A is referred in the judgment—in this case also A. A is worthy, that is to say, on A's own account. This is Mr. Picard's analysis, not mine; but I do not see that it even follows necessarily that there is any worth involved in such a situation. The judgment may be incorrect, false, and A may not in any sense be worthy. My thinking that it is will surely not make A valuable; why should it make it worthy?— either in itself worthy, or as a means? In fact, if A is frankly a means to B, and the case is one of contributory value, which Mr. Picard finds has the same triadic structure as intrinsic worth, the triadic relation, if it holds, is simply a judgment. The first term is the individual doing the judging, the second term is A, and the third term is B, to which A is, in Mr. Picard's analysis, referred as cause. More simply, the judging individual stands in relation to two terms, A and B, and to the universal which actually relates A and B. The judging individual stands in relation to the complex consisting of the terms A and B and the relation connecting them. The judgment is expressed in the form "A *causes* B." Now when we value anything as a means, it is true that we are most likely to have made such a judgment, and there are at least three terms involved in the situation. But it is equally clear that we may be mistaken in the judgment, as we may be in the case of the judgment of intrinsic worth above. A may thus have no value at all. It may also be the case that the judgment "A *causes* B" is correct, and still that A has no value. For it may turn out that our end B is not liked by us, and so that the means A, which we correctly judged to be a cause of B, has no value. According to Mr. Picard, A would have worth in both of these cases; and if this be so, worth may be entirely valueless. It is at least an extraordinary use of language that thus identifies worth with what an object must have because we have made the mistake either of thinking it causally connected with that of which it is not a cause, or of thinking that that with which it is actually connected is valuable when it is not.

My discussion does not attempt to cover all the ground which Mr. Picard covers, much less to refute his theory of value; it only attempts to indicate that what he takes to be an uncritical assumption on my part was what I considered an integral portion of a thesis to be made clearly intelligible and so far as might be generally acceptable. It seems to me also to offer a very strong reason for ruling out the suggested use of the term *worth* for *standard value,* which is either a case of genuine value, past or present, for so many people or for such a length of time that it has come to be considered standard without being necessarily felt as a value at all; or which is not a case of value, but either the assertion that something or other should be valued, or that some one or other considers it valuable, or wishes it so considered. In Dr. Pepper's paper, read before the Philosophical Association in December, 1921, but not published, which Mr. Picard cites,[16] the suggestion is less, I think, that intrinsic worth is constituted in or by judgment, as that what he calls standard-value (Mr. Picard's intrinsic—and triadic—worth) is not really a case of value at all. To use *worth* as a designation for this, which is in no sense a value, seems to me to give up one of the main clarifications which modern value theory offers to ethics; namely, that value is one thing, conformity another; so that duty ethics, Puritan ethics, formal ethics, Kantian ethics, is seen to have no right to the conception "moral worth" at all, no right to talk about anything but *conformity* of acts. The value of such conformity, if I may speak a little loosely and still not be interpreted as adhering to the myth of a social mind—the value of such conformity is constituted in that relation in which society observes the pattern of the act as it is performed and likes it or dislikes it as it sees it embellishing the edifice of civilization or disfiguring it. The relation in which such liking joins the terms (the socially minded individual and the contemplated act) constitutes the goodness of the act, its moral value, its intrinsic, and as I should say, necessarily *esthetic* worth—*or value.*

So much for my first objection. My second is merely that Mr. Picard has apparently misread *disinterested* as *un*interested in the passage which he quotes as my unconscious illustration of a distinction which he thinks I should make, but which as I have shown above appears to me to be either irrelevant or mistaken.[17] That disinterested attentiveness not only may be, but characteristically is —indeed that it is the very type of—"the interest of which we speak when we discuss affective relations" seems to me quite clear. At any rate the estheticians all think so, from Kant down; and it would be a strange criticism of the "disinterested esthetic attitude" of Kant and Croce and Bosanquet and Santayana and Mr. Clive Bell to say that it lacked feeling-tone or was not essentially a specific sort of feeling-tone. Whether the Christian mystics were

16 This JOURNAL, Vol. XIX, No. 18, P. 485.
17 *Ibid.,* p. 480.

altogether disinterested or not is something of a question, but in their visions there was no lack of affective tone; and in the typical contemplation of esthetic objects it is generally agreed that the emotional content, the liking, not to say loving, adoring, worshipping, is the essential, and as I should assert *constitutive*, character of the disinterested attitude.

D. W. PRALL.

UNIVERSITY OF CALIFORNIA.

The Journal of Philosophy

VALUES, LIKING, AND THOUGHT

SPEAKING literally, there *are* no such things as values, the first word of the title. There are things, all sorts of things, having the unique, the experienced, but undefinable, quality of value. Values in the plural, or *a* value in the singular, is merely a convenient abbreviation for an object, event, situation, *res*, possessing the quality. Calling the thing a value is like calling a ball struck in baseball, a hit or a foul. Verbally the usage may save a long explanation. But while in discussing baseball a sense of the concrete context will save one from making independent entities out of hits and fouls, discussion of the theory of values and goods, whether moral or esthetic, manifests a tendency to forget the concrete things to which the value-quality is attached. Thus it is said that liking constitutes values. Since liking does not constitute the *things,* the poems, sounds, pictures, persons, flowers, or whatever they are, it is clear that what is really meant is either (*a*) that liking is a *condition* of a thing acquiring the quality of valuity or valueness (if I may coin words to assist in avoiding the ambiguity), or (*b*) that liking is an ingredient, a constituent part of the total situation possessing the quality. There are, as far as I can see, no other alternatives. The following article is in effect an expansion of this remark.

I

Mr. Prall's recent contribution in this JOURNAL, entitled "In Defense of a 'Worthless' Theory of Value," in part a criticism of some views previously expressed by me, illustrates to my mind the ambiguity in question. What does the word "value" in the title signify? Does it mean the quality of valuity or the thing having value? The point at issue between us is the relation of a kind of judgment, called valuative, to values. As I apprehend the article the truth in it is that judgment does not constitute the quality. This I admit. But nothing else constitutes the quality, either—constitutes it, that is, in the sense of *being* it. The quality is itself and nothing else. The only intelligible subject of discussion is whether judgment helps constitute *values*, that is, whether it is a condition of the acquisition of valuity by things, or is a constituent part of the total complex situation having valuity. And the theme of this article is that in both of these senses the relation of judgment or reflection to things having value is as direct and integral as that of liking.

As the body of the discussion will consist of a running commentary upon selected passages of Mr. Prall's article,[1] it may assist comprehension if we summarize the main points at the outset.

1. Because of the ambiguity pointed out, there is a double meaning in Mr. Prall's assertion that value is constituted by a motor-affective act. If he is talking about value in the strict sense, the quality, then his statement signifies that the motor-affective attitude *is* the quality. But this statement appears obviously false, or rather meaningless. If he is talking about a thing or situation having the quality, then the natural interpretation is that this attitude is a condition of the acquisition or possession of the quality by anything. This is an intelligible proposition, and taken in a restricted sense, to mean that liking is a necessary but not sufficient condition of the occurrence of a thing with value-quality, it is to my mind true. But it is a proposition about the occurrence of a thing or quality, and as such is a causal proposition. Since Mr. Prall admits that judgment may also be a causal condition of the existence of things having value, it forms no basis for drawing a hard and fast line between liking and judgment with respect to values.

2. This admission is fatal to that part of Mr. Prall's theory which holds that there is always a difference in kind in the relationship of liking and judgment to values. But I shall go further than to hold that judgment is *sometimes* a condition of the occurrence of things possessed of valuity. I hold that thought as well as liking, an affective thought or a thoughtful affection, is always the condition of the occurrence of value-things. There is no reason for assuming the factual incompatibility of thought and a motor-affective act; on the contrary, a motor-affective act that has no element of judgment in it is a purely animal act. Exclusive of integration with thought, such acts are events of appetitive assimilation accompanied, we may imagine, by pleasurable quality; events like the gorging of food, sexual conjugation, *etc.* Only when the act contains discriminating *meaning* does it constitute an act capable of being called taste, appreciation, or that sort of a motor-affective act which determines the existence of *a* value. There is nothing in the nature of a motor-affective act which prevents integration within it of reflective meaning; only when the two are incorporated together, only when the motor-affective act carries meanings due to prior valuations, do appreciation and a value exist. This conception does not imply that *all* judgments about values determine their occurrence. Judgments about an

[1] This JOURNAL, Vol. XX, No. 5, pp. 128–136 (1922).

esthetic object—about an object which is primarily or usually esthetic,—are not necessarily esthetic; they may not be valuations. One may form judgments about the historic origin, technical construction, dimensions, *etc.*, of the Parthenon which do not differ in the least from judgments about a locomotive or a potato. But even such judgments may *become* evaluative; they may be factors in generating an object with enriched esthetic meaning. They then are integral constituents in a fuller appreciation.

II

We now come to the details of Mr. Prall's argument. Using the type of instance suggested by me in a previous article, namely, such judgments as that it is worth while to study music to improve one's musical taste, he admits that such judgments may lead to the existence of values which would not otherwise exist for a person since he may thereby come to like different arrangements of sounds. But he goes on to say that "the making of the judgment will have been [a] but one step in a long causal sequence, at the end of which there will occur a value situation, a situation caused by the judgment no more than by the various activities of eyes, ears, and other organs, violins and bows. . . . There will occur at the end of all this [b] a situation in which I . . . contemplate with pleasure and satisfaction . . . the sounds of the music which fell on them [ears] before so unacceptably. And in the occurring of this relation the value of music occurs. . . . [c] So that the last stage in the process, which is not judging, but is contemplating and liking, constitutes the value in a very different sense from that in which the value situation is constituted by the 'proximate' valuation judgment, . . . that I had better listen to music or study music. . . . " (*Op. cit.*, pp. 131–132.)

I may point out in passing that the articles of mine which Mr. Prall criticized were not concerned with the nature of value, either the quality or things having the quality, but with the nature of valuation as a judgment. And my point was that such judgments are "practical," that is, they concern cases where the value of things or acts is uncertain, indeterminate, and relate to an act to be performed as a condition of the existence of something with determinate value. It happens that Mr. Prall is interested in his writing in value, while my interest was logical—that is, was in a certain type of judgment. This difference of interest is accountable, I think, for some writing at cross-purposes on both sides, and I am not sure yet how far Mr. Prall concedes my point as to valuation judgments. So I will pass over the matter of judgment and take the matter from Mr. Prall's side, the nature of a value.

In passage (a) Mr. Prall is dealing with the conditions of the *occurrence* of a situation having value, the causation of *a* value. Judgment is admitted in some cases at least to be one such causal condition.[2] In (b) values (things with valuity) are identified with a complex situation, namely, sounds contemplated with pleasure and liking. In (c) we are told that contemplation with liking "constitutes the value" in a very different sense from that in which judging constitutes it.

I do not believe that Mr. Prall would even appear to have reached this conclusion if it were not for the ambiguity between value as a quality of something and value as a metaphorical term for a thing with the quality. Three cases are possible. (1) Mr. Prall may mean that liking constitutes the quality as quality, not in any causal sense, but in the sense of being it. This meaning is, I take it, what his argument requires. But how liking can *be* the quality I do not understand, and until Mr. Prall expressly asserts that this is what he intends I shall not believe him to mean it. (2) "Constitutes" is an ambiguous term. It may signify either to be a constituent in a thing or to cause the thing to be. That liking is a factor in causing the thing to acquire value, a cause of the occurrence of the value-situation, I do not deny. It was part of the point of my article on value-judgment that judgment determines the existence of a value by determining a certain liking to exist which would not otherwise exist. But there is here no "very different" kind of constituting on the part of liking and judgment; there is precisely the same kind, liking being the nearer and judgment the more remote causal condition. (3) Mr. Prall may mean to assert that contemplation with liking is a constituent portion of the situation having value, that situation being complex, musical sounds being one constituent and contemplative liking another. Valuity, the quality, on this notion may be undefinable and simple, like any ultimate empirical quality, but the thing which possesses the undefinable is two things-in-relation, one the object, the other the human attitude.

I have no objections to this third conception, any more than I have to the second. But unless Mr. Prall confuses either or both the second and third with the first, his conclusion does not seem to be established. For the fact that contemplative liking is an ingredient or constituent in the complex situation possessing value in no way precludes an act of thought being also an ingredient or constituent factor; it may be included within the motor-affective

---

2 Mr. Prall's statement that judgment is no more a causal condition than eyes and ears, violins, *etc.*, hardly meets my point. According to my conception a certain use of eyes, ears, violin, *etc.*, is the subject-matter of the valuation judgment; consequently, being the material of judgment, they can hardly be contrasted with it.

act. Mr. Prall's own account suggests that it is so included. It is not mere liking that he relies on, like the liking of a pig for his swill; the motor affective attitude by description includes contemplation. And how there can be contemplation without thought I do not understand. The other factor in the complex is some recognized object, some *thing* contemplated and liked, such as sound. And a recognized, an identified and discriminated, object assuredly involves an act of thought.

A phrase employed in the quotation by Mr. Prall seems to make it the more likely that Mr. Prall has confused being a constituent part in a complex whole (value quality is not the other constituent, it must be remembered; the other constituent is an object, like sound) with constituting the quality. He says that "in the occurring of this *relation* the value of music occurs" (italics mine). Of course, this may mean only the view just considered, that the situation *having* value is complex, consisting of related things. But, except upon the basis of the wholly undemonstrated position (and one inconceivable in point of fact) that contemplative liking excludes thought, this does not imply that thought is not also within the relationship. Somehow the passage intimates that since the quality occurs when the relation occurs, the quality *is* a relation to liking. But to identify qualities with relations seems meaningless; value is not one of the related terms of the complex situation; it is either the situation itself, if *a* value is meant, or it is a quality of a situation consisting of related things.

We pass on to another quotation. He goes on to say of the "values of my theory" that "in so far as they have any common elements or characteristics to justify grouping them under the term *value* at all, they can be shown to be constituted in the motor-affective *relation* which constitutes immediate *value*" (*op. cit.*, p. 132, italics mine). Here there can be no question of Mr. Prall's confusing different things. The following specific questions may be asked: (1) Does the plural "they" in the first clause signify the same thing as the following "value" in the singular? Or does "they" refer to what strictly are not values at all, but only certain objects (like sounds) having value-quality, while the singular value refers to the latter? (2) What does the final term "immediate value" refer to, value or *a* value? (3) And when he says that a motor-affective *relation* constitutes this immediate value, in what sense is he using the word "constitutes": in the sense (*a*) of being it, (*b*) of a causal condition of a thing's acquiring value-quality, or (*c*) in the sense of being one constituent in a complex? If Mr. Prall would be good enough to answer these questions, I am sure it will conduce to the clearing up of the issue.

A further passage reads: "A valuation judgment helps, as do a thousand other things and activities, to enstate the value, to bring me to the point, that is, of being able to do the actual valuing." Here the ambiguity is in a verb instead of in substantive form. "Valuing" as distinct from valuation is an unfortunate word. It suggests that we value values, and thus suggests that valuation is something radically different from judgment. Substitute for "actual valuing" some word like prizing, or appreciating, or contemplative liking, and it becomes clear that the question at issue is open, not even touched. For that question is whether appreciation, enjoyed contemplation, or whatever term be used, does or does not include an element of reflective apprehension. The true contrast is not between appreciation and thought, but between mere appetitive liking that excludes thought and the kind of liking that includes a thoughtful factor; between an appreciation which embodies a minimum of thought and one which embodies the results of much thoughtful interest.

This fact throws light upon Mr. Prall's comment in a passage in which he says that he can not see that the study of judgments which help enstate a value situation is "particularly important for understanding values, or for learning to value justly." The study of judgments of valuation is, indeed, of no importance in understanding value as a *quality*. But neither is the study of anything else. As a quality it is ultimate, simple, and undefinable. But "values" in the plural means things having the quality: sounds, colors, friends, birds, flowers, *etc., etc.* Now since the cultivation of judgment about these things is the means by which liking is transferred from some of them to others of them, it would seem to be a primary business of any theory of criticism, ethical or esthetic, to recognize this fact.

Mr. Prall insists upon the importance of the cultivation of taste; he speaks about learning "to value justly," where value clearly means not valuating, but liking, appreciating. This is, of course, an admission that we may like wrongly, and that some likings do *not* properly determine the existence of things with value. He says that values are "satisfactory or unsatisfactory according as a subject's faculties are acute or not, and his training in specific fields thorough." Just how by his theory a value can possibly be unsatisfactory—or not a value—I don't know. But all these sayings may be taken as an indication that Mr. Prall's subconsciousness works more truly than his theorizing. For all the statements testify to acknowledgment of a factor in determining what things have value other than a *bare* affecto-motor attitude. And what is this other factor operative in cultivation of taste, in making faculties acute and sensitive, likings just, and training thorough, save thought?   JOHN DEWEY.

COLUMBIA UNIVERSITY.

Vol. XXI., No. 5   February 28, 1924

VALUE AND THOUGHT-PROCESS

IN the nature of the case the questions that Mr. Dewey has put so specifically in his comment [1] on an article of mine on the subject of value,[2] seem to me in part gratuitous. The answering of them, however, will doubtless conduce, as he says, to clearing up the issue. But Mr. Dewey's first sentence, "Strictly speaking there *are* no such things as values," is so very much to the point that I may be

[1] This JOURNAL, Vol. XX, No. 23, pp. 617–622 (1923).
[2] This JOURNAL, Vol. XX, No. 5, pp. 128–136 (1923).

excused at the beginning for adding a comment which seems to me significant, a comment which Mr. Dewey apparently thinks it not necessary to make. Things are never values: they are said to have value, which is thus an adjective of things. But this seems to mean for Mr. Dewey that values in the strict sense of the term *are* not at all; for he italicizes *are,* and when he says broadly that there are no such things as values, *things* would seem to be used in its widest sense, as meaning entities, realities, individuals. There are, of course, no such existent things as values; but there are such entities, such realities, such individual forms as values. If there were not it would be foolish, as Mr. Dewey perhaps thinks it is—I am not sure of his opinion here—to discuss anything but the one question to which he chiefly confines himself, *viz.,* What brings about or is responsible for the fact that things come to be valuable? But values in the strictest terms of discourse *are;* they have no existence, but they have being and reality, which is to say that they are natures or characters or qualities—essences, if we are to use the term of such metaphysical logicians as Plato and Leibniz and Spinoza and of Mr. Santayana.

Plato, indeed, made essence into a sort of transcendent existence; Leibniz, while he tried to keep it a pure possibility, still gave it a place in God's existence and a right to demand attention as worthy of existence, an actual tendency to exist on its own account, "each possible thing having the right to claim existence in proportion to the perfection which it involves."[3] Spinoza kept the distinction clearer. Attribute, for example, was that which the intellect perceives as the essence of Substance, but Substance as such, in its existence, or even in all its essense, intellect must fail to perceive. It is true that the essence of Substance involves its existence; but the case of Substance is unique, and the true definition in the case of each existent *thing* involves nothing but its nature,—involves, that is to say, only its essence, leaving its existence entirely unaccounted for.[4] Mr. Santayana is still more insistent on the distinction; it is maintained from the very beginning of *The Life of Reason:* "What exists at any instant, if you arrest and name it, turns out to have been an embodiment of some logical essence such as discourse might define."[5] It is only such a defining of value that I have ever attempted; but such defining seems to me important.

So far as I know, I have always been careful to use *value* as the properly abstract noun that I take it to be. Mr. Dewey considers it legitimate to use the word in a looser sense, not, as I should think, warranted in any accurate discussion, to mean *things valued.* It is

[3] *Monadology,* 51, 54.
[4] Spinoza, *Ethics,* Part I, Proposition VIII, note 2.
[5] *Op. cit.,* Vol. I, p. 24.

by taking my use of the word to carry this sense, a usage which he now and then permits himself, that he very generously puts into my sentences a meaning that he considers sound. He wishes not to believe that I mean to assume the "wholly undemonstrated and in point of fact inconceivable position" that my theorizing distinctly indicates, until I assert that I do. By thus generously giving me the benefit of the ambiguity, however, he is very easily able to show that what he takes to be the main issue between us, which he states several times with precision, resolves itself in the proposition that judgment is as definitely constitutive of value as is "an appreciation that embodies a minimum of thought," "a liking that excludes thought," "the liking of a pig for his swill," if you choose.

This issue Mr. Dewey has certainly made clear, and I may as well make it equally clear that this seems to me not "the only intelligible subject of discussion," and furthermore that while I do—and, as Mr. Dewey's quotations show, *did* in the article discussed by him—not only admit, but very specially assert, that judgment may help in the acquisition of the values [6] that things may acquire, I do not admit that in the total complex situation in which alone value occurs, judgment plays the kind of part that is played by an attitude that excludes judgment. This is beside the point for much of Mr. Dewey's argument, but it seems to me an intelligible and significant assertion. If it is trite and obvious, it is for all that not generally admitted. That is the only excuse for the present essay in repetition.

Before I answer Mr. Dewey's specific questions, let me, however, make perfectly unambiguous the proposition above in which I said that Mr. Dewey resolved the issue, *viz.*, that judgment is as definitely constitutive of value as bare liking. *To be constitutive* means here *to go to make up* as an essential element or part in a total situation. *Value* has only its abstract meaning—the meaning of an abstract noun, that is; and when I use the plural *values* I mean also the plural of the same abstract noun. One says color and colors, red and reds, redness and rednesses, beauty and beauties; and such terms are, of course, used very frequently to indicate things "having" the qualities. But the plurals are just as important and just as accurately used to indicate (*a*) a number of cases of the quality, or, if the term includes many qualities having this more general quality in common, to indicate (*b*) the quality in its various kinds (instead of number) of occurrences. There are under *a* the different values of my pen and my typewriter; and there are ordinarily supposed to be not only numerically different cases of value, but also various kinds of value. Thus there are under *b* moral, ethical, and esthetic values, again in the plural and again not meaning things at all. So that this plural

---

[6] *Valuity* seems to me not a happy coinage, and at least here unnecessary.

need involve no ambiguity. I am sorry if I have seemed to be speaking ambiguously in the use of the term in this way, even though such usage has given the opportunity for generosity in interpretation. The values are not the pen or the typewriter itself, nor moral acts, but the values that these are said to have, as a book may be said to have its own style, and authors their various styles; if the style is the man, surely it is his character or essence; not his existence, but his way of existence, his quality.

Now, having indicated an answer in general, let me be more specific. First there are the three questions which Mr. Dewey puts at the bottom of page 621, and which he specifically asks to have answered. The sentence which he finds so full of ambiguity and which demands these answers to clear it, is to the following effect: "The values of my theory in so far as they have any common elements to justify grouping them under the term *value* at all can be shown to be constituted in the motor-affective relation which constitutes immediate value." The answers to the numbered questions are enough, I think, to show what the questions were. (1) The plural, *values*, at the beginning has the same signification as the singular, *value*, in italics. (2) The term *immediate value* refers to value in precisely the same sense of the word. (3) *Constitutes* is used in the sense of *being*, Mr. Dewey's first alternative possibility. For since I was asserting that the motor-affective relation constitutes the value, and since I had been careful to explain—Mr. Dewey quotes the clause—that "in the occurrence of this relation the value . . . occurs," I felt at liberty to say that the relation constituted the value, thinking that my analysis of the situation made my meaning clear. The relation means the situation, the constituted relation with the two terms present. Further, this relation can not occur without the attitude of the subject, while any object whatever will do for the other term; for any object whatever may conceivably be liked, while only a particular kind of subject with a particular kind of attitude can do the liking. Hence it seemed to me not very ambiguous to say that the liking-relation constitutes the value. At least I hope that there can be no ambiguity in my present statement.

"But how can a relation *be* a quality?" Mr. Dewey asks. "To identify qualities with relations seems meaningless; value is not one of the related terms of the . . . situation . . . it is a quality of a situation consisting of related things." My answer is that the two things in the relation are an animal organism and something to which the organism reacts. And it is when this reaction takes place that the relation is established and that that which the organism takes as its object is said in ordinary parlance to have value. As Mr. Dewey enunciates the alternatives open to me on page 620, the same point is involved. No. 1 here is not only the meaning required for my argument, as he sees and notes, but the meaning intended, a meaning which Mr. Dewey says he does not understand. The issue then comes to be, since we are agreed on the situation as involving the same three factors, *viz.*, a subject, an object, and an attitude which relates them, just what this attitude is and whether judgment is included in it or not. My contention is that it is not; that for value to occur or to arise, and to arise in the occurrence itself, there must be an attitude; but I wish to say at the same time that this attitude is like the pig's towards his swill,—not a thoughtful attitude, like Mr. Dewey's towards a problem he is engaged upon.

But Mr. Dewey here takes my description of the attitude as "contemplative liking," so that he finds it easy to indicate my real difficulty, one which he finds insuperable because meaningless. "How," he asks—and the question is obviously rhetorical—"how can contemplation fail to be thoughtful; how can it exclude judgment?" This I shall even have the temerity to try and make clear, for above all others this seems to me the issue at stake. Mr. Dewey's greater interest is in what causes things to become valuable, and in his solution of this problem I follow him; except that I feel that in laying such stress on judgment and thought he is over-emphasizing their importance, the importance of a logical and practical activity. So far as I know, what causes anything to take on value is very largely just such thinking as he indicates in the last sentence of his article; but what I should wish to emphasize is a non-practical, non-intellectual activity. Since he admits the importance of both kinds, there is no serious theoretical issue between us here. Certainly Mr. Dewey's practical judgments, as he calls them, are a large part of the process that "enstates" values, as he has previously put it. Since, however, desires, likings, bare motor-affective attitudes also help, I can not see why he finds *valuing* as distinct from *valuation* an unfortunate word. It would be so in his context, perhaps; it seems to me not so in mine. But he would be right at this point in saying that the issue which he wishes resolved is still open, *viz.*, the issue as to "whether appreciation . . . does or does not include an element of reflective apprehension." If *reflective* means thoughtful or logical or judgmental, I think that such an element is not included. This is, if I have followed at all, what I must now make clear.

The question then is, what does the occurrence of the value-quality consist in? What is the nature of what happens, if value is to occur in the happening? What are the elements of the situation we have agreed to talk about?

To answer this question is, of course, to define the indefinable, if definition must always be of the Leibnizian form—red is a color. But there is another sort of definition which empiricists have always used, the kind that is of the form—this is red, accompanied by a gesture that points to something that *is* red. It is in this sense only that red exists, and it is in this sense that value exists. Neither of them exists, I suppose, in the sense that the substance of nature itself exists, a moving chaos in which we knock against other chaotic elements. As Mr. Santayana puts it, nothing given exists; and I had made up my mind to that long ago. But I have not made up my mind to the impossibility of empirical definitions, nor to the impossibility of so framing causal laws and descriptions of functions that discourse becomes intelligible, communicable, and useful. So I can say that value is there where the relation above described comes to be. The value is there as the quality of this spatio-temporal happening. And it only comes to be there when the substance of an animal so reacts upon the substances about it that the animal feels pleased or displeased. Value is thus constituted in tropisms, if you like. For value, esse *is* percipi; values to be such are felt, and the feeling of the animal that has any feeling is all that is needed to give a situation where there is value, for feelings are had only by reaction to stimulus, and stimulus comes from an independent substantial source—perhaps within the animal's own body—whose *esse* is not *percipi* at all, but whose qualities are empirically *what* they are because the stimulus is what it is and the animal's attitude what *it* is.

Mr. Dewey's pig and his swill is as good an illustration as any, although I should prefer, since I must give a meaning to the term *contemplation,* a cat in the sun or a ruminating cow. Here by good luck we have the very synonym for contemplative. In human beings the attitude is the attitude of a habitually more practical and thoughtful animal, but an animal attitude it remains; and the ruminating cow, the cud she chews, and the feeling of acceptance instead of riddance that keeps her chewing, comprise a very good case of a situation in which value occurs. As she keeps on chewing the value recurs—an esthetic value, I hope; for I suppose that the cow is not grinding predigested corn into milk, nor even preparing supplies to keep up her necessary strength. She is having elementary esthetic enjoyment in each chew, or perhaps more strictly in each impulse to go on chewing, ruminating, contemplating; as an infant is having such enjoyment when it chews on a teething ring, or Aristotle's God when he contemplates the universe. For while this species of contemplation was certainly akin to psychological process, Aristotle's God was surely not doing what Mr. Dewey calls thinking.[7] As Mr.

---

[7] See *How We Think,* p. 9, where Mr. Dewey says that there are involved in every reflective act ''a state of perplexity, hesitation, doubt'' and ''an act of search,'' etc.

Taylor translates, God, instead of really thinking, was only "thinking of thought," in an "activity of immobility."[8] How, indeed, could he have been thinking, with the whole moving universe which he knew by heart immediately present to his mind, seen by him in pure intuition, in the one case in which there could be immanent knowledge, the case, that is, where there could be no knowledge at all? All the relativity of the actual motion was lost, I suppose, and the whole paradox of an Unmoved Mover seems on this basis a very plausible, nay intelligible, idea. What would be *un*intelligible, what always has been unintelligible, is a *moving* mover. What indeed could call forth thought in such a situation? Plato has described this same thrilling, but thoughtless, contemplation in the *Phædrus*. Montaigne's neat eulogy of the permanent pleasure of sex intercourse, Dr. Johnson's equally pat notion of the perfect life as driving with a pretty woman, and Browning's sentimental, but barbarous, *Last Ride* all give us the same notion of heaven. It is a thoughtless place; there is no judging in heaven; the Last Judgment has been made. Even the Christian God has stopped thinking, and there is only the timeless music of the twanging harps, which is eternal without needing to endure.

Value occurs instantaneously. It is an occurrence that defies literal analysis, but symbolically language can indicate, *i.e.*, point out, the kind of an occurrence that it is.

If this is a "wholly undemonstrated" position, it is because it could not conceivably be demonstrated except by just this kind of careful indication. And if it is "in point of fact inconceivable," that is true of all occurrences as such, whether they are occurrences of quality or of philosophical opinions upon the nature of a particular quality called value. Can Mr. Dewey *demonstrate* occurrence except by pointing to it? Or can he—can logic itself?—make transition conceivable? The occurrence of value is a case of the occurrence of quality, of a transition, and is *therefore* not literally conceivable.

But put it more simply—in psychological terms. What Mr. Dewey says that I need to prove is that contemplative liking excludes thought. This, I understand him, would effectively refute the one part of his double contention at the bottom of page 617, which asserts that judgment is a necessary "constituent part of the total complex situation having valuity." The other part of his contention I do not deny, as I have made clear above. But why need there be judgment in contemplative liking? When we listen to music, and in the few moments when our attention recurs in strong enough pulsations so that we really hear it, we do not think. There are no problems; there is no need to think; there is no "thought-provoking

---

[8] A. E. Taylor, *Aristotle*, p. 50.

situation" to force us on. Rather we rest in the barest feeling. We rest as the pig would rest with his swill if there were no other pigs to get ahead of him, and if he did not have to perform so many difficult practical operations to devour it. But we rest also as Aristotle's God does,—unmoved, not thinking; or as any mortal does in the face of beauty which is really his. One does not thoughtfully contemplate works of art unless one is trying to re-express them in another medium or thinking up things to say about them, or trying to remember what some one else has already said. One is simply struck with them, with form itself; art moves us instantaneously or not at all. It may take years before we see anything very complex as beautiful; but when we do, it is at a glance, between breaths. So esthetic trances have been mistaken for eternity,[9] which occurs, I suppose, instead of enduring. It has been clearly seen by poets, and now at last by philosophers in Italy, that poetry is essentially lyrical, of a moment. This is why Goethe says that art for most of us is fragments, and only for great minds the one immediately present whole which it is to the poet himself. And it is this type of experience, entirely undemonstrated, as any experience must needs be to be experience at all, that I mean by contemplative liking.

If, as Mr. Woodworth seems to think,[10] feeling is the body's instantaneous impulse to accept or to be rid of, then this is the hint of a psychological account of esthetic contemplation at its root. But I am not explaining how it can happen, but trying to say what the essential nature of the happening itself is—to define it by pointing it out.

Mr. Dewey has treated my article with careful consideration. Perhaps it seems ungracious to refuse the charity he offers by way of my "ambiguities"; but the central point on which we differ seems to me of the greatest significance, and we differ by a world. For I can not help finding in Mr. Dewey's insertion of thought and judgment into value, even into the process that makes things valuable one over against another, the process that he calls evaluation,—I can not help seeing here a suggestion that value is not the creation of irrational preference, but is somehow at bottom rational. I have indeed spoken of just preferences and values; those which, when one is all that a human being can come to be by training in perception and feeling, one will naturally have or appreciate. There is no difficulty in having the word *justice* mean something here, which it really does mean. On the contrary, it is only by the admission of preference as the beginning of reason and justice that one can be a naturalist at all, or a scientific student of morals. For if evolution means

---

[9] A minor and modern instance is Rupert Brooke's *Dining-Room Tea.*
[10] R. S. Woodworth, *Psychology*, pp. 177–178.

anything, if biological science has validity or value, then mind occurs in nature, and reason is born of the irrational; it is an irrational existence before it is anything else and in order to be anything else. As beginnings are never conceivable, Hume to the contrary notwithstanding, so the beginnings of rationality can only be what was not rational and became so, an obviously "inconceivable" occurrence. The first step to make the thought process what it is was not a thoughtful step. It was an animal attitude, accepting or rejecting appearances, as it felt them good or bad. Value came first.

But this is not the place to dilate upon the theme of reason and its ordered universe, floating in an inconceivably vaster irrational and unknown chaos of possibilities. I can only hope that Mr. Dewey will think that I mean to hold the inconceivable position that I do with at least as much ground in my well-working subconsciousness—I take it to be my natural soul, which does all my thinking and theorizing too—as in my expressed argument. One of his questions I have failed to answer. How can there be values which are not valuable? There can not be. But there can be dislikes as well as likes, and so negative values as well as positive. Mr. Dewey may find that the present discourse has only the former sort of value. It seems to me, however, that I have at least shown that I mean quite unambiguously something; that most of what I mean does not interfere with accepting Mr. Dewey's doctrine of valuation judgments, except in so far as this doctrine suggests that such judgments are integral to the occurrence of value itself; and that the rest of what I mean bears on the nature of value, however indefinable value may be because it is an ultimate category, a mere event, the occurrence of one specific sort of quality, or more rigorously, the specific sort of quality that is present to mind as the essence of the thoughtless situation indicated.

D. W. PRALL.

UNIVERSITY OF CALIFORNIA.

THE JOURNAL OF PHILOSOPHY

"OBJECTIVITY" IN VALUE JUDGMENTS

IT seems unlikely that most men are incurably committed to the quest for certainty. Where philosophical criticism does not disillusion them, practical failure if often enough repeated may. Yet giving up the quest for certainty does not entail abandonment of the search for a related but more modest thing often called "objectivity." Even many empiricists, long reconciled to the tentativeness and fallibility of all beliefs, wish to discover a foundation for value judgments which will approximate the degree of probability attained by scientific judgments. Or if we must generally be content with a lower degree of probability than is usually obtainable in, say, physics, we still wish to found our value judgments on evidence and on hypothetico-inductive inference from evidence. Unless we can do so, the alternatives are either some form of apriorist absolutism or a subjectivism which makes valuations dependent on the momentary feeling or whim of the individual.

Absolutism is no solution for our time. The supposedly self-evident axioms or intuitions to which it appeals are seen to be even more variable from individual to individual and from culture to culture than are sense-perceptions themselves; and so the rationalist attitude leads to a scepticism which is more devastating than that which results from empiricism at its crudest. Furthermore, the *a priori* methods of rationalism have been thoroughly discredited in other fields of inquiry which deal with the world of existence. And values, whatever their ontological status, at least manifest themselves in, and control, the realm of existence.

There is an equally persistent effort to escape from the extreme forms of subjectivism and relativism, such as are currently represented by those logical positivists who hold that values are wholly relative to the opinion or the immediate feeling of the individual, hence that any alleged statements about them are mere "ejaculations of emotion."

It is in reaction to such views that we find contemporary students of value seeking an objective basis for value judgments. The meanings offered for the term "objectivity"—notoriously one of the danger-signals of philosophical terminology—vary with the solutions proposed. I shall deal only with those that are relevant to an empirical approach to value, for empiricism in this field will stand or fall by its ability to solve this problem. Unless it can do so, it can not serve as a guide in living.

Objectivity with respect to values is currently being sought in the following principal directions: (1) in the properties of valued objects themselves; (2) in universal validity of the rules which guide conduct; (3) in the universal concepts with an objective foundation in reality; (4) in agreement, or the social dimension of valuation; (5) in knowledge of the "conditions" of value experience. It is not my intention to show that all these approaches are worthless, for the resulting analyses have clarified many aspects of valuation. The negative thesis of this essay is, rather, that none of these five by itself, nor all of them together, suffice to answer the basic question, which is: How can we avoid the vicious relativism which makes "x is good" mean merely "A given individual, or a given group, thinks—or feels—that x is good (or desirable, or satisfying, etc.)"?

(1) *Value as a character of the valuable object.* The simplest way of attributing objective status to valuations is that of naïve realism, according to which values are properties of things in the same way that squareness, roundness, and (according to this school) blueness and loudness characterize them. The value properties are carried over into perception just as are the other properties. The mind merely selects them. If any one fails to perceive a value when it is really present, this is due to a failure in his capacity of discrimination.[1]

This position is subject to all the difficulties of naïve realism as a general epistemological position: e.g., failure to explain hallucination and error, failure to take into account the complexity of the perceptual process including the rôles of the medium and the responding organism, and neglect of the part that interpretation and reflection play in discrimination.

There are also certain difficulties peculiar to value properties. When an object is valuable to a given person at one time, and not valuable to him at a later time, it is implausible to explain this situation in all cases by saying that he fails to discriminate the value at the later time. For he has already shown his capacity to discriminate the value, and he may on the later occasion deliberately search for it. These conditions usually suffice to reveal

---

[1] The classic statement of this position is to be found in G. E. Moore's *Principia Ethica*, and its standard refutations in Santayana's *Winds of Doctrine*, Ch. IV, and R. B. Perry's *General Theory of Value*, Ch. II.

other properties of the object that have persisted. But suppose that the interests and emotional habits of the person in question can be shown to have changed. Here is a verifiable alteration in the situation, whereas the supposed change in the value properties of the object is merely conjectural.

An allied position which seeks to take the interests of the experiencer of value into account, and at the same time to place the value in the object, is that of objective relativism. Mr. Eliseo Vivas as spokesman for this view acknowledges that "the value of the object arises out of the interaction of the desiring self and the desired object," and that "the value is not in the object for the self when the self does not desire it." Yet he holds that "value is objective for the valuing organism" in the sense that the "value resides in the outside or object-term of a relational complex which is a value situation, the inside term of which is a self."[2] His principal ground for locating the value in the outside term, or object, is that human beings sometimes, and animals presumably always, may value objects without being explicitly aware of the feelings of satisfaction that accompany the perception of the object. Thus it is asserted to be the bouquet of the cigar or the taste of the milk (these also are assumed to be in the object) to which value attaches, not the satisfaction that accompanies these. Mr. Vivas admits that we can desire, and therefore value, the satisfaction or enjoyment, but he tends to dismiss this attitude as a vagary of hedonists. His position could be attacked on such psychological and epistemological grounds as that the affective element—which is admittedly present and essential—is not itself in the object, and that consequently at least one of the principal ingredients of the value is not in the object. An even more important objection is that this position does not afford an escape from relativistic scepticism. For the objectification of the value may be illusory; on the view in question, the value is in the object only for a given organism, or group of organisms, which may be mistaken in locating it there. Even though the value should in the objective relativist's sense be "in the object," this does not ensure that our *judgments* about the object will be objective. So much is tacitly admitted by Mr. Vivas, when he goes on to find the kind of objectivity we are seeking in the social dimension of value experience. But this will be discussed under (4) and (5).

(2) and (3) *Objectivity as residing in universal rules or concepts.* Certain moral rules, such as "Do not kill," and certain concepts such as "beauty" and "security," are observed to have

―――――――

[2] Eliseo Vivas: "Value and Fact," *Philosophy of Science,* Vol. 6 (1939), p. 435.

gained the allegiance of many individuals and of widely varying cultures. Consequently it is hoped to state these rules and define these concepts in such a way as to make them absolutely universal in their compulsiveness. Objectivity, so it is assumed, means primarily universality. But when the rules and concepts are clarified, several obstacles are encountered. The rules or values are found to conflict. "Do not kill" may be found to be incompatible in a particular situation with the rule "Act so as to preserve the lives of your children and friends"; or we may have a choice between beauty and security. Casuistry then gets to work and modifies the rule so as to remove the contradiction: e.g., "Do not kill except when necessary to defend your children and friends." But this rule in turn may conflict with others, and it may be too vague about the circumstances in which it is applied to be of use. When the rule takes all the relevant circumstances into account, it is no longer universal, for every moral situation is unique. Consequently upon analysis the most that can be claimed for rules by empiricists is wide generality, not strict universality. A widely general rule is one that furnishes guidance in a large number of similar and frequently recurring situations; a "value" that claims general allegiance is one that corresponds to basic needs and interests which manifest themselves in many individual lives and cultures. These are rooted in common human biological structure and in the fundamental structural patterns of human association. In so far as we can discover and formulate these, we have found guide-posts toward objectivity in our judgments. But these do not afford a complete solution of our problem. We are not enabled to determine which rule or value is applicable in a given particular situation, or whether any hitherto discovered will suffice. Nor is it always the common human or social element that is decisive: the idiosyncratic factors in a man or a culture may be the source of the value. For man's biological nature has a large degree of plasticity, and his environment and his social patterns change.

(4) *Agreement or "social objectivity" as the criterion of value.* When it is perceived that strict universality is not to be found in rules or value concepts, then universality is sought in agreement: "x is good" means "Persons A, B, C . . . will find x good" (the agreement may be restricted to a specified group or extended to all mankind). Thus Mr. Vivas, in the article quoted: "When I say that something is good, and I do not mean merely that I like it . . . I mean not only that it will satisfy an isolated interest, but that it will not interfere with the other interests which will make up my system, but will rather aid and foster them. But I

also mean that the other members of the social group with which I identify myself will concur with this judgment."[3] The value judgment in this case may be a singular one, "This is good," as well as a universal rule. The universality is one of assent rather than logical universality.

But here again the constitution and interests of the individuals concerned may vary, even within a single social group. In any case, agreement is at most a rough test of value, not the basis of its objectivity. For the sum of a number of judgments can not be objective unless there is a basis of objectivity in each; and further, you can fool all the people some of the time. Consequently the social dimension of value may be appealed to in a different fashion:

(5) *Objectivity as residing in the "publicly observable" conditions and results of value experiences.* Thus Professor Dewey: "Judgments about values are judgments about the conditions and results of experienced objects; judgments about that which should regulate the formation of our desires, affections and enjoyments."[4] The dominant note in Dewey's discussion of value is an emphasis that reflective inquiry into means is important to the choice of ends: we must know which ends are realizable in the actual world, and this knowledge modifies our ends-in-view. Since the material and social conditions which make the achievement of a given set of values possible or impossible are open to public inspection, these supply an "objective" foundation for our values in opposition to the reliance of extreme "subjectivist" theories on private feeling.

This emphasis of Dewey's has been a useful corrective to such theories as artificially separate means and ends, and then treat ends as chosen purely by feeling. But Dewey admits that "liking" or "enjoyment" is a constituent of the value experience itself. Since the individual has direct access to this through self-observation, and others may have some access to it indirectly, it would seem to be a grave sin of omission for an empiricist to exclude this phase of the act from study when seeking evidence for valuations. In no other field do we rule out attention to the phenomenon under study itself, to concentrate exclusively on its conditions and results.

Thus although, as I shall argue later, Dewey is moving in the right direction when he seeks objectivity in the *evidence* for value judgments, his social behaviorism leads him to ignore one very

---

3 *Ibid.*, pp. 437–438.
4 *The Quest for Certainty*, p. 265; see also his *Theory of Valuation, passim.*

important kind of evidence, namely, that concerning the immediate quality of the experience of value itself.

To oppose, or to supplement, these five inadequate approaches, I wish to suggest the following primary meaning of objectivity:

(6) A value judgment may be said to be objective without qualification when it is *true*.

This answer is so simple that it has been all but overlooked. As baldly stated, it may seem either obvious or question-begging. That it is not obvious, however, will appear from the fact that none of the above five theories explicitly put the answer in this way, even though they may presuppose it. Does it beg the question? It may be declared to do so on either of the following grounds:

(*a*) That the theories in question are themselves concerned with the criteria or conditions of truth in value judgments. E.g., it may be asserted that a value judgment can be true only if values are properties of objects, or if universal value concepts have a foundation in reality. But let us remember the problem from which we started, which was, how we could escape from ethical scepticism, how we could find propositions about values sufficiently reliable to serve as guides in living. Surely, then, the answer we have suggested, if it is valid, must be the direct and primary answer to our problem. For if we can guide our conduct by true judgments we have no grounds for scepticism. Our question, then, is primarily an epistemic question. We are seeking *knowledge* with regard to valuations. It may be that ontological questions, such as some of the above, are involved, and I for one should insist that "truth" is a term containing an ontological reference. But the nature of this reference is an auxiliary question.

(*b*) The proposed solution may be declared question-begging also for the following reason: that, on empiricist principles, we can never *know* that any proposition is true. All we can assert confidently is that there is evidence which gives the proposition a high degree of probability. These statements are correct, but are compatible with the view offered. Even though we can not with certainty know any valuational proposition to be true, it is only in terms of the ideal of truth that we can define the ideal of objectivity.

But this second objection points to a needed application of the view proposed.

A value judgment is objective *without qualification,* it was said, when it is true. It follows that the judgment can be *known* to be objective only in the degree that it can be *known* to be true.

For practical purposes, then, we can escape from scepticism with regard to values to the extent that we can obtain empirical evidence which is relevant to the truth or probability of value judgments. The sceptic is the man who believes that there is *no* evidence that is relevant to the truth or probability of any proposition, that no proposition has more evidential weight than any other. The non-sceptical empiricist, on the other hand, holds that, while no proposition involving existence can be known with certainty to be true, nevertheless some possess much more evidential support than others, hence possess a much higher degree of probability. And the degree of probability may be so high in many cases that the proposition supplies a reliable guide for action.

Do value judgments, then, conform to the canons of empirical logic? In other words, are they verifiable by the hypothetico-inductive method?

Let us consider the species of value judgment which we encounter most often in ethics. The difficulty arises over the term "ought," or some equivalent, which is always found in the ethical judgment. It is often said that the "ought" can never be reduced to an "is," that "value" is irreducible to "fact." For example, "I ought to do x," or "x is good," can not be equated with "x is desired by me," or "I like x."

If the "ought" is analyzed in this oversimple way, then empiricism in ethics is indeed untenable, and the "ought" becomes something very mysterious. But the meaning of an ethical judgment is capable of analysis in a more complicated and, I believe, more adequate fashion. When I say that I ought to do x, I am referring to something beyond my desire or liking of the moment.

Let us consider the matter first at the purely egoistic level of conduct. When I say that x is good for me, I mean that it will fit in with the whole pattern of my interests and my potential satisfactions. I mean that in the long run act x will promote the system of my interests to a greater extent than any feasible alternative, and also that the resulting satisfactions will be qualitatively superior to those resulting from any other interest pattern.

Similarly on the social or altruistic level. When I say that an act is right or good, I mean that it will promote the interest pattern, actual or potential, of the group, and that this pattern will supply the group with richer intrinsic quality of experience than any alternative.

Briefly, on this view "I ought to do x" means "x will promote the maximum of integration plus qualitative satisfaction."

What we have, then, in the ethical judgment is not a simple descriptive proposition concerning present or past fact, but a predictive judgment involving the potentialities of human nature as well as its actuality. In the large sense of fact, the future is also a fact, and the nature of the world includes what it can be as well as what it is so far. The judgment of value is, then, in this very special sense a judgment of fact.

Is the ethical judgment, so conceived, subject to empirical verification?

I believe that it is. We can obtain empirical evidence both as to the tendency of a given act to promote integration of interests, and also as to its fitness to produce a qualitatively rich experience. Our scientific knowledge, such as our medical knowledge, and our practical experience of the way certain types of act fit into a given context of interests, supply us with evidence as to the integrative or disintegrative tendency of an act. Likewise our observation, largely introspective, of the "inner" quality of various types of satisfaction in the past, and our imaginative experiments with comparatively novel types of act, give us some basis on which to forecast the affective quality of experience, both our own and others'.

To the extent that we have relevant evidence of these kinds, the ethical judgment is "objective." It rests on observed fact and inductive inference from such fact. In so far as introspection plays a part in the knowledge of qualitative satisfaction, the evidence is in the psychological sense "subjective," i.e., it is directly accessible to one observer alone. But it is still evidence, and it is to some extent capable of intersubjective confirmation by indirect means. Even without confirmation, the evidence of one witness has some weight.

One peculiarity of value judgments, then, is that the evidence on which they rest, although it is a matter of empirical observation, is partly of this "private" character. But this fact need not lead, as it is sometimes held to lead, to the extreme relativist position that such evidence is of no worth. For propositions about feelings are themselves true or false, though sometimes only one person from the nature of the case can directly determine their truth or falsity with any adequacy.

Another peculiarity of value judgments is that the basic judgment, and theoretically the only type of judgment that can have complete truth or objectivity, is the *singular* judgment. Each art object is ultimately unique, and so is each ethical situation. So I can say that *"This x* is beautiful (or good)," with more evidential weight than *"All x* is beautiful (or good)."

Objectivity in value judgments, then, attaches primarily to singular judgments, judgments about an individual person in an individual situation. This is why the second meaning of objectivity expounded in the early part of this essay is misleading. By a thorough analysis of the situation, I may assert much more confidently that "This wine is good" than that "All wine is good," and that "For Joe Doakes to kill John Smith under these circumstances is wrong" than that "For any person x to kill any other person y under all circumstances is wrong." Singular judgments of value *can* be either true or false without qualification, though it is necessary to repeat that as empiricists we must say that we can never certainly know them to be true or false. Reputedly universal judgments or rules, however, in this field are more or less rough generalizations possessing at most statistical truth, since they can not take into account the complexities of individual situations involving competing values and disvalues.[5] We need such rules, and we need them in the analysis of particular situations themselves. So far as they serve to guide us here, they have a degree of objectivity. But from the nature of the ethical situation, the proposition which directs an ethical choice is singular, and prescribes a particular line of conduct in an individual situation.

On this view there is a kind of relativism involved in value judgments. When we say that this x is good, we mean that it is good for a given individual or group within a specifiable situation, or at most that an object or action of the type in question is roughly adequate in many or most situations that are similar. But it can not be asserted to be good for all individuals in all situations. For value always involves a *relation* between men and their world, and these latter are highly variable terms.

But this kind of relativism is not "vicious," i.e., it does not lead to scepticism. "x is good for person A in situation m" does

---

[5] I am referring here to those ethical maxims which prescribe a specific value-content, such as those given above, "All wine is good," or "All killing is wrong." Their terms belong to what roughly corresponds to Carnap's "object-language" in science, and in ethics we may call such a language EL_1. But there is also a "metalanguage" in which ethical theory itself is written, which we may call EL_n. This consists of the definitions and theorems which state the meanings of ethical terms, and which formulate the syntax of EL_1. An example of expressions in EL_n would be the definition of good given above: "'x is good' means 'x will promote the maximum of integration plus qualitative satisfaction.'" Although expressions in EL_n are not exclusively syntactical, or completely lacking in content—since they refer to general aspects of the value situation, that is, of men in relation to their world—they do not suffice to direct action in particular situations. They may, however, indirectly influence action, in so far as ethical dialectic affects specific valuations. Universal propositions in EL_n may be true or false without qualification, though of course they can never be known with certainty to be so, and though a completely adequate formulation of them may be a remote, even an impossible, ideal.

not mean "x is *thought* or *felt* by person A, or by some other person, to be good for A in situation m." This would lead to as many possible truths as there are observers of the situation, and hence would destroy objectivity in any relevant sense. On the contrary, the judgment means "x will promote the maximum of integration plus qualitative satisfaction for A (and—if we are speaking on the level of social morality—for the others affected) in situation m." Now x either will or will not do this. If it will, the proposition is true; if it will not, the proposition is false—regardless of what A or anyone else thinks or feels. The person who is most likely to be right is the person who has the most evidence and interprets it most ably. Sometimes the individual most immediately concerned is the least qualified to judge, even though he may have better access to certain types of relevant evidence.

This view of objectivity will suffice for those who are willing to examine each important situation on its merits. It will not satisfy those who persist in demanding rules and value concepts that will prescribe the duties of all individuals in all cultures. But I have not been seeking an objectivity which obviates the necessity for reflection on the nuances of life. Such objectivity would be a moral juggernaut.

Nor is the view of objectivity here presented a comforting doctrine. Evidence concerning the qualitative aspect of different types of experience or patterns of life, obtained as it is through ruthless self-observation and through dramatic rehearsal of the probable experience of others, is slippery and difficult knowledge. The critical person will often have to suspend judgment, or to make a choice from evidence that is heart-rendingly scant, or to act on "hunches" cast up by his subconscious perceptions of fitness. But this would seem to be an inescapable predicament of the human tragi-comedy.

PHILIP BLAIR RICE.

KENYON COLLEGE.

THE JOURNAL OF PHILOSOPHY

VALUATION JUDGMENTS AND IMMEDIATE QUALITY

THERE is much in Mr. Rice's recent article in this JOURNAL with which a neo-empiricist is happy to agree.[1] He will agree, on the critical side, with opposition to the metaphysical "realism" that locates the "objectivity" of value in "objects" that are so-called because of lack of any connection whatever with human behavior. He will agree also with the opposition to those views which admit a human factor in values, but which interpret it in such a way that the result is sceptical denial of the possibility of any genuine judgments about them. These agreements are based upon those positive aspects of Mr. Rice's paper which (1) identify the problem of the possibility of genuine judgments of value with the problem of the possibility of reaching conclusions about value that are capable of providing guidance to life-behavior; and (2) which identify the "objectivity" of judgments with verifiability by empirical evidence. The view that value-judgments are "objective" for the same reason that other judgments are accepted as valid,—because, that is, they are verifiable by the hypothetico-inductive method,[2] is that upon which the neo-empiricist stands.

I

The greater one's satisfaction with these points of Mr. Rice's article, the greater, however, will be one's disappointment that Mr. Rice introduces an element of "subjectivity" which is reached by a different method and depends upon a different kind of criterion than that used in defining "objectivity." The method and criterion are so fundamentally different that they cease to be correlative. For *subjective* is defined in terms of a special order of Being, viz., one that is directly open to observation only by one person, and by a special kind of knowing called "introspection," or *"self-knowledge"*—an order of Being which accordingly is "inner" and "private." It is defined, then, by falling back upon an assump-

[1] "Objectivity" in Value Judgments, Vol. XL (1943), pp. 5–14.

[2] *Op. cit.*, p. 12. In view of this emphasis upon verifiability, it seems a matter of regret that no allusion is made to the articles by Dr. Lepley dealing with this point.

tion of a certain sort of epistemological-metaphysical "reality" while "objective," on the other hand, is defined on the basis of evidential support depended upon in all scientific inquiry. Not only does Mr. Rice use a method and criterion that are explicitly rejected in the case of "objectivity," but he further complicates matters by holding that this introspective approach to a private and inner material provides a special kind of verifying evidence with respect to valuation judgments, a kind which can and should be *added on* to the evidence supplied by common and public observation, such as is used in arriving at non-valuation propositions—a view which renders the "subjective" itself "objective" on the basis of the definition given of objectivity!

Before dealing with this latter matter, I shall say something about the definition of "subjectivity" that would be arrived at on the basis of parity of reasoning and criterion with that used in the case of "objectivity." It would run something as follows: Propositions (judgments, beliefs, or whatever) are *subjective* when they are produced by causal conditions which fail to possess genuine evidential capacity and verifying power, but which nevertheless are taken at the time to possess them and hence to provide acceptance and assertion of the propositions in question. The only "assumption" in this definition is the empirically verifiable fact that all beliefs, right and wrong, valid and invalid, have concrete causal conditions which, under the given circumstances, *produce* judgments, but which in some cases are conditions that warrant or justify the proposition that is generated, while in other cases they are found not to be such as to furnish justifying ground. Epistemological philosophers make a great ado about illusions, hallucinations, forms of insanity. But science proceeds on the basis that there are concrete conditions for their occurrence, and that these conditions are capable of being detected and eliminated, or discounted, as far as capacity to produce acceptance of a given proposition and belief is concerned. It was perhaps "natural" in a backward state of science to lump together concrete and specifiable conditions of error and mistake under the general and supposedly unanalyzable assumption of "a subject," as a name for a general peculiar order of Being. But scientific inquiry has progressed by searching for and detecting specific concrete conditions which are subject to exactly the same kind of public observation and test as are the conditions that warrant and justify sound and valid propositions (judgments, beliefs, or whatever). It is the peculiarity of Mr. Rice's view of evaluative judgments that he has completely rejected the epistemological-metaphysical assumption in the case of "objectivity" while retaining it in the case of the "subjective."

The consistent empirical view is that viewed as *events*, as occurrences, the *subjective* and *objective* are both of the same nature. They differ (and differ basically) with respect to the capacity of their respective causal conditions to serve as valid *grounds*,—in their ability, that is, to stand up in the exercise of the verifying evidential function.

II

Mr. Rice offers no direct evidence or argument for holding to the existence of material that is private and inner and hence (by its very nature) accessible directly only to observation by a "self" which is single, exclusive, and non-public and non-social. He engages, however, in a discussion of another view whose defects are supposed to provide ground for the position he takes. As this other view is attributed to me, consideration of it may have the disadvantage of seeming to be purely an argument *pro domo*. But I hope the discussion will turn out, as it develops, to deal with two points of much more than personal importance. One of them concerns the matter of subjectivity; the other concerns the capacity of a "value experience" (as described by Mr. Rice) to serve as supplementary or "plus" evidence in verification of value-*judgments*.

Mr. Rice attributed to me, quite correctly, the view that evaluative judgments are conclusions of inquiries into the "conditions and results of experienced objects." He also points out, quite correctly, that this view is equivalent to holding that "objectivity" resides in "the publicly observable conditions and consequences of value-experiences." And he further states that I am moving in the right direction in seeking objectivity in the evidence for value judgments. The trouble is that I do not go far enough with respect to what is evidential and verifying material. My "social behaviorism leads [me] to ignore one very important kind of evidence, namely, that concerning the immediate quality of the experience of value itself." [3] This statement does not of itself expressly assert that this "immediate quality" is private and subjective. In so far, it is possible to discuss the question of the evidential value of an immediately experienced quality apart from the question of its alleged subjective nature.

Mr. Rice's statement that "value-judgments are concerning the immediate quality of the experience of value itself," is joined to a statement that since I *admit* "that 'liking' or 'enjoyment' is a constituent of the value experience itself," it is the more strange

[3] *Op. cit.*, pp. 9–10.

that I ignore the evidential and verifying force of the experience of liking and enjoyment.[4]

Now I do a good deal more than hold that qualitative "enjoyment," "satisfaction," is a *constituent* of the experienced material which the valuation judgment is about or "is concerning." I hold that it is the *entire* material that judgment is about. But it is an essential part of my view of valuation judgments that the satisfaction, liking, enjoyment, they are about is not itself a *value* save in a figurative way, a way illustrated in the figure of speech in which a man is called a candidate. For it is not asserted that he is inherently and *per se* a *candidate,* but that he is one in connection with an on-going course of events of which a future election is an indispensable part—that is, in a prospective reference. And so an enjoyment is called a *value* with reference to being potentially the material for an evaluative judgment, or in connection with events still to occur. This designation is innocent as a figure of speech; it confuses the entire issue when taken literally.

The strange part of Mr. Rice's criticism of my view is that he himself explicitly insists upon the prospective reference of an evaluation judgment as far as its "objectivity" is concerned—and I fail to see how any statement can be regarded as a *judgment* unless it lays claim to objectivity in the sense of evidential support. The following considerations quoted from Mr. Rice's article certainly read as if they were in complete harmony with my view that the mere enunciation that something, as a matter of fact, is enjoyed or liked is not a *judgment* of the value of what is enjoyed. For in defining "objectivity" (without a claim to which, as I have just said, no form of words can be termed *judgment*) he says expressly that an ethical judgment is *not* a simple descriptive judgment concerning present or past fact, but "is a *predictive* judgment concerning the *potentialities* of human nature as well as its actuality." And he explicitly states that to say an act, x, is good refers to it not in isolation, but in connection with a whole system or "pattern of interests"; and that it has "objectivity," in case it will promote the *pattern* of interests "in the long run . . . to a greater extent than any feasible alternative";[5] and that x has objectivity because it refers "to something *beyond my desire or liking at the moment.*"[5] And while he does not go further than say that my emphasis upon "conditions and consequences" is "in the right direction," he does not indicate on what basis alternative possibilities can be compared and investigated with respect to connection with a system of interests save on the ground of "conditions and consequences."

---

[4] P. 9. The word "admits" is not italicized in Mr. Rice's text. My reason for italicizing will be readily gathered from what follows.

[5] *Op. cit.*, p. 11, my italics.

III

What then is the difference between us? Why does Mr. Rice find my view to be seriously defective, since he agrees with the two main points of my theory as to *judgments* that are evaluations, namely, as to the points (1) that the problem of *objectivity* of such judgments amounts to the problem of whether intelligent guidance of the course of life-conduct is possible, and (2) that *objectivity* is possible because value-judgments concern a set, system, or pattern of interests, beyond the immediate occurrence of a given liking or satisfaction? As far as I can make out, the difference is two-fold. My critic holds that the occurrence of a liking or satisfaction affords an added or "plus" verifying *evidence;* and he holds that since what is liked is qualitative, it is subjcetive in the sense of being directly open only to *self*-observation or introspection, or is private and inner. I take up first his view that the immediate quality of a satisfaction is a necessary part of the *evidence* that the satisfaction is a value. This view seems quite incompatible with Mr. Rice's doctrine that the question of value has to do with the connection of a satisfaction with a system of interests, involving the future and a comparison of alternative acts with respect to their integrative function.

Hence the force of his statement that my "social behaviorism leads me to ignore one very important kind of evidence, namely, that concerning the immediate quality of the experience of value itself" seems to rest upon an equivoke. I am so far from "ignoring" it that, according to my view, the entire valuation process is precisely and exclusively about or concerning this quality in its immediate occurrence. And the statement of Mr. Rice himself to the effect that valuation is not a description of what has happened, but is *predictive in reference,* reads like an explicit endorsement of the same doctrine. The equivoke consists in taking evidence *concerning* an immediately experienced quality to be identical with evidence *supplied* by that very immediate qualitative satisfaction (enjoyment, liking) although its *doubtful* status with respect to its connection with a whole pattern of interests is the occasion and the ground for a valuation-*judgment!* The equivoke is clear in the assumption made in the following passage. He says that since "Dewey admits that 'liking' or 'enjoyment' is a constituent of the value experience itself . . . it would seem to be a grave sin of omission for an empiricist to exclude this phase of the act from study when seeking evidence for valuations" (p. 9). The clear implication is that the exclusion of an immediately experienced quality from possession of *evidential and verifying function in judgment* is equivalent to excluding it from all recognition or attention whatever—although in fact this phenomenon is precisely that which judgment is about, or "is concerning" in the attempt to determine its standing *qua* value! And when he says, as a criticism of my view, that "in no other field do we rule out attention to the phenomenon under study itself, to concentrate exclusively upon its conditions and results" (p. 9), it seems to me clear that there is an illicit transfer from the problem of the *evidential* force and function of a given phenomenon over to the fact that a liking has taken place: A transfer that is illicit because it unwittingly substitutes possession of evidential force for the fact of the bare occurrence of that which evokes and demands judgment with respect to its value-status. It is not easy to understand why and how an inquiry, in the case of a given event, into *its* conditions and results is a case of ruling out attention to it. So much for the question of the evidential worth, with respect to determination of value, of the bare occurrence of an event which as an event is undeniably immediately *qualitative*.

IV

I turn now to the other question, the assumption of Mr. Rice that since what is enjoyed is immediately qualitative it is therefore "subjective." For there is no doubt that it is this assumption that leads him to believe that definition in terms of causes and effects, conditions and consequences, is only a partial definition, being confined to factors admittedly "objective" in Mr. Rice's, as well as my own, sense of the word. I point out that in my general doctrine about judgment and verification *situation* is the key word, and that a situation is held to be *directly and immediately qualitative*. And it is held that a situation evokes inquiry, terminating in *judgment*, when it is *problematic* in its immediate quality, because of confusing, conflicting, relatively disordered qualities. Hence any inquiry which is evoked is successful in the degree in which further observation succeeds in discovering facts by means of which inquiry terminates in an ordered, unified situation (as immediately qualitative as the original problematic situation). What is discovered in effecting this kind of transformation from one type of quality to another constitutes its *verifying* status with respect to any theory of hypothesis that is involved in the conduct of observations: the hypothetico-inductive method to which reference was earlier made.

Since the present matter of discussion does not concern the truth of my theory but its nature, I content myself with a single quotation. A transformed qualitative situation is said to be the *end* of inquiry "in the sense in which 'end' means *'end-in-view'* and in the sense in which it means 'close.' " [6]

Now Mr. Rice gives no argument at all in support of his position that the immediate qualitative material of liking (satisfaction, enjoyment) is *subjective*. Apparently he takes it to be self-evident. But Mr. Rice holds that the reason my theory is defective is because I hold that valuation judgments are determined in terms of "conditions and consequences," thus leaving out of account evidence supplied by material which is "subjective." Hence, it is more than pertinent for me to point out that, according to my theory, while the initial problematic situation and the final transformed resolved situation are equally immediately qualitative, no situation is subjective nor involves a subject-object relation. While this fact shows that my theory is at the opposite pole from "ignoring" qualitative immediacy, its pertinence here lies in the fact that if Mr. Rice wishes to engage in relevant criticism of my theory, he should give arguments in support of his view that qualities, at least in the case of phenomena of liking and satisfaction, are open to direct inspection or observation only by an act of introspection or "self-observation" of material which is inherently "inner and private." And he should give reasons for holding that the events which provide the primary datum are (1) not of the nature of *situations*, and/or (2) that there is satisfactory evidence for holding that situations with respect to their qualitative immediacy, are "subjective" instead of being prior to, neutral to, and inclusive of, any distinction and relation that can be legitimately instituted between subject and object. For *denial* of the primacy and ultimacy of this relation (supposed to be the inherent epistemological-metaphysical basis and background from which philosophical theory must proceed) is the basic feature of my general theory of knowledge, of judgment and verification, my theory of value-judgments being but a special case of this general theory.

And in calling my theory on this matter a special case of my *general* theory I intend to call attention to the fact that I have denied that as judgments, and in respect to method of inquiry, test, and verification, value-judgments have any peculiar or unique features. They differ from other judgments, of course, in the specific material they have to do with. But in this respect inquiries and judgments about potatoes, cats, and molecules differ from one another. The genuinely important difference resides in the fact of the much greater *importance with respect to the conduct of life-behavior* possessed by the special subject-matter of so-called value-

6 *Logic: The Theory of Inquiry*, p. 158.

judgments. For in comparison with the deep and broad *human* bearing of their subject-matter, the subject-matter of other judgments is relatively narrow and technical.

V

I am grateful to Mr. Rice not only for his agreement, as far as it goes, with some of the main tenets of my theory, but for the opportunity his article gives me for making clear my actual position on the secondary and derived nature of the "subject-object" distinction and relation, and the primary character of situations that are completely neutral to this distinction and relation, for the latter, in my view, is intermediate, transitive, and instrumental in the transformation of one type of immediately qualitative situation into a situation of another type in respect to ordering and arrangement of qualities, but of the same type with respect to its immediate qualitative nature, which is neither subjective, nor objective, nor a relation of the two.

I am grateful because I have come increasingly to the conclusion that failure to grasp my view on this matter and its fundamental position in my discussion of special topics, is the chief factor in producing misapprehension of my view of many special topics I have discussed. A recent article in this JOURNAL by Mr. Brotherston is in point. His article on "The Genius of Pragmatic Empiricism"[7] sets out by saying that this theory holds that "the subject-object relation . . . [obtains] in a field of common sense and scientific procedure which at the very beginning of enquiry is given as an on-going concern" (p. 14). Representatives of the theory have made, according to him, an advance in showing that there is no explicit awareness of this relation until reflective analysis set in. But they have made the mistake of not expressly pointing out that it is there from the beginning, with primacy attached to the "subject" factor. Now whether or not we *should* have taken this view, it is in fact so different from that we have taken that it may be called "the *evil* genius" of pragmatic empiricism.[8]

[7] Vol. XL (1943), pp. 14–21 and pp. 29–39.

[8] Another article by A. F. Bentley on "Truth, Reality, and Behavioral Fact" states the actual position correctly, and in particular effects a correction of Mr. Brotherston's misconception of James's "neutral entities" (this JOURNAL, Vol. XL, 1943, pp. 169–187. I may refer to an earlier article of mine, "How is Mind to be Known," this JOURNAL, Vol. XXXIX (1942), pp. 29–35. In an earlier article of mine, "The Objectivism-subjectivism of Modern Philosophy" (this JOURNAL, Vol. XXXVIII, 1941, pp. 533–542), I fear I did not make it sufficiently clear that in speaking of organic and environmental factors as conditions of a situation, what is meant is that they are

I now recur to the matter of the connection of immediate quality with value-judgments. The view that the bare occurrence of *any* kind of satisfaction is evidence of value seems to me to involve a relapse into that prescientific method which Peirce called the method of *congeniality*. Nor is it at all clear to me how a quality said to be private and inner can be added on to qualities which are public to form an evidential whole. Such an addition or joining seems to be something like a contradiction *in adjecto*. But these considerations are not at all incompatible with the fact that marked satisfaction, amounting at times to positive excitement, may qualify situations in which terminate judgments of value are *verified by evidential facts*. But the quality of a satisfaction that arises because of attainment of adequate verification is *toto coelo* different from the quality of a satisfaction that happens to occur independent of evidence as to its status *qua* value. One of the main benefits of a genuine education in use of scientific method is that it produces immediate sensitiveness to the difference between these two kinds of satisfaction.

John Dewey

Columbia University

The Journal of Philosophy

TYPES OF VALUE JUDGMENTS

I AM grateful to Professor Dewey for giving, in his "Valuation Judgments and Immediate Quality,"[1] such detailed attention to an article of mine,[2] and for the clarification which his paper affords of certain very important points in his theory of valuation. It is also gratifying to have Mr. Dewey's confirmation of my opinion that we are in agreement on certain essential points of an empirical approach to values—for which, indeed, my own views are so largely indebted to his. In what follows, I shall confine myself to those points on which there has been misunderstanding or disagreement.

The central issue is whether data or aspects of events that are "subjective," in the sense that they are directly accessible only to self-observation, can serve as evidence for value judgments. And more specifically, whether introspection of that phase of the value situation which is called "enjoyment" or "satisfaction" can supply evidence relevant to decisions about values. Mr. Dewey holds that it can not; my paper criticized him for this view, and advanced the thesis that it can. My position is that an adequate empiricism with regard to values must take account of such evidence; Mr. Dewey holds that such a view is incompatible with empiricism.

Bearing upon this main issue are four related points of dispute, with which I shall deal in turn:

(1) *Two meanings of the antithesis "subjective-objective."* Mr. Dewey points out that in one context I use the term "'subjective" in a sense which is not correlative with the principal use of the term "objective," so that what is subjective by one criterion can be objective by another. Such was my explicit intention. My problem is to find out why Mr. Dewey finds this procedure "disappointing" or *prima facie* paradoxical. The assumption of my paper was that of the many senses in which the antithesis "subjective-objective" is used there are two distinct senses, both of which are pertinent to a study of valuation. These two senses

---

[1] This Journal, Vol. XL (1943), pp. 309–317.

[2] "'Objectivity' in Value Judgments," this Journal, Vol. XL (1943), pp. 5–14.

I shall call, in this discussion, (a) the logical sense, (b) the psychological sense.

(a) The logical sense. Mr. Dewey is substantially correct in stating that the primary sense of "objectivity" in my paper identifies it with "verifiability by empirical evidence." Actually and strictly, I identified objectivity with truth rather than with verifiability. I take verifiability to be a criterion (though not the sole criterion) of meaning rather than of truth. Truth is more closely related to verification than to verifiability. I identified *"known* to be true" with "verified," and thus equated for practical purposes an objective judgment with a verified judgment. But this qualification is not important for the present issue, since Mr. Dewey's definition is in the same universe of discourse as mine.

The correlative sense of the term "subjective" is "false," or (on the practical level) "unverified." With qualifications similar to those stated above, I should accept Mr. Dewey's definition of the logically subjective: "Propositions (judgments, beliefs, or whatever) are *subjective* when they are produced by causal conditions which fail to possess genuine evidential capacity and verifying power, but which nevertheless are taken at the time to possess them. . . ." His examples are beliefs of those suffering from illusions, hallucinations, and insanity.

(b) The psychological sense. My statement to which Mr. Dewey takes exception was: "In so far as introspection plays a part in the knowledge of qualitative satisfaction, the evidence is *in the psychological sense* 'subjective,' i.e., it is directly accessible to one observer alone." The italics were not in the original, but my clear intent was to state that "objective" (sense a) and "subjective" (sense b) were compatible predicates.[3]

I do not see anything logically or linguistically scandalous in this procedure. The antithesis "strong-weak" also has at least two senses, but it is not contradictory to assert that the same man is both physically strong and mentally weak. If there has been a confusion, then, it would seem plausible that Mr. Dewey is confused when he holds that anything which is psychologically subjective is also logically subjective.

If "subjective" (sense b) means that which can directly be observed only through introspection, and thus is directly accessible to one observer alone, then "objective" in a correlative sense means

[3] Strictly speaking, the terms in sense a apply to propositions, and in sense b primarily to data or evidence. Thus it would be accurate to state that data that are subjective in sense b may be used to confer objectivity (sense a) on propositions.

that which is perceived by non-introspective or "external" observation, and is equally accessible to more than one observer.

Mr. Dewey asserts, without citing evidence from my paper, that I conceive the subjective (sense b) to refer to a "special order of Being," which constitutes "a certain sort of epistemological-metaphysical reality." From similar criticisms of introspection elsewhere in Mr. Dewey's writings, I presume that he is imputing to me something like a Cartesian dualism of mental and material substance. My distinction, however, was quite neutral with regard to metaphysical assumptions, and if any epistemological tenets are involved they are not presuppositions of this view but consequences of it together with other premises.

The distinction was intended to be exclusively one of psychological procedure. It refers to the fact that each individual stands in a unique relation to certain aspects of his own experience, a relation which is not shared by other observers with regard to those aspects of that person's experience. "Introspection" was here used in the sense employed by the late Professor Mead when he said that psychology "does make use of introspection, in the sense that it looks within the experience of the individual for phenomena not dealt with in any other sciences—phenomena to which only the individual has experiential access." [4] It is such phenomena, or rather aspects of phenomena, which I call subjective in the psychological sense. I say aspects of phenomena because I agree with Mead and with Mr. Dewey himself that the ultimate unit of conduct is most usefully conceived as the total act, or process, or event, and I hold that this is adequately treated only in terms of a total situation involving factors that are both subjective and objective in sense b.

Examples of aspects of events which are subjective in this sense are muscular sensations, thoughts which are not uttered or enacted, and feelings or "affective" tones. Both the occurrence and the quality of these aspects of phenomena can be directly observed only by the individual in whose organism they are occurring, though others may sometimes infer their occurrence from external symptoms, and consequently may infer their quality from associated "subjective" events which occur under similar conditions within their own experience. The sensory nerves directly concerned in perceiving subjective phenomena are the proprioceptors and interoceptors.[5]

The individual has no such unique vantage-point in observing

[4] *Mind, Self and Society*, pp. 4–5.
[5] Cf. R. B. Perry, *General Theory of Value*, pp. 270–271.

the "objective" aspects of events and acts (whether others' or his own), such as shapes, colors, and overt movements.[6] These are perceived by use of the exteroceptors, such as the optic and auditory nerves. Persons B, C, and D are on an equality with regard to observation of the color of person A's complexion, his dancing, and his spoken words, so far as bare difference of personal identity goes. A is even at a slight disadvantage in observing these aspects of his own behavior, although he can overcome this disadvantage to some extent by such means as the use of mirrors. A does, however, have a kind of access to the subjective aspects of these phenomena which is denied to B, C, and D, although the latter may be more nearly correct than A in their interpretation of the total act or situation. This is because the total situation includes both subjective and objective aspects, and both are relevant to the judgment on it as a totality. Furthermore, A, B, C, and D may erroneously interpret their psychologically objective data: hence objectivity in sense b and in sense a need not coincide.

Mr. Dewey states that my paper "offers no direct evidence for the existence of material that is private and inner and hence (by its very nature) accessible directly only to observation by a self which is single, exclusive, and non-public and non-social." I did not state nor imply that the self is "non-public and non-social." I do hold that it has its sequestered and idiosyncratic aspects. From the nature of the case, I can not offer to anyone else "direct" evidence for the occurrence of such aspects. For this, I must ask Mr. Dewey to examine his own joys, pains, and secret thoughts. If he should tell me that he does not have any such, nothing that I might say could refute him. However, as I understand his position from his other writings, he does not deny that experience has such aspects, but merely that they can possess evidential weight.

[6] The data or sensations involved in the perception of such phenomena are not necessarily objective in a common epistemological sense in which "primary" qualities are declared to be objective in contrast with subjective or "secondary" qualities, i.e., as asserting that primary qualities resemble certain corresponding properties of their objects, whereas secondary qualities are not thus iconic. This is a third distinct meaning of the antithesis, according to which shapes, e.g., are held to be objective and colors subjective. Furthermore, according to all epistemological schools except the naïve or direct realists, the *sensa* or *data* in the case of "objective" phenomena (sense b) are accessible only to the person to whose stream of consciousness they belong, and hence are "subjective" in still a fourth sense, which is partly psychological, partly epistemological. I have dealt with the relation between the second sense of the antithesis (sense b) and this fourth sense in another paper, " 'Public' and 'Private' Factors in Valuation," which has been accepted for publication by *Ethics*. But here I am trying to avoid epistemological issues.

(2) *How immediate qualities are perceived.* From the above discussion it should be clear that I do not hold, as Mr. Dewey took me to be saying, that all qualities are perceived by introspection. "Subjective" qualities (sense b), which include affective tones, are apprehended directly by introspection, and "objective" qualities (sense b) are perceived by external or behavioristic observation. The two kinds of qualities are closely associated, and a relation of dependence may subsist between them, so that we may with some probability infer the existence of one from the other in particular cases. In the experience of a painting, for example, the affective tone is derived from, and felt as fused with, the design and color. But the two kinds of qualities are distinguishable even though, in most cases, they are not separable. And the two methods of observation collaborate. Since, as Mr. Dewey holds, values are affective-motor phenomena, affective qualities are of special importance to a theory of value. It is for this reason that in my previous paper I emphasized the rôle of introspection in perception of qualities.[7] In Mr. Dewey's writings on value we read much about the motor element in value experience, but little about the affective element.

(3) *"Public" and "private" as aspects of the "problematic situation."* The above definitions of "public" and "private" (for the sake of brevity I shall henceforth use these terms for "objective" and "subjective" respectively, in sense b), are, so far as I can see, compatible with analysis of valuation in terms of the *positive* features of Mr. Dewey's "problematic situation." (As I shall suggest below, the conception of the "problematic situation" becomes Procrustean when the attempt is made to fit all valuational and cognitive situations into it, to treat them all in terms of a "motor block.") Let us consider the situation "toothache" or "something-wrong-with-tooth." The "difficulty" which initiates the problem may be either publicly or privately detected. Usually in this case it is detected privately: I observe introspectively a "pain," and this suggests to me the hypothesis "I ought to visit a dentist," or—though with less initial probability—"I ought to have a cavity filled." The ache is not, as Mr. Dewey seems to hold, merely a "dubious" element in the situation, but, together with my previous knowledge of similar situations, it constitutes *prima facie* evidence for these value judgments. However, I seek further evidence to confirm them. This further evidence may consist of non-introspective observation to see if a brown speck can be found on my tooth. Such observation can be carried out by a

---

7 See also my "Quality and Value," this JOURNAL, Vol. XL (1943), pp. 337–348.

number of other persons, including my dentist, or by myself with a mirror. If there is a conflict between the public and the private evidence, usually I trust the dentist's public evidence, and permit him to act accordingly. (I should assign superior evidential weight to the private evidence only if the dentist told me that there was nothing wrong with me, or that the pain was good in itself.) The difficulty is fully "resolved" only if the external manifestations of dental trouble disappear, and also if after an appropriate time the pain vanishes. I use the introspectively observed disappearance of the pain as an important part of the evidence that the situation has been resolved, and hence that the value judgment was correct. If the pain is still with me, I use it as initial evidence for a new hypothesis, namely, that the trouble was neuralgia and not decay. The two types of evidence, therefore, may reinforce or correct each other. Just why Mr. Dewey holds that the perception of the ache has no evidential weight is not clear to me.

Mr. Dewey's account of the problematic situation *abstracts from* the aspects of the situation which I have been considering; it ignores the alternative psychological perspectives from which observations can be made. So I do not know how to interpret his statement that the "immediate qualitative nature" of the situation is neither "subjective, nor objective, nor a relation of the two," if the terms in question are used in sense *b*. Nor do I see that a reference to the immediate quality of the situation is relevant if the terms are used in sense *a*. There is, I suppose, a sense in which the situation as a *gestalt* is perceived as having a unitary quality of its own. But our knowledge of the *total* quality, so far as we can achieve it, is not "immediate," but the result of construction and inference. We can, however, get perspectives upon this total quality by either external observation or introspection, or by both together; the idea of its quality as a whole is put together from the various partial perspectives and the immediate qualities which they supply.

In reading Mr. Dewey's account of mind, I have long been puzzled by what seems to me to be his *standpointless* psychology. I can see why he rejects both introspectionism and Watsonian behaviorism as adequate approaches by themselves, and also why he is dissatisfied with a parallelism which tries to put private and public data together mechanically. His emphasis on the total act is a useful one, and for the purpose of stating psychological laws it is often desirable to ignore the partial perspectives used in particular observations, and to speak in terms of "functions" and other behavioral concepts which cut across the distinction between introspection and external observation. But why this should entail that a distinction between these two chief types of perspective is illegitimate for a descriptive analysis of actual psychological procedures is not clear.

(4) *Evidence "about" enjoyment and evidence "supplied by"* enjoyment. Mr. Dewey holds (*a*) that valuational propositions "concern" enjoyment, but denies (*b*) that such propositions may draw upon evidence "supplied by" observation of enjoyment. He interprets a statement of mine in such a way that he understands me to "identify" these two propositions, and he believes that my view rests upon this supposed "equivoke." I did not intend to assert a logical identity or equivalence between propositions (*a*) and (*b*), although I do hold that they are closely related materially.

When I predict that a certain experience will have value, I do not use introspection of *that* experience to obtain evidence. (Such a view would truly involve the "equivoke" in question.) *That* experience, by hypothesis, has not yet occurred, so I can not introspect it. I may, however, found my prediction in part on introspection of my present *anticipation* of the future experience, and on my *remembrance* of the affective qualities of similar experiences in the past. This view is based, not upon any deductive argument, but upon my empirical analysis of what I—and other persons— actually *do* when making decisions in such matters. If I predict that the experience of a Beethoven concerto, or a baseball game between the Dodgers and the Reds, will bring me "satisfaction" or "enjoyment" and hence value, it is in part because I remember that similar occasions in the past have been accompanied by enjoyment, and because I discover introspectively that my imaginative rehearsal of the probable experience ahead of me is now accompanied by relish. Such predictions have shown themselves to be sufficiently reliable that I continue to use this type of evidence, with discrimination and in conjunction with other kinds. Of course memory and anticipation are fallible with respect to affective qualities, and hence the private evidence is not conclusive. But neither, according to empiricism, is any other kind of evidence conclusive.

Mr. Dewey's second argument against the evidential function of introspectively obtained evidence is that this is incompatible with my view that ethical judgments are predictive in character,[8]

---

[8] I do not hold that *all* judgments of value are predictive in the sense that they refer to or are "about" a future event; in the earlier paper I took this position only with regard to a certain type of ethical judgment. Nor do I

that they take into account "the connection of a satisfaction with a system of interests, involving the future and a comparison of alternative acts with respect to their integrative function." That there should be such an incompatibility I do not see, and Mr. Dewey offers no reasons for this view. My decision in such a case as the concert or the baseball game takes account of public factors—the state of my bank account, the demands of other interests beside my musical or sporting interests upon my time, and the fitness of a soloist or a star pitcher—as well as private factors; both may be used for the purposes of prediction. If such public evidence excludes private evidence of the kind that has been mentioned in the preceding paragraph, the burden of proof that this is so rests upon Mr. Dewey. He should show this by analysis of concrete instances of such experiences and not by deduction from general assumptions concerning empirical method. For it is precisely the adequacy of these assumptions that is in question.

If we had at the present time an adequate doctrine of the logical syntax of empirical knowledge, I believe that the above analysis of valuation could be fitted into it, with resulting clarification of the whole field. Much of the controversy over theory of value among empiricists in recent years has sprung from the failure to recognize that there are many different types of value situations, and consequently that there is a great variety of kinds of "value judgments," with extremely various logical structures. The discussion of value theory by Mr. Dewey, R. B. Perry, and the late D. W. Prall, carried on intensively in this JOURNAL between 1914 and 1925, and prolonged by more or less desultory firing between Dewey and Perry since then, will illustrate the point. Thus Mr. Dewey in the course of that discussion wrote: ". . . The articles of mine which Mr. Prall criticized were not concerned with the nature of value, either the quality or the things having the quality, but with the nature of valuation as a judgment. . . . It happens that Mr. Prall is interested in his writings in value, while my interest was logical—that is, was in a certain type of judgment." [9] Perhaps it is because he has recognized the oddity of trying to construct a theory of "valuation" without at the same time offering a theory of "value" that Mr. Dewey on several later occasions has made at least casual attempts to define the latter concept. Thus, in his most recent article, he states that he holds that "qualitative 'enjoyment,' 'satisfaction,' " is "the *entire* material" that a valuation judgment is about. But he goes on to say that enjoy-

believe that such judgments depend exclusively upon evidence to be obtained in the future.

[9] This JOURNAL, Vol. XX (1923), p. 619.

ment is equated with value here only in a "figurative" sense; that enjoyment is properly called a value only "with reference to being potentially the material for an evaluative judgment, or in connection with events still to occur." Now here, as in his earlier discussion of the subject, Mr. Dewey has been concerned only with those types of judgment which he calls judgments of practice, and which seek to determine a particular future course of action in the presence of a "difficulty" or motor block. Here the judgment or reflection does create or modify the value involved. On the other hand, Prall, Perry, and most other empirical writers on value start from a simpler type of judgment asserting "valuable" as a predicate, and take this as the archetypal value judgment.

Now I should like to suggest that it is linguistically naïve to continue to dispute about *the* meaning of value, or the characteristics of *the* value judgment. If we should attempt to construct a logical syntax of valuation, we should have to take into account a number of different types of judgments that have been called value judgments. Among these is what might be called an elementary judgment of intrinsic value. The scheme for such a judgment is "x is intrinsically valuable to person A at time t (or in situation m)," and this is equivalent to "A enjoys x at time t (etc.)." This is one common meaning of "valuable"; propositions of this type are true or false and therefore significant, and their verification rests on observation. The label "*elementary judgments of intrinsic value*" is not intended to suggest that such judgments are logically atomic, although they are the simplest propositions which make explicit the three terms—an object, an organism, and a situation—to which a value is relative. The evidence upon which such judgments rest is reported by still simpler propositions analogous to Carnap's "protocol sentences" or, better, Russell's "basic propositions."[10] Some of these simpler propositions are usually based upon introspection, others on external observation. A himself takes into account observations formulable as "Enjoyment now," or "This is enjoyed." Other persons use such indirect evidence as "A looks happy" or "A says he likes this." Both A and the others, furthermore, use public evidence of the type involved in time determination or in description of the other objective factors of the situation.

Another fundamental type of value judgment would be "x has instrumental value in situation m," and this when expanded is equivalent to "x in situation m has such properties that it is capable of promoting intrinsic value y for A in situation n." (Or,

[10] *An Inquiry into Meaning and Truth*, chapters X, XI.

in many cases, "x will promote the removal or avoidance of disvalue z. . . .") Likewise, there are elementary judgments of comparative value, either intrinsic or instrumental. Thus "x has more simple intrinsic value than y for A . . ." would mean "x gives A more enjoyment than does y. . . ." (The definition of "more enjoyment" here is not easy.)

Ethical and esthetic judgments each include a number of subspecies, and are always more complex than the judgments hitherto discussed. In one of the commonest types of esthetic judgment, which we may call the critical judgment, "x has esthetic value" means "x would give perceptual enjoyment to anyone sharing cultural tradition k who was trained to discriminate properties a, b, and c of x." In a common type of ethical judgment, "A ought to do act x" means "x will produce more integration of interests, together with resulting satisfaction, for A and the other persons affected than will any feasible alternative." An adequate treatment of the logical structure of such ethical propositions would show that they in turn rest upon elementary propositions both of simple intrinsic and of simple instrumental value, and perhaps also on esthetic judgments of several types. All these types of judgment would go back for their evidential support to protocol sentences or basic propositions recording observations, introspective or external, and hence would be empirical.

In conclusion, I should like to say a word about Mr. Dewey's identification of "neo-empiricist" or "scientific" method with the instrumentalist position. Empiricism, as I understand the term, is the view that all existential propositions derive their probability from observation. It holds that laws and other complex propositions in any field are obtained by observation, hypothesis, deductive prediction, and verification. Exponents of scientific method have at various times made two further assumptions derived from the study of the methods of the physical sciences: (a) that science must be metric, that it can deal only with quantitative aspects of the subject-matter; (b) that only "public" evidence is admissible. Mr. Dewey rejects the first of these assumptions as essential to empirical or scientific method in the broad sense. What I am suggesting is that instrumentalism and neo-positivism should reexamine the second of these assumptions also. If it should prove too restricting to enable us to deal properly with values, then empiricism as a general doctrine of method can be preserved only by rejecting the assumption. But if empiricism continues to be defended in such a way as to exclude the affective evidence that most men take into account in making value judgments, then the result will be to aggravate that "new failure of nerve" of which

Mr. Dewey has written elsewhere, and to turn many of those who are especially concerned with values away from the promising but incomplete contemporary versions of empiricism, to find refuge in some form of intuitionism or apriorism or authoritarianism.

PHILIP BLAIR RICE

KENYON COLLEGE

FURTHER AS TO VALUATION AS JUDGMENT [1]

I AM grateful to Mr. Rice for giving me further opportunity to clear up points in my view which I have failed to make sufficiently clear in the past. I shall in my present attempt confine myself to two leading theses put forth by Mr. Rice. One of them is that there are certain events which are intrinsically of such a nature that they can be observed only "introspectively," or by the single person or self in whom they occur, such events being so "sequestered and idiosyncratic" as to be private and, psychologically, "subjective." The second proposition is that in spite of their subjective intrinsic nature, they are capable of being used as evidence in the case of judgments of value along with facts of a public and "objective" nature, thus being logically "objective" although subjective in existence.[2]

I

The first of these two propositions concerns a question of fact. The fact involved is of such a fundamental nature that it has no more bearing upon or connection with the logical question of the evidence that validity supports judgments of valuation than it has with a multitude of other philosophic questions. I shall discuss it, then, *as* a question of fact, noting, however, that in Mr. Rice's

[1] The present paper is called out by the article of Professor Rice on *Types of Value Judgment*, this JOURNAL, Vol. XL (1943), pp. 533–543. I add here the remark that while I occasionally use the words "valuation judgments," I regard the phrase as pleonastic, *valuation* being judgment. (*Valuing*, as I pointed out long ago, is an ambiguous word standing both for judgment or evaluation and for direct liking, cherishing, relishing, holding dear, etc.) Since Mr. Rice in his present paper attributes to me an identification of what I called *neo*-empiricism—to distinguish it from traditional sensationalist empiricism—and scientific method with "instrumentalism," I also add the remark that the only identification I made was—and is—with the "hypothetico-inductive method."

[2] There is a third point in Mr. Rice's paper which, apparently, gives its caption to his article. It is sufficiently independent of the points just mentioned to merit consideration on its own account and, accordingly, is not touched upon in this reply.

view the fact, as he interprets it, plays an important part in judgments about "values." Mr. Rice holds that such events as "shapes, colors, overt movements" have qualities which are open to observation on equal terms by a number of observers, and hence are public and "objective" in their mode of existence. In contrast with such events, stand events such as "muscular sensations," thoughts not uttered or enacted, feelings having affective tone, etc. The latter can be observed only by a single person, or "introspectively," and hence are private, subjective. It is expressly held that "both the occurrence and the quality of these events can be directly observed only by the individual in whose organism they are occurring." Physiologically, they are said to be conditioned by proprioceptors and interoceptors, while events of a public and "objective" nature are conditioned by exteroceptors.

There is one difficulty in discussing this question of fact. The kind of event whose character is in dispute can not, by definition, be had by any two observers in common, and hence not by Mr. Rice and myself. Mr. Rice accordingly refers me, quite logically, to "my own" (exclusively my own) "joys, pains, and secret thoughts" for evidence of the existence of privately observed events. Now the bald statement that while I recognize the existence of such events as Mr. Rice gives examples of, I do *not* find them to be "private" or inner as observed and known, does not carry discussion far; it seems rather to leave it at a dead end.

The matter at issue may, however, be approached indirectly. Mr. Rice objects to my characterizing his position as "epistemological-metaphysical." I gave no reasons for that characterization. For I did not intend it to apply in any invidious way to Mr. Rice's view. On the contrary, I intended it to apply to a traditional and still generally accepted doctrine which originated and developed in modern epistemological discussions, and which is "metaphysical" in the sense that it has to do with the inherent nature of two kinds or orders of existence. Since Mr. Rice accepts and promulgates the view, if I understand him aright, that there are two such orders, one psychological and "individual," the other not, I used the characterization in question.[3]

---

[3] This matter is somewhat complicated in Mr. Rice's last paper by the fact that he freely refers to "subjective" and "objective" as *aspects;* aspects it would seem of "experience," which is taken to have two sides or faces, x, one private and one public. I should still regard this view as "metaphysical" in the sense of involving generalizations of the highest degree of generality about the nature of what exists. In any case, since I can not suppose that Mr. Rice is hedging in using the word "aspects," the word seems to need explanation. Mr. Rice's discussion of "muscular sensations,

In any case, I wish to repeat my expression of gratitude to Mr. Rice for giving me an opportunity to state my position on this matter as explicitly as possible, since, as I remarked in my earlier article, failure to grasp my actual view seems to account for misapprehension of many points in my general philosophical theory. In this restatement of my view, I begin by stating the conclusion I have arrived at. It is as follows: The undeniable *centering* of the events which are the more immediate condition of the occurrence of events in the way of observation and of knowledge generally, within a particular organism, say that of John Smith, has been taken as proof that the resulting *observation* is itself "individual." I believe further that this conversion of a condition of the occurrence of an event into an inherent and intrinsic property of the event itself (that of observation) is not due to anything in the facts, but is derived from the holdover of an earlier doctrine, of pre-scientific and largely theological origin, of an individual soul as the knower—even though the "soul" part has been thinned down into "mind," "consciousness," or even that supposedly scientific *Ersatz*, the brain of a single organism.

I do not deny, in other words, that the immediate or last conditions of the *occurrence* of a pain, say of a toothache, and the immediate and last conditions of the occurrence of an event in the way of knowing a given event *as* a toothache, are *centered* in particular organic bodies. But I do deny that causal conditions of the *occurrence* of an event are *ipso facto* qualities or traits of the event. I hold that they are extrinsic to the event itself although strictly relevant to its occurrence. And I also hold that while the temporally and spatially terminal conditions of an observation are *centered* in a particular organism, they are not *located* under the skin of the organism. For events outside the skin as well as under it are directly involved in the production of either a pain or an observation of it *as* pain.

I begin with the last point. In making a distinction between what I have called the *centering* of an event and its *location,* I have nothing recondite in mind. Every event that takes place has a certain extensive durational and spatial spread, as long and as wide as all the interacting conditions involved. Environmental conditions are surely as much a part of the occurrence of a toothache as are organic conditions; to *know* the event *as* the toothache it actually is depends on knowledge of the former. The sole difference that exists between environmental conditions and organic conditions is that the former occupy a relatively initial place and

secret thoughts, feelings of affective tone," seems to treat them as events on their own account.

the latter a relatively terminal position in the series of occurrences forming a single total event. The operative presence of both environing and organic conditions, on equal terms, is found in events Mr. Rice terms "private" as it is in those he calls "public." The notion that language in the cases when it is not heard by others (is not "uttered or enacted") is on that account private in origin, occurrence, and quality is so extreme that it is hard for me to believe that it is held by any except extreme solipsists. Moreover, if the fact that certain occurrences center in a particular organism justifies the conclusion that the event thus conditioned is private and "subjective," the doctrine that colors and overt movements *as perceived* are also private seems logically to follow. Mr. Rice has corrected my impression that he holds qualities *as such* to be "subjective." But I think the logic of the matter as far as concerns the grounds for holding that *all* qualities are subjective is with those who make no difference between perceived colors and perceived pains.

As far as the logic of the matter is concerned, why not hold that *all events* have an exclusive, sequestered, private, self-centered aspect? A fire, for example, does not occur at large. It takes place in a particular house and may be confined to a single house: that is, according to the logic employed in behalf of the subjectivistic doctrine, it is "individual." All, except confirmed pan-psychists, who hold that this fact does not render the fire subjective while a similar fact causes the perception of a toothache to be private, seem to have a responsibility for indicating the difference in the two cases—pan-psychists not having that responsibility because they use the same logic all the way through.

Finally and most conclusively, the qualified and restricted relative sense in which a pain-event, say, may properly be said to be *centered*, with respect to its occurrence, in a particular organism has nothing to do with *observational knowledge* of it *as* pain and *as* the pain of a toothache. The fact that under ordinary conditions some one else can see "my own" teeth much more readily than I can, will not, I suppose, be taken to prove that after all what is seen by him belongs to him in a "private" way. Nor will the fact that I can not, under ordinary conditions, see the back of my own head be taken to militate against the fact that, after all, it is the back of "my own" head that is involved. Nor will the fact that from where I now sit I can observe certain things not observable by others from the positions they now occupy be taken as evidence that the things in question are private and subjective.

The examples I have chosen will, presumably, call out the retort that the conditions of perception and non-perception in the cases cited are wholly extrinsic, not affecting the nature or quality of the things perceived. Exactly so. My position is that the causes why a toothache is "felt" directly by one and not by another human being are of a similar extrinsic kind, not at all affecting the observed nature of the event as pain and as pain of a toothache. We are brought back to the matter of the distinction between conditions for the occurrence of a given event and the observed qualities of that event.

We have to *learn* to see, hear, and to feel when "feeling" is taken to mean an identification and demarcation of an event as having the qualities that define it as a kind of event—as happens in the case of identifying and distinguishing an event as pain and as toothache. It is to be hoped, though not too confidently asserted, that, in another generation or so, facts ascertained in biology, anthropology, and other sciences will displace the influence now exerted upon theories of observation and knowledge by doctrines that were framed before the sciences attained anything approaching their present estate. As things now stand, much that still passes as sound psychological knowledge is the result of the seeping in of doctrines it was "natural" enough to hold in earlier conditions, but which are now scientifically nullified.

In recurring to the confusion of events which, in a relative and restricted sense, are conditions of the occurrence of an event with the properties of that event as observed, I mentioned that under ordinary circumstances we do not perceive our own teeth or the backs of our own heads. Nevertheless it is easily "done with mirrors." In principle, though not in practical ease, the same thing holds in the case of a toothache. In case a certain grafting of the proprioceptor nerve-tissues of two organisms could be successfully effected (and events as strange as this have actually taken place) there would exist the conditions for observation on equal terms by different observers—the criterion for that which is said to be "public."

And in connection with the other point, that perception and observation are affairs of identifying and distinguishing an event as *such-and-such*, Mr. Rice evinces a sound sense of fact in his admission that a perception based upon knowledge of the public kind—as in the case of observation by a dentist—is more likely to be valid than the observation of one with less technical knowledge, even though the conditions of occurrence of what is observed happen to center in the organism of the latter. In fact this admission on the part of Mr. Rice comes so close to taking the view I have been presenting that the matter might be left there.

I add, however, that I believe detailed examination of the case represented by "muscular sensations" would prove especially instructive. At what time and under what circumstances was it that the existence of qualities, which, on the physiological side, are mediated by changes of the nervous tissues in muscular structures, was first detected? I believe that the facts of the case would show that instead of their presence being an affair of direct and easy observation on the part of the one in whose organism the immediately conditioning events take place, it was an affair, at the outset, of a conclusion reached by knowledge of other facts —a hypothetical conclusion which was then tested by setting up special conditions (in principle like the use of a mirror in perceiving the back of one's own head) that enabled direct observation to be made.

I add also that examination of the case of language, whether uttered or "secret," would supply, in my judgment, evidence that is all but crucial. That language is something *learned*, and learned under social or public conditions, hardly needs argument. If we eliminate the influence exerted by traditional doctrines owing their present currency to the force of tradition rather than to scientifically ascertained facts, we shall, I believe, have no difficulty in accepting the view that instead of their first being "thoughts" which are private and which become public by being clothed externally in language, it is by language, by communication, that events otherwise dumb become possessed of "meanings" which, when they are studied in a cut-off way, are called "thoughts." I can imagine that this reference to language deciding the meanings *"pain, toothache"* will seem irrelevant to Mr. Rice. The issue is too large to argue at length here. But the question at issue is accessibility to *observation*. To defend the position of irrelevancy it would be necessary to show that observation of an event as *such-and-such* is possible without use of characteristics determined publicly in language, and/or that conditions without which an event can not occur are not relevant to its characterization.[4]

---

4 Dr. Rice was kind enough to send me a copy of his rejoinder, published in the same issue, to this article. Accordingly I append a few brief comments bearing upon the foregoing section. (1) I began the present article by saying that the first thesis of Mr. Rice which I should criticize is the view of the *"intrinsic,"* and *"unique,"* inaccessibility of certain events to public (i.e., dual or plural) observation. For I understood Mr. Rice to hold to the *intrinsic* character of the inaccessibility of certain events to dual observation. And I do not find in his rejoinder any disavowal of this position. It is retracted, however, if I understand him, in one case, a case usually cited as typical, that of the pain of a toothache. But, if I understand him, there is still not the retraction of the view of *intrinsic* inaccessibility which seems to

II

The previous section concerns a matter of fact. While the conclusion reached affects the theory of valuation, it affects it only in the way in which it bears upon discussion of any philosophic topic. Its discussion takes up as much space as is given it in the present paper because the question raised and the criticisms made in previous articles seem to make it necessary. The conclusion I have reached appears at first sight to have left, as far as I am concerned, the question having to do with evidence for valuation in a total *impasse*. For if there are no "subjective" events of the kind indicated, then of course subjective events are not evidential with respect either to valuation or anything else.

The actual question, with respect to valuations, however, is not disposed of in this rather cavalier manner. I do not deny the existence of the kind of *subject-matter* which is called private and inner by Mr. Rice. On the contrary, we agree that this kind of material (whether subjective or objective) is that which valuations are about or concern. The question as to the evidential status for judgment of this material is accordingly still before us. The logical issue as distinct from that of fact needs discussion. Moreover, in his last article Mr. Rice has given illustrations that help define the issue.

follow. (2) My point was that cases like this one proved that the number of observers to whom a given event is observable is an *extrinsic* matter, just as with the fact that *under present conditions* I am the only observer to whom events in the room where I am now writing are "accessible." (3) I was so far from attributing to Mr. Rice the view that *he* bases *his* distinction between public and private events upon the causal conditions of their occurrence," that I pointed out that his failure to do so was a case of his regarding inaccessibility under specifiable conditions of time and place as *intrinsic* and absolute—if I understand the words "intrinsic" and "unique" correctly. (4) Hence, instead of taking the position that "external relations can not be used as the 'defining properties' of events" (and of classes of events), my argument is that spatial-temporal *differences* in such "external relations" make the entire difference between the events and classes of events set *intrinsically* apart by Mr. Rice. So that the distinction is as *extrinsic* as is my inability to see, under *usual* space-time conditions, the back of my own head. (5) I am not sure whether Mr. Rice intended to attribute to me the view that I base the distinction between the classes of events in question "on their centering in the organism." But to avoid the possibility of misunderstanding, I add that I do not. On the contrary, my point is that *all* events in the way of observations are *centered* in an organism, while *all* events, those Mr. Rice calls private as well as those he calls public, extend, spatially and temporally, far beyond the skin of the organism in which they come to a head. This consideration adds to the relevancy of reference to language in the matter of observation in which an event is characterized as *such-and-such*.

Let me begin, then, by repeating as emphatically as possible that the occurrence of events in the way of prizing, cherishing, admiring, relishing, enjoying, is not in question. Nor is their primary importance for human life in any way depreciated; the events are what make life worth having. Nor is it held that they must be taken out of their qualitative immediacy and be subjected to judgment. On the contrary, my thesis, as respects valuation, is that only when conditions arise that cause doubt to arise as to their value (not their occurrence) are they judged. There is no single word that covers the entire range of events of the kind mentioned. It is convenient to use a single word to save constant repetition of things admired, enjoyed, liked, held dear, relished, cherished; this list being far from covering their entire range. I shall use the word "the enjoyeds." I use that term rather than "enjoyments" because it emphasizes the fact that actual events are involved; we do not enjoy enjoyments, but persons, scenes, deeds, works of art, friends, conversations with them, and ball games and concertos, to mention Mr. Rice's illustrations.

In his original article, Mr. Rice criticized my view that valuation-judgments proceed by placing the enjoyeds in the context (provided of course by inquiry) of conditions that produce them and consequences that result from them. Mr. Rice did not deny that this operation furnishes evidence, but charged me with neglecting the evidence which is supplied by the very occurrence of the enjoyeds. In fact he even went so far as to imply that I paid no attention to their occurrence in my pre-occupation with conditions and consequences. My reply was that so far from neglecting this fact, my theory holds that such are the events the *subject-matter* of valuations; but that since their unsettled or dubious state *qua* value is precisely that which calls out judgment, it is an equivoke to treat them, *in their bare occurrence*, as capable of providing evidence.

In his present reply, Mr. Rice cites the case of a toothache, saying that its immediately dis-enjoyed qualities may, and often do, furnish part of the evidence for the judgment of value: " 'I ought to visit a dentist,' or—though with less initial probability—'I ought to have a cavity filled.' " He continues "The ache is not, as Mr. Dewey seems to hold, merely a 'dubious' element in the situation, but, together with my previous knowledge of similar situations, it constitutes *prima facie* evidence for these value judgments." I do not know just what Mr. Rice has in mind by saying that I seem to hold that the ache is "merely a dubious element in the situation." I do not, however, suppose that he means to impute to me the view that its existence is in doubt. So I repeat that *if* there is a pause for valuation-judgment, it is because there is some doubt, in the total situation, of just what it indicates as to what it is better to do; what *should* or ought to be done. And I insert the *if* because it is by no means necessary that judgment intervene. One having the ache may make it a rule to visit a dentist; the event in question then operates as a direct stimulus— and unfortunately many persons react just by standing an ache until it ceases.

The nub of Mr. Rice's position, however, is found in the sentence containing the phrase "together with," in saying that the qualities of the ache provide, *along with previous knowledge,* evidence. Now there is a meaning of the words "together with" in which the statement made seems just as sensible and evident to me as it does to Mr. Rice. But this meaning is just not that which Mr. Rice gives the words. "Together with" is an ambiguous phrase. Mr. Rice gives it the meaning his own theory requires; that it is itself evidence as far as it goes, evidence which is then *added on* to evidence supplied by previous knowledge of similar situation. My understanding of the words is that which, I believe, would occur to one independent of any theory. When the event of an enjoyed is judged with respect to estimating its value, its occurrence *qua* value is passed upon by means of taking it out of its isolated occurrence and bringing it into connection with the other facts, primarily those supplied by memory-knowledge of what has happened in the past in similar situations. By being viewed "together with" such facts, judgment is formed as to what the event indicates to be better or as to what should be. From my point of view, then, the meaning Mr. Rice gives the phrase repeats the equivoke with which he was charged in my previous article.

Mr. Rice's sense for fact leads him, even so, to qualify the evidential status of the event; he calls it *"prima facie* evidence," and goes on to speak of the need of "further evidence" being sought for to confirm (or, I suppose, perhaps to refute) evidence that is only *prima facie.* My point is that this further evidence is "together with" the enjoyed in question in precisely the same sense in which the knowledge of previous situations is together with it: the means of determining a valuation of it.

Mr. Rice gives some further examples of the same general type, referring to valuations regarding events to happen in the future. He says in the case of a judgment that it will be enjoyable to go to a Beethoven concerto or a ball game between the Dodgers and the Reds, "it is in part because I remember that similar occasions in the past have been accompanied by enjoyment, and because I discover introspectively that my imaginative rehearsal of the probable experience ahead of me is now accompanied by relish.'' No one can doubt that evidence supplied by the fact that similar events in the past have proved enjoyable is good evidence of the fact that, under like conditions, the same sort of event will be enjoyed in the future. Instead of proving Mr. Rice's contention that the present relish of the prospect is *added* evidence it goes to show that evidence provided by *other* events is summoned to pass upon the quality *qua* value, of the relish in question. I repeat that I don't hold that valuation-judgment *must* intervene. One may react directly by going to the ball-park or the concert-hall. Unless perchance Mr. Rice holds that every case of an enjoyed is, *ipso facto,* also a case of occurrence of a valuation-judgment, what are the conditions which according to him, evoke judgment of an enjoyed event in case there is no doubt as to its status *qua* value?

But the reader can analyze for himself the examples cited by Mr. Rice, and decide whether they are in fact instances that what is directly enjoyed are cases of providing additional, even *prima facie,* evidence in *judgments* regarding value, or whether the evidence to which it is said to be *added* is in fact that which decides the *value* of an enjoyed event. And if we were engaged merely in controversy and not in discussion of an issue, I would add that introduction of the *phrase prima facie* is itself a sufficient indication that the latter of the two alternatives describes the facts of the case.

JOHN DEWEY

COLUMBIA UNIVERSITY

THE JOURNAL OF PHILOSOPHY

SOME QUESTIONS ABOUT VALUE

WHEN I analyze the discouragement I have experienced lately in connection with discussion of value, I find that it proceeds from the feeling that little headway is being made in determining the questions or issues fundamentally involved rather than from the fact that the views I personally hold have not received general approval. The clear-cut quality of the recent paper by Dr. Geiger [1] moves me to try to do something by way of clarifying underlying issues, with only that degree of attention to answers and solutions as may serve to make the nature of the questions stand out. I do not suppose that any formulation of questions which I can make will be uninfluenced by the answers I would give them. But if others will state the issues that seem to *them* to be basic, perhaps discussion of solutions will be more fruitful in the way of approach to agreement than has been the case. [2]

I begin with a preliminary rough listing.

I. What connection is there, if any, between an attitude that will be called prizing or holding dear and desiring, liking, interest, enjoying, etc.?

II. Irrespective of which of the above-named attitudes is taken to be primary, is it by itself a *sufficient* condition for the existence of values? Or, while it is a necessary condition, is a further condition, of the nature of *valuation* or *appraisal*, required?

III. Whatever the answer to the second question, is there anything in the nature of appraisal, evaluation, as judgment or/and proposition, that marks them off, with respect to their logical or their scientific status, from other propositions or judgments? Or are such distinctive properties as they possess wholly an affair of their subject-matter—as we might speak of astronomical and geological propositions without implying that there is any difference between them *qua* propositions?

[1] "Can We Choose between Values?" this JOURNAL, Vol. XLI, pp. 292–298.

[2] I should add that no attempt is made to list all the questions upon which division in conclusions rests. The view that gives value a *transcendent* character has been omitted, so what is said will not appeal to those who hold that view.

IV. Is the scientific method of inquiry, in its broad sense,[3] applicable in determination of judgments and/or propositions in the way of valuations or appraisals? Or is there something inherent in the nature of values as subject-matter that precludes the application of such method?

I

It can not be assumed that the meaning of the words "prizing" and "desiring" (or of any of the words of the first question) is evident on their face. To attempt to define them all is impossible and unnecessary. The word "prizing" is here used to stand for a *behavioral* transaction. If its force is reduced from overt action to an *attitude*, then the attitude or disposition in question must be understood to be taken toward things or persons, and as having no shadow of meaning if it be isolated from that which it is *towards*. Equivalent names would be nourishing, caring for, looking out after, fostering, making much of, being loyal or faithful to, clinging to, provided these words are taken in an active behavioral sense. If this meaning belongs to "prizing," then the first question concerns the connection (or lack of connection) which holds between the way of behaving that is specified and such states, acts, or processes, as "desiring," "liking," "interest," "enjoying," *no matter how the latter are defined.*

That is to say, *if* the latter words are given a behavioral description, the problem is that of the connections sustained to one another by various attitudes or dispositions which are homogeneous in dimension, since all are behavioral. It might, for example, be held that, since what is called *prizing, holding dear,* is a way of behaving tending to maintain something in factual (space-time) existence, *interest* stands for an enduring, or long-time-span, disposition of this nature, one which holds together in system a variety of acts otherwise having diverse directions. *Desire* might then be the behavioral attitude that arises when prizings are temporarily blocked or frustrated, while *enjoying* would be the name for the consummatory phase of prizing.[4] If, however, *desire, interest,* etc., are given a non-behavioral meaning, then it seems that they must

---

[3] The phrase "in its broad sense" is inserted to make it clear that "scientific" is not assumed in advance to signify reduction to physical or biological terms, but, as is the case with scientific investigations of concrete matters generally, leaves the scope of the subject-matter to be determined in the course of inquiry.

[4] The word "might" is used in the text to indicate that the particular descriptions given are intended to serve as sample illustrations of homogeneous behavioral interpretation, not as finalities.

stand for something "internal," "mentalistic," etc. In this case, the issue at stake would be a choice between a view which holds that *valuing* is basically a mode of behavior that serves to keep in being a thing that exists independently of being valued, and the view that some kind of a mental state or process suffices to generate value as an uniquely complete product.

Upon the first-mentioned view, "prizing" (as here understood) has definite biological roots, such as, for example, are manifest in the behavior of a mother-bird in nourishing its young or of a mother-bear in attacking animals that threaten her young. The intensity of the "prizing" involved is then measured by the amount of energy that goes into the nourishing or the protecting behavior. Upon this view there is always an event or thing having existence independently of being prized (or valued) to which the quality or property of "value" is added under specified conditions of space-time. From the view that the desire, liking, interest, or whatever, that generates value is solely "internal" or "mental," it seems to follow that if the value in question is then attached to an event or object (something in space-time), it is because of an external more or less accidental association. For if desire or liking is an "internal" state complete in itself, then the fact that it hits upon or bears upon, say, a diamond, or a young woman, or holding an official position, is assuredly so external as to be relatively a matter of accident.

II

Another issue that seems to be basic in current literature concerns the question of the connection or lack of connection between *valuing* and *valuation* in the sense of *evaluating*. Do values come into existence (no matter how they are understood and accounted for) apart from and prior to anything whatever in the way of an evaluating condition? In case they do so arise, what is the relation of subsequent evaluations to a value having prior existence? *How* does a valuation supervene? And *why* does it supervene—that is to say, what is its function, if any?

The statements in the foregoing paragraph are based upon belief that examination of current discussions will show that some hold that nothing having the properties of value can arise save as some factor of appraisal, of measuring and comparing, enters in, while others hold that values may and do exist apart from any operation of this latter sort so that valuation is always wholly *ex post facto* as far as existence of values is concerned.

It is true, I think, that holding dear and valuing are used interchangeably. As far as usage goes, this fact might seem on its face to point to valuing being complete apart from evaluating. But the fact that valuation and valuing are also often used as synonyms is enough to give pause to such a conclusion. Appraisers in the field of taxation, for example, are said to value real estate, and there are expert appraisers in almost every field having to do with buying and selling property. And it is just as true that they *fix* value as it is that they pass upon it. The underlying issue here is whether "value" is a noun standing for something that is an entity in its own right or whether the word is adjectival, standing for a property or quality that belongs, under specifiable conditions, to a thing or person having existence independently of being valued. If the first view is adopted, then to say that a diamond, or a beloved person, or holding an official position, has or is a value, is to affirm that a connection somehow has been set up between two separate and unlike entities. If the second view is held, then it is held that a thing, in virtue of identifiable and describable events, has acquired a quality or property not previously belonging to it. As a thing previously hard becomes soft when affected by heat, so, on this view, something previously indifferent takes on the quality of value when it is actively cared for in a way that protects or contributes to its continued existence. Upon this view, a value-quality loses the quasi-mystical character often ascribed to it, and is capable of identification and description in terms of conditions of origin and consequence, as are other natural events.[5]

When it was suggested above that *appraising* (*evaluating*) is often used interchangeably with *valuing,* there was no intention of intimating that there is no difference between the direct behavioral operation of holding dear and such operations as valuations of real estate and other commodities. There is a decided difference. The point in calling attention to the fact of common usage is twofold. It definitely raises the question of the relation of *valuation* and *value* to one another. Does *valuation* affect or modify things previously valued in the sense of being held dear (desired, liked, enjoyed), or does a valuation-proposition merely communicate the fact that a thing or person has in fact been held dear (liked, enjoyed, esteemed)? If the latter, what is the function of deliberation? Is it or is it not true that at times questions arise as to whether things previously highly esteemed (desired, liked, etc.) *should* be so viewed and treated? In the latter case, it would seem

---

[5] If this line of interpretation were carried out, it would indicate that the appearance of value-quality is genetically and functionally continuous, not only with physiological operations that protect and continue living processes, but with physical-chemical interactions that maintain stability amid change on the part of some compounds.

that reflective inquiry (deliberation) is engaged in for the sake of determining the value-status of the thing or person in question.

The other point in calling attention to occasional interchangeable use of *valuing* and *valuation* is to raise the question whether the undeniable difference between direct valuing and the indirectness of evaluation is a matter of *separation* or of *emphasis*. If there is in direct valuing an element of recognition of the properties of the thing or person valued as *ground* for prizing, esteeming, desiring, liking, etc., then the difference between it and explicit evaluation is one of emphasis and degree, not of fixed kinds. *Ap-praising* then represents a more or less systematized development of what is already present in *prizing*. If the valuing is *wholly* a-rational, if there is nothing whatever "objective" as its ground, then there is complete separation. In this case the problem is to determine whether valuation (i) is simply a "realistic" apprehension of something already completely there, or (ii) is simply a verbal communication of an established fact but not in any sense a proposition, or (iii) if it does enter at all into formation of subsequent valuings, how does it manage to do so.

III

The third problem grows quite directly out of the one just considered. It may be stated as follows: Is there anything unique or distinctive about valuation-propositions *as propositions?* (If they merely enunciate to others facts already in existence, this question does not arise, since such communications are, *ipso facto*, not *propositions*. Outright statements that valuation-propositions *qua* propositions and not just because of their subject-matter are of a distinctive kind are not usual in the literature that discusses the subject of value. But positions are frequently taken and topics introduced that do not seem to have any meaning unless that position has been assumed without explicit statement. I give one typical example.

Articles frequently appear that discuss the relation of *fact* and *value*. If the subject discussed under this caption were the relation of value-facts to *other* facts, there would not be the assumption of uniqueness just mentioned. But anyone reading articles devoted to discussion of this issue will note that it is an issue or problem just because it is held that propositions about values are somehow of a unique sort, being *inherently* marked off from propositions about facts. I can think of nothing more likely to be clarifying in the present confused state of the subject than an explicit statement of the *grounds* upon which it is assumed that propositions about values are *not* propositions about space-time facts, together with explicit discussion of the *consequences* of that position. If a question were raised about the relation of geological propositions to astronomical propositions, or of meteor-propositions to comet-propositions, it would not occur to anyone that the "problem" was other than that of the connection between two sets of facts. It is my conviction that nothing would better clarify the present unsatisfactory state of discussion of value than definite and explicit statement of the reasons why the case is supposed to be otherwise in respect to value.

IV

Of late, there has appeared a school of theorists insisting with vigor that genuine propositions (and/or judgments) about values are impossible, because the latter have properties that render them wholly recalcitrant to cognitive treatment. In brief, this school holds that verbal expressions about values are of the nature of exclamations, expressing only the dominant emotional state of the one from whom the ejaculation issues. The ejaculation may be verbally extended into a sentence expressing a desire or liking or an interest. But, so it is said, the only question of a cognitive or intellectual nature that can be raised is whether the verbal expression in question (whether it be a shorter ejaculation or an expanded sentence) actually expresses the emotional state of the speaker or is meant to mislead others by concealing or distorting his actual state.

The practical import of this position may be inferred from the fact that according to it differences as to value can not be adjudicated or negotiated. They are just ultimate facts. In the frank words of one who has taken this position, serious cases of ultimate difference can be settled, if at all, only by "bashing in of heads." I shall not ask here how far this view carries to its logical conclusion the view that some "internal" or mentalistic state or process suffices to bring value-events into existence. I limit myself to pointing out that at the present time serious differences in valuing are in fact treated as capable of settlement only by recourse to force and in so far the view in question has empirical support. This is the case in recourse to war between nations, and in less obvious and complete ways, in domestic disputes between groups and in conflict of classes. In international relations short of war, the view is practically taken in acceptance of an ultimate difference between "justiciable" and "non-justiciable" disputes.

It can not be denied that this particular question is of immense practical import. Using the word "bias" without prejudice, I think it may be stated as follows: Are value-facts bias-facts of such intensity and exclusiveness as to be unmodifiable by any possible consideration of grounds and consequences? The question at issue is not whether some values are now actually treated as if they were of this kind. It is whether the cause of their being so treated inheres in them as value-facts or is a cultural-social phenomenon. If the latter is the case they are capable of modification by socio-cultural changes. If the former is the case, then differences in valuing which are of serious social importance can not be brought within the scope of investigation so as to be settled in a reasonable way. They may not always lead to open conflict. But if not it will be because it is believed that the latter will not be successful, or will be too costly, or that the time is not ripe, or that some more devious method will accomplish a wished-for triumph more effectively.

This fourth question is evidently connected with those previously discussed. If valuing consists *wholly* and exclusively of something inherently recalcitrant to inquiry and adjudication, then it must be admitted that it can not rise about the brute-animal level—save with respect to the *means* most likely to secure its victory over conflicting valuations and values. But if, in answer to the third question, it is decided that there is some element or aspect of valuation on "objective" grounds in every case of prizing, desiring, etc., etc., then it is possible that this element or aspect may itself become so prized, desired, and enjoyed that it will gain in force at the expense of the brute and non-rational factor.

In this connection it seems worthy of note that those writers who hold to the completely a-rational character of valuing begin by accepting the "internal" mentalistic theory of value, and then proceed to endow this quasi-gaseous stuff with powers of resistance greater than are possessed by triple-plate steel. While the four questions that have been formulated are those which seem to me to be more or less openly expressed in current discussion, the fact I have just stated leads me to raise, on my own account, another question which does not often appear in the literature on value, and which, nevertheless, may be more fundamental than those which do appear. Are values and valuations such that they can be treated on a psychological basis of an allegedly "individual" kind? Or are they so definitely and completely socio-cultural that they can be effectively dealt with only in that context? [6]

JOHN DEWEY

COLUMBIA UNIVERSITY

[6] Since the above text was written, I find this question explicitly raised as basic to economic theory, in the book of Ayres, *The Theory of Economic Progress*, especially pp. 73–85, 90, 97.

THE JOURNAL OF PHILOSOPHY

ETHICAL SUBJECT–MATTER AND LANGUAGE

I

DISCUSSION of the topic indicated by the caption of this article centers about a particular thesis put forward by Professor Stevenson in his recent book.[1] Since my article is definitely critical as to this particular thesis, I feel the more bound to indicate at the outset certain points in which I think his book as a whole should command not only the attention but the support of students of ethical theory. Among points of agreement are the following: (i) There is great need for more attention to the language that characterizes specifically ethical judgments or sentences. (ii) Ethical inquiries should "draw from the *whole* of a man's knowledge," since the materials of such inquiries lend "themselves very poorly to specialization." (iii) Ethical inquiry has suffered from "quest for ultimate principles, definitively established"—a procedure that "not only hides the full complexity of moral issues, but puts static, other-worldly norms in the place of flexible, realistic ones." (iv) Finally since "ethical *issues* differ from scientific ones," there should be careful attention to the *way* in which they differ.[2]

There is such ambiguity in the word "issues" that grasp upon its double reference is indispensable. In one sense of the word, that moral and scientific issues differ is not just to be admitted as a concession, but is to be insisted upon as characteristic of ethical subject-matter and ethical sentences *qua* ethical. The sense in which *issues* differ, if not a commonplace, is commonly acknowledged in calling ethics a practical or "normative" subject. But in this sense "issue" is equivalent to office, function, use, force; it concerns the contextual "practical" reference, the *objective* of

---

[1] *Ethics and Language* by Charles L. Stevenson, Yale University Press, 1944. I wish to express my indebtedness to a review of the book by Dr. Henry Aiken published in this JOURNAL, Vol. XLII (1945), pp. 455–470. Since his discussion of what Stevenson says about the relation of attitudes and beliefs seems to me conclusive I say nothing on that point, and am enabled to adopt a different line of approach.

[2] The quoted passages are all from page 336 of *Ethics and Language;* "*whole*" is italicized in the original text while "*issues*" and "*way*" are not. The reason why I have italicized these words is central in my discussion, as will appear as it proceeds.

ethical sentences. As far as accomplishment of this function and use is intended on the part of those who engage in forming, accepting, or rejecting ethical sentences, a differential *interest* marks them off from sentences having what is conventionally called a scientific interest. While difference determines the specific facts *selected* as the distinctive content or subject-matter of ethical sentences, it does not constitute a component part of that subject-matter. It is one thing to say that, because of the differential use or function of ethical sentences, certain facts rather than others are selected and that they are arranged or organized in a given way rather than in some other way. A like proposition applies to differences that mark off the sciences from one another—physics, for example, from physiology. It is quite another thing to convert the difference in function and use into a differential component of the structure and contents of ethical sentences. This conversion marks, in effect, Stevenson's treatment.

I may further anticipate the tenor of the discussion which follows by saying that I do not see how it can be denied that the subject-matter which is selected as appropriate and required for sentences which will fulfill the proper office or function of ethical sentences is charged (and properly so) with facts designated by such names as greed-generosity, love-hate, sympathy-antipathy, reverence-indifference. It is usual to give such facts, taken collectively, the name "emotions," or, slightly more technically, the name "affective-motor." It is one thing to acknowledge (and insist) upon this feature of ethical sentences as one demanded by their function or the use they are put to. It is quite another thing to hold that this subject-matter is not capable of and does not need *description,* and description of the kind belonging to sentences having "scientific" standing. I believe that examination of Stevenson's specific treatment of the "emotional" (or the "emotive" in his terminology) will show that he takes the fact that factually grounded reasons are employed in genuinely ethical sentences in order to modify affective-motor attitudes which influence and direct conduct, to be equivalent to the presence of an extra-cognitive constituent in the sentences in question. In short, the very fact that factual grounds (which are capable of description) are the means used in genuine ethical sentences to affect the springs of conduct and thereby to direct and redirect conduct, is employed as if it introduced into the specific subject-matter of ethical sentences a factor completely recalcitrant to intellectual or cognitive consideration.[3] One can agree fully that ethical sentences (as far as their

[3] The word "genuine" is used in the text because there can be no doubt that sentences *claiming* to be ethical often use an extra-cognitive "emotive"

end and use is concerned) "plead and advise" and speak "to the conative-affective natures of men." [4]   Their use and intent is practical. But the point at issue concerns the means by which this result is accomplished. It is, I repeat, a radical fallacy to convert the end-in-view into an inherent constituent of the means by which, in genuinely moral sentences, the end is accomplished. To take the cases in which "emotional" factors *accompany* the giving of reasons as if this accompaniment factor were an inherent part of the judgment is, I submit, both a theoretical error and is, when widely adopted in practice, a source of moral weakness.[5]

II

While the previous paragraphs anticipate to some extent the conclusion to be reached in the following discussion, they are chiefly designed to indicate the nature of the problem by telling what it is *not*. Strangely enough (save perhaps on the ground of the ambiguity which has been mentioned) it is not easy to quote isolated sentences in which there is explicit statement that ethical sentences as such contain two independent components, one cognitive, the other non-cognitive. It is easy enough to find sentences like the following: "For the contexts that are most typical of normative ethics, the ethical terms have a function that is *both* emotive and descriptive." [6]   But in such passages the word "function" appears. Accordingly, I come directly to discussion of the particular grounds upon which Stevenson bases his conclusion about the non-cognitive constituent of ethical sentences. His statement of this ground or reason appears in connection with a discussion of signs and *meanings*. The evidence brought forward for the existence of signs and meanings which are exclusively "emotive" consists of an account (i) of such non-linguistic events as sighs, groans, smiles, etc., and (ii) of linguistic events such as interjections. Unless the occurrence of emotive meanings in a sense which excludes a descriptive reference (and descriptive meaning) can be independently established, there can, of course, be no

factor to influence conduct, thereby cooking the factual evidence adduced. Moreover, some theories, like Kant's, have gone so far as to make a directly and exclusively "imperative" factor the very core of all ethical judgments.

4 *Op. cit.*, p. 13.

5 I would not overemphasize the matter, but I get the impression that Stevenson is influenced at times in connection with the "meaning" of moral judgments, by that ambiguity in which "meaning" has the sense of both design or purpose and that which a sign indicates.

6 *Op. cit.*, p. 84. We do have, however, such phrases as "the independence of emotive meaning," in the sense of its remaining the same when "descriptive" meaning changes (p. 73).

question of such an element being found in ethical sentences. Hence further discussion centers on this point.

I quote a key passage *in extenso:*

The emotive meaning of words can best be understood by comparing and contrasting it with the expressiveness of laughs, sighs, groans, and all similar manifestations of the emotions, whether by voice or gesture. It is obvious that these ''natural'' expressions are direct behavioristic symptoms of the emotions or feelings to which they testify. A laugh gives direct ''vent'' to the amusement which it accompanies, and does so in such an intimate, inevitable way that if the laugh is checked, some degree of amusement is likely to be checked as well. In much the same way a sigh gives immediate release to sorrow; and a shrug of the shoulders integrally expresses its nonchalant carelessness. One must not, merely on this account, insist that laughs, sighs, and so on, are literally a part of language, or that they have an emotive meaning; but there remains an important point of analogy: Interjections, which *are* a part of language, and which do have an emotive meaning, are *like* sighs, shrieks, groans, and the rest in that they can be used to ''give vent'' to the emotions or attitudes in much the same way. . . . Emotive words, then, whatever else must be said of them, are suitable for ''venting'' the emotions, and to that extent are akin not to words which denote emotions, but rather to the laughs, groans, and sighs that ''naturally'' manifest them. . . . Why is it that ''natural'' manifestations of emotions are ascribed meaning only in this broader sense [viz., the sense in which a natural event like ''reduced temperature may at times mean convalescence,'' a sense said to be ''wider'' than any found in linguistic theory], whereas interjections, so like them in function, may be ascribed meaning in a narrower sense? [7]

Discussion of the answer given by Stevenson to this last question, that as to why the meaning of ''natural'' signs is different from that of linguistic signs, will be postponed until what is said about interjections, and sighs, groans, and so on, as being alike in that both are merely expressive of emotions and hence have no ''referent,'' has been taken up. On the one hand, the events in question are said to *vent,* to *release;* on the other hand, they are said to be *symptomatic,* and to *manifest,* and to *testify.* In the latter capacity they are assuredly signs in a cognitive sense. When the word ''express'' is used there seems to be an intermediate and ambiguous term; as far as ''express'' means *convey* a cognitive sign is undoubtedly involved; as far as to *express* means to ''squeeze out'' it is akin to *venting.*

Now while I have classified venting and manifestings under two heads, one of which concerns signs while the other one does not, it is characteristic of Stevenson's treatment that he identifies the bald fact of venting or releasing with being a sign. Moreover, he treats a venting as a sign not only of emotion in general but as a sign of specific emotions—a groan of discomfort and a sigh of sor-

[7] *Op. cit.,* pp. 37–39 *passim.*

row, etc. How they can be viewed or treated as such apart from aid and support given by a developed system of known things (which are designated linguistically) I am unable to see. And by this remark I do not mean the trivial or tautological fact that one needs language to give a name to them; I mean that giving them a name as events of a genus, namely, emotion, and as events of species of that genus, is not possible without identifications and discriminations which involve connection with events that are outside the bare occurrence of what is said to be a venting. They are, indeed, so far outside that they can be made and understood only by adults; that is, by those having a rather wide acquaintance with things to which "description" is applicable.

The point here made comes out even more forcibly, if possible, in discussion of interjections as *linguistic* signs. This discussion occupies a central strategic position. For since they are linguistic signs, if it can be established that they have meaning and yet a meaning that is exclusively "emotive," there is in so far a factual basis for the view that "meanings" of this type are ingredients of ethical sentences. The evidence offered by Stevenson is indicated in a passage in which, after saying that there is one sense in which "the 'meaning' of a sign is that *to which* people refer when they use the sign," a kind of meaning for which the word "referent" may be substituted and which is *descriptive*, he goes on to say that there is, however, another sort of meaning possessed by some linguistic signs. Some words (such as "alas") have no referent, but do have a kind of meaning, namely, "emotive meaning." [8] Here we have at least a negative specification of what it is to be a linguistic sign that is "emotive." Its distinctive characteristic is lack of a *referent*. It expresses a meaning; like a sigh it gives vent to a feeling. Thus it shows that there are some signs which are "akin not to words which denote emotions, but rather to the laughs, groans, and sighs that 'naturally' manifest them." [9] And yet this very passage, and the whole discussion of which it is a part, refers to "something called emotion" in general and to different emotions in particular (amusement, sorrow, etc.) as that of which interjections are signs! If this is not to "denote," to designate, or name, I do not know what it is. And the denoting in question occurs only by virtue of identifications and discriminations without which the sounds called interjections are at best but events in the way of vocalizations—and, of course, to identify an event even as a "vocalization" is to name it in a way that is made possible only through a set or system of "referents."

[8] *Op. cit.*, p. 42.
[9] *Op. cit.*, p. 38.

It is convenient to introduce further discussion by reference to a cough as a "natural" sign. That "a cough may mean a cold" is an undeniable fact. But when it is said that as a natural sign it lacks "the elaborate conditioning developed for purposes of communication," we are given pause.[10] That, as a *natural* event, a cough may *not* be a sign of a cold is, I should say, an undeniable fact. That a cough can be taken and used as a sign without rather elaborate "conditioning" is, I should say, impossible; at least it seems to be possible only if it is in a class with that cake of Alice in Wonderland which bore on its face the words "Eat me." Consider, for example, the ground upon which a physician breaks up coughs of the common or garden variety into signs of a number of different physiological conditions. It does not follow, of course, that a cough is a linguistic sign in the conventional sense of linguistic. But it does follow that in its capacity or status as *sign*, or with respect to *signness*, it does not differ from a linguistic sign. And that a cough can become a sign of a cold, save in and because of a *context* of linguistic signs which enable it to stand for something beside itself, seems most doubtful. By means of its presence in a total context of which language is another member it acquires an ability to refer beyond its mere occurrence. Without such reference it lacks the properties of a sign. And it is worth noting that a *word* is originally a natural event, a sound or spatial marking before and independently of being a sign.

So far, emphasis has fallen upon the respect in which some natural events, groans, etc., are said to be signs *like* some linguistic signs, namely, interjections. It is worth while to notice the reasons given by Stevenson for holding that they are unlike in one important respect, that which renders an interjection linguistic. In giving answer to the question cited above as to why "natural manifestations" of emotion have meaning in the "broader sense" in which other natural events have meaning we find the following: "The expressiveness of interjections, unlike that of groans or laughs, depends upon conventions that have grown up in the history of their usage. . . . People groan, in all languages, so to speak, but say 'ouch' only in English." In the same connection it is said that interjections, being recognized grammatical forms of speech, "are of interest to the etymologist and phonetician, whereas the latter [groans, etc.] are of scientific interest only to the psychologist or physiologist." [11] Yet the words "*only* to the physiologist and psychologist" occur in a passage in which they are discussed as of defi-

10 *Op. cit.*, p. 57.

11 The passage first quoted is from page 39; the latter passage is found on page 38.

nite interest to the student of signs, namely, as proof of a certain theory about them! What is to be proved concerns their status as *signs,* with respect to *signness;* what is adduced concerns the particular group that investigates them. The specific kind of "training" or "conditioning" involved in the case of what is meant to the grammarian, etc., and to the physiologist is different. But so is the kind of training that is involved in calling the same thing H_2O and *water.*

Stevenson treats a groan as an inherent manifestation, an expression, and as a sign of something, namely, an emotion. He does so only by assuming that there is given at and from the outset of its occurrence *two* things; one an emotion, the other its venting or release. But there is in the first instance but a single total event of the same order as, say, urination, the turning over of a baby in its crib, its gurgling, its shedding of tears. There are total behavioristic acts, not an emotion and its release. Any one of the events mentioned may come to be taken and used as a sign. But it *becomes* a sign; it is not a sign in its original bare occurrence. The problem of how it becomes a sign, under what conditions it is taken as standing for something beside itself, is not even raised in Mr. Stevenson's treatment. If it were discussed, I think it would be clear that the conditions in question are those of a behavioral transaction in which *other* events (those called "referents" or, more commonly, "objects") are joint partners along with the event which as bare event is *not* a sign.

The conditions under which "alas" and "helas" become, respectively, signs to different social groups are not at all those under which both of them have the character of being signs, and signs of the same event, a sorrowful one. I would not cite a dictionary as final authority. But a dictionary statement has suggestive force. In the *Oxford Dictionary* I find the following: "Alas; an exclamation expressive of unhappiness, grief, pity, or concern." Is it expressive of any of these conditions apart from having a specified position in a complex situation in which occur also the things the "emotions" are *at, about,* or *of?* Moreover, the four words are not synonyms. Apart from the co-presence of the "objects" they are of and about, apart from a descriptive context, that is, how can it be told which one of these four "alas" is expressive of? And just as certain intonations, gestures, facial expressions are simulated in order to mislead a spectator or listener, and just as such cases need to be discriminated from genuine cases if the "practical" response is to be appropriate to the facts of the case, so with discriminating actual from a pretended "meaning" of an interjection. The *Oxford Dictionary* follows the passage quoted above with the words: "Occ. with dat. obj., or with for." I submit that the word "occasional" refers only to explicit linguistic usage; that when the dative object is not *linguistically* specified it is because it is such a part of the situation shared by speaker and listener that it is superfluous to speak of it. As to the use of "for," we find among the illustrative quotations the following: " 'Las, I could weep for your calamity," and "Alas, both for the deed and its cause." Is there any case in which "alas" has meaning apart from something that is of the nature of a calamity, a loss, a tragic event, or some cause or deed which is mourned? I imagine that when a reader sees the word "emotive," he is likely to think of events like anger, fear, hope, sympathy, and in thinking of them he thinks necessarily of other things—the things with which they are integrally connected. Only in this way can an event, whether a sigh or a word like "alas," have identifiable and recognizable "meaning." And yet this is just what Stevenson's theory excludes!

In connection with his theory that all meaning is a case of a "psychological response," Mr. Stevenson, with his usual care and candor, leaves us no doubt of the kind of psychological response, which is definitely characteristic in his theory of the emotive response. Here are his words: After he has spoken of feeling and emotion as synonyms he says: "The term 'feeling' is to be taken as designating an affective state *that reveals its full nature to immediate introspection,* without use of induction." [12] It certainly must be so taken if there is to be a type of meaning which is exclusively "emotive," because of having no "referent," no *to which.* Only on the ground of the allegation that an emotion self-reveals its full nature in the bare fact of its occurrence, including not only the fact that it *is* an emotion but the fact that it is sorrow, anger, etc., can the fact designated by the words "of, about, to" etc., be ruled out as irrelevant. It is out of the question here to go into the question of "the psychological" in general and of "introspective" self-revelation in particular. I must content myself here with pointing out (i) the central position held by these assumptions in Stevenson's doctrine, and (ii) the fact that they *are* assumptions, made as if they were such a matter of course as to be universally acceptable, and hence not in need of evidence nor argument but only of exposition.[13]

[12] *Op. cit.,* p. 60; italics not in original text.

[13] In the title of Mr. Stevenson's third chapter, the words "psychological" and "pragmatic" are used as synonyms. In treating them as such he relies upon the authority of Morris's extraordinary interpretation of Peirce's theory of signs and meanings. I shall discuss Peirce's theory and Morris's misrepresentation in a future article in this JOURNAL in which I shall take the opportunity to deal with points here left out of consideration.

III

Discussion up to this point is preliminary to consideration of the main theme of Stevenson's book, ethical language. The latter theory loses its main prop (as far as duality of meaning is ascribed to ethical language) if his account of emotive manifestations, "natural" and linguistic, is invalid. But it is worth while to discuss the effect of his theory on ethical language. His general point of view is fairly presented in the following passage: "For the contexts that are most typical of normative ethics, the ethical terms have a function that is *both* emotive and descriptive."[14] In admitting the "descriptive," Stevenson goes beyond those writers who have denied all descriptive force to moral expressions.[15] In so far, Stevenson's treatment constitutes a decided advance upon them. I begin by stating what the point at issue is not. Stevenson says "Ethical terms cannot be taken as fully comparable to scientific ones. They have a quasi-imperative *function*."[16] Now (as was said earlier) the point at issue does not concern the last of the two sentences quoted. Nor does it concern the correctness of the statement that "Both imperative and ethical sentences are *used* more for encouraging, altering, or redirecting people's aims and conduct than for simply describing them."[17] The point at issue is whether the facts of *use* and *function* render ethical terms and sentences not fully comparable with scientific ones as respects their subject-matter and content. As far as concerns *use* it would not, I believe, be going too far to say the word "more" in the above passage is not strong enough. Of ethical sentences as ordinarily used, it may be said, I believe, that their *entire* use and function of ethical sentences is directive or "practical." The point at issue concerns another matter: It concerns how this end is to be accomplished if sentences are to possess distinctively and genuinely *ethical* properties. The theoretical view about ethical sentences which is an alternative to that put forward by Stevenson is, that as far as non-cognitive, extra-cognitive, factors enter into the subject-matter or content of sentences purporting to be legitimately ethical, those sentences are by just that much deprived of the properties sentences should have in order to be genuinely *ethical*.

Let us note a somewhat analogous case. The practices, often resorted to by a skilled lawyer in defending a client charged with a

[14] *Op. cit.*, p. 84. I pass over the use of the word "function" as its ambiguity has already been considered.

[15] Footnotes on pp. 256–257 of his work give references to the more important among these writers.

[16] *Op. cit.*, p. 36; italics not in original.

[17] *Op. cit.*, p. 21; italics not in original text.

criminal act, often contain non-cognitive elements and these may sometimes be more influential, more directive, of what the jury does than evidence of the matter-of-fact or descriptive sort. Would one say in this case that these means, such as intonations, facial expressions, gestures, etc., are a *part* of legal propositions *qua* legal? If not in this case, why in the case of ethical propositions? And in this connection it is worth noting that in some cases at least (possibly in all cases) scientific propositions have a practical office and function. Such is assuredly the case in which a scientific theory is in current dispute because opposite views are entertained. Surely evidence adduced is *used* and is *intended* to be used so as to confirm, weaken, modify, redirect propositions accepted by others. But I doubt if one would hold that the *heat* that sometimes accompanies the putting forth of reasons for changing old views is a part of the *subject-matter* of the propositions *qua* scientific.

Extra-cognitive devices are without doubt employed to effect a result which in consequence is moral only in the sense in which the word "*im*moral" is included in the scope of "moral." Many propositions which are now taken to be immoral have had positive moral property ascribed to them at former times. There is here a strong indication that extra-rational factors played an undue part in forming the earlier propositions and in getting them accepted. It would be foolish to deny that partisanship, "wishful thinking," etc., plays today a great rôle in not only getting propositions accepted but in determining the *subject-matter* of *what* is accepted. But I should suppose it to be evident that such facts are "ethical" only in the sense in which that word covers the anti-ethical and the pseudo-ethical. If moral theory has any distinctive province and any important function it is, I would say, to criticize the language of the *mores* prevalent at a given time, or in given groups, so as to eliminate if possible this factor as a component of their subject-matter; to provide in its place sound matter-of-fact or "descriptive" grounds drawn from any relevant part of the *whole* knowledge possessed at the time.

I conclude with a point which, as far as it is personal, is of minor importance, but which may be used to illustrate the position or principle taken in the foregoing discussion. Stevenson takes up my use of "to be" in my discussion of evaluative judgments—of which ethical judgments are one species. He finds in my use of "to be" a definite indication that I am compelled to admit a quasi-imperative "force" in ethical propositions.[18] Since I did not explicitly give them a directive force, it seems to Mr. Stevenson that I must give a predictive force to "to be." So he concludes that

---

[18] *Op. cit.,* pp. 255 ff.

what I say about evaluative judgments owes its plausibility in considerable degree to the fact that I permit "hortatory to be's" to be absorbed, as it were, "into an elaborate conjunction of predictive ones."

I begin by saying that whatever I have said about "will be," or of a "predictive sort," is of the same kind as what I have said, in connection with evaluations, about what *has* been and what is *now* going on; that is, it is concerned exclusively with giving reasons or grounds, of the matter-of-fact sort, open to description, for taking a specific ground about some *to-be* in the sense of what *should* be done. I had supposed that my pretty continued mention of the need of inquiry into "*conditions and consequences,*" drawing upon the whole of *knowledge* of fact that is relevant, made it clear that their office was to determine in a reasonable way cases of *to be's.* Since, apparently, I did not make that point clear, I am glad to state again, in the present context, that *evaluative* statements concern or have reference to what ends are to-be-chosen, what lines of conduct are to-be-followed, what policies are to-be-adopted. But it is morally necessary to state grounds or reasons for the course advised and recommended. These consist of matter-of-fact sentences reporting what has been and now is, as conditions, and of estimates of consequences that will ensue if certain of them are used as means. For in my opinion sentences about what *should* be done, chosen, etc., are sentences, propositions, judgments, *in the logical sense* of those words only as matter-of-fact grounds are presented in *support* of what is advised, urged, recommended to be done—that is, worthy of being done on the basis of the factual evidence available.

It is unfortunately true that many moral *theories,* some of them of considerable prestige in philosophy, have interpreted moral subject-matter in terms of norms, standards, ideals, which, according to the authors of these theories, have no possible factual standing. "Reasons" for adopting and following them then involve a "reason" and "rational" in a sense which is expressly asserted to be transcendent, *a priori,* supernal, "other-worldly." According to theorists of this type, to give reasons of the kind found in inquiries and conclusions in other subjects eliminates what is genuinely moral, reducing it, say, to the "prudential" and the expediently "politic." On this basis, ethics can be "scientific" only in a sense which gives the word "science" a highly esoteric significance—a sense in which some writers hold philosophy to be *the* supreme science, having methods and depending upon faculties that are beyond the possible reach of humbly subordinate "natural" sciences. In view of the vogue of this type of moral theory, it was probably inevitable, historically speaking, that in the course of time writers would arise who would take theorists of this type at their word as far as concerns the negative part of their theories; and hence would announce that *all* moral judgments and theories are wholly extra-scientific. It is the merit of Stevenson's treatment that he has seen that there is *one* component of ethical sentences that demands and is capable of the same kind of development and test that are found in inquiry into other subjects. It is because of this positive contribution that it has seemed to me desirable to subject to criticism that part of his theory in which he has gone but half-way in this direction.

JOHN DEWEY

COLUMBIA UNIVERSITY

Vol. XXVI, No. 12. June 6, 1929

BOOK REVIEWS

The Public and its Problems. JOHN DEWEY. New York: Henry Holt & Company. 1927. Pp. vi + 224.

Those admirable essays which Professor Dewey has contributed from time to time through a long series of years to public problems have whetted a healthy appetite for a systematic study of political philosophy from his pen. This book, brief as it is, will do not everything, but a great deal, in this direction. If anyone's writing deserves the name "pregnant," it is Dewey's; he always accomplishes more than his title implies. The main intention of this book is to diagnose the predicament of contemporary democracy, to show how it arose, and to indicate a way out: but the four chapters in which this is done are preceded by two chapters, on the public and on the state, which constitute a rapid sketch of a general theory of political order.

This theory is set in direct contrast to all theories which would account for the state by "special causal forces or agencies," whether by deliberate invention or contract or divine institution or specific human instinct or some peculiar and constant nisus in human nature, such as an interest in the rational solution of quarrels. Such causal theories commonly mistake for a cause what is really an effect: men who are molded by any sort of institution develop an accustomed-ness-to, and so a pseudo-need for, that sort of institution. Dewey proposes to base his theory on observable behavior and its consequences, without reference to any *ad hoc* dispositions.

He contrasts his theory also with all theories which would make the state a matter of inclusive or primary social importance. The state is important, but its importance is residual and variable. If other social groupings take good care of their by-products, the state may have little to do; if they leave many secondary results of their activities unattended to, the state may be highly necessary. But in any case, these other groupings are first both in time and in importance; and the state only arises when the remoter consequences of these original dealings become so "extensive and enduring" that they can not well be ignored.

The parameters, then, of Dewey's theory are these: (1) the fact of association, taken as a datum; (2) the consequent fact that actions affect other persons; (3) the distinction between direct, intended effects and the indefinitely extended fringe of indirect, unintended effects,—let us say, the extra-effects; (4) the further distinction among the extra-effects of the sporadic from the extensive and enduring; (5) the presumption that persons reached by these significant extra-effects will be similarly affected and will have similar judgments as to whether the effects are desirable or undesirable, and therefore (if they observe this fact) have a common interest in dealing with them. (6) The public is defined as the group of all persons who recognize themselves as having a common interest in the significant extra-effects of action. (7) When such a public acquires representatives or officers for controlling these extra-effects, it has become a political state.

These parameters are for the most part matters of fact. The hypothetical element is the conception of the public. It is not John Locke's "body politic"; for it requires no act of agreement to bring it into being, but only an act of mutual recognition. Furthermore, it is not composed of separable individuals, but of already associated, tradition-bearing men and groups. Otherwise, its discovered concerns resemble those of Locke's body politic, namely, the effective regulation of social incidents by officers rather than by each man for himself, and the normal subordination of these officers to that definable purpose. So far as they are legitimate, "all governments are representative" (76).

These premises provide a notably simple and pertinent account of the meaning of political democracy; it is, in essence, nothing more than a set of devices for holding governments to their business as representatives of the public. "Democracy is not an alternative to other principles of associated life. It is the idea of community life itself'' (p. 148). This does not mean that democracy was created for this express purpose: for, as Dewey repeatedly reminds us, democracy is no more a result of a drive toward democracy than states are the result of a plan or instinct to make states. "It is mere mythology to attribute such unity of result as exists to single force or principle.'' There were long-standing evils to be remedied —especially the bedevilled, irrelevant methods of getting officers, and the use of office for private rather than for public ends—evils which grew naturally not more out of original sin than out of the drift of all concentration of power in the absence of any clear theory of the function of the state. But these evils had existed, and had been more or less clearly felt, throughout the course of political experience: if a particular and successful series of efforts to get rid of them is made at a particular epoch in history, that result is not to be explained by any new clarity in the aim, but by the fact that the social elements which most felt the pinch of those evils at that time were opportunely endowed with power and prestige.

It was primarily the new economic motives which animated the disposition to assert rights. Machinery in the hands of a capable middle class, conscious of new enjoyments and of new powers, is an energy that can not be restrained by a network of obsolete rules. Thus the ideology of individual rights and suffrage becomes an instrument for bringing government to book in the interest of industry and property. Modern liberalism was developed under conditions which checked its emancipating influences at the point where they brought the maximum benefit to those forces which have since been making big business. The philosophy of individualism reflected the new-born energies of the entrepreneur group; and hence we have the paradox that the isolated individual and his rights were most widely celebrated in theory while the system was brewing in which the masses are now most thoroughly submerged. For now we are members, less of one another, and less of the state, than of those "great impersonal concerns" which, with vast social utility and with some disutilities, stand between us and the sky.

So far, the argument has been that democracy as a partially realized fact is an incidental result of changing conditions of life in which economic forces have taken a primary hand; while the ideology of democracy has played a rôle, at first passive ("reflecting" new conditions) and then active, but never active enough and never as broad as the nominal scope of the ideas. And while the ideas worked out their logic (I trust Dewey will not seriously object to this way of expressing the process whereby the working classes deduced in their own behalf the corollaries of the "rights of man"), other consequences not contemplated by anybody have created new publics, while obscuring the old outlines and not revealing the new; and they have done this faster than the liberating process could run its course. With all the development of political machinery that has gone on in the last century, we are farther from democracy, farther from a genuine control by the public of the conditions of its life, than we were in 1832. There is, in a sense, a Great Society, greater than ever before; but it is a society of standardized individuals linked by way of abstract functions in an organization of abstract interests: it is not a Community, and democracy can not exist until it becomes one.

It is evident that the account of the history of modern democracy which leads to this penetrating, and I believe just, diagnosis of the major malady of contemporary politics, concedes a great deal to one form of the economic interpretation of the history of thought. It is equally evident that in so far as the economic interpretation is accepted, instrumentalism is set aside. For if ideas are instruments they must do work; that is, they must bring their users where they intend to go: that is, again, so far as ideas are instrumental, there is a conscious directionality in history. Without doubting the reality of those contexts of liberalism which Dewey so skilfully exhibits, I would raise the question whether he has not surrendered too much of the original instrumentality of these ideas, which were born, after all, in an era of keen political self-consciousness. The important truth that men always produce *other than* they intend is the shadow of the truth that they always produce *something of* what they intend, and that this passage from intent to achievement is what makes history go, and always constitutes its central current. Of such purposiveness in the use of ideas the rise of modern democracy would seem to furnish some of the most striking instances, perhaps more so in the early demands for freedom of conscience, and in the revolutions in America and France, than in eighteenth- and nineteenth-century England.

I wonder if I am right in thinking that in emphasizing the rôle of economic conditions, Dewey is speaking to some extent under reserve. For even while pointing out that the notion of individual liberty was chiefly effective in the hands of merchants and manufacturers who had to struggle against the rigidity and intrusiveness of governments, he notes that "the need of some control over them (these new modes of association) was the chief agency in making the government of these states democratic . . ." (p. 98). Of course, if democracy is primarily a result of the struggle of the public to control the results of business, it is not primarily a result of the struggle of business to control government: and in so far as it is a result of conscious struggle at all, the instrumental ideas were weapons, and not "reflections" of conditions brought about by other forces.

In any case, Dewey has no intention of yielding the main issue to economic determinism. However much the result to which history has led may be unintended, the existing situation must be faced with intention: the problem of creating a genuinely democratic community is "primarily and essentially an intellectual problem" (p. 126). The cure for the ills of democracy is, for Dewey also, more democracy—not in the sense of more machinery, but in the sense of a more adequate grasp of the idea. The Great Community must be ushered in by more day-to-day knowledge of socially significant truth, by a current social enquiry freely pursued and freely disseminated, and by the enlisting of art in the presenting of that scientific self-knowledge whose fascination, in our present jaded state of interest, our public does not understand. These are presently pertinent means to a goal which Dewey evidently regards as persistent, simply because it is "the idea of community life itself" and can not be abandoned. It is only in this sense that he can say "Invent the railway, the telegraph, mass manufacture, and concentration of population in urban centers, and some form of democratic government is humanly speaking inevitable" (p. 110). These things, taken by themselves, have (unlike Carlyle's printing press) tended to produce an un-democracy; and it is just this undemocracy that is intolerable, and toward whose remedy we can now deliberately aim.

It is impossible to present here the substance of the final chapters, freighted as they are with wise counsel toward methods of equipping the public for its moral task of achieving an adequate intelligence. I wish, rather, to revert to the general political principles outlined at the beginning, raising certain questions which, at their best success, may lead to further definitions of that theory.

1. Do the extra-effects of action outline a public, or does a pre-existing public delimit the range of extra-effects?

No two actions have the same range of extra-effects, and no two kinds of action. In the prairie country a citizen must not light a grass fire in his back-yard, nor in the old days must he provide Indians with fire-water: each deed had an obvious physical spread of extra-effects, but these spreads were not identical. A forgery committed in the same settlement would also have a spread of after-effect, like a stroke in a bunch of nine-pins, but its outline would again differ, and would probably leap more rapidly over local limits. If there is a common multiple or containant of a large number of such spreads, it would seem to be roughly outlined (and, of course, never strictly confined) by barriers of language, custom, and geography—that is, by a pre-existent community.

2. Is the public concerned merely, or even primarily, with extra-effects of action; or is it primarily concerned with those same direct effects which are the objects of the individual agents?

A murder, a theft, the forgery we mentioned, any felony within a primary social group concerns the public. Does this concern exist *only* because of the possible spread of such deeds? In that case, no murder is punished because of itself, which is absurd: and further, the possible spread, not merely through the possible further activities of the murderer, but through suggestion and imitation, is unlimited by any boundary save that of rumor itself. On the face of things, the state is not concerned with actual extra-effects of crime: it acts on the assumption that "this sort of thing won't do," each case of it being bad in the direct incidence of its fall. In the long run, the state is concerned with extra-effects, because it is concerned with the total meaning of actions; but it would appear to be concerned first of all with precisely those immediate effects which the individual means to have, and therefore, in various cases, it enquires particularly into his intention.

3. The outlining of states can, indeed, never be understood by alleging any universal disposition of human nature. These outlines are particular, and bear the impress of particular deeds. As a matter of history, is it not true in general, that these outlines exist because publics had something to *do,* rather than because they had something to *suffer or enjoy?*

The common interests in effects and extra-effects never stop at political boundaries, and have never stopped there. Trade with all its common concerns has straddled community lines from the beginning. Neither our prairie fire, nor our drunken Indian, nor our plague-bearing rat, nor our inspired Mahdi, respect the outlines of nations. Common interests are only feebly checked in their spread by the political outlines of primitive or of modern times. But there has always been a limit to the group that could realize an impulse to *common action.* That limit has varied with the capacities of leaders to create a common set of will, and with the facilities for organization. The tribes of inner Arabia in the sixth century, dispersed and quarreling among themselves, have many tangible common interests, but can get no community out of them. Mohammed appears and makes a state of them, not by devising a system of inner administration (though that has to be worked out by degrees), but by training their imaginations to a common achievement, in the course of which the body within which those elementary common interests echoed was enlarged many times. Historically speaking, states appear to have been outlined, not by the scope of judicial business, but by the shore line of some maximal commotive impulse or cultural idea, an incentive to community enterprise in what we now call the executive department of government. The fact that these enterprises have frequently been wars ought not, I think, to conceal the fact that they have often had, and are capable of having, quite other motivation.

From either view of the historical meaning of political boundaries, we would infer their very relative importance, and the wisdom of keeping them open to revision. But it seems evident that the judicial community of mankind is capable of a more rapid extension than the executive community; and the world may become a Public, in Dewey's sense, long before it is capable of becoming a state. Perhaps the conception of the Public, as Dewey has expounded it, will prove to be the more significant conception for the future of mankind.　　　　　　　WILLIAM ERNEST HOCKING.

HARVARD UNIVERSITY.

THE JOURNAL OF PHILOSOPHY

THE FUTURE OF LIBERALISM [1]

THE emphasis of earlier liberalism upon individuality and liberty defines the focal points in discussion of the philosophy of liberalism to-day. This earlier liberalism was itself an outgrowth, in the late eighteenth and nineteenth centuries, of the earlier revolt against oligarchical government, one which came to its culmination in the "glorious revolution" of 1688. The latter was fundamentally a demand for freedom of the taxpayer from government arbitrary action in connection with a demand for confessional freedom in religion by the Protestant churches. In the later liberalism, expressly so called, the demand for liberty and individual freedom of action came primarily from the rising industrial and trading class and was directed against restrictions placed by government, in legislation, common law and judicial action, and other institutions having connection with the political state, upon freedom of economic enterprise. In both cases, governmental action and the desired freedom were placed in antithesis to each other. This way of conceiving liberty has persisted; it was strengthened in this country by the revolt of the colonies and by pioneer conditions.

Nineteenth-century philosophic liberalism added, more or less because of its dominant economic interest, the conception of natural laws to that of natural rights of the Whig movement. There are natural laws, it held, in social matters as well as in physical, and these natural laws are economic in character. Political laws, on the other hand, are man-made and in that sense artificial. Governmental intervention in industry and exchange was thus regarded as a violation not only of inherent individual liberty but also of natural laws—of which supply and demand is a sample. The proper sphere of governmental action was simply to prevent and to secure redress for infringement by one, in the exercise of his liberty, of like and equal liberty of action on the part of others.

Nevertheless, the demand for freedom in initiation and conduct

[1] This article and Professor Hocking's which follows it are taken from the symposium held at the meeting of the Eastern Division of the American Philosophical Association, December, 1934. In the next issue of this JOURNAL will appear an article by Professor J. H. Randall, Jr., which, though not part of the symposium, is based on the discussions of that occasion.

of business enterprise did not exhaust the content of earlier liberalism. In the minds of its chief promulgators there was included an equally strenuous demand for the liberty of mind, freedom of thought and its expression in speech, writing, print, and assemblage. The earlier interest in confessional freedom was generalized, and thereby deepened as well as broadened. This demand was a product of the rational enlightenment of the eighteenth century and of the growing importance of science. The great tide of reaction that set in after the defeat of Napoleon, the demand for order and discipline, gave the agitation for freedom of thought and its expression plenty of cause and plenty of opportunity.

The earlier liberal philosophy rendered valiant service. It finally succeeded in sweeping away, especially in its home, Great Britain, an innumerable number of abuses and restrictions. The history of social reforms in the nineteenth century is almost one with the history of liberal social thought. It is not, then, from ingratitude that I shall emphasize its defects, for recognition of them is essential to an intelligent statement of the elements of liberal philosophy for the present and any nearby future. The fundamental defect was lack of perception of historic relativity. This lack is expressed in the conception of the individual as something given, complete in itself, and of liberty as a ready-made possession of the individual, only needing the removal of external restrictions in order to manifest itself. The individual of earlier liberalism was a Newtonian atom having only external time and space relations to other individuals, save that each social atom was equipped with inherent freedom. These ideas might not have been especially harmful if they had been merely a rallying cry for practical movements. But they formed part of a philosophy and of a philosophy in which these particular ideas of individuality and freedom were asserted to be absolute and eternal truths; good for all times and all places.

This absolutism, this ignoring and denial of temporal relativity, is one great reason why the earlier liberalism degenerated so easily into pseudo-liberalism. For the sake of saving time, I shall identify what I mean by this spurious liberalism, the kind of social ideas represented by the "Liberty League" and ex-President Hoover. I call it a pseudo-liberalism because it ossified and narrowed generous ideas and aspirations. Even when words remain the same, they mean something very different when they are uttered by a minority struggling against repressive measures and when expressed by a group that, having attained power, then uses ideas that were once weapons of emancipation as instruments for keeping the power and wealth it has obtained. Ideas that at one time are means of producing social change assume another guise when they are used as means of preventing further social change. This fact is itself an illustration of historic relativity, and an evidence of the evil that lay in the assertion by earlier liberalism of the immutable and eternal character of their ideas. Because of this latter fact, the *laissez-faire* doctrine was held by the degenerate school of liberals to express the very order of nature itself. The outcome was the degradation of the idea of individuality, until in the minds of many who are themselves struggling for a wider and fuller development of individuality, individualism has become a term of hissing and reproach, while many can see no remedy for the evils that have come from the use of socially unrestrained liberty in business enterprise, save change produced by violence. The historic tendency to conceive the whole question of liberty as a matter in which individual and government are opposed parties has borne bitter fruit. Born of despotic government, it has continued to influence thinking and action after government had become popular and *in theory* the servant of the people.

I pass now to what the social philosophy of liberalism becomes when its inheritance of absolutism is eliminated. In the first place such liberalism knows that an individual is nothing fixed, given ready-made. It is something achieved, and achieved not in isolation, but the aid and support of conditions, cultural and physical, including in "cultural" economic, legal, and political institutions as well as science and art. Liberalism knows that social conditions may restrict, distort, and almost prevent the development of individuality. It therefore takes an active interest in the working of social institutions that have a bearing, positive or negative, upon the growth of individuals who shall be rugged in fact and not merely in abstract theory. It is as much interested in the positive construction of favorable institutions, legal, political, and economic, as it is in the work of removing abuses and overt oppressions.

In the second place, liberalism is committed to the idea of historic relativity. It knows that the content of the individual and freedom change with time; that this is as true of social change as it is of individual development from infancy to maturity. The positive counterpart of opposition to doctrinal absolutism is experimentalism. The connection between historic relativity and experimental method is intrinsic. Time signifies change. The significance of individuality with respect to social policies alters with change of the conditions in which individuals live. The earlier liberalism in being absolute was also unhistoric. Underlying it there was a philosophy of history which assumed that history, like time in the Newtonian scheme, means only modification of external relations; that it is quantitative, not equalitative and internal. The same thing is true of any theory that assumes, like the one usually attributed to Marx, that temporal changes in society are inevitable—that is to say, are governed by a law that is not itself historical. The fact is that the historicism and the evolutionism of nineteenth-century doctrine were only half-way doctrines. They assumed that historical and developmental processes were subject to some law or formula outside temporal processes.

The commitment of liberalism to experimental procedure carries with it the idea of continuous reconstruction of the ideas of individuality and of liberty in intimate connection with changes in social relations. It is enough to refer to the changes in productivity and distribution since the time when the earlier liberalism was formulated, and the effect of these transformations, due to science and technology, upon the terms on which men associate together. An experimental method is the recognition of this temporal change in ideas and policies so that the latter shall coördinate with the facts instead of being opposed to them. Any other view maintains a rigid conceptualism and implies that facts should conform to concepts that are framed independently of temporal or historical change.

The two things essential, then, to thorough-going social liberalism are, first, realistic study of existing conditions in their movement, and, secondly, leading ideas, in the form of policies for dealing with these conditions in the interest of development of increased individuality and liberty. The first requirement is so obviously implied that I shall not elaborate it. The second point needs some amplification. Experimental method is not just messing around nor doing a little of this and a little of that in the hope that things will improve. Just as in the physical sciences, it implies a coherent body of ideas, a theory, that gives direction to effort. What is implied, in contrast to every form of absolutism, is that the ideas and theory be taken as methods of action tested and continuously revised by the consequences they produce in actual social conditions. Since they are operational in nature, they modify conditions, while the first requirement, that of basing them upon realistic study of actual conditions, brings about their continuous reconstruction.

It follows finally that there is no opposition in principle between liberalism as social philosophy and radicalism in action, if by radicalism is signified the adoption of policies that bring about drastic instead of piece-meal social changes. It is all a question of what kind of procedures the intelligent study of changing conditions discloses. These changes have been so tremendous in the last century, yes, in the last forty years, that it looks to me as if radical methods were now necessary. But all that the argument here requires is recognition of the fact that there is nothing in the nature of liberalism that makes it a milk-water doctrine, committed to compromise and minor "reforms." It is worth noting that the earlier liberals were regarded in their day as subversive radicals.

What has been said should make it clear that the question of method in formation and execution of policies is the central thing in liberalism. The method indicated is that of maximum reliance upon intelligence. This fact determines its opposition to those forms of radicalism that place chief dependence upon violent overthrow of existing institutions as the method of effecting desired social change. A genuine liberal will emphasize as crucial the complete correlation between the means used and the consequences that follow. The same principle which makes him aware that the means employed by pseudo-liberalism only perpetuate and multiply the evils of existing conditions, makes him also aware that dependence upon sheer massed force as the means of social change decides the kind of consequences that actually result. Doctrines, whether proceeding from Mussolini or from Marx, which assume that because certain ends are desirable therefore those ends and nothing else will result from the use of force to attain them is but another example of the limitations put upon intelligence by any absolute theory. In the degree in which mere force is resorted to, actual consequences are themselves so compromised that the ends originally in view have in fact to be worked out afterwards by the method of experimental intelligence.

In saying this, I do not wish to be understood as meaning that radicals of the type mentioned have any monopoly of the use of force. The contrary is the case. The reactionaries are in possession of force, in not only the army and police, but in the press and the schools. The only reason they do not advocate the use of force is the fact that they are already in possession of it, so their policy is to cover up its existence with idealistic phrases—of which their present use of individual initiative and liberty is a striking example.

These facts illustrate the essential evil of reliance upon sheer force. Action and reaction are equal and in opposite directions, and force as such is physical. Dependence upon force sooner or later calls out force on the other side. The whole problem of the relation of intelligence to force is much too large to go into here. I can only say that when the forces in possession are so blind and stubborn as to throw all their weight against the use of liberty of inquiry and of communication, of organization to effect social change, they not only encourage the use of force by those who want social change, but they give the latter the most justification they ever have. The emphasis of liberalism upon the method of intelligence does not commit it to unqualified pacifism, but to the unremitting use of every method of intelligence that conditions permit, and to search for all that are possible.

In conclusion, I wish to emphasize one point implied in the early part of the paper. The question of the practical significance of liberty is much wider than that of the relation of government to the individual, to say nothing of the monstrosity of the doctrine that assumes that under all conditions governmental action and individual liberty are found in separate and independent spheres. Government is one factor and an important one. But it comes into the picture only in relation to other matters. At present, these other matters are economic and cultural. It is absurd to conceive liberty as that of the business entrepreneur and ignore the immense regimentation to which workers are subjected, intellectual as well as manual workers. Moreover, full freedom of the human spirit and of individuality can be achieved only as there is effective opportunity to share in the cultural resources of civilization. No economic state of affairs is merely economic. It has a profound effect upon presence or absence of cultural freedom. Any liberalism that does not make full cultural freedom supreme and that does not see the relation between it and genuine industrial freedom as a way of life is a degenerate and delusive liberalism.

JOHN DEWEY.

COLUMBIA UNIVERSITY.

LIST OF PAGE REFERENCES

INDEX OF AUTHORS AND TITLES

Names of contributors to this volume are printed in small capitals. Authors are those who are quoted or considered at some length. Titles are by John Dewey, unless otherwise noted; books in italics, articles in quotes. Articles published in THE JOURNAL OF PHILOSOPHY are not included.

703